The
UNTOLD
HISTORY
of the
UNITED
STATES

Oliver Stone
and Peter Kuznick

EBURY
PRESS

1 3 5 7 9 10 8 6 4 2

Published in 2012 by Ebury Press, an imprint of Ebury Publishing
A Random House Group company
Published in the USA by Simon and Schuster in 2012

A full list of credits and permissions appears on page 711

The Random House Group Limited Reg. No. 954009

Addresses for companies within the Random House Group can be found at
www.randomhouse.co.uk

A CIP catalogue record for this book is available from the British Library

The Random House Group Limited supports The Forest Stewardship Council (FSC®), the
leading international forest certification organisation. Our books carrying the FSC label are
printed on FSC® certified paper. FSC is the only forest certification scheme endorsed by the
leading environmental organisations, including Greenpeace. Our paper procurement
policy can be found at www.randomhouse.co.uk/environment

MIX
Paper from
responsible sources
FSC
www.fsc.org   FSC® C016897

Printed and bound in Great Britain by Clays Ltd, St Ives PLC

ISBN 9780091949297 (hardback)
ISBN 9780091949303 (trade paperback)

To buy books by your favourite authors and register for offers visit www.randomhouse.co.uk

To our children—Tara, Michael, Sean, Lexie, Sara, and Asmara—
and the better world that they and all children deserve.

CONTENTS

FOREWORD

This book and the documentary film series it is based on challenge the basic narrative of U.S. history that most Americans have been taught. That popular and somewhat mythic view, carefully filtered through the prism of American altruism, benevolence, magnanimity, exceptionalism, and devotion to liberty and justice, is introduced in early childhood, reinforced throughout primary and secondary education, and retold so often that it becomes part of the air that Americans breathe. It is consoling; it is comforting. But it only tells a small part of the story. It may convince those who don't probe too deeply, but like the real air Americans breathe, it is ultimately harmful, noxious, polluted. It not only renders Americans incapable of understanding the way much of the rest of the world looks at the United States, it leaves them unable to act effectively to change the world for the better. For Americans, like people everywhere, are in thrall to their visions of the past, rarely realizing the extent to which their understanding of history shapes behavior in the here and now. Historical understanding defines people's very sense of what is thinkable and achievable. As a result, many have lost the ability to imagine a world that is substantially different from and better than what exists today.

Thus, the book we have written, though inspired by and based upon the documentary film series, is in many ways independent. We see the book and documentary as complementary but not the same. We hope documentary viewers will read the book to get a fuller sense of this history and that readers will watch the documentary to get the full power of the visual and dramatic presentation. We offer both book and film series to the forces of progressive change around the world in the hopes that the information we provide will prove useful in their fight for a more just, humane, democratic, and equitable world.

INTRODUCTION:

Roots of Empire: "War Is a Racket"

We write this book as the curtain slowly draws down on the American Empire. It was 1941 when magazine magnate Henry Luce declared the twentieth century the "American Century." Little could he have imagined how true that would be, writing before the defeat of Germany and Japan, the advent of the atomic bomb, the boom in U.S. postwar production, the rise and institutionalization of the military-industrial complex, the development of the Internet, the transmogrification of the United States into a national security state, and the country's "victory" in the Cold War.

Luce's vision of untrammeled U.S. hegemony has always been a contested one. Vice President Henry Wallace urged the United States to instead usher in what he called "the Century of the Common Man." Wallace, whom realists dismissed as a "dreamer" and a "visionary," laid out a blueprint for a world of science- and technology-based abundance, a world banning colonialism and economic exploitation, a world of peace and shared prosperity. Unfortunately, the postwar world has conformed much more closely to Luce's imperial vision than Wallace's progressive one. More recently, in 1997, a new generation of proponents of U.S. global supremacy, who would go on to constitute the neoconservative "brain trust" of the disastrous George W. Bush presidency, called for the establishment of a "new American Century." It was a perspective that gained many adherents in the earlier years of the twenty-first century, before the calamitous consequences of the United States' latest wars became widely recognized.

The United States' run as global hegemon—the most powerful and dominant nation the world has ever seen—has been marked by proud achievements and terrible disappointments. It is the latter—the darker side of U.S. history—that we explore in the following pages. We don't try to tell all of U.S. history. That would be an impossible task. We don't focus extensively on many of the things the United States has done right. There are libraries full of books dedicated to that purpose and school curricula that trumpet U.S. achievements. We are more concerned with focusing a spotlight on what the United States has done wrong—the ways in which we believe the country has betrayed its mission— with the faith that there is still time to correct those errors as we move forward into the twenty-first century. We are profoundly disturbed by the direction of U.S. policy at a time when the United States was recently at war in three Muslim countries and carrying out drone attacks, best viewed as targeted assassinations, in at least six others. Why does our country have military bases in every region of the globe, totaling more than a thousand by some counts? Why does the United States spend as much money on its military as the rest of the world combined? Why does it still possess thousands of nuclear weapons, many on hair-trigger alert, even though no nation poses an imminent threat? Why is the gap between rich and poor greater in the United States than in any other developed country, and why is the United States the only advanced nation without a universal health care program?

Why do such a tiny number of people—whether the figure is currently 300 or 500 or 2,000—control more wealth than the world's poorest 3 billion? Why are a tiny minority of wealthy Americans allowed to exert so much control over U.S. domestic politics, foreign policy, and media while the great masses see a diminution of their real power and standards of living? Why have Americans submitted to levels of surveillance, government intrusion, abuse of civil liberties, and loss of privacy that would have appalled the Founding Fathers and earlier generations? Why does the United States have a lower percentage of unionized workers than any other advanced industrial democracy? Why, in our country, are those who are driven by personal greed and narrow self-interest empowered over those who extol social values like kindness, generosity, compassion, sharing, empathy, and community building? And why has it become so hard for the great majority of Americans to imagine a different, we would say a better, future than the one defined by current policy initiatives and social values? These are only a few of the questions we will address in these pages. Although we can't hope to answer all of them, we hope to present the historical background that will enable readers to explore these topics more deeply on their own.

Along the way, we will also highlight some of the forces and individuals who have endeavored, sometimes heroically, to put the country back on the right track. We take seriously President John Quincy Adams's July 4, 1821, condemnation of British colonialism and declaration that the United States "goes not abroad, in search of monsters to destroy" lest she "involve herself beyond the power of extrication, in all the wars of interest and intrigue, of individual avarice, envy, and ambition, which assume the colors and usurp the standard of freedom. The fundamental maxims of her policy would insensibly change from *liberty* to *force.*" The United States, Adams warned, might "become the dictatress of the world [but] she would be no longer the ruler of her own spirit."[1]

Adams presciently foresaw what would befall the United States if it sacrificed its republican spirit on the altar of empire. Compounding the problem is Americans' persistent denial of their nation's imperial past and the ways in which it shapes present policy. As historian Alfred McCoy observes, "For empires, the past is just another overseas territory ripe for reconstruction, even reinvention."[2] Americans refuse to live in history, even though, as novelist J. M. Coetzee understands, empire must always do so. In *Waiting for the Barbarians,* he wrote, "Empire dooms itself to live in history and plot against history. One thought alone preoccupies the submerged mind of Empire: how not to end, how not to die, how to prolong its era. By day it pursues its enemies. It is cunning and ruthless, it sends its bloodhounds everywhere. By night it feeds on images of disaster: the sack of cities, the rape of populations, pyramids of bones, acres of desolation. A mad vision yet a virulent one."[3]

Americans believe they are unbound by history. Historian Christopher Lasch saw this as a reflection of their "narcissism." It is also, for many, a way to avoid grappling with what their nation has become over the past century. It was easier, while U.S. dominance lasted, for citizens to comfort themselves with consoling fables of U.S. benevolence while real historical knowledge steadily declined. Americans' continuing separation from the rest of the multilingual and integrated world only exacerbates the problem. Seclusion has not only bred ignorance; it has also bred fear, which we have seen manifested repeatedly in the exaggerated assessment of enemy threats and recurrent panics about alien intruders, domestic and foreign radicals, and, more recently, menacing Islamic terrorists.

U.S. citizens' ignorance of their country's history was once again driven home when the results of a nationwide test, known as the Nation's Report Card, were unveiled in June 2011. The test of fourth, eighth, and twelfth graders revealed that U.S. students are, according to the *New York Times,* "less proficient in their nation's history than in any other subject." The National Assessment of Educational Progress found that only 12 percent of high school seniors demonstrated proficiency. And even the "proficiency" of that 12 percent was called into question when, shockingly, only 2 percent could identify the social problem that the *Brown v. Board of Education* decision was meant to correct, even though the answer was evident in the wording of the question.[4]

This gaping historical void has largely been filled with myth. Among those myths is the self-serving idea that, in the words of John Winthrop aboard the

Arbella in 1630, America shall be as a divinely ordained "city upon a hill"—a beacon for the rest of the world to follow. According to such reasoning, the United States is measurably superior to the rest of the corrupt and venal world. At certain moments, that has been true. There have been times when American values and achievements have led the way to major advances in human history and social progress. But there have been just as many occasions, if not more, when the United States has undermined human progress in pursuing its policies. Though the belief that the United States is fundamentally different from other nations—that others act out of self-interest to achieve power or economic gain while the United States, motivated only by a commitment to freedom and liberty, altruistically sacrifices for mankind—was buried for many in the ruins of Hiroshima and Nagasaki and in the jungles of Vietnam, it has reemerged in recent years as a staple of right-wing historical revisionism.

This myth of American exceptionalism was perhaps best reflected in the post-Versailles comment by President Woodrow Wilson that "at last the world knows America as the savior of the world!"[5] U.S. leaders have expressed that sentiment repeatedly over the years, although usually with a little more humility.

Such humility is completely missing from declarations by Tea Party xenophobes who have made obeisance to the notion of American exceptionalism the sine qua non of patriotism and take President Barack Obama's more nuanced comments to confirm their suspicion that, even if he was born in the United States, as most now grudgingly admit, he's still not really an American. They take great umbrage at his 2009 comment that "I believe in American exceptionalism, just as I suspect that the Brits believe in British exceptionalism and the Greeks believe in Greek exceptionalism."[6]

That Obama refuses to trumpet the notion that the United States is history's gift to humanity has become an article of faith among Republican leaders who, knowing that 58 percent of Americans believe that "God has granted America a special role in human history," have opportunistically used Obama's less-than-full-throated assent to bludgeon him. Former Arkansas Governor Mike Huckabee charged that Obama's "worldview is dramatically different than any president, Republican or Democrat, we've had. . . . He grew up more as a globalist than an American. To deny American exceptionalism is in essence to deny the heart and soul of this nation."[7]

The importance of developing an uncorrupted view of U.S. history and a cogent critique of U.S. imperialism has been an article of faith among left-leaning historians and activists dating back to the New Left in the 1960s. Conservatives, on the other hand, have routinely denied that the United States has any imperial pretensions. It is only recently that neoconservatives have broken with this pattern, proudly proclaiming not only that America is an empire but that it is the most powerful and most righteous empire the world has ever seen. To most Americans this is still blasphemy. To the neocons it reflects muscular-ity—the United States playing the dominating role for which God prepared it. In the euphoria following the October 7, 2001, invasion of Afghanistan, before the folly of the United States' latest imperial adventures came crashing down on premature celebrants, conservative pundits jumped on the empire bandwagon. William Kristol's *Weekly Standard* boldly headlined the cover of its October 15 edition, "The Case for American Empire." *National Review* editor in chief Rich Lowry called for "a kind of low-grade colonialism" to topple dangerous govern-ments beyond Afghanistan.[8] A few months later columnist Charles Krautham-mer took note of the fact that "people are now coming out of the closet on the word 'empire.'" He thought it timely, given the complete U.S. domination "cultur-ally, economically, technologically and militarily."[9] The *New York Times* Sunday magazine cover for January 5, 2003, read, "American Empire: Get Used To It."

Although many neoconservatives see the empire as a recent development, U.S. expansionist impulse shaped settlement, growth, and conquest from the establishment of the earliest British colonies, an impulse later embodied in the notion of "manifest destiny" and reflected in the Monroe Doctrine. As Yale histo-rian Paul Kennedy put it, "From the time the first settlers arrived in Virginia from England and started moving westward, this was an imperial nation, a conquer-ing nation."[10] This sometimes genocidal hunger for others' land and resources was always couched in the highest of motives—a commitment to altruistically advancing freedom, progress, and civilization—and continues to be so today. As William Appleman Williams, one of the earliest and most insightful students of the American Empire, explained, "The routine lust for land, markets, or security became justifications for noble rhetoric about prosperity, liberty, and security."[11] U.S. leaders have accordingly denied, though not always convincingly, the racist assumptions that justified this expansionist impulse.

They have also denied the means by which it was accomplished. But remind-ers have often come from the most unexpected of places. It was Samuel Hunting-ton, progenitor of the reductionist and wrongheaded "clash of civilizations" the-sis, who astutely pointed out: "The West won the world not by the superiority of its ideas or values or religion (to which few members of other religions were converted) but rather by its superiority in applying organized violence. Western-ers often forget this fact; non-Westerners never do."[12]

Wall Street Journal editor and Council on Foreign Relations senior fellow Max Boot understood better than most that U.S. imperial designs were not of recent vintage. He chided Donald Rumsfeld for his sharp response to an Al-Jazeera reporter who asked him if the United States was "empire building." Boot quipped that Rumsfeld "reacted as if he'd been asked whether he wears women's underwear." "We don't seek empires," Rumsfeld snapped. "We're not imperialistic. We never have been." Boot disagreed, citing the expansion across the continent that began with the Louisiana Purchase; moving abroad with the late-nineteenth-century acquisitions of Puerto Rico, the Philippines, Hawaii, and Alaska; followed by the post–World War II "bout of imperialism" in Germany and Japan; and capped off with the "recent 'nation-building' experiments in Somalia, Haiti, Bosnia, Kosovo and Afghanistan[, which] are imperialism under another name." But, unlike critics on the left, Boot applauded U.S. expansionary policies. "U.S. imperialism," he argued, "has been the greatest force for good in the world during the past century."[13]

Harvard historian Niall Ferguson, a sometime apologist for the British Empire, understood that Americans' pretension to superiority was, to say the least, self-serving. Ferguson wryly observed, "To those who would still insist on American 'exceptionalism,' the historian of empires can only retort: as exceptional as all the other sixty-nine empires."[14]

Although apologists' claims to moral superiority were certainly overblown, their claims to military superiority seem defensible. Few have more perspective on this topic than Paul Kennedy, whose award-winning 1987 book *The Rise and Fall of the Great Powers* noted that the U.S. Empire was in decline, following the habitual pattern of imperial overreach. But, like others, he was dazzled and, one might say, blinded by the ease with which the United States obliterated Afghanistan following the terrorist attacks of September 11, 2001. "Nothing has ever existed like this disparity of power; nothing," he wrote, reversing his earlier judgment. "I have returned to all of the comparative defence spending and military personnel statistics over the past 500 years . . . and no other nation comes close. The Pax Britannica was run on the cheap, Britain's army was much smaller than European armies, and even the Royal Navy was equal only to the next two navies—right now all the other navies in the world combined could not dent American maritime supremacy." Kennedy was awestruck by the fierce power of the country's twelve carrier groups. No other empire could compare: "Charlemagne's empire was merely Western European in its reach. The Roman empire stretched farther afield, but there was another great empire in Persia, and a larger one in China. There is, therefore, no comparison," he concluded.[15]

But even these claims deserve closer scrutiny. The United States certainly possesses the greatest firepower, the best trained and equipped and most capable troops, and the most technologically sophisticated weaponry of any military power in history. But this has not easily translated into victory on the battlefield when the enemy employs asymmetrical tactics and the objective is winning hearts and minds.

Confusion over U.S. imperial status has resulted from the fact that the United States exercises the power and functions of an empire but does not take on the traditional trappings of one. Clearly, it has not followed the path of European colonial empires, although it has occasionally dabbled in colonial ventures. These have, for the most part, been adjuncts to overseas economic penetration constituting what some have called an "open-door" empire, one more concerned with control of markets and other forms of economic domination than with controlling subject populations and actual territory. The United States has, however, repeatedly resorted to military force and even prolonged occupations to deal with threats to those economic interests and private investments. More recently, U.S. control has been exercised through what Chalmers Johnson aptly described as an "empire of bases" that are a substitute for the colonies of days gone by. By 2002, Pentagon figures indicated that the United States had some form of military presence in 132 of the UN's then 190 member nations.[16] Add to that the multibillion-dollar carrier battle groups, and the U.S. military presence is truly global. Plus, the United States retains the world's most potent nuclear arsenal, capable, despite reductions in recent years, of ending life on the planet several times over.

The latest frontier has been military domination of space as part of what the United States calls "full-spectrum dominance." It was outlined in the U.S. Space Command's 1997 publication "Vision for 2010" and fleshed out further in the Pentagon's "Joint Vision 2020."[17] It portends unchallenged U.S. military domination on land and sea and in space.

The American Empire has evolved over the course of more than a century. After fulfilling what journalist John L. O'Sullivan termed its "Manifest Destiny" by spreading across North America, the United States looked overseas. William Henry Seward, Secretary of State to both Abraham Lincoln and Andrew Johnson, articulated a grandiose vision that incorporated Alaska, Hawaii, Canada, parts of the Caribbean and Colombia, and Midway Island.

While Seward dreamed, the Europeans acted, gobbling up everything they could get their hands on in the late nineteenth century. Britain led the way, adding 4.75 million square miles of territory—an area significantly larger than the United States—in the last thirty years of the century.[18] France added 3.5 million.[19] Germany, off to a late start, added 1 million. Only Spain's colonization was in decline. By 1878, the European powers and their former colonies controlled 67 percent of the earth's surface and, by 1914, an astounding 84 percent.[20] By the 1890s, Europeans had divided up 90 percent of Africa, the lion's share claimed by Belgium, Britain, France, and Germany. Massachusetts Senator Henry Cabot Lodge, the leading proponent of an American Empire, observed, "The great nations are rapidly absorbing for their future expansion and their present

*During the late nineteenth century, European countries vastly
expanded their empires. As illustrated in these maps, by 1878, the
European powers and their former colonies controlled 67 percent
of the earth's surface and, by 1914, an astounding 84 percent.*

defense all the waste places of the earth" and urged the United States to move
quickly to make up for lost time.[21]

But such an empire was anathema to most Americans, who were struggling
to defend a nineteenth-century vision of a producer's republic from a ravenous
industrial capitalist order. The enormous gulf between opulent capitalists and
struggling masses shook the foundations of Americans' democratic and egalitarian ideals. Most farmers and workers deplored the idea that a handful of bankers
and industrialists, along with their stable of rubber-stamp legislators and judges,
should run the country. Poet Walt Whitman captured that feeling when he
described the excesses of capitalism as "a sort of anti-democratic disease and
monstrosity."[22]

The 1870s, 1880s, and 1890s witnessed some of the bloodiest labor struggles
in the nation's history. In 1877, striking railroad workers and their myriad supporters from all parts of the working class paralyzed much of the nation's rail

This August 1883 Puck *magazine cartoon depicts the unequal late nineteenth-century battle between labor and monopolists. A number of robber barons are portrayed in the stands at left, including (from left to right) financier and telegraph innovator Cyrus Field, railroad magnate William Vanderbilt, shipbuilder John Roach, and railroad magnate Jay Gould.*

traffic as capitalists, haunted by memories of the revolutionary workers who created the Paris Commune of 1871, conjured up their own nightmare visions when several cities, including Chicago and St. Louis, were shut down by general strikes. In Washington, D.C., the *National Republican* newspaper ran an editorial titled "The American Commune," which stated, "The fact is clearly manifest that communistic ideas are very widely entertained in America by the workmen employed in mines and factories and by the railroads." The railroad strike "is nothing less than communism in its worst form, not only unlawful and revolutionary, but anti-American."[23] St. Louis's leading newspaper, the *Republican*, concurred: "It is wrong to call this a strike; it is a labor revolution."[24] When local militias proved unwilling or unable to quell the uprising, President Rutherford B. Hayes, who owed his office in part to the railroad magnates, sent in the U.S. Army. The ensuing battles left over a hundred workers dead and a nation bitterly divided.

The struggles intensified in the 1880s as the Knights of Labor exploded on the scene, successfully striking Jay Gould's 15,000-mile railroad network in 1885. Gould was no ordinary robber baron. Having once boasted that he could "hire one half of the working class to kill the other half," he was perhaps the

*"Haymarket Riot," May 4, 1886. Authorities used the death of
policemen in Haymarket Square to crush not only the anarchists,
who were involved in the incident, but also the Knights of
Labor. Soon radicals across the nation were under attack.*

most hated man in the nation.[25] And the Knights, with their appeal to class unity
and democratic socialist philosophy, was no ordinary labor federation. Gould's
capitulation to the Knights' demands, in what the business newspaper *Brad-
street's* called a "complete surrender," shocked the nation.[26] Knights membership
skyrocketed around the country, jumping from 103,000 on July 1, 1885, to over
700,000 a year later. The movement was dealt a crushing blow, however, when
authorities nationwide used the death of seven policemen in Chicago's Haymarket Square in May 1886 as an excuse to not only destroy the anarchists, who
were involved in the incident, but to go after the Knights, who forswore violence
and were completely uninvolved in the Haymarket events. Radicals everywhere
were targeted in the ensuing Red Scare.

Looking back on the period, reformer Ida Tarbell recalled that "the eighties
dripped with blood."[27] Though the decade did not quite drip with blood, workers did question the legitimacy of a system that empowered the wealthy—the
new corporate and banking elite—and marginalized the overwhelming majority
of workers and farmers, who experienced limited advances in good times and
often devastating setbacks in bad.

Discontent was regularly expressed by angry farmers as well, particularly the

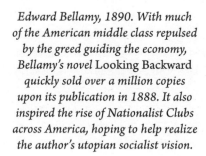

*Edward Bellamy, 1890. With much
of the American middle class repulsed
by the greed guiding the economy,
Bellamy's novel* Looking Backward
*quickly sold over a million copies
upon its publication in 1888. It also
inspired the rise of Nationalist Clubs
across America, hoping to help realize
the author's utopian socialist vision.*

ones who organized the Farmers Alliances in the 1880s and the People's Party in the early 1890s. Historians continue to debate just how radical farmers were, but there is no doubt that most opposed the growing reach of the corporate state, and many of their leaders roused audiences with anti–Wall Street rhetoric. The People's Party adopted a platform at its first convention in Omaha, Nebraska, in 1892 that declared, "The fruits of the toil of millions are boldly stolen to build up colossal fortunes for a few, unprecedented in the history of mankind; and the possessors of these, in turn, despise the republic and endanger liberty. From the same prolific womb of governmental injustice we breed the two great classes—tramps and millionaires."[28]

Although the Populists' appeal was limited to parts of the South, Midwest, and West, the People's Party won almost 9 percent of the presidential vote in 1892, carrying five midwestern and western states and electing over 1,500 candidates, including three governors, five senators, and ten congressmen. The Populists doubled their vote in 1894, electing seven congressmen and six senators.

Much of the middle class shared the revulsion toward an economy predicated upon the notion that individuals motivated by private greed would somehow produce a greater social good. Middle-class Americans not only sided with the railroad strikers in the Great Strike of 1877, they devoured Edward Bellamy's enormously popular 1888 utopian socialist novel *Looking Backward*, which quickly sold over a million copies, making it the second most popular American novel of the nineteenth century, behind Harriet Beecher Stowe's *Uncle Tom's Cabin.*

The financial panic on Black Friday—May 5, 1893—triggered the nation's worst depression to date. It would last five long years. Within months, 4 million workers lost their jobs. Unemployment soon approached 20 percent.

The nation debated the depression's causes and sought ways to avoid future economic collapse. Those who believed that the 1893 depression resulted from overproduction argued that the United States needed more markets abroad to absorb its growing surplus. Socialists, trade unionists, and reformers, on the other hand, believed that the 1890s crisis resulted from *under*-consumption and proposed a different solution: redistributing wealth at home so that working people could afford to buy the products of America's farms and factories. But few capitalists endorsed that approach, choosing instead to involve the United States in world affairs in ways that would fundamentally transform the nation.

Before the United States could stake its claim to foreign markets and natural resources, it needed a modern steam-powered navy and bases around the world to supply it. The United States annexed the harbor of the Pacific island of Pago Pago in 1889 and built a new navy between 1890 and 1896.

Pago Pago was just the start. In 1893, American sugar planters, working with the U.S. minister in Honolulu and supported by U.S. marines and sailors, toppled Hawaiian Queen Liliuokalani and installed American Sanford Dole, a cousin of pineapple magnate James Dole, as president. The United States annexed Hawaii in 1898. President William McKinley called it "Manifest Destiny."[29]

The United States declared war against Spain on April 25, 1898, purportedly to deliver Cuba from Spanish tyranny. The fighting began thousands of miles away in Manila Bay, where, on May 1, Commodore George Dewey destroyed the Spanish fleet. One anti-imperialist noted, "Dewey took Manila with the loss of one man—and all our institutions."[30] The war was over in three months.

Secretary of State John Hay called it "a splendid little war."[31] Not everyone thought the war so splendid. On June 15, 1898, the Anti-Imperialist League tried to block U.S. annexation of the Philippines and Puerto Rico. Its ranks included such prominent individuals as Andrew Carnegie, Clarence Darrow, Mark Twain, Jane Addams, William James, William Dean Howells, and Samuel Gompers. But anti-imperialists' efforts were no match for a nation imbued with the glory of war and the thrill of easy victory in a righteous cause.

When the dust of war settled, the United States had secured the beginnings of an overseas empire, having annexed Hawaii and acquired Puerto Rico, Guam, and the Philippines from Spain. The Philippines were viewed as an ideal refueling stop for China-bound ships. After wavering about what to do with the islands, walking the White House floor night after night and praying to "Almighty God"

Satirizing both the emerging American imperialism and the nation's ongoing cruelties, this January 1899 Puck *magazine cartoon depicts the Philippines, Hawaii, Puerto Rico, and Cuba as children being lectured to by Uncle Sam. In the back rows sit children reading books labeled with the names of various U.S. states. In the far corner of the room a Native American child holds his book upside down, while a Chinese child stands at the "Open Door." In the upper left corner an African American is left the menial task of washing the classroom window. The blackboard reads, "The consent of the governed is a good thing in theory, but very rare in fact. —England has governed her colonies whether they consented or not. By not waiting for their consent she has greatly advanced the world's civilization. —The U.S. must govern its new territories with or without their consent until they can govern themselves."*

for guidance, McKinley opted for annexation, seizing upon the opportunity to civilize one of the world's "inferior" races, which Rudyard Kipling referred to as the "white man's burden."[32]

Under the leadership of Emilio Aguinaldo, the Filipinos had been rebelling against Spanish rule for years, and they naively believed the United States would help them gain independence. They drafted a constitution and established a republic on January 23, 1899, with Aguinaldo as president. On February 4, U.S. forces opened fire in Manila. U.S. newspapers reported this as an unprovoked Filipino attack on unarmed U.S. soldiers in which 22 were killed and 125 to 200 wounded. Filipino losses were estimated in the thousands. Newspapers predicted that the attack would rally support for the imperial cause and ensure Senate approval of the bitterly contested treaty, according to which the United States was to pay Spain

$20 million for the Philippines. The *New York World* observed that the United States was "suddenly, without warning, face to face with the actualities of empire. . . . To rule, we must conquer. To conquer, we must kill."[33] Pressure mounted on treaty opponents to support the troops. General Charles Grosvenor, a congressman from Ohio, declared, "They have fired on our flag. They have killed our soldiers. The blood of the slain cries from the ground for vengeance."[34]

The *Chicago Tribune* described the Senate debate as the bitterest contest "since the impeachment trial of Andy Johnson."[35] Senator George Frisbie Hoar of Massachusetts warned that the United States would become "a vulgar, commonplace empire founded upon physical force, controlling subject races and vassal states, in which one class must forever rule and the other classes must forever obey."[36] After much arm-twisting and assurances that this did not entail permanent U.S. control of the Philippines, the treaty was ratified by a margin of one vote over the two-thirds needed. Hoar later observed, the United States "crushed the Republic that the Philippine people had set up for themselves, deprived them of their independence, and established there, by American power, a Government in which the people have no part, against their will."[37] Senator Richard Pettigrew called the betrayal of Filipino independence "the greatest international crime of the century."[38]

Filipinos overwhelmingly supported the rebels and provided them food and shelter. The Americans, some of whom employed the tactics they had perfected fighting Native Americans, responded with extraordinary brutality. Following one ambush, General Lloyd Wheaton ordered all towns within a twelve-mile radius destroyed and all their inhabitants killed. When rebels surprised the Americans stationed at Balangiga on the island of Samar, killing fifty-four of the seventy-four men there, Colonel Jacob Smith ordered his troops to kill everyone over the age of ten and turn the island into "a howling wilderness."[39] Some of the soldiers happily obliged. One wrote home, "Our fighting blood was up, and we all wanted to kill 'niggers.' . . . This shooting human beings beats rabbit hunting all to pieces."[40] U.S. officers put hundreds of thousands into concentration camps.

One of the most vigorous backers of the U.S. takeover of the Philippines was Senator Albert Beveridge of Indiana. Beveridge visited the Philippines to get a firsthand look at the situation. The only senator to have actually visited the Philippines, his views were eagerly anticipated. He addressed a crowded Senate chamber in early January 1900, offering one of the most colorful, blunt, and chauvinistic defenses on record of U.S. imperial policy:

> The Philippines are ours forever. . . . This island empire is the last land left
> in all the oceans. . . . Our largest trade henceforth must be with Asia. The
> Pacific is our ocean. More and more Europe will manufacture the most it
> needs, secure from its colonies the most it consumes. Where shall we turn

for consumers of our surplus? Geography answers the question. China is our natural customer. . . . The Philippines give us a base at the door of all the East. . . . Most future wars will be conflicts for commerce. The power that rules the Pacific, therefore, is the power that rules the world. And, with the Philippines, that power is and will forever be the American Republic. . . . God . . . has marked the American people as His chosen nation to finally lead in the regeneration of the world. This is the divine mission of America, and it holds for us all the profit, all the glory, all the happiness possible to man. We are trustees of the world's progress, guardians of its righteous peace. The judgment of the Master is upon us: "Ye have been faithful over a few things; I will make you ruler over many things."[41]

But for McKinley the real prize was the fabled China market, which Japan and the European powers had been carving into exclusive areas for investment. Fearing that the United States would be frozen out of the China market, Secretary of State John Hay issued his first "open-door" note in 1899, asking other nations to grant equal access to commercial activity in their spheres of influence. Although the responses were often ambiguous, Hay declared the following March that all had assented to the open-door principle. Chinese nationalists, however, resenting all foreign domination, sparked a massive uprising against foreign occupiers and their missionary allies. Five thousand U.S. troops joined those from Europe and Japan in suppressing the Boxer Rebellion.

Thus, the 1900 presidential election between McKinley and William Jennings Bryan took place with U.S. troops tied down in China, Cuba, and the Philippines. At the Democratic National Convention, Bryan defined the contest as a fight between "democracy on the one hand and plutocracy on the other," and he launched into an impassioned attack on imperialism. In his booming baritone, he aligned his opposition to imperial conquest with the philosophies of Thomas Jefferson and Abraham Lincoln, quoting Jefferson: "If there be one principle more deeply rooted than any other in the mind of every American, it is that we should have nothing to do with conquest."[42] The voting public, by a narrow margin, seemed to at least acquiesce in the new imperial course laid out by McKinley and his advisors. Socialist Eugene Debs barely registered in the polls.

After the election, Philippine atrocity stories began to circulate, replete with lurid accounts of murder, rape, and a kind of torture now called waterboarding. In November 1901, the *Philadelphia Ledger*'s Manila correspondent reported:

The present war is no bloodless, fake, opera bouffé engagement. Our men have been relentless; have killed to exterminate men, women, children, prisoners and captives, active insurgents and suspected people, from lads

The presidential election of 1900 pitted Republican William McKinley (left), a proponent of American Empire and a staunch defender of the eastern establishment, against Democrat William Jennings Bryan (right), a midwestern populist and outspoken anti-imperialist. With McKinley's victory, Bryan's warnings against American Empire would, tragically, be ignored.

of ten and up, an idea prevailing that the Filipino, as such, was little better than a dog . . . whose best disposition was the rubbish heap. Our soldiers have pumped salt water into men to "make them talk," have taken prisoner people who held up their hands and peacefully surrendered, and an hour later, without an atom of evidence to show that they were even insurrectos, stood them on a bridge and shot them down one by one, to drop into the water below and float down as an example to those who found their bullet riddled corpses.[43]

One soldier sent the following account to the *Omaha World-Herald:*

Lay them on their backs, a man standing on each hand and each foot, then put a round stick in the mouth and pour a pail of water in the mouth and nose, and if they don't give up pour in another pail. They swell up like toads. I'll tell you it is a terrible torture.[44]

Fighting persisted for three and a half years before President Theodore

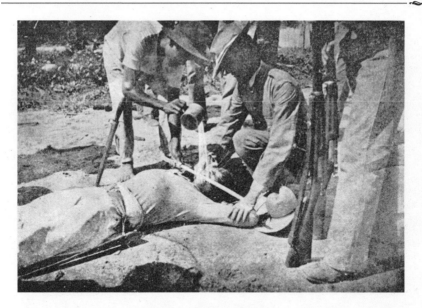

U.S. troops employed the torture we now call waterboarding. One reporter wrote "our soldiers have pumped salt water into men to 'make them talk.'"

Roosevelt declared the islands pacified. The United States deployed a total of 126,000 troops, 4,374 of whom did not make it back alive.[45] The toll among Filipinos was much higher—perhaps 20,000 guerrillas and at least 200,000 civilians, many from cholera.[46] Americans comforted themselves with the thought that they had spread civilization to a backward people, but at a hefty price—$400 million. Senator Beveridge felt it was money well spent. But Beveridge underestimated the real cost. The republic of Washington and Jefferson, which had long inspired democratic and revolutionary movements around the world, had started down the road that would soon make it the foe of meaningful change and the defender of the status quo.

In February 1901, while U.S. troops were, in McKinley's words, uplifting, civilizing, and Christianizing the Filipinos, the U.S. Congress dispelled any lingering illusions regarding Cuban independence. It passed the Platt Amendment, which asserted the United States' right to intervene in future Cuban affairs, limited the amount of debt Cuba could accumulate, restricted Cuba's power to sign treaties, and gave the United States a naval base at Guantánamo Bay, which would secure the eastern approach to the Isthmus of Panama. The United States made clear that the army would not leave until the amendment was incorporated into the Cuban Constitution.

The bodies of dead Filipinos.

After the war, American businessmen swooped in, grabbing all the assets they could seize. United Fruit Company gobbled up 1.9 million acres of land for sugar production at 20 cents per acre. By 1901, Bethlehem Steel and other U.S. businesses may have owned over 80 percent of Cuban minerals.

In September 1901, a twenty-eight-year-old anarchist, Leon Czolgosz, shot McKinley at the Pan-American Exposition in Buffalo. One of his anarchist acquaintances reported that Czolgosz had complained about the "outrages committed by the American government in the Philippine islands."[47] Ironically, the assassination brought to office a much more committed imperialist, Teddy Roosevelt.

The new president savored the prospect of a canal through the Isthmus of Panama that would connect the Caribbean with the Pacific. But Panama was a province of Colombia, which refused to relinquish sovereignty for the $10 million the United States offered. Roosevelt took matters into his own hands and seized the canal route from those "cut-throats of Bogota."[48] The United States orchestrated a revolution, sent in warships to keep the Colombian army at bay, and quickly recognized Panama's independence. In addition to the Canal Zone, the United States received the same right to intervene in Panamanian affairs that it had extorted from Cuba. Secretary of War Elihu Root warned that building the canal would force the United States to police the region for the foreseeable future.

ABOVE: *Plowing on a Cuban sugar plantation.*

RIGHT: *The United Fruit Company office building in New Orleans. The Spanish-American War proved quite profitable for American businessmen. Once the war in Cuba ended, United Fruit took 1.9 million acres of Cuban land at 20 cents an acre.*

The United States began policing the region long before completion of the canal in 1914. As U.S. investment in Central America grew by leaps and bounds in the late nineteenth and early twentieth centuries, United Fruit Company and other U.S. corporations insisted on stable, compliant governments that would protect their interests. Americans took over banana and coffee plantations, mines, railroads, and similar enterprises. So much land was devoted to commodity production for export that the countries became dependent on food imports to feed their citizens. The revenue at least enabled them to service their mounting debt to foreign banks.

Defending American businessmen's growing investments required the constant involvement of the military to prop up corrupt and dictatorial governments and suppress revolutionary movements. As early as 1905, Root, who had become secretary of state, wrote candidly, "The South Americans now hate us, largely because they think we despise them and try to bully them."[49] Between 1900 and 1925, the United States repeatedly intervened militarily in Latin America. It sent troops to Honduras in 1903, 1907, 1911, 1912, 1919, 1924, and 1925; to Cuba in 1906, 1912, and 1917; to Nicaragua in 1907, 1910, and 1912; to the Dominican Republic in 1903, 1914, and 1916; to Haiti in 1914; to Panama in 1908, 1912, 1918, 1921, and 1925; to Mexico in 1914; and to Guatemala in 1920.[50] The only reason it didn't intervene more frequently was that it often stayed, occupying countries for extended periods of time: Nicaragua from 1912 to 1933, Haiti from 1914 to 1933, the Dominican Republic from 1916 to 1924, Cuba from 1917 to 1922, and Panama from 1918 to 1920.

Honduras was dominated first by the Spanish, then by the British, and then by the Americans. By 1907, its foreign debt stood at $124 million, its national income at $1.6 million.[51] Between 1890 and 1910, foreign banana companies transformed the nation. First the Vaccaro brothers and then Sam "the Banana Man" Zemurray bought up vast plantations and the government officials needed to make sure things ran smoothly. They were soon joined by United Fruit Company of Boston. Beginning in 1907, political instability afforded the United States a pretext to intervene militarily and reinstall the supine government of Manuel Bonilla. U.S. bankers also replaced their British counterparts in controlling Honduran debt. With the political climate improved, United Fruit increased its holdings from 14,000 acres in 1918 to 61,000 in 1922 to 88,000 in 1924.[52] In 1929, Zemurray sold out to United Fruit and became the company's top official. The people of Honduras have remained impoverished ever since.

The Nicaraguans fared no better. U.S. marines, under the command of Smedley Butler, intervened in 1910 to establish a government friendly to U.S. interests. When growing U.S. domination provoked the ire of Nicaraguans, Butler's marines again intervened to defeat the rebels, killing two thousand Nicaraguans in the fighting. Butler was beginning to understand that his mission was essentially to protect U.S. commercial and banking interests. As he wrote to his wife during the fighting, "It is terrible that we should be losing so many men fighting the battles of these d . . . d spigs—all because Brown Bros. have some money down here."[53] When the Central American Court, which Roosevelt had established with much fanfare in 1907 to peacefully adjudicate conflicts in the region, condemned the U.S. intervention, U.S. authorities ignored that ruling, effectively destroying the court's authority. U.S. troops would occupy the country for the next twenty years.

In 1922, *The Nation* ran a scathing editorial titled "The Republic of Brown Bros.," which echoed Butler's assertion that the marines were there to do Brown Brothers' bidding. The piece detailed how the bankers had systematically secured control over Nicaragua's customs, railroad, national bank, and internal revenues with "the State Department in Washington and the American Minister in Managua acting as private agents for these bankers, using American marines when necessary to impose their will." [54]

Augusto Sandino was among the many Nicaraguans committed to throwing off the yoke of U.S. tyranny in their country. In 1927, he and his guerrillas engaged in a bloody battle with U.S. marines before retreating into the mountains. He reemerged the next year and, with popular backing, waged a guerrilla campaign against the occupying forces and their Nicaraguan National Guard surrogates. One U.S. planter wrote Secretary of State Henry Stimson that the military intervention had "proved a calamity for the American coffee planters. Today we are hated and despised. This feeling has been created by employing the American marines to hunt down and kill Nicaraguans in their own country." [55] Understanding this and fearing that U.S. military involvement in Central America was undermining his ability to protest Japanese actions in Manchuria, Stimson pulled the marines out of Nicaragua in January 1933, leaving things in the hands of the National Guard under the leadership of Anastasio Somoza. With the marines withdrawn, Sandino announced his readiness to negotiate but was captured and executed by Somoza's National Guard. In 1936, Somoza seized the presidency, brutally exercising power that he and his two sons would not relinquish for another forty-three years until they were overthrown by the Sandinista revolutionary movement, named after Sandino, triggering another war with the United States under the presidency of Ronald Reagan.

No one had more firsthand experience intervening in other countries than Major General Smedley Butler. Butler enlisted in the marines at age sixteen when the 1898 war against Spain began. He first fought against the Filipino insurgents and then helped put down the Boxer Rebellion in China. Before long he was commanding one Central American intervention after another. Having already received two Medals of Honor, Butler commanded the 13th Regiment in France during the First World War. For that service he received the Army Distinguished Service Medal, the Navy Distinguished Service Medal, and the French Order of the Black Star. A tiny bulldog of a man, Butler wrote a book titled *War Is a Racket,* which is still quoted and admired by many military men.

General Smedley Butler fought in the Philippines, China, and Central America. He wrote that he was "a high class muscle-man for Big Business, for Wall Street and for the Bankers . . . a gangster for capitalism."

At the end of his long and highly decorated service, he reflected upon his years in uniform:

> I spent thirty-three years and four months in active military service as a member of this country's most agile military force, the Marine Corps. I served in all commissioned ranks from Second Lieutenant to Major-General. And during that period, I spent most of my time being a high class muscle-man for Big Business, for Wall Street and for the Bankers. In short, I was a racketeer, a gangster for capitalism.
>
> I helped make Mexico, especially Tampico, safe for American oil interests in 1914. I helped make Haiti and Cuba a decent place for the National City Bank boys to collect revenues in. I helped in the raping of half a dozen Central American republics for the benefits of Wall Street. The record of racketeering is long. I helped purify Nicaragua for the international banking house of Brown Brothers in 1909–1912. I brought light to the Dominican Republic for American sugar interests in 1916. In China I helped to see to it that Standard Oil went its way unmolested. . . .

During those years, I had, as the boys in the back room would say, a swell racket. Looking back on it, I feel that I could have given Al Capone a few hints. The best he could do was to operate his racket in three districts. I operated on three continents.[56]

Long after Butler's retirement, war would remain a "racket" as U.S. troops and intelligence operatives fanned out across the globe to defend the economic and geopolitical interests of American capital. They would occasionally improve the lives of those they left behind. But more often, as we detail in the following pages, they would leave misery and squalor. The record of the American Empire is not a pretty one. But it is one that must be faced honestly and forthrightly if the United States is ever to undertake the kind of fundamental structural reforms that will allow it to play a leading role in advancing rather than retarding the progress of humanity.

Chapter 1

WORLD WAR I:

Wilson vs. Lenin

The election of 1912 found Woodrow Wilson, a former president of Princeton University and governor of New Jersey, in a hard-fought four-party race against two former presidents—Theodore Roosevelt and William Howard Taft—and Socialist Eugene Debs. Though Wilson won the electoral college vote handily, the popular vote was closer: he received 42 percent to 27 percent for Roosevelt, the Progressive Party candidate, and 23 percent for Taft. Debs, running for a fourth time, tallied 6 percent of the vote.

Wilson would put his personal stamp on the office and the country to a much greater extent than his immediate predecessor or his successors. Descended from Presbyterian ministers on both sides of the family, Wilson could be strongly moralistic and infuriatingly and self-righteously inflexible. His rigidity was often fueled by the dangerous belief that he was carrying out God's plan. He shared his predecessors' sense of the United States' global mission. In 1907, the Princeton president declared, "The doors of the nations which are closed must be battered down. . . . Concessions obtained by financiers must be safeguarded by ministers of state, even if the sovereignty of unwilling nations be outraged in the process."[1] In keeping with that sentiment, he would repeatedly transgress against the sovereignty of unwilling nations. And he shared his southern forebears' sense of white racial superiority, taking steps to resegregate the federal government during his tenure in office. Wilson even screened D. W. Griffith's pioneering though notoriously racist film *Birth of a Nation* at the White House in 1915 for cabinet members and their families. In the film, a heroic Ku Klux Klan gallops in just in time to save white southerners, especially helpless women, from the clutches of brutish, lascivious freedmen and their corrupt white allies—a perverse view of history that was then being promulgated in less extreme terms by William

Dunning and his students at Columbia University. Upon viewing the film, Wilson commented, "It is like writing history with Lightning and my only regret is that it is all so terribly true."[2]

As Richard Hofstadter noted over seventy years ago, Wilson's "political roots were Southern, his intellectual traditions were English." Among the English thinkers, he was most taken with the conservative views of Walter Bagehot. Bagehot's influence was apparent in Wilson's 1889 study *The State,* in which Wilson wrote, "In politics nothing radically novel may safely be attempted. No result of value can ever be reached . . . except through slow and gradual development, the careful adaptations and nice modifications of growth." What he liked about the American Revolution was that, in his view, it wasn't revolutionary at all. The French Revolution, on the other hand, was an abomination. He deplored Thomas Jefferson's embrace of revolution in general and the French Revolution in particular. He disapproved of labor and agrarian radicalism and expressed greater sympathy for business than for labor. Overall, Wilson had a deep abhorrence of radical change in any form.[3]

Wilson's hatred of revolution and staunch defense of U.S. trade and investment would color his presidency and influence his policies both at home and abroad. "There is nothing in which I am more interested than the fullest development of the trade of this country and its righteous conquest of foreign markets," he told the Foreign Trade Convention in 1914.[4]

Together these views shaped Wilson's policy toward Mexico, where American bankers and businessmen, particularly oilmen, had a major stake in the outcome of the revolution. Between 1900 and 1910, U.S. investments in Mexico doubled to nearly $2 billion, giving Americans ownership of approximately 43 percent of Mexican property values, 10 percent more than Mexicans themselves owned.[5] William Randolph Hearst alone held over 17 million acres.

U.S. and British corporations had thrived under Porfirio Díaz's three-decade dictatorship, laying siege to almost all of Mexico's minerals, railroads, and oil.[6] They had reason for concern when Francisco Madero's revolutionary forces overthrew Díaz in 1911. Many U.S. businessmen quickly soured on the new regime and applauded when Victoriano Huerta, with the support of U.S. Ambassador to Mexico Henry Lane Wilson, ousted Madero in the waning days of the Taft administration.[7] But Woodrow Wilson, upon coming to power, not only refused to recognize the new government, whose legitimacy he questioned, he sent tens of thousands of troops to the Mexican border and warships to the oil fields near Tampico and the port of Vera Cruz.

Wilson, who had once voiced a desire to teach Latin Americans "to elect good men,"[8] itched for an excuse to intervene directly, overthrow Huerta, and tutor the backward Mexicans in good government. He got what he wanted on

April 14, 1914, when U.S. sailors who rowed to Tampico were arrested for being in a war zone without a permit. When the Mexican commanding officer released them a couple hours later, he apologized both to them and to their U.S. commanding officer, Admiral Henry Mayo, who refused to accept the apology in the face of such an insult. Mayo demanded that the Mexican forces give a twenty-one-gun salute to the American flag. Instead, General Huerta added his apology and promised to punish the responsible Mexican officer. Over the objections of Secretary of State William Jennings Bryan and Secretary of the Navy Josephus Daniels, Wilson backed Mayo. He rejected Huerta's offer of a reciprocal salute by the two sides and asked Congress to authorize the U.S. military to exact "the fullest recognition of the rights and dignity of the United States."[9] Congress eagerly complied. Wilson sent a force of seven battleships, four fully manned marine troop transports, and numerous destroyers to Mexico. When Mexicans at Vera Cruz resisted U.S. seizure of a customhouse, over 150 were killed. Six thousand marines occupied Vera Cruz for seven months.

In August 1914, U.S.-backed Venustiano Carranza replaced Huerta. But Carranza, a staunch nationalist, refused to bargain with Wilson, who then threw his support behind Pancho Villa, beginning a bungled series of political and military interventions into the Mexican Revolution.

While the United States was busy policing its neighbors to the south, far more ominous developments were occurring in Europe. The assassination of Archduke Franz Ferdinand of Austria by a Serbian fanatic on June 28, 1914, triggered a chain of events that, in August, plunged the world into the most brutal orgy of bloodshed and destruction humanity had yet seen. That predominantly European bloodletting—the Great War, World War I—would be only the start of a century of unending warfare and horrific violence, human and technological barbarism on an unimaginable scale, that would later come to be known as the American Century.

The twentieth century dawned with a rush of optimism. War seemed a distant relic of a cruel and primitive past. Many people shared the optimistic belief propounded by Norman Angell in his 1910 book *The Great Illusion* that civilization had advanced beyond the point where war was possible. Such optimism proved illusory indeed.

Europe was awash in imperial rivalries. Great Britain, with its powerful navy, had reigned supreme in the nineteenth century. But its economic model of cannibalizing the economies of increasing parts of the globe and not investing in its own homegrown manufacturing was failing. Reflecting Great Britain's ossified social order and lack of investment at home was the fact that, in 1914, only 1 percent of young Brits graduated from high schools compared with 9 percent of their U.S. counterparts.[10] As a result, Great Britain was being eclipsed by the United States in terms of industrial production, and, more ominously, its continental rival Germany was competing in the production of steel, electrical power, chemical energy, agriculture, iron, coal, and textiles. Germany's banks and railroads were growing, and in the battle for oil, the newest strategic fuel that was necessary to power modern navies, Germany's merchant fleet was rapidly gaining on Great Britain's. Great Britain was now 65 percent dependent on U.S. oil and 20 percent on Russian and was coveting potential new reserves of the Middle East, which were part of the tottering Ottoman Empire.

A latecomer to the imperial land grab, Germany felt cheated of its due. It intended to right that wrong. Its economic and political penetration of the Ottoman Empire worried Great Britain. It set its sights on Africa. It wanted more.

Other troubling signs appeared. A European arms race was occurring on land and, especially, at sea, where Great Britain and Germany battled for naval dominance. Great Britain's big-gun dreadnought class of battleships gave it the upper hand—for now. And European nations conscripted young men into vast standing armies.

Entangling alliances threatened to turn local conflicts into global conflagrations. And in August 1914, when Austria-Hungary declared war against Serbia, what looked like a third Balkan war quickly spiraled out of control. The Central Powers—Germany, Turkey, and Austria-Hungary—lined up against the Triple Entente—France, Great Britain, Italy, Japan, and Russia. Others would soon join. The battlefields would run red with blood.

Only Europe's large socialist and labor parties and trade unions could prevent the slaughter. Many belonged to the socialist Second International. They knew that the most important conflict was between capital and labor, not German workers and their British counterparts. They pledged that if the capitalists went to war, the workers would refuse to follow. Why, they asked, should workers die to enrich their exploiters? Many supported a general strike. The more radical, like Vladimir Lenin and Rosa Luxemburg, vowed, if war started, to overthrow the capitalist regimes. Hopes of stopping the madness rested with Germany, where the Social Democrats were the largest party in parliament, and with France.

But those hopes were crushed when German socialists, claiming they had to defend the country against the Russian hordes, voted for war credits and the French, vowing to defend against the autocratic Germans, did the same. Only in Russia and Serbia did the socialists stand true. In country after country, nationalism trumped internationalism, loyalty to nation outweighed loyalty to class. Europe's naive young men marched off to die for God, glory, greed, and defense of the fatherland. Humanity was dealt a blow from which it has never fully recovered.

The slaughter was on as civilization plunged into what Henry James described as "this abyss of blood and darkness."[11] American social reformer Reverend John Haynes Holmes expressed the crushing impact it had on reformers everywhere: "suddenly, in the wink of an eye, three hundred years of progress is tossed into the melting-pot. Civilization is all gone, and barbarism come."[12]

Most Americans sympathized with the Allies against the Central Powers, but few clamored to join the fight. Americans of all political persuasions feared getting dragged into Europe's bloodletting. Eugene Debs urged workers to oppose the war, wisely observing "Let the capitalists do their own fighting and furnish their own corpses and there will never be another war on the face of the earth."[13] As reports of the fighting filtered in, antiwar sentiment held strong. The most popular song of 1915 was "I Didn't Raise My Boy to Be a Soldier."

Despite overwhelming sympathy for the Allies, the United States declared neutrality in the war. But many Americans, particularly those of German, Irish, and Italian heritage, sided with the Central Powers. "We have to be neutral," Wilson explained, "since otherwise our mixed populations would wage war on each other."[14] It was, however, a neutrality in principle more than in practice. Economic interests clearly placed the United States in the Allied camp. Between 1914, when the war began, and 1917, when the United States entered, U.S. banks loaned $2.5 billion to the Allies but only $27 million to the Central Powers. The House of Morgan was especially involved, serving as the British government's sole purchasing agent between 1915 and 1917. Eighty-four percent of Allied munitions bought in the United States during those years passed through Morgan hands.[15] Overall, the $3 billion the United States was selling to Great Britain and France by 1916 dwarfed the miniscule $1 million it sold to Germany and Austria-Hungary. Although deep-seated resentments toward Great Britain, stemming from the Revolutionary period and the War of 1812, had not completely abated, most Americans identified the Allied nations as democracies and Germany as a repressive autocracy. Czarist Russia's involvement on the Allied side made it difficult to draw such clear lines. And both sides regularly violated the United States' neutral rights. Great Britain, relying on its superior naval power, launched a blockade of northern European ports. Germany retaliated with a U-boat (the German word for "submarine" was *Unterseeboot*) campaign that threatened neutral shipping. Wilson accepted the Allied blockade but protested vigorously against Germany's actions. Bryan foresaw clearly that Wilson's tilt toward the Allies would drag the United States into the war and tried to maintain a more evenhanded approach. He had opposed allowing loans to the combatants, warning Wilson, "Money is the worst of all contrabands because it commands everything else."[16] Though intent on remaining neutral so that he could help mediate an end to the war, Wilson rejected Bryan's effort to bar U.S. citizens from traveling on belligerents' ships.

In May 1915, Germany sank the British liner *Lusitania,* leaving 1,200 dead, including 128 Americans. Roosevelt called for war. Despite initial disclaimers, the ship was in fact carrying a large cargo of arms to Great Britain. Bryan demanded that Wilson condemn the British blockade of Germany as well as the German attack, seeing both as infringements of neutral rights. When Wilson refused, Bryan resigned in protest. Though Wilson had won reelection in 1916 on the slogan "He kept us out of war," he was increasingly coming to believe that if the United States didn't join the war, it would be denied a role in shaping the postwar world.[17]

On January 22, 1917, Wilson dramatically delivered the first formal presidential address to the Senate since the days of George Washington. He laid bare his soaring vision for peace and the future. He called for "peace without victory" based on core American principles: self-determination, freedom of the seas, and an open world with no entangling alliances. The centerpiece of such a world would be a league of nations that could enforce the peace, a demand initially advanced by groups within America's peace movement such as the Woman's Peace Party.

When he concluded, the Senate erupted in applause. Senator John Shafroth of Colorado called it "the greatest message of a century."[18] The *Atlanta Constitution* wrote, " 'Startling,' 'staggering,' 'astounding,' 'the noblest utterance that has fallen from human lips since the Declaration of Independence,' were among the expressions of senators. The president himself after his address said: 'I have said what everybody has been longing for, but has thought impossible. Now it appears to be possible.'"[19] Despite the Republicans' carping, Wilson's peace message struck the right chord with most Americans. But the Europeans, having shed rivers of blood in two and a half years of fighting, were not feeling so magnanimous. French writer Anatole France observed that "peace without victory" was like "bread without yeast," "a camel without humps," or "a town without brothel . . . an insipid thing" that would be "fetid, ignominious, obscene, fistulous, hemorrhoidal."[20]

Germany's resumption of submarine warfare on January 31, 1917, after a hiatus of almost a year, and its clumsy appeal to Mexico for a wartime military alliance that would facilitate a Mexican reconquest of Texas, New Mexico, and Arizona, intensified anti-German sentiment and heightened the pressure on Wilson to intervene. But Wilson's real motive was his belief that only by entering the war could he be guaranteed a voice in negotiations.[21] When Jane Addams and other leaders of the Emergency Peace Federation visited Wilson at the White House on February 28, the president explained that "as head of a nation participating in the war, the President of the United States would have a seat at the Peace Table, but that if he remained the representative of a neutral country he could at best only 'call through a crack in the door.' The appeal he made was, in substance, that the foreign policies which we so extravagantly admired could have a chance if he were there to push and to defend them, but not otherwise." [22]

On April 2, 1917, Wilson asked Congress for a declaration of war, saying, "the world must be made safe for democracy." Six opposed it in the Senate, including Robert La Follette of Wisconsin, and fifty voted against it in the House, including Jeannette Rankin of Montana, the first woman elected to Congress. Opponents attacked Wilson as a tool of Wall Street. "We are about to put the dollar sign on the American flag," charged Senator George Norris of Nebraska.[23] La Follette exaggerated when claiming that the American people would vote against the war by more than a ten-to-one margin, but opposition did run deep. Despite government appeals for a million volunteers, reports of the horrors of trench warfare and poison gas dampened enthusiasm. Only 73,000 signed up in the first six weeks, forcing Congress to institute a draft. Among those who did volunteer was future historian William Langer, who later remembered "the eagerness of the men to get to France and above all to reach the front. One would think," he reasoned,

> that, after almost four years of war, after the most detailed and realistic
> accounts of murderous fighting on the Somme and around Verdun, to say
> nothing of the day-to-day agony of trench warfare, it would have been all
> but impossible to get anyone to serve without duress. But it was not so.
> We and many thousands of others volunteered. . . . I can hardly remember
> a single instance of serious discussion of American policy or of larger war
> issues. We men, most of us young, were simply fascinated by the prospect
> of adventure and heroism. Most of us, I think, had the feeling that life, if
> we survived, would run in the familiar, routine channel. Here was our one
> great chance for excitement and risk. We could not afford to pass it up.[24]

Among those offering to serve was fifty-eight-year-old Teddy Roosevelt, who visited Wilson on April 10 and requested permission to lead a division of volunteers into battle. Roosevelt was so eager to go to the front that he even promised to cease his attacks on Wilson. Wilson denied his request. Roosevelt accused him of basing his decision on political calculations. Among those who criticized Wilson's decision was soon-to-be French prime minister Georges Clemenceau, who thought Roosevelt's presence would be inspirational.

Imbued with the martial spirit and patriotism of their father, all four of Roosevelt's sons did enlist and see combat. Ted, Jr., and Archie were wounded in action. Ted was also gassed at Cantigny. Twenty-year old Quentin, the youngest of the children, was killed when his plane was shot down in July 1918, a blow from which his father would never recover. Theodore Roosevelt's health declined rapidly and he died within six months at age sixty, having been able to witness, from a safe distance, the horrors of modern warfare.

Unfortunately for Wilson, not all Americans were as gung ho as the Roosevelts. Because antiwar sentiment had run so deep in much of the country, the Wilson administration felt compelled to take extraordinary measures to convince the skeptical public of the righteousness of the cause. For that purpose, the government established an official propaganda agency—the Committee on Public Information (CPI)—headed by Denver newspaperman George Creel. The committee recruited 75,000 volunteers, known as "four-minute men," who delivered short patriotic speeches in public venues across the country, including shopping districts, streetcars, movie theaters, and churches. It flooded the nation with propaganda touting the war as a noble crusade for democracy and encouraged newspapers to print stories highlighting German atrocities. It also asked Americans to inform on fellow citizens who criticized the war effort. CPI advertisements urged magazine readers to report to the Justice Department "the man who spreads pessimistic stories . . . cries for peace, or belittles our efforts to win the war."[25]

Underlying Wilson's wartime declarations and the CPI's emphasis on promoting "democracy" was the realization that for many Americans democracy had become a kind of "secular religion" that could exist only within a capitalist system. Many also associated it with "Americanism." It meant more than a set of identifiable institutions. As Creel said on one occasion, it is a "theory of spiritual progress." On another occasion, he explained, "Democracy is a religion with me, and throughout my whole adult life I have preached America as the hope of the world."[26]

Newspapers voluntarily fell in line behind the propaganda effort as they had in 1898 and would in all future U.S. wars. Victor Clark's study of the wartime press for the National Board for Historical Service (NBHS) remarkably but revealingly concluded that the "voluntary co-operation of the newspaper publishers of America resulted in a more effective standardization of the information and arguments presented to the American people, than existed under the nominally strict military control exercised in Germany."[27]

Historians also rallied to the cause. Creel established the CPI's Division of Civic and Educational Cooperation under the leadership of University of Minnesota historian Guy Stanton Ford. Several of the nation's leading historians, including Charles Beard, Carl Becker, John R. Commons, J. Franklin Jameson, and Andrew McLaughlin, assisted Ford in simultaneously promoting U.S. aims and demonizing the enemy. Ford's introduction to one CPI pamphlet decries the "Pied Pipers of Prussianism," declaring, "Before them is the war god, to whom they have offered up their reason and their humanity; behind them the

The Committee on Public Information, the government's official wartime propaganda agency, recruited 75,000 volunteers, known as "four-minute men," to deliver short patriotic speeches across the country. They flooded the nation with pro-war propaganda and urged Americans to inform on "the man who spreads pessimistic stories . . . cries for peace, or belittles our efforts to win the war."

misshapen image they have made of the German people, leering with blood-stained visage over the ruins of civilization." [28]

The CPI's penultimate pamphlet, "The German-Bolshevik Conspiracy," proved to be its most controversial. Based on documents obtained by the head of the CPI's foreign section and former Associate Chairman Edgar Sisson, the pamphlet alleged that Lenin and Trotsky and their associates were paid German agents who were betraying the Russian people on behalf of the imperial German government. The documents, for which Sisson paid lavishly, were widely known to be forgeries in Europe and were similarly suspected by the State Department. Wilson's chief foreign policy advisor, Colonel Edward House, wrote in his diary that he told the president that their publication signified "a virtual declaration of war upon the Bolshevik Government" and Wilson said he understood. Publication was withheld for four months. Wilson and the CPI ignored all warnings and released them to the press in seven installments beginning on September 15, 1918.[29] Most U.S. newspapers dutifully reported the story uncritically and unquestioningly. The *New York Times*, for example, ran a story under the headline "Documents Prove Lenine and Trotzky [*sic*] Hired by Germans."[30] But controversy quickly erupted as the *New York Evening Post* challenged their authenticity, noting that "the most important charges in the documents brought forward by Mr. Sisson were published in Paris months ago, and have, on the whole, been discredited."[31] Within a week, the *Times* and the *Washington Post* were both reporting charges by S. Nuorteva, the head of the Finnish Information Bureau, that the documents were widely known to be "brazen forgeries."[32] Sisson and Creel defended their authenticity. Creel responded angrily to Nuorteva's allegations: "That is a lie! The government of the United States put out these documents and their authenticity is backed by the government. This is bolshevik propaganda and when an unsupported bolsheviki attacks them it is hardly worth bothering about."[33] He flailed wildly in a threatening letter to the editor of the *Evening Post*:

> I say to you flatly that the New York Evening Post cannot escape the charge
> of having given aid and comfort to the enemies of the United States in
> an hour of national crisis. These documents were published with the full
> authority of the Government behind them. They were not given out until
> there was every conviction that they were absolutely genuine. . . . I do not
> make the charge that the New York Evening Post is German or that it has
> taken German money, but I do say that the service it has rendered to the
> enemies of the United States would have been purchased gladly by those
> enemies, and in terms of unrest and industrial stability this supposedly
> American paper has struck a blow at America more powerful [than] could
> possibly have been dealt by German hands.[34]

Acceding to Creel's request, the NBHS set up a committee, comprised of Jameson, the head of the Department of Historical Research of the Carnegie Institution, and Samuel Harper, a professor of Russian language at the University of Chicago, to review the documents. They confirmed the authenticity of most of the fraudulent documents. *The Nation* charged that the documents and NBHS report spoiled "the good name of the Government and the integrity of American historical scholarship."[35] In 1956, George Kennan proved once and for all what most suspected: the documents were indeed forgeries.[36]

Historians' and other academics' complicity in selling wartime propaganda brought well-deserved opprobrium down on their heads during the interwar period. In 1927, H. L. Mencken's *American Mercury* deplored the knee-jerk patriotic conformity that sullied all the country's top colleges and universities. Charles Angoff wrote, "Bacteriologists, physicists and chemists vied with philosophers, philologians and botanists in shouting maledictions upon the Hun, and thousands took to snooping upon their brethren as entertained the least doubt about the sanctity of the war. . . . Such guilt against American idealism was sufficient cause, in the eyes of all patriotic university presidents and boards of trustees, for the immediate dismissal of the traitors."[37]

Despite the well-deserved criticism, controlling public opinion became a central element in all future war planning. Harold Lasswell identified its importance in his 1927 book *Propaganda Technique in the World War*. Lasswell wrote:

During the war period it came to be recognized that the mobilization of
men and means was not sufficient; there must be a mobilization of opinion.
Power over opinion, as over life and property, passed into official hands,
because the danger from license was greater than the danger of abuse.
Indeed, there is no question but that government management of opinion
is the unescapable corollary of large-scale modern war. The only question is
the degree to which the government should try to conduct its propaganda
secretly, and the degree to which it should conduct it openly.[38]

Campuses became hotbeds of intolerance. University professors who spoke
against the war were fired. Others were cowed into silence. As Columbia University President Nicholas Murray Butler exclaimed in announcing the end of academic freedom on campus:

What had been tolerated before became intolerable now. What had
been wrongheadedness was now sedition. What had been folly was now
treason . . . there is and will be no place in Columbia University, either on
the rolls of its Faculties or on the rolls of its students, for any person who
opposes or counsels opposition to the effective enforcement of the laws
of the United States, or who acts, speaks, or writes treason. The separation
of any such person from Columbia University will be as speedy as the
discovery of his offense.[39]

This was no idle threat. The following October, Columbia announced the
firing of two prominent faculty members for their outspoken opposition to the
war. Professors James McKeen Cattell, one of the nation's leading psychologists,
and Henry Wadsworth Longfellow Dana of the Department of English and
Comparative Literature, a grandson of the poet, were condemned by the faculty
and trustees as well as by Butler. The official university statement charged that
they "had done grave injury to the university by their public agitation against
the conduct of the war." The *New York Times* commented, "Since the declaration of war against Germany Professor Cattell has been especially obnoxious to
the Columbia Faculty because of his unhesitating denunciation of a war policy
by our Government." Dana was ousted because of his active role in the antiwar
People's Council.[40] Applauding Columbia's action, the *Times* editorialized, "The
fantasies of 'academic freedom' . . . cannot protect a professor who counsels
resistance to the law and speaks, writes, disseminates treason. That a teacher of
youth should teach sedition and treason, that he should infect, or seek to infect,
youthful minds with ideas fatal to their duty to the country, is intolerable."[41]

The following week, Professor Charles Beard, arguably the nation's leading historian in the first half of the twentieth century, resigned in protest. Although an early and fervent supporter of the war and a harsh critic of German imperialism, he condemned the control of the university by a "small and active group of trustees who have no standing in the world of education, who are reactionary and visionless in politics, narrow and mediaeval in religion." Beard explained that, despite his own enthusiastic support for the war, "thousands of my countrymen do not share this view. Their opinions cannot be changed by curses or bludgeons. Arguments addressed to their reason and understandings are the best hope."[42] Beard had already incurred the ire of several trustees the previous spring when he declared at a conference, "If we have to suppress everything we don't like to hear, this country is on a pretty wobbly basis. This country was founded on disrespect and the denial of authority, and it is no time to stop free discussion." At least two other faculty members also resigned in solidarity, and historian James H. Robinson and philosopher John Dewey condemned the firings and expressed regret at Beard's resignation.[43] In December, Beard charged that reactionary trustees saw the war as an opportunity "to drive out or humiliate or terrorize every man who held progressive, liberal, unconventional views on political matters in no way connected with the war." Similar purges of left-wing professors, as well as the application of "very strong" pressure on grammar and high school teachers, occurred throughout the country.[44]

The War Department went one step further, turning the docile campuses into military training grounds. On October 1, 1918, 140,000 students on more than five hundred campuses across the country were simultaneously inducted into the army as part of the Student Army Training Corps (SATC). Given the rank of private, they were thereafter educated, housed, clothed, equipped, and fed at government expense.[45] They also received privates' pay. The *Chicago Tribune* reported, "Rah-rah days are over for American college boys. . . . College hereafter is to mean business—largely intensive preparation for the business of war."[46] Eleven hours per week were slated for military drills, on top of forty-two hours of courses on largely military-oriented "essential" and "allied" subjects. As part of this training, students at participating institutions were required to take a propaganda-laden "War Issues Course."[47]

Having drawn blood in his personal campaign to make the universities "safe for democracy," Butler set his sights higher, calling for the ouster of Robert La Follette from the U.S. Senate for his treasonous opposition to the war. Butler told three thousand wildly cheering delegates to the annual convention of the American Bankers Association in Atlantic City that they "might just as well put poison into the food of every boy" who went to war "as to permit this man to make war upon the nation in the halls of congress."[48] La Follette was also targeted by members of the University of Wisconsin faculty, over 90 percent of

Wisconsin's Robert "Fighting Bob" La Follette was one of six senators who voted against U.S. entry into World War I.

whom signed a petition condemning his antiwar position and several of whom began a drive to "put La Follette and all his supporters out of business," according to one of the campaign's leaders.[49]

La Follette survived the national campaign to force his ouster, but the Bill of Rights didn't fare as well. Congress passed some of the most repressive legislation in the country's history. The Espionage Act of 1917 and the Sedition Act of 1918 curbed speech and created a climate of intolerance toward dissent. Under the Espionage Act, people faced $10,000 fines and up to twenty years in jail for obstructing military operations in wartime. It targeted "Whoever, when the United States is at war, shall willfully cause or attempt to cause insubordination, disloyalty, mutiny, or refusal of duty in the military or naval forces of the United States, or shall willfully obstruct the recruiting or enlistment service of the U.S."[50] The act empowered Postmaster General Albert Burleson, who, socialist Norman Thomas said, "didn't know socialism from rheumatism," to ban from the mail any literature he believed advocated treason or insurrection or opposed the draft.[51] The following year, Attorney General Thomas W. Gregory convinced Congress to expand the act to ban anyone who might "utter, print, write, or publish any disloyal, profane, scurrilous, or abusive language about the form of government of the United States or the Constitution of the United States, or the military or naval forces of the United States . . . and whoever shall by word or act support or favor the cause of any country with which the United States is at war or by word or act oppose the cause of the United States." [52]

The agents hired to enforce this crackdown on dissent were part of a burgeoning federal bureaucracy. The federal budget, which was less than $1 billion in 1913, had ballooned to over $13 billion five years later.

Hundreds of people were jailed for criticizing the war, including IWW leader "Big Bill" Haywood and Socialist Eugene Debs. Debs spoke out repeatedly against the war and was finally arrested in June 1918 after addressing a large crowd outside the prison in Canton, Ohio, where three Socialists were being held for opposing the draft. Debs ridiculed the idea that the United States was a democracy when it jailed people for expressing their views: "They tell us that we live in a great free republic; that our institutions are democratic; that we are a free and self-governing people. This is too much, even for a joke." [53] He spoke only briefly of the war itself: "Wars throughout history have been waged for conquest and plunder. . . . And that is war in a nutshell. The master class has always declared the wars; the subject class has always fought the battles." [54]

The U.S. attorney for northern Ohio, E. S. Wertz, ignoring the advice of the Justice Department, had Debs indicted on ten violations of the Espionage Act. In solidarity with his jailed comrades around the world, Debs pleaded guilty to the charges. He told the jury, "I have been accused of obstructing the war. I admit it. Gentlemen, I abhor war. I would oppose war if I stood alone. . . . I have sympathy with the suffering, struggling people everywhere. It does not make any difference under what flag they were born, or where they live." Prior to sentencing, he addressed the judge:

> Your honor, years ago I recognized my kinship within all living beings, and
> I made up my mind that I was not one bit better than the meanest on earth.
> I said then, and I say now, that while there is a lower class, I am in it; while
> there is a criminal element, I am of it; while there is a soul in prison, I am
> not free. [55]

Upbraiding those "who would strike the sword from the hand of this nation while she is engaged in defending herself against a foreign and brutal power," the judge sentenced Debs to ten years in prison. [56]

Socialist publications were banned from the mail. Patriotic thugs and local authorities broke into socialist organizations and union halls. Labor organizers and antiwar activists were beaten and sometimes killed. The *New York Times* called the Butte, Montana, lynching of IWW Executive Board member Frank

Under the 1917 Espionage Act, the U.S. imprisoned hundreds of draft protesters and war critics, including IWW leader "Big Bill" Haywood and the Socialist Eugene Debs. Debs (pictured here addressing a crowd in Chicago in 1912) had urged workers to oppose the war, proclaiming "Let the capitalists do their own fighting and furnish their own corpses and there will never be another war on the face of the earth."

Little "a deplorable and detestable crime, whose perpetrators should be found, tried, and punished by the law and justice they have outraged." But the *Times* was far more upset by the fact that IWW-led strikes were crippling the war effort and concluded, "The IWW agitators are in effect, and perhaps in fact, agents of Germany. The Federal authorities should make short work of these treasonable conspirators against the United States."[57]

All things German were vilified in a wave of intolerance masquerading as patriotism. Schools, many of which now demanded loyalty oaths from teachers, banned the German language from their curricula. Iowa, not taking any chances, went further and, under the 1918 "Babel Proclamation," banned the speaking of all foreign languages in public and over the telephone. Nebraska followed suit. Libraries across the country discarded German books, and orchestras dropped German composers from their repertoires. Just as French fries would later be renamed "freedom fries" by a know-nothing Congress furious at French opposition to the 2003 invasion of Iraq, their World War I counterparts renamed hamburgers "liberty sandwiches," sauerkraut "liberty cabbage," German measles "liberty measles," and German shepherds "police dogs."[58] German Americans faced discrimination in all aspects of life.

Given the widespread pressure for "100 percent Americanism," it is no surprise that dissidents were not only ostracized, they were occasionally murdered by patriotic mobs.[59] The *Washington Post* assured its readers that occasional lynchings were a small price to pay for a healthy upsurge of patriotism. The *Post* editorialized in April 1918, "In spite of excesses such as lynchings, it is a healthful and wholesome awakening in the interior part of the country. Enemy propaganda must be stopped, even if a few lynchings may occur."[60]

The nation's heartland had indeed been slow to rally to the cause. Early on, the conservative Akron, Ohio, *Beacon-Journal* noted that there was "scarcely a political observer . . . but what will admit that were an election to come now a mighty tide of socialism would inundate the Middle West." The country had "never embarked upon a more unpopular war," it contended. Antiwar rallies drew thousands. Socialist Party candidates saw their votes increase exponentially in 1917 in cities throughout the country. Ten Socialists won seats in the New York State Legislature.[61]

Despite the ostracism, mass arrests, and organized violence, the Socialists and radical laborites known as Wobblies would not be silenced. While some Americans marched off to war to the strains of the hit song "Over There," the Wobblies responded with a parody of "Onward Christian Soldiers" titled "Christians at War," which began "Onward, Christian soldiers! Duty's way is plain; Slay your Christian neighbors, or by them be slain." And ended with "History will say of you: 'That pack of God damned fools.'"[62]

Wilson's lofty rhetoric and assurances about fighting a war to end all wars seduced many of the nation's leading progressives, including John Dewey, Herbert Croly, and Walter Lippmann. They convinced themselves that war afforded a unique opportunity to implement long-desired reforms at home. Antiwar midwestern progressives like Senators La Follette and Norris more accurately understood that war presaged the death knell of meaningful reform.

Among those who seized the opportunity to implement long-sought changes were the moral reformers, especially those who viewed the war as an opportunity to combat sexual vice. Ostensibly concerned about the health of the soldiers, they waged an aggressive campaign against prostitution and venereal disease. Red-light districts around the country were shut down, driving prostitutes underground and into the hands of pimps and other exploiters.[63] The crackdown intensified after the passage of the Chamberlain-Kahn Act in 1918, according to which any woman walking alone near a military base was subject to arrest, incarceration, and a forced gynecological exam, which reformers condemned as "speculum rape." Those found to have venereal disease were quarantined in federal institutions.[64]

The Commission on Training Camp Activities (CTCA) also endeavored to rein in male sexuality with an abstinence campaign that impugned the patriotism of soldiers who contracted venereal disease. The CTCA plastered training camp

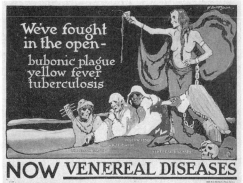

*WWI anti-venereal disease posters. Moral reformers seized on
the war as an opportunity to implement long-sought changes. The
Commission on Training Camp Activities (CTCA) endeavored to
rein in male sexuality with an abstinence campaign that impugned
the patriotism of soldiers who contracted venereal disease.*

walls with posters reading "A German Bullet is Cleaner than a Whore" and "A Soldier who gets a dose is a Traitor." One pamphlet asked, "How can you look the flag in the face if you were dirty with gonorrhea?"[65] While VD rates among soldiers did not rise as rapidly as some feared, pregnancy rates among high school girls living in the vicinity of military bases certainly did.

General John "Black Jack" Pershing, who commanded the American Expeditionary Forces (AEF) during the war, tried to ride herd on troops when they got to France—a task that proved more difficult than defeating the Germans on the battlefield. CTCA head Raymond Fosdick took notice of the vast difference between French and American sexual attitudes. The French, he observed, "felt that an army could not get along without sexual indulgence and that to attempt to carry out such a policy was to court discontent, a lowering of morale and health standards, and perhaps even mutiny." French Premier Clemenceau offered to set up licensed brothels for U.S. soldiers like the ones that serviced his own fighting men. Upon receiving the letter with Clemenceau's offer, Secretary of War Newton Baker reportedly blurted out, "For God's sake ... don't show this to the President or he'll stop the war."[66]

The warnings proved futile. Those afflicted were segregated and ostracized. Moral reformers feared the veterans would return home and infect American women. But that was only one concern. Reformers also worried that the troops, having discovered what some called the "French Way," would foist their new-found appetite for oral sex on innocent American girls. Colonel George Walker of the urological department fretted, "When one thinks of the hundreds and hundreds of thousands of young men who have returned to the United States with those new and degenerate ideas sapping their sources of self-respect and thereby lessening their powers of moral resistance, one indeed is justified in becoming alarmed."[67]

For the most part, reformers' efforts to use the war as a laboratory for social and economic experimentation were cut short by the limited duration of U.S. involvement. The war years did, however, bring unprecedented collusion between large corporations and the government in an attempt to rationalize and stabilize the economy, control unfettered competition, and guarantee profits— something that the top bankers and corporate executives had striven for decades to achieve. As a result, American banks and corporations thrived during the war, with munitions makers leading the pack. Randolph Bourne, who decried fellow progressives' fraudulent rationales for defending the war in his scathing article "Twilight of Idols," observed elsewhere that "war is the health of the state."[68]

While reformers were hard at work, U.S. troops finally began arriving in Europe, where they contributed significantly to the Allied victory. Their arrival boosted Allied morale, and they assisted in winning some major battles. Arriving late, they managed to avoid the most brutal trench warfare Europeans on both sides had endured during the darkest times in 1916, when Great Britain suffered 60,000 casualties in a single day at the Somme. France and Germany together suffered almost a million casualties during the Battle of Verdun. Ordered to charge into the teeth of German machine guns and artillery, France lost half of its young men between the ages of fifteen and thirty. Americans first saw mean-ingful action in May 1918, six months before the war's end, when they helped beleaguered French forces turn the tide and repulse the Germans along the Marne. In September, 600,000 Americans fought valiantly to break through the German lines. The Germans surrendered on November 11, 1918. In all, of the 2 million U.S. soldiers who reached France, over 116,000 died and 204,000 were wounded. By comparison, European casualty figures were truly staggering— perhaps as many as 10 million dead soldiers and 20 million dead civilians, the latter due mostly to disease and starvation.

Had the war dragged on, the casualty figures might have been much higher. The unprecedented wartime mobilization of science and technology had already begun to transform the nature of warfare. Even more frightening innovations appeared to be imminent.

Atop that list was a new generation of chemical weapons. The taboo against using chemical weapons and other poisons in war dates back to the Greeks and Romans. Various efforts were made to codify this ban over the centuries. In 1863, the U.S. War Department's Lieber Code of Conduct prohibited "the use of poison in any manner, be it to poison wells, or food, or arms."[69] Just one year earlier, in 1862, John W. Doughty, a New York schoolteacher, had sent Secretary of War Edwin Stanton a design for a projectile filled with explosives in one compartment and liquid chlorine in the other that could be used to drive Confederate troops out of their fortifications. The War Department didn't pursue that suggestion or a later one by Forrest Shepherd, formerly a professor of economic geology and agricultural chemistry at Western Reserve University, to incapacitate Confederate soldiers with hydrogen chloride vapors. Other ideas for chemical weapons were also afoot during the Civil War. An 1862 article in *Scientific American* informed readers that "several incendiary and asphyxiating shells have been invented for the purpose of scattering liquid fire and noxious fumes around the space where they explode." The 1905 *Washington Evening Star* obituary of chemist William Tilden contained the followed intriguing tidbit: "Tilden had a scheme for producing chemically a means of settling wars quickly by making them terribly destructive. He is said to have interested General Grant in this matter, and at the suggestion of the latter finally abandoned it, because, as General Grant said, such a terrific agency for destroying human life should not be permitted to come into use by the civilized nations of the world."[70]

Others shared Grant's sense of how "civilized" nations should behave. The Hague Declaration Concerning Asphyxiating Gases of 1899 outlawed the wartime use of "projectiles" whose "sole object" was "the diffusion of asphyxiating or deleterious gases."[71]

Germany broke the spirit if not the letter of the Hague Convention when it first successfully used poison gas at the Second Battle of Ypres on April 22, 1915, following an abortive attempt at Bolimów on the eastern front. A yellowish green plume of chlorine gas blanketed French troops along four miles of trenches with catastrophic results. Over six hundred soon lay dead. Many more were temporarily blinded and a good number taken prisoner. The *Washington Post* headlined its front-page article "Crazed by Gas Bombs" and reported German threats that more potent gas weapons were on the way.[72] The Germans accused France of having been the first to use such weapons. The French had in fact made prior use of a chemical irritant on a limited scale at the start of the war. But Ypres represented a new departure. The *Post* reported that French soldiers died from "agonizing suffocation," their bodies turned black, green, or yellow, and were driven insane. "This use of poison gases," the *Post* predicted, "will doubtless go on record as the most striking and distinguishing novelty of the present war, just as every great war of the past has been marked by some peculiarly surprising method of destroying life."[73] The *New York Times* editorially condemned the use of poison gas not because it killed people more cruelly than other methods but because of the suffering of survivors, which was, "according to the victims and to expert observers, of a severity unparalleled in the dreadful annals of conflict." After this harsh condemnation, the *Times* threw up its hands and accepted that if one side used such weapons, "others will be obliged in self-defense to imitate the deplorable example. That, as everybody says, is war."[74] The British did indeed retaliate with poison gas at Loos in September, only to see the winds shift and the gas blown back into the British trenches, resulting in more British casualties than German.

European armies devised fairly effective countermeasures against these initially milder varieties of gases that at least reduced the number of fatalities. Between April 1915 and July 1917, British forces suffered 21,908 casualties and 1,895 deaths from gas warfare. On July 12, 1917, Germany unleashed much more potent mustard gas weapons against the British, again at Ypres. From that point until the end of the war the following November, British forces suffered 160,970 casualties and 4,167 deaths. Hence, by the time U.S. troops joined the fighting, deadlier varieties were being used by both sides, including those with phosgene, hydrogen cyanide, and mustard agents. Casualties skyrocketed, but, in relative terms, the number of fatalities declined sharply.[75] American chemists were determined to change that.

The United States launched a large-scale chemical warfare research program run initially under the aegis of several different departments until centralized under the newly established Chemical Warfare Service on June 28, 1918. Research programs were initially dispersed on a number of campuses before being consolidated in the Experiment Station at American University in Washington, D.C., in September 1917. Most of the nation's leading chemists descended on the campus to conduct the research. The effort eventually employed over 1,700 chemists, working out of more than sixty buildings, many hastily constructed. By war's end, 5,400 chemists were serving in the military in what was being labeled "the Chemist's War."[76]

In rushing to serve their country, American chemists were following in the footsteps of their European colleagues. Germany's chemical warfare research was centered in its prestigious Kaiser Wilhelm Institute for Physical Chemistry and Electrochemistry, where such luminaries as Fritz Haber, James Franck, Otto Hahn, Walther Nernst, and Richard Willstätter all lent their services. Institute Director Haber rallied the others behind the notion that "science . . . belonged to humanity in peacetime and the fatherland in war."[77] In Great Britain, scientists at thirty-three laboratories tested 150,000 organic and inorganic compounds in an effort to discover ever deadlier concoctions. The largest facility alone employed over a thousand scientists.[78]

Scientists of all nations were eager to do their part to assist the war effort.

Johns Hopkins physicist J. S. Ames wrote, "For the first time in the history of science men who are devoting their lives to it have an immediate opportunity of proving their worth to their country. It is a wonderful moment; and the universities of the country are seizing it." University of Chicago physicist Robert Millikan gushed, "the world has been waked up by the war to a new appreciation of what science can do."[79]

The Chemical Warfare Service prioritized speed over safety. As a result, numerous deaths were recorded, according to electrical engineer George Temple, who had been head of motor maintenance at "Camp American University." In an interview years later with the American University student newspaper, the *Eagle,* Temple recounted several incidents. In one, "three men were burned by a deadly dose of gas. The bodies were hauled away on a cart, the flesh 'jiggling off their bones.'"[80] Each morning, during roll call, workers were asked to volunteer for burning with experimental gases. Temple volunteered seven times. In the laboratories, leaks often occurred. Canaries were kept nearby. The death of a canary meant that it was time to evacuate the building.[81]

Temple described what it was like when researchers headed home after a day in the laboratories: "At the end of the day the camp personnel, their clothes impregnated by gas, would pile into the trolleys. As the trolley cars neared the downtown area, civilians began boarding them. Soon they were all sneezing or crying, depending upon the type of gas the soldiers had been working with."[82] Living near campus was not particularly safe either, as former U.S. Senator Nathan Scott discovered. Scott, his wife, and his sister were "gassed" by a "cloud" that escaped from one of the campus labs. Scott and his sister sought treatment from the Experiment Station doctor and then at a local hospital.[83]

Among those at American University was young Harvard chemist James Conant, who would go on to head U.S. scientific research during the next world war. His successful research on lewisite earned him a promotion in July 1918. The newly appointed twenty-five-year-old major was deployed to a Cleveland suburb to oversee a project to mass-produce lewisite. Working out of the factory of the Ben Hur Motor Company in Willoughby, Conant's team produced artillery shells and aerial bombs packed with the deadly substance, of which contact with even the smallest amount was believed to cause "intolerable agony and death after a few hours."[84]

The CWS established its largest production facility adjacent to the Aberdeen, Maryland, proving ground. In early 1919, the *New York Times* detailed the massive operation at the site officially known as the Edgewood Arsenal, which it described as "the largest poison gas factory on earth," producing three to four times as much as the British, French, and Germans combined. Reporter Richard Barry, who toured the facility, wrote, "I went through the hospitals and saw the men who had been struck down by the fiendish gases while at work; some with arms and legs and trunks shriveled and scarred as by a horrible fire, some with the deep suppurations still oozing after weeks of careful nursing." Barry guessed that the casualty rate might have exceeded that of any division in France.[85]

The facility was enormous, containing almost three hundred buildings serviced by twenty-eight miles of railway and fifteen miles of roads. It produced 200,000 chemical bombs and shells daily. Twelve hundred researchers and seven hundred assistants studied more than four thousand potentially poisonous substances.[86] Barry interviewed Colonel William H. Walker, the former chair of MIT's chemical engineering department, who served as commanding officer of the proving grounds. Walker reported that two months before the armistice, the United States had perfected a new deadly approach to using chemical weapons. The United States was prepared to have its planes drop one-ton mustard gas containers over fortified German cities. One ton of gas would engulf an area of an acre or more and, Walker assured readers, "not one living thing, not even a rat, would live through it." The new weapons were ready to deploy in September 1918, but the Allies balked at their use. England finally acceded, but France, fearing reprisals, withheld approval until the Allies had advanced sufficiently that the gas couldn't blow back into French territory and the Allies commanded "the air so as to insure safety from possible reprisals." Those conditions would not have been met until spring 1919.

At that point, Walker indicated, the United States would have had thousands of tons of mustard gas in France for the assault. "We could have wiped out any German city we pleased . . . and probably several of them, within a few hours of giving the release signal." Walker concluded that the Germans' knowledge of Allied plans was "a very big factor in [their] capitulation." On Armistice Day, the CWS shuttered its Edgewood operations with 2,500 tons of mustard gas sitting on the piers ready for shipment. "Somehow we had been cheated of our prey," Walker regretted, but he took comfort in his belief that the gas had expedited Germany's surrender.[87]

In the 1920 Army Reorganization Hearings, Assistant Secretary of War Benedict Crowell made clear how central the use of chemical warfare had been to the United States' planned 1919 offensive. Crowell testified, "Our offensive in 1919, in my opinion, would have been a walk to Berlin, due to chemical warfare. Of course, that was kept as a secret."[88]

During the war, the combatants used a total of 124,000 metric tons of thirty-nine different toxic agents, dispersed, for the most part, by 66 million artillery shells. Among the German casualties in October 1918 was Lance Corporal Adolf Hitler, who described the incident in *Mein Kampf*: "My eyes were transformed into glowing coals and the world had grown dark around me."[89]

Barry reported that when he visited the Edgewood plant in December 1918, it was "being dismantled. The machinery is being carefully taken apart, oiled, and wrapped and stored away—ready for the next war, should there ever be one." Disposing of the contaminated parts and gas would be a little more complicated, he mused, especially because the United States had produced enough gas to kill everyone in both North and South America.[90]

Walker understood that chemical weapons could be made much more deadly if dropped by airplanes. Science fiction writers like Jules Verne in his novel *Clipper of the Clouds* (1886) and H. G. Wells in *The War in the Air* (1908) foresaw the frightening potential for conventional aerial bombardment in future wars. The world got a small taste of what this would be like prior to World War I: aerial attack from hot-air balloons can actually be traced back to late-eighteenth-century France, and Austria later used hot-air balloons to bomb Venice in 1849. Between 1911 and 1913, Italy, France, and Bulgaria employed aerial bombardment on a small scale in local skirmishes.[91] The prospect of using planes to drop chemical weapons was even more frightening.

World War I provided the first real showcase of air warfare, though it only offered a small glimpse of what was to come. Germany struck first on August 6, 1914. Its zeppelins dropped bombs on Liège, Belgium. Germany was the first country to bomb civilians from the air when an August 1914 attack on a Parisian railway station missed its target and killed a woman. In September, during the First Battle of the Marne, German airmen bombed Paris on several occasions. The first Allied urban aerial bombing came in December, when French airmen bombed Freiburg. By spring 1918, German bombing had injured over four thousand British civilians and left more than one thousand dead. Though used on a limited scale, the potential for air warfare was apparent. British forces had only 110 warplanes when the war began. But Great Britain, along with France, produced 100,000 more before the war was over. Germany produced 44,000.[92]

During the 1920s, Great Britain made extensive use of aerial bombardment to defend and police its far-flung empire in places as disparate as Afghanistan, Egypt, India, Yemen, Somaliland, and especially Iraq, which British forces occupied following the defeat of the Ottoman Empire. Under the euphemism of "air policing," the Royal Air Force conducted an extensive bombing campaign against Iraqis resisting British colonialism. The commander of the 45th Squadron reported, "They [i.e., the Arabs and the Kurds] now know what real bombing means, in casualties and damage; they now know that within 45 minutes a full sized village . . . can be practically wiped out and a third of its inhabitants killed or injured by four or five machines."[93]

In the 1920s, Italian airpower strategist Giulio Douhet argued that aerial bombing now held the key to military victory and differentiating between soldiers and civilians was no longer possible. The United States' leading advocate of airpower, General William "Billy" Mitchell, was thinking along similar lines. In his 1925 book *Winged Defense,* he warned, "If a nation ambitious for universal conquest gets off to a 'flying start' in a war of the future, it may be able to control the whole world. . . . Should a nation, therefore, attain complete control of the air, it could more nearly master the earth than has ever been the case in the past."[94] Others tried to couch their fascination with aerial warfare in more positive terms. CWS director General Amos Fries coined the following fanciful slogan for his agency: *"Every development of science that makes warfare more universal and more scientific makes for permanent peace by making warfare more intolerable"* (italics in original).[95]

While some planned for war, others planned for peace, fearing that another war augured even greater devastation. Will Irwin's 1921 book *The Next War* went through twelve printings that year. Irwin, a journalist who had worked with the Committee for Public Information, painted a bleak picture of future prospects. He reminded readers that at the time of the armistice, the United States was manufacturing lewisite gas. He described the qualities that made it so effective and so terrifying:

> It was invisible; it was a sinking gas, which would search out the refugees
> of dugouts and cellars; if breathed, it killed at once—and it killed not
> only through the lungs. Wherever it settled on the skin, it produced a
> poison which penetrated the system and brought almost certain death.
> It was inimical to all cell-life, animal or vegetable. Masks alone were of
> no use against it. Further, it had *fifty-five times* the "spread" of any poison
> gas hitherto used in the war. An expert has said that a dozen Lewisite air
> bombs of the greatest size in use during 1918 might with a favorable wind
> have eliminated the population of Berlin. Possibly he exaggerated, but
> probably not greatly. The Armistice came; but gas research went on. Now
> we have more than a hint of a gas beyond Lewisite. . . . A mere capsule of
> this gas in a small grenade can generate square rods and even acres of death
> in the absolute.[96]

Chemists, the most conservative segment of the scientific community and, not coincidentally, the one most closely tied to industry, took pride in their contribution to the war effort. That contribution didn't go unnoticed by others. The *New York Times* announced that chemists' efforts "should be gratefully acknowledged by the lay public. Our chemists are among the best soldiers of democracy" and "the most effective of our national defenders."[97]

Chemists joined with their military and industrial allies in resisting postwar

Italian, British, and German bombers. Militaries first bombed targets,
including civilians, during World War I. Germany began to do so in
1914, over Liege, Belgium. By spring of 1918, German bombs had
injured over 4,000 British civilians and left over 1,000 dead.

efforts to ban future uses of chemical warfare. In 1925, the League of Nations adopted the Geneva Protocol, outlawing the use of chemical and bacteriological weapons in war. The Coolidge administration supported it. Veterans' groups, the American Chemical Society (ACS), and chemical manufacturers led the opposition. Meeting in Los Angeles in August, the ACS council unanimously resolved to go "strongly on record against the ratification of the Geneva protocol on poisonous gases, as against both National safety and on the grounds of humanity."

The chemists, five hundred of whom were still in the Chemical Warfare Officers' Reserve Corps or the CWS, tried to convince the public that chemical weapons were actually more humane than other weapons, that the United States needed to be prepared for their use in the next war, and that the treaty might place the League of Nations in control of the U.S. chemical industry. Senator Joseph Ransdell of Louisiana hoped that the resolution would "be sent back to the Committee on Foreign Relations and buried so deep it would never appear before us again."[98] He got his wish. The committee never released it for a floor vote. In the ten years that followed, forty countries—including every great power besides the United States and Japan—ended up ratifying the treaty.[99]

Gas warfare scored its greatest successes against the poorly equipped Russian troops on the eastern front, who suffered 425,000 gas-induced casualties and 56,000 deaths.[100] For Russia, with 2 million dead and 5 million wounded, the war proved disastrous in all regards. Finally fed up with the tsar's indifference to their hardships, the Russian people overthrew Nicholas II's regime in March 1917. But many felt further betrayed when, with Wilson's support, the reformist government of Alexander Kerensky opted to keep Russia in the war. The Russian masses demanded a sharper break with the past.

On November 7, 1917, the Bolsheviks, led by Vladimir Lenin and Leon Trotsky, seized power, dramatically changing the course of world history. They were inspired by Karl Marx, a nineteenth-century German-Jewish intellectual who believed that class struggle would eventually result in an egalitarian socialist society. Marx, ironically, had doubted that a successful socialist revolution could occur in economically and culturally backward Russia. Ignoring Marx's warnings, the Bolsheviks set out to reorganize Russian society at its roots, nationalizing banks, distributing landed estates to the peasants, putting workers in control of factories, and confiscating church property. Lenin's Red Guard ransacked the old Foreign Office and brazenly published what it found: a web of secret agreements between the Allies from 1915 and 1916 that divided the postwar map into exclusive zones of influence. Much as the United States would react to the WikiLeaks publications of its diplomatic cables in 2010, the Allies were outraged at this brazen violation of the old diplomatic protocol, which now exposed the hollowness of Wilson's call for "self-determination" after the war. Among the treaties was the Sykes-Picot Agreement, which divided up the Ottoman Empire among Great Britain, France, and Russia. Carving out new nations with little regard for historical and cultural affinities, it planted the seeds of future conflict in the oil-rich Middle East.

Not since the French Revolution some 125 years before had Europe been so profoundly shaken and changed. Lenin's vision of worldwide Communist revolution captured the imagination of workers and peasants around the globe, posing a direct challenge to Wilson's vision of liberal capitalist democracy.

U.S. soldiers undergoing anti-gas training at Camp Dix, New Jersey. Despite being proscribed by civilizations for centuries, chemical warfare became widespread during World War I. Thousands died from poison gas attacks.

Wilson's Anglophile secretary of state Robert Lansing reported disappointedly that Lenin's Communist message was resonating with workers. He warned Wilson on January 1, 1918, that Lenin's appeal was directed "to the proletariat of all countries, to the ignorant and mentally deficient, who by their numbers are urged to become masters. Here seems to me to lie a very real danger in view of the present social unrest throughout the world." [101]

Wilson decided to make his own bold move in an attempt to steal Lenin's thunder. He announced his Fourteen Points on January 8, 1918. This liberal, open, anti-imperialist peace plan endorsed self-determination, disarmament, freedom of the seas, free trade, and a League of Nations. Only such an exalted mission would justify continuing "this tragical and appalling outpouring of blood and treasure." "The day of conquest and aggrandizement is gone by; so is also the day of secret covenants," he declared in what later would turn out to be a boldfaced lie. [102] But suddenly two competing new visions for the postwar world were on the table.

Vladimir Lenin and the Bolsheviks seized power in Russia on November 7, 1917, dramatically altering the course of world history. Lenin's vision of worldwide Communist revolution would capture the imagination of workers and peasants around the globe, posing a direct challenge to Woodrow Wilson's vision of liberal capitalist democracy.

Lenin again caught the capitalist world off guard. On March 3, eight months before the armistice, he signed a peace treaty with Germany, pulling Russian troops from the war. Lenin was so desirous of peace that he acceded to the harsh terms of the Treaty of Brest-Litovsk even though it meant relinquishing Russian control over Poland, Finland, the Baltic States, Ukraine, Georgia, and more—over 300,000 square miles of territory and 50 million people. Wilson and the Allies were furious. They reacted quickly.

The conservative counterrevolution against the Bolsheviks was ferocious. Separate armies attacked the new Russia from all directions—native Russians and Cossacks, the Czech legion, Serbs, Greeks, Poles in the west, the French in Ukraine, and some 70,000 Japanese in the Far East. In reaction, Lenin's co-revolutionary leader Leon Trotsky ruthlessly put together a Red Army of approximately 5 million men. The outspoken ex–Lord of the Admiralty Winston Churchill spoke for capitalists everywhere when he said that Bolshevism should be strangled in its cradle.

An estimated 40,000 British troops arrived in Russia, some deployed to the Caucasus to protect the oil reserves at Baku. Though most of the fighting would

*President Woodrow Wilson speaking at the Greek Theatre in Berkeley,
California, September 1919. Reelected president in 1916 on the slogan
"He kept us out of war," Wilson entered World War I in 1917, hoping
to give the United States a hand in shaping the postwar world.*

be over by 1920, pockets of resistance persisted until 1923. In a foreshadowing
of what was to come some sixty years later, Muslim resistance in Central Asia
lasted into the 1930s.

Japan, France, Great Britain, and several other nations sent tens of thousands of troops to Russia, in part to assist conservative White Russians
attempting to overthrow the fledgling Bolshevik regime. The United States initially hesitated to join them but finally sent over 15,000 troops to eastern and
northern Russia with the hope of maintaining a limited eastern front against
Germany and limiting Japanese gains. Wilson rejected proposals by British
cabinet officer Winston Churchill, commander in chief of the Allied armies,
Marshal Ferdinand Foch, and other Allied leaders for a direct military intervention to overthrow the Bolsheviks. Wilson resisted Foch's ongoing entreaties, explaining "any attempt to check a revolutionary movement by means of
deployed armies is merely trying to use a broom to sweep back a high tide.
Besides, armies may become impregnated with the very Bolshevism they are
sent to combat."[103] Still, U.S. troops remained in the country until 1920, long
after the original military rationale had ceased to exist. U.S. participation in

this operation poisoned its relations with the new Soviet government from the start.[104] It also deepened mistrust toward Wilson and his motives on the part of a crucial group of mostly midwestern progressive senators—a mistrust that would come back to haunt him when he struggled to achieve his crowning vision, a league of nations.

These "peace progressives," as Robert David Johnson and other historians have labeled them, held differing views of Russia's new revolutionary government, but they all recoiled at the notion of a U.S. military intervention. California Republican Senator Hiram Johnson took the lead. He argued that the United States should deal with the issues that had given rise to Bolshevism—"oppression, and poverty, and hunger"—rather than intervening militarily to overthrow the new government, an undertaking he saw as part of Wilson's "war against revolution in all countries." He desired "no American militarism to impose by force our will upon weaker nations." Mississippi Senator James Vardaman charged that the intervention had been conducted on behalf of international corporations that wanted to collect the $10 billion that the imperial Russian government had owed them. Robert La Follette deplored it as a "mockery" of the Fourteen Points—"the crime of all crimes against democracy, 'self-determination,' and the 'consent of the governed.'"[105] Idaho Senator William Borah reported that people who returned to the United States after spending months in Russia were telling a very different story about conditions there than the Wilson administration was presenting. Borah had been hearing "that the Russian people very largely support the Soviet Government." And, he continued, "If the Soviet Government represents the Russian people, if it represents 90 percent of the Russian people, I take the position that the Russian people have the same right to establish a socialistic state as we have to establish a republic."[106] Johnson introduced a resolution to stop funding for the intervention, which gained strong support, deadlocking at 33–33.[107]

While growing numbers were beginning to question aspects of Wilson's diplomacy at home, he still seemed to offer a beacon of hope for war-weary Europeans. Adoring crowds mobbed him when he arrived in Europe on December 18, 1918, for the Paris Peace Conference. H. G. Wells recalled, "For a brief interval Wilson stood alone for mankind. Or at least he seemed to stand for mankind. And in that brief interval there was a very extraordinary and significant wave of response to him throughout the earth. . . . He ceased to be a common statesman; he became a Messiah."[108]

The Germans had surrendered on the basis of Wilson's Fourteen Points, believing that they would be treated fairly. One German town greeted returning troops with a banner reading "Welcome, brave soldiers, your work has been done; God and Wilson will carry it on."[109] The Germans even deposed the kaiser and adopted a republican form of government as a sign of good faith. But the ill-defined Fourteen Points proved a weak foundation on which to base negotiations. And Wilson mistakenly failed to get his allies to concur during the war when he had more leverage. He had naively told Colonel Edward House, "When the war is over, we can force [England and France] to our way of thinking, because . . . they will be financially in our hands."[110]

Despite their indebtedness, the Allies balked at Wilson's terms. Having paid such a high price for victory, they had little interest in Wilson's lofty rhetoric about making the world safe for democracy, freedom of the seas, and "peace without victory." They wanted revenge, new colonies, and naval dominance. Wilson had already betrayed one of the central tenets by intervening in the Russian Civil War and maintaining forces in the country. More betrayals would follow. The British made it clear that they had no intention of abiding by Wilson's call for freedom of the seas, which would have limited their navy's ability to enforce British trade routes. The French made it equally clear they would not accept a nonpunitive treaty. France had lost well over a million soldiers and Great Britain just under a million. British Prime Minister David Lloyd George noted that in the United States "not a shack" had been destroyed.[111] The French also remembered their defeat in the Franco-Prussian War, further fueling their desire to debilitate and dismember Germany.

Twenty-seven nations met in Paris on January 12, 1919. The task ahead of them was enormous. To varying degrees, the Ottoman, Austro-Hungarian, German, and Russian empires were collapsing. New countries were emerging. Revolutionary change was encroaching. Starvation was rampant. Disease was spreading. Displaced populations were seeking refuge. Visionary leadership was desperately needed. But Lloyd George, Clemenceau, and Italian Prime Minister Vittorio Orlando found Wilson, who considered himself the "personal instrument of God," to be absolutely insufferable.[112] Clemenceau supposedly commented, "Mr. Wilson bores me with his 14 Points; why, God Almighty has only ten!"[113] Lloyd George took great pleasure in Clemenceau's response to Wilson: "If the President took a flight beyond the azure main, as he was occasionally inclined to do without regard to relevance, Clemenceau would open his great eyes in twinkling wonder, and turn them on me as much as to say: 'Here he is off again.' I really think that at first the idealistic President regarded himself as a missionary whose function was to rescue the poor European heathen." Lloyd George applauded his own performance under the difficult circumstances, "seated as I was between Jesus Christ and Napoleon Bonaparte."[114]

Few of Wilson's Fourteen Points remained in the final treaty. The victors, particularly Great Britain, France, and Japan, divided the former German colonies and holdings in Asia and Africa along the lines established by the secret 1915 Treaty of London. They also carved up the Ottoman Empire. They sanitized their actions by calling the colonies "mandates." Wilson resisted but ultimately went along. He rationalized his acquiescence by arguing that the Germans had "ruthlessly exploited their colonies," denying their citizens basic rights, while the Allies had treated their colonies humanely[115]—an assessment that was greeted with incredulity by the inhabitants of those Allied colonies, like French Indochina's Ho Chi Minh. Ho rented a tuxedo and bowler hat and visited Wilson and the U.S. delegation to the conference, carrying a petition demanding Vietnamese independence. Like most of the other non-Western world leaders in attendance, Ho would learn that liberation would come through armed struggle, not colonialist largesse. Mao Zedong, then working as a library assistant, expressed similar frustration: "So much for national self-determination," he vented. "I think it is really shameless!"[116] Wilson went so far in compromising his principles that he even accepted a U.S. mandate over Armenia, leading Clemenceau to comment wryly, "When you cease to be President, we will make you Grand Turk."[117]

Allied leaders did little to hide the racism that underlay their continued subjugation of dark-skinned peoples. This was most apparent when Japan's representatives—Baron Nobuake Makino and Viscount Chinda—proposed that a clause on racial equality be included in the Covenant of the League of Nations. The clause read, "The equality of states being a basic principle of the League of Nations, the High Contracting Parties agree to accord, as soon as possible, to all alien nationals of States members of the League, equal and just treatment in every respect, making no distinction, either in law or fact, on account of their race or nationality." The Japanese proposal was rejected outright by defenders of the British Empire, including British Foreign Secretary Arthur James Balfour and Australian Prime Minister William Hughes. As one British cabinet member, Lord Robert Cecil, explained, the clause raised "extremely serious problems" for the British Empire.[118]

Having admitted to Lloyd George before the proceedings began that he was less interested in the details of the settlement than in the League of Nations— which he considered crucial to preventing future war—Wilson's attempt to secure the kind of nonpunitive treaty he publicly advocated failed miserably. The treaty dealt very harshly with Germany. It included a "war guilt clause," drafted by future secretary of state John Foster Dulles, that placed the entire blame on Germany for starting the war and required Germany to pay extremely heavy reparations. Wilson, intently focused on the League, repeatedly compromised on these and other crucial matters, disappointing even his strongest supporters. Clemenceau snidely remarked that Wilson "talked like Jesus Christ but acted like Lloyd George."[119] Economist John Maynard Keynes condemned Wilson's capitulation to this "Carthagenian Peace"—a tragic repudiation of his Fourteen Points—and predicted that it would lead to another European war.[120]

Ho Chi Minh rented a tuxedo and bowler hat and visited Wilson and the U.S. delegation to the Paris Peace Conference, carrying a petition demanding Vietnamese independence. Like most of the other non-Western world leaders in attendance, Ho would learn that liberation would come through armed struggle, not the colonizers' largesse.

Although Lenin wasn't invited to Paris, Russia's presence cast a pall over the meetings, like "the Banquo's ghost sitting at every Council table," according to Herbert Hoover.[121] Lenin had dismissed Wilson's Fourteen Points as empty rhetoric and said that the capitalist powers would never abandon their colonies or accept the Wilsonian vision of peacefully adjudicating conflicts. His call for worldwide revolution to overthrow the entire imperialist system was finding a receptive audience. Colonel House wrote in his diary in March, "From the look of things the crisis will soon be here. Rumblings of discontent every day. The people want peace. Bolshevism is gaining ground everywhere. Hungary has just succumbed. We are sitting upon an open powder magazine and some day a spark may ignite it."[122] The Allies were so worried about Communist revolutions in Eastern Europe that they inserted a clause in the armistice agreement forbidding the German army to evacuate the countries on its eastern frontier until "the Allies think the moment suitable."[123] Though Béla Kun's Communist government in Hungary would soon be toppled by invading Romanian forces and an attempt to seize power by the Communists in Germany failed, House and Wilson had reason to be alarmed at the radical tide sweeping Europe and beyond.

American workers also participated in the radical upsurge; 365,000 striking

From left to right: British Prime Minister David Lloyd George, Italian Premier Vittorio Orlando, French Premier Georges Clemenceau, and Wilson at the Paris Peace Conference. At the conference, most of the lofty rhetoric of Wilson's "Fourteen Points" was rejected by the other Allies, who were out for revenge, new colonies, and naval dominance in the postwar world.

steelworkers led the way, followed by 450,000 miners and 120,000 textile workers. In Boston, police voted 1,134–2 to strike, leading the *Wall Street Journal* to warn, "Lenin and Trotsky are on their way." Wilson called the strike "a crime against civilization."[124] And a general strike in Seattle was led by a Soldiers', Sailors', and Workmen's Council modeled on the Russian Revolution. Seattle Mayor Ole Hanson denounced it as "an attempted revolution." The strikers, he charged, "want to take possession of our American Government and try to duplicate the anarchy of Russia."[125] Over 5 million workers struck that year alone. When strikebreakers, protected by armed guards, local police, and newly sworn in deputies, were not sufficient to defeat the strikes, state militias and even federal troops were called in to finish the job, sending the labor movement into a tailspin from which it would not recover for well over a decade. Though the use of federal troops on behalf of powerful capitalists had been highly controversial in 1877, workers had increasingly learned that police, courts, troops, and the entire apparatus of the state would be arrayed against them when they struggled for higher wages, better working conditions, and the right to join unions.

Having badly weakened the Left during the war, government officials now

In 1919, over 4 million U.S. workers struck for higher wages, better conditions, and organizing rights. As illustrated by this leaflet from the Seattle General Strike, the Russian Revolution helped inspire this intensified labor militancy.

tried to finish it off. In November 1919 and January 1920, Attorney General A. Mitchell Palmer used a spate of largely ineffectual anarchist bombings as an excuse to unleash federal agents to raid radical groups and labor organizations across the country. Though called the Palmer Raids, the operation was actually run by the twenty-four-year-old director of the Justice Department's Radical Division, J. Edgar Hoover. Over five thousand alleged radicals were arrested, many incarcerated without charges for months. Russian-born Emma Goldman and hundreds of other foreign-born activists were deported. This flagrant abuse of civil liberties not only devastated the progressive movement, it deliberately identified dissent with un-Americanism. But for Hoover, it was just the beginning. By 1921, his index-card system, cataloguing all potentially subversive individuals, groups, and publications, contained 450,000 entries.[126]

After the Paris conference, Wilson gushed, "At last the world knows America as the savior of the world!"[127] Back in the United States, Wilson was greeted like anything but a savior by treaty opponents, who attacked from both the left and the right. Wilson fought back, touring the country. He argued that the United States needed to ratify the treaty so it could join the League of Nations, which was the only way it could rectify the problems created by the treaty. Senator Borah, leading the opposition among progressives like Senators La Follette, Norris, and Johnson, denounced Wilson's proposed international body as a league of "imperialists" bent upon defeating revolutions and defending their own imperial designs. Borah thought the treaty, despite Wilson's efforts to soften it, was "a cruel, destructive, brutal document" that had produced "a league to guarantee the integrity of the British empire." [128] Norris condemned the treaty provision handing Shandong, the birthplace of Confucius, to Japan as "the disgraceful rape of an innocent people." [129] They were joined by isolationists and others who wanted guarantees that the United States wouldn't be drawn into military actions without authorization by Congress.

Ironically, Wilson's own wartime policy had deprived him of many of his best allies. CPI head Creel pointed this out to the beleaguered president in late 1918, telling him "All the radical, or liberal friends of your anti-imperialist war policy were either silenced or intimidated. The Department of Justice and the Post Office were allowed to silence and intimidate them. There was no voice left to argue for your sort of peace. The Nation and the Public got nipped. All the radical and socialist press was dumb." [130] Wilson's obstinacy made a bad situation worse. Rather than compromise on proposed treaty modifications, Wilson watched the treaty and the League go down to defeat, finally falling seven votes short of ratification.

The peace proved particularly onerous for Germany. Reparations totaled $33 billion—less than one-fifth what France demanded but more than double what Germany had expected, at a time when its ability to pay was severely compromised by its loss of colonies and Polish-speaking territories. Germany also surrendered the port of Danzig and the Saar coal region. And the German people were embittered by the "war guilt clause."

The House of Morgan's fingerprints were all over the treaty's economic clauses. As award-winning Morgan biographer Ron Chernow noted, "Morgan men were so ubiquitous at the Paris Peace Conference in 1919 that Bernard Baruch grumbled that J. P. Morgan and Company was running the show." The most prominent among the Morgan men was Thomas Lamont, the House of Morgan's leading partner, upon whom Wilson relied. Another Morgan partner, George Whitney, observed that Wilson appeared to trust Lamont's financial views more than anyone else's. Lamont advocated setting German reparations at $40 billion and later held to the belief that, if anything, the Germans had gotten off easy. At Paris, he and the other bankers made sure that Morgan's interests were well protected. [131]

Although the reparations and the "war guilt clause" created a hostile and unstable environment in postwar Germany, their impact has sometimes been exaggerated. The reparations were more onerous on paper than in practice. Beginning in 1921, the actual payments were repeatedly revised downward based on Germany's ability to pay. And the "war guilt clause"—Article 231— does not actually mention "guilt." It holds Germany accountable for reparations for "all the loss and damage" resulting from "a war imposed upon them by the aggression of Germany and her allies." [132] It is certainly true, however, that Hitler and other right-wing Germans exploited the postwar sense of victimization that

THE GAP IN THE BRIDGE.

As this December 1919 Punch *cartoon shows, the Senate's rejection of U.S. participation in the League of Nations rendered the League largely ineffectual. Wilson had helped guarantee the League's defeat by silencing potential anti-imperialist allies in the U.S. during the war.*

came with defeat and Allied retribution. The fact that little of the fighting took place on German soil and that wartime government propaganda had led most Germans to believe that victory was imminent made the settlement even more difficult to swallow and lent credibility to Hitler's allegations.

Economic, social, and political instability also rocked postwar Italy, where armed *fascisti*—followers of Benito Mussolini—repeatedly clashed with leftist demonstrators and strikers. U.S. Ambassador Robert Johnson warned of the dangers of a takeover by Mussolini's extreme right-wing forces. The U.S. Embassy reported in June 1921: "the fascisti seem to be the aggressors, while the communists . . . have . . . shift[ed] the imputation of lawlessness and violence from the party of 'Red' revolution to the self-constituted party of 'law and order.'" Later, when Richard Child, Warren G. Harding's ambassador to Italy, replaced Johnson, he did an about-face, praising Mussolini and castigating the Communists. Child and other embassy officials downplayed Mussolini's right-wing extremism, extolling instead his anti-Bolshevism and willingness to use strong-arm methods to defeat labor. U.S. support continued even after Mussolini's imposition of a Fascist dictatorship. Mussolini's defenders included American business leaders like Secretary of the Treasury Andrew Mellon, Thomas Lamont of J. P. Morgan, and Ralph Easley of the National Civic Federation.[133]

Historians have long since discredited the myth that revulsion caused by the war and European entanglements plunged the United States into isolationism in the 1920s. In fact, World War I marked the end of European dominance and the ascendancy of the United States and Japan, the war's two real victors. The twenties saw a rapid expansion of American business and finance around the globe. New York replaced London as the center of world finance. The era of U.S. domination of the world economy had now begun. Among the leaders in this effort were the oil companies.

The war proved that controlling oil supplies was central to projecting and exercising power. Great Britain and Germany tried to cut off each other's oil supplies during the war. Great Britain, hurt by German attacks on its oil supply ships, first expressed concern about an oil shortage in early 1916. The Allies also blockaded Germany's access to oil resources, and British Colonel John Norton-Griffiths attempted to lay oil supplies in Romania to waste when Germany moved to seize them in late 1916. Underscoring the importance of these developments, Britain's Lord Curzon pronounced soon after the armistice that "the Allied cause had floated to victory upon a wave of oil." The United States was key to that victory, having met 80 percent of the Allies' wartime petroleum needs.[134] But once the war ended, oil companies were poised to grab whatever new oil-rich territories they could. As Royal Dutch Shell asserted in its 1920 annual report, "We must not be outstripped in this struggle to obtain new territory . . . our geologists are everywhere where any chance of success exists."[135]

Royal Dutch Shell trained its sights on Venezuela, where General Juan Vicente Gómez's government offered friendly, stable conditions that seemed much more hospitable than the ongoing volatility and declining production in Mexico.[136] Concerned about Great Britain's predominance in Venezuela and believing that production during World War I had largely depleted U.S. domestic supplies, U.S. companies soon joined the competition for Venezuelan oil.[137] In *The Prize,* Daniel Yergin's pioneering book on the oil industry, the author describes Gómez as a "cruel, cunning, and avaricious dictator who, for twenty-seven years, ruled Venezuela for his personal enrichment."[138] Indeed, according to historian Steven Rabe, Gómez essentially made the country "his private *hacienda*" as he "amassed a personal fortune estimated at $200 million and landholdings of 20 million acres." Tellingly, the dictator's passing in 1935 would be greeted in Venezuela with a weeklong "spontaneous popular outburst" in which demonstrators vented their rage by ravaging "his portraits, statues, and buildings," and even "massacred" some of his "sycophants."[139]

Gómez's power rested upon local *caudillos* (strongmen), an army staffed by his loyalists, and a network of domestic spies. Detractors faced harsh persecution. U.S. Chargé d'Affaires John Campbell White reported that prisoners in

Venezuela were treated with "medieval severity." The United States was always ready to step in if needed. In 1923, the United States sent a Special Service squadron to the country as a show of support in response to what turned out to be unfounded rumors of an impending revolution.[140]

With an economy increasingly dependent on petroleum revenues, Gómez enlisted the oil companies to write parts of Venezuela's business-friendly 1922 Petroleum Law. The companies reaped massive profits. Oil company workers and the environment fared less well. Spills and accidents occurred frequently. One oil well blowout in 1922 spread twenty-two miles, releasing nearly a million barrels of oil into Lake Maracaibo.[141]

While Gómez was busy enjoying his wealth and fathering his alleged ninety-seven illegitimate children, his family and hangers-on, known as *Gomecistas,* bought up the choice properties and then sold them to foreign companies, accumulating vast fortunes for themselves and their leader, while their countrymen remained mired in poverty. In the process, Venezuelan oil production jumped from 1.4 million barrels in 1921 to 137 million in 1929, trailing only the United States in total output and first worldwide in exports. Of the three companies dominating the Venezuelan market, two were American-owned—Gulf and Pan American, which had been purchased in 1925 by Standard Oil of Indiana.[142] Combined, the two companies replaced Great Britain's Royal Dutch Shell as Venezuela's majority oil producers in 1928 and were responsible for 60 percent of production in the country by the time of Gómez's death.[143]

But left-wing opposition to the dictatorships of Gómez and his successors was growing. Oil workers occasionally went on strike for better conditions and pay, and in 1928 students at the Universidad Central in Caracas, known as the "Generation of '28," staged an uprising condemning the dictatorship and calling for a more democratic government. After years of struggle, in 1945, Rómulo Betancourt's leftist Democratic Action (AD) succeeded in overthrowing the regime of Isaías Medina Angarita. Betancourt forged a relationship with the oil companies that was more representative of Venezuela's interests. He was ousted in a 1948 military coup. While acknowledging the need for outside investment, these progressive reformers established a legacy of radical nationalist and anti-imperialist resistance to exploitation of Venezuelan resources by foreign oil interests.[144]

By 1920, Americans had wearied of Wilsonian "idealism." They were ready for what Warren G. Harding labeled a "return to normalcy," which, in terms of the decade's first two Republican presidents, meant a return to mediocrity. The Harding, Coolidge, and Hoover administrations sought ways to expand U.S. economic interests in Latin America without resorting to the heavy-handed gunboat diplomacy that marked the Roosevelt, Taft, and Wilson regimes. During the 1920 presidential campaign, Harding seized upon vice presidential candidate Franklin

The Venezuelan dictator General Juan Vicente Gómez's brutal and rapacious reign made his country a favorite of American and British oil companies. While amassing his own fortune, Gómez employed local caudillos (strongmen), an army staffed by his loyalists, and a network of domestic spies to ensure that Venezuela remained stable and hospitable to Western oil interests.

D. Roosevelt's remark that as assistant secretary of the navy, he had personally written the constitution of Haiti to assure listeners that as president, he, Harding, would not "empower an Assistant Secretary of the Navy to draft a constitution for helpless neighbors in the West Indies and jam it down their throats at the point of bayonets borne by United States Marines." He enumerated other things Wilson had done that he would not repeat: "Nor will I misuse the power of the Executive to cover with a veil of secrecy repeated acts of unwarranted interference in domestic affairs of the little republics of the Western Hemisphere, such as in the last few years have not only made enemies of those who should be our friends, but have rightfully discredited our country as their trusted neighbor."[145]

In fact, Harding and his Republican successors made more friends among U.S. bankers than among the inhabitants of those little republics. In May 1922, *The Nation* reported, revolutionaries sparked an uprising against "Brown Bros.' extremely unpopular President of Nicaragua." When the revolutionaries captured a fort overlooking the capital, the U.S. marine commander simply alerted them that he would use artillery if they didn't relinquish control. *The Nation* saw this as typical of what was happening throughout Latin America, where U.S. bankers ruled through puppet governments backed up by U.S. troops. The magazine inveighed against this deplorable situation:

> There are, or were, twenty independent republics to the south of us. Five
> at least—Cuba, Panama, Haiti, Santo Domingo, and Nicaragua—have
> already been reduced to the status of colonies with at most a degree of
> rather fictitious self-government. Four more—Guatemala, Honduras,

Costa Rica, and Peru—appear to be in process of reduction to the same status. Mr. Hughes is not treating Mexico as a sovereign, independent state. How far is this to go? . . . Is the United States to create a great empire in this hemisphere—an empire over which Congress and the American people exercise no authority, an empire ruled by a group of Wall Street bankers at whose disposal the State and Navy Departments graciously place their resources? These are the questions which the people, the plain people whose sons die of tropic fever or of a patriot's bullet, have a right to ask.[146]

Far from having become isolationist following the Great War, the United States found more effective ways than warfare to expand its empire. In fact, the war left an increasingly bitter taste in the mouths of most Americans. Although U.S. involvement in the First World War had been relatively brief and, by most measures, enormously successful, the nature of the fighting, marked by trench and chemical warfare, and the shaky postwar settlement combined to undermine the glory of the war itself. In its aftermath, Americans became increasingly disillusioned. A war fought to make the world safe for democracy seemed to have failed in its purpose. Nor was there much hope that this war would end all wars. Though some people nevertheless clung to the belief that the United States had engaged in a great crusade for freedom and democracy, for others the phrase rang hollow. A postwar literature of disillusionment emerged in the works of E. E. Cummings, John Dos Passos, Ernest Hemingway, Ezra Pound, Thomas Boyd, William Faulkner, Laurence Stallings, Irwin Shaw, Ford Madox Ford, Dalton Trumbo, and other writers as the nation learned once again that the initial euphoria of war would be erased by the reality of what the war actually achieved. In Dos Passos's 1921 novel *Three Soldiers,* his wounded protagonist, John Andrews, suffers through a visit from a YMCA representative, intent on lifting his spirits, who says, "I guess you're in a hurry to get back at the front and get some more Huns. . . . It's great to feel you're doing your duty . . . [Huns] are barbarians, enemies of civilization." Andrews recoils at the notion that "the best that had been thought" was reduced to this. Dos Passos wrote, "Furious, hopeless irritation consumed him. . . . There must be something more in the world than greed and hatred and cruelty."[147]

Some expressed anger at the war. Others just expressed a profound sense of postwar malaise. In 1920, in *This Side of Paradise,* F. Scott Fitzgerald wrote of Amory Blaine and his young friends that "here was a new generation . . . grown up to find all Gods dead, all wars fought, all faiths in man shaken."[148] Gertrude Stein saw that same sense of ennui in Ernest Hemingway and his drunken friends and commented, "All of you young people who served in the war. You are a lost generation."[149]

Not to be outdone, Hollywood produced several successful antiwar movies, some of which are still classics. Rex Ingram's *The Four Horsemen of the Apocalypse* (1921) brought instant stardom to Rudolph Valentino. King Vidor's *The Big Parade* was the top box-office draw in 1925. William Wellman's *Wings* (1927) was the first film to win the Academy Award for Best Picture, and Lewis Milestone's powerful *All Quiet on the Western Front* (1930) remains one of the great antiwar films of all time.

The war proved demoralizing in a myriad of subtle ways as well. The prewar march of civilization grounded in a faith in human progress had been negated by a war that seemed to showcase barbarism and depravity. Put simply, the faith in human capability and human decency had disappeared. This was understandably evident on both sides of the Atlantic. Sigmund Freud, who became a household name in the United States during the 1920s, is a case in point. Freud's prewar emphasis on the tension between the pleasure principle and the reality principle gave way to a postwar pessimism about human nature grounded in his focus on the death instinct.

Negative views of human nature were reflected in a loss of faith in essential human capabilities. The army presented psychologists with a vast laboratory on which to conduct experiments in human intelligence and the 3 million inductees provided an extraordinary pool of human guinea pigs. Working with army personnel, many of whom were trained in testing at Fort Oglethorpe, Georgia, psychologists administered intelligence tests to 1,727,000 recruits, including 41,000 officers. The data accumulated about educational levels were eye-opening. Some 30 percent of the recruits were illiterate.[150] The amount of education varied widely among the different groups, ranging from a median of 6.9 years for native whites and 4.7 years for immigrants to 2.6 years for southern blacks. The results of intelligence tests were even more sobering. The tests—albeit crude and culturally biased—found an astounding 47 percent of white draftees and 89 percent of blacks to be "morons."[151]

Nowhere was the subsequently degraded view of human intelligence more evident than in postwar advertising. The 1920s is often viewed as the golden age of advertising—the decade in which the industry really blossomed into the principal capitalist art form. As Merle Curti showed in his study of the advertising industry journal *Printer's Ink*, before 1910, advertisers, by and large, assumed that consumers were rational and self-interested and could be appealed to on that basis. Between 1910 and 1930, however, the majority of comments indicated that advertisers were viewing consumers as nonrational. As a result, advertisements increasingly abandoned the reason-why approach and appealed to fantasies and emotions.[152] A speaker at a 1923 advertising convention in Atlantic City captured this sense when he warned, "Appeal to reason in your advertising, and you appeal to about four percent of the human race." [153] This sentiment became accepted wisdom among advertisers. William Esty of the J. Walter Thompson agency instructed colleagues that all experts believed "that it is futile to try to appeal to masses of people on an intellectual or logical basis." [154] John Benson, the president of the American Association of Advertising Agencies, observed in 1927, "To tell the naked truth might make no appeal. It may be necessary to fool people for their own good. Doctors and even preachers know that and practice it. Average intelligence is surprisingly low. It is so much more effectively guided by its subconscious impulses and instincts than by its reason." [155]

Nowhere was this postwar pessimism more apparent than in the writings of Walter Lippmann, who was, in many respects, the nation's outstanding public intellectual during the decade. A leading socialist and progressive in the prewar period, Lippmann's faith in human rationality steadily declined after the war. In his 1922 classic *Public Opinion,* he introduced the term "stereotypes" to describe the images in people's minds that did not correspond to reality. He proposed substituting scientifically trained experts for the democratic public, for whom the world had become too complex. By the time he published *The Phantom Public* two years later, his faith in democracy had eroded further. The best people could do, he believed, was choose good leaders to guide them. Then, in his 1929 classic *A Preface to Morals,* he despaired over the very purpose of human existence in a meaningless universe, a view reflective of the United States' broader existential crisis of 1929–1930.

The most acerbic of democracy's critics was certainly H. L. Mencken, "the sage of Baltimore." Mencken referred to the common man, mired in religion and other superstitions, as a "boob," a member of the species "boobus Americanus." He expressed contempt for the same yeoman farmers whom Jefferson anointed the backbone of democracy, exclaiming "we are asked to venerate this prehensile moron as . . . the citizen par excellence, the foundation-stone of the state! . . . To Hell with him, and bad luck to him." [156]

By the early 1920s, the America of Jefferson, Lincoln, Whitman, and the young William Jennings Bryan had ceased to exist. It had been replaced by the world of McKinley, Teddy Roosevelt, J. Edgar Hoover, and Woodrow Wilson. Wilson's failures, in many ways, provide a fitting capstone to a period in which the United States' unique mixture of idealism, militarism, avarice, and realpolitik propelled the nation toward becoming a world power. Wilson proclaimed, "America is the only idealistic nation in the world" and acted as if he believed it were true.[157] He hoped to spread democracy, end colonialism, and transform the world. His record is much less positive. While supporting self-determination and opposing formal empire, he intervened repeatedly in other nations' internal affairs, including Russia, Mexico, and throughout Central

America. While encouraging reform, he maintained a deep mistrust of the kind of fundamental, and at times revolutionary, change that would actually improve people's lives. While championing social justice, he believed that property rights were sacrosanct and must never be infringed upon. Though endorsing human brotherhood, he believed that nonwhites were inferior and resegregated the federal government. While extolling democracy and the rule of law, he oversaw egregious abuses of civil liberties. While condemning imperialism, he sanctioned the maintenance of the global imperial order. And while proclaiming a just, nonpunitive peace, he acquiesced in a harsh, retributive peace that inadvertently helped create the preconditions for the rise of Hitler and the Nazis. Wilson's stunningly inept performance at Versailles and his combative intransigence upon his return home contributed to Senate defeat of the treaty and the League.

Thus the war would have consequences that went far beyond the horrors on the battlefield. The United States never joined the League of Nations, rendering that body impotent in the face of Fascist aggression in the 1930s. Revelations that the United States had entered the First World War on false pretenses, while bankers and munitions manufacturers—later labeled "merchants of death"—had raked in huge profits, created widespread skepticism about foreign involvements at a time when the United States needed to contend with a real "axis of evil": Germany, Italy, and Japan. By the time the United States acted, it was much too late. The necessity of finally combating fascism would, however, afford the United States an opportunity to reclaim some of that democratic, egalitarian heritage on which its earlier greatness and moral leadership had rested. And, though late in entering World War II, the United States provided crucial assistance in defeating Europe's fascists and played the decisive role in defeating Japan's militarists. But by setting off the atomic bombs in Hiroshima and Nagasaki at the end of the war, the United States, once again, proved itself unready to provide the kind of leadership a desperate world cried out for.

Chapter 2

THE NEW DEAL:

"I Welcome Their Hatred"

The world Franklin Delano Roosevelt confronted when he was inaugurated president on March 4, 1933, bore strikingly little resemblance to the one in which he ran for vice president thirteen years earlier. In 1920, the world was on the mend following the Great War. In 1933, the problems seemed insurmountable. The United States was mired in the fourth year of the worst depression in its history. Unemployment stood at 25 percent. GNP had fallen by 50 percent. Farm income plummeted by 60 percent. Industrial production was down by more than 50 percent. The banking system had collapsed. Breadlines formed in every town and city. Homeless walked the streets. Misery was ubiquitous, despair pervasive.[1]

Most of the world was in even worse shape than the United States. Unlike the United States, which had experienced a period of relative prosperity in the 1920s, most belligerents had never fully recovered from the devastation of the world war. Their citizens had less of a cushion to buffer them from the impact of the global economic meltdown. Trouble loomed everywhere.

Benito Mussolini was firmly ensconced in power in Italy after eleven years of dictatorial rule. Adolf Hitler and his National Socialists had come to power in Germany by exploiting both postwar grievances and economic hardship. Only a week before Roosevelt took office, Hitler had used the Reichstag fire to consolidate his dictatorial stranglehold over the country, unleashing vicious attacks on German Communists, Social Democrats, trade unionists, and left-wing intellectuals.

Trouble was also brewing in Asia. In September 1931, Japanese forces had seized Manchuria, a resource-rich and contested region situated between the Soviet Union, China, and Korea, and renamed it Manchukuo in 1932. In response to international protests, Japan left the League of Nations in 1933.

Despite the devastation wrought by the Depression, the mood was decidedly more upbeat in the United States. On the day of Roosevelt's inauguration, a *New York Times* editorial captured the excitement that surrounded the change of administrations:

> Americans are a people of invincible hope. . . . But seldom can their
> eagerness to see a new President inaugurated have equaled that of this year.
> . . . they have exhibited an extraordinary patience in enduring hardships
> which millions of them have somehow come to believe will be mitigated or
> removed by the mere fact of Mr. ROOSEVELT'S entering the White House.
> . . . Mr. ROOSEVELT has . . . given an impression of buoyant optimism in
> the face of a great complex of knotty problems awaiting him. . . . Even citizens
> sunk in gloom . . . will preserve a remnant of admiration for a President who
> begins his turn by acting on the belief that "nothing is impossible for the
> United States." . . . no President of the United States ever came to greater
> opportunities amid so great an outpouring of popular trust and hope.[2]

Roosevelt decided to act boldly. The country was behind him. The Democrats controlled both houses of Congress and people wanted action. Will Rogers commented on the president's early days: "If he burned down the capitol, we would cheer and say, 'Well, we at least got a fire started anyhow.'"[3]

Roosevelt's much-anticipated inaugural address rallied the nation to the fight. His declaration that "the only thing we have to fear is fear itself" seems, in retrospect, to have been out of touch with reality, given the magnitude of the problems. But Roosevelt connected with a deeper reality: Americans' desperate need for renewed hope and confidence. And that he set out to restore.

He identified those responsible for the current dismal state of affairs: "The money changers have fled from their high seats in the temple of our civilization. We may now restore that temple to the ancient truths. The measure of the restoration lies in the extent to which we apply social values more noble than mere monetary profit." He called for "strict supervision of all banking and credits and investments" and "an end to speculation with other people's money."[4]

Roosevelt had given little indication of the kind of policies he would adopt once in office. At times, during the campaign, he attacked President Herbert Hoover from the right for spending too aggressively and unbalancing the budget. At other times, he acknowledged the suffering of the people and called for a "new deal." Now he had to solve some very real and very practical problems. Hoover accused him of deliberately making a bad situation worse by ignoring Hoover's pleas for joint action during the four-month interregnum between the

Franklin Delano Roosevelt and Herbert Hoover en route to the
U.S. Capitol for Roosevelt's inauguration, March 4, 1933. The
inauguration incited much optimism. Will Rogers commented on
Roosevelt's early days, "If he burned down the capitol, we would
cheer and say, 'Well, we at least got a fire started anyhow.'"

election and Roosevelt's taking office in March. Now the waiting was over. First up was the banking system.

Between 1930 and 1932, one-fifth of U.S. banks had failed. Many others were tottering. On October 31, 1932, with the Nevada governor off in Washington seeking a federal loan, Lieutenant Governor Morley Griswold declared a twelve-day bank holiday, preventing depositors from withdrawing their funds and thereby safeguarding against a run on the banks. Mayors and governors across the nation anxiously eyed the situation, hesitating to follow suit. Things began to unravel when Michigan declared an eight-day bank holiday on February 14, closing 550 state and national banks. The *New York Times* assured nervous readers that "there is no reason why [Michigan] should be taken as a precedent." Maryland and Tennessee saw sufficient reason to act, as did Kentucky, Oklahoma, and Alabama, as panicky depositors lined up to get their money out while they still could.[5] By the time Roosevelt was inaugurated, banking had been halted completely or sharply limited everywhere.

Conditions were ripe for dramatic changes in the banking system. Public anger against bankers had been building since the stock market crash. The year before, in February 1932, *New York Times* reporter Anne O'Hare McCormick had described the widespread antipathy toward Wall Street bankers afoot throughout the land: "In a country which suffered more than 2,000 bank failures last year . . . the tendency is to blame the bankers for almost everything that has happened at home and abroad. . . . Not in a generation at least has the feeling against money barons been so bitter. . . . The average citizen always suspected the morals of the financial hierarchy, but now his distrust goes further: he doubts its intelligence."[6]

A year later, mistrust of Wall Street financiers was at an all-time high, fueled by Senate inquiries into the banks' role in precipitating the economic collapse. Peter Norbeck, the chair of the Senate Committee on Banking and Currency, appointed former New York County Assistant District Attorney Ferdinand Pecora to run the hearings. Pecora blistered the nation's leading bankers. When announcing, in early February, that Charles E. Mitchell, the powerful chairman of the board of National City Bank, the world's largest bank, was being called to testify, Norbeck, a Republican from South Dakota, issued a statement: "The investigation so far shows that some of the large banks were highly responsible for the wild stock market boom . . . some banks were in on the promotion scheme. . . . It was just a polite way of robbing the public." Norbeck added that when the Federal Reserve Board in Washington tried to slow down the stock market boom, Mitchell, chair of the New York Federal Reserve Bank, had "defied the board and speeded up the boom. He took a 'go-to-hell' attitude toward the Board and got away with it."[7]

News of the hearing was splashed across the front pages of newspapers. Pecora exposed fraud and wrongdoing on the part of the nation's top bankers, including obscene salaries, unpaid taxes, hidden bonuses, unethical loans, and more. Mitchell, one of the most powerful men in the country, was forced to resign. He managed, however, to win acquittal on charges of defrauding the government of $850,000 in income taxes, narrowly escaping a possible ten-year prison sentence.

Magazines began calling bankers "banksters." *The Nation* observed, "If you steal $25, you're a thief. If you steal $250,000, you're an embezzler. If you steal $2,500,000, you're a financier."[8] In this climate, Roosevelt had pretty much a free hand to do what he wanted. Brain Truster Raymond Moley noted, "If ever there was a moment when things hung in the balance, it was on March 5, 1933—when unorthodoxy would have drained the last remaining strength of this capitalist system." Senator Bronson Cutting concluded that Roosevelt could have nationalized the banks "without a word of protest." Rexford Guy Tugwell, director of the Agricultural Adjustment Administration, and other advisors urged Roosevelt to do just that.

*A run on a bank, February 1933. Between 1930 and 1932, one-fifth
of U.S. banks failed. By the time Roosevelt was inaugurated, banking
had been halted completely or sharply limited everywhere.*

But Roosevelt chose a much more conservative course of action. He declared
a four-day national bank holiday, conferred with the nation's top bankers on his
first full day in office, called a special session of Congress to pass emergency legislation, and calmed citizens' fears with the first of his famous fireside chats. Congress
passed and Roosevelt signed the Emergency Banking Act, written largely by the
bankers themselves. The banking system had been restored without radical change.
Congressman William Lemke remarked, "The President drove the money-changers
out of the Capitol on March 4th—and they were all back on the 9th."[9] Roosevelt's
solution to the banking crisis would serve as a template for how he would handle
most issues. His instincts were fundamentally conservative. He would save capitalism from the capitalists. As Secretary of Labor Frances Perkins, the first female
cabinet officer in the nation's history, explained, Roosevelt "took the status quo in
our economic system as much for granted as his family . . . he was content with
it."[10] But the means he would use to save capitalism would be bold, visionary, and
humane. They would transform American life for decades. Perhaps longer.

Though clearly not a radical, Roosevelt laid out an ambitious recovery program during his first hundred days in office. It included the Agricultural Adjustment Administration, to save farming; the Civilian Conservation Corps (CCC),
to put young men to work in the forests and parks; the Federal Emergency Relief

Administration (FERA) under Harry Hopkins, to provide federal assistance to the states; the Public Works Administration (PWA) under Harold Ickes, to coordinate large-scale public works projects; the Glass-Steagall Banking Act, which separated investment and commercial banking and instituted federal insurance of bank deposits; and the National Recovery Administration (NRA) to promote industrial recovery.

Established by the National Industrial Recovery Act (NIRA), which Roosevelt considered "the most important and far reaching legislation ever enacted by the American Congress," the NRA was modeled, in part, on the War Industries Board (WIB), which Bernard Baruch had directed during World War I.[11] The NRA suspended antitrust laws, effectively sounding the death knell for laissez-faire capitalism. Centralized planning would instead revitalize the shattered economy. Under the NRA, each industry drew up its own code covering wages, prices, production, and working conditions. The largest corporations dominated the code-setting process in their respective industries, with labor and consumer groups playing, at best, a minor role.

The initial NIRA legislation was hastily cobbled together and did not provide clear guidelines for what was to follow. Many liberals applauded it. *The Nation* welcomed it as a step toward a "collectivized society."[12] It was Roosevelt's choice of General Hugh Johnson to administer the NRA that gave it its distinctive coloration. Johnson was Baruch's man. They had worked closely together on the WIB. After retiring from the army, Johnson became an advisor to Baruch in his business dealings. Johnson's leadership of the NRA has fueled allegations that the New Deal was fascistic—a dangerous notion later peddled by Ronald Reagan and more recently touted by conservative writer Jonah Goldberg. Reagan touched a raw nerve when he said during the 1976 presidential campaign that "fascism was really the basis of the New Deal."[13]

Johnson was the exception rather than the rule. He did not hide his fascist sympathies. In September 1933, he reviewed the 2 million–strong NRA parade down New York's Fifth Avenue. *Time* magazine reported, "General Johnson, his hand raised in a continuous Fascist salute, had declared the parade to be 'the most marvelous demonstration I have ever seen.'"[14] Johnson gave Frances Perkins a copy of Raffaello Viglione's fascist tract *The Corporate State*. Roosevelt finally removed him because of his erratic behavior, abrasive personality, heavy drinking, and penchant for antagonizing labor. In his deeply emotional farewell speech, he celebrated the "shining name" of Benito Mussolini.[15]

There was great uncertainty about where Roosevelt was taking the country, leading some observers to compare the United States with Fascist Italy. The *Quarterly Review of Commerce* wrote in autumn 1933, "Some see in his programme a movement toward a form of American fascism. In fact the tremendous

(**TOP**) *Civilian Conservation Corps (CCC) crew at work in Idaho's Boise national forest.* (**ABOVE**) *Public Works Administration (PWA) had carriers carry bricks for the construction of a high school in New Jersey. The CCC and PWA were part of Roosevelt's ambitious recovery plan laid out during his first one hundred days in office.*

concentration of power in the hands of the president, the new codes under the National Industrial Recovery Act regulating competition, the fixing of minimum wage rates, of maximum working hours in industry, and the general policy of economic planning and co-ordination of production, all strongly suggest essential features of the Italian fascist programme." The writer described Johnson's

*Established by the National Industrial Recovery Act (NIRA),
which Roosevelt considered "the most important and far reaching
legislation ever enacted by the American Congress," the NRA
sounded the death knell for laissez-faire capitalism by suspending
antitrust laws and endorsing centralized planning.*

anti-labor proclivities, including his delivering, on October 10, "a warning to labour in no uncertain terms that 'strikes were unnecessary' under the Roosevelt plan and that no opposition of any kind would be tolerated." [16]

Although a plethora of right-wing groups emerged during the 1930s, the fascist threat that Sinclair Lewis warned about in his 1935 novel *It Can't Happen Here* never took hold in the United States. That is not to say that Mussolini and Hitler lacked admirers. *Time* and *Fortune* were unabashed supporters of Mussolini. In 1934, the editors of *Fortune* magazine extolled Italian fascism, which embodied "certain ancient virtues of the race [including] discipline, duty, courage, glory, sacrifice." [17] Many American Legionnaires felt the same way. Legion Commander Alvin Owsley declared in 1923 that "the *Fascisti* are to Italy what the American Legion is to the United States," and the organization invited Mussolini to address its national convention in 1930. [18] Elected officials including Pennsylvania Senator David Reed praised Mussolini and proclaimed, "if this country ever needed a Mussolini it needs one now." [19]

Hitler, too, had more than his share of U.S. defenders. Among the more notorious was Republican Congressman Louis T. McFadden of Pennsylvania. He took to the floor of the House in May 1933 to decry the international Jewish conspiracy, reading passages from *The Protocols of the Elders of Zion,* an anti-Semitic screed purporting to prove a Jewish conspiracy to take over the world, into the *Congressional Record* and announcing that the president's abandonment of the gold standard "had given the gold and lawful money of the country to

the international money Jews of whom Franklin D. Roosevelt is the familiar."
"This country has fallen into the hands of the international money changers,"
he charged. "Is it not true," McFadden asked, "that in the United States today
the Gentiles have the slips of paper while the Jews have the gold and the lawful
money? And is not this repudiation bill a bill specifically designed and written by
the Jewish international money changers in order to perpetuate their power?"[20]

The infamous "radio priest" of Royal Oak, Michigan, Father Charles Coughlin, took to the airwaves to proclaim his corporatist and increasingly anti-Semitic
vision. His weekly publication *Social Justice* serialized *The Protocols* and urged
followers to join the Christian Front armed militia. Gallup reported in 1938 that
10 percent of American families owning radios listened to Coughlin's sermons
on a regular basis and 25 percent did so occasionally. Eighty-three percent of the
steady listeners approved of the priest's messages.[21] Even in 1940, *Social Justice*
had over 200,000 readers weekly.[22]

Even farther to the right were the so-called shirt movements, which took
their inspiration from Mussolini's black shirts and Hitler's brown shirts. William
Dudley Pelley's Silver Legion may have enlisted as many as 25,000 members in
1933. In Kansas, Gerald Winrod, the "Jayhawk Nazi," whose *Defender* newspaper reached a hundred thousand readers, garnered 21 percent of the Republican
vote in the Kansas U.S. Senate primary in 1938.[23] With West Virginia's Knights
of the White Camelia, Philadelphia's Khaki Shirts, Tennessee's Crusader White
Shirts, and New York City's Christian Mobilizers, the country was awash in
extremists.[24] One of the most violent of these organizations was the Midwest-
based Black Legion, which had split off from the Ku Klux Klan in 1925. Wearing
black robes instead of the Klan's white sheets, the Legion had a membership estimated at between 60,000 and 100,000 in 1935. Its head, electrician Virgil Effin-
ger, spoke openly about the need for mass extermination of American Jews[25]
before the federal government cracked down on the group in 1937. Although
not a "shirter," a failed haberdasher, Harry Truman, had earlier applied for membership in the Klan before thinking the better of it.

In reality, Hugh Johnson's influence on the New Deal was fleeting and the
far Right's nonexistent. Not only did the New Deal reject fascist solutions, it
resisted attempts to impose any unified, coherent philosophy. It was more of a
hodgepodge of agencies. Raymond Moley wrote that viewing the New Deal as
the product of a consistent plan "was to believe that the accumulation of stuffed
snakes, baseball pictures, school flags, old tennis shoes, carpenter's tools, geom-
etry books, and chemistry sets in a boy's bedroom could have been put there by
an interior decorator." Roosevelt was more pragmatic than ideological. And he
was willing to allow government to play a vastly bigger role than any of his predecessors could have imagined.[26]

Roosevelt focused from the outset on jump-starting the U.S. economy and getting Americans back to work. Solving international problems would take a backseat. He made that abundantly clear at the World Economic Conference in London in July 1933. He had already issued executive orders to release U.S. monetary policy from the constraints of gold in April but held out the prospect of returning the United States and, if possible, the rest of the world to the gold standard. By the summer, however, he had had a change of heart. So when confronted with the choice between an inflationary economic recovery program at home and going along with the Europeans' demand for currency stabilization and a restored international gold standard, Roosevelt opted for the former. Fully expecting that Roosevelt would go along with the joint declaration by Great Britain and the gold-bloc nations to return to the gold standard and halt speculation in exchange rates, the fifty-four world leaders attending the London summit were taken aback by Roosevelt's July 3 announcement that the United States would be party to neither exchange rate stabilization nor a gold standard. The conference broke up, leaving most European leaders bitterly disappointed. Many, including Hitler, concluded that the United States was withdrawing from world affairs.

Back home, Roosevelt received a mixed response. Certain business and banking titans, including Frank A. Vanderlip, J. P. Morgan, and Irénée du Pont, offered measured support, at least in public.[27] Moley surmised that nine out of ten bankers—"even those in the lower part of Manhattan"—supported Roosevelt's rejection of the gold standard.[28] But former Democratic presidential candidate turned New Deal critic Al Smith dismissed Roosevelt's monetary policy, calling it a commitment to "baloney dollars" instead of "gold dollars." Smith expressed astonishment that "the Democratic party is fated to be always the party of greenbackers, free silverites, rubber dollar manufacturers, and crackpots."[29]

Moley's assurances notwithstanding, many bankers adamantly opposed Roosevelt's currency measures. The Federal Reserve advisory council, made up of leading bankers throughout the nation, warned the Federal Reserve Board that economic recovery required a gold standard. "Demands for currency inflation and further credit inflation," the council instructed, ". . . rest upon reasoning again and again proved . . . to be a tragic illusion."[30] The most scathing condemnation of both Roosevelt and his currency decisions, however, came from the Chamber of Commerce. After rejecting a resolution offering support for Roosevelt's monetary policy, the New York State Chamber applauded when railroad magnate Leonor F. Loree declared that "the ending of the gold standard was as great a violation of trust and a denial of what is printed on that bill as was Germany's wartime disregard for Belgium's neutrality."[31] By the next May, having been bludgeoned with a constant barrage of criticism, Roosevelt felt compelled to send a letter to the U.S. Chamber of Commerce's annual convention, asking members to "stop crying wolf" and to "cooperate in working for recovery."[32] But businessmen's attacks on Roosevelt and his New Deal policies intensified. In October 1934, *Time* noted that businessmen's enmity toward Roosevelt had become quite personal: "It was no longer a matter of Business v. Government but of Business v. Franklin Delano Roosevelt."[33]

Roosevelt's inward-looking approach was apparent across the board. He repudiated his earlier support for joining the League of Nations and willingly sacrificed foreign trade in order to stimulate domestic recovery. He even took steps to reduce the country's 140,000-man army, which prompted a visit by Secretary of War George Dern. Dern brought along General Douglas MacArthur, who told the president that he was endangering the country's safety. In his memoirs, MacArthur recalled:

> The President turned the full vials of his sarcasm upon me. He was a scorcher when aroused. The tension began to boil over. . . . I spoke recklessly and said something to the general effect that when we lost the next war, and an American boy, lying in the mud with an enemy bayonet through his belly and an enemy foot on his dying throat, spat out his last curse, I wanted the name not to be MacArthur, but Roosevelt. The President grew livid. "You must not talk that way to the President!" he roared.

MacArthur, overwrought, apologized, offered his resignation as chief of staff, rushed outside, and vomited on the White House steps.[34]

Openly opposing Wall Street and the military made for smart politics in 1930s America, and Roosevelt was nothing if not an astute politician. The 1934 midterm elections showed how far to the left the country had moved. In fact, much of the electorate was to the left of the New Deal. In a remarkable break with normal voting patterns, the party in power drubbed the opposition. The Democrats won twenty-six of thirty-five Senate races, giving them a 69–25 advantage over Republicans in the upper chamber, with one seat being held by a Progressive and one by a Farmer-Laborite. Their lead in the House jumped to 322–103, with seven Progressives and three Farmer-Laborites. The *New York Times* called it "the most overwhelming victory in the history of American politics[, giving] the President a clear mandate . . . and . . . literally destroy[ing] the right wing of the Republican party."[35]

Viewing the election as a wake-up call for Republicans, Idaho Republican Senator William Borah told reporters that "unless the Republican party is delivered from its reactionary leadership and reorganized in accordance with its one-time liberal principles it will die like the Whig party of sheer political cowardice."

He criticized his party's leadership for opposing the New Deal "without offering a program of their own in place of it." Borah complained that when Republicans around the country ask their leaders for an alternative to the New Deal, "they are offered the Constitution. But people can't eat the Constitution." [36]

Radical ideas were in the air. Upton Sinclair, author of *The Jungle*, almost won election as governor of California with a campaign called "End Poverty in California" that proposed handing uncultivated farms to farmers and idle factories to workers for productive use. California physician Francis Townsend's call for giving people over age sixty $200 a month to stimulate the economy won numerous adherents. And Louisiana Governor Huey Long's "Share the Wealth" program, with its "soak-the-rich" tax plan, offered another vision for redistribution of wealth and a more just and egalitarian society.

The Soviet Union, which would later become such an albatross around the necks of American leftists when the almost unfathomable depths of Stalinist cruelty became known, actually strengthened the appeal of left-wing reform in the early 1930s. Soviet communism seemed to be producing a dynamic egalitarian society that offered a viable alternative to the moribund capitalist economic order. Soviet leaders sparked the interest of American intellectuals in 1928 by announcing their first Five-Year Plan, which promised a rational, centralized economy that would create abundance by unleashing science and technology. Socialists and progressives had long favored intelligent planning over a seemingly anarchic system in which individual capitalists made decisions based on maximizing profits. The concept of planning had inspired works as disparate as Edward Bellamy's 1888 socialist masterpiece *Looking Backward* and Walter Lippmann's 1914 *Drift or Mastery*, the bible of the Progressive movement. Many intellectuals agreed with editor of *The Nation* Oswald Garrison Villard, who, in late 1929, described the Soviet Union as "the greatest human experiment ever undertaken." [37]

The results seemed to justify that description. While the United States and the rest of the capitalist world plunged deeper into depression, the Soviet economy appeared to be booming. In early 1931, the *Christian Science Monitor* reported that not only was the Soviet Union the only country to have escaped the Depression, its industrial production had jumped an astronomical 25 percent the previous year. In late 1931, *The Nation's* Moscow correspondent described the Soviet frontier as "a charmed circle which the world economic crisis cannot cross. . . . While banks crash . . . abroad, the Soviet Union continues in an orgy of construction and national development." [38] *The Nation* could be dismissed as a liberal publication, but similar reports in *Barron's*, *Business Week*, and the *New York Times* were harder to disregard. As the U.S. unemployment rate approached 25 percent, a *Times* report that the Soviet Union intended to hire foreign workers caused desperate jobless Americans to stampede Soviet offices in the United States. Despite official Soviet disclaimers, *Business Week* reported that the Soviets planned to import 6,000 Americans and that 100,000 had applied. Soviet society seemed to be undergoing an incredible transformation from agrarian backwardness to industrial modernization before people's eyes.[39]

Many American intellectuals had also begun to see the Soviet Union as a place of intellectual, artistic, and scientific vibrancy compared with the United States' stultifying bourgeois culture. In 1931, economist Stuart Chase wrote, "For Russians the world is exciting, stimulating, challenging." The next year, he asked, "Why should Russians have all the fun of remaking a world?"[40] *New Republic* literary editor Edmund Wilson noted that when visiting the Soviet Union, he felt as if he were "at the moral top of the universe where the light never really goes out." Socialized medicine for all, remarkable scientific breakthroughs, dazzling economic growth—Soviet progress, many Americans believed, was vastly eclipsing that of its economically struggling capitalist competitors.[41]

Indications of Soviet success added enormously to the appeal of the Communist Party of the United States of America (CPUSA) at a time when so many Americans were looking for alternatives. An invigorated Communist Party would contribute significantly to the growth of 1930s radicalism, but it was only one piece in a much larger puzzle. Many groups, some having nothing to do with the CP, became radicalized during this decade. Radicalization proceeded at different paces for different groups. The first to respond were the unemployed. Hundreds of thousands demonstrated for jobs and relief all over the country on March 6, 1930. Intellectuals followed suit, rejecting the shallow materialism of American life in the 1920s and the anti-intellectualism that had driven so many writers and artists to Europe for cultural salvation. Edmund Wilson captured this perfectly when he wrote in 1932:

> to the writers and artists of my generation who had grown up in the Big
> Business era and had always resented its barbarism . . . these years were
> not depressing but stimulating. One couldn't help being exhilarated at the
> sudden and unexpected collapse of the stupid gigantic fraud. It gave us a
> new sense of freedom and it gave us a new sense of power to find ourselves
> still carrying on while the bankers, for a change, were taking a beating.[42]

The upsurge among workers started in 1933, as the economy showed early signs of recovery, and continued throughout the decade. The year 1934 saw major strikes in Toledo, Minneapolis, and San Francisco as well as a national textile strike as workers turned to Musteites, Trotskyists, and Communists for

*Unemployed march, Camden, New Jersey. The year 1934
saw major strikes in Toledo, Minneapolis, and San Francisco,
as well as a national textile strike, as workers turned to
radical groups for leadership. Unemployed workers supported
the strikers rather than take jobs as strikebreakers.*

leadership. Unemployed Councils and Unemployed Leagues brought in job-less workers to support the strikes rather than take jobs as strikebreakers. With broad support from all sectors of the working class, these strikes often spread to other industries, even shutting down entire cities, as happened in San Fran-cisco. The *Los Angeles Times* reported, "The situation in San Francisco is not cor-rectly described by the phrase 'general strike.' What is actually in progress there is an insurrection, a Communist-inspired and led revolt against organized gov-ernment."[43] The Portland *Oregonian* called for presidential intervention: "San Francisco, paralyzed, is in the throes of violent insurrection. Portland faces the practical certainty of a general strike within a few days that will similarly paralyze this city." The *San Francisco Chronicle* complained, "The radicals have wanted no settlement. What they want is revolution."[44]

This was a welcome change after thirteen years in which the unions had taken a pounding and suffered sharp declines in membership. Aided by New Deal leg-islation that helped level the playing field between management and labor, the labor movement even began to penetrate heavy industry with the formation of the Congress of Industrial Organizations in 1935. Communists played a major role in the organizing. Corporate resistance often resulted in violent and bloody

Evicted sharecroppers along Highway 60, New Madrid County, Missouri. During the Depression, African Americans' economic hardship was exacerbated by racism and discrimination.

confrontations. But militant workers adopted new tactics like sit-down strikes that proved particularly effective in the right circumstances.

African Americans' economic hardship was exacerbated by racism and discrimination. Black unemployment skyrocketed as the Depression effectively eliminated an entire category of "Negro jobs." Urban black unemployment reached over 50 percent in the South in 1932. The North was not much better; in Philadelphia, black unemployment topped 56 percent. Many blacks, struggling for both jobs and civil rights, thought the legalistic approach of the NAACP was too slow given the tenor of the times and turned instead to the CP and its front organizations. Though the national party leaders may have taken their marching orders from Moscow, that information often did not trickle down to the grass-roots level.

And scientists, who were among the most conservative groups in the country at the start of the decade—in 1933, sociologist Read Bain called them "the worst citizens of the Republic" because of their apathy and social irresponsibility—had been transformed into one of the most radical by decade's end, standing in the forefront of the antifascist movement and questioning whether capitalism thwarted the socially beneficial application of science and technology.[45] In the December 1938 election for president of the American Association for the Advancement of Science, the nation's largest body of scientists, the five leading vote getters were leaders of the left-wing science and society movement and the winner, renowned Harvard physiologist Walter Cannon, was one of the most openly left-wing scientific activists in the country.[46]

During those turbulent years, many liberals began calling themselves socialists or radicals. Minnesota Governor Floyd Olson proclaimed, "I am not a liberal. . . . I am a radical."[47] For many on the left, even liberalism connoted a moderation that bordered on cowardice. Lillian Symes wrote in *The Nation* in 1934, "No worse insult [than being called a liberal] could be hurled at any-one's mentality at a time like this."[48] Many felt the same way about joining the Socialists when the Communist Party seemed to offer a viable and more radical alternative. John Dos Passos explained his support of the Communists in 1932: "Becoming a Socialist right now would have just the same effect on anybody as drinking a bottle of near beer."[49]

Ironically, during the 1935–39 Popular Front period, when the Communists garnered their greatest support, Norman Thomas's Socialists were often to the left of the Communists, who deliberately toned down their rhetoric in hope of build-ing a broad coalition against fascism. Hundreds of thousands of Americans joined the Communist Party or worked with its affiliated organizations. Among them were many of the country's best writers, including Ernest Hemingway, Erskine Caldwell, John Dos Passos, Edmund Wilson, Malcolm Cowley, Sinclair Lewis, Langston Hughes, Sherwood Anderson, James Farrell, Clifford Odets, Richard Wright, Henry Roth, Lillian Hellman, Theodore Dreiser, Thomas Mann, William Carlos Williams, Nelson Algren, Nathanael West, and Archibald MacLeish.

But as the 1930s advanced, Western intellectuals' early enthusiasm for Soviet communism began to wane. Encircled by hostile capitalist nations and fearing a new war, Josef Stalin embarked upon a policy of breakneck industrialization that would claim many victims. Reports filtered out of the Soviet Union of fam-ines and starvation, political trials and repression, ham-fisted bureaucracy, secret police, brutal prisons, and ideological orthodoxy. Kulaks were slaughtered for resisting forced collectivization of agriculture. More than 13 million people died under Stalin's despotic rule. Organized religion was stifled. Military leaders were purged.[50] And even those who refused to believe the horrific reports filtering out of the Soviet Union were shocked by Stalin's apparent treachery in concluding the Non-Aggression Pact with Germany in 1939. Communists left the party in droves at that point, but diehards blamed Stalin's about-face on Western capital-ist nations' refusal to assist the Soviet Union in stopping Hitler despite Stalin's persistent calls for collective defense.

The combination of a left-leaning Congress, an energized, progressive popu-lace, and a responsive and caring president made possible the greatest period of social experimentation in U.S. history, especially after the upsurge in mid-decade radicalism drove the New Deal farther left. In December 1935, Harold Ickes told the president that he "believed the general sentiment of the country to be much more radical than that of the Administration." Roosevelt agreed and sharpened his attack on the business community. He saved his heaviest artillery for his annual message to Congress on January 3, 1936, which he delivered at night over national radio. The only previous time that a president had addressed an evening session was on April 2, 1917, when Wilson read his war message to the House. Roosevelt lashed out at his enemies on the right: "We have earned the hatred of entrenched greed. They seek the restoration of their selfish power. . . . Give them their way and they will take the course of every autocracy of the past—power for themselves, enslavement for the public."[51]

Having been pushed to the left by the progressive upsurge, Roosevelt kept up his harsh attack on business throughout the 1936 campaign. He trumpeted the list of progressive achievements. The Works Progress Administration (WPA) and other government programs put millions of unemployed back to work in government jobs. The economic and banking systems had been reformed. The government, for the first time, sided, however tentatively, with labor against the employers and nurtured the growth of unions. Social Security guaranteed a modicum of comfort in old age that few workers had previously enjoyed. The tax burden was shifted increasingly to the wealthy.

On the eve of the election, Roosevelt took his defiantly antibusiness message to supporters at Madison Square Garden, declaring,

> We had to struggle with the old enemies of peace—business and financial monopoly, speculation, reckless banking class antagonism, sectionalism, war profiteering. They had begun to consider the Government of the United States as a mere appendage to their own affairs. We know now that Government by organized money is just as dangerous as Government by organized mob . . . They are unanimous in their hate for me—and I welcome their hatred.[52]

When election day came around, the revitalized Democrats gave the Republicans the political thrashing of their lives at every level. Roosevelt defeated Kansas Governor Alf Landon 523–8 in the Electoral College, winning every state except Maine and Vermont. Democrats gleefully amended the old saying that "as goes Maine, so goes the country" to declare, "as goes Maine, so goes Vermont."[53] The Democrats controlled the House 331–89 and the Senate 76–16, after accounting for the Farmer-Laborites and George Norris's switch to Independent.

The *Chicago Tribune* saw the lopsided vote as an unambiguous endorsement of the president's agenda. "The result of the election is a vote of confidence in Mr.

Roosevelt and the New Deal . . . he will enter upon his second term with what amounts to a blank check signed yesterday by an overwhelming majority of the American people." The conservative *Tribune* worriedly pointed to the coalition Roosevelt had formed with the Farmer-Labor, American Labor, Socialist, and Communist parties: "How Mr. Roosevelt will discharge his obligations to his radical partners becomes a matter of intense interest."[54]

But the near universal hopes for further reform would be frustrated by political and economic miscalculation on the part of the usually savvy president. Roosevelt lost momentum following the election with his ill-fated scheme to pack the Supreme Court with progressive judges out of frustration with the Court's repeated vetoing of New Deal programs. If the New Deal stumbled over the Supreme Court, it was knocked flat by the economic crisis of 1937, which critics quickly dubbed the "Roosevelt recession." Believing incorrectly that economic progress was self-sustaining and the Depression's end in sight, administration officials decided to cut spending and balance the budget. Roosevelt particularly targeted the WPA and PWA for deep cuts. The economy plummeted almost overnight. In fact, the collapse was so stunning that Roosevelt and other administration officials believed it was deliberately staged by businessmen seeking to bring Roosevelt down. Stocks rapidly lost one-third of their value, and corporate profits fell by 80 percent. Unemployment skyrocketed anew as millions lost jobs.

Reformers were now on the defensive. Despite that, many Americans realized that one essential human need had yet to be addressed and set out to correct that oversight. Few people appreciate how close the United States came to adopting a national health care program in 1938 and 1939. The Committee of Physicians for the Improvement of Medical Care, an insurgent group of progressive physicians, largely based at the nation's most prestigious medical schools, acting in defiance of the conservative American Medical Association, sparked a national movement to create a sweeping national health care system. The administration threw its weight behind the effort, arguing that health care was a right, not a privilege, a position strongly supported by labor and a broad range of reform-minded organizations. In fact, administration support was so strong that the editors of *The Nation* were convinced that "no government would" so mobilize public opinion or "put such expert effort and the time and attention of more than half of its cabinet officials into the development of such a program and then abandon it."[55] In late February 1939, New York Senator Robert Wagner submitted his administration-backed bill for a national health program, claiming that no legislation had received "more widespread approval" from the American people.[56] But faced with vehement AMA opposition and seeking to avoid a nasty fight with elections approaching, Roosevelt decided to abandon the effort. New Deal reform was over once and for all.[57]

The progressive reforms that the New Dealers had been able to implement provoked sharp opposition from the still powerful business community. Roosevelt and advisor Rexford Guy Tugwell, agency heads Harry Hopkins and David Lilienthal, and progressive cabinet members like Henry Wallace, Harold Ickes, and Frances Perkins incurred the wrath of much of the business and banking communities. Though some businessmen, like Joseph Kennedy, thanked Roosevelt for rescuing capitalism from shortsighted capitalists, most considered him the enemy and fought the New Deal every step of the way. A U.S. Chamber of Commerce membership survey registered 97 percent opposition to the philosophy of the New Deal.[58]

The most extreme of these right-wing businessmen set out to prove that the *New York Times'* obituary for the Republican Right was premature. They announced formation of the American Liberty League in August 1934, a few months before the midterm elections, although they had begun gathering forces long before that.

The American Liberty League was the brainchild of members of the du Pont family, including brothers Irénée, Pierre, and Lammot, and in-law and top executive Robert "Ruly" Carpenter. Carpenter alleged that Roosevelt was being controlled by "[Felix] Frankfurter and his thirty-eight hot dogs—a gang of fanatical and communistic Jew professors." He recruited John Raskob, former chairman of the Democratic National Committee, to the cause. Raskob, a strong proponent of shifting the tax burden from the wealthy to the working class, had engineered du Pont's purchase of General Motors and had simultaneously served as chief financial officer in both corporations. Others brought on board included GM President Alfred Sloan, former Democratic presidential candidates Al Smith and John Davis, National Steel Corporation President Ernest Weir, Sun Oil Company President J. Howard Pew, and General Foods Chairman E. F. Hutton. Charles Lindbergh turned down the League's offer to serve as president.[59]

The American Liberty League went public on August 22, 1934, announcing its intention to combat radicalism, defend property rights, and uphold the Constitution. Headed by Jouett Shouse, former chairman of the Democratic Executive Committee, the five-member executive committee included Irénée du Pont, Al Smith, John Davis, former New York Republican Governor Nathan Miller, and New York Republican Congressman James Wadsworth, Jr. Shouse announced plans to recruit 2 million to 3 million members and hundreds of thousands of contributors. The League unfurled a massive, though largely ineffectual, "education" campaign over the next few years in a concerted effort to stem the liberal tide. It fell far short, however, of its recruitment and fund-raising targets, claiming 125,000 members and 27,000 contributors. But most of the members were inactive, and most of the funds came from the du Ponts and a handful of other right-wing businessmen. Its reputation was also tarnished by two damning congressional investigations of 1934 and 1935.[60]

The first investigation was short-lived but shocking in its implications. In November 1934, highly decorated retired Marine General Smedley Butler told the House Special Committee on Un-American Activities that William Doyle, commander of the American Legion's Massachusetts branch, and bond salesman Gerald MacGuire had tried to recruit him to organize a military coup against the Roosevelt administration. Paul Comly French, a reporter for the *New York Evening Post* and the *Philadelphia Record,* corroborated Butler's account, testifying that he overheard MacGuire say at one point, "We need a Fascist government in this country to save the Nation from the Communists who want to tear it down and wreck all that we have built in America. The only men who have patriotism to do it are the soldiers and Smedley Butler is the ideal leader. He could organize one million overnight." MacGuire had gone to France to study fascist veterans' movements, which he envisioned as a model for the force Butler could organize in the United States.

Butler rejected MacGuire's entreaties. "If you get the 500,000 soldiers advocating anything smelling of Fascism," he warned, "I am going to get 500,000 more and lick the hell out of you, and we will have a real war right at home." Testimony revealed that Doyle and MacGuire were fronting for many of the same Morgan and du Pont–linked bankers and industrialists who had formed the American Liberty League. MacGuire denied the charges, and New York Mayor Fiorello LaGuardia mockingly dismissed the episode as a "cocktail putsch." Morgan partner Thomas Lamont called the allegations "Purest moonshine! Too utterly ridiculous to comment upon!" But James Van Zandt, national commander of the American Legion and a future congressman, lent support to Butler's testimony, reporting that "agents of Wall Street" had also approached him.[61]

After hearing the testimony, the House committee, chaired by John McCormack of Massachusetts, reported that it had been "able to verify all the pertinent statements made by General Butler" except for MacGuire's direct solicitation of his services, which it accepted as fact. It concluded that "attempts to establish a fascist organization in the United States . . . were discussed, were planned, and might have been placed in execution when and if the financial backers deemed it expedient."[62] The committee, strangely, chose not to call many of those implicated to testify, including Colonel Grayson Murphy, General Douglas MacArthur, Al Smith, former American Legion Commander Hanford MacNider, John Davis, Hugh Johnson, and Thomas Lamont. Butler decried the fact that their names had been omitted from the final report.

The second set of hearings, which began earlier but lasted longer, was conducted by North Dakota Senator Gerald Nye. Nye had been appointed to the

Senate upon the death of his predecessor and twice reelected. He immediately identified with the Progressives, including George Norris, William Borah, and Robert La Follette, sharing their desire to avoid overseas entanglements that might involve the United States in foreign wars and their opposition to using the military to protect American businessmen's overseas investments. In February 1934, Nye proposed what would become one of the most remarkable congressional investigations in U.S. history. He called upon the Senate Foreign Relations Committee to investigate individuals and corporations involved in manufacturing and selling arms, munitions, and other implements of war. Its targets would include steel, airplane, and automobile manufacturers, arms and munitions makers, and shipbuilders. The focus on arms merchants rather than bankers represented a departure from the views of Harry Elmer Barnes and other revisionist historians who had written blistering critiques of U.S. involvement in the war. Barnes wrote in 1934 that arms dealers "never exerted so terrible an influence upon the promotion of warfare as did our American bankers between 1914 and 1917."[63]

The idea for the hearings had come from Dorothy Detzer, a tireless peace activist who served as the National Executive Secretary of the U.S. chapter of the Women's International League for Peace and Freedom. Detzer's twin brother had been a victim of mustard gas in the Great War. Needing someone to sponsor the proposal in the Senate, she approached twenty senators. All turned her down. George Norris suggested that she try Nye, who agreed to do it. Peace groups around the country organized support for the resolution. In April, the Senate authorized hearings into the "munitions trust," focusing on war profiteering, the role of weapons makers' propaganda in pushing the government toward war, and whether the government should have a monopoly of all weapons manufacturing in order to remove the profit motive from war fighting. The resolution's cosponsor, Senator Arthur Vandenberg, pledged to find out if the country would be allowed "to live at peace among ourselves and with our neighbors and without artificial encouragement to friction and misunderstanding and then to conflict, and then to disaster." Vandenberg wanted to find out if "these sordid intrigues which we know to exist elsewhere" were also occurring in the United States.[64]

Nye, Vandenberg, and Vice President John Nance Garner selected four Democrats—Homer Bone of Washington, Bennett Champ Clark of Missouri, Walter George of Georgia, and James Pope of Idaho—and three Republicans—Nye, Vandenberg, and W. Warren Barbour of New Jersey. Clark nominated Nye as chairman of the Special Committee Investigating the Munitions Industry, and Pope seconded the nomination. Hearings were delayed to give the committee time to begin its research, which was coordinated by Stephen Rauschenbusch, son of the renowned Social Gospel minister Walter Rauschenbusch. A young

Harvard law graduate named Alger Hiss served as a legal assistant, on loan from Jerome Frank of the Agricultural Adjustment Administration.[65]

Progressives rallied to the cause. An article in the *Railroad Telegrapher* captured the festering anger that many workers still felt toward the munitions makers a decade and a half after the end of the World War: "the American people are showing signs of awakening to the system which encourages wars, slays and tortures millions to build a few swollen fortunes, and leaves the common man and woman staggering under crushing debts. . . . Labor's millions are called on to fight all wars, to suffer the mud, lice and blood of the trenches while the bosses gather their dollars and the bosses' sons become officers. And, after the war is over, labor pays and pays and pays." In an editorial titled "Murder Incorporated," the *New Republic* stated that the investigators would have to follow "the torturous track of blood money . . . the track is there, the blood-dripping profits are there, a vast, worldwide network of incorporated murder is there."[66]

While the nation waited for the hearings to commence, two important and timely books appeared that fueled public anger and provided more grist for the inquisitors. *Merchants of Death* by H. C. Engelbrecht and F. C. Hanighen, which was chosen as a Book-of-the-Month Club selection, and *Iron, Blood, and Profits* by George Seldes were released on the same day in April 1934. They detailed not only the sordid dealings of U.S. munitions makers but those of their compatriots in other parts of the world. Doubleday also reprinted in pamphlet form the startling exposé of the European arms industry from the March issue of *Fortune* titled "Arms and the Men." That article also seethed with visceral anger. It began:

> According to the best accountancy figures, it cost about $25,000 to kill a
> soldier during the World War. There is one class of Big Business Men in
> Europe that never rose up to denounce the extravagance of its governments
> in this regard—to point out that when death is left unhampered as an
> enterprise for the individual initiative of gangsters the cost of a single
> killing seldom exceeds $100. The reason for the silence of these Big
> Business Men is quite simple: the killing is their business. Armaments
> are their stock in trade; governments are their customers; the ultimate
> consumers of their products are, historically, almost as often their
> compatriots as their enemies. That does not matter. The important point is
> that every time a burst shell fragment finds its way into the brain, the heart,
> or the intestines of a man in the front line, a great part of the $25,000,
> much of it profit, finds its way into the pocket of the armament maker.[67]

Roosevelt voiced approval of the hearings and urged stronger international steps to curb what he called the "mad race in armament which, if permitted to

Republican Senator Gerald Nye of North Dakota led the 1934 hearings on the U.S. arms industry that revealed the nefarious practices and enormous wartime profits of American munitions companies. "The committee listened daily to men striving to defend acts which found them nothing more than international racketeers, bent upon gaining profit through a game of arming the world to fight itself," he said. Among the more damning details brought to light by the hearings was that U.S. companies were helping Nazi Germany rearm.

continue, may well result in war." "This grave menace to the peace of the world," he added, "is due in no small part to the uncontrolled activities of the manufacturers and merchants of engines of destruction."[68]

The committee's eighty researchers and accountants combed the books of the United States' leading corporations. Committee members were astonished by the findings. Senator Pope promised that the people will be "amazed by the story of greed, intrigue, war scare propaganda and lobbying which will be made public" during the hearings. He added that the information would "shock the entire Nation when disclosed."[69] Just before the start of hearings, the *New York Times* reported that a majority of the seven committee members favored complete government operation of war materials manufacturing plants. Pope expressed optimism that the evidence would be so disturbing that there would be "almost universal demand" for such actions.[70]

On September 12, Felix, Irénée, Lammot, and Pierre du Pont took the stand together and were grilled about the firm's enormous profits during the war years. The company had received orders of $1.245 billion between 1915 and 1918, a 1,130 percent increase over company orders in the four years prior to the war.[71] During the war, du Pont had paid 458 percent dividends on original par value stock. The hearings that day also revealed that in 1932 Army Chief of Staff General Douglas MacArthur had gone to Turkey, where, according to a letter from an executive of the Curtis Wright Corporation, he had "apparently talked up American military equipment to the skies in discussions which he had with the Turkish general staff." At that point, Nye interjected, "It looks to me like Gen. MacArthur was pretty much of a salesman. It makes one begin to wonder if the Army and Navy is just a sales organization for private industry."[72]

The hearings produced troubling revelation after troubling revelation. U.S. and foreign arms dealers had divided foreign markets through cartel arrangements, sharing secrets and profits and designing German submarines that were busy sinking Allied ships during World War I. More recently, American companies had been helping Nazi Germany rearm. Officials of United Aircraft and Pratt and Whitney testified that they had sold planes and aircraft equipment to Germany for, they claimed, commercial, not military, use. Nye was incredulous. "Do you mean to say," he asked, "that through all of these negotiations you hadn't the ghost of an idea that Germany was buying for military purposes?"[73] U.S. policy since 1921, Secretary of State Cordell Hull reiterated, had been to oppose the sale of any military equipment to Germany.

Support for the hearings came in from across the political spectrum as the committee landed blow after blow. In late September, John Thomas Taylor, the legislative representative of the American Legion, announced that he supported the plan proposed by the earlier War Policies Commission to have the government seize 95 percent of any abnormal profits in wartime.[74] Nye promptly announced that he would introduce legislation raising income taxes to 98 percent on all incomes above $10,000 on the day the United States entered a war in order to entirely eliminate war profits.[75] Nye said that he and two other committee members actually preferred to nationalize the entire arms industry in the event of another war.[76]

Public interest in the hearings was tremendous. England made plans to hold its own hearings. Hearings were already under way in several Latin American countries, spurred by disturbing revelations about nefarious dealings between those countries and the arms makers. Nye had received more than ten thousand congratulatory letters and telegrams. He was being flooded with speaking requests. The adulation made the *Washington Post* nervous. It editorialized that the outpouring of support was no surprise because "The inquiry revealed much information of a sensational character and gave to the average citizen a new conception of the uncontrolled forces which combat in effect, if not in intent, the efforts to secure world peace. To see glaring publicity given to what has been essentially a secret traffic, evoked a responsive chord among all who desire a better world order." The *Post* begrudgingly praised the committee's "excellent work."[77]

In early October, Nye gave a national address over NBC radio in which he defended his plans for nationalizing the arms industry and sharply increasing wartime taxes. "Do that and then observe the number of jingoists diminish," he suggested. If such steps were taken, he confirmed, "war may not be as unpreventable as pictured." He summarized the committee hearings to that point: "The committee listened daily to men striving to defend acts which found them nothing more than international racketeers, bent upon gaining profit through a game of arming the world to fight itself."[78]

Calls for nationalization by Nye and other committee members sparked a vigorous national debate in late 1934. In December, the *Washington Post* pooh-poohed Nye's proposals and referred readers to an op-ed piece insisting that the topic had been thoroughly vetted in Geneva for the past fifteen years and that it was "an undisputed fact" that "enlightened opinion" was against it. The du Ponts and others weighed in along similar lines.[79] Commentators pointed out the problems with Nye's plan. If the weapons industry were nationalized, Walter Lippmann asked, how would the United States decide about exporting weapons to other countries? If the United States nationalized its weapons industry, would other countries follow suit? If so, what would happen to countries with no munitions plants? How would determination be made about the many products that could be used for commercial as well as military purposes? The *Chicago Tribune* pointed specifically to Japan's buying scrap metal in the United States and cited the du Ponts' contention that bales of cotton could be munitions of war. Others asked what would happen to the war industries during peacetime. And, if the factories were obsolescent and unused, would the nation be able to gear up quickly enough to meet an emergency?[80]

With public pressure building for decisive action, Roosevelt decided to get out ahead of and defuse the issue. On December 12, he announced that he had asked a high-powered group of government and industrial leaders to come up with a plan to end war profiteering. Roosevelt told the reporters, "The time has come to take the profits out of war." Three hours later the group met at the White House to begin its work. Arriving arm in arm were none other than the commission chairman, Bernard Baruch, and Hugh Johnson, the commission's executive director. Others asked to assist with drafting the legislation included the secretaries of state, war, labor, agriculture, treasury, and navy, Rail Coordinator Joseph B. Eastman, Army Chief of Staff MacArthur, Assistant Secretary of the Navy Roosevelt, Assistant Secretary of Agriculture Tugwell, Assistant Secretary of Labor Edward F. McGrady, and George Peck, the head of the Export-Import Bank. Nye Committee members erupted in anger, accusing the administration of trying to restrict their inquiry before the investigation was completed.[81]

Others also voiced skepticism about Roosevelt's motives. *Washington Post* columnist Raymond Clapper listed several explanations that were circulating around Washington. One was that the president wanted to steal the spotlight from Nye and Vandenberg, the Republican senators who were making headlines with their investigations. Another was that the "munitions interests have got to the Administration and that it is trying to take them off of the spot."[82]

Nye thought Roosevelt was up to no good. "The departments of our government are really codefendents with the munitions industry and the profiteers," he exclaimed, having only recently become sensitive to the degree of government complicity in international arms sales.[83]

Refusing to let the administration steal its thunder, the Nye Committee came out with more headline-grabbing exposés. The du Ponts remained in Nye's crosshairs. Alger Hiss revealed more evidence of untrammeled greed. The *Washington Post* headlined one December 1934 front-page article "800% War Profit Told at Inquiry; Du Pont Deal Up." Hiss released a list of companies involved in various aspects of war production and the gaudy returns on their investments. He also released names of the 181 individuals who reported incomes exceeding $1 million in 1917 and noted that 41 of them had appeared for the first time. The list included six du Ponts, four Dodges, three Rockefellers, three Harknesses, two Morgans, two Vanderbilts, two Whitneys, and only one Mellon.[84]

The more blood Nye drew, the shriller the attacks on the committee became. The *Chicago Tribune* condemned the committee's method of damning witnesses as "unjust, dishonorable, and disgusting."[85] But support for the investigation remained strong. Nye met with Roosevelt in late December. The committee had received over 150,000 friendly letters by that point. Afterward, Nye assured reporters that he had mistaken Roosevelt's motives. The president was entirely behind the investigations, he said, and no new legislation would be forthcoming until the investigation had run its course.[86]

• Members of the committee tried to warn the public about what they feared was an impending European war. Pope thought it "paradoxical" that governments around the world were aiding munitions manufacturers. Countries, he regretted, "seem to be in the grip of some monster that is driving them to destruction. Preparations for the next war are feverishly under way. That it is inevitable is widely assumed."[87]

In early February 1935, Representative John McSwain of South Carolina introduced legislation that would freeze prices at the level they were at on the day war was declared. Baruch and Johnson both testified on behalf of the legislation and both opposed Nye's more sweeping nationalization proposals.

Meanwhile, at the hearings, Eugene Grace, president of Bethlehem Steel Corporation and the Bethlehem Shipbuilding Corporation, admitted that his company's profits jumped from $6 million before the war to $48 million once the war started and that he had received personal bonuses of $1,575,000 and $1,386,000. Senator Bone aggressively questioned him about Treasury Department charges that "Bethlehem profits . . . were unconscionable and unjust," the subject of an $11 million suit that had been tied up in the courts for years.[88]

In February, the committee weighed a request to open up a new line of inquiry. The annual convention of the Department of Superintendence of the National Education Association (NEA) heard a powerful indictment of the "insidious influences" of press magnate William Randolph Hearst by former president of the American Historical Association Charles Beard. Beard claimed that Hearst "has pandered to depraved tastes and has been an enemy of everything that is noblest and best in our American tradition." According to the *Times,* when Beard finished, the thousand educators in attendance "rose to their feet and applauded for several minutes." The association passed a resolution declaring that NEA members had been "shocked and outraged by the iniquitous greed for profits on the part of American munitions manufacturers [as] has been revealed in all the grossness of their corruption by the Nye Committee." The resolution called upon the committee to also investigate "the propaganda in newspapers, schools, motion pictures and radio carried forward to increase the fear of war and promote the sale of munitions," specifically including the Hearst newspapers. Nye responded that such an investigation did fall within the purview of his committee and requested more information. But, after further consideration, he decided against the inquiry.[89]

In late March, a Senate bill to ban war profits started to take shape. The *New York Times* described it as "a plan that is admittedly the most radical in the history of the government." The *Washington Post* concurred, describing it as "a plan so drastic in its confiscatory features that six months ago it would have been scoffed at. . . . It went beyond anything that Senator Gerald P. Nye, dapper chairman and most radical member of the committee, ever thought of recommending." Staff researcher John Flynn laid it out for committee members, who met with the president to discuss it. Roosevelt surprised them by responding positively. Secretary of State Cordell Hull, however, advised Roosevelt against supporting any specific legislation eliminating war profits.

But, given the president's backing, committee members decided to put their proposals into legislative form. The tentative provisions included a tax of 100 percent on all incomes over $10,000 and hefty taxes on lower incomes, a 50 percent tax on the first 6 percent of corporate profits and 100 percent on profits over 6 percent, drafting corporate officials into the army, shuttering all stock exchanges for the duration of the war, prohibiting all commodity speculation, and commandeering of all essential industries and services. Flynn told the committee, "The profits in war, the spiraling of prices, the uncivilized scrambling for the shameful fruits of national disaster, can be prevented in only one way, and that is to prevent inflation at the beginning. In 1917 and 1918 we had our war and we sent the bill to our children and grandchildren. In the next war we must resolve, as intelligent as well as civilized beings, that while one part of the population—the army—fights in the field, the other part, that stays at home, will pay the bills."[90]

The slightly amended Flynn proposal was introduced as the Emergency Wartime Act in early April. The bill would mandate government seizure of all profits above 3 percent and all individual earnings above $10,000. Nye commented, "The bill is drastic because war is a drastic thing. The tax collector who comes for one man's money is not nearly so solemn and forbidding as the draft officer who knocks at another man's door and calls for his young son."[91]

When the House was ready to vote on the more moderate McSwain bill, pandemonium broke out. Opposition rang down from all sides. The *New York Times* reported, "Anti-war sentiment so swept the House that the original McSwain proposal was amended beyond recognition." Amendments included an excess war profits tax of 100 percent, government control of the financial and material resources of the country, and conscripting officials in industry, commerce, transportation, and communications.[92] The bill passed the House with provisions to draft all men between the ages of twenty-one and forty-five but with conscription of management officials stripped out. The bill was framed so that it would be easy to add provisions from the more radical Nye bill in the final version.

Arthur Krock inveighed against both bills in the *New York Times*. "The McSwain bill," he charged, "is colored with pacifism, the Nye bill with syndicalism, socialism or communism . . . the two measures seek to discourage war by providing the certainty that the well-to-do would be ruined when war was declared. Only labor and passive objectors have been treated with consideration. All the provisions of the bills are designed to prevent limiting the wage or strikes of the one and the conscription of the other."[93] Baruch also weighed in against features of the Nye bill, claiming it would increase inflation, paralyze war production, and leave the country defenseless against a major attack. Nye accused Baruch of being business's mouthpiece and not really wanting to eliminate war profits.[94]

Nye introduced his bill in the Senate in early May as an amendment to the McSwain War Profits Bill. He promised that this would be only the first of several bills to come out of his committee, explaining, "We believe the opinion of the American people is behind this bill. We think that now, when the whole world is troubled by rumors of wars, is the time to serve notice on our own people and on the world that America does not intend to use another war as an instrument to make a foolish and futile effort to make a few people rich."[95]

The committee presented three resolutions to the Senate. One prohibited making loans to warring nations or their citizens. A second denied passports to citizens entering war zones. And a third embargoed arms shipments to warring nations if such shipments might involve the United States in conflicts. The Senate

Foreign Relations Committee approved the first two measures and was debating the third when Hull convinced committee members to keep U.S. options open in dealing with other nations. With the developing Ethiopia crisis on their minds, they decided to reconsider all three measures before finalizing their actions.

When Congress adjourned in September, the differences between the House and Senate versions of the war profits bill had not yet been resolved. That was a relief to the *Chicago Tribune,* which called it a "communistic defense act" that in the event of war would allow the president to "communize the American nation as completely as Lenin communized Russia."[96]

At that point, with pressure building for dramatic action, Wilson's former Secretary of War Newton Baker threw a monkey wrench into the proceedings. He responded to a letter to the *New York Times* by William Floyd, the head of Peace Patriots, by denying that there had been any discussion of protecting private U.S. commercial or financial interests in the run-up to the United States' entry into the World War and averred that "America's safety from future wars cannot be secured by muzzling bankers or disabling munitions makers."[97] Four days later, banker Thomas Lamont wrote, challenging Floyd's evidence and blaming German aggression, not U.S. commercial interests, for U.S. entry.[98]

These very issues formed the crux of renewed committee investigations in early 1936. Was it true that the House of Morgan and other Wall Street firms had pushed the United States to war in order to recoup the enormous sums they had lent to the Allies? Both sides readied for the battle. The much-anticipated showdown occurred on January 7, when J. P. Morgan appeared before the committee along with his partners Lamont and George Whitney, as well as Frank Vanderlip, a former president of National City Bank. John W. Davis came along as Morgan's counsel. The committee moved the hearings to the Caucus Room of the Senate Office Building in order to accommodate the record number of requests for seats. Nye Committee researchers had been poring over the books and files of the banking behemoth for almost a year, examining more than 2 million letters, telegrams, and other documents. The night before the hearings, the firm invited reporters to its forty-room suite at the Shoreham Hotel for an off-the-record background briefing by Lamont and Whitney. Nye took to the radio to lay out his position to a national audience. "After we had started stretching our American neutrality policy to accommodate commercial interests to the extent of permitting loans," he reasoned, "the Allied powers were never in doubt as to what America would ultimately do. They knew what we didn't seem to realize, namely that where our pocketbook was, there would we and our hearts ultimately be."

Morgan released a nine-page statement denying such allegations. It read, "We call particular attention to the secured nature of these loans, because there has been an impression fostered in certain quarters to the effect that the Allied loans were worthless unless America entered the war; that the holders of these loans urged our Government into the war 'to make the loans good.' There was nothing in the facts remotely justifying this fantastic theory. The loans were always good. No one feared for their safety." The statement argued that U.S. business was already thriving from supplying the Allies and there was no material advantage to having the United States enter the war.[99]

Losing the debate could have enormous consequences. Nye and Clark recognized that the evidence presented about U.S. entry into the past war could determine the fate of the important neutrality bill they were introducing that week.

At that first hearing, the committee released documents showing that President Wilson had sided with Secretary of War Robert Lansing over Secretary of State William Jennings Bryan's sharp opposition and decided to allow bankers to float loans to belligerents in 1914, long before the policy change was publicly announced. Before adjourning, Senator Clark asked one last question of Vanderlip: "Do you think Great Britain would have paid her debts if she had lost the war?" Vanderlip replied, "Yes, even had she lost the war she would have paid." [100]

In subsequent hearings, Nye and other committee members endeavored to show that the United States had never been neutral in the war and that German submarine warfare was just the pretext Wilson seized upon as an excuse to intervene. Nye dropped one last bombshell: he alleged that Wilson learned about the Allies' secret treaties before the United States entered the war and then "falsified" the record by telling members of the Senate Foreign Relations Committee that he had found this out only later, at Versailles.

The Nye Committee investigations showed that Wilson had, in effect, lied the country into war. He had undermined neutrality by allowing loans and other support to the Allies, deliberately exaggerated claims of German atrocities, and covered up the fact of his knowledge of the secret treaties. Far from being a war to further democracy, it had been a war to redivide the spoils of empire.

Aspersions on the integrity of Woodrow Wilson proved to be the final straw for many Senate Democrats, who rose in fevered denunciations of the committee chairman in what the Washington Post described as "a tornado of protest and resentment." Senator Tom Connally of Texas led the charge, declaring, "I do not care how the charges were made; they are infamous. Some checker-playing, beer-drinking back room of some low house is the only place fit for the kind of language the Senator from North Dakota, the chairman of the committee—this man who is going to lead us out toward peace—puts into the record about a dead man—a great man, a good man, and a man who, when alive, had the courage to meet his enemies face to face and eye to eye." Connally accused Nye and the committee of an "almost scandalous effort to besmear and besmut the records of America in the World War." The controversy split the committee itself. Two of the members, Senators Pope and George, left the hearing in protest. Pope returned and read a statement in which he and Gregory expressed resentment at "any effort to impugn the motives of Woodrow Wilson and to discredit his great character." They regretted that the purpose of the investigation was being lost sight of and feared that the chance of securing "remedial legislation" was slipping away. They questioned the integrity of the committee's investigation: "Such efforts to disparage Wilson and Lansing . . . disclose the bias and prejudice with which the investigation is being carried on." They made it clear that they were not resigning from the committee and would return for a vote on the final report. Another committee member, Senator Vandenberg, added that he, too, admired Wilson but that economic motives had provided "an inevitable and irresistible impulse" for getting the United States into the war. He wanted to make sure that never happened again and said he took pride in what the committee had accomplished: "History has been rewritten in the last 48 hours. It is important that history should be revealed in all its nakedness, no matter what it shows." Nye assured Pope and George that he had no malice toward Wilson and had even voted for him in 1916, promising to persevere "as long as there is a possibility of lessening the chances of our being drawn into war."[101]

The bloodletting continued the next day in the Senate. Seventy-eight-year-old Carter Glass of Virginia, who had served as Wilson's secretary of the Treasury in the last months of his administration, accused Nye of an "infamous libel," an "unspeakable accusation against a dead President, dirt-daubing the sepulchre [sic] of Woodrow Wilson." Pounding his hand on the desk so hard that blood spurted all over his papers, Carter cried out, "Oh, the miserable demagogy, the miserable and mendacious suggestion, that the House of Morgan altered the neutrality course of Woodrow Wilson!" Nye finally got his chance to respond on the floor of the Senate. He said that what surprised him was that there had not been "an earlier concerted effort" to stop his committee's work and that the hostility only became apparent with the appearance of Morgan and his partners. He offered no apologies, instead reading letters and documents that, he reiterated, showed that "the United States entered the war knowing the spoils had been agreed upon. Yet we were told news of secret treaties came as a bombshell at the peace conference."[102]

Two days later, Nye informed Morgan and his partners that they need not appear as scheduled the following week for further examination. The committee had hit a roadblock, and the prospects of Senate appropriation of the $9,000 needed to continue its work looked bleak. He accused his detractors of using the Wilson issue as a "smoke screen." Their real intention, he insisted, was to "seize upon any weapon and resort to any subterfuge to kill legislation which threatens the bloody profits to be made from war."[103]

To everyone's surprise and Nye's delight, the hearings were not aborted. On January 30, the Senate unanimously approved $7,369 to finish the probe. Even Connally reversed his previous position and voted for the added funding, but he urged the committee to stick to living people and not invade the "cemeteries and catacombs" of the dead.[104] The *New York Times* explained the Senate's change of heart: "When Wilsonians resentful of slurs against their World War chieftain threatened to interrupt the inquiry by stripping it of funds, mail sacks on Capitol Hill bulged with letters urging that the full story of 1914–18 be told. That demonstration of an anti-war mood explains why an inquiry which had provoked more bitterness than any similar affair in many years was allowed to survive." The *Times* credited the committee with having already achieved "notable reforms." "It helped to place on the books a statute requiring munitions makers to obtain licenses and report all shipments to the State Department. It resulted in the framing of bills to remove exorbitant profits from the arms and shipbuilding industries, and it is expected that these proposals will eventually become law in one form or another. But its major accomplishment is the churning of public opinion on the subject of war, peace and profits."[105]

During the final sessions, representatives of the House of Morgan did their best to fend off charges that their loans to the Allies had influenced U.S. participation in the war. The *New York Times* headlined its February 5 article "Morgan Leaves Happy, 'Cleared' by Friend Nye." The *Times* breathed a sigh of relief. It titled its February 9 editorial "An Inquiry Ends Well." The committee's efforts to show that Morgan had made "enormous profits out of the sale of munitions" and had "used its powerful influence" to secure American entry were completely discredited, the *Times* noted, and "the inquiry ended on a sort of jovial note of congratulation between MR. MORGAN and his 'friend NYE.'" The editorial concluded, "Such an outcome is of great public benefit. . . . It is easy to imagine the disturbing effect if a contrary result had been reached. People would despairingly have concluded that there was something rotten in the whole banking business."[106]

Nye immediately took issue with the *Times*' portrayal. "There is not a single member of the Senate committee of inquiry that believes that the inquiry has afforded a clean bill of health for the banking house of Morgan." Although Morgan couldn't be blamed for inducing U.S. entry into the war to protect its investments, Nye noted that it was "altogether fair to say that these bankers were in the heart and center of a system that made our going to war inevitable." Once Wilson allowed Morgan to become banker to the Allies, Nye added, "the road to war was paved and greased for us."[107]

Dramatic evidence that the committee hearings were having the desired impact appeared in a Gallup Poll released on March 7. When asked, "Should the manufacture and sale of war munitions for private profit be prohibited?"

82 percent of Americans responded yes and only 18 percent no. The strongest support came from Nevada, where 99 percent favored abolishing profits. The weakest came from Delaware, the home of Du Pont, where only 63 percent answered affirmatively. George Gallup reported that since the company had begun polling the previous October, only old-age pensions had received more support in any of its surveys. Gallup quoted a grocer in western Pennsylvania who said, "The profit system in munitions has been leading us to war for generations." [108] Even Nye had considered such ideas farfetched when he began his hearings seventeen months earlier. "I thought," he admitted, "that nationalization of munitions manufacturers was about the wildest idea we had under consideration." [109] The *Washington Post,* among others, congratulated Nye and his committee for educating the public on "the abuses which have developed in the munitions trade and . . . the relation between war and the accessibility of arms." [110] The next day, Eleanor Roosevelt, speaking in Grand Rapids, Michigan, called for taking all profits out of the munitions industry. The *New York Times,* which had so recently come to the defense of Morgan and the munitions manufacturers, did not even report that the Gallup Poll had been released.

In April, the Nye Committee issued its long-awaited third report. It concluded, "While the evidence before this committee does not show that wars have been started solely because of the activities of munitions makers and their agents, it is also true that wars rarely have one single cause, and the committee finds it to be against the peace of the world for selfishly interested organizations to be left free to goad and frighten nations into military activity." [111] Four of the seven members of the committee—Nye, Clark, Pope, and Bone—called for outright government ownership of the munitions industry. The minority—George, Barbour, and Vandenberg—called for "rigid and conclusive munitions control." [112] But the bill to remove the profits from war had been assigned to a subcommittee chaired by Connally, one of Nye's biggest critics. There it languished, and when it was finally introduced in watered-down form, it failed to get the requisite votes. Similar bills introduced by Nye and others over the next five years also failed to gain traction.

Among the issues raised by the hearings that continue to rankle investigators is U.S. businessmen's contribution to Germany's economic and military revitalization long after they had become aware of the repugnant nature of Hitler's regime. Since 1933, Hitler had been imprisoning and murdering Communists, Social Democrats, and labor leaders. His vicious anti-Semitism was apparent, although the campaign to exterminate the Jews was still several years away. Close ties between U.S. businessmen and bankers and their German counterparts had been forged in the years prior to Hitler's rise to power. U.S. loans, largely organized by the Morgan and Chase banking interests, propped up the faltering German economy of the 1920s. IBM, headed by Thomas Watson, purchased a controlling interest in the German firm Dehomag. Sloan's General Motors purchased German car manufacturer Adam Opel between 1929 and 1931. Ford increased investment in its German subsidiary, Ford Motor Company Aktiengesellschaft, declaring that this move would build a bridge between countries.[113] Watson shared that vision. "World Peace through World Trade!" he was fond of proclaiming.[114]

World peace, however noble, was no more the capitalists' primary concern than was achieving wealth and power through a competitive marketplace. Through a dizzying array of formal and informal business agreements, a network of multinational corporations based in the United States, England, and Germany colluded to capture markets and control prices. A trade agreement reached in Düsseldorf between the Federation of British Industries and Reichsgruppe Industrie was announced in March 1939, proclaiming, "It is agreed that it is essential to replace destructive competition, wherever it may be found, by constructive cooperation designed to foster world trade to the mutual benefit of Great Britain, Germany, and all other countries."[115] It was only after the war that most observers became aware how extensive such arrangements had been. As Theodore Kreps of Stanford University observed in May 1945, "The word 'cartel' has recently been catapulted from the obscure technical jargon of economic treatises to the front pages of daily newspapers."[116] Typical of these arrangements, Edsel Ford sat on the board of the German chemical firm IG Farben's U.S. subsidiary, General Aniline and Film, while Farben General Manager Carl Bosch sat on the board of Ford's European subsidiary. Similar arrangements tied together Farben, Du Pont, GM, Standard Oil, and Chase Bank.

After meeting Hitler in 1937, Watson dutifully and credulously relayed the führer's message to a gathering of the International Chamber of Commerce in Berlin: "There will be no war. No country wants war, no country can afford it."[117] A few days later, on his seventy-fifth birthday, he accepted the Grand Cross of the German Eagle, which Hitler bestowed on him for the welcome assistance that Dehomag's punch-card machines were providing the German government in tabulating its 1930 census and, as a result, identifying Jews. Dehomag's counting machines represented an unprecedented breakthrough in the organization of data that later, when the company was under Nazi control, helped make the trains to Auschwitz run on time.

Henry Ford also attested to Hitler's pacific intentions. On August 28, 1939, just four days prior to the invasion of Poland, Ford assured the *Boston Globe* that Hitler was just bluffing. The Germans "don't dare have a war and they know it," he said. A week later, after the German invasion had begun, he had the temerity to remark to a friend, "There hasn't been a shot fired. The whole thing has just been made up by Jew bankers."[118]

Ford and Watson should both have known better. In 1937, Ford's German subsidiary was manufacturing heavy trucks and troop carriers for the German Wehrmacht. In July 1939, the subsidiary changed its name to Ford-Werke. Farben, which was later convicted of crimes against humanity for operating the Buna rubber plant at Auschwitz and supplying the notorious Zyklon-B tablets used to exterminate Jews, owned 15 percent of the company. When the war started in 1939, Ford and GM still controlled their German subsidiaries, which dominated the German auto industry. Despite their subsequent disclaimers, they refused to divest themselves of their German holdings and even complied with German government orders to retool for war production, while resisting similar demands from the U.S. government to retool their factories at home. Sloan justified such behavior in March 1939, following the Nazi occupation of Czechoslovakia, based on the fact that the German operations were "highly profitable." Germany's internal politics, he insisted, "should not be considered the business of the management of General Motors." Opel converted the 432-acre complex in Russelsheim to production of Luftwaffe warplanes, providing fully 50 percent of the propulsion systems for Germany's JU-88 medium-range bombers while also helping to develop the world's first jet fighter, the ME-262, which was capable of speeds a hundred miles per hour faster than the United States' P-510 Mustangs. In appreciation of their efforts, the Nazi government decorated Henry Ford with the Grand Cross of the German Eagle in 1938, four months after Germany had annexed Austria, and similarly honored James D. Mooney, GM's chief overseas executive, one month later. Ford's parent company lost effective control of the company during the war years, when Ford-Werke supplied the regime with arms, employing prisoners from nearby Buchenwald concentration camp as slave labor. When a former prisoner Elsa Iwanowa brought suit against the company in 1998, the Ford Motor Company hired a small army of researchers and lawyers to investigate its past behavior and promote its preferred image as part of the "arsenal of democracy." Just after the war, however, a report by U.S. Army investigator Henry Schneider called Ford-Werke an "arsenal of Nazism." [119] And, as Bradford Snell discovered during his congressional investigation into the monopolistic practices of the auto industry, through "their multinational dominance of motor vehicle production, GM and Ford became principal suppliers for the forces of fascism as well as for the forces of democracy." [120]

Henry Ford did more than supply trucks for the German military; he also helped the Nazis hone their hateful ideology. In 1921, he published a collection of anti-Semitic articles titled *The International Jew,* which was widely read by future Nazi leaders. He also sponsored the printing of a half-million copies of the *Protocols of the Elders of Zion.* The fact that the *Protocols* had been widely exposed as a forgery didn't deter Ford. Baldur von Schirach, former head of the Hitler Youth organization and wartime governor of Nazi-occupied Vienna, testified at Nuremberg:

> The decisive anti-Semitic book which I read at that time was Henry Ford's book, *The International Jew*. I read it and became anti-Semitic. This book made . . . a great impression on my friends and myself, because we saw in Henry Ford the representative of success, also the representative of a progressive social policy. In the poverty-stricken and wretched Germany of the time, youth looked toward America, and . . . it was Henry Ford who, to us, represented America. . . . If he said Jews were to blame, naturally we believed him.[121]

Hitler hung a portrait of Ford in his Munich office and confided to a *Chicago Tribune* reporter in 1923, "I wish I could send some of my shock troops to Chicago and other big American cities to help in the elections. We look on Heinrich Ford as the leader of the growing Fascist Party in America." In 1931, he told readers of the *Detroit News*, "I regard Henry Ford as my inspiration."[122]

The Germans also drew inspiration from the ill-fated U.S. flirtation with eugenics and "racial hygiene" in the 1920s and 1930s. California paved the way in forced sterilizations, with more than a third of the sixty thousand performed, but other states were not far behind.[123] Rockefeller and Carnegie money helped fund the research that gave these efforts a patina of respectability. These developments did not go unnoticed in Germany. In *Mein Kampf*, Hitler lauded American leadership in the field of eugenics. He later informed his Nazi colleagues, "I have studied with great interest the laws of several American states concerning prevention of reproduction by people whose progeny would, in all probability, be of no value or be injurious to the racial stock."[124]

Among those states was Virginia, whose decision to sterilize a "feeble-minded" young woman prompted the famous 1927 Supreme Court ruling in the case of *Buck v. Bell*. In writing the majority opinion, eighty-six-year-old Justice Oliver Wendell Holmes, a Civil War veteran, argued that Buck's sacrifice of procreative freedom was comparable to soldiers sacrificing their lives in wartime: "We have seen more than once that the public welfare may call upon the best citizens for their lives. It would be strange if it could not call upon those who already sap the strength of the State for these lesser sacrifices . . . in order to prevent our being swamped with incompetence." Holmes concluded, "It is better for the entire world, if instead of waiting to execute degenerate offspring for crime, or to let them starve for their imbecility, society can prevent those who are manifestly unfit from continuing their kind. . . . Three generations of

A German edition of Henry Ford's The International Jew, *a collection of anti-Semitic articles that was widely read by future Nazi leaders.*

imbeciles are enough." [125] Although Virginia was second only to California in forced sterilizations, some felt it was not aggressive enough. In pushing the state legislature to broaden its sterilization law, Dr. Joseph DeJarnette complained in 1934, "The Germans are beating us at our own game." [126]

Although most U.S. companies doing business in Hitler's Germany removed American officials in 1939 or 1940, control often remained in the hands of the same German businessmen who had run the companies as subsidiaries of U.S. firms. Profits, meanwhile, piled up in blocked bank accounts.

Prominent among the American capitalists with ties to Nazi counterparts was Prescott Bush, the father of one president and grandfather of another. Researchers have been trying for years to determine the precise nature of Bush's ties to Fritz Thyssen, the wealthy German industrialist who played a crucial role in bankrolling Hitler, as revealed in his 1941 memoirs *I Paid Hitler.* Thyssen ultimately repudiated the Nazi dictator and was himself imprisoned.

While incarcerated, Thyssen's vast wealth was protected overseas, much of it by the investment firm of Brown Brothers Harriman, through the holding company Union Banking Corporation. The account was managed by senior partner Prescott Bush. In 1942, the U.S. government seized Union Banking Corporation under the Trading with the Enemy Act for its association with the Thyssen-owned Bank voor Handel en Scheepvaart NV of Rotterdam. The government also seized four other Thyssen-linked companies whose accounts Bush handled: the Holland-American Trading Company, the Seamless Steel Equipment Corporation, the Silesian-American Corporation, and the Hamburg-Amerika Line shipping company. [127]

Following the war, most of this Nazi-tainted money was released. Union

Banking Corporation shares were returned to Bush; Dehomag's frozen profits were taken by IBM; and Ford and GM both reabsorbed their German subsidiaries—even receiving reparations for the European factories that had been destroyed by Allied bombing, up to $33 million in the case of GM.[128]

These businessmen were not alone. Many American companies continued doing business with Nazi Germany right up to the Japanese attack on Pearl Harbor. As Ford Motor Company was happy to point out in its 2001 investigation into the activities of Ford-Werke, at the start of the war, 250 American firms owned more than $450 million worth of German assets, with 58.5 percent being owned by the top ten. Among the companies were familiar names like Standard Oil, Woolworth, IT&T, Singer, International Harvester, Eastman Kodak, Gillette, Coca-Cola, Kraft, Westinghouse, and United Fruit. Ford ranked sixteenth, holding only 1.9 percent of the total U.S. investment. Standard Oil and GM topped the list, holding 14 and 12 percent, respectively.[129]

Many of these companies were represented by the corporate powerhouse law firm Sullivan and Cromwell, headed by future Secretary of State John Foster Dulles. His brother Allen Dulles, future head of the CIA, was a partner. Among their clients was the Bank for International Settlements (BIS), which had been set up in Switzerland in 1930 to channel war reparations between the United States and Germany.

After war was declared, the bank continued to offer financial services to the Third Reich. The majority of gold looted during the Nazi conquests of Europe ended up in BIS vaults, and the transfer of capital allowed the Nazis access to money that would have been normally trapped in blocked accounts under the Trading with the Enemy Act. Several Nazis and supporters were involved at high levels, including Hjalmar Schacht and Walther Funk, who both ended up in the dock at the Nuremberg trials, though Schacht was acquitted. American lawyer and chairman of the bank, Thomas McKittrick, facilitated the process, claiming "neutrality" but effectively aiding the Nazis. The BIS's operations were so vile that Secretary of the Treasury Henry Morgenthau charged that twelve of the bank's fourteen directors were "Nazi or Nazi-controlled." [130]

Chase, Morgan, Union Bank, and the Bank for International Settlements all managed to obfuscate their collaboration with the Nazis. Chase and Morgan continued to work with Vichy France. Its deposits doubled during the war years. In 1998, Holocaust survivors sued the banks, claiming they held blocked accounts from that era. Morgan quickly settled. Chase contested the charges.

While American capitalists piled up the earnings from their overseas investments and did everything possible to ingratiate themselves to the German government,[131] Gerald Nye and his crack team of investigators succeeded brilliantly in revealing sordid truths about the influence and machinations of arms manufacturers and moneylenders, exposing the ugly reality hidden beneath the lofty refrains to which the GIs had marched off to war. But the hearings had two other effects that, with the wisdom of hindsight, we can justly regret. First, they tended to oversimplify the causes of the war. And, second, they reinforced the country's isolationist tendencies at precisely the worst time imaginable—when U.S. influence might have helped avert disaster. The hearings justified the widespread belief that the United States should steer clear of entangling alliances and involvement in world affairs. For perhaps the only time in U.S. history, powerful antiwar sentiment was actually misplaced in light of the true threat to humanity posed by fascistic and other dangerous forces. Cordell Hull later wrote that the Nye Committee hearings had had the "disastrous effects" of catalyzing "an isolationist sentiment that was to tie the hands of the Administration just at the time when our hands should have been free to place the weight of our influence in the scales where it would count." [132] In January 1935, *Christian Century* observed, "Ninety-nine Americans out of a hundred would today regard as an imbecile anyone who might suggest that, in the event of another European war, the United States should again participate in it." [133]

Events in Europe would soon prompt some to reconsider. First Hitler repudiated the arms limitations imposed at Versailles. Then, in October 1935, Mussolini invaded Ethiopia. Hampered by recently passed neutrality legislation imposing an embargo on arms sales to all belligerents and a domestic population whose loyalties were sharply divided, with Italian Americans generally supporting Mussolini and African Americans supporting Ethiopia, the United States stayed on the sidelines. Nor did the international community strongly condemn the invasion. The League of Nations denounced the Italian aggression and looked to impose an oil embargo with potentially devastating consequences. The League's Coordination Committee asked nonmember nations if they would comply. At the time, the United States supplied more than half the world's oil. U.S. cooperation could have done much to deter fascist aggression. But Roosevelt, bowing to the isolationist sentiment at home, opted not to participate. Roosevelt instead announced a "moral embargo" on shipments of oil and other important resources. The "moral embargo" proved completely ineffectual as U.S. resource shipments to Italy nearly tripled over the next few months. [134] The League passed limited and toothless sanctions that it watered down out of deference to British and French timidity and fear of provoking Italy.

Mussolini's gambit succeeded. Hitler and the Japanese concluded that Great Britain, France, and the United States had no stomach for war and would rather acquiesce than face military action. In January 1936, Japan walked out of the London Naval Conference and began an ambitious militarization program. In March 1936, German troops occupied the Rhineland. It was both Hitler's big gamble and his big bluff. But it worked. He later admitted that armed resistance would have forced him to back down. "The forty-eight hours after the march into the Rhineland were the most nerve-wracking in my life," he said. "If the French had then marched into the Rhineland, we would have had to withdraw with our tails between our legs, for the military resources at our disposal would have been wholly inadequate for even a moderate resistance." [135]

The feeble international response to the Spanish Civil War was even more disheartening. Fighting broke out in July 1936 as Francisco Franco's forces set out to topple the elected Spanish government and establish a fascist regime. The republic had made enemies among U.S. officials and corporate leaders by its progressive policies and tight regulation of business. Some alleged Communist influence and expressed fear that a republican victory would result in Communist domination. American Catholics and church officials, angered by the republic's aggressive anticlericalism, rallied to Franco's support, as did Hitler and Mussolini, who provided abundant aid, including aircraft, pilots, and thousands of troops. Germany would use the war to test the weapons and tactics it later deployed against Poland and the rest of Europe. Stalin sent planes and tanks to the democratic forces but couldn't come close to matching the massive assistance from Berlin and Rome. But Roosevelt did nothing to assist the Republican forces. Nor did Great Britain or France. The United States, following the British and French lead, banned the shipment of weapons to both sides, which weakened the beleaguered and outgunned government forces. Ford, GM, Firestone, and other U.S. businesses provided the fascists with trucks, tires, and machine tools. Texaco Oil Company, headed by pro-Fascist Colonel Thorkild Rieber, promised Franco all the oil he needed—on credit. Roosevelt, furious, threatened an oil embargo and slapped Texaco with a fine. But Rieber persisted undeterred, supplying oil to Hitler and being lionized in the pages of *Life* magazine. [136]

Progressive Americans rallied to the republican cause. Surprisingly to some, it was antiwar stalwart Gerald Nye who led the Senate fight to send desperately needed arms to Republican forces. Some three thousand brave American volunteers went to Spain to battle the Fascists, traveling first to France and then sneaking across the Pyrenees into Spain. Four hundred fifty men formed the legendary Communist-backed Abraham Lincoln Brigade, which suffered 120 dead and 175 wounded. Paul Robeson, the extraordinarily talented African-American athlete, intellectual, actor, and singer, went to the battlefield to entertain the troops.

The fighting dragged on for three years. The republic fell in spring 1939, burying with it not only over 100,000 republican soldiers and 5,000 foreign volunteers but the hopes and dreams of much of humanity. By 1938, Roosevelt realized how foolish his policies had been and tried to send covert aid to the

*A ceremony during the first gathering of Veterans of the
Abraham Lincoln Brigade, the legendary Communist-backed
group of volunteers who went to fight Franco's Fascists in Spain.
The brigade suffered 120 dead and 175 wounded.*

republic. It was too little too late. His policy had been "a grave mistake," Roosevelt told his cabinet. He warned that they would soon all pay the price.[137]

The world did little to impede Japanese aggression in China in 1937, though many onlookers were horrified at the reports of the fighting. Beginning with the Marco Polo Bridge incident in July 1937, fighting spread to other parts of the country. With Jiang Jieshi's (Chiang Kai-shek's) forces fleeing in retreat, Japan brutalized Chinese civilians. The atrocities, including an orgy of rape, looting, and murder, were most egregious in Shanghai and Nanjing.

With fascistic and militaristic forces on the march, the world was hurtling rapidly toward war. Motivated in some cases by sympathy for the fascists, in others by hatred of Soviet communism, and in others by fear of plunging into the same abyss that had caused such suffering in the previous world war, the Western democracies stood on the sidelines as Italy, Japan, and Germany set about to forcibly change the balance of global power.

Chapter 3

WORLD WAR II:

Who Really Defeated Germany?

Most Americans view World War II nostalgically as the "good war," in which the United States and its allies triumphed over German Nazism, Italian fascism, and Japanese militarism. The rest of the world remembers it as the bloodiest war in human history. By the time it was over, more than 60 million people lay dead, including 27 million Russians, between 10 million and 20 million Chinese, 6 million Jews, 5.5 million Germans, 3 million non-Jewish Poles, 2.5 million Japanese, and 1.5 million Yugoslavs. Austria, Great Britain, France, Italy, Hungary, Romania, and the United States each counted between 250,000 and 333,000 dead.

Unlike World War I, World War II began slowly and incrementally. The opening shots were fired in 1931, when Japan's Kwantung Army overwhelmed Chinese forces in Manchuria.

While the Western powers expanded their colonial empires in the late nineteenth century, the rapidly modernizing and industrializing Japan sought its proper place among the world's leading nations. Japan demonstrated its new military prowess by defeating China in the Sino-Japanese War of 1894–1895 and then delivering a stunning defeat to Russia in the Russo-Japanese War exactly a decade later. It was the first time in almost seven hundred years—since the days of Genghis Khan—that an Eastern power had defeated a Western one. The loss devastated the Russian regime, sparking a revolutionary upsurge in 1905. This radical ferment, fueled by tsarist injustice and heavy losses to Germany in World War I, would culminate in the Russian Revolution in 1917. The Russo-Japanese War also created a bitterness between Russia and Japan that would fester for decades.

Meanwhile, Germany, thirsting to avenge its own devastating defeat in World War I, was on the march in the West. Hitler and Mussolini formed the Axis in 1936 and began assisting General Francisco Franco's overthrow of the Spanish Republic. The Western democracies' spineless response to Fascist aggression in Ethiopia and Spain emboldened Hitler to believe that he could pursue his plans to conquer the rest of Europe. It also convinced Stalin that Great Britain, France, and the United States had no interest in taking collective action to slow the Nazi advance.

In 1937, full-scale war erupted in China as the powerful Japanese army captured city after city. In December 1937, Japanese soldiers brutalized the citizens of Nanjing, killing 200,000 to 300,000 civilians and raping perhaps 80,000 women. Japan soon controlled the east coast of China, with its population of 200 million.

The international situation deteriorated further in 1938 when the Germans annexed Austria and the Allies capitulated to Hitler at Munich, giving Germany the Sudetenland in Czechoslovakia. British Prime Minister Neville Chamberlain infamously proclaimed that the settlement had brought "peace in our time."[1] Roosevelt knew better. The British and French, he insisted, had abandoned the helpless Czechs and would "wash the blood from their Judas Iscariot hands."[2] But Roosevelt also knew that the United States itself was offering little support to those who wanted to stand up to the Nazi dictator. Nor did the United States do enough to help Germany and Austria's desperate Jewish communities. In 1939 the United States admitted its full quota of 27,300 German and Austrian immigrants—the only year in which it did so. But with hundreds of thousands of Jews seeking refuge, U.S. assistance proved woefully inadequate. And Roosevelt made no effort to raise the low quota established by discriminatory immigration legislation in 1924.[3]

Hitler struck again in March 1939, invading Czechoslovakia. Stalin understood that the Soviet Union's turn was coming soon. For years the Soviet dictator had implored the West to unite against Hitler and Mussolini. The Soviet Union even joined the League of Nations in 1934. But Soviet pleas for collective security against the fascist aggressors were repeatedly ignored. Following Hitler's assault on Czechoslovakia, Stalin again urged England and France to join in defense of Eastern Europe. His entreaties fell on deaf ears.

Fearing a German-Polish alliance to attack the USSR, he decided to buy time. In August, he struck an unsavory deal with his mortal enemy. Hitler and Stalin shocked the world by signing a nonaggression pact with a secret protocol dividing Eastern Europe between them. In fact, the Soviet dictator had proposed a similar alliance with Britain and France, but neither would accept Stalin's demand to place Soviet troops on Polish soil as a way of maximizing the deterrent effect. Hitler invaded Poland on September 1. The Allies declared war on Germany. The Soviet Union invaded Poland on September 17. The Soviets soon thereafter asserted control over the Baltic states of Estonia, Latvia, and Lithuania and invaded Finland.

After a brief respite, in April 1940, Hitler unleashed his furious blitzkrieg.

*Hitler and Mussolini formed the Axis in 1936 and began
a campaign of aggression in Ethiopia and Spain. Initially,
the Western democracies did little to stop them.*

In rapid succession, Denmark, Norway, Holland, and Belgium all fell. On June 22, France, its younger generation having been decimated in World War I and its conservative ruling class anti-Semitic to the core, surrendered after only six weeks of fighting, leaving Great Britain isolated. During the Battle of Britain in summer 1940, prospects looked bleak. But Germany's failure to destroy Great Britain's Royal Air Force made the cross-channel invasion of Great Britain planned for September 1940 impossible. Still, the German Luftwaffe's pummeling of British cities continued.

Roosevelt wanted to help, but with neutrality legislation on the books, military preparedness at a low level, and isolationist sentiment running high, there was little he could do. He also encountered resistance from cabinet members and military leaders who thought that Great Britain was lost and resources should be concentrated on defending the homeland. He maneuvered to get Great Britain as much military aid as he could. Opening himself up to attacks that he was acting illegally, he bypassed the Senate and unilaterally decided to provide Great Britain with fifty old naval destroyers in exchange for ninety-nine-year leases of air and naval bases on eight British possessions in the Western Hemisphere. As the Battle of Britain raged on, Roosevelt was willing to absorb such attacks to bolster British resolve.[4]

World leaders condemned Japanese aggression but did little to help China as Japan relentlessly bombed Chinese cities. In July 1939, the United States tightened the noose around the Japanese economy by terminating its 1911 commercial treaty with Japan, which cut off the flow of vital raw materials, and banning U.S. exports critical to the Japanese war machine. Meanwhile, in Manchuria, Soviet and Japanese armies battled over the disputed border, leading to Soviet General Georgi Zhukov's first victory and heightening tensions in the East.

In September 1940, Germany, Italy, and Japan formally concluded the Tripartite Pact, establishing the "Axis powers" alliance. Hungary, Romania, Slovakia, and Bulgaria joined soon thereafter.

Seeing the war clouds gathering on the horizon, Roosevelt decided to break with precedent and run for a third term. The Republicans nominated a corporate attorney from Indiana, Wendell Willkie, a political moderate who supported much of the New Deal legislation and advocated military aid to Great Britain. The fact that Willkie, a recent convert to the Republican Party, had garnered the nomination angered party diehards like former Senator James Watson, who commented, "If a whore repented and wanted to join the church, I'd personally welcome her and lead her up the aisle to a pew. But, by the Eternal, I'd not ask her to lead the choir the first night."[5]

Roosevelt gave serious thought to choosing a running mate. The stakes were high. The nation might soon be at war. He weighed his options and chose his Secretary of Agriculture: Henry A. Wallace. He knew that there would be strong opposition to Wallace, who came from a line of prominent Iowa Republicans. His grandfather had founded *Wallaces' Farmer*, a leading farm journal dedicated to scientific agriculture. His father served as secretary of agriculture under Harding and Coolidge until his death in 1924. Although he supported Smith in 1928 and Roosevelt in 1932, Wallace didn't officially switch parties until 1936, leading some party officials to question his loyalty, much as Republicans were questioning Willkie's.

Roosevelt had no such doubts. He knew where Wallace stood on the issues. Wallace had been a stalwart as secretary of agriculture, overseeing an extraordinary return to agricultural prosperity. Farmers, who still constituted a quarter of the population in 1933, were in miserable shape when Wallace became secretary. Production of farm commodities had flooded the markets, driving down prices. The problem, which persisted throughout the 1920s, reached crisis proportions after 1929. Total farm income in 1932 stood at one-third of what it had been in 1929. By 1933, desperation stalked rural America. Roosevelt understood that the overall success of the New Deal depended on the restoration of farm prosperity. Wallace's solution proved extremely controversial. He proposed paying farmers to reduce agricultural production on the assumption that lowered supply would increase demand and thereby raise prices. But in 1933, he was forced to take even more drastic action. The price of cotton had dropped to 5 cents per pound. Warehouses were bursting. Export markets had evaporated. And another large crop was sprouting. Wallace decided to pay farmers to destroy 25 percent of the crop that was then in the ground. For Wallace, who had spent years perfecting a strain of hybrid corn and who believed that abundant food supplies were essential for a peaceful world, the thought was almost inconceivable. "To have to destroy a growing crop," he lamented, "is a shocking commentary on our civilization." That August, more than 10 million acres of cotton were plowed under.

But what came next was even more difficult. Wallace still had to deal with an abundance of hogs. On the advice of hog farmers, Wallace supported a program of slaughtering 6 million baby pigs weighing under one hundred pounds, approximately half the normal two-hundred-pound market weight of adults. Critics lambasted Wallace's "pig infanticide" and "pig birth control." Wallace retorted, "Doubtless it is just as inhumane to kill a big hog as a little one. . . . To hear them talk, you would have thought that pigs are raised for pets." Wallace made sure that some good came of this program. He distributed one hundred million pounds of pork, lard, and soap to needy Americans. "Not many people realized how radical it was—," he reflected, "this idea of having the Government buy from those who had too much, in order to give to those who had too little."

Wallace's much-maligned policies produced the desired effect. The price of cotton doubled. Farm income jumped by 30 percent in one year. Still, Wallace regretted the unfortunate message such policies sent: "The plowing under of 10 million acres of cotton in August 1933, and the slaughter of 6 million little pigs in September, 1933, were not acts of idealism in any sane society. They were emergency acts made necessary by the almost insane lack of world statesmanship during the period from 1920 to 1932."[6] Wallace's clarifications notwithstanding, the seemingly wanton destruction of crops and livestock in the midst of hunger and poverty turned people's empty stomachs and saddled the New Deal with an image of callousness and a reputation of espousing a philosophy of recovery through scarcity.

Overall, as Arthur Schlesinger, Jr., later wrote, "Wallace was a great secretary of agriculture. . . . In time he widened his concern beyond commercial farming to subsistence farming and rural poverty. For the urban poor, he provided food stamps and school lunches. He instituted programs for land-use planning, soil conservation and erosion control. And always he promoted research to combat plant and animal diseases, to locate drought-resistant crops and to develop hybrid seeds in order to increase productivity."[7]

During his eight years as secretary of agriculture, Wallace not only solidified his reputation as one of the New Deal visionaries on domestic policy, he carved credentials as an outspoken antifascist. In 1939, he lent his support to the American Committee for Democracy and Intellectual Freedom (ACDIF). The ACDIF had been organized by Franz Boas, America's leading anthropologist, and like-minded left-leaning scientists earlier that year. In late 1938, Boas released his Manifesto on Freedom of Science. Signed by 1,284 scientists, it condemned Nazi racism and treatment of scientists and teachers and urged a vigorous defense of democracy and intellectual freedom in the United States. Scientists held Wallace in high regard, considering him the most scientifically literate member of the Roosevelt administration and the scientific community's best ally. They invited him to participate in an October 1939 ACDIF panel discussion on "How the Scientist Can Help Combat Racism" at the New York World's Fair. Wallace defined "racism" as "the attempts of individuals in certain groups to dominate others through the building up of false racial theories in support of their claims." Drawing on his background in plant genetics, he focused on "the role that scientists can play in combating such false theories and preventing the use of these theories for the destruction of human liberty." He appealed to scientists to lead the fight:

> For the combating of "racism" before it sinks its poison fangs deep in
> our body politic, the scientist has both a special motive and a special
> responsibility. His motive comes from the fact that when personal liberty
> disappears scientific liberty also disappears. His responsibility comes from
> the fact that only he can give the people the truth. Only he can clean out
> the falsities in our colleges, our high schools and our public prints. Only he
> can show how groundless are the claims that one race, one nation, or one
> class has any God-given right to rule.[8]

Now, with European democracy on life support, Roosevelt demanded a champion of freedom and democracy as his running mate. But party bosses and party conservatives opposed Wallace for the very reasons Roosevelt wanted him. They feared his radical views. They mistrusted his devotion to principles over politics. It looked as though the Wallace nomination would go up in flames. Roosevelt, angry and frustrated, wrote a remarkable letter to the assembled delegates, a letter of which contemporary Democrats would be wise to take heed, in which he flatly turned down the presidential nomination. He explained:

> the Democratic Party [must] champion . . . progressive and liberal policies
> and principles. . . . The party has failed . . . when . . . it has fallen into the
> control of those [who] think in terms of dollars instead of . . . human
> values. . . . Until the Democratic Party . . . shakes off all the shackles

of control fastened upon it by the forces of conservatism, reaction
and appeasement, . . . it will not continue its march to victory . . . the
Democratic Party . . . cannot face in both directions at the same time.
[Therefore, I] declin[e] the honor of the nomination for the Presidency.[9]

Eleanor Roosevelt saved the day. The first wife of a nominee ever to address a
convention, she told disgruntled delegates that "we face now a grave and serious
situation" and reminded them that this was "no ordinary time."[10] Under intense
pressure, the party bosses, who dominated the nominating process, and the convention delegates buckled and put Wallace onto the ticket. They would, however, later seek an opportunity to exact revenge.

In November, Roosevelt and Wallace handily defeated Wendell Willkie and
Charles McNary, winning 55 percent of the vote. Before the vote, Roosevelt
promised that he would keep the United States out of the war. He told an overflow crowd in Boston Garden, "I have said this before but I shall say it again. Your
boys are not going to be sent into any foreign wars."[11] But the United States was
indeed inching closer to the conflict and was already supplying Great Britain
with much of its military needs, including artillery, tanks, machine guns, rifles,
and thousands of planes.

In early January 1941, Roosevelt upped the ante further by proposing lend-
lease aid to Great Britain in a bill patriotically numbered H.R. 1776. This would
give him enormous discretion in providing assistance short of war to the increasingly desperate British without worrying about the "silly, foolish dollar sign."[12]
The response to Roosevelt's message showed the challenge he faced in convincing the country that war was in the United States' best interest. At a press conference the next day, Eleanor Roosevelt said she was "astonished and saddened" by
the cold Republican response to the president's message.[13]

Republican critics were indeed more incensed than ever. Thomas Dewey,
who would later run for president, warned that the bill "would bring an end to
free government in the United States and would abolish the Congress for all
practical purposes." Alf Landon called it "the first step toward dictatorship by
Mr. Roosevelt."[14] Landon saw the handwriting on the wall: "Step by step, he
is working us into war," he charged. Gerald Nye contended that if lend-lease
passed, "war is almost inevitable."[15]

Critics feared that loans and other ties to Great Britain would again draw
the United States into war as they had in 1917. A heated debate erupted in Congress. Democratic Senator Burton Wheeler of Montana dismissed the thought
that Hitler would ever declare war on the United States and charged that the
lend-lease-give program was "the New Deal's Triple A foreign policy—plow
under every fourth American boy."[16] Roosevelt shot back, saying that Wheeler's

comment was "the most untruthful . . . the most dastardly, unpatriotic . . . the rottenest thing that has been said in public in my generation."[17]

Roosevelt's defenders agreed that aiding Great Britain was the United States' best chance to avoid being drawn into the war. Senator Joshua Lee of Oklahoma came to the president's defense: "Hitler is a madman standing at the switch of the most powerful and destructive machine that the human brain ever devised. The charred ruins of an entire continent stand as grim proof that he does not hesitate to throw that switch. . . . America has only one chance to escape total war and that chance is England. England is the only barrier between America and a baptism of blood."[18]

Lend-lease passed Congress in early March with an amendment banning the U.S. Navy from providing protection for the convoys carrying the goods. Congress appropriated the first $7 billion out of what would eventually total $50 billion to fund the shipments. Senator Arthur Vandenberg vented, "We have torn up 150 years of traditional American foreign policy. We have tossed Washington's Farewell Address in the discard. We have thrown ourselves squarely into the power politics and power wars of Europe, Asia and Africa. We have taken the first step upon a course from which we can never hereafter retreat."[19]

Prime Minister Churchill thanked the Americans profusely. He telegrammed the president, "Our blessings from the whole of the British Empire go out to you." The British soon realized, however, that there were limits to Roosevelt's largesse and his support for the perpetuation of Churchill's empire. Roosevelt included provisions in the Lend-Lease Act that would allow the United States to penetrate the British Empire's closed trading sphere and prevent its reestablishment after the war. The British were less than thrilled at the prospect or at the forced sale of British assets. Churchill complained, "we are not only to be skinned, but flayed to the bone." But he understood that, much as Roosevelt's critics feared, the United States was on the path to war. "I would like to get them hooked a little firmer," he confessed, "but they are pretty on now."[20]

The American people, it turned out, were increasingly willing to hook themselves. Their sympathies lay entirely with the Allies. A Gallup Poll released in October 1939 found that 84 percent wanted Great Britain and France to win the war. Only 2 percent were rooting for Germany. Still, at that point, 95 percent wanted the United States to stay out of the war.[21]

Ironically, it was Hitler who helped end Great Britain's isolation, as history took another dramatic turn on June 22, 1941. Breaking its 1939 treaty with the USSR, Germany launched Operation Barbarossa—a full-scale invasion of the Soviet Union. Stalin, who had earlier purged much of his general staff, ignored repeated warnings that an attack was imminent. His forces were caught completely

*American-made howitzers ready for transport to Great Britain
in 1941 as part of the lend-lease program to aid the British war
effort. Lend-lease deepened U.S. involvement in the European
war, outraging isolationist Republicans in Congress.*

off guard as 3.2 million German troops attacked along a two-thousand-mile front.[22] Germany quickly pushed deep into the Soviet Union. The Luftwaffe destroyed Soviet air units and the Wehrmacht encircled Soviet forces, inflicting terrible losses. The Nazis advanced toward Leningrad, Smolensk, and Kiev. The crippling blow dealt to the Red Army by the Nazi blitzkrieg sparked fears in London and Washington that Stalin would conclude a separate peace with Hitler, as Lenin had done with Germany in 1918.

The Soviet Union certainly felt little allegiance toward Great Britain, France, and the United States, each of which had, in its own way, tried to undermine the Russian Revolution. Beginning in 1925 with the publication of *Mein Kampf,* Hitler had repeatedly expressed his enmity toward the Soviet Union. As his expansive intentions became clear in the mid-1930s, Stalin's appeals to England and France for a military alliance against Germany proved fruitless. When the Soviets aided the republican forces in Spain, who were locked in bitter combat with the German- and Italian-backed army of General Francisco Franco, British conservatives, including Winston Churchill, sympathized with Franco's Fascist rebels. The Soviets also deplored the Allies' craven performance at Munich, which effectively gave the Germans free rein to destroy the Soviet Union.

Few people believed that the Soviets could withstand the Nazi onslaught. The U.S. Army calculated that they could hold on for no more than three months and might even fold in four weeks. Roosevelt and Churchill desperately sought to keep the Soviets in the war, knowing that Great Britain's survival might depend on it. Swallowing his long-standing hatred of communism, Churchill pledged support for the Soviet Union and urged his allies to do the same. He promised "to destroy Hitler and every vestige of the Nazi regime."[23] Acting Secretary of State Sumner Welles issued a statement on behalf of the president indicating that material assistance to the Soviet Union might be forthcoming but left the question of lend-lease up in the air for the time being. Some tried to nip that idea in the bud. Missouri Senator Harry Truman fanned the flames of mistrust toward the Soviet Union, recommending, "If we see that Germany is winning we ought to help Russia, and if Russia is winning we ought to help Germany, and that way let them kill as many as possible."[24]

Ignoring Truman's advice, Roosevelt asked the Soviet ambassador to compile a list of items the United States might provide. In July, Roosevelt sent Harry Hopkins to Moscow to take the Soviets' pulse and assess their staying power. He instructed Stalin to treat Hopkins "with the same identical confidence you would feel if you were talking to me." Stalin acknowledged the German military superiority but said that the Soviets would take advantage of the winter lull to be ready to fight by spring: "Give us anti-aircraft guns and the aluminum [for planes and] we can fight on for three or four years." Hopkins believed him.[25] By August, Roosevelt ordered delivery of the first hundred fighter planes. More supplies were on the way.

U.S. military leaders, intent upon building up U.S. defenses, impeded Roosevelt's efforts. The British also objected to diversion of their supplies. Seeing the bigger picture, Roosevelt ordered Secretary of War Henry Stimson and other cabinet members to speed delivery to the Soviet Union. His announcement that W. Averill Harriman would be leading a U.S. delegation to Moscow to confer on providing more military aid drew an outraged response from Robert McCormick's right-wing *Chicago Tribune:*

> A national emergency does not require that an American mission go to
> the bloody Kremlin to consider the needs of the greatest barbarian of
> modern times. We are not required by our national interests or our national
> dangers to join hands with a system of government which professes
> undying contempt for everything we regard as necessary in our way of
> living and plans unremitting and unrelenting warfare against such people as
> constitute the American nation.[26]

German cavalry leave a Russian village in flames during Operation Barbarossa, the full-scale German invasion of the Soviet Union in June 1941.

Given the depth of anti-Soviet sentiment in the United States, Roosevelt felt he had to move gingerly in providing tangible assistance to the Soviet government. A Gallup Poll found that only 35 percent of respondents favored aiding the Soviets on the same basis as that offered to Great Britain three months earlier. On November 7, 1941, the twenty-fourth anniversary of the Russian Revolution, Roosevelt announced that the United States would extend lend-lease aid to the Soviet Union. The president offered a billion-dollar interest-free credit to be repaid starting five years after the end of the war.

But when promised U.S. aid failed to arrive, Soviet elation turned bitter. The *New York Times* reported that U.S. shipments in October and November had fallen "far, far short" of "the specified tonnage of materials of war" the United States had committed. In fact, the United States had delivered less than half of what it had offered. Arthur Krock attributed this to special circumstances but failed to mention deliberate foot-dragging by some who disapproved the entire enterprise.[27] The failure to deliver the promised equipment dealt a crushing blow to Soviet prospects, with Moscow and Leningrad under siege, Ukraine occupied, and the Red Army suffering debilitating losses, and did little to convince the Soviets of U.S. goodwill.

Roosevelt wanted the United States in the war and, like Wilson before him, maneuvered quietly to make that happen. He believed that Hitler was intent on world domination and must be stopped. In early 1941, U.S. and British military officers met to devise a strategy for first defeating Germany and then engaging Japan that they would implement upon the U.S. entry into the war. In the meantime, Germany's U-boat campaign was undermining U.S. efforts to supply Great Britain, sinking an inordinate number of British ships. In April, Roosevelt began allowing U.S. ships to provide vital intelligence to the British about the presence of enemy ships and planes and soon authorized transporting supplies to British soldiers in North Africa, precipitating direct confrontations with German U-boats. After one incident, a German communiqué charged Roosevelt with "endeavoring with all the means at his disposal to provoke incidents for the purpose of baiting the American people into the war." [28] In September, after one of these allegedly unprovoked attacks, Roosevelt announced a "shoot on sight" policy toward German and Italian ships in U.S. waters. [29]

In August 1941, Roosevelt met secretly with Churchill in Newfoundland. The two leaders drew up the Atlantic Charter, which, much like Wilson's Fourteen Points, articulated a democratic and progressive set of war aims. It would remain to be seen if the United States could deliver better this time around. The charter disavowed territorial aggrandizement and territorial changes without the consent of the governed. It proclaimed self-government, equal access to trade and resources for victors and vanquished alike, a peace allowing "freedom from fear and want," freedom of the seas, disarmament, and a permanent system of general security. Fearing that Roosevelt's proposed wording threatened Great Britain's colonial sphere, Churchill added a clause stipulating that equal access to international wealth would be guaranteed only "with due respect for . . . existing obligations."

Roosevelt turned down Churchill's request to have the United States join the war immediately. But Churchill's account of the talks captures Roosevelt's true intentions: Roosevelt, he told his cabinet, "said he would wage war, but not declare it, and that he would become more and more provocative. If the Germans did not like it, they could attack American forces. Everything was to be done to force an 'incident' that could lead to war." [30] Though some people might excuse Roosevelt's deceptive behavior in the lead-up to the war as a necessary manipulation of public opinion in a righteous cause, future presidents would also take it upon themselves to play fast and loose with the truth in manipulating the nation into wars, as Woodrow Wilson had done a quarter century earlier. Such a policy in the hands of less scrupulous and less farsighted presidents, much like Roosevelt's wartime abuse of civil liberties, would pose a grave threat to the nation and its republican system of governance.

The president ultimately got his wish, but it was not triggered by an incident in Europe, as most were anticipating. On December 7, 1941, the day President Roosevelt said would "live in infamy," the Japanese navy attacked the U.S. naval

Churchill and Roosevelt aboard the Prince of Wales *during the*
Atlantic Charter conference in August 1941. The charter renounced
a number of imperialist practices and proclaimed such themes as self-
government and disarmament. But, afraid that Roosevelt's wording
could eliminate Great Britain's colonial sphere, Churchill added
the condition that equal access to international wealth would be
guaranteed only "with due respect for . . . existing obligations."

base at Pearl Harbor, Hawaii, leaving almost 2,500 dead and sinking or disabling much of the U.S. fleet. The Americans were caught literally sleeping on a Sunday morning. They knew an attack from Japan was coming, but they didn't anticipate that it would be in Hawaii. It was an intelligence failure on a colossal scale. Given the abundance of warning signs and the degree of ineptitude involved, much as with the attacks on September 11, 2001, many believed then and now that Roosevelt must have abetted the attack in order to draw the United States into the war. The evidence, however, does not support that charge.[31]

The next day, Great Britain and the United States declared war on Japan. Three days later, Germany and Italy declared war on the United States. The bloodletting and chaos would soon engulf the globe.

The United States had stood in the way of Japan's plans for conquest. Japanese leaders had been eyeing the rich French and Dutch colonies that the German subjugation of continental Europe had made ripe for the plucking. Though

*The U.S. naval base at Pearl Harbor during the
Japanese bombardment on December 7, 1941.*

some army officers argued that Japan should join Germany and first knock out its old Russian antagonist to the north, other strategists prevailed. As a result, Japan invaded French Indochina to the south in July 1941, seeking the resources and bases needed to fortify its position in the region. The United States responded by completely embargoing petroleum exports to Japan. Its supplies dwindling, Japan's leaders decided to secure oil from the Dutch East Indies, but they feared that the U.S. fleet at Pearl Harbor could interfere with their efforts.

With the United States and its allies focused on the European theater, the Japanese conquest proceeded largely unimpeded: Thailand, Malaya, Java, Borneo, the Philippines, Hong Kong, Indonesia, Burma, Singapore. Citizens of those countries often greeted the Japanese as liberators from European colonial oppressors. President Roosevelt said privately, "Don't think for a minute that Americans would be dying in the Pacific . . . if it hadn't been for the short-sighted greed of the French and the British and the Dutch." [32] Subjugated peoples' embrace of the Japanese "liberators" would prove short-lived.

Japan failed to deliver the knockout blow at Pearl Harbor that it desperately sought. The Allies began a counteroffensive led by General Douglas MacArthur and Admiral Chester Nimitz. In June 1942, U.S. forces defeated the Japanese navy at Midway and initiated their island-hopping strategy.

In some ways, this war would change the world even more dramatically than the First World War. Anticipating the creation of a new world order, influential

Americans began offering their visions of what might emerge and the role the United States could play to make that happen. One of the most compelling visions was outlined in early 1941 by publishing magnate Henry Luce in an editorial in *Life* magazine. Luce, who also published *Time* and *Fortune,* had apparently recovered from his earlier infatuation with Mussolini and now anointed the twentieth century the "American Century." He wrote, "We must accept wholeheartedly our duty and our opportunity as the most powerful and vital nation in the world and in consequence to exert upon the world the full impact of our influence, for such purposes as we see fit and by such means as we see fit." [33]

Some applauded this statement as an affirmation of democratic values within an evolving international capitalist market. Former New Deal administrator Raymond Moley knew better and urged Americans to disavow this "temptation to drift into empire." [34]

Vice President Henry Wallace deplored all empires—whether British, French, German, or American. In May 1942, Wallace repudiated Luce's nationalistic and, arguably, imperial vision and proposed a progressive, internationalist alternative:

> Some have spoken of the "American Century." I say . . . the century . . . which will come of this war—can and must be the century of the common man. . . . No nation will have the God-given right to exploit other nations . . . there must be neither military nor economic imperialism. . . . International cartels that serve American greed and the German will to power must go. . . . The march of freedom of the past 150 years has been a . . . great revolution of the people, there were the American Revolution of 1775, the French Revolution of 1792, the Latin American revolutions of the Bolivian era, the German Revolution of 1848, and the Russian Revolution of 1917. Each spoke for the common man. . . . Some went to excess. But . . . people groped their way to the light. . . . Modern science, which is a by-product and an essential part of the people's revolution, has made it . . . possible to see that all of the people of the world get enough to eat. . . . We shall not rest until all the victims under the Nazi yoke are freed. . . . The people's revolution is on the march. [35]

When the bloodiest war in human history finally drew to a close three years later, Americans would choose between these diametrically opposed visions: Luce's American Century versus Wallace's Century of the Common Man.

The United States' entry into the war following the attack at Pearl Harbor only complicated the fight over scarce resources. Meeting the United States' own defense requirements made it that much more difficult for it to fulfill its

commitments to the Soviet Union. In late December, Averill Harriman estimated that the United States had shipped only a quarter of the tonnage of supplies promised and much of what had been sent was defective. In late February,
Lend-Lease Administrator Edward Stettinius wrote to Assistant Secretary of
War John McCloy, "As you are aware, the relations between this Government
and the Soviet Government have been constantly disturbed by the failure of
this Government to meet its commitments." Roosevelt understood the terrible
position the U.S. failure to deliver was putting the Soviet Union in and what it
might mean for future relations. In March, he admitted his apprehensions about
a "Russian collapse" because of U.S. negligence: "I do not want to be in the same
position as the English[, who] promised the Russians two divisions. They failed.
They promised them help in the Caucasus. They failed. Every promise the English have made to the Russians, they have fallen down on." [36]

In May 1942, Roosevelt told General MacArthur, "I find it difficult . . . to
get away from the simple fact that the Russian armies are killing more Axis personnel and destroying more Axis materiel than all the other twenty-five United
Nations put together. Therefore, it has seemed wholly logical to support the great
Russian effort in 1942 by seeking to get all munitions to them that we possibly
can." [37] Roosevelt knew that delays in delivering the promised military equipment had cost him an opportunity to win Stalin's trust. But other opportunities
would present themselves. Stalin made two additional requests of his allies. Perhaps delivering on these would allow the United States to regain the initiative.

Stalin sought territorial concessions. He wanted to retain the gains the Red
Army had seized after his 1939 pact with Hitler: the Baltic states of Lithuania,
Latvia, and Estonia, eastern Poland, and parts of Romania and Finland. The British were inclined to go along but felt caught in a difficult bind, pulled between
U.S. and Soviet interests, needing Soviet help to survive the war and U.S. assistance to preserve their empire after the war. Churchill pressed Roosevelt to allow
him to offer Stalin the territorial concessions he desired. He warned Roosevelt
that a break with the Soviets would bring down his government, which would be
replaced by a "Communist, pro-Moscow" government. The Americans refused to
budge and instructed British Foreign Secretary Anthony Eden to make no postwar
commitments during his trip to Moscow in late December 1941. Stalin responded
angrily to Eden's rebuff of his demands, leading Churchill to appeal to Roosevelt
again. "The Atlantic Charter," he insisted, "ought not to be construed so as to deny
to Russia the frontiers which she occupied when Germany attacked." [38]

Having failed to receive either the promised aid or territorial gains, Stalin
pressed even harder for his third and most significant demand: rapid establishment of a second front in Europe to alleviate pressure on his beleaguered military. He urged the British to invade northern France. In September 1941, he

pressed them to send twenty-five or thirty divisions to the Soviet Union. Questioning the sincerity of Great Britain's commitment, he said, "By her passive attitude Britain is helping the Nazis. Do the British understand this? I think they do. What is it then they want? It seems they want us to be weakened."[39]

The lack of outside support may have left the Soviets weak, but they refused to collapse. Despite suffering catastrophic losses in the early months of the war, the Red Army defeated Germany in the Battle of Moscow in the fall and winter of 1941–1942. For the first time, the mighty German war machine had been stopped.

To Roosevelt, territorial concessions smacked of the secret treaties that had tied Wilson's hands during the First World War. They contradicted the spirit of the Atlantic Charter. He preferred to launch an invasion of Western Europe at the earliest possible date. In early 1942, General Dwight D. Eisenhower, working for Army Chief of Staff General George C. Marshall, drew up plans for an invasion of Europe by spring 1943 at the latest and by September 1942 if necessary to stave off Soviet defeat, which was still a possibility. As Eisenhower stated emphatically in July 1942, "We should not forget that the prize we seek is to keep 8,000,000 Russians in the war."[40] Eisenhower, Marshall, and Stimson all saw this as the only way to defeat Germany. Roosevelt agreed. He sent Harry Hopkins and General Marshall to convince Churchill to go along. He wrote to Churchill, "Your people and mine demand the establishment of a front to draw off pressure on the Russians, and those peoples are wise enough to see that the Russians are killing more Germans and destroying more equipment than you and I put together."[41] Churchill understood how important this plan was to Roosevelt and his advisors. He cabled the president, "I am in entire agreement in principle with all you propose, as so are the Chiefs of Staff."[42]

Convinced that he had British support, Roosevelt asked Stalin to send Minister of Foreign Affairs Vyacheslav Molotov and a trusted general to Washington to discuss a proposal that would ease the pressure on the western front. On the way, Molotov stopped in London, where Churchill was anything but reassuring about the second front. Molotov arrived in the U.S. capital in late May 1942. He asked Roosevelt bluntly if the United States indeed planned to open up another front that coming summer. Roosevelt turned to Marshall, who assured him that the United States was prepared to do so. The two sides issued a joint public communiqué stating that "in the course of the conversations full understanding was reached with regard to the urgent tasks of creating a second front in Europe in 1942."[43] Roosevelt also laid out a breathtaking vision for postwar collaboration. The victors, he explained, would "keep their armaments" and form "an international police force."[44] The "four policemen"—the United States, United Kingdom, USSR, and China—would disarm the Germans and their allies and "preserve peace by force." Stalin was delighted by the plans but far less pleased by

Roosevelt's insistence that preparing the second front would necessitate cutting aid to the Soviet Union to 60 percent of what he had originally promised. Still, the second front was the Soviet Union's main priority, and Roosevelt planned to deliver. He notified Churchill, "I have a very strong feeling that the Russian position is precarious and may grow steadily worse during the coming weeks. Therefore, I am more than ever anxious that BOLERO [the first phase of the operation] proceed to definite action beginning in 1942."[45]

The Soviet people were elated by the news. The *New York Herald Tribune* reported that they had been gathering around their radios every morning hoping for news that the invasion had begun, only to have their hearts sink when they discovered it hadn't.[46] Pulitzer Prize–winning Moscow correspondent Leland Stowe reported that if the front were postponed, the "disillusionment of the great mass of Russian people would be almost immeasurable. The present steadily mounting and invaluable cooperation between the Soviet, British and American governments and leaders would suffer such a setback as to constitute, diplomatically, materially and psychologically, a major disaster for the Allied cause."[47] The U.S. ambassador in Moscow similarly warned that postponement would make the Russian people doubt U.S. sincerity and do "inestimable harm."[48]

Despite reaching a similar agreement with Molotov regarding the second front, the British had no intention of going along with the plans. Arguing that they lacked sufficient troops due to the crisis in the Middle East—33,000 British troops had just humiliatingly surrendered to an enemy force half that size at Tobruk in Libya—and that they could not muster enough ships to transport invading forces across the English Channel, Churchill convinced Roosevelt to postpone the promised invasion and instead mount an invasion of Vichy-occupied North Africa, which was the key to the oil-rich Middle East, where the British had important colonial interests that were being threatened by Hitler's forces. The Soviet leaders were furious about this reversal, which many considered part of a conscious strategy of allowing the Soviet Union to be bled dry fighting the Nazis while its capitalist allies secured their global interests and then marched in to set the peace terms at the end of the war. To make matters worse from the Soviet standpoint, during his stop in London, Molotov, in gratitude for the pledged second front, had not pressed his territorial demands. The Soviets now felt as if all three of their major demands had been denied. Relations among the Soviets, Americans, and British hit rock bottom in the fall of 1942 with the Nazi onslaught against Stalingrad. Symptomatic of the Soviets' acute mistrust of their Western allies was the fact that Molotov, when traveling in the West, always slept with a gun under his pillow.[49]

Furious with this British-imposed change of plans, Marshall lobbied unsuccessfully against the invasion of North Africa, which he dismissed as "periphery pecking." The United States had delayed major operations in the Pacific in order to expedite victory in Europe. Now those plans had been abandoned in an apparent attempt to secure British "imperial" interests in the Middle East, South Asia, and southern Europe. Marshall was so angry that he proposed reversing course and taking on the Japanese before confronting the Germans. Chief of Naval Operations Admiral Ernest King enthusiastically agreed. The British would never invade Europe, he sneered, "except behind a Scotch bagpipe band." Marshall's disgust reverberated down the ranks. General Albert Wedemeyer told Marshall that the British war plans had "been designed to maintain the integrity of the British Empire." General Henry "Hap" Arnold, chief commander of the Army Air Forces, suggested to Marshall that perhaps the Americans should start dealing with the British the same way that the Germans treated the Italians. U.S. military leaders believed that the British, unlike the Soviets, were afraid to take on the Germans. As Secretary of War Stimson mused the next year, "The shadows of Passchendale [*sic*] and Dunkerque still hang too heavily over the imagination of [Churchill's] government." [50]

Eisenhower, Stimson, Hopkins, and the military chiefs continued to push forcefully for a second front, but to no avail. In June 1942, the U.S. chiefs of staff reluctantly agreed to the TORCH campaign in North Africa under Eisenhower's command. Although a case could indeed have been made that the Allies lacked the landing craft, air cover, and sufficient number of troops to pull off a second front in late 1942 or early 1943, such arguments were not convincing to the Soviets or, at the time, to U.S. military leaders. Eisenhower predicted that the day they decided to proceed with TORCH would go down as the "blackest day in history." [51]

But whether deterred by fear or not, the British never had any intention of directly engaging the powerful Wehrmacht and had instead designed a strategy based on sea power and attacking Hitler's vulnerable southern flank, which was protected by weaker Italian forces. Great Britain decided to secure North Africa, the Mediterranean, and the Middle East, in order to hold on to Persian and Iraqi oil reserves and maintain its access to India and the rest of the empire through the Suez Canal and Gibraltar. The discovery of enormous oil reserves shortly before the war in Saudi Arabia, Kuwait, and Qatar further drove home the importance of this region, where much of the early fighting between British, German, and Italian forces had occurred. Great Britain was so intent upon keeping the Axis powers out of the Middle East that it diverted troops and tanks there even though they were desperately needed to defend the homeland against an imminent German attack.

During these months, the American people's attitude toward the Soviet Union was undergoing a profound shift. For many Americans, the Nazi-Soviet Pact had confirmed their worst suspicions about Soviet communism, causing an outpouring of anti-Soviet feeling between 1939 and 1941. But much of that disappeared as the Soviets' courageous resistance against the Nazis captured Americans' imagination and sympathy. The resulting outpouring of goodwill toward the Soviet Union would lay the basis, many hoped, for friendship and collaboration in the war's aftermath as well.

Within days of the attack on Pearl Harbor, Soviet diplomat Maxim Litvinov visited the State Department. Secretary of State Cordell Hull used the occasion to applaud the Soviet Union's "heroic struggle" against the Nazis.[52] Before long, the notion of Soviet "heroism" was ubiquitous. In April 1942, *New York Times* correspondent Ralph Parker commended "how rapidly and how completely the Russian people" had "adapted themselves to war conditions." He applauded their willingness to sacrifice and their extraordinary work ethic. "The whole people are caught up with an enthusiastic passion to be doing something constructive for the common task." He proclaimed, "It would need a Tolstoy to describe the heroic endurance of the men and women who have made these things possible."[53] In June 1942, the month marking the first anniversary of Soviet resistance to the German invaders, Orville Prescott, the *New York Times'* principal daily book reviewer, was already crediting the Red Army with winning the war and saving humanity. "The vast armaments, the fighting skill and magnificent courage of the Red Army may prove to have been the decisive factors in the salvation of the human race from Nazi slavery," Prescott gushed. "Our debt of gratitude to the millions of Russian soldiers who have fought and died in this war and who will continue to do so is beyond estimation or expression."[54] General MacArthur credited the Red Army with "one of the greatest military feats in history."[55]

Hollywood pitched in too. Though it had once scrupulously avoided making films about the Soviet Union, in July 1942, at least nine movies about the Soviet Union were in production or under consideration by such major studios as MGM, Columbia, United Artists, Twentieth Century–Fox, and Paramount.[56] Five significant motion pictures eventually appeared: *Mission to Moscow, North Star, Song of Russia, Three Russian Girls,* and *Days of Glory.*

A consensus was building that without the second front the war could not be won. After acknowledging that "the Russians have done most of the fighting and most of the dying," the *Atlanta Constitution* contended that though a second front would bring tragedy to many American homes, it "must . . . be done if the war is to be won." Leland Stowe reminded readers that the Soviet Union could not hold out alone forever: "In 13 months the Russians have suffered more than 4,500,000 in killed, wounded, and prisoners . . . probably six or seven times Great Britain's losses in nearly three years of war . . . 20 times the total American casualties in the first World War."[57] He stressed that "Soviet Russia is the one great power which is indispensable as an ally of the United States—if we are

American observers took special notice of the "heroic" struggle to repel the Nazi invaders by both the Red Army and Soviet civilians. Clockwise from top: A group of women and elderly men dig a trap to halt the German advance on Moscow; a group of distraught women in Kiev, Ukraine, gather during a Nazi attack; frightened children look up from a bunker in Kiev during a German air raid; Red Army soldiers in the Soviet Union.

going to win the war. . . . If Russia's fighting millions were suddenly removed from the scene, they alone would be irreplaceable."[58]

With the steady barrage of pro-Soviet and pro–second front coverage, the American public rallied to the cause. In July 1942, Gallup reported that 48 percent of Americans wanted the United States and Great Britain to attack immediately, while only 34 percent wanted to wait until the Allies were stronger.[59] Americans pasted bumper stickers reading "Second Front Now" on their cars. Readers flooded newspapers with letters calling for an immediate attack on Hitler's forces in Europe. Among the many published by the *Washington Post*, one, inspired by the "spectacle of a courageous ally who alone has withstood and forced back the Nazi hordes," demanded that Great Britain and the United States "divide the forces of Hitler by opening a western front and together with our Russian ally crush this menace to world freedom and civilization."[60]

Support was building in all directions. Thirty-eight leaders of the CIO told Roosevelt that "only immediate land invasion of Western Europe will guarantee winning the war."[61] Five days later the organization hosted a pro–second front rally in New York City's Madison Square Park.[62] Several AFL affiliates lent their support. Elected officials jumped on the bandwagon, including Senators James Mead of New York and Claude Pepper of Florida, New York City Mayor Fiorello LaGuardia, and New York State Representative Vito Marcantonio.[63] In September, author Dashiell Hammett released the names of five hundred writers who, under the banner of the League of American Writers, declared themselves "enthusiastically behind President Roosevelt for the immediate opening of a second front now."[64] Twenty-five thousand people rallied in New York's Union Square as Representative Marcantonio and Communist Party head Earl Browder addressed the crowd.[65] The 1940 Republican Party presidential candidate Wendell Willkie added his endorsement following a meeting in Moscow with Stalin.[66]

But despite the public demand for a second front in Europe, U.S. and British troops headed off to North Africa. Left to its own devices, the resurgent Red Army reversed the course of the war, vanquishing the Nazis at Stalingrad. More than a million soldiers were engaged on each side. The Germans, under General Friedrich Paulus, were pushing to take control of the Soviet Union's rich oil fields in the Caucasus. The Soviets, under Marshall Georgi Zhukov, were determined to stop them at all costs. The six-month battle was fierce, the human toll horrific. Casualties exceeded three-quarters of a million on each side, and civilian deaths totaled over 40,000. After that colossal defeat, the German army began a full-scale retreat from the eastern front. Hitler, stunned by the surrender of twenty-three generals and the Sixth Army's 91,000 troops, lamented, "The God of War has gone over to the other side."[67]

*Echoing Americans across the country, twenty-five thousand rallied in
New York's Union Square on September 24, 1942, to demand that the
United States open a second front in the war in Western Europe to relieve
some of the tremendous pressure on Russia in its fight against Germany.*

By the time Roosevelt and Churchill met in Casablanca in January 1943, the
momentum had shifted. The Red Army was on the offensive and moving west.
Roosevelt's strategy of resisting Soviet territorial demands by substituting massive aid and an early second front had foundered. The Americans and the British
would henceforth be on the defensive in trying to deny Stalin's gains. To make
matters worse, Roosevelt and Churchill decided to land in Sicily, again postpon-
ing the second front and relegating their nations to further irrelevance in determining the outcome of the war.

The Red Army continued its advance, but at an enormous cost. In November 1943, Stalin commemorated the anniversary of the Russian Revolution with
a speech celebrating the survival and future resurgence of the Soviet state. He
decried the Nazis' murder and pillage and promised revenge against the German
invaders: "In the districts they seized, the Germans have exterminated hundreds
of thousands of our citizens. Like the Medieval barbarians of Attila's hordes, the
German fiends trample the fields, burn down villages and towns, and demolish
industrial enterprises and cultural institutions. . . . Our people will not forgive
the German fiends for these crimes."[68]

The U.S. president and the Soviet premier met for the first time in Tehran in November 1943. Roosevelt had told Churchill in March 1942, "I can personally handle Stalin better than either your Foreign Office or my State Department. Stalin hates the guts of all your top people. He thinks he likes me better and I hope he will continue to do so."[69] After trying unsuccessfully to exclude Churchill from the meeting, Roosevelt accepted Stalin's offer to stay in the Soviet Embassy. Roosevelt had indicated informally beforehand that he was open to establishing the Curzon Line as Poland's eastern border. Despite these gestures, he found Stalin cold and aloof during the first three days of meetings and feared he would not succeed in developing the rapport he hoped for. He decided to try to reach Stalin on a more human level, employing the kind of charm and humor that would allow him to create a personal bond—the trademark of Rooseveltian diplomacy. He explained to Labor Secretary Francis Perkins:

> I thought it over all night and made up my mind I had to do something desperate. . . . I had a feeling that the Russians did not feel right about seeing [Winston and me] conferring together in a language which we understood and they didn't. On my way to the conference room that morning we caught up with Winston and I had just a moment to say to him, "Winston, I hope you won't be sore at me for what I am going to do." Winston just shifted his cigar and grunted. . . . I began almost as soon as we got into the conference room. I talked privately with Stalin. I didn't say anything that I hadn't said before, but it appeared quite chummy and confidential, enough so that the other Russians joined us to listen. Still no smile. Then I said, lifting my hand up to cover a whisper (which of course had to be interpreted) "Winston is cranky this morning, he got up on the wrong side of the bed." A vague smile passed over Stalin's eyes, and I decided I was on the right track. As soon as I sat down at the conference table, I began to tease Churchill about his Britishness, about John Bull, about his cigars, about his habits. It began to register with Stalin. Winston got red and scowled, and the more he did so, the more Stalin smiled. Finally Stalin broke out into a deep, hearty guffaw, and for the first time in three days I saw light. I kept it up until Stalin was laughing with me, and it was then that I called him "Uncle Joe." He would have thought me fresh the day before, but that day he laughed and came over and shook my hand. From that time on our relations were personal, and Stalin himself indulged in an occasional witticism. The ice was broken and we talked like men and brothers.[70]

Roosevelt made important headway at Tehran. The United States and Great Britain promised to open the long-delayed second front the following spring.

Stalin agreed to enter the war against Japan once Germany had been crushed. Roosevelt acceded to the Soviet-desired territorial changes in Eastern Europe, requesting that Stalin implement them judiciously and not offend world opinion. He also proposed that the Soviets hold plebiscites in the Baltic states, but Stalin rejected that request. Roosevelt indicated that he would allow the Soviets considerable latitude in shaping those countries' future. He came away from the conference encouraged that the trust he had established with Stalin would moderate the Soviet leader's demands and convince him to hold free elections in Eastern Europe that would produce governments friendly to the USSR.

The Red Army advanced into Poland in January 1944. That month, Stimson discussed Poland's future with Secretary Hull, who thought it essential to establish the principal of "no acquisition by force." Stimson recounted, "I thought we had to consider other things more realistic than that, such as the feelings which would actuate Russia: (a) that she had saved us from losing the war; (b) that she prior to 1914 had owned the whole of Poland including Warsaw and running as far as Germany and that she was not asking for restitution of that."[71]

The Soviet Union quickly set up a friendly government in Lublin, Poland, that excluded representatives of the exile government in London. Later that year, the Red Army moved into Romania, Bulgaria, and Hungary. When the United States and Great Britain complained that they were only allowed a token role in the occupation, Stalin replied that the Soviet Union had been given only a token role in the occupation of Italy.

Finally, on June 6, 1944, the long-awaited second front was opened one and a half years later than promised. Over 100,000 Allied troops and 30,000 vehicles landed on the beach at Normandy, France. Nine thousand died during the landing. By that point, the Soviets, despite having suffered catastrophic casualties, were occupying much of Central Europe. Now the Allied forces would approach Germany from both the east and the west. Victory would soon be at hand.

Up to that point, the Soviet Union had almost singlehandedly battled the German military. Until the invasion of Normandy, the Red Army was regularly engaging more than two hundred enemy divisions while the Americans and British together rarely confronted more than ten. Churchill admitted that it was "the Russian Army that tore the guts out of the German military machine." Germany lost over 6 million men on the eastern front and approximately 1 million on the western front and in the Mediterranean.[72]

As the fighting intensified on the battlefield, the pace of planning picked up in the boardrooms. The United States invited friendly governments to Bretton Woods in New Hampshire to design the postwar capitalist economic order. Conferees approved U.S. plans to establish two major economic institutions: the development-minded World Bank, with initial funding of $7.6 billion, and the finance-minded International Monetary Fund, with $7.3 billion. The United States, which controlled two-thirds of the world's gold, insisted that the Bretton Woods system rest on both gold and the U.S. dollar, ensuring that U.S. economic hegemony would continue for the foreseeable future and the United States would be banker to the world. Soviet representatives attended the conference but later declined to ratify the final agreements, charging that the institutions they had created were "branches of Wall Street."[73] A Soviet official commented that "at first sight," the Bretton Woods institutions "looked like a tasty mushroom, but on examination they turned out to be a poisonous toadstool."[74] The British understood that the new order would further erode their special sphere. Although Churchill had fulminated in late 1942, "I have not become the King's First Minister to preside over the liquidation of the British Empire," the balance of power had irrevocably shifted.[75]

Some people have questioned the sincerity of Roosevelt's anticolonial efforts during the war, and although he was certainly never the passionate crusader against colonialism that Vice President Wallace was, he did repeatedly express outrage at the colonizers' unjust and inhumane treatment of subject populations. Elliott Roosevelt reported his father's stern words to an "apoplectic" Churchill in 1941. "I can't believe," he said, "that we can fight a war against fascist slavery, and at the same time not work to free people all over the world from a backward colonial policy." He pressed Churchill to end Britain's rule in India and beyond.[76] During a press conference in February 1944, Roosevelt publicly excoriated British colonial rule in Gambia in West Africa, which he had visited the previous year. "It's the most horrible thing I have ever seen in my life," he declared. "The natives are five thousand years back of us. . . . The British have been there for two hundred years—for every dollar that the British have put into Gambia, they have taken out ten. It's just plain exploitation of those people."[77]

Roosevelt spoke repeatedly about a postwar trusteeship system that would prepare the colonies for independence. One of the initial beneficiaries would be Indochina, which he insisted not be given back to the French after the war, as Churchill and Charles de Gaulle demanded it be. "Indo-China should not go back to France," he told Secretary of State Cordell Hull in October 1944. "France has had the country—thirty million inhabitants—for nearly one hundred years, and the people are worse off than they were at the beginning. . . . The people of Indo-China are entitled to something better than that."[78] Churchill feared that Roosevelt would use Indochina as a wedge to force full-scale decolonization. Churchill made it clear that he would not contemplate such a possibility. He told Eden in late 1944, "There must be no question of our being hustled or seduced into declarations affecting British sovereignty in any of the Dominions or Colonies. . . . 'Hands off the British Empire' is our maxim, and it must not be weakened or smirched to please sob-stuff merchants at home or foreigners of any hue." Despite having Stalin's support for his decolonization efforts, Roosevelt backed off from aggressively pressing the point out of fear of rupturing the wartime alliance with Great Britain. With even less justification and more tragic consequences in the long run, he even backed off from decisively pressing the point on Indochina. However, in what turned out to be his last press conference, on April 5 in Warms Springs, Georgia, exactly one week before his death, Roosevelt, accompanied by Philippine President Sergio Osmeña, promised that once Japanese troops had been ousted from the Philippines, the United States would grant the Filipinos "immediate" independence.[79] Churchill did withstand U.S. pressure to grant India its independence after the war, but even that victory would prove ephemeral as the Indian people took matters into their own hands.

Although the world of formal empires and closed trading spheres would not vanish overnight, the U.S. economic juggernaut would brook no rivals from among the war-shattered economies of Europe and Asia. And undergirding the newly strengthened dollar would be the enormous power of the U.S. military. Roosevelt allowed his military advisors to play a central role in policy making. In early 1942, he created the Joint Chiefs of Staff. In July, he appointed Admiral William Leahy to be his personal chief of staff and liaison to the Joint Chiefs. He also leaned heavily on Army Chief of Staff General George C. Marshall for advice.

The War Department required an imposing new home that would come to symbolize its new role and the United States' vast military power. In the summer of 1941, the War Department's 24,000 civilian and military employees were operating out of seventeen different buildings. Brigadier General Brehon Burke Somervell informed Stimson that having everyone under the same roof would increase their efficiency by 25 to 40 percent.[80] Construction on a new headquarters in Arlington, Virginia, began on September 11, 1941. The builders kept the five-sided shape that had been chosen to fit the original site even though the location had been switched. The first occupants began moving in April 1942, although construction wasn't completed until January of the following year. The man in charge of this massive construction project—Colonel Leslie Groves—would later make an even greater mark on the war effort. When finished, the largely windowless Pentagon was the biggest office building in the country, covering 29 acres and containing 17.5 miles of corridors. Visitors routinely got lost, and deliverymen were rumored to have wandered the halls for three days before being rescued.[81]

Halfway around the globe, Churchill and Stalin met in Moscow in October 1944. The meeting was code-named Tolstoy. Churchill hoped to resolve the impasse over Poland. U.S. Ambassador to the Soviet Union Averill Harriman tagged along as an "observer" but was not present when the two leaders conducted the most important business. Sitting in front of a fireplace in the Kremlin, Churchill cracked some of his favorite Polish jokes. The two leaders then set about defining British and Soviet spheres of influence in the Balkans and laying the groundwork for Western recognition of Soviet interests in Poland. On the back of a scrap of paper, Churchill proposed the share of influence each nation would exert: the Soviet Union would get 90 percent in Romania and 75 percent in Hungary and Bulgaria; Great Britain would get 90 percent in Greece. Yugoslavia would be split fifty-fifty. Stalin took the paper, paused, and made a large check with a blue pencil before handing it back to Churchill, who commented, "Might it not be thought rather cynical if it seemed we had disposed of these issues, so fateful to millions of people, in such an offhand manner? Let us burn the paper." But Stalin urged Churchill to hold on to the historic scrap of paper, which Churchill called a "naughty document." [82]

It was exactly the kind of deal that Roosevelt had set out to prevent. Hull protested the establishment of "spheres of interest." Churchill decried U.S. hypocrisy: "Is having a Navy twice as strong as any other power 'power politics'? . . . Is having all the gold in the world buried in a cavern 'power politics'? If not, what is 'power politics'?" [83]

Stalin quickly delivered on his part of the bargain. He stood aside in December 1944 as British troops brutally repressed a left-wing uprising in Greece, where the Communists, who had led the underground resistance to the Nazis, were battling for power with reactionary forces who wanted to restore the monarchy. Great Britain supported the monarchists. Stalin refused to support the leftists, despite the fact that they had the backing of much of the Greek population. The U.S. public was shocked by Great Britain's behavior.

Roosevelt, Stalin, and Churchill met for a second time at Yalta on the Black Sea in early February 1945. Though the Battle of the Bulge was still raging in Belgium and fighting had intensified in the Pacific, the war had clearly turned in the Allies' favor. The time had come to finalize postwar plans. The Soviet Union was in a commanding position. The Red Army occupied Poland, Romania, Czechoslovakia, Hungary, Bulgaria, and Yugoslavia and was approaching Berlin. Deep rifts had appeared among the Allies, reflecting fundamentally different geopolitical and strategic views. The Soviet Union was preoccupied with security. Great Britain sought to preserve its empire. The United States wanted Soviet assistance in ending the Pacific war, fashioning a world economy that would be open to U.S. trade and investment, and establishing a United Nations to preserve the peace.

The USSR had paid an enormous price in repulsing the German invasion. Many millions of its soldiers and citizens lay dead, and much of the nation was in ruins. The United States and Great Britain had helped the Soviets defeat Germany, but their efforts and resulting losses paled beside those of their Soviet ally.

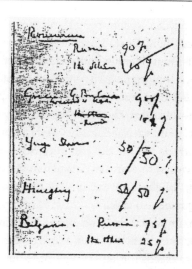

During a secret meeting in Moscow in October 1944, Churchill and Stalin outlined an agreement for British and Soviet spheres of influence in postwar Europe on this scrap of paper.

The United States had, in fact, come out of the war economically and militarily stronger than ever. But its diplomatic leverage was compromised by its failure to deliver the relief and assistance it had promised Stalin during the darkest hours of the war. The United States still had one major card to play: the promise of postwar economic assistance to help the Soviets rebuild their shattered nation. The once powerful British were in the weakest position, no longer able to press their claims independently. Great Britain now depended on U.S. goodwill and largesse to retain its status as a major power in the postwar world. The conflicts that surfaced at Yalta would eventually tear the alliance apart. But those tensions would not be apparent in the public display of unity or in the exuberant response by citizens around the world desperate for good news after many long years of war.

These differences played out in the debate over Poland, which was the focus of seven of Yalta's eight plenary sessions. Stalin declared, "the question of Poland is not only a question of honor but also a question of security. Throughout history, Poland has been the corridor through which the enemy has passed into Russia." It was a matter "of life and death for the Soviet Union."[84]

Stalin demanded recognition of the Communist-led government operating out of the eastern city of Lublin that was provisionally ruling Poland. Its crackdown on internal opposition had sparked the beginning of a civil war. Roosevelt and Churchill backed the London-based government in exile, most of whose members were virulent anti-Communists. Stalin accused them of being terrorists. It was to weaken the London Poles that Stalin committed the dual atrocities of killing thousands of Polish army officers in the Katyn Forest in 1940 and having the Red Army stop on the banks of the Vistula in 1944 while the Germans put down the Warsaw Rising.

The three leaders compromised on setting up a Polish Provisional Government of National Unity. The agreement stated, "The Provisional Government which is now functioning in Poland should therefore be reorganized on a broader democratic basis with the inclusion of democratic leaders from Poland itself and from Poles abroad." Then the British, U.S., and Soviet ambassadors were to consult with the Polish leaders, and free elections, open to all "democratic and anti-Nazi parties," were to be held.[85] The three leaders agreed on the Curzon Line as the eastern border, despite the objections of the London Poles, but disagreed on Poland's western boundary, which was left for future resolution. The agreements were admittedly vague. Admiral Leahy, a veteran of the Spanish-American and First World Wars, who had spent time in the Philippines, China, Panama, and Nicaragua before returning from retirement to serve as Roosevelt's chief of staff, warned Roosevelt, "this is so elastic that the Russians can stretch it all the way from Yalta to Washington without technically breaking it." Roosevelt agreed, "I know, Bill—I know it. But it's the best I can do for Poland at this time."[86]

At Tehran, Roosevelt had written Stalin a personal note promising that "the United States will never lend its support in any way to any provisional government in Poland that would be inimical to your interests."[87] Yet the London Poles, being hard-line anti-Communists, were clearly inimical to Stalin's perception of Soviet interests.

Roosevelt understood that he had little leverage at Yalta. He was more excited about getting Stalin to agree to the "Declaration on Liberated Europe," which promised to establish broadly representative governments through free elections.

Though they didn't see eye to eye on Germany, the Big Three agreed to divide the soon-to-be-conquered nation into four military zones, with one to be controlled by France. Unable to reach an accord on postwar German reparations, they decided to establish a reparations commission, which could base discussions on a figure of $20 billion, with half going to the Soviet Union. Stalin agreed to come into the war against Japan three months after the end of the war in Europe. In return, the United States promised territorial and economic concessions in East Asia that largely restored what Russia had lost to Japan in the 1904–05 Russo-Japanese War.

The news of Yalta ignited a kind of optimism that hadn't been seen for decades. Former President Herbert Hoover called the conference a "great hope to the world." CBS war correspondent William Shirer, who later authored the renowned best seller *The Rise and Fall of the Third Reich*, declared it a "landmark in human history."[88] Roosevelt addressed the Congress upon his return, concluding:

The conference in the Crimea was a turning point, I hope, in our history, and therefore in the history of the world. . . . We shall have to take the responsibility for world collaboration, or we shall have to bear the responsibility for another world conflict. . . . And I am confident that the Congress and the American people will accept the results of this conference as the beginning of a permanent structure of peace upon which we can begin to build, under God, that better world in which our children and grandchildren, yours and mine, the children and grandchildren of the whole world, must live and can live. And that, my friends, is the only message I can give you, for I feel very deeply, and I know that all of you are feeling it today and are going to feel it in the future.[89]

Harry Hopkins, Roosevelt's advisor and confidant, shared the post-Yalta enthusiasm:

We really believed in our hearts that this was the dawn of the new day we had all been praying for and talking about for so many years. We were absolutely certain that we had won the first great victory of the peace—and by "we," I mean all of us, the whole civilized human race. [The Soviets had proved] reasonable and farseeing and there wasn't any doubt in the minds of the President or any of us that we could live with them and get along with them peacefully for as far into the future as any of us could imagine. But I have to make one amendment to that—I think we all had in our minds the reservation that we could not foretell what the results would be if anything should happen to Stalin. We felt sure that we could count on him to be reasonable and sensible and understanding—but we never could be sure who or what might be in back of him there in the Kremlin.[90]

The Soviets shared in the post-Yalta ebullience but could not be sure about the man next in line behind Roosevelt. Observers of Roosevelt's speech to Congress noticed how rapidly the president's health was failing. Exhausted from his trip, for the first time in his presidency he addressed the Congress sitting, not standing. Over the next weeks, disagreements with the Soviets surfaced over Poland and other issues, raising vexing questions for the president about the future of the relationship. But he never lost hope that the three nations would continue to work together in peace and friendship. In his last cable to Churchill, Roosevelt wrote, "I would minimize the general Soviet problem as much as possible because these problems, in one form or another, seem to arise every day and most of them straighten out."[91]

On April 12, 1945, Harry Truman, who had succeeded Wallace as vice

*The Big Three at Yalta, February 1945, where they overcame serious
differences over the future of Poland and the rest of Europe to reach a series
of agreements, igniting optimism in both the U.S. and the Soviet Union.*

president after the 1944 elections, went to House Speaker Sam Rayburn's office
in the Capitol to play poker and make a dent in his latest shipment of whisky.
Upon arrival, he was instructed to call Steve Early at the White House immediately. Early told him to rush right over. At the White House, Eleanor Roosevelt informed Truman that the president had died. After regaining his bearings,
Truman expressed his regrets and asked if there was anything he could do. Mrs.
Roosevelt replied, "Is there anything we can do for you? For you are the one in
trouble now." [92]

Truman was shockingly unprepared for that moment. He had met with
Roosevelt only twice during his eighty-two days as vice president, and they had
not spoken about any of the substantive issues facing the nation. In fact, most
astoundingly, neither Roosevelt nor any of the other top officials had even
informed Truman that the nation was building an atomic bomb. On his first day
in office, the new president ran into a group of reporters outside the Capitol.
One asked how his first day on the job was going, to which Truman replied,
"Boys, if you ever pray, pray for me now. I don't know whether you fellows ever
had a load of hay fall on you, but when they told me yesterday what had happened, I felt like the moon, the stars and all the planets had fallen on me. I've got

*Harry S. Truman taking the oath of office at the White
House following Roosevelt's death. The new president
was shockingly unprepared for the moment.*

the most terribly responsible job a man ever had." When a reporter yelled out,
"Good luck, Mr. President," Truman responded, "I wish you didn't have to call
me that."[93] It was not false humility on Truman's part. He sincerely felt he was in
way over his head and told everyone he met with that it was all a mistake and he
was not qualified to be president.

Stimson, Wallace, and others were afraid that Truman, given his own inclina-
tions and lack of preparation, would be putty in the hands of some of the hard-
liners. Stimson anticipated that the greatest pressure would come from Churchill
and warned Marshall that they "ought to be alert now that a new man was at the
helm in the Presidency to see that he was advised as to the background of the
past differences between Britain and America on these matters."[94]

Roosevelt had spelled out perhaps the most crucial difference at his March
16 cabinet meeting. Forrestal missed the meeting but had Assistant Secretary
H. Struve Hensel attend and take notes, which Forrestal included in his diary:
"The President indicated considerable difficulty with British relations. In a semi-
jocular manner of speaking, he stated that the British were perfectly willing for
the United States to have a war with Russia at any time and that, in his opinion,
to follow the British program would be to proceed toward that end."[95]

The first to see him, on April 13, was Secretary of State Edward Stettinius. The former lend-lease administrator jumped at Truman's request to be educated about what was going on in the world. Stettinius had had little influence with Roosevelt. In fact, many considered him a complete lightweight. A friend of Roosevelt complained, "A Secretary of State should be able to read and write and talk. He may not be able to do all of these, but Stettinius can't do any of them." [96] Stettinius painted a picture for Truman of Soviet deception and perfidy. Since Yalta, he explained in a memo later that day, the Soviets have "taken a firm and uncompromising position on nearly every major question." He charged them with acting unilaterally in the liberated areas and said that Churchill felt even more strongly than he did on these matters. [97] Churchill wasted little time confirming that view both in cables and in a hurried visit to Washington by Foreign Secretary Anthony Eden. The British ambassador to the United States, Lord Halifax, sized Truman up and decided that the new president was "an honest and diligent mediocrity . . . a bungling if well meaning amateur" surrounded by "Missouri County court-house calibre" friends. [98]

That afternoon Truman met with his old Senate mentor James F. "Jimmy" Byrnes. Admitting his abject ignorance, Truman implored Byrnes to tell him about everything "from Tehran to Yalta" and "everything under the sun." [99] Because Byrnes had been part of the U.S. delegation at Yalta, Truman assumed he had accurate knowledge about what transpired. It would be many months before Truman discovered that that was not the case. In this and subsequent meetings, Byrnes reinforced Stettinius's message that the Soviets were breaking the Yalta Agreement and that Truman needed to be resolute and uncompromising with them. He also gave Truman his first real briefing about the atomic bomb, which, he conjectured, "might well put us in a position to dictate our own terms at the end of the war." [100] He did not specify exactly to whom the United States would be dictating terms. Truman so trusted Byrnes that he made clear his intention to appoint him secretary of state as soon as Stettinius had gotten the United Nations off the ground. Truman's close friend and appointments secretary Matthew Connelly later wrote, "Mr. Byrnes came from South Carolina and talked to Mr. Truman and immediately decided that he would take over. Mr. Truman to Mr. Byrnes, I'm afraid, was a nonentity, as Mr. Byrnes thought he had superior intelligence." [101] Superior intelligence, perhaps, but, between this unlikely pair, who would do so much to shape the postwar world, Truman had more formal education, having at least graduated from high school, whereas Byrnes had dropped out at age fourteen.

Ambassador Harriman paid a call on Stalin at the Kremlin and found the Soviet leader profoundly saddened by Roosevelt's death. Stalin held Harriman's hand as he bemoaned humanity's loss in Roosevelt's passing and asked Harriman

Truman with James Byrnes (left) and Henry Wallace at Roosevelt's funeral. Having been Truman's mentor as a senator, Byrnes became the new president's closest advisor on foreign policy. He would later help convince Truman to fire Wallace from his cabinet.

to convey his deepest condolences to Mrs. Roosevelt and the Roosevelt children. Harriman tried to assure Stalin that he would develop an equally strong relationship with President Truman, whom Harriman described as "a man of action and not of words." Stalin responded, "Roosevelt has died but his cause must live on. We will support President Truman with all our forces and all our will." [102] The usually skeptical Harriman was moved by the depth of Stalin's emotion.

Molotov stopped off in Washington before heading to San Francisco for the opening of the United Nations. He was eager to speak directly with the new president. Harriman rushed to Washington too, intent upon reaching Truman prior to his meeting with the Soviet foreign minister. Arriving in time, he warned Truman that the United States was facing a "barbarian invasion of Europe" and urged him to stand firm and tell Molotov that "we would not stand for any pushing around on the Polish question." [103] Harriman reinforced the advice that Truman had been receiving from Churchill and Eden. As soon as the Soviet Union extended control over a country and imposed its system, he declared, the secret police moved in and wiped out free speech. He felt certain that the Soviets wouldn't risk a break with the United States because they desperately sought the postwar reconstruction aid that Roosevelt had dangled before them. Stettinius and Secretary of the Navy James Forrestal generally concurred with that assessment. All three encouraged a tough stand over Poland.

On April 23, Truman gathered his foreign policy advisors for a final meeting before sitting down with Molotov. Stimson, Marshall, and Leahy offered a different point of view. Leahy again noted the opaque elasticity of the Yalta Agreement and the difficulty of alleging bad faith on that basis. In fact, he said, after the understanding at Yalta, he would have been surprised had the Soviets behaved differently than they had. The esteemed Marshall, whom *Time* magazine had named Man of the Year for 1943, contended that a break with the Soviet Union would be disastrous, given U.S. dependence on it to help defeat the Japanese. Stimson showed the clearest understanding of the Soviet predicament and urged greater circumspection on the part of the inexperienced president. He explained that the Soviet Union had been a trustworthy ally, often delivering even more than had been promised, especially in important military matters. He reminded the president of Poland's importance to the Soviets and said that "the Russians perhaps were being more realistic than we were in regard to their own security." He added that outside the United States and Great Britain, including countries under U.S. influence, very few countries shared the United States' understanding of free elections.[104] Truman, true to form, tried to mask his limited understanding of the issues with bluster and bravado. He promised to stand up to Molotov and demand that the Soviets stop breaking the Yalta Agreement. As far as the United Nations was concerned, the United States would "go on with plans for the San Francisco conference and if the Russians did not wish to join us they could go to hell."[105] He acknowledged to Harriman that he didn't expect to get 100 percent of what he wanted from the Soviets, but he did expect to get 85 percent.[106]

Perhaps not surprisingly, the most vociferous critics of the Soviet Union shared a similar class background that inclined them to mistrust the Soviets' motives and intentions and revile anything that smacked of socialism. Harriman, the son of a railroad millionaire, had founded Brown Brothers Harriman. Forrestal had made a fortune on Wall Street. And Stettinius had been chairman of the board of U.S. Steel, the nation's largest corporation. They would join with other wealthy international bankers, Wall Street and Washington lawyers, and corporate executives, who had also inherited or made their fortunes during the interwar years, to shape postwar U.S. policy. These men included Dean Acheson of Covington and Burling; Robert Lovett of Brown Brothers Harriman; John McCloy of Cravath, Swain and Moore; Allen and John Foster Dulles of Sullivan and Cromwell; oil and banking magnate Nelson Rockefeller; Paul Nitze of Dillon, Read; Ferdinand Eberstadt of Dillon, Read and F. Eberstadt and Co.; and General Motors President Charles E. Wilson, who, in 1944, as the director of the War Production Board, told the

Army Ordnance Board that in order to prevent a return to the Depression, the United States needed "a permanent war economy." [107] Although these people also served in the Roosevelt administration, they had exerted much less influence on Roosevelt, who acted largely as his own secretary of state.

In his meeting with Molotov later that day, Truman put on his tough-guy act and wasted little time accusing the Soviets of having broken the Yalta Agreement, particularly in Poland. When Molotov tried to explain that Poland, being on the Soviet Union's border, was a vital security issue for the Soviets and that the agreement called for including friendly Poles, not the London group that was virulently hostile to the Lublin government, Truman rudely dismissed his clarifications. When Molotov tried to raise other issues, Truman snapped, "That will be all, Mr. Molotov. I would appreciate it if you would transmit my views to Marshal Stalin." [108] Molotov replied, "I've never been talked to like that in my life." Truman fired back, "Carry out your agreements and you won't get talked to like that." [109] Molotov, indignant at such treatment, stormed out of the room. Years later, Molotov remembered Truman's "imperious tone" and "rather stupid" effort to show "who was boss." [110]

Truman soon thereafter boasted to Joseph Davies, the former ambassador to the Soviet Union, "I gave it to him straight. I let him have it. It was the straight one-two to the jaw." [111]

Stalin wasted no time in responding to Truman's undiplomatic dressing down of Molotov. Having been invaded by Germany twice in twenty-five years through Poland and Eastern Europe, he insisted on having friendly governments to his west and especially on his border. He cabled Truman the following day, outlining what had actually occurred at Yalta. He contended that Roosevelt had agreed that the Lublin government would form the kernel of the new Polish government. Because "Poland borders on the Soviet Union," the Soviets had the right to a friendly government there. He said he didn't know if the governments of Belgium or Greece were really democratic, but he wouldn't make a stink because they were vital to British security. He wrote, "I am ready to fulfill your request and do everything possible to reach a harmonious solution. But you demand too much of me . . . you demand that I renounce the interests of security of the Soviet Union, but I cannot turn against my country." [112]

Stalin believed that he and Roosevelt had reached an understanding about Poland that respected the Soviet Union's security needs. In fact, when Harriman wanted to make an issue of Poland at the Foreign Ministers Conference in Moscow in October 1943, Secretary of State Hull rebuked him and reminded him of the United States' real priorities, commenting, "I don't want to deal with these piddling little things. We must deal with the main issues." [113] But under Truman the anti-Soviet hard-liners were driving policy. Stalin felt betrayed.

The opening of the United Nations in San Francisco on April 25 should have been an occasion to celebrate a new era in international peace and reconciliation. Instead, the early sessions were marred by tension between the principal wartime allies. On the opening day, Harriman met with members of the U.S. delegation to make sure, he said, that "everyone understands that the Soviets . . . were not going to live up to their post-war agreements." They would, he insisted, use any devious means at their disposal to dominate Eastern Europe. When Harriman repeated the charges in off-the-record press conferences, several reporters walked out and accused him of being a "warmonger." [114] The U.S. delegates showed no such skepticism. Molotov's request to have the Lublin government seated to represent Poland was rejected. But the United States rallied Latin American representatives to support seating the Argentine government despite its Nazi sympathies.

Realizing that his get-tough tactics with the Soviet Union had not produced the desired results, Truman met twice with Joseph Davies to seek his counsel. As ambassador to the Soviet Union, Davies, a conservative corporate attorney, had surprised liberal critics by sympathizing with the Soviet experiment. Truman confessed to Davies that after his tirade, Molotov "was visibly shaken, blanched and went pale." He concluded that "the tough method" clearly worked because the Soviets backed down at San Francisco and didn't demand recognition of the Lublin government. But after that, relations had deteriorated rapidly. "What do you think," he asked. "Did I do right?"

Davies explained that Molotov had come to see him before his April 23 meeting with Truman and asked if Truman knew all the facts about Yalta. He said that Roosevelt's death had been "a great tragedy" to them because "Stalin and Roosevelt understood each other." Davies explained to Truman that the Soviets had always been "sticklers for reciprocity . . . between allies." So they accepted British-imposed governments in Africa, Italy, and Greece, even though they didn't represent the antifascist forces in those countries, because they understood that they were "vital interests" to the United States and Great Britain. They expected similar consideration for their vital security interests in Poland. Davies reminded Truman that while the United States and Great Britain were planning global strategy, the Soviet Union was doing all the fighting. Truman was surprised to learn that the Soviets had even agreed not to press their territorial claims with Churchill "out of consideration for Roosevelt." Truman promised he would "clean out" the people in the State Department who were so anti-Soviet that they'd been misleading him. Davies noted how fundamentally the relationship had changed in the last six weeks, with the British acting as instigators.

Davies warned Truman that if the Soviets decided that the United States and Great Britain were "ganging up on them," they would respond by out-toughing the West, as they had in concluding the pact with Hitler when it became clear that the West would not help them stop the Nazis. But he assured Truman that "when approached with generosity and friendliness, the Soviets respond with even greater generosity. The 'tough' approach induces a quick and sharp rejoinder that 'out toughs' anyone they consider hostile." Davies agreed to set up a meeting between Truman and Stalin. Truman admitted that he was in over his head and had mishandled things. Davies recorded Truman's self-deprecating comments in his diary: "It's no wonder that I'm concerned over this matter. It is a terrible responsibility and I am the last man fitted to handle it and it happened to me. But I'll do my best." "Here lies Joe Williams, he did his best./Man can do no more./But he was too slow on the draw," Truman quipped revealingly.[115]

Another former ambassador to the Soviet Union, Admiral William H. Standley, who had served in 1942 and 1943, spoke out publicly to counter those who believed Stalin was up to no good. Writing in *Collier's*, Standley insisted that Stalin genuinely desired to cooperate with the United States to establish a durable world peace. The Soviet Union not only "desperately" needed a stable peace, he believed, "but I am certain that [Stalin] desires it sincerely and fervently." "The world," he added, "simply cannot stand another war."[116]

Things had been going well on the battlefield in Europe. On April 26, U.S. and Soviet soldiers met on the Elbe River near Torgau, 4,500 miles from the shores of the United States and 1,400 bloody miles from the ruins of Stalingrad. The occasion was joyous. Food abounded, and liquor flowed—champagne, vodka, cognac, wine, beer, scotch. Private First Class Leo Kasinsky called it "the best time I ever had in my life. . . . [The Soviets] gave us a wonderful meal and we had about sixty toasts." "Boy," he added, "they don't even drink like that in Brooklyn."[117] The *New York Times* reported "toasts and songs and expressions of hope for the future in which America, Russia and Britain would stand together for enduring peace."[118]

On May 7, 1945, Germany surrendered. Hitler and Eva Braun had committed suicide in their bunker a week earlier. A U.S. diplomat wrote that the Soviet people's joy was "indescribable." Crowds gathered in front of the U.S. Embassy in Moscow and shouted, "Hurrah for Roosevelt!"[119] Stalin addressed 2 to 3 million people in Red Square.

Americans returned that feeling of goodwill toward the Soviets, acknowledging the immensity of their sacrifice and suffering. In June, C. L. Sulzberger wrote in the *New York Times* that their losses strained the imagination: "In terms of misery and suffering, of malady and disaster, of wasted man hours in a land where work is glorified, the loss is incalculable. It cannot be gauged by the scarcely touched peoples of America. It cannot be measured by the sadly battered people of England. It perhaps cannot be fully realized even by the masses of Russian people themselves." Sulzberger understood that such devastation would have enduring consequences: "this terrible suffering and unprecedented destruction" will "leave its marks not only upon the people and lands of the U.S.S.R. but upon future decisions and policies as well as psychological attitudes." This meant that the Soviets would demand "allies of the surest sort" in Eastern Europe, the permanent debilitation of German military power, and the forging of friendly relations with the nations of Central Asia and the Far East that bordered the Soviet Union. He predicted that Soviet citizens, despite the fact that they were eager for "the better things of life," would patiently sacrifice material comforts for a return to the sense of security that had been shattered by the war years.[120]

Charitable efforts to ease Soviet deprivation proliferated throughout the year. On New Year's Day, the editors of the *Washington Post* urged Americans to remember Russian children as they celebrated their holiday and "send them a tithe of our good fortune," commemorating "the sense of community we have come to feel toward the Russian people."[121] Even First Lady Bess Truman lent a hand. In July, she became honorary chairman of the English Classics Collection of Books for Russian War Relief, which commenced a nationwide drive to collect a million books to replace those destroyed by the Nazis. Each donated volume would bear the flags of the two nations along with a frontispiece inscription, reading "To the heroic people of the Soviet Union from the people of America."[122]

Numerous stories circulated about the bravery and generosity of Soviet soldiers and average citizens. The *Washington Post* detailed the story of Captain Ernest M. Gruenberg, a paratroop surgeon, on D-Day. Upon escaping from a POW camp, Gruenberg and two other U.S. officers made the journey to Moscow in just fourteen days. Gruenberg recounted, "We hardly ever walked. Always there was a truck or train to haul us and no one ever asked for money or tickets. We were Americans and nothing, apparently, was too good for us. Everywhere people took us in. We rode in trucks and box cars but we made a grand entry into Moscow in the car reserved for Russian officers—free, of course." The Soviets and Poles were so willing to share their meager food supplies that Gruenberg believed he gained back the twenty-five pounds he had lost in prison.[123]

The comradely feelings toward the Soviet people translated into optimism about postwar comity between the two nations. A March Gallup Poll revealed that 55 percent of Americans believed that the Soviet Union could be trusted to cooperate with the United States after the war.[124]

Although many of Truman's advisors assumed that Stalin would set up Communist regimes throughout the territories occupied by the Red Army, Stalin was in no rush to institute revolutionary change. He recognized that the Communists represented a minority element in most of these nations, though they had often played a leading role in anti-Nazi resistance movements. He had once remarked that communism fit Poland like a saddle fit a cow.[125]

And Soviet soldiers did little to ingratiate themselves with the German

*Led by the Russian War Relief,
Americans gave generously to
their struggling Soviet allies.*

people. Seeking revenge for the havoc, devastation, and humiliation that German soldiers had wreaked on the Soviet Union, they behaved brutally toward the vanquished Germans. German women paid an especially high price for Germany's crimes. In just a few weeks, over 100,000 sought medical care for rape.

Although such behavior was unconscionable and inexcusable, it can be understood as more than simply the "barbarian invasion" alleged by Harriman. Soviet troops had not only witnessed German atrocities inside the Soviet Union; their rage had been fueled by what they had seen while liberating concentration camps, including Majdanek, Sobibor, Treblinka, and Auschwitz, en route to Berlin. As the war correspondent Alexander Werth described it, "As the Red Army advanced to the west, it heard these daily stories of terror, and humiliation and deportation; it saw the destroyed cities; it saw the mass-graves of Russian war prisoners, murdered or starved to death . . . in the Russian soldiers' mind, the real truth on Nazi Germany, with its Hitler and Himmler and its *Untermensch* philosophy and its unspeakable sadism became hideously tangible." [126] Soldiers described the horrors they had witnessed. V. Letnikov wrote to his wife in 1945:

> Yesterday we examined a death camp for 120,000 prisoners. Posts
> two meters high with electric fencing enclose the camp. In addition,
> the Germans mined everything. Watchtowers for armed guards and
> machineguns stand fifty meters apart. Not far away from the death barracks
> is the crematorium. Can you imagine how many people the Germans have
> burned there? Next to this exploded crematorium, there are bones, bones,
> and piles of shoes several meters high. There are children's shoes in the pile.
> Total horror, impossible to describe. [127]

Soviet newspapers, including those read by the soldiers, went out of their way to publish grisly accounts of the atrocities. By the time they reached German soil, Soviet troops' anger could barely be contained. Stalin, neither condoning nor condemning such behavior, did nothing to stop it.

Far from initially imposing Communist regimes, Stalin tried to restrain those seeking revolutionary change in both Western and Eastern Europe, urging them to establish broader democratic coalitions. More of a nationalist than an international revolutionary, he thought first about what was in the interests of the Soviet Union. He expected the United States' support for postwar reconstruction, and he needed the Allies' cooperation to guarantee against the restoration of German power, which he still saw as the primary threat to the Soviet Union. He told his Communist allies not to follow the Bolshevik model but to move toward socialism under other "political systems—for example by a democracy, a parliamentary republic and even by a constitutional monarchy." [128] He wanted nothing to disrupt his alliance with the United States and Britain. Hence, the governments he set up in Soviet-liberated Eastern and Central Europe were friendly to the Soviet Union but not Communist-dominated.

Truman was also feeling more conciliatory. After his meetings with Davies and conversations with Harry Hopkins and Secretary of Commerce Henry Wallace, he made an effort to improve relations with the Soviets. He and his military leaders resisted Churchill's pressure to maintain troops in their advanced positions until they had wrested concessions from the Soviets. Truman gradually discovered that Stalin's interpretation of the Yalta Agreement conformed more closely to the truth than his own. Byrnes admitted that he had left Yalta before the final agreement was concluded and that he had not participated in many of the critical meetings. Truman also learned that Roosevelt had indeed acceded to a Soviet sphere of influence in Eastern Europe and that there were no grounds for demanding a new government in Poland. He sent Harry Hopkins to meet with Stalin in late May, and they worked out an agreement on Poland that was similar to the formula established for Yugoslavia. The reorganized cabinet would include former Prime Minister Stanislaw Mikolajczyk as deputy prime minister and three other non-Communists, along with the seventeen posts accorded to the Communists and their allies. Truman told journalists that this represented a "very pleasant yielding" on the part of Stalin, which augured well for future cooperation between the United States and the Soviet Union.[129]

As Truman left for Potsdam in July, there was a much greater basis for optimism regarding the postwar alliance than there had been only two months earlier. But some raised a cautionary note. *Life* magazine in July 1945—just two years after it had put Stalin on the cover as a hero—cautioned that "Russia is the No. 1 problem for America because it is the only country in the world with the dynamic power to challenge our own conceptions of truth, justice and the good life."[130]

The Potsdam meeting, though amicable on the surface, would prove a setback to long-term cooperation. News of the successful atomic bomb test convinced Truman that the United States could get along just fine without catering to Soviet concerns, and his behavior toward Stalin conveyed that message. On his way back from Potsdam on the USS *Augusta,* he told a group of officers that it didn't matter if the Soviets were obstinate "because the United States now had developed an entirely new weapon of such force and nature that we did not need the Russians—or any other nation."[131]

Chapter 4

THE BOMB:

The Tragedy of a Small Man

A young second lieutenant, Paul Fussell, was about to be transferred from Europe to the Pacific when he received the news of the atomic bombing of Hiroshima. In 1988, he published *Thank God for the Atom Bomb.* "For all the fake manliness of our facades," he wrote, "we cried with relief and joy. We were going to live. We were going to grow up to adulthood after all." [1]

Generations of Americans have been taught that the United States reluctantly dropped atomic bombs on Japan at the end of World War II to save the lives of hundreds of thousands of young men like Fussell who were poised to die if the U.S. invaded. But the story is really more complicated—and much more disturbing.

With its sights trained on first defeating the Nazis, the United States threw the lion's share of its resources into the European war. Roosevelt had insisted on the Europe-first strategy. He opposed "an all-out effort in the Pacific." Defeating Japan, he argued, would not defeat Germany, but defeating Germany would mean defeating Japan, "probably without firing a shot or losing a life." [2]

Following the surprise attack at Pearl Harbor, the Japanese took the offensive early in the war. But the United States scored a major victory at Midway in June 1942 and then began the island-hopping strategy that would continue for more than three years. The Japanese fought fiercely, ensuring that U.S. victory would come at an enormous cost. U.S. industrial production gave the U.S. forces tremendous advantages. By 1943, U.S. factories were churning out almost 100,000 planes a year, dwarfing the 70,000 Japan produced during the entire war. By the summer of 1944, the United States had deployed almost a hundred aircraft carriers in the Pacific, far more than Japan's twenty-five for the entire war.

Science also figured prominently in the war effort. Development of radar and the proximity fuze contributed to the Allied victory. But it was the development of the atomic bomb that would change the course of history.

Science fiction writers and scientists had long pondered the possibility of atomic energy for both peaceful and military purposes. Beginning in 1896, a series of scientific discoveries by Henri Becquerel, Marie and Pierre Curie, and Frederick Soddy and Ernest Rutherford ignited public curiosity about radioactivity. In the early 1900s, comments by Rutherford, Soddy, and others about the enormous energy locked in matter and the possibility of blowing up the universe aroused futuristic apprehension. But they and others also fantasized about the positive uses to which such energy might be put and the utopian societies that could emerge.

While awaiting the advent of atomic power to create a new Garden of Eden, the public became enamored of the healing powers of radium and other radioactive ingredients. Promoters claimed that their products could heal all sorts of maladies, ranging from baldness to rheumatism to dyspepsia to high blood pressure. One list contained eighty patent medicines with radioactive ingredients that could be inhaled or injected or taken in tablets, bath salts, liniments, suppositories, or chocolate candy. William Bailey claimed that the products produced at the Bailey Radium Laboratories in East Orange, New Jersey, would cure everything from flatulence to sexual debility. Among his products was the Radioendocrinator, which could be worn around the neck to rejuvenate the thyroid, around the trunk to stimulate the adrenals and ovaries, or under the scrotum in a special jockstrap. He did a thriving business, especially with his liquid Radithor, whose saddest and most noteworthy victim was wealthy Pittsburgh manufacturer and playboy Eben Byers. Byers's physician recommended he try Radithor for his injured arm, and Byers began drinking several bottles a day in December 1927. Not only did it work for his arm, Byers claimed, it gave him new vitality and sexual energy. Believing it was an aphrodisiac, Byers pressed the substance on his lady friends. By 1931, he himself had consumed between 1,000 and 1,500 bottles and started feeling sick. He lost weight, experienced bad headaches, and watched his teeth fall out. Experts decided that his body was slowly decomposing. His upper jaw and most of his lower jaw were removed, and holes appeared in his skull. From there the end came quickly as he succumbed to radioactive poisoning.[3]

Among those who warned of atomic energy's dystopian possibilities was H. G. Wells, who wrote the first atomic war novel—*The World Set Free*—in 1914. Wells prophesied an atomic war between Germany and Austria on one side and England, France, and the United States on the other in which over two hundred cities were destroyed by the "unquenchable crimson conflagrations of the atomic bombs."[4] He later proposed his own epitaph: "God damn you all, I told you so."

A brilliant, quirky, Hungarian physicist named Leo Szilard was influenced by Wells's writing. Szilard, who left Germany soon after the Nazi takeover, had

H. G. Wells wrote the first atomic war novel, The World Set Free, in 1914. He prophesied an atomic war between Germany and Austria, on one side, and England, France, and the United States, on the other, in which over two hundred cities were destroyed by the "unquenchable crimson conflagrations of the atomic bombs." He later proposed his own epitaph: "God damn you all, I told you so."

given extensive thought to the possibility of atomic energy. He tried to discuss the feasibility with Rutherford, who dismissed it as the "merest moonshine" and threw Szilard out of his office.[5] Undaunted, Szilard took out a patent in 1934 on how a nuclear chain reaction would work, citing beryllium as the most likely element rather than uranium.

In December 1938, two German physicists stunned the scientific world by splitting the uranium atom, making the development of atomic bombs a theoretical possibility. Those in the United States who were most alarmed by this development were the scientists who had escaped from Nazi-occupied Europe, who feared the consequences should Hitler get his hands on such a weapon. Proposing that the United States build its own atomic bomb as a deterrent, the émigré scientists tried but failed to arouse the interest of U.S. authorities. Feeling desperate, in July 1939, Szilard and fellow Hungarian physicist Eugene Wigner solicited the help of the universally admired Albert Einstein, who agreed to write to President Roosevelt, urging him to authorize a U.S. atomic research program. Einstein later regretted the action, admitting to chemist Linus Pauling, "I made one great mistake in my life—when I signed the letter to President Roosevelt recommending that the atom bombs be made."[6] He actually wrote three letters to Roosevelt on the subject.

The scientists were right about one thing. Germany did begin an atomic research program. But, unbeknown to the Americans until late in the war, Germany abandoned its atomic research early on to focus on more immediately available weapons like the V-1 and V-2 rockets. Hitler and Albert Speer had little interest in putting manpower and resources into a weapon they might not be able to use in the current war.

Despite Roosevelt's commitment, U.S. research developed at a glacial pace. It languished until fall 1941, when the United States officially received the British MAUD report, which corrected the erroneous belief that five hundred tons of pure uranium might be required to make a bomb—an amount that would stop the program in its tracks. In fact, wartime science administrator James Conant thought it unwise to commit so many resources to the project. Nobel Prize–winning physicist Arthur Holly Compton reported that by the summer of 1941, "The government's responsible representatives were . . . very close to dropping fission studies from the war program."[7] However, the new calculations showed that only five to ten kilograms were needed and that a bomb was achievable within two years.

With the new report in hand, Vannevar Bush, the country's other top science administrator, went to see Roosevelt and Vice President Henry Wallace on October 9. Based on the new information, Roosevelt gave Bush the resources he requested.

Bush put Compton in charge of bomb design. Compton set up the Metallurgical Laboratory at the University of Chicago. The goal was to produce a self-sustaining chain reaction in an atomic pile. Compton asked J. Robert Oppenheimer, the brilliant and charismatic theoretical physicist, to bring together a team of extraordinary theoreticians to grapple with a number of important questions. Among Oppenheimer's "luminaries," as he called them, were Edward Teller and Hans Bethe, who shared a compartment on the train west to Berkeley, where they were to gather in the summer of 1942. Teller confided what was really on his mind. Bethe recalled, "Teller told me that the fission bomb was all well and good and, essentially, was now a sure thing. In reality, the work had hardly begun. Teller likes to jump to conclusions. He said that what we really should think about was the possibility of igniting deuterium by a fission weapon—the hydrogen bomb."[8] Teller was so gung ho on the fusion bomb that his fellow scientists had a difficult time getting him to focus on the problem at hand—building an atomic bomb. Thus, from nearly the outset of the project, the leading scientists were aware that what lay at the end of the road was not just an atomic bomb, which would vastly multiply human destructive capabilities, but a hydrogen bomb, which could threaten all life on the planet.

That summer they had a scare so profoundly unsettling that it forced them to halt the project. During their deliberations, the physicists suddenly realized that an atomic detonation might ignite the hydrogen in the oceans or the nitrogen in

Albert Einstein
Old Grove Rd.
Nassau Point
Peconic, Long Island

August 2nd, 1939

F.D. Roosevelt,
President of the United States,
White House
Washington, D.C.

Sir:

Some recent work by E.Fermi and L. Szilard, which has been communicated to me in manuscript, leads me to expect that the element uranium may be turned into a new and important source of energy in the immediate future. Certain aspects of the situation which has arisen seem to call for watchfulness and, if necessary, quick action on the part of the Administration. I believe therefore that it is my duty to bring to your attention the following facts and recommendations:

In the course of the last four months it has been made probable - through the work of Joliot in France as well as Fermi and Szilard in America - that it may become possible to set up a nuclear chain reaction in a large mass of uranium,by which vast amounts of power and large quantities of new radium-like elements would be generated. Now it appears almost certain that this could be achieved in the immediate future.

This new phenomenon would also lead to the construction of bombs, and it is conceivable - though much less certain - that extremely powerful bombs of a new type thus may be constructed. A single bomb of this type, carried by boat and exploded in a port, might very well destroy the whole port together with some of the surrounding territory. However, such bombs might very well prove to be too heavy for transportation by air.

-2-

The United States has only very poor ores of uranium in moderate quantities. There is some good ore in Canada and the former Czechoslovakia, while the most important source of uranium is Belgian Congo.

In view of this situation you may think it desirable to have some permanent contact maintained between the Administration and the group of physicists working on chain reactions in America. One possible way of achieving this might be for you to entrust with this task a person who has your confidence and who could perhaps serve in an inofficial capacity. His task might comprise the following:

a) to approach Government Departments, keep them informed of the further development, and put forward recommendations for Government action, giving particular attention to the problem of securing a supply of uranium ore for the United States;

b) to speed up the experimental work,which is at present being carried on within the limits of the budgets of University laboratories, by providing funds, if such funds be required, through his contacts with private persons who are willing to make contributions for this cause, and perhaps also by obtaining the co-operation of industrial laboratories which have the necessary equipment.

I understand that Germany has actually stopped the sale of uranium from the Czechoslovakian mines which she has taken over. That she should have taken such early action might perhaps be understood on the ground that the son of the German Under-Secretary of State, von Weizsäcker, is attached to the Kaiser-Wilhelm-Institut in Berlin where some of the American work on uranium is now being repeated.

Yours very truly,
(Albert Einstein)

One of three letters Albert Einstein wrote to President Roosevelt urging him to authorize a U.S. atomic research program. Einstein later regretted this action, admitting to Linus Pauling, "I made one great mistake in my life—when I signed the letter to President Roosevelt recommending that the atom bombs be made."

the atmosphere and set the planet afire. Nuel Pharr Davis, in his study of Oppenheimer and physicist Ernest Lawrence, describes the abject fear that engulfed the room: "Oppenheimer stared at the blackboard in wild surprise, and the other faces in the room, including Teller's, successively caught the same look. . . . Teller had correctly calculated the heat production of a fission bomb; Oppenheimer saw it, with or without a deuterium wrapper, setting afire the atmosphere of the entire planet, and no one at the conference could prove he was wrong."[9] Oppenheimer rushed east to confer with Compton. In his memoirs, *Atomic Quest,* Compton explains that he and Oppenheimer agreed that "unless they came up with a firm and reliable conclusion that our atomic bombs could not explode the air or the sea, these bombs must never be made." Compton reflected, "Better to accept the slavery of the Nazis than to run a chance of drawing the final curtain on mankind!"[10] Back at Berkeley, Bethe performed some additional calculations and discovered that Teller hadn't accounted for the heat that would be absorbed by radiation, which lowered the odds of blowing up the world to three in 1 million—a risk they were willing to chance.

On December 2, 1942, the scientists at Met Lab succeeded in creating the first sustained nuclear chain reaction. Given the lack of safety precautions, it's lucky they didn't blow up the city of Chicago. Szilard and Italian émigré Enrico

Artist's rendition of the first sustained nuclear chain reaction on December 2, 1942, at the Met Lab at the University of Chicago. Leo Szilard and Enrico Fermi shook hands in front of the reactors as the scientists toasted with Chianti in paper cups to salute Fermi's leadership. Szilard, however, appreciated what a bittersweet moment it actually was and warned Fermi that the date would go down in history as a black mark against mankind.

Fermi shook hands in front of the reactors as the scientists toasted with Chianti in paper cups to salute Fermi's leadership. Szilard, however, appreciated what a bittersweet moment it actually was and warned Fermi that December 2 "would go down as a black day in the history of mankind."[11] He was right.

Slow out of the gate, the United States now embarked on a crash program— the Manhattan Project—under Brigadier General Leslie Groves in late 1942. Groves appointed Oppenheimer to organize and head the project's main laboratory at Los Alamos in New Mexico's beautiful Sangre de Cristo Mountains. Most onlookers assumed that the relationship between Groves and Oppenheimer would be a marriage made in Hell. They were opposites in every imaginable way. Groves weighed more than twice as much as the pencil-thin scientist, who, despite being over six feet tall, weighed 128 pounds at the start of the Project and 115 by the end. Groves came from poverty, Oppenheimer from wealth. They were different in religion, taste in foods, smoking and drinking habits, and especially politics. Groves was a staunch conservative, Oppenheimer an unapologetic leftist, most of whose students, friends, and family members were Communists. He admitted that he was a member of every Communist Party front group on the West Coast. At one point, he had given 10 percent of his monthly salary to the Communist Party to support the republican forces in Spain.

Oppenheimer and Groves were also opposites in temperament. Whereas

Groves and Oppenheimer at ground zero of the Trinity test. The two leaders of the Manhattan Project were opposites in every imaginable way—in stature, religion, taste in foods, smoking and drinking habits, and especially politics. The two were also opposites in temperament. Whereas Oppenheimer was beloved by most of those who knew him, Groves was universally despised. But Groves's gruff, bullying, take-no-prisoners style actually complemented Oppenheimer's ability to inspire and get the most out of his colleagues in driving the project forward to completion.

Oppenheimer was beloved by most of those who knew him, Groves was universally despised. Groves's assistant, Lieutenant Colonel Kenneth Nichols, said that his boss was "the biggest S.O.B. I have ever worked for." He described him as "demanding," "critical," "abrasive and sarcastic," "intelligent," and "the most egotistical man I know." Nichols admitted that he "hated his guts and so did everyone else." [12] But Groves's gruff, bullying, take-no-prisoners style actually complemented Oppenheimer's ability to inspire and get the most out of his colleagues in driving the project forward to completion.

That is not to suggest that the scientists and the military didn't clash over security provisions and other matters. Where possible, Oppenheimer ran interference for the scientists and eased the suffocating grip of military control. Sometimes Oppie, as his friends called him, made his point humorously. On one occasion, Groves told Oppenheimer that he didn't want him to wear his signature porkpie hats because they made him too recognizable. When Groves next entered Oppenheimer's office, he found him wearing a full Indian headdress, which Oppenheimer proclaimed he would continue to wear until the end of the war. Groves ultimately relented.

As the bomb project progressed steadily, so did the Allied effort in the Pacific. By 1944, the United States was capturing more and more Japanese-occupied territories, eventually bringing Japan itself within range of U.S. bombers. In July

1944, the Combined Chiefs of Staff, under General George Marshall, a future secretary of state and Nobel Peace Prize winner, adopted a two-pronged strategy to win the Pacific war: first strangle Japan with an air and sea blockade and pummel the country with "intensive air bombardment";[13] then, with Japan's military weakened and morale lowered, invade.

In June 1944, as Allied forces advanced in both the European and Pacific theaters, Churchill and Roosevelt finally delivered on the long-delayed second front, landing 100,000 troops on the beach at Normandy, France. German forces, retreating from the Soviet advance, would now have to fight a real two-front war.

On July 9, U.S. forces took Saipan. The toll was enormous. Thirty thousand Japanese troops and 22,000 civilians were killed or committed suicide. The United States counted almost 3,000 dead and over 10,000 wounded in the nearly month-long combat—its highest battle toll to date in the Pacific. For most Japanese leaders, the calamitous defeat offered definitive proof that military victory could not be won. On July 18, Prime Minister Hideki Tojo and his cabinet resigned.

The next day, just as news of Tojo's resignation began to circulate, the Democratic National Convention opened in Chicago. Franklin D. Roosevelt easily secured the nomination for an unprecedented fourth term. The real contest was over the vice presidency. Henry Wallace had incurred the wrath of party conservatives by calling for a worldwide "people's revolution," toward which end the United States and Soviet Union would work together,[14] and by championing the cause of labor unions, women, African Americans, and the victims of European colonialism. His enemies included Wall Street bankers and other anti-union business interests, southern segregationists, and defenders of British and French colonialism.

William Stephenson, head of British intelligence in New York, even deployed Roald Dahl to spy on Wallace when the RAF lieutenant and future writer was posted to Washington, D.C. In 1944, Dahl got hold of a draft of Wallace's forthcoming pamphlet "Our Job in the Pacific." What he read, he said, "made my hair stand on end." Wallace called for the "emancipation of . . . colonial subjects" in British India, Malaya, and Burma, French Indochina, the Dutch East Indies, and many small Pacific islands. Dahl secreted the manuscript out of Wallace's friend's home and rushed it to British officials to copy and transmit to British intelligence and Churchill. "I was later told," Dahl reminisced, "that Churchill could hardly believe what he was reading." Wallace wrote in his diary that "the entire British Secret Service was shaking with indignation as well as the British Foreign Office." British leaders pressured Roosevelt to censure and part ways with his vice president. Stephenson remarked, "I came to regard Wallace as a menace and I took action to ensure that the White House was aware that the British Government would view with concern Wallace's appearance on the ticket at the 1944 presidential elections." Dahl, whose main job in Washington was monitoring

Wallace's activities—the two regularly walked and played tennis together—said his "friend" was "a lovely man, but too innocent and idealistic for this world." [15]

It was precisely because most of the world did not agree with Dahl's assessment that Wallace posed such a threat. In March 1943, Wallace embarked on a forty-day, seven-nation goodwill tour of Latin America. Speaking in Spanish, he electrified his audiences. He stopped first in Costa Rica, where 65,000 people, 15 percent of that nation's population, turned out to greet him. "The reception accorded Mr. Wallace was the greatest in the history of Costa Rica," the *New York Times* reported. But that was just the beginning. Three hundred thousand greeted his plane in Chile. More than a million cheered him as he walked through the streets of Santiago arm in arm with President Juan Antonio Rios. One hundred thousand people, 20,000 over capacity, packed the stadium to hear him speak. Ambassador Claude Bowers reported to Washington: "Never in Chilean history has any foreigner been received with such extravagance and evidently sincere enthusiasm.... His simplicity of manner, his mingling with all sorts of people, his visit to the workers' quarters without notice ... and his inspection of the housing projects absolutely amazed the masses who responded almost hysterically."

In Ecuador, he spoke movingly of the postwar future at the University of Guayaquil. "If the liberation of the people for which the fight is going on today with the blood of youth and the sweat of workers results in imperialism and oppression tomorrow, this terrible war will have been in vain," he declared. "If this sacrifice of blood and strength again brings a concentration of riches in the hands of a few— great fortunes for the privileged and poverty for the people in general—then democracy will have failed and all this sacrifice will have been in vain." Two hundred thousand welcomed him to Lima. The trip was not only a personal triumph; it was a diplomatic tour de force. When it was over, a dozen Latin American countries had declared war on Germany and twenty had broken diplomatic relations. [16]

Wallace was equally popular back home. While he was away, Gallup asked Democratic voters whether they viewed favorably or unfavorably each of the four leading contenders to replace Roosevelt if he decided not to run again. Wallace's 57 percent favorability rating more than doubled that of his nearest competitor. [17]

Wallace's acclaim made it even more urgent for his detractors to make their move. Knowing that Roosevelt's failing health meant he would not survive a fourth term, the party bosses decided to oust Wallace from the ticket and replace him with someone more amenable to the party's conservative factions. In 1944, they staged what was known among insiders as "Pauley's coup," named after Democratic Party Treasurer and oil millionaire Edwin Pauley. [18] Pauley had once quipped that he went into politics when he realized that it was cheaper to elect a new Congress than to buy up the old one. Pauley's co-conspirators included Edward Flynn

Harry Truman (pictured here at age thirteen) overcame a very difficult childhood, one that took a great toll on his psyche. He struggled to win the approval of his roughneck father. And he was forced to wear Coke-bottle-thick glasses, so he couldn't play sports or roughhouse with the other boys, who picked on and bullied him. "To tell the truth, I was kind of a sissy," Truman remembered.

of the Bronx, Mayor Edward Kelly of Chicago, Mayor Frank Hague of Jersey City, Postmaster General and former Party Chairman Frank Walker, Party Secretary George Allen, and national Democratic Party Chairman Robert Hannegan.

After going through the list of potential candidates, the party bosses chose undistinguished Missouri Senator Harry Truman to replace Wallace. They picked Truman not because he had any substantial qualifications for the position but because he had been sufficiently innocuous as a senator that he had made few enemies and he could be counted on not to rock the boat. They gave little, if any, thought to the attributes that would be necessary to lead the United States and the world in the challenging times ahead, when decisions would be made that would shape the course of history. Thus Truman's ascent to the presidency, like much of his career, was a product of backroom deal-making by corrupt party bosses.

Although Harry Truman left office with approval ratings so low that only George W. Bush has come close, he is now widely viewed as a nearly great president and routinely showered with praise by Republicans and Democrats alike. Former National Security Advisor and Secretary of State Condoleezza Rice, whom George W. Bush credited with telling "me everything I know about the Soviet Union," named Truman her man of the century to *Time*.[19] Some historians have fallen into the same trap, none more than David McCullough, whose hagiographic biography of Truman won him a Pulitzer Prize.

The real Harry Truman is more interesting than McCullough's one. Truman overcame a very difficult childhood, one that took a great toll on his psyche. Growing up on his family's Missouri farm, he struggled to win the affection of his father, John "Peanuts" Truman. The elder Truman, though only five foot four, relished beating up much taller men to show how tough he was. He wanted that same toughness in his sons. He found it in Harry's younger brother Vivian. Harry, however, was diagnosed with hypermetropia, or "flat eyeballs," and forced to wear Coke-bottle-thick glasses, so he couldn't play sports or roughhouse with the other boys. "I was afraid my eyes would get knocked out if there was too much of a rough and tumble play," he explained. "To tell the truth, I was kind of a sissy." [20] He was picked on and bullied by the other boys, who called him "four-eyes" and "sissy" and chased him home after school. To make matters worse, when he arrived home trembling and out of breath, his mother would comfort him by telling him not to worry because he was meant to be a girl anyway. He wrote about one incident in a 1912 letter, "That sounds rather feminine, doesn't it. Mamma says I was intended for a girl anyway. It makes me pretty mad to be told so but I guess it's partly so." He later reflected that being regarded as a "sissy" was "hard on a boy. It makes him lonely, and it gives him an inferiority complex, and he has a hard time overcoming it." [21] Not surprisingly, gender issues plagued him for years. He often referred to his feminine features and attributes. He would later prove that not only was he not a sissy, he could stand up to Stalin and show him who was boss.

Economic hardship also plagued him. Although he was a good student, with a serious interest in history, his family's economic circumstances made it impossible for him to attend college. After graduating from high school, he bounced around for a while before returning to work on his father's farm. He also got involved in three failed business ventures and didn't experience real success until his service in the First World War, when he served bravely and honorably in France.

His final business venture, a haberdashery that went belly up in 1922, left the thirty-eight-year-old Truman with a wife to support and limited prospects. It was at that low point that party boss Tom Pendergast offered to get Truman elected judge in Jackson County. During the campaign, Truman, who was always bigoted and anti-Semitic, sent a $10 check to the Ku Klux Klan but was denied membership because he would not promise to stop hiring Catholics. [22]

Truman remained a loyal member of the notorious Pendergast machine throughout the 1920s and early 1930s but felt as if he were getting nowhere in life. On the eve of his forty-ninth birthday in 1933, he mused, "Tomorrow I'll be forty-nine, but for all the good I have done the forty might as well be left off." [23] The following year, just when Truman had wearied of machine politics and was contemplating a return to the farm, Boss Pendergast picked him to run for the Senate— his first four choices had turned him down—and engineered his election. When asked why he had chosen someone as unqualified as Truman to run, Pendergast replied, "I wanted to demonstrate that a well oiled machine could send an office boy to the senate." [24] Known derisively among his new Senate colleagues as "the Senator from Pendergast" and shunned by most of them, Truman worked hard to gain respectability in Washington, a stature he finally achieved during his second term in the Senate.

Failing to garner President Roosevelt's endorsement in 1940, Truman barely won reelection to the Senate with the help of the St. Louis Hannegan-Dickmann Democratic machine, while his old party boss Tom Pendergast languished in prison. Truman now owed favors to two corrupt urban machines.

He almost didn't get that second term. Failing to win Roosevelt's endorsement, Truman eked out reelection to the Senate in 1940 by a razor-thin margin with the help of the St. Louis Hannegan-Dickmann machine while Pendergast languished in federal prison. Truman now owed favors to two corrupt urban machines. Roosevelt, meanwhile, was staking his own political future on the choice of the high-minded Wallace as his vice presidential running mate, taking comfort in the knowledge that Wallace's progressive ideals would help steer the country through the rocky times ahead.

The American people showed much better judgment than the party bosses. When Gallup asked likely Democratic voters in a Gallup Poll released on July 20, 1944, during the Democratic National Convention in Chicago, who they wanted on the ticket as vice president, 65 percent selected Henry Wallace. Jimmy Byrnes of South Carolina, who would later exert so much influence over Truman's Cold War thinking and atomic bomb decision, received 3 percent of the vote, with Wallace even trouncing him by a six-to-one margin in the South. Truman came in eighth out of eight candidates, with the support of 2 percent of those polled. But Roosevelt, tired, ailing, and dependent on the bosses for reelection, was not willing or able to fight for Wallace as he had in 1940. He simply announced that were he a delegate, he would vote for Wallace.

Party leaders made sure they had an iron grip on the convention. Yet the rank-and-file Democrats would not go quietly, staging a rebellion on the convention floor. The groundswell of support for Wallace among the delegates and attendees was so great that despite the bosses' stranglehold over the proceedings and strong-arm tactics, Wallace's supporters almost carried the day as an uproarious demonstration for Wallace broke out on the convention floor. In the midst of the demonstration, Florida Senator Claude Pepper realized that if he got Wallace's name into nomination that night, Wallace would sweep the convention. Pepper fought his way through the crowd to get within five feet of the microphone when the nearly hysterical Mayor Kelly, purporting that there was a fire hazard, got the chairman, Senator Samuel Jackson, to adjourn the proceedings. Had Pepper made it five more feet and nominated Wallace before the bosses forced adjournment against the will of the delegates, Wallace would have become president in 1945 and the course of history would have been dramatically altered. In fact, had that happened, there might have been no atomic bombings, no nuclear arms race, and no Cold War. Wallace was far ahead in the initial balloting. But the bosses further restricted admission and made the requisite backroom deals. Truman finally prevailed on the third ballot. Ambassadorships, postmaster jobs, and other positions were offered. Cash payoffs were made. Bosses called every state chairman, telling them that the fix was in and Roosevelt wanted the Missouri senator as his running mate. On Roosevelt's urging, Wallace agreed to remain in the cabinet as secretary of commerce.

Jackson apologized to Pepper the next day. "I knew if you made the motion," he explained, "the convention would nominate Henry Wallace. I had strict instructions from Hannegan not to let the convention nominate the vice president last night. So I had to adjourn the convention in your face. I hope you understand." "What I understood," Pepper wrote in his autobiography, "was that, for better or worse, history was turned topsy-turvy that night in Chicago."[25]

Meanwhile, the bomb project was progressing rapidly. Scientists, still worried that they might trail the Germans, worked feverishly on two types of atom bombs—one using uranium, the other plutonium. It was not until late 1944 that the Allies discovered that Germany had abandoned its bomb research in 1942. Although the original rationale for the bomb project—as a deterrent to a German bomb—no longer applied, only one scientist, Polish-born Joseph Rotblat, left the Manhattan Project at that point. The rest, fascinated by the research and believing they could speed the end of the war, pushed even harder to finish what they had started.

If Wallace's ouster from the ticket represented the first major setback to hopes for a peaceful postwar world, fate would soon deliver a second devastating blow. On April 12, 1945, with German surrender imminent, the United States' beloved wartime leader—President Franklin Delano Roosevelt—passed away after more than twelve years in office. The longest-serving president in U.S. history, he had seen the country through its hardest times: the Great Depression and World War II. The nation mourned and wondered about Roosevelt's successor.

Events unfolded at a dizzying pace over the next four months, forcing the new president to make some of the most momentous decisions in the nation's history. After an emergency cabinet meeting on April 12, Secretary of War Henry Stimson finally let Truman in on the bomb secret. Truman received a fuller briefing

Polish-born physicist Joseph Rotblat was the only scientist to leave the Manhattan Project when it was discovered in late 1944 that Germany had abandoned atomic bomb research in 1942. Although the original rationale for the bomb—as a deterrent against a German bomb—no longer applied, other scientists, fascinated by the research and believing they could speed the end of the war, pushed even harder to finish what they had started.

the following day from Byrnes, his old Senate mentor, whom Secretary of the Navy James Forrestal had flown up from South Carolina in his private plane. A former Supreme Court Justice, Byrnes had expected the vice presidential nomination in 1944, but party leaders considered his staunch segregationist views too great a liability. At that meeting, Byrnes told Truman that the United States was building an explosive "great enough to destroy the whole world."[26]

Truman received a fuller briefing on the atom bomb on April 25 from Stimson and Groves. They explained that they expected, within four months, to have "completed the most terrible weapon ever known in human history, one bomb of which could destroy a whole city." Soon other nations would develop their own bombs. "The world in its present state of moral advancement compared with its technical development would be eventually at the mercy of such a weapon. In other words, modern civilization might be completely destroyed."[27] They warned that the fate of humanity would depend upon if and how such bombs were used and what was subsequently done to control them. In an account of the meeting published posthumously by his daughter, Truman wrote, "Stimson said gravely that he didn't know whether we could or should use the bomb, because he was afraid that it was so powerful that it could end up destroying the whole world. I felt the same fear."[28]

Caught between the advancing Soviet troops, who had entered Berlin from the east, and the Allied forces approaching from the west, Germany surrendered on May 7. That meant that the Soviet Union, as agreed at Yalta, would enter the Pacific war around August 7, almost three months before the November 1 start date for the invasion of Japan.

Japanese soldiers fought fiercely and valiantly. Few ever surrendered. They believed that death on the battlefield would bring the highest honor: eternal repose at Yasakuni Shrine. At Tarawa, of 2,500 Japanese defenders, only 8 were taken alive. In just five weeks of combat at Iwo Jima, 6,281 U.S. sailors and marines were killed and almost 19,000 wounded. At Okinawa, the biggest battle of the Pacific War, 13,000 Americans were killed or missing and 36,000 wounded. As many as 70,000 Japanese soldiers and more than 100,000 Okinawan civilians died, many of them taking their own lives.[29] Americans were also shocked to watch wave after wave of kamikaze pilots suicidally crash their planes in a last-ditch effort to sink or damage U.S. ships.

As prospects worsened in 1945, some Japanese leaders began calling loudly for "100 million deaths with honor," preferring that the nation fight to the death rather than surrender. But U.S. top leaders, including Marshall and Stimson, dismissed such rantings, remaining convinced that when defeated, Japan would surrender. The "Proposed Program for Japan" that Stimson presented to Truman in early July stated that despite Japan's capacity for "fanatical resistance to repel an invasion," he believed that "Japan is susceptible to reason in such a crisis to a much greater extent than is indicated by our current press and other current comment. Japan is not a nation composed wholly of mad fanatics of an entirely different mentality from ours."[30]

The debate over just how costly an invasion would have been has raged for decades. The Joint Staff Planners prepared a paper for the Joint Chiefs' June 18 meeting with the president, estimating 193,500 dead and wounded in taking Japan. Some estimates were higher, some lower. Truman initially said that thousands would have died but then steadily raised the number. He later claimed that Marshall had told him that a half-million men could be lost in an invasion. But the basis for this assertion has never been found. Marshall's own estimates were much lower as were those of General MacArthur, who was in charge of planning for the invasion.

But as the war dragged on month after bloody month, the prospects for an invasion dimmed. By the end of 1944, the Japanese navy was decimated, having lost 7 of 12 battleships, 19 of 25 aircraft carriers, 103 of 160 submarines, 31 of 47 cruisers, and 118 of 158 destroyers. The air force was also badly weakened. With the rail system in tatters, food supplies shrank and public morale plummeted. Some Japanese leaders feared a popular uprising. Prince Fumimaro Konoe, who had served three times as prime minister between 1937 and 1941, sent a memo to Emperor Hirohito in February 1945: "I regret to say that Japan's defeat is inevitable." He warned, "What we must worry about is a Communist revolution that might accompany defeat."[31] Since at least the previous August, in the aftermath of the U.S. victory at Saipan, Japan had quietly commenced studies on how to end the war. Japanese desperation was growing by the day, as was apparent to publishing magnate Henry Luce, who visited the Pacific for a firsthand look in spring 1945. He wrote, "A few months before Hiroshima, I was with Admiral Halsey's Navy as it assaulted the coast of Japan. Two things seemed clear to me—as they did to many of the top fighting men I talked to: first, that Japan was beaten; second, that the Japanese knew it and were every day showing signs of increasing willingness to quit."[32] Even Richard Frank, whose book *Downfall* presents the most authoritative defense of the atomic bombings, observed, "It is reasonable to assume that even without atomic bombs, the destruction of the rail-transportation system, coupled to the cumulative effects of the blockade-and-bombardment strategy, would have posed a severe threat to internal order and subsequently thus impelled the Emperor to seek to end the war."[33]

Why, then, if Japan was not a nation of suicidal fanatics and its prospects for military victory had vanished, did its leaders not surrender and ease the suffering of their soldiers and citizens? The answer to that lies, in large measure, in the U.S. surrender terms, though the emperor and his advisors must bear their share of the blame.

At Casablanca in January 1943, President Roosevelt called for the "unconditional surrender" of Germany, Italy, and Japan.[34] He later claimed to have done so spontaneously, catching even Churchill by surprise. In a letter to his biographer Robert Sherwood, Churchill supported that interpretation: "I heard the words 'unconditional surrender' for the first time from the President's lips at the [news] conference."[35] Though "unconditional" had not been included in the official communiqué of the press conference, it had clearly been discussed beforehand and agreed upon by Roosevelt and Churchill. The ramifications of adhering to that demand would be enormous.

The Japanese assumed that "unconditional surrender" meant the destruction of the *kokutai* (imperial system) and the likelihood that the emperor would be tried as a war criminal and executed. For most Japanese, such an outcome was too terrible to contemplate. They had been worshipping the emperor almost as a god since Jimmu in 660 B.C. A study by MacArthur's Southwest Pacific Command explained, "to dethrone, or hang, the Emperor would cause a tremendous and violent reaction from all Japanese. Hanging of the Emperor to them would be comparable to the crucifixion of Christ to us. All would fight to die like ants."[36] Realizing that, many urged Truman to soften the surrender terms. Acting Secretary of State Joseph Grew, who had previously served as ambassador to Japan and knew the Japanese better than any other top administration official, wrote in April 1945, "Surrender by Japan would be highly unlikely regardless of military defeat, in the absence of a public undertaking by the President that unconditional surrender would not mean the elimination of the present dynasty if the Japanese people desire its retention."[37] Grew joined with Stimson, Forrestal, and

Assistant Secretary of War John McCloy in urging Truman to change the surrender terms. U.S. military leaders also felt strongly about the wisdom of giving the Japanese assurances about the emperor. Admiral Leahy told a June meeting of the Joint Chiefs of Staff that he feared that "our insistence on unconditional surrender would result only in making the Japanese desperate and thereby increase our casualty lists." [38]

U.S. officials understood how critical the question of surrender terms was to the Japanese because they had broken Japanese codes even before the United States entered the war and were intercepting Japanese communications that repeatedly emphasized the surrender issue. In May, Japan's Supreme War Council met in Tokyo. The council, also known as the Big Six, consisted of Prime Minister Kantaro Suzuki, Foreign Minister Shigenori Togo, Army Minister Korechika Anami, Army Chief of Staff Yoshijiro Umezu, Navy Minister Mitsumasa Yonai, and Navy Chief of Staff Soemu Toyoda. They decided to solicit the help of the Soviet Union to get better surrender terms from the United States, offering the USSR territorial concessions in return. Japan's initial contacts were enough to convince Soviet officials that the Japanese were looking for a way out of the war. That news did not please the Soviet leaders, who wanted to secure the concessions the Allies had promised in return for the Soviets entering the Pacific War, which was still a couple months off. On June 18, the emperor informed the Supreme War Council that he favored quick restoration of the peace. The council concurred, agreeing to ascertain the Soviet Union's willingness to broker a surrender that would safeguard the emperor and preserve the imperial system.

A series of cables in July from Foreign Minister Togo in Tokyo to Ambassador Naotake Sato in Moscow made that crystal clear. On July 12, Togo cabled Sato, "It is His Majesty's heart's desire to see the swift termination of the war. . . . [However,] as long as America and England insist on unconditional surrender, our country has no alternative but to see it through in an all-out effort for the sake of survival and the honor of the homeland." [39] The following day, Togo cabled, "His Majesty the Emperor, mindful of the fact that the present war daily brings greater evil and sacrifice upon the peoples of all the belligerent powers, desires from his heart that it may be quickly terminated." [40]

Despite the mounting evidence that changing surrender terms could bring the war to a swift end, Truman listened instead to Byrnes, who insisted that the American public would not tolerate compromising surrender terms and warned the president that he would be crucified politically if he tried. [41]

Though dropping two atomic bombs on an already defeated nation in order to avoid domestic political repercussions would seem morally reprehensible under any circumstances, there was little reason to think that Truman would have had to pay a price for letting the emperor remain on the throne. In fact,

Republican leaders had provided Truman all the political cover he needed. On July 2, 1945, Senate Minority Leader Wallace White, a Republican from Maine, addressed his Senate colleagues, urging President Truman to clarify what he meant by "unconditional surrender" in the hope of expediting Japan's surrender. If Japan ignored or rejected the president's offer to surrender on more favorable terms, he reasoned, "it will not have increased our losses or otherwise have prejudiced our cause. Much might be gained by such a statement. Nothing could be lost." White's Republican colleague from Indiana, Homer Capehart, held a press conference later that day to support White's request. Capehart informed the press that the White House had received an offer by Japan to surrender solely on the grounds that Emperor Hirohito not be deposed. "It isn't a matter of whether you hate the Japs or not. I certainly hate them. But what's to be gained by continuing a war when it can be settled now on the same terms as two years from now?"[42] In a June editorial, the *Washington Post* condemned "unconditional surrender" as a "fatal phrase" that was conjuring up such fears among the Japanese people that it was proving an impediment to ending the fighting.[43]

Changing the surrender terms was not the only way to expedite Japanese surrender without using atomic bombs. What the Japanese dreaded above all else was the Soviet Union's entry into the war. In early April 1945, the Soviet Union informed Japan that it was not renewing the 1941 Neutrality Pact, raising Japanese fears that the Soviets would declare war. All parties understood what that would mean. On April 11, the Joint Intelligence Staff of the Joint Chiefs predicted, "If at any time the USSR should enter the war, all Japanese will realize that absolute defeat is inevitable."[44] In May, Japan's Supreme War Council drew a similar conclusion: "At the present moment, when Japan is waging a life-or-death struggle against the U.S. and Britain, Soviet entry into the war will deal a death blow to the Empire."[45] On July 6, the Combined Intelligence Committee issued a top secret report on the "Estimate of the Enemy Situation" for the Combined Chiefs of Staff, who would be meeting at Potsdam. The section assessing the "Possibility of Surrender" described the effect Soviet entry would have on the already hopeless Japanese:

> The Japanese ruling groups are aware of the desperate military situation and are increasingly desirous of a compromise peace, but still find unconditional surrender unacceptable. The basic policy of the present government is to fight as long and as desperately as possible in the hope of avoiding complete defeat and of acquiring a better bargaining position in a negotiated peace.... We believe that a considerable portion of the Japanese population now consider absolute military defeat to be probable. The increasing effects of sea blockade and cumulative devastation wrought by strategic bombing, which has already rendered millions homeless and has destroyed from 25% to

50% of the built-up areas of Japan's most important cities, should make this realization increasingly general. An entry of the Soviet Union into the war would finally convince the Japanese of the inevitability of complete defeat. Although individual Japanese willingly sacrifice themselves in the service of the nation, we doubt that the nation as a whole is predisposed toward national suicide.... The Japanese believe, however, that unconditional surrender would be the equivalent of national extinction.[46]

The Japanese *ketsu-go* strategy entailed preparing for an Allied invasion, with the hope of inflicting such heavy casualties that the war-weary Allies would offer more lenient surrender terms. Japanese leaders had correctly identified Kyushu as the intended landing site and beefed up their forces. Civilians armed with sharpened bamboo spears were instructed to fight to the death along with the soldiers.

Clearly, U.S. leaders knew that retention of the emperor was the main obstacle to Japanese surrender and that the dreaded Soviet entry was drawing closer. Why, under those circumstances, would the United States use two atomic bombs against an almost helpless population? To make sense of that, one has to understand the moral climate within which that decision was made.

Americans felt a profound hatred toward the Japanese. Pulitzer Prize–winning historian Allan Nevins wrote after the war, "Probably in all our history, no foe has been so detested as were the Japanese."[47] Whereas U.S. wartime propaganda took pains to differentiate between evil Nazi leaders and "good Germans," no such distinction was made among the Japanese. As *Newsweek* reported in January 1945, "Never before has the nation fought a war in which our troops so hate the enemy and want to kill him."[48]

Historian John Dower has shown that Americans thought of the Japanese as vermin, cockroaches, rattlesnakes, and rats. Simian imagery abounded. Admiral William "Bull" Halsey, commander of the South Pacific Force, was notorious in this regard, urging his men forward to kill the "yellow monkeys" and "get some more monkey meat." People questioned whether the Japanese were really human. *Time* wrote, "The ordinary, unreasoning Jap is ignorant. Perhaps he is human. Nothing ... indicates it." The British Embassy in Washington reported back to London that the Americans viewed the Japanese as a "nameless mass of vermin," and the ambassador described Americans' "universal 'exterminationist' anti-Japanese feeling." When popular war correspondent Ernie Pyle was transferred from Europe to the Pacific in February 1945, he observed, "In Europe we felt that our enemies, horrible and deadly as they were, were still people. But out here I soon gathered that the Japanese were looked upon as something subhuman and repulsive; the way some people feel about cockroaches or mice."[49]

Some of this sentiment can certainly be attributed to racism. But other

*Americans felt a profound hatred toward the Japanese. As Newsweek
reported in January 1945, "Never before has the nation fought a
war in which our troops so hate the enemy and want to kill him."
Whereas U.S. wartime propaganda took pains to differentiate
between evil Nazi leaders and "good Germans," no such distinction
was made among the Japanese, who were portrayed as vermin,
cockroaches, rattlesnakes, and rats. Simian imagery abounded.*

powerful forces were also at work in producing this hatred of the Japanese. Even
before the United States entered the war, Americans had heard about Japanese
bombing, rape, and brutality toward the Chinese, especially in Nanjing. Americans' rancor toward Japan soared with the "sneak attack" at Pearl Harbor. Then,
in early 1944, the government released information about the sadistic treatment
of U.S. and Filipino prisoners during the Bataan death march two years earlier.
Soon stories about unspeakable Japanese cruelty—torture, crucifixion, castration, dismemberment, beheading, burning and burying alive, vivisection, nailing

prisoners to trees and using them for bayonet practice—flooded the media.
Hence, what had been anger toward the Japanese earlier in the war turned to
abject hatred just as U.S. military action was heating up in the Pacific.[50]

But President Truman's bigotry toward Asians long antedated reports of Japanese savagery. As a young man courting his future wife, he wrote, "I think one man
is as good as another so long as he's honest and decent and not a nigger or a Chinaman. Uncle Will says that the Lord made a white man of dust, a nigger from mud,
then threw up what was left and it came down a Chinaman. He does hate Chinese
and Japs. So do I. It is race prejudice I guess."[51] Truman regularly referred to Jews as
kikes, to Mexicans as greasers, and to other groups with equally derogatory names.
His biographer Merle Miller reported, "Privately Mr. Truman always said 'nigger';
at least he always did when I talked to him."[52]

Truman's racism notwithstanding, it is right to criticize Japan's unconscionable behavior during the war. However, it is also worth noting that Americans
often behaved wretchedly as well. U.S. Pacific war correspondent Edgar Jones
detailed U.S. atrocities in a February 1946 article in *The Atlantic Monthly:* "What
kind of war do civilians suppose we fought, anyway? We shot prisoners in cold
blood, wiped out hospitals, strafed lifeboats, killed or mistreated enemy civilians, finished off the enemy wounded, tossed the dying into a hole with the dead,
and in the Pacific boiled the flesh off enemy skulls to make table ornaments for
sweethearts, or carved their bones into letter openers."[53]

Racism also reared its ugly head in the treatment of people of Japanese descent
living in the United States when the war broke out. Japanese Americans had faced
discrimination in voting, jobs, and education for decades. The Immigration Act of
1924 denied Japanese who had settled in the United States after 1907 the right to
become naturalized U.S. citizens and prohibited further immigration from Japan.
Even before Pearl Harbor, some on the West Coast began conjuring up fanciful scenarios of Japanese-American sabotage in the event of war. One journalist
wrote, "When the Pacific zero hour strikes, Japanese Americans will get busy at
once. Their fishing boats will sow mines across the entrances of our ports. Mysterious blasts will destroy navy shipyards and flying fields and part of our fleet. . . .
Japanese farmers, having a virtual monopoly of vegetable production in California, will send their peas and potatoes and squash full of arsenic to the markets."
Following Pearl Harbor, rumors and ugliness proliferated. One California barber-
shop offered "free shaves for Japs," but added, "not responsible for accidents." A
funeral parlor announced, "I'd rather do business with a jap than an American."[54]

California Attorney General Earl Warren led the charge to remove Japanese
Americans from the western states. Warren warned that the Japanese in southern
California might be "the Achilles heel of the entire civil defense effort."[55] Lieu-
tenant Colonel John L. DeWitt, commander of the Fourth Army and head of the

Western Defense Command, who had worked on the 1921 War Plans Division strategy to intern all "enemy aliens" on the islands of Hawaii, seconded Warren's efforts. On December 9, DeWitt announced that Japanese warplanes had flown over San Francisco the previous night and the city was in imminent danger of Japanese attack. DeWitt told a Civil Defense Council meeting, "Death and destruction are likely to come to this city any moment." Rear Admiral John Greenslade informed the audience that they had been "saved from a terrible catastrophe" by "the grace of God." "Why bombs were not dropped," DeWitt admitted, "I do not know." One reason might have been that the Japanese flyover never occurred, which might also explain why U.S. forces never shot down any of the planes and why the army's and navy's searches for the Japanese aircraft carriers came up empty. But DeWitt was furious with San Franciscans who did not take the blackout orders seriously enough, denouncing them as "inane, idiotic and foolish," and threatened, "If I can't knock these facts into your heads with words, I will have to turn you over to the police to let them knock them into you with clubs." [56]

DeWitt's mistrust of San Franciscans was benign. His mistrust of Japanese was pathological. DeWitt had initially characterized talk of large-scale evacuations as "damned nonsense." But public pressure continued to mount, reinforced by the late-January release of a government report on the bombing of Pearl Harbor that was prepared by Supreme Court Justice Owen Roberts. Espionage, the report alleged, had facilitated the attack. While most of the information was conveyed by Japanese consular agents, other Hawaiians of Japanese descent also played a role. The report reinforced public doubts about the loyalty of Japanese Americans. The resulting outcry apparently changed DeWitt into a passionate advocate of relocation. DeWitt argued that the fact that the Japanese, citizens and noncitizens alike, had not engaged in sabotage proved that they were plotting a future assault. Others, including Stimson and McCloy, echoed his sentiments, pressuring Roosevelt to take action before it was too late. [57]

Defectors from the "Japs-can't-be-trusted" line included one very unlikely individual: FBI Director J. Edgar Hoover. Hoover told Attorney General Francis Biddle that mass evacuations weren't necessary. All known security risks had already been rounded up. Biddle informed Roosevelt that "there were no reasons for mass evacuations." [58]

Roosevelt ignored their advice. Despite the fact that there was no evidence of Japanese-American sabotage, on February 19, 1942, Roosevelt signed Executive Order 9066, which laid the groundwork for the evacuation and incarceration of Japanese and Japanese Americans from California, Oregon, and Washington, two-thirds of whom were U.S. citizens by birth. Although the executive order made no explicit mention of race or ethnicity, its intended target population was unmistakable.

Despite the fact that there was no evidence of Japanese-American sabotage, on February 19, 1942, Roosevelt signed Executive Order 9066, which laid the groundwork for the evacuation and incarceration of Japanese and Japanese Americans from California, Oregon, and Washington, two-thirds of whom were U.S. citizens by birth. Although the executive order made no explicit mention of race or ethnicity, its intended target population was unmistakable.

U.S. authorities abandoned the sweeping evacuation plans made for Hawaii's large Japanese population when wealthy white sugarcane and pineapple plantation owners complained that they would lose their labor force. However, the government did impose martial law, suspend the writ of habeas corpus, and locked up some two thousand *kibei,* people of Japanese descent who had visited Japan for education and acculturation.

On the mainland, especially in California, where the Japanese represented only slightly above 2 percent of the population, the situation was very different. Executive Order 9066 forced some 120,000 to evacuate their homes and settle outside the prohibited defense zones. But their entry was blocked by surrounding states. The governor of Idaho, Chase Clark, spewed, "The Japs live like rats, breed like rats and act like rats. We don't want them." The governor of Wyoming warned that if the Japanese were moved to his state, "There would be Japs hanging from every pine tree." The attorney general of Idaho recommended that "all Japanese . . . be put in concentration camps." "We want to keep this a white man's country." [59]

By February 25, 1942, the FBI had incarcerated all adult males of Japanese ancestry on Terminal Island, California. The U.S. Navy gave all other residents of Japanese ancestry forty-eight hours to clear out. Between March and October 1942, the Wartime Civil Control Administration (WCCA) opened temporary camps, known as assembly centers, to hold Japanese inmates, who were registered and given numbers. In Santa Anita and Tanforan, California, families were housed in horse stables, a single stall accommodating five or six people. They were later moved to more permanent relocation centers, referred to at the time as "concentration camps." Conditions in the camps were deplorable; they often lacked running water, bathroom facilities, decent schools, insulated cabins, and proper roofs. The camps did, however, have adequate barbed-wire fencing, machine-gun installations, and guard towers. Appalled by the treatment of the prisoners, Milton Eisenhower resigned as director of the War Relocation Authority (WRA).[60]

Some westerners were motivated by greed in supporting the evacuations. Because evacuees were allowed to take away only what they could carry, their former neighbors eagerly bought their property at a fraction of its real value or seized what was left behind, including abandoned crops. A leader of the Grower-Shipper Vegetable Association of Central California admitted, "We're charged with wanting to get rid of the Japs for selfish reasons. We might as well be honest. We do. It's a question of whether the white man lives on the Pacific Coast or the brown man." The Japanese lost an estimated $400 million in personal property—worth perhaps $5.4 billion today.[61]

Starting in March 1942, the War Relocation Authority moved prisoners to ten hastily constructed relocation centers in Arizona, Arkansas, California, Colorado, Idaho, Utah, and Wyoming. The Poston and Gila River Relocation Centers in Arizona soon housed populations of 17,814 and 13,348, respectively, making them the third and fourth largest cities in the state virtually overnight. Heart Mountain became the third largest city in Wyoming.[62]

Inside the camps, Japanese toiled under scorching desert sun in Arizona and California, swamplike conditions in Arkansas, and bitter cold in Wyoming, Idaho, and Utah, and were paid a paltry $12 per month for unskilled labor and $19 for skilled. Japanese doctors earned $228 per year, while a white senior medical officer earned $4,600. White nurses who earned $80 per month at Yellowstone County Hospital received $150 at Heart Mountain, eight to ten times as much as their Japanese counterparts.[63] Federal authorities sent photographers Ansel Adams and Dorothea Lange to capture images of daily camp life, instructing them to take no photos showing barbed wire, watchtowers, or armed soldiers. Still Adams, Lange, and a Japanese inmate, Toyo Miyatake, captured a few of the banned images.[64]

In February 1943, the U.S. government pulled a shameless about-face. Needing more manpower to fight the war, Roosevelt called upon American-born Nisei to join the segregated 442nd Regimental Combat Team, in conjunction with the 100th Battalion Hawaii already stationed in Camp Shelby, Mississippi. The "One PukaPuka," as the Hawaiian members called their unit, had volunteered early in the war and had had to struggle long and hard to be recognized as worthy to serve. The 442nd Regiment became one of the most decorated units in U.S. military history, fighting bravely in Italy and France and suffering 1,072 casualties, including 216 deaths in October 1944.[65]

That Japanese Americans were capable of such sacrifice for their country

Japanese Americans arrive at the Santa Anita Assembly Center from San Pedro, California, where they were housed in horse stables before being moved to more permanent relocation centers.

Inside relocation centers, Japanese toiled under scorching desert sun in Arizona and California, swamplike conditions in Arkansas, and bitter cold in Wyoming, Idaho, and Utah, and were paid minuscule wages for their efforts.

was apparently beyond the comprehension of the head of the Western Defense Command. In April 1943, DeWitt told the House Naval Affairs Subcommittee that he wasn't worried about Germans or Italians, "but the Japs we will be worried about all the time until they are wiped off the face of the map." "A Jap's a Jap," he informed them, whether a U.S. citizen or not. DeWitt's racist remarks rankled the *Washington Post,* which shot back, "The general should be told that American democracy and the Constitution of the United States are too vital to be ignored and flouted by any military zealot. . . . Whatever excuse there once was for evacuating and holding them indiscriminately no longer exists." [66]

Many Americans agreed. Some drew parallels with Nazi policies, although the differences, admittedly, were much greater than the similarities. In June 1942, *Christian Century* wrote, "The whole policy of resort to concentration camps is headed . . . toward the destruction of constitutional rights . . . and toward the establishment of racial discrimination as a principle of American government. It is moving in the same direction Germany moved." Eugene V. (Victor Debs) Rostow published a scathing piece in the *Yale Law Journal* in 1945, arguing, "We believe that the German people bear a common political responsibility for outrages secretly committed by the Gestapo and the SS. What are we to think of our own part in a program which violates every democratic social value, yet has been approved by the Congress, the President and the Supreme Court?" [67]

In June 1943, the Supreme Court ruled unanimously in the government's favor in the first two cases to come before it. Although the ruling in *Hirabayashi v. United States* did not address the fundamental issues of evacuation and incarceration, Justice Frank Murphy's concurring opinion came very close to doing so:

> To say that any group cannot be assimilated is to admit that the great
> American experiment has failed. . . . Today is the first time, so far as I am
> aware, that we have sustained a substantial restriction of the personal
> liberty of citizens of the United States based upon the accident of race
> or ancestry. . . . In this sense, it bears a melancholy resemblance to the
> treatment accorded to members of the Jewish race in Germany and in
> other parts of Europe.[68]

On January 2, 1945, the WRA "ended" forced incarceration but provided little assistance as prisoners tried to rebuild their shattered lives. Some decided to migrate as far away from the West Coast as possible. According to the National Park Service, the Japanese received only "$25 per person, a train ticket, and meals on route for those with less than $500 in cash." [69]

It was not until the passage of the Immigration and Naturalization Act of 1952 that many of the older Japanese, the *Issei,* were deemed "fit to be citizens."

Moreover, it took over forty years for a national apology and monetary redress of $1.5 billion for survivors of the incarceration centers.[70]

The United States' moral threshold—particularly its indifference to inflicting civilian casualties on a massive scale—had also been dramatically lowered by years of bombing civilian populations, particularly in the air war against Japan. Urban area bombing had begun during the First World War. The Germans, British, French, Italians, and Austrians had all bombed one another's cities, and some of this continued in brutal fashion during the interwar period. To its credit, the United States strongly condemned the Japanese bombing of Chinese cities in 1937. When war began in Europe in 1939, Roosevelt implored the combatants to refrain from the "inhuman barbarism" involved in bombing defenseless civilians.[71]

Undeterred, Germany began bombing British cities. The British responded with thousand-plane bombing raids on urban targets in Germany. By the mid-1940s, great cities such as Barcelona, Madrid, Shanghai, Beijing, Nanjing, Warsaw, London, Rotterdam, Moscow, Stalingrad, Leningrad, Cologne, Hamburg, Berlin, and many others had been severely bombed.

The United States, by contrast, concentrated almost entirely on precision bombing of key industries and transportation networks until late in the European war. In August 1942, Captain Paul Tibbets, who would later pilot the B-29 that dropped the atomic bomb on Hiroshima, expressed apprehension at the possibility of causing civilian casualties as he prepared to lead the first daytime raid by U.S. bombers against German targets in occupied France. He told a reporter that he felt "sick with thoughts of the civilians who might suffer from the bombs dropped by this machine." Watching the bombs fall, he thought, "My God, women and children are getting killed!"[72] But as the war continued, Americans' scruples began to soften. The October 1943 area-bombing raid on Münster was an important turning point. The most tragic exception to the earlier standards was U.S. participation in the Allied bombing of Dresden in February 1945.

The United States adopted a far more ruthless bombing policy in Japan. When Major General Haywood Hansell, head of the 21st Bomber Command, resisted orders to use incendiaries against large urban areas, Air Force General Henry "Hap" Arnold replaced him with General Curtis LeMay. Nicknamed "Iron Ass" by his men because he was so relentless and demanding, LeMay had made his reputation in the air war in Europe. In Japan, he revolutionized bombing tactics and took what was already being referred to as "terror bombing" to an entirely different level.

On the night of March 9–10, 1945, LeMay sent 334 planes to attack Tokyo with incendiary bombs consisting of napalm, thermite, white phosphorus, and other inflammable materials. The bombs destroyed sixteen square miles, killing perhaps 100,000 people and injuring even more. The scalding inferno caused

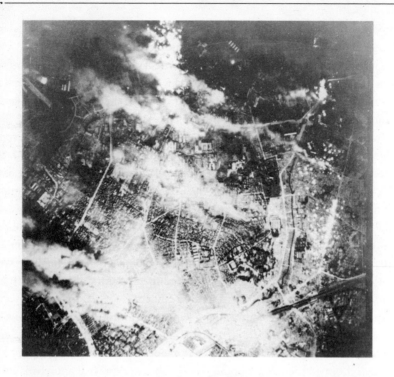

ABOVE AND OPPOSITE: *On the night of March 9–10, 1945, General Curtis LeMay sent 334 planes to attack Tokyo with incendiary bombs consisting of napalm, thermite, white phosphorus, and other inflammable materials. The bombs destroyed sixteen square miles, killing over eighty thousand and injuring close to a million. The scalding inferno caused canals to boil, metal to melt, and people to burst spontaneously into flames. The victims, LeMay reported, were "scorched and boiled and baked to death."*

canals to boil, metal to melt, and people to burst into flames spontaneously. The victims, LeMay reported, were "scorched and boiled and baked to death." By May, 75 percent of bombs dropped were incendiaries designed to burn down Japan's "paper cities." According to Japanese scholar Yuki Tanaka, the United States firebombed over a hundred Japanese cities.[73] Destruction reached 99.5 percent in the city of Toyama, driving Secretary of War Henry Stimson to tell Truman that he "did not want to have the US get the reputation of outdoing Hitler in atrocities," though Stimson did almost nothing to halt the slaughter. He had managed to delude himself into believing Arnold's promise that he would limit "damage to civilians."[74] Future Defense Secretary Robert S. McNamara, who was on LeMay's staff in 1945, agreed with his boss's comment that if the United States lost the war, they'd all be tried as war criminals and deserved to be convicted.[75]

Hatred toward the Japanese ran so deep that almost no one objected to the

mass slaughter of civilians. Oppenheimer recalled Stimson's disappointment over Americans' indifference: "I remember Mr. Stimson saying to me that he thought it appalling that there should be no protest over the air raids which we were conducting against Japan, which in the case of Tokyo led to such extraordinarily heavy loss of life. He didn't say that the air strikes shouldn't be carried on, but he did think there was something wrong with a country where no one questioned that."[76] Brigadier General Bonner Fellers called it "one of the most ruthless and barbaric killings of non-combatants in all history."[77] Arnold felt that "90% of Americans would have killed every Japanese."[78]

General Groves's Target Committee decided that the atomic bombs would be dropped on military facilities surrounded by workers' homes in previously unbombed cities. The committee decided to make the initial use so spectacular that people everywhere would appreciate the weapons' significance. When members of Stimson's Interim Committee, which examined a number of issues surrounding the use of the atomic bombs, raised alternatives, including a demonstration, Byrnes, as Truman's personal representative on the committee, overrode them.

At its May 31 meeting, the Interim Committee also addressed the future of nuclear weapons. Scientists understood that the bombs under production were the most rudimentary, primitive prototypes of what was to follow. The prospect terrified them. Oppenheimer informed the nation's top military and civilian officials that within three years the United States could have weapons of between 10 and 100 megatons—potentially almost seven thousand times as powerful as the bomb that would soon be dropped on Hiroshima.[79]

In late May, Szilard, Nobel Prize–winning chemist Harold Urey, and astronomer Walter Bartky attempted to see Truman to caution against using the bomb. They were rerouted to Spartanburg, South Carolina, to speak with Byrnes, whose response appalled Szilard: "Mr. Byrnes did not argue that it was necessary to use the bomb against the cities of Japan in order to win the war. He knew at that time, as the rest of the government knew, that Japan was essentially defeated. . . . At that time Mr. Byrnes was much concerned about the spreading of Russian influence in Europe; [insisting] that our possessing and demonstrating the bomb would make Russia more manageable in Europe."[80] Groves also admitted that in his mind the Soviet Union had always been the enemy: "There was never from about two weeks from the time I took charge of this Project any illusion on my part that Russia was our enemy, and the Project was conducted on that basis."[81] Groves shocked Joseph Rotblat when he said over dinner in March 1944, "You realize of course that the main purpose of this project is to subdue the Russians."[82] Byrnes's and Groves's statements shed crucial light on Byrnes's April 13 remark to Truman that the atomic bomb "might well put us in a position to dictate our own terms at the end of the war."[83]

While Los Alamos scientists worked feverishly to complete the bomb, others began to have doubts about the wisdom of what they had done. In June, Chicago Met Lab scientists set up a series of committees to explore various aspects of atomic energy. The Committee on Social and Political Implications, chaired by the Nobel Laureate James Franck, issued a report, greatly influenced by Leo Szilard, questioning the wisdom of using atomic bombs in the current war. It warned that a surprise attack on Japan would not only destroy the United States' moral position, it could instigate a nuclear arms race with the Soviet Union, creating the prospect of "total mutual destruction."[84] The report also noted that because there was no secret to the scientific principles behind the bomb, the Soviet Union would soon catch up.

Szilard understood the dangers better than anyone else. He desperately attempted to prevent the bombs' use. He circulated the Franck Committee report to scientists at other laboratories. After security officers had it classified and banned its circulation, Szilard drew up a petition warning the president:

> The atomic bombs at our disposal represent only the first step in this direction, and there is almost no limit to the destructive power which will become available in the course of their future development. Thus a nation which sets the precedent of using these newly liberated forces of nature for the purposes of destruction may have to bear the responsibility of opening the door to an era of devastation on an unimaginable scale.[85]

One hundred fifty-five scientists at Chicago's Met Lab and the uranium plant in Oak Ridge signed the petition. Oppenheimer banned its circulation at Los Alamos and alerted Groves, who made sure it didn't reach Stimson and Truman until it was too late to stop the bomb's use. Groves's security agents had been conducting extensive surveillance of Szilard throughout the war. At one point, Groves went so far as to draft a letter to the attorney general labeling Szilard an "enemy alien" and requesting that he "be interned for the duration of the war." Fortunately, Compton persuaded him not to send it. Groves ordered his own poll among scientists and was chagrined to see that 83 percent favored demonstrating the bomb before using it against Japan.[86] He hushed up the results.

Others also tried to prevent the bombs' use but, sadly, had no more success than Szilard. On June 27, Undersecretary of the Navy Ralph Bard, the navy representative to the Interim Committee, wrote Stimson a memo, stating, "During recent weeks I have also had the feeling very definitely that the Japanese Government may be searching for some opportunity which they could use as a medium of surrender." He urged that the United States, "as a great humanitarian nation," warn Japan about the Soviet entry into the war and the development of the atomic bomb and clarify the surrender terms. Some historians believe that after leaving the government a few days later, Bard met with the president to press those points, but the record is ambiguous. It is clear, however, that when Truman met with the Joint Chiefs on June 18, Assistant Secretary of War John McCloy recommended that he tell the Japanese "that they would be permitted to retain the Emperor and a form of government of their own choosing" and "that we had another and terrifyingly destructive weapon which we would have to use if they did not surrender."[87]

Things came to a head when Allied leaders gathered in Potsdam, a suburb of bombed-out Berlin. The target date for the first atomic bombing was less than a month away. Truman arrived on July 15, nervously anticipating his first meeting with Churchill and Stalin. Reports poured in confirming the Japanese desire to quit if allowed to surrender conditionally. The evidence that top U.S. officials recognized the signals emanating from Tokyo is unassailable. Truman unambiguously characterized the intercepted July 18 cable that stated, "Uncon-ditional surrender is the only obstacle to peace" as "the telegram from the Jap emperor asking for peace."[88] Forrestal wrote about "evidence of a Japanese desire to get out of the war," Stimson about "Japanese maneuverings for peace," and Byrnes about "Japanese peace feelers."[89] In his 1966 book *The Secret Surrender,* OSS official and later CIA head Allen Dulles recalled, "I went to the Potsdam Conference and reported there to Secretary Stimson on what I had learned from Tokyo—they desired to surrender if they could retain the Emperor and the con-stitution as a basis for maintaining discipline and order in Japan after the devas-tating news of surrender became known to the Japanese people."[90] The Pacific Strategic Intelligence Summary for the week of the Potsdam meeting reported, "it may be said that Japan now, officially if not publicly, recognizes her defeat. Abandoning as unobtainable the long-cherished goal of victory, she has turned to the twin aims of (a) reconciling national pride with defeat, and (b) finding the best means of salvaging the wreckage of her ambitions."[91] As the head of the War Department Operations Division Policy Section, Colonel Charles "Tick" Bon-esteel, recalled, "the poor damn Japanese were putting feelers out by the ton."[92]

Truman's principal reason for going to Potsdam, he claimed, was to make sure the Soviets were coming into the war as promised. Knowing that their entry would deliver the final crushing blow, he rejoiced when Stalin reassured him, writing in his diary on July 17, "He'll be in the Jap War on August 15. Fini Japs when that comes about."[93] The next day, Truman wrote to Bess, "We'll end the war a year sooner now, and think of the kids who won't be killed!"[94]

Truman had one more card to play, but the timing had to be precise. Stimson understood that. He wrote in his diary on May 15 that the bomb was a crucial diplomatic tool but that it wouldn't be tested before Potsdam: "We think it will be shortly afterwards, but it seems a terrible thing to gamble with such big stakes in diplomacy without having your master card in your hand."[95]

Truman had pushed the start of the summit back two weeks and hoped the bomb would be tested before negotiations with Stalin began. Oppenheimer confessed, "we were under incredible pressure to get it done before the Potsdam meeting."[96] It turned out, from Truman's perspective, to be worth the wait.

On July 16, while Truman was touring Berlin and preparing for the next day's meeting with Stalin, scientists exploded the first atomic bomb in the des-ert outside Alamogordo, New Mexico. The Trinity test exceeded expectations. Given the enormous power of the 18.6-kiloton blast and the brightness of the sky, some scientists feared they had indeed set the atmosphere on fire. Oppen-heimer said that a phrase from the Bhagavad Gita flashed through his mind: "I am become death, destroyer of worlds." Deputy Director Kenneth Bainbridge put it more simply: "Now we're all sons-of-bitches."[97]

Groves cabled the preliminary results to Stimson, who rushed to brief Truman and Byrnes. They were elated. On July 21, Groves sent a much fuller and more dramatic report, which stated, "The test was successful beyond the most optimistic expectations of anyone." Groves estimated the energy released to be equivalent to 15 to 20 kilotons of TNT, an amount that so far exceeded anything previously achieved that it was almost inconceivable. Stimson read it to the president and secretary of state. Along with Groves's report came one by Brigadier General Thomas Farrell, who described a "strong, sustained awesome roar which warned of doomsday."[98] When Churchill read this report, he exclaimed, "this is the Second Coming in Wrath."[99]

Truman, Byrnes, and Groves believed they now had a way to speed Japanese surrender on U.S. terms without Soviet help and thereby deny the Soviet Union the promised territorial and economic concessions. Stimson observed, "The President was tremendously pepped up by [the report] and spoke to me of it again and again when I saw him. He said it gave him an entirely new feeling of confidence."[100] Truman, who had allowed Churchill and Stalin to dominate the early sessions, now rode roughshod over the proceedings. Winston Churchill described the scene at the next plenary session: "I couldn't understand it. When he got to the meeting after having read this report he was a changed man. He told the Russians just where they got on and off and generally bossed the whole meeting."[101] McCloy too noted the role the bomb played in bucking up Truman's confidence: "Throughout it all the 'big bomb' is playing its part—it has stiffened both the Prime Minister and the President. After getting Groves' report they went to the next meeting like little boys with a big red apple secreted on their persons."[102]

Though never able to stand up to his father or Boss Pendergast or the other bullies, Truman could now stand up to Stalin himself. If, as was said, the revolver made all men six feet tall, the successful atomic bomb test made the diminutive Truman a giant who towered over the world's most fearsome dictators. But Truman's public bravado masked a deeper understanding of the world he was about to usher in with the use of the atomic bomb. He wrote in his Potsdam diary, "We have discovered the most terrible bomb in the history of the world. It may be the fire destruction prophesied in the Euphrates Valley Era, after Noah and his fabulous Ark."[103] Unfortunately, Truman's apocalyptic forebodings did not impel him to seek alternatives as the day of reckoning approached.

Unlike the other principal decision makers—Truman, Byrnes, and Groves—Stimson did have serious misgivings about using the atomic bomb. He referred to it as "the dreadful," "the terrible," "the dire," "the awful," and "the diabolical." He considered it not merely a new weapon but "a revolutionary change in the relations of man to the universe . . . that might even mean the doom of civilization . . . it might be a Frankenstein which would eat us up."[104] He tried repeatedly to convince Truman and Byrnes to assure the Japanese about the emperor. But trying to convince them was an exercise in futility. When Stimson complained to Truman about being ignored on this point at Potsdam, Truman told his elderly, frail secretary of war that if he didn't like it, he could pack his bags and go home.

At Potsdam, Stimson informed General Dwight Eisenhower, the supreme allied commander, that the bomb's use was imminent. Eisenhower reacted strongly. He described his response in a *Newsweek* interview: "So then he told me they were going to drop it on the Japanese. Well, I listened, and I didn't volunteer anything because, after all, my war was over in Europe and it wasn't up to me. But I was getting more and more depressed just thinking about it. Then he asked for my opinion, so I told him I was against it on two counts. First, the Japanese were ready to surrender and it wasn't necessary to hit them with that awful thing. Second, I hated to see our country be the first to use such a weapon." [105] Eisenhower told historian Stephen Ambrose that he had expressed his opposition directly to Truman and his top advisors. Historian Barton Bernstein finds reason to doubt Eisenhower's account, but General Omar Bradley supports Ike's version. [106]

Now that the bomb had been successfully tested, Truman, Byrnes, and Stimson no longer welcomed the Soviet Union's entry into the war, which would entitle the Soviets to the concessions Roosevelt had promised at Yalta. Churchill observed on July 23, "It is quite clear that the United States do not at the present time desire Russian participation in the war against Japan." [107] Byrnes acknowledged, "Neither the President nor I were anxious to have them enter the war after we had learned of this successful test." He explained to his assistant Walter Brown that he was "hoping for time, believing that after [the] atomic bomb Japan will surrender and Russia will not get in so much on the kill." [108] For Truman and his advisors, the way to accomplish this seemed obvious: use the atomic bomb. Truman spelled it out: "Believe Japs will fold up before Russia comes in. I am sure they will when Manhattan appears over their homeland." [109]

Before the conference ended, Truman sidled up to Stalin and casually mentioned that the United States had developed a "new weapon of unusual destructive force." Unaware that Soviet intelligence had kept Stalin informed of the Manhattan Project, Truman was surprised by his seemingly disinterested response and wondered if Stalin had grasped what he was telling him. Stalin understood far more than Truman realized. He knew that the test had been scheduled. Now he concluded that it had succeeded. He immediately phoned Soviet security and Secret Police Chief Lavrenti Beria and berated him for not having known that the test had occurred. Andrei Gromyko reported that when Stalin returned to his villa he remarked that the Americans would use their atomic monopoly to

Stalin and Truman with Secretary of State James F. Byrnes and Soviet Foreign Minister Vyacheslav Molotov at the Potsdam Conference in July 1945. While at Potsdam, Truman and his advisors learned of the successful Trinity test of the atomic bomb. Now armed with the new weapon and hoping to deny the Soviets promised territorial and economic concessions, Truman, Byrnes, and Secretary of War Henry Stimson no longer welcomed the Soviet Union's entry into the war in the Pacific.

dictate terms in Europe but that he wouldn't give in to their blackmail.[110] He ordered Soviet military forces to speed the country's entry into the war, and he ordered Soviet scientists to pick up the pace of their research.

Truman never issued a direct order to drop the bomb. At Potsdam, on July 25, he approved a directive signed by Stimson and Marshall ordering that the atomic bombs be used as soon after August 3 as weather permitted. He knew there was little chance that the final Potsdam Declaration, which contained neither a significant modification of surrender terms, a warning about the bomb, or notice of Soviet entry into the war, would be accepted by Japan. Still, it is important to note that contrary to later claims by Truman and Stimson, the authorization was given before, not after, the Japanese rejected the Potsdam Declaration. Truman did not invite Stalin to sign the declaration, even though Stalin came intending to sign it and even brought a draft of his own. Stalin's signature would have notified the Japanese that the Soviet Union was about to come into the war. The absence of his signature encouraged the Japanese to continue their futile effort to gain Soviet assistance in securing better surrender terms while the hours ticked off until the bomb was ready to use.

Truman's behavior at Potsdam reinforced Stalin's belief that the United States intended to end the war quickly and renege on its promised concessions. During the conference, he told Truman that Soviet troops would be ready to attack by the middle of August. Soviet Chief of Staff Aleksei Antonov informed his U.S. counterparts that the actual start date was more likely the end of the month. Stalin ordered Marshal Aleksandr Vasilevski to prepare to invade ten to fourteen days earlier.[111]

Although Truman always took responsibility for the decision, Groves, who had drafted the July 25 memo, contended that Truman didn't really decide; he simply acquiesced. "As far as I was concerned," he wrote, "his decision was one of non-interference—basically, a decision not to upset the existing plans. . . ." "Truman did not so much say 'yes' as not say 'no.'" Groves described Truman scornfully as "a little boy on a toboggan."[112]

Truman left Potsdam on August 2. The following day, Byrnes's assistant wrote in his diary, "Aboard Augusta/President, Leahy, JFB agrred [sic] Japas [sic] looking for peace."[113] Truman also wanted peace. But first he wanted to use the atomic bomb.

General Douglas MacArthur, the supreme commander of Allied forces in the Pacific and the second-highest-ranking active-duty officer in the U.S. Army, considered the bomb "completely unnecessary from a military point of view" and became both angry and depressed when he learned that the United States was about to use it. He held a press conference on August 6, before the bomb drop was announced, and told reporters that the Japanese were "already beaten" and that he was thinking about "the possibilities of a next war with its horrors magnified 10,000 times."[114]

On August 6, at 2:45 A.M., three B-29s took off for Japan from the island of Tinian in the Marianas, 1,500 miles away. The lead plane, the *Enola Gay,* carried the uranium bomb, Little Boy, which exploded at 8:15 A.M. with a yield now estimated at 16 kilotons of TNT. Hiroshima's approximately 300,000 civilians, 43,000 soldiers, 45,000 Korean slave laborers, and several thousand Japanese Americans, mostly children whose parents were interned in the United States, were just beginning their day. The target was the T-shaped Aioi Bridge, near the center of the city. Hiroshima, despite its port and Second General Army Headquarters, had not been considered a priority military target for earlier bombing. The bomb totally destroyed an area extending approximately two miles in all directions. Watching the city of Hiroshima disappear horrified the *Enola Gay's* crew members. The pilot, Paul Tibbets, who named the plane after his mother, described the scene below: "The giant purple mushroom had already risen to a height of 45,000 feet, 3 miles above our own altitude, and was still boiling upward like something terribly alive. Even more fearsome was the sight on the ground

Pilot Paul Tibbets (center with pipe) with his crew and the Enola Gay.

below. Fires were springing up everywhere amid a turbulent mass of smoke that had the appearance of bubbling hot tar." [115] On another occasion, he reflected, "If Dante had been with us on the plane, he would have been terrified. The city we had seen so clearly in the sunlight a few minutes before was now an ugly smudge. It had completely disappeared under this awful blanket of smoke and fire." Tail gunner Bob Caron called it a "peep into hell." Copilot Robert Lewis wrote in his flight log, "My God! What have we done?" [116]

Radioman Abe Spitzer watched from the accompanying plane, the *Great Artiste,* and thought he was hallucinating. He provided the most graphic and terrifying description of what crew members witnessed and one worth quoting at length:

> Below us, spread out almost as far as I could see, was a great fire, but it was like no ordinary fire. It contained a dozen colors, all of them blindingly bright, more colors than I imagined existed, and in the center and brightest of all, a gigantic red ball of flame that seemed larger than the sun. Indeed, it seemed that, somehow, the sun had been knocked out of the sky and was on the ground below us and beginning to rise again, only coming straight up toward us—and fast.
>
> At the same time, the ball itself spread outward, too, until it seemed to

cover the entire city, and on every side the flame was shrouded, half-hidden by a thick, impenetrable column of grey-white smoke, extending into the foothills beyond the city and bursting outward and rising toward us with unbelievable speed.

Then the ship rocked again, and it sounded as if a giant gun—some large artillery or cannons—were firing at us and hitting us from every direction.

The purple light was changing to a green-blue now, with just a tinge of yellow at the edges, and from below the ball of fire, the upside down sun, seemed to be following the smoke upward, racing to us with immeasurably fast speed—although, we at the same time, though not so quickly—were speeding away from what was left of the city.

Suddenly, we were to the left of the pillar of smoke, and it continued rising, to an estimated height, I later learned, of 50,000 feet. It looked like a kind of massive pole that narrowed toward the top and reached for the stratosphere. The scientists later told us they believed the pole was as much as four or five miles wide at its base and a mile and a half or more wide at the top.

As I watched, hypnotized by what I saw, the column of smoke changed its color, from a grey-white to brown, then amber, then all three colors at once, mingled into a bright, boiling rainbow. For a second it looked as though its fury might be ending, but almost immediately a kind of mushroom spurted out of the top and traveled up, up to what some say was a distance of 60,000 or 70,000 feet . . . the whole column seethed and spurted, but the mushroom top shot out in every direction, like giant waves during an ocean storm.

Then, quite suddenly, the top broke off the column, as if it had been cut away with a sharp blade, and it shot still further up; how far I don't know; nobody did or does; not even the pictures show that, and none of the apparatus could measure it exactly. Some said it was 80,000 feet, some 85,000 feet, some even more. . . . After that, another mushroom, somewhat smaller, boiled up out of the pillar.[117]

Spitzer heard someone say, "I wonder if maybe we're not monkeying around with things that are none of our business."[118]

The view from the ground was very different and far more harrowing. At the hypocenter, where temperatures reached 5,400° F, the fireball roasted people "to bundles of smoking black char in a fraction of a second as their internal organs boiled away."[119] Tens of thousands were killed instantly. An estimated 140,000 were dead by the end of the year and 200,000 by 1950. The United States officially reported that only 3,242 Japanese troops were killed. Among the casualties

A mushroom cloud rises over the Japanese city of Hiroshima following the atomic bombing on August 6, 1945. The view from the ground was very different and far more harrowing. At the hypocenter, where temperatures reached 5,400° F, the fireball roasted people "to bundles of smoking black char in a fraction of a second as their internal organs boiled away."

at Hiroshima were approximately a thousand American citizens, mostly second-generation Japanese-Americans, and twenty-three U.S. prisoners of war, some of whom survived the blast only to be beaten to death by bomb survivors. Several U.S. prisoners of war were killed by the bomb.

Injured and burned survivors suffered immensely. *Hibakusha* (bomb-affected persons) described it as walking through Hell. The streets were filled with an endless ghostlike procession of horribly burned, often naked people, whose skin hung off their bones. Desperately seeking help for their wounded bodies, searching for family members, and trying to escape from the encroaching fires, they tripped over dead bodies that had been seared into lumps of charcoal, often frozen in midstep. Hiroshima's most renowned atomic bomb poet, Sankichi Toge, who died in 1953 at age thirty-seven, wrote a poem titled "August Sixth" that reads in part:

> How could I ever forget that flash of light!
> In an instant thirty thousand people disappeared from the streets;
> The cries of fifty thousand more
> Crushed beneath the darkness. . . .
>
> Then, skin hanging like rags,
> Hands on breasts;
> Treading upon shattered human brains. . . .
> Crowds piled on the river bank, and on rafts fastened to the shore,
> Turned gradually into corpses under the scorching sun. . . .

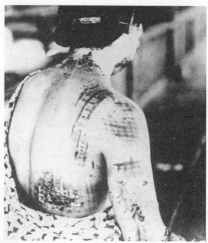

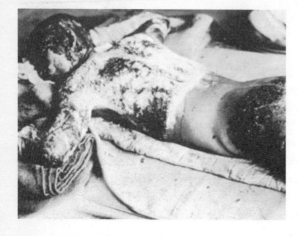

*Injured and
burned survivors
suffered immensely.
Hibakusha (bomb-
affected persons)
described it as
walking through Hell.*

The conflagration shifts . . .
Onto heaps of schoolgirls lying like refuse
So that God alone knew who they were. . . .

How could I forget that quiet
Which descended over a city of three hundred thousand?
The calm
How could I forget those pleas
Of a dying wife and child
Emitted through the whiteness of their eyes,
Piercing our minds and souls![120]

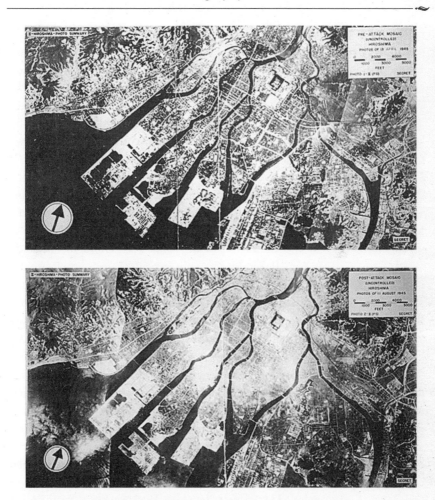

*These before and after photos from the U.S. Strategic Bombing
Survey help demonstrate the magnitude of destruction
leveled on the city of Hiroshima by the atomic bomb.*

The crew members sat silently on the flights back to Tinian. Some took solace in the belief that what they had witnessed was so horrific that it would definitely end the war. *Great Artiste* tail gunner Al "Pappy" DeHart said he wished he hadn't seen what he had just witnessed, adding, "I won't be mentioning it to my grandchildren. Not ever. I don't think it's the kind of thing to be telling kids. Not what we saw." [121]

Truman was dining on board the USS *Augusta* on his way back from Potsdam when he learned of Hiroshima. He jumped up and exclaimed, "This is the greatest thing in history." [122] He shortly thereafter said that announcing the news of Hiroshima was the "happiest" announcement he had ever made.

Truman's reported jubilation made some uncomfortable. One Democratic committeeman admonished him by telegram two days later: "no president of the United States could ever be jubilant over any device that could kill innocent human beings. Please make it clear that it is not destruction but the end of destruction that is the cause of jubilation."[123]

Soviet leaders were anything but jubilant. Knowing that the bomb was not needed to defeat a nation already on life support, they concluded that the Soviet Union was the real target. The Americans, they figured, wanted to speed the Japanese surrender in the hope of preempting Soviet gains in Asia. Even more disconcerting, they concluded that the Americans, by using it on Hiroshima when it was clearly not necessary, were signaling that the United States wouldn't hesitate to use it against them too if they threatened U.S. interests.

The Russians got the message. *Sunday Times* correspondent Alexander Werth, who spent 1941 to 1948 in Moscow, observed, "the news [of Hiroshima] had an acutely depressing effect on everybody. It was clearly realized that this was a New Fact in the world's power politics, that the bomb constituted a threat to Russia, and some Russian pessimists I talked to that day dismally remarked that Russia's desperately hard victory over Germany was now 'as good as wasted.'"[124]

It was precisely the gratuitous nature of the bombings that haunted Marshal Zhukov's memories twenty-six years later and made clear to him what their real intention was. He reflected, "It was clear already then that the U.S. Government intended to use the atomic weapon for the purpose of achieving its Imperialist goals from a position of strength in 'the cold war.' This was amply corroborated on August 6 and 8. Without any military need whatsoever, the Americans dropped two atomic bombs on the peaceful and densely populated Japanese cities of Hiroshima and Nagasaki." Other military leaders were also aghast. Gromyko's son Anatoly recalled his father telling him that Hiroshima "set the heads of the Soviet military spinning. The mood in the Kremlin, in the General Staff was neurotic, the mistrust towards the Allies grew quickly. Opinions floated around to preserve a large land army, to establish controls over extended territories to lessen potential losses from atomic bombings."[125]

Political leaders, including Stalin and Foreign Minister Vyacheslav Molotov, were equally alarmed. Physicist Yuli Khariton recalled that "The whole Soviet government interpreted [Hiroshima] as atomic blackmail against the U.S.S.R., as a threat to unleash a new, even more terrible and devastating war." Nuclear physicists were summoned to the Kremlin for daily reports on their progress. Within days, Stalin had launched a crash program to build a Soviet bomb.[126]

Following Hiroshima, Japanese leaders pressed for a quick response from the Soviets on their willingness to mediate. They received a clear answer, when, in the early hours of August 9, the powerful Red Army smashed through

Japan's forces in Manchuria, Korea, Sakhalin, and the Kurils, encountering little resistance.

On the morning of August 9, the four top Foreign Ministry officials went to Prime Minister Suzuki's residence to deliver the bad news. "What we feared has finally come," Suzuki responded.[127]

Later that morning, before Japan had time to react to the Soviet invasion, the United States dropped an implosive plutonium bomb, nicknamed Fat Man, on the city of Nagasaki. Poor visibility over the primary target—Kokura—forced the pilot, Charles Sweeney, to switch to downtown Nagasaki. The bomb landed two miles off target in the Urakami district, exploding over the largest Catholic cathedral in Asia with a force of 21 kilotons. Forty thousand people died immediately, including about 250 soldiers. Seventy thousand died by the end of 1945, perhaps 140,000 in five years. Spitzer said that he and other crew members of the *Great Artiste*, after watching Hiroshima disappear, could not believe that a second city had been wiped off the face of the earth: "There was no need for more missions, more bombs, more fear and more dying. Good God, any fool could see that."[128] Telford Taylor, the chief prosecutor at the Nuremberg trials, observed, "The rights and wrongs of Hiroshima are debatable, but I have never heard a plausible justification of Nagasaki," which he considered a war crime.[129]

Japanese officials, despondent over the Soviet attack, held an emergency cabinet meeting at which they learned about Nagasaki. Neither that announcement nor Army Minister Anami's fallacious report that the United States had a hundred more atomic bombs and Tokyo was the next target moved the participants closer to surrendering unconditionally. Most saw little difference between the United States wiping out entire cities with three hundred planes and thousands of bombs or doing so with one plane and one bomb. That the United States could and would burn down Japanese cities was an established fact. The Soviet invasion, however, totally demoralized the Japanese leaders. It proved the absolute bankruptcy of both Japan's diplomatic approach to the Soviet Union and its *ketsu-go* strategy of fiercely resisting a U.S. invasion. For Japanese leaders contemplating surrender, the atomic bombs provided an added inducement but not the decisive one, although some of them latched on to them as a convenient excuse. The emperor announced his willingness to surrender, accepting the Potsdam Declaration, but only as long as it "does not comprise any demand which prejudices the prerogatives of His Majesty as a Sovereign Ruler."[130]

Suzuki recognized that there was no choice: Japan must surrender immediately, he declared, or "the Soviet Union will take not only Manchuria, Korea, Karafuto, but also Hokkaido. This would destroy the foundation of Japan. We must end the war when we can deal with the United States."[131] Once the emperor's decision was clear, the three recalcitrant members of the Big Six, who had been holding out

Ruins in Nagasaki, where 40,000 people died immediately during the atomic bombing; 70,000 died by the end of 1945 and 140,000 in five years. Telford Taylor, the chief prosecutor at the Nuremberg trials, observed, "The rights and wrongs of Hiroshima are debatable, but I have never heard a plausible justification of Nagasaki."

for three additional demands—self-disarmament, no war crimes trials, and no occupation—dropped their opposition to surrender. Thus, with the Red Army rapidly approaching the Japanese mainland, the Japanese leaders decided to surrender to the Americans, whom they viewed as much more likely to allow them to keep the emperor. They also feared that the advancing Red Army would trigger pro-Communist uprisings inside Japan, as they had in parts of Europe.

Truman and his advisors weighed the Japanese offer to surrender. Byrnes warned that retaining the emperor would lead to "crucifixion of the President." Stimson disagreed, arguing that "even if the question hadn't been raised by the Japanese we would have to continue the Emperor ourselves . . . in order to get into surrender the many scattered armies of the Japanese who would own no other authority and . . . to save us from a score of bloody Iwo Jimas and Okinawas." In his diary, Stimson expressed his frustration with Byrnes: "There has been a good deal of uninformed agitation against the Emperor . . . by people who know no more about Japan than has been given them by Gilbert and Sullivan's 'Mikado,' and I found today that curiously enough it had gotten deeply embedded in the minds of influential people in the State Department." [132] After further debate, they compromised on a vague statement that promised, "The ultimate form of government shall, in accordance with the Potsdam Declaration, be established by the freely expressed will of the Japanese people." [133]

After the war, Japanese leaders attributed the surrender to both the atom bombs and the Soviet invasion. Although the interviews were carried out by U.S. occupation authorities, several still gave primacy to the Soviet invasion—not the atomic bomb or other U.S. actions. Deputy Chief of Staff General Torashiro Kawabe explained:

> It was only in a gradual manner that the horrible wreckage which had been
> made of Hiroshima became known. . . . In comparison, the Soviet entry
> into the war was a great shock when it actually came. Reports reaching
> Tokyo described Russian forces as "invading in swarms." It gave us all the
> more severe shock and alarm because we had been in constant fear of it
> with a vivid imagination that "the vast Red Army forces in Europe were
> now being turned against us." [134]

Admiral Toyoda agreed: "I believe the Russian participation in the war against Japan rather than the atom bombs did more to hasten the surrender." Lieutenant General Sumihisa Ikeda, the director of Japan's General Planning Agency, said that "upon hearing of the Soviet entry into the war, I felt that our chances were gone." The Army Ministry responded similarly to a direct question from General Headquarters, stating, "The Soviet participation in the war had the most direct impact on Japan's decision to surrender." [135] A study conducted by the U.S. War Department in January 1946 came to the same conclusion, finding "little mention . . . of the use of the atomic bomb by the United States in the discussions leading up to the . . . decision . . . it [is] almost a certainty that the Japanese would have capitulated upon the entry of Russia into the war." [136]

Erroneously convinced that the bombs had ended the war, 85 percent of the American public approved of their use. Almost 23 percent wished that the Japanese hadn't surrendered so quickly, so that the United States could have dropped more atom bombs on them. But unknown to most of the public, many U.S. top military leaders considered the bombings either militarily unnecessary or morally reprehensible. Truman's chief of staff, Admiral William Leahy, who chaired the meetings of the Joint Chiefs, was the most impassioned, classifying the bomb with chemical and bacteriological weapons as violations of "every Christian ethic I have ever heard of and all of the known laws of war." He proclaimed that the "Japanese were already defeated and ready to surrender. . . . The use of this barbarous weapon at Hiroshima and Nagasaki was of no material assistance in our war against Japan. In being the first to use it we adopted an ethical standard common to the barbarians of the dark ages. I was not taught to make war in that fashion and wars can not be won by destroying women and children." [137] Leahy angrily told the journalist Jonathan Daniels in 1949, "Truman told me it was agreed that they would use it . . . only to hit military objectives. Of course, then they went ahead and killed as many women and children as they could which was just what they wanted all the time." [138]

General Douglas MacArthur always maintained that the war would have ended months earlier if the United States had modified its surrender terms. In 1960, he told former President Hoover that if Hoover's "wise and statesmanlike" memo to Truman of May 30, 1945, advocating change in surrender terms, had been acted on, it "would have obviated the slaughter at Hiroshima and Nagasaki in addition to much of the destruction . . . by our bomber attacks. That the Japanese would have accepted it and gladly I have no doubt." [139]

General Henry "Hap" Arnold wrote, "it always appeared to us that, atomic bomb or no atomic bomb, the Japanese were already on the verge of collapse." [140] Shortly after the war ended, General Curtis LeMay argued, "Even without the atomic bomb and the Russian entry into the war, Japan would have surrendered in two weeks." "The atomic bomb had nothing to do with the end of the war." [141] General Carl "Tooey" Spaatz, commander of the U.S. Strategic Air Forces in the Pacific, wrote in his diary two days after the bombing of Nagasaki, "When the atomic bomb was first discussed with me in Washington I was not in favor of it just as I have never favored the destruction of cities as such with all inhabitants being killed." [142]

Many Naval officers agreed with the air chiefs. Admiral Ernest King, commander in chief of the U.S. Navy, told his aide, "I don't think we should do it at this time. It is not necessary." He told an interviewer, "I didn't like the atom bomb or any part of it." [143] Admiral Chester Nimitz, commander in chief of the Pacific Fleet, told a gathering at the Washington Monument shortly after the war, "The Japanese had, in fact, already sued for peace before the atomic age was announced to the world with the destruction of Hiroshima and Nagasaki and before the Russian entry into the war." [144] Admiral William "Bull" Halsey, commander of the South Pacific Fleet, said the following year, "The first atomic bomb was an unnecessary experiment.... It was a mistake to ever drop it.... It killed a lot of Japs, but the Japs had put out a lot of peace feelers through Russia long before." [145]

As Brigadier General Carter Clarke, who was in charge of preparing summaries of intercepted diplomatic cables, stated, "we brought them down to an abject surrender through accelerated sinking of their merchant marine and hunger alone, and when we didn't need to do it, and we knew we didn't need to do it, and they knew we knew we didn't need to do it, we used them as an experiment for two atomic bombs." [146]

Six of the United States' seven five-star officers who received their final star in World War II—Generals MacArthur, Eisenhower, and Arnold and Admirals Leahy, King, and Nimitz—rejected the idea that the atomic bombs were needed to end the war. Sadly, though, there is little evidence that they pressed their case with Truman before the fact.

But Groves knew their views. Before Hiroshima, Groves had prepared an order requiring U.S. commanders in the field to first clear all statements on the bombings with the War Department, because, as Groves admitted, "We didn't want MacArthur and others saying the war could have been won without the bomb." [147]

In late August, even Jimmy Byrnes admitted that the bomb wasn't needed to end the war. The *New York Times* reported that Byrnes had "cited what he called Russian proof that the Japanese knew that they were beaten before the first atomic bomb was dropped on Hiroshima." [148]

The Vatican quickly condemned the bombing. *Catholic World* described the bombs' use as "atrocious and abominable . . . the most powerful blow ever delivered against Christian civilization and the moral law." Federal Council of Churches leader John Foster Dulles, Eisenhower's future hawkish secretary of state, worried, "If we, a professedly Christian nation, feel morally free to use atomic energy in that way, men elsewhere will accept that verdict. Atomic weapons will be looked upon as a normal part of the arsenal of war and the stage will be set for the sudden and final destruction of mankind." [149]

Others also deplored the bombings. University of Chicago President Robert Hutchins participated in a University of Chicago Round Table discussion on "Atomic Force—Its Meaning for Mankind" broadcast on NBC on August 12, just three days after the bombing of Nagasaki. Hutchins declared: "This is the kind of weapon that should be used, if at all, only as a last resort and in self-defense. At the time this bomb was dropped, the American authorities knew that Russia was going to enter the war. It was said that Japan was blockaded and its cities burned out. All the evidence points to the fact that the use of this bomb was unnecessary. Therefore, the United States has lost its moral prestige."[150]

Brave young Americans like Paul Fussell and their Soviet and British counterparts defeated Japan in World War II. Many lost their lives in the process. Yet the myth has been promulgated by Truman, Stimson, and others that the atomic bomb was responsible for the Allied victory and that it saved hundreds of thousands of American lives by ending the war without a U.S. invasion. In 1991, former President George Herbert Walker Bush went so far as to defend Truman's "tough, calculating decision, [which] spared millions of American lives."[151] The facts show otherwise. Though the atomic bombs certainly contributed to the Japanese decision to surrender, they were ancillary to U.S. island hopping, bombing, and blockade and to the dramatic impact of the Soviet invasion, which convinced the Japanese leaders that even holding on for the last decisive battle on the Japanese mainland was no longer a viable option. Nor was it for the Americans. As Leahy confessed, "I was unable to see any justification, from a national-defense point of view, for an invasion of an already thoroughly defeated Japan."[152]

Nor did dropping atomic bombs on Hiroshima and Nagasaki make the Soviet Union more pliable. It merely convinced Stalin that the United States would stop at nothing to impose its will and that the Soviets must speed the development of their own atomic bomb as a deterrent to the bloodthirsty Americans.

And in what many consider a cruel irony, the United States allowed Japan to keep the emperor, whose retention, most experts believed, was essential to postwar social stability. Contrary to Byrnes's admonitions, Truman suffered no political repercussions from that decision.

The nuclear arms race that Szilard and others feared was now under way. Truman had helped make real his nightmarish vision of a world poised on the brink of annihilation. Stimson made the same point in his 1947 defense of the bombing, writing, "In this last great action of the Second World War we were given final proof that war is death. War in the twentieth century has grown steadily more barbarous, more destructive, more debased in all its aspects. Now, with the release of atomic energy, man's ability to destroy himself is very nearly complete."[153]

Truman always claimed that he felt no remorse, even bragging that he "never lost any sleep over that decision."[154] When television interviewer Edward R. Murrow asked him, "Any regrets?" he responded, "Not the slightest—not the slightest in the world."[155] When another interviewer asked if the decision had

General Douglas MacArthur with Emperor Hirohito. In what many consider a cruel irony, the United States allowed Japan to keep the emperor, whose retention, most experts believed, was essential to postwar social stability. Contrary to Byrnes's admonitions, Truman suffered no political repercussions from that decision.

been morally difficult to make, he responded, "Hell no, I made it like that," snapping his fingers.[156]

Truman met Oppenheimer for the first time on October 25, 1945, and asked him to guess when the Soviets would develop a bomb. When Oppenheimer admitted that he didn't know, Truman declared that he did: "Never." Unnerved by this truculent display of ignorance, Oppenheimer said at one point, "Mr. President, I feel I have blood on my hands." Truman responded angrily. "I told him the blood was on my hands—to let me worry about that." Afterward Truman told Dean Acheson, "I don't want to see that son-of-a-bitch in this office ever again." He later called Oppenheimer a "cry-baby scientist."[157]

The horrors and bloodshed of World War II hardened a lot of people to the suffering of others. Future renowned physicist Freeman Dyson, who was then ready to go to Okinawa as part of the Tiger Force fleet of three hundred British bombers, tried to illuminate the process:

> I found this continuing slaughter of defenseless Japanese even more
> sickening than the slaughter of well-defended Germans. But still I did not
> quit. By that time I had been at war so long that I could hardly remember
> peace. No living poet had words to describe that emptiness of the soul
> which allowed me to go on killing without hatred and without remorse.

But Shakespeare understood it, and he gave Macbeth the words: ". . . I am in blood/Stepp'd in so that, should I wade no more,/Returning were as tedious as going o'er." [158]

Writer and social critic Dwight Macdonald captured this dehumanization even before Hiroshima's devastation. He traced the transformation from the "unbelieving horror and indignation" people felt when Franco's planes killed hundreds of Spanish civilians in 1938 to the abject indifference to hundreds of thousands of victims in Tokyo: "We have grown callous to massacre. King Mithridates is said to have immunized himself against poison by taking small doses which he increased slowly. So the gradually increasing horrors of the last decade have made each of us to some extent a moral Mithridates, immunized against human sympathy." [159]

Not all were immunized against human sympathy. Many of the scientists involved in the bomb project became lifelong antinuclear activists, like Leo Szilard, who switched from physics to biology and founded the Council for a Livable World; Albert Einstein, who became the chair of the Emergency Committee of Atomic Scientists in 1946; and Joseph Rotblat, who campaigned tirelessly for nuclear abolition until his death at age ninety-six and won the Nobel Peace Prize in 1995.

Even British Prime Minister Winston Churchill recognized the difficulty of defending the atomic bombings. Churchill visited Truman toward the end of his presidency. Truman threw a small dinner to which he invited Robert Lovett, Omar Bradley, Harriman, and Acheson. Margaret, the president's daughter, described the scene: "Everyone was in an ebullient mood, especially Dad. Without warning, Mr. Churchill turned to him and said, 'Mr. President, I hope you have your answer ready for that hour when you and I stand before Saint Peter and he says, "I understand you two are responsible for putting off those atomic bombs. What have you got to say for yourselves?"'" [160] The atomic bombings would not be the only thing Churchill and Truman would have to answer for as the United States and Great Britain charged toward confrontation with the Soviet Union.

The person who did the most to try to stop that confrontation, Henry Wallace, has been largely lost to history. Few people remember how close Wallace came to getting the vice presidential nomination on that steamy Chicago night in July 1944. What might this country have become had Wallace succeeded Roosevelt in April 1945 instead of Truman? Would atomic bombs still have been used in World War II? Could we have avoided the nuclear arms race and the Cold War? Would civil rights and women's rights have triumphed in the immediate postwar years? Might colonialism have ended decades earlier and the fruits of science and technology been spread more equitably around the globe? We'll never know.

Chapter 5

THE COLD WAR:

Who Started It?

"Men and women a century from now will very likely find the Cold War as obscure and incomprehensible as we today find the Thirty Years War—the terrible conflict that devastated much of Europe not too long ago. Looking back at the 20th century," Arthur Schlesinger, Jr., wisely observed, "our descendants will very likely be astonished at the disproportion between the causes of the Cold War, which may well seem trivial, and the consequences, which could have meant the veritable end of history."[1] Did the Cold War have to be fought the way it was—with U.S. and Soviet nuclear weapons poised to destroy each other and wipe out all of the rest of humanity as collateral damage? Could the Cold War have been avoided entirely? Were there statesmen who offered a dramatically different vision of a postwar world based on peaceful and friendly competition that would uplift all of humanity?

The early Cold War would be animated by the clash between two fundamentally different visions of the U.S. role in the world—Henry Luce's hegemonic vision of the twentieth century as the "American Century" and Henry Wallace's utopian vision of the "Century of the Common Man." The stakes would be enormous.

On September 2, 1945, the Second World War officially ended. Though Americans everywhere were cheered by that news, a strange pall hung over the nation as Americans envisioned their own future in the burned-out ruins of Hiroshima and Nagasaki. On August 12, CBS newsman Edward R. Murrow observed, "Seldom, if ever, has a war ended leaving the victors with such a sense of uncertainty and fear, with such a realization that the future is obscure and that survival is not assured." Public discourse was rife with apocalyptic forebodings, as Americans were struck by what historian Paul Boyer describes as a "primal fear of extinction."[2] The *St. Louis Post-Dispatch* worried that science may have "signed the mammalian world's death certificate." John Campbell, editor of *Astounding Science Fiction* magazine, admitted that he had been contemplating this development for fifteen years and added, "Frankly, I am scared." This was not just a new bomb; it was, he explained, "the power to kill the human race."[3] The *New York Times* regretted that humans could now "blow ourselves and perhaps the planet itself to drifting dust."[4] The *Washington Post* lamented that the life expectancy of the human species had "dwindled immeasurably in the course of two brief weeks."[5]

War's end left much of Europe and Asia in tatters. As many as 70 million people lay dead. Civilian deaths outnumbered military deaths by more than three to two. The Soviet losses were unparalleled, as retreating German troops destroyed everything in their path. President John F. Kennedy later remarked, "No nation in the history of battle ever suffered more than the Soviet Union in the Second World War. At least 20 million lost their lives. Countless millions of homes and families were burned or sacked. A third of the nation's territory, including two-thirds of its industrial base, were turned into a wasteland—a loss equivalent to the destruction of this country east of Chicago."[6]

Only the United States escaped such destruction. The U.S. economy was booming. GNP and exports more than doubled prewar levels. Industrial production soared, growing during the war at a record 15 percent annually. The United States held two-thirds of the world's gold reserves and three-quarters of its invested capital. It produced a phenomenal 50 percent of the world's goods and services. Yet businessmen and planners worried that the end of wartime spending augured a return to prewar depression conditions. They particularly feared the consequences should Europe adopt economic spheres closed to American trade and investment.

With Franklin Roosevelt at the helm, the United States skillfully steered a middle course between Great Britain and the Soviet Union. Most Americans looked askance at British imperialism and disapproved of Great Britain's repressive policies in Greece, India, and elsewhere. Many also mistrusted Soviet-style socialism and decried the Soviet Union's heavy-handed treatment of Eastern Europe. After the war, the United States used a $3.75 billion credit to pry open the British Empire, gaining equal access for American capital and goods. It also canceled Great Britain's lend-lease debt. The United States disappointed the Soviet Union by not offering similar aid, although it had dangled the prospect of

OPPOSITE: *Ruins in London, Warsaw, and Kiev. The end of World War II left much of Europe and Asia in tatters. Perhaps as many as 70 million lay dead. Civilian deaths outnumbered military deaths by more than three to two.*

a large credit during wartime discussions. Harry Truman, unfortunately, showed none of Roosevelt's dexterity in navigating an independent course as he tacked increasingly toward the British camp, ignoring Soviet concerns at a time of maximum U.S. strength and relative Soviet weakness.

In mid-September, Secretary of State James Byrnes traveled to London to confer with Vyacheslav Molotov and other foreign ministers. Before leaving, he made clear his intention to use the U.S. atomic monopoly to force Soviet compliance with U.S. demands. But whenever Byrnes insisted the Soviets open up Eastern Europe, Molotov pointed to exclusionary U.S. policies in Italy, Greece, and Japan. Tired of Byrnes's belligerence, Molotov finally asked if he was hiding an atomic bomb in his coat pocket, to which Byrnes replied, "You don't know southerners. We carry our artillery in our pocket. If you don't cut out all this stalling . . . , I'm going to pull an atomic bomb out of my hip pocket and let you have it."[7]

U.S. atomic diplomacy, in its first iteration, had clearly failed to produce the desired results. Secretary of War Henry Stimson objected to such crude intimidation. In a September memo, Stimson had advised Truman that bullying the Soviets with atomic weapons would backfire and only speed the Soviet Union's efforts to attain its own atomic arsenal:

> our satisfactory relations with Russia [are] not merely connected with
> but . . . virtually dominated by the problem of the atomic bomb . . . if we . . .
> hav[e] this weapon rather ostentatiously on our hip, their suspicions and
> their distrust of our purposes and motives will increase. . . . The chief lesson
> that I have learned in a long life is that the only way you can make a man
> trustworthy is to trust him; and the surest way to make him untrustworthy
> is to distrust him and show your distrust.[8]

Stimson boldly called for halting U.S. development of atomic bombs if Great Britain and the Soviet Union did likewise and impounding those the United States had already built. Truman dedicated the September 21 cabinet meeting to Stimson's urgent appeal to strengthen the U.S. friendship with the Soviet Union before it developed its own atomic bombs. The meeting, occurring on Stimson's seventy-eighth birthday, would be the last for the retiring statesman. The cabinet split sharply over Stimson's proposals, with Secretary of Commerce Henry Wallace rallying supporters and Secretary of the Navy James Forrestal leading the opposition. Forrestal would play an important role in the hardening of U.S. policy toward the Soviet Union. He had earned a fortune on Wall Street and married a former Ziegfeld Follies girl before joining the White House staff in 1939. Like most other Wall Streeters, he deeply distrusted the Soviet Union. He leaked a phony account of the cabinet discussion to the press. The next day, the *New York Times* reported that Wallace had proposed sharing "the secret of the atomic bomb" with the USSR.[9] Though Truman immediately repudiated this flagrant falsehood and set the record straight, Wallace could see the writing on the wall.

Having just returned from a conference on atomic energy at the University of Chicago, Wallace understood the real stakes better than Truman and other administration officials. The experts agreed that whatever secret there might have been to the atomic bomb had vanished when the United States dropped the first one on Hiroshima. They also knew, as the Franck Committee had warned in June, that the Soviet Union would soon develop its own atomic arsenal. The scientists in attendance drove home the fact that the current generation of atomic weapons paled by comparison to what would soon be available. Therefore, they concluded, steps to curb an arms race were essential and urgent. Wallace had told the gathering that "any nation that violates the international moral law, sooner or later gets into trouble—the British have done that in relation to colonial peoples and the United States [is] in danger of doing it with the atomic bomb." He conveyed that same message to his fellow cabinet members.[10]

A few days later, Wallace received a letter from physicist Arthur Holly Compton. Compton alerted Wallace to ominous developments at the weapons laboratories. "There is a reasonable chance," he reported, "that a concentrated scientific and technical effort, comparable with that spent on the development of the present atom bomb, could develop a super bomb" of staggering destructive capability. He expressed the deeply held view among the members of the Scientific Panel of the Interim Committee. "We feel that this . . . should *not* be undertaken . . . because we . . . prefer defeat in war to a victory obtained at the expense of the enormous human disaster that would be caused by its . . . use." Compton presented some rough figures to show just how powerful a bomb he was talking about: The "area completely destroyed by 1 atomic bomb, 4 square miles. Area completely destroyable by 1000 atomic bombs, as in a future war, 4000 square miles. Area completely destroyable by 1000 super bombs, about 1,000,000 square miles. Area of continental United States, about 3,000,000 square miles." What worried Compton was that "the theoretical basis of the super bomb has arisen spontaneously with at least four persons working on our project who have independently brought the idea to me. This means that it will occur likewise to those in other nations engaged on similar developments. If developed here, other great powers must follow suit." Wallace and Compton both felt that only some form of world government could meet such a challenge.[11]

Wallace fought a rearguard action against the powerful forces propelling the country toward war with the Soviet Union. Truman's ouster of the few remaining

New Dealers from his cabinet, left Wallace increasingly isolated. Now Stimson too was gone. As Soviet intelligence noted, the rightward shift in Truman's economic and foreign policy advisors was unmistakable.

Wallace, undeterred, met with Truman on October 15 to press him on softening his tone toward the Soviet Union, and gave him a report he had written titled "The Significance of the Atomic Age." Truman read it sentence by sentence in his presence. It warned, "When many nations have atomic bombs [it] will require only the smallest spark to set off a worldwide humanity-destroying explosion. Steps should be taken at once to call into being a vital international organization based on the elimination of all weapons of offensive warfare, the pooling of the constructive aspects of atomic energy, and the adoption of the principle of international trusteeship for certain areas of the world." Truman agreed completely, telling Wallace that "this was what he had been trying to say right along." He also remarked, somewhat overgenerously, that "Stalin was a fine man who wanted to do the right thing." Truman even agreed with Wallace's statement that "the purpose of Britain was to promote an unbreachable break between us and Russia."[12] Wallace's efforts bore fruit. In the fall of 1945, Truman told a press conference, "Russia's interests and ours do not clash, and never have. We have always been friends, and I hope we always will be."[13]

With the nuclear issue looming large, scientists descended on Washington to promote international control of atomic energy and prevent military control of atomic research. Wallace supported their efforts, testifying before the Senate Special Committee on Atomic Energy that the May-Johnson bill, by providing for military oversight of peacetime nuclear research, would set up the "most undemocratic, dictatorial arrangements that have ever . . . been proposed to the Congress in a major legislative measure."[14] Its passage would threaten to deliver the American people into the hands of "military fascism."[15] Wallace further pressed Truman to remove control of U.S. atomic weapons from Leslie Groves and require authorization of the president, secretary of state, secretary of war, and secretary of the navy before they could be used. Wallace feared that given Soviet-hater Groves's unilateral control over the nuclear arsenal, he might launch an atomic attack on his own authority.

Such a fear was not as farfetched as it might seem. In late 1945, Groves openly advocated a preemptive attack against the Soviet Union. He reasoned that the United States had two choices. It could quickly reach an agreement with the Soviets ensuring that nobody use atomic bombs under any circumstances. But such an agreement, he believed, would necessarily entail "the abandonment of all rights of privacy—that of the home, the laboratory and the industrial plant throughout the world including the United States." Failure to reach an agreement, however, would mean the United States, Great Britain, and the

Soviet Union all having atomic bombs. In that case, he contended, "The United States must for all time maintain absolute supremacy in atomic weapons, including number, size and power, efficiency, means for immediate offensive use and defensive against atomic attack. We must also have a worldwide intelligence service which will keep us at all times completely informed of any activities of other nations in the atomic field and of their military intentions." That would lead to an atomic arms race. But he didn't think that "the world could . . . long survive such a race." Therefore, he concluded, the United States should not permit any potential rival "to make or possess atomic weapons. If such a country started to make atomic weapons we would destroy its capacity to make them before it had progressed far enough to threaten us." [16]

The scientists, in their efforts to achieve international control of atomic power and to ensure civilian control at home, always viewed Wallace as their most trustworthy ally in the administration. Oppenheimer visited him in October and voiced the scientists' distress over the growing tension with the Soviet Union and the fact that Byrnes was using "the bomb as a pistol to get what we wanted in international diplomacy." He knew the Russians would respond by very quickly developing their own bomb. Oppenheimer complained that "the heart has completely gone out of" the scientists. "All they think about now are the social and economic implications of the bomb." Wallace was shaken by seeing Oppenheimer so agitated: "I never saw a man in such an extremely nervous state as Oppenheimer. He seemed to feel that the destruction of the entire human race was imminent." Wallace shared Oppenheimer's concern about the precarious nature of the international situation and encouraged him to speak directly with Truman. Unsettled by the encounter with Oppenheimer, Wallace commented, "The guilt consciousness of the atomic bomb scientists is one of the most astounding things I have ever seen." [17]

Oppenheimer took Wallace's advice and met with Truman six days later. The meeting could not have gone worse. Truman stressed national considerations in passing an atomic energy act; Oppenheimer pressed for international control. The meeting ended disastrously with Oppenheimer's confession of guilt over the bomb.

Wallace persevered in his effort to mitigate the influence of Truman's conservative advisors, who preferred confrontation with the Soviet Union over continuing the wartime alliance. They saw malign intent in every Soviet action. Wallace encouraged Truman to understand how his words and actions looked to Soviet leaders. Following the cabinet meeting the day after Truman's unfortunate encounter with Oppenheimer, Wallace stayed behind to speak with the president. He again urged Truman to be evenhanded with Great Britain and the Soviet Union and to offer the Soviet Union a loan comparable to the one the United States had offered Great Britain. He compared U.S. dictating election results in Cuba and Mexico to the way the Soviets exerted control over the Balkan states. Truman, as always, agreed completely with Wallace's analysis of events.

The effects of Wallace's repeated interventions were usually short-lived. Truman's other advisors discerned a more threatening pattern in Soviet actions and succeeded in convincing the president to view the world through their prism. By November, they were referring to Wallace and Truman's progressive friends as "Reds" and telling Truman, "Don't pay any attention to what those 'Reds' want you to do."[18]

Meanwhile, Soviet leaders were pursuing their own agenda: securing their gains in Eastern Europe and Asia, rebuilding their shattered economy, and making certain that Germany and Japan never again posed a threat to Soviet security. They were well positioned to act on those interests. With Communists having played a leading role in antifascist resistance movements, beleaguered Europeans often welcomed Soviet troops as liberators. Communist party membership soared across Europe. Communists won more than 20 percent of the vote in France, Italy, and Finland in 1945. With European populations uprooted, homeless, hungry, and unemployed, the prospect seemed ripe for further Communist gains. In Italy, where 1.7 million joined the party, real wages in 1945 were barely a quarter of 1913 levels and GNP was at 1911 levels. Undersecretary of State Dean Acheson worried that Europe would turn toward socialism, leaving the United States isolated: "They have suffered so much and they believe so deeply that governments can take some action which will alleviate their sufferings, that they will demand that the whole business of state control and state interference shall be pushed further and further."[19]

But the Soviet Union, adhering to wartime understandings and hoping to maintain the wartime alliance, went out of its way to restrain its frustrated Communist allies in China, Italy, France, and Greece. In early 1946, a Gallup Poll found that only 26 percent of Americans thought the Soviets sought world domination. Thirteen percent thought the British did.[20]

During these early postwar months, Truman vacillated in his attitude toward Stalin, often likening him to Boss Pendergast in Kansas City. Others did likewise. Even Averell Harriman, a fierce critic who worked with Stalin as ambassador during the war, recognized the complexity of his personality:

> It is hard for me to reconcile the courtesy and consideration that
> he showed me personally with the ghastly cruelty of his wholesale
> liquidations. Others, who did not know him personally, see only the tyrant
> in Stalin. I saw the other side as well—his high intelligence, that fantastic
> grasp of detail, his shrewdness and his surprising human sensitivity that he

was capable of showing. . . . I found him better informed than Roosevelt, more realistic than Churchill, in some ways the most effective of the war leaders . . . for me Stalin remains the most inscrutable and contradictory character I have ever known.[21]

With tensions over Poland having eased, Germany would provide an early test case for postwar cooperation. After Germany's surrender, the Allies divided the country into Soviet, U.S., British, and French zones. Roosevelt had first supported the Morgenthau Plan for "pastoralization" of Germany to ensure that it never again posed a threat to its neighbors. "We have to be tough with Germany," he told Morgenthau in August 1944. "We either have to castrate the German people or you have got to treat them in such a manner so they can't just go on reproducing people who want to continue the way they have in the past."[22] But the United States reversed itself once it became convinced that restoration of the German economy would be key to overall European recovery. This placed the Western powers at odds with the Soviets, who feared German revitalization and were busy stripping the eastern zone of assets to ship back to the Soviet Union. These conflicting interests impeded the creation of a unified Germany, thereby planting the seeds for later conflict, while Germans struggled to eke out a living regardless of which zone they lived in.

The first major superpower conflict erupted in the Middle East, not Europe, as Stalin moved to expand Soviet influence in Iran and Turkey at declining Britain's expense. The Middle East had assumed increased strategic significance following completion of the Suez Canal in 1869 and the introduction of long-distance air routes in the early twentieth century. English historian Arnold Toynbee described it as "the shortest route between the two chief concentrations of population and power in the world of the twentieth century": India, East Asia, and the Pacific on the one hand, and Europe, America, and the Atlantic on the other. He explained that "command of the Middle East carried with it the power of keeping open the direct routes between those two geographical poles, or closing them, or forcing them open again."[23] The Soviet Union had long coveted the Turkish Straits, which would have allowed it access to the Mediterranean, and Stalin believed that he had won that concession from Roosevelt and Churchill during the war. He now pressured Turkey to build joint military bases in the straits. The ensuing conflict, like everything else in the Middle East, revolved around oil. At the start of the war, the United States accounted for 61 percent of overall world oil production. Great Britain controlled 72 percent of Middle Eastern oil, the United States only 10 percent. The United States now sought a bigger share in the Middle East. Saudi Arabia held the key to U.S. ambitions. In 1943, the United States extended lend-lease aid to the oil-rich sheikdom. The following year, Saudi King Ibn Saud granted the United States permission to construct an air base at Dharan.[24]

In a 1944 meeting with British Ambassador Lord Halifax, Roosevelt drew a map of Middle Eastern oil holdings and informed Halifax that Iranian oil belonged to Great Britain, Saudi oil to the United States, and Iraqi and Kuwaiti oil to both. The following year, Roosevelt concluded a deal with Ibn Saud pledging U.S. support in return for exclusive access to Saudi oil. Truman understood the importance of maintaining U.S. control of this vital resource. In August 1945, Gordon Merriam, Chief of the State Department Near East Division, alerted Truman to the fact that Saudi Arabia's oil resources were "a stupendous source of strategic power, and one of the greatest material prizes in human history."[25]

Iran was another prize. In September 1941, tired of Reza Shah Pahlavi's erratic behavior and questionable loyalties, Britain and the USSR invaded and occupied the country, forcing Reza Shah into exile and replacing him with his twenty-one-year-old son.[26]

Having eyed Iran's rich oil reserves since the 1920s, the United States now maneuvered to expand its influence, offering lend-lease aid and sending in civilian and military advisors. In 1943, Secretary of State Cordell Hull explained to Roosevelt why it was essential to limit British and Soviet power: "It is to our interest that no great power be established on the Persian Gulf opposite the important American petroleum developments in Saudi Arabia."[27]

Like Great Britain and the United States, the Soviet Union did indeed have designs on Iranian oil. Stalin wanted to develop the oil fields in northern Iran. He also worried about the security of the Soviet Union's Baku oil fields, which were only a hundred miles north of the Russo-Iranian border. Stalin pressed Iran for oil concessions comparable to those granted to Great Britain and the United States and, with troops remaining in the country from World War II, supported a separatist uprising in Iran's northern provinces to force Iran's hand.

Churchill, meanwhile, itched for a confrontation with the Soviet Union. A rabid anti-Communist and unabashed imperialist, Churchill had tried to draw the United States into military engagement with the Soviet Union as far back as 1918. Though forced to defer his long-sought confrontation during the war, he pounced as soon as the opportunity presented itself. Soviet probes in Iran and Turkey had threatened the British sphere in the Middle East and Mediterranean, and Great Britain's hold on India seemed precarious. The exposure of a Soviet atomic espionage ring in Canada in early February added credibility to warnings issued by Forrestal, Leahy, and other hard-liners. A speech that month by Stalin raised further hackles, though it was actually much less inflammatory than Soviet expert George Kennan and others contended.

Anti-Soviet sentiments were clearly on the rise in early March 1946 when

*Truman and Churchill gesture from a train en route to
Fulton, Missouri, where Churchill would deliver his bellicose
"Iron Curtain" speech in early March 1946.*

Churchill spoke in Fulton, Missouri, with Truman sitting on the platform. His bellicose words delivered a sharp, perhaps fatal, blow to any prospects for postwar comity:

> From Stettin in the Baltic to Trieste in the Adriatic, an iron curtain has descended across the Continent. . . . Police governments are prevailing . . . in a great number of countries . . . the Communist parties or fifth columns constitute a growing challenge and peril to Christian civilization. . . . I do not believe that Soviet Russia desires war. What they desire is the fruits of war and the indefinite expansion of their power and doctrines. [28]

Stalin responded angrily, accusing Churchill of being in bed with the "warmongers" who followed the "racial theory" that only English speakers could "decide the fate of the whole world." [29]

The speech aroused intense passions on all sides. Major newspapers were mixed in their reactions. The *New York Times* applauded Churchill's harsh rhetoric, spoken "with the force of the prophet proved right before." [30] The *Washington Post* also found elements to applaud but criticized Churchill's "illogical" call for an "international police force," as "overdo[ing] the emphasis on force." [31]

The *Chicago Tribune* agreed with Churchill's analysis of what was occurring in Eastern Europe but sharply disagreed with his remedy and pounced upon his defense of British imperialism: "He proposes an alliance, half slave and half free, with the British empire representing slavery. He comes really as a suppliant, begging assistance for that old and evil empire and frankly expecting to get it on his own terms." Such an alliance would require U.S. acceptance of "the enslavement and exploitation of millions of British subjects." The *Tribune* lectured sternly that the United States should not use its power "to maintain British tyranny thruout the world. We cannot become partners in slave holding." [32]

Several senators vigorously denounced Churchill's defense of empire. Maine Republican Owen Brewster proclaimed, "We cannot assume the heritage of colonial policy represented by the British foreign and colonial office. Nine-tenths of the world is not Anglo-Saxon. We must consider how we are going to gain the confidence of the world that is not Slav or Anglo-Saxon. I fear an alliance with Britain would be the catalyst that would precipitate the world against us. We should orient American policy independently with the Russians." Florida's Claude Pepper observed, "He spoke beautifully for imperialism—but it is always British imperialism. I think his tory sentiments make him as much opposed to Russia as to a labor government in his own country. We want Anglo-American cooperation, but not at the exclusion of the rest of the world." Pepper later joined fellow Democrats Harley Kilgore of West Virginia and Glen Taylor of Idaho in issuing a statement rejecting Churchill's proposal for "an old fashioned, power politics, military alliance between Great Britain and the United States" that would "cut the throat of the UNO." [33] Pepper told reporters, "It is shocking to see Mr. Churchill . . . align himself with the old Chamberlain Tories who strengthened the Nazis as part of their anti-Soviet crusade . . . the people of the world who really want peace [must] take note of this Tory clamor in Britain and the United States which is building up war. The new British-American imperialism which Mr. Churchill proposes and defends makes us false to the very ideals for which both Nations fought." [34]

Nor did the public clamor to support Churchill's belligerent call. As one *Washington Post* reader asserted, "Senator Pepper and his colleagues should be congratulated on their courageous reply to the war-mongering speech of Churchill. Who is the President of the United States, Truman or Churchill? Why should Churchill tell us what our policies should be when even the British people repudiated Churchill's policies in the last election. Churchill is a warmonger and it is time that Senator Pepper told him so. We need a second Declaration of Independence from British rule." [35]

Riding on the train to Missouri with Churchill, Truman had read Churchill's speech in its entirety and heartily approved of its contents. But, in light of the outcry against Churchill's pugnacity, he denied having advance knowledge of what Churchill would say. Truman's boldfaced lies were quickly exposed by journalists.

Led by members of the Roosevelt family, New Deal progressives condemned Churchill and beseeched Truman to change course before it was too late. Speaking publicly, Eleanor Roosevelt deplored Churchill's inflammatory remarks. James Roosevelt, Franklin and Eleanor's oldest son, did likewise at a meeting of the Independent Citizens' Committee of the Arts, Sciences and Professions. He declared, "Let us make clear to all the world that the Right Hon. Winston Churchill—now a guest in our country—speaks only for himself when he attacks world peace—when he proposes once again that mankind divide itself into two camps. Too often in the past his cronies—both here and abroad—have been outright reactionaries. It is up to us and to every peace-loving man and woman in the world to stand up now and repudiate the word, the schemes and the political allies of the Hon. Winston Churchill." Roosevelt knew what Truman could do if he wanted to ease tensions: "I would like to see the Secretary of Commerce, Henry Wallace, fly to Russia." Because of his reputation "for fairness and integrity," Roosevelt explained, a personal mission from him to Stalin could do more for peace and understanding "than any number of sharply worded notes or communiqués."[36]

James Roosevelt had been introduced by Harold Ickes, Roosevelt's former long-standing secretary of the interior, who, as a stalwart New Deal progressive, had consistently been a thorn in Truman's side. Truman had finally rid himself of Ickes the previous month, after earlier denigrating him in front of reporters as "shitass Ix."[37] Ickes's resignation came over his opposition to Truman's nominating California oil millionaire Edwin Pauley, to whose nefarious activities Truman owed his office, as assistant secretary of the navy. But Ickes stood in the way, accusing Pauley of lying when he testified that he had not lobbied against the government's suit to assert federal title to the oil along the nation's coasts. Ickes alleged that Pauley had offered "the rawest proposition ever made to me": oilmen would contribute $300,000 to the Democratic Party in 1944 if the government dropped the tidelands suit that Ickes had brought. Ickes reported that at a special cabinet meeting the previous week, Truman had implored him to "Be as gentle as you can with Ed Pauley" and that party chairman Robert Hannegan had "been moving heaven and earth" to get Pauley confirmed. Ickes chose integrity over gentleness. He lashed out, "I don't care to stay in an Administration where I am expected to commit perjury for the sake of the Party." He released his acerbic exchange of letters with Truman over the resignation. He warned that unless the administration changed its unsavory ways, it would bring about a scandal reminiscent of Teapot Dome. The Department of the Interior, he reminded Truman, "must always be on guard against any association of money with politics." Ickes also told reporters that no oilman should be allowed to hold a government office that dealt with oil policy.[38] The *Los Angeles Times* headlined its front-page article "Ickes Blowup Rocks Capital like Atom Bomb," describing what reporter Bill Henry called "the biggest press conference in the history of Washington."[39]

In introducing James Roosevelt, Ickes offered some sage advice to his former boss on dealing with the Soviets: "The people . . . want President Truman to stand up aggressively for the foreign policies of President Roosevelt. They do not feel comfortable with the sniping at Russia, which is being indulged in. They know that without Russia we would still be fighting the war. They cannot envisage a peaceful future without an understanding with Russia."

The following month, on the first anniversary of Roosevelt's death, Wallace spoke in New York's City Hall, repudiating Churchill and proposing a different vision of competition between the two nations:

> The only kind of competition we want with the Soviets is to demonstrate that we can raise our standard of living faster during the next 20 years than Russia. We shall compete with Russia in serving the spiritual and physical needs of the common man. . . . The only way to defeat Communism in the world is to do a better and smoother job of maximum production and optimum distribution. . . . Let's make it a clean race, a determined race but above all a peaceful race in the service of humanity. . . . Russia can't ride roughshod over eastern Europe and get away with it any more than we can do the same in Latin America or England in India and Africa. . . . The source of all our mistakes is fear. . . . Russia fears Anglo-Saxon encirclement. We fear Communist penetration. If these fears continue, the day will come when our sons and grandsons will pay for these fears with rivers of blood. . . . Out of fear great nations have been acting like cornered beasts, thinking only of survival. . . . A month ago Mr. Churchill came out for the Anglo Saxon century. Four years ago I repudiated the American century. Today I repudiate the Anglo Saxon century with even greater vigor. The common people of the world will not tolerate a recrudescence of imperialism even under enlightened Anglo-Saxon, atomic bomb auspices. The destiny of the English speaking people is to serve the world, not dominate it.[40]

Following Churchill's speech, U.S.-Soviet relations deteriorated rapidly. At the United Nations, the United States pressed for a confrontation over Iran, despite the Soviet Union's agreement to withdraw its troops. When Soviet troops stayed beyond the March 2 deadline for their removal, Truman threatened war. He wrote, "If the Russians were to control Iran's oil, either directly or indirectly, the raw material balance of the world would undergo serious damage and it would be a serious loss for the economy of the western world." Forrestal afterward noted that "whoever sits on the valve of Middle East oil may control the destiny of Europe." Truman decided to send a clear message that the United States—not the Soviet Union—would sit on that valve.[41]

Former Columbia President Nicholas Murray Butler, the 1931 Nobel Peace Prize winner and president of the Carnegie Endowment for International Peace, made it clear that the issue involved was oil, not democracy. "Iran is wholly a question of oil," he explained. "Large commitments have been proposed and made to Great Britain. A way ought to be found for Russia to have a share of the oil without carrying on a political military disturbance." Some found that suggestion quite plausible. In an editorial on the crisis, the *Washington Post* suggested that "Russia may have legitimate claims to make on Iran. On the oil situation, for instance, we have repeatedly argued that a joint plan for the exploitation of the oil resources of the Middle East is definitely in order."[42]

Claude Pepper got a closer look at the unfolding crisis in his tour of the Middle East, which included an interview with Stalin. After returning to the United States, Pepper addressed the Senate, exonerating the Soviet Union and condemning British imperial overreach: "It comes with ill grace from a certain world power whose people are stationed in every nation from Egypt to Singapore to make a world conflagration out of the movement of a few troops a few miles into some neighboring territory to resist an oil monopoly which they enjoy." "If American foreign policy is made the scapegoat for such imperialism, it is more stupid than I thought is possible for it to be." The *Washington Post* reported that after Pepper finished, several senators and House members walked over to shake his hand.[43]

The public was not enthusiastic about confronting the Soviet Union over Iranian oil. The *Washington Post* carried a particularly illuminating letter identifying the stakes in Iran and disavowing military action:

> I do not believe that the fate of the oil deposits of Iran justifies war with Russia. If this oil were located in North or South America, the . . . United States would both protect these oil deposits for our use in any future war and guarantee that no other strong power could seize these oil fields. If the Iranian oil occupied a geographic position near any of the British dominions, as it does next to the Soviet states, I believe Great Britain would secure or protect this oil. . . . The support of Iranian freedom has never before been suggested as justifying an overseas war for Americans. Iranian freedom as we understand freedom has never existed, so those who suggest war in support of such freedom are without a real cause. . . . I am firmly convinced that the vast majority of Americans do not want to fight Russia for any cause that has yet developed. I also believe that a majority of Americans hope and think that left alone with her own borders reasonably

secure that Russia will work to help support the peace of the world and to develop her own great natural resources for generations to come.[44]

Pressured by the United States and Great Britain, Soviet forces withdrew from Iran. Truman later told Senator Henry "Scoop" Jackson that he had summoned Soviet Ambassador Andrei Gromyko to the White House and informed him that if Soviet troops weren't out in forty-eight hours, "We're going to drop it on you." They were out, he claimed, in twenty-four hours.[45] Although the real story behind Soviet withdrawal is much more complicated, Truman drew the lesson that when confronted with superior force, the Soviets would back down. The United States decided to press its advantage. In May, it halted reparations shipments from western Germany that the Soviets desperately needed. In July, it decided to keep troops in South Korea and the following month to maintain a naval presence in the eastern Mediterranean.

While Truman was making atomic threats, the public quaked at the prospect of atomic war. In early 1946, *Ladies' Home Journal* instructed readers, "Over and above all else you do, the thought you should wake up to, go to sleep with and carry with you all day" is prevention of nuclear war.[46] Henry Wallace agreed and pushed Truman to pursue international control of atomic weapons more aggressively. In January 1946, Truman appointed Acheson, who had voiced similar concerns, to head a committee to tackle the problem. Acheson named Tennessee Valley Authority (TVA) Administrator David Lilienthal to chair a board of scientific advisors. Acheson confided to Lilienthal that Truman and Byrnes had neither "the facts nor an understanding of what was involved in the atomic energy issue, the most serious cloud hanging over the world." Commitments had been made, and, with Byrnes then in London, new ones were being made "without a knowledge of what the hell it is all about—literally!" Acheson bemoaned the fact that "the War Department, and really one man in the War Department, General Groves, has, by the power of veto on the ground of 'military security,' really been determining and almost running foreign policy."

The resulting Acheson-Lilienthal report, which the hardheaded Acheson described as "a brilliant and profound document," was largely the work of Oppenheimer.[47] Under the plan, an international Atomic Development Authority would oversee the mining, refining, and utilization of all the world's atomic raw materials, denaturing all fissionable material and making it available for peaceful uses. National activity in these "dangerous" areas would be outlawed. The plan intentionally minimized the need for on-site inspections to increase the chances that the Soviet Union would accept it.

Hopes for an international agreement were dashed when Truman and Byrnes appointed Byrnes's fellow South Carolinian, seventy-five-year-old financier

Bernard Baruch, to present the plan to the United Nations. Paying off another old political debt, Truman empowered him to revise it as he saw fit. Baruch had bankrolled Truman when he trailed in his 1940 Senate reelection bid and desperately needed funds. All involved, including Acheson, Lilienthal, and Oppenheimer, were furious, knowing that Baruch, an outspoken anti-Communist who viewed the bomb as the United States' "winning weapon," would reformulate the plan so that the Soviets would reject it out of hand. Lilienthal wrote in his journal, "When I read this news last night, I was quite sick. . . . We need a man who is young, vigorous, not vain, and who the Russians would feel isn't out simply to put them in a hole, not really caring about international cooperation. Baruch has none of these qualifications." Baruch's choice of fellow businessmen as advisors further infuriated those who had labored so hard to come up with a plan that would work. He decided not to include scientists because, he later explained, "I concluded that I would drop the scientists because as I told them, I knew all I wanted to know. It went boom and it killed millions of people." Vannevar Bush, who had served on the Acheson-Lilienthal Committee, dismissed Baruch's advisors as "Wall Streeters." He let Baruch know that he considered him and the rest of the crew completely unqualified for the job. Baruch announced that he would turn to Groves and the industrialists for advice on technical matters. Facing widespread criticism, Baruch finally relented and asked Oppenheimer to come on board as chief scientific advisor. "Don't let those associates of mine worry you," he told the physicist. "Hancock is pretty 'Right,' but [winking] I'll watch him. Searls is smart as a whip, but he sees Reds under every bed." He said they would have to begin "preparing the American people for a refusal by Russia." Oppenheimer declined the invitation.[48]

Baruch proceeded to amend the original proposal, larding it with inspections and other provisions that the Soviets would be certain to reject. Not only did Acheson and Lilienthal try to convince him to remove those provisions, Truman and Byrnes did too. Baruch remained adamant, threatening to resign if his plan was not adopted, and Truman, in a colossal failure of presidential leadership, backed down. On the eve of Baruch's submitting the plan to the United Nations on June 14, Byrnes admitted to Acheson that appointing Baruch was "the worst mistake I have ever made." Even Truman later privately admitted that appointing Baruch was "the worst blunder I ever made."[49]

Soviet leaders waited ten days before lashing out at the U.S. proposal. *Pravda* charged that the Baruch plan was "a product of atomic diplomacy, [and] reflects the obvious tendency toward world domination." The plan made it clear that the United States intends "to consolidate [its] monopoly" on the production of "atomic weapons." *Pravda* pointed out that the U.S. government had contracted production of bombs "to private monopolistic firms such as E. I. du Pont de

Financier Bernard Baruch (pictured here in 1920), whom Truman appointed to present the U.S. plan for international atomic control to the United Nations. Baruch rejected input from scientists and amended the original proposal, larding it with inspections and other provisions that the Russians would be certain to reject.

Nemours, whose entire pre-war outlook was connected by a thousand threads to the German I. G. Farbenindustrie."[50] The Soviets submitted a counterplan of their own, which would ban production, stockpiling, and use of atomic weapons. Existing stockpiles would be destroyed within three months.

The U.S. decision to proceed with its July 1 atomic bomb test in the Bikini Atoll in the Marshall Islands sent the Soviets another chilling message about U.S. intentions. The General Assembly of the Universalist Church denounced the tests as being "offensive to the very purpose of the Christian spirit."[51] Ickes described the Bikini tests as "diplomacy by intimidation" and noted that if it were the Soviets carrying them out, "Americans would find cause for deep concern about the future peace of the world." Raymond Gram Swing told his ABC Radio listeners that many Americans, including atomic scientists and members of Congress, had protested the decision. "On the one hand we're striving to rid the world of a weapon which may set back civilization for centuries. . . . On the other hand we're training ourselves in the use of this very weapon. So we strive to save civilization, and we learn how to wreck it, all on the same weekend." The Soviets, predictably, responded in similar fashion. *Pravda*'s Boris Izakov wondered why the Americans would go to such lengths to improve their bombs if they were serious about disarmament.[52]

There was indeed a madness to the unfolding nuclear arms race that no one expressed better than Lewis Mumford when he first learned that the test was to occur. In an article in Norman Cousins's *Saturday Review* titled "Gentlemen, You Are Mad!" Mumford wrote:

> We in America are living among madmen. Madmen govern our affairs in the name of order and security. The chief madmen claim the titles of

Explosion during the July 1946 Bikini atomic bomb tests, which Harold Ickes described as "diplomacy by intimidation" designed to impress the Soviet Union.

general, admiral, senator, scientist, administrator, Secretary of State, even President. And the fatal symptom of their madness is this: they have been carrying through a series of acts which will lead eventually to the destruction of mankind, under the solemn conviction that they are normal, responsible people, living sane lives, and working for reasonable ends.

Soberly, day after day, the madmen continue to go through the undeviating motions of madness: motions so stereotyped, so commonplace, that they seem the normal motions of normal men, not the mass compulsions of people bent on total death. Without a public mandate of any kind, the madmen have taken it upon themselves to lead us by gradual stages to that final act of madness which will corrupt the face of the earth and blot out the nations of men, possibly put an end to all life on the planet itself.[53]

Henry Wallace tried to stop the madness. In July 1946, he wrote a long memo to Truman, repudiating the "growing feeling . . . that another war is coming and the only way that we can head it off is to arm ourselves to the teeth . . . all of past history indicates that an armament race does not lead to peace but to war." He saw the coming months as very possibly "the crucial period which will decide whether the civilized world will go down in destruction after the five or ten years needed for several nations to arm themselves with atomic bombs." He urged Truman to consider how "American actions since V-J Day appear to other nations," pointing to "$13 billion for the War and Navy Departments, the Bikini tests of the atomic bomb and continued production of bombs, the plan to arm Latin America with our weapons, production of B-29s and planned production of B-36s, and the effort to secure air bases spread over half the globe from which the other half of the globe can be bombed.... [This] make[s] it appear either (1) that we are preparing ourselves to win the war which we regard as inevitable or (2) that we are trying to build up a predominance of force to intimidate the rest of mankind. How would it look to us if Russia had the atomic bomb and we did not, if Russia had 10,000-mile bombers and air bases within a thousand miles of our coastlines and we did not?"

Wallace called for sharply cutting defense spending, because maintaining peace by a "predominance of forces is no longer possible." In 1938, the United States spent less than $1 billion on national defense. Now, he calculated, the War and Navy Departments, war liquidation, and interest on public debt and veterans' benefits, representing the cost of past wars, consumed $28 billion, or 80 percent, of the current $36 billion budget. Wallace reiterated scientists' warnings that "atomic warfare is cheap" and even having ten times as many bombs as one's enemy gives no decisive advantage. "And most important, the very fact that several nations have atomic bombs will inevitably result in a neurotic, fear-ridden, itching-trigger psychology. . . . In a world armed with atomic weapons, some incident will lead to the use of those weapons." He forcefully dismissed those advocating a "preventive war," whose "scheme is not only immoral but stupid." The only solution, he concluded, "consists of mutual trust and confidence among nations, atomic disarmament, and an effective system of enforcing that disarmament." [54]

Wallace's peace offensive was aided by two significant publications that summer. In late August, *The New Yorker* devoted an entire issue to John Hersey's "Hiroshima" that did more to humanize the victims of the atomic bombings than any other contemporary English-language publication. In September, *Look* magazine began publishing a four-part series by Elliott Roosevelt that detailed how his father's and Stalin's plans for postwar peace and collaboration were derailed by Truman and Churchill. Truman would later dismiss Roosevelt's son as the "product of a piss erection."

Wallace understood the urgency of the situation. He looked forward to a major address on September 12 in New York's Madison Square Garden. Before delivering the speech, Wallace went over it with Truman, who repeatedly expressed his agreement. Truman told reporters beforehand that he had read it and concurred entirely with its sentiments. In New York, with twenty thousand in attendance, Wallace sat on stage with Paul Robeson as Claude Pepper told the crowd, "With conservative Democrats and reactionary Republicans making our foreign policy as they are today, it is all we can do to keep foolish people from having us pull a Hitler blitzkrieg and drop our atomic bombs on the Russian people." [55] When Wallace's turn came, he delivered a powerful plea for peace:

> Tonight I want to talk about peace—and how to get peace. Never have the common people of all lands so longed for peace. Yet, never . . . have they feared war so much. . . . We cannot rest in the assurance that we invented the atom bomb. . . . He who trusts in the atom bomb will sooner or later perish by the atom bomb. . . . The British imperialistic policy in the Near East alone, combined with Russian retaliation, would lead the United States straight to war. . . . We are reckoning with a force which cannot be handled successfully by a "Get tough with Russia" policy. . . . This does not mean appeasement. We want to be met halfway. . . . And I believe that we can get cooperation once Russia understands that our primary objective is neither saving the British Empire nor purchasing oil in the Near East with the lives of American soldiers. We cannot allow national oil rivalries to force us into war . . . we have no more business in the political affairs of eastern Europe than Russia has in the political affairs of Latin America, western Europe, and the United States. We may not like what Russia does in eastern Europe. Her type of land reform, industrial expropriation, and suppression of basic liberties offends the great majority of the people of the United States. . . . But at the same time we have to recognize that the Balkans are closer to Russia than to us—and that Russia cannot permit either England or the United States to dominate the politics of that area. . . . Russian ideas of social-economic justice are going to govern nearly a third of the world. Our ideas of free-enterprise democracy will govern much of the rest. The two ideas will endeavor to prove which can deliver the most satisfaction to the common man in their respective areas of political dominance. . . . Under friendly peaceful competition the Russian world and the American world will gradually become more alike. The Russians will be forced to grant more and more of the personal freedoms and we shall become more and more absorbed with the problems of social-economic justice. Russia must be convinced that we are not planning for war against her and we must be certain that Russia is not carrying on territorial expansion or world domination . . . the United Nations should have . . . control of the strategically located air bases with which the United States and Britain have encircled the world. And not only should individual nations be prohibited from manufacturing atomic bombs, guided missiles, and military aircraft for bombing purposes, but no nation should be allowed to spend on its military establishment more than perhaps 15 percent of its budget . . . we who look on this war-with-Russia talk as

Secretary of Commerce Henry Wallace arrives at the White House. After his call for a more conciliatory approach to dealing with the Soviet Union in his September 12, 1946, speech at Madison Square Garden, Truman fired him. Cold War hard-liners such as James Byrnes helped convince Truman that Wallace had to go.

criminal foolishness must carry our message direct to the people—even though we may be called communists because we dare to speak out.[56]

The speech was absolutely incendiary. Republican Senator Robert Taft accused Truman of betraying Byrnes, who was irate over being so publicly repudiated. The *New York Times'* James Reston wrote that Truman was the only person in Washington who saw no difference between what Wallace advocated and what Truman and Byrnes had been proposing.[57] The State Department let it be known that this was more embarrassing to Byrnes than if someone had yanked off his pants in the middle of the Paris conference. British officials were furious. Experts in the British Foreign Office said, "there is no such thing as the government of the United States" and the London press sneered that American foreign policy is still "in the hillybilly stage."[58]

Many rallied to Wallace's defense. Eleanor Roosevelt approved Wallace's remarks: "he tried to make clear that we neither approved of British imperialism nor of Soviet aggression. He stated that we wanted to be friendly with Russia, that we wanted to meet her half-way, but that she also had to meet us half-way."[59]

Having become an object of international derision, Truman attempted to tell reporters that he meant only to defend Wallace's right to express his opinions, not the content of his speech. He later denied that he had read and approved the entire speech in advance.

In the midst of the controversy, someone leaked Wallace's July 23 memo to Truman in which he identified the "fatal defect" in the Baruch plan. Several Soviet newspapers published it in its entirety.

That defect is the scheme ... of arriving at international agreements by 'easy stages,' of requiring other nations to enter into binding commitments not to conduct research into the military uses of atomic energy and to disclose their uranium and thorium resources while the United States retains the right to withhold its technical knowledge of atomic energy until the international control and inspection system is working to our satisfaction.

Is it any wonder that the Russians did not show any great enthusiasm for our plan? ... I think we would react as the Russians appear to have done. We would have put up counterproposal for the record, but our real effort would go into trying to make a bomb so that our bargaining position would be equalized....

... Realistically, Russia has two cards which she can use in negotiating with us: (1) our lack of information on the state of her scientific and technical progress on atomic energy and (2) our ignorance of her uranium and thorium resources. These cards are nothing like as powerful as our cards—a stockpile of bombs, manufacturing plants in actual production, B-29s and B-36s, and our bases covering half the globe. Yet we are in effect asking her to reveal her only two cards immediately—telling her that after we have seen her cards we will decide whether we want to continue to play the game.[60]

Truman insisted that Wallace stop talking about foreign policy while the postwar conference of the Council of Foreign Ministers was taking place. Byrnes had cabled Truman from Paris to complain that Wallace's speech and memo had thrown the meeting into complete disarray. Byrnes and Baruch were both threatening to resign. Truman feared that Forrestal and Secretary of War Robert Patterson would do likewise. He decided to fire Wallace and wrote a scathing letter demanding his resignation. Wallace immediately phoned the president to say that the letter would not reflect well on Truman if it got out. Truman immediately sent someone over to pick it up. No copy remains. Only Truman's diary entry that night gives some indication of what he might have written. He described Wallace as

a pacifist one hundred percent. He wants us to disband our armed forces, give Russia our atomic secrets and trust a bunch of adventurers in the Kremlin Politbureau. I do not understand a "dreamer" like that. The German-American Bund under Fritz Kuhn was not half so dangerous. The Reds, phonies and "parlor pinks" seem to be banded together and are becoming a national danger. I am afraid they are a sabotage front for Uncle Joe Stalin.[61]

With Wallace's departure, the last chance to avert the Cold War and nuclear arms race disappeared. That night, September 20, 1946, Wallace told a national radio audience:

> Winning the peace is more important than high office. It is more important than any consideration of party politics. The success or failure of our foreign policy will mean the difference between life and death for our children and our grandchildren. It will mean the difference between the life and death of our civilization. It may mean the difference between the existence and the extinction of man and of the world. It is therefore of supreme importance, and we should every one of us regard it as a holy duty, to join the fight for winning the peace. . . . I wish to make it clear again that I am against all types of imperialism and aggression, whether they are of Russian, British, or American origin. . . . The success of any policy rests ultimately upon the confidence and the will of the people. There can be no basis for such success unless the people know and understand the issues, unless they are given all the facts and unless they seize the opportunity to take part in the framing of foreign policy through full and open debate. In this debate, we must respect the rights and interests of other peoples, just as we expect them to respect ours. How we resolve this debate, as I said in my New York speech, will determine not whether we live in "one world" but whether we live at all. I intend to carry on the fight for peace.[62]

Support for Wallace had poured in throughout the controversy. Albert Einstein wrote, "I cannot refrain from expressing to you my high and unconditional admiration for your letter to the President of July 23rd. There is a deep understanding concerning the factual and psychological situation and a far-reaching perception of present American foreign policy. Your courageous intervention deserves the gratitude of all of us who observe the present attitude of our government with grave concern."[63]

With Wallace gone, the United States plunged headlong into Cold War both at home and abroad. On September 24, the long-awaited report from White House counsel Clark Clifford and his assistant George Elsey arrived. The comprehensive review of Soviet actions, intentions, and capabilities was intended to show that the Soviets had regularly violated their agreements. It painted a dire picture of Soviet efforts "to weaken the position and to destroy the prestige of the United States in Europe, Asia, and South America" so they could rule the world, while sowing discord in the United States through the Communist Party. The United States needed to respond by beefing up its atomic arsenal, expanding its network of overseas bases, strengthening its military capabilities, and mobilizing its resources to "assist all democracies which are in any way menaced or endangered by the U.S.S.R." They failed, however, to document Soviet perfidy in regard to treaty obligations, admitting that "it is difficult to adduce direct evidence of literal violations."[64]

In a penetrating critique of the report's distortions, historian Melvyn Leffler wrote, "Clifford and Elsey ignored actions that might have injected hues of gray into their black-and-white characterization of Soviet foreign policy," such as all the instances where the Soviets had honored or exceeded their agreements, withdrawn their troops, allowed free elections, and discouraged insurrectionary activity. "Double standards and self-deception repeatedly crept into the Clifford-Elsey report," he noted, adding

> Truman's advisors did not ask how America's own questionable record
> of compliance affected Soviet behavior. They did not acknowledge that
> [General Lucius] Clay and other War Department officials consistently
> identified France, not Russia, as the principal source of U.S. problems in
> Germany. They suspected that any Soviet interest in German unification
> masked the Kremlin's quest to gain leverage over all of Germany, but
> conveniently dismissed the American desire to dilute Soviet influence in
> the east and to orient all of Germany to the West. Likewise, Clifford and
> Elsey pointed to the retention of Russian troops in Iran as irrefutable proof
> of the Soviet desire to dominate Iran and gain control of Middle Eastern
> oil. They did not say (and may not have known) that, at the very time they
> were writing their report, State Department officials and military planners
> were contending that the U.S. troops must remain beyond the stipulated
> deadlines for their withdrawal in Iceland, the Azores, Panama, the
> Galapagos, and other locations in order to augment American bargaining
> leverage for postwar base and military transit rights.

Leffler also accused them of presenting "a totally misleading rendition of Soviet capabilities." Clifford later admitted that it was the kind of "black and white" analysis that Truman liked.[65]

Clifford and Elsey ruled out further efforts to negotiate with the Soviets. "The language of military power," they wrote, "is the only language" the Soviets understand. Hence, they warned ominously, "the United States must be prepared to wage atomic and biological warfare" against the Soviet Union.[66] Truman ordered Clifford to round up all ten copies of the report and lock them up. "If this got out," he snapped, "it would blow the roof off the White House, it would blow the roof off the Kremlin." It would also prove that Wallace, whom Truman had fired four days earlier, had been correct in all his warnings about the hard-line, confrontational direction of U.S. policy.[67]

In his response to Clifford and Elsey's questions, Admiral Leahy provided Truman and Clifford with copies of the will of Tsar Peter the Great, in which he urged the Russians to conquer large parts of Asia and Europe and maintain a constant war footing. No one questioned the veracity of this notorious eighteenth-century forgery. Truman cited it on several occasions, drawing continuities between tsarist policies and those of the present Stalinist regime.[68]

While the Soviets were imposing friendly left-wing governments in their sphere, the British were imposing right-wing governments in theirs. In Greece, the British army toppled the popular leftist National Liberation Front and restored the monarchy and right-wing dictatorship. Jailing of critics and other repressive measures soon sparked a Communist-led uprising. The Yugoslavs provided support but the Soviets did not, as Stalin abided by his wartime agreement with Churchill that placed Greece within the British sphere of influence.

Following the severe winter of 1946–1947, financially strapped Great Britain asked the United States to take the lead in defeating the Greek insurgents and modernizing the Turkish army. One State Department official later commented, "Great Britain had within the hour handed the job of world leadership . . . to the United States."[69] But the war-weary public and the Republican-controlled Congress, which was intent upon reducing taxes and cutting back U.S. international commitments, stood in Truman's way. The Republicans had trounced the Democrats in the November 1946 congressional elections, employing the kind of Red-baiting tactics that would become so familiar over the next decade. The Republican National Committee chairman declared the election a choice between "communism and Republicanism" and charged that "alien-minded radicals" had seized control of the Democratic Party.[70]

Congress was reluctant to foot the bill for Truman's costly Greek and Turkish initiatives. Soviet military probes in the Mediterranean had largely ceased, and tensions between the United States and the Soviet Union had again abated. Senator Arthur Vandenberg told Truman that he would have to "scare the hell out of the country" if he hoped to win approval for a global anti-Communist campaign that would change foreign policy "from top to bottom." Dean Acheson took the lead in crafting the administration's message, framing it as a struggle between freedom and totalitarianism. Only a few months earlier, he had complained about supporting the "reactionary regime" in Greece. But the Turkish crisis had convinced him otherwise.[71] The son of a clergyman, Acheson believed that life was a "pilgrimage from birth to death through a battleground between good and evil."[72] He told a group of congressional leaders, "Like apples in a barrel infected by one rotten one, the corruption of Greece would infect Iran and then all to the east. It would also carry infection to Africa through Asia Minor and Egypt, and to Europe through Italy and France, already threatened by the

Truman addresses a joint session of Congress in March 1947. The president asked for $400 million to finance efforts in Greece and Turkey and, in what came to be known as the Truman Doctrine, declared that the United States must support "free peoples who are resisting subjugation by armed minorities or outside pressure."

strongest domestic Communist parties in Western Europe." He called it an "Armageddon."[73]

George Kennan, who was head of the State Department policy planning staff, and others, including George C. Marshall, whom Truman had picked to replace Byrnes as secretary of state, George Elsey, and Soviet expert Chip Bohlen, found this farfetched. Truman sided with Acheson against those who advised him to tone down the rhetoric. Addressing both houses of Congress, Truman appealed for $400 million to finance efforts in Greece and Turkey and declared that the United States must support "free peoples who are resisting subjugation by armed minorities or outside pressure,"[74] thence to be known as the Truman Doctrine.

After a heated debate, Congress fell into line. Many members, however, were troubled by Truman's call to arms and support for blatantly undemocratic and unpopular governments. Bernard Baruch described the speech as "tantamount to a declaration of . . . ideological or religious war."[75] Marshall criticized Truman's exaggerations. Walter Lippmann was so upset with the Truman Doctrine's overblown rhetoric and apparently open-ended commitment to intervention that he and Acheson almost came to blows at a Washington dinner party. Some, including Kennan, rejected Truman's justification for aiding Turkey, which faced no overt Soviet threat, and feared that Stalin would respond the way Truman would if the Soviets sent military aid to Mexico.

Once again, Henry Wallace led the opposition. The day after Truman's speech, he took to the airwaves on the NBC radio network to decry the "utter nonsense" of describing the Turkish or Greek governments as democratic and accused Truman of "betraying" Roosevelt's vision for world peace. "When President Truman proclaims the world-wide conflict between east and west," he warned, "he is telling the Soviet leaders that we are preparing for eventual war." People the world over were feeling hungry and insecure and demanding change.

Trying to thwart that change was not only futile, it was counterproductive. "Once America stands for opposition to change," he prophesied, "we are lost. America will become the most hated nation in the world." Military aid was not the answer. "Truman's policy," he predicted, "will spread communism in Europe and Asia. When Truman offers unconditional aid to King George of Greece, he is acting as the best salesman communism ever had."[76]

The Soviets responded angrily. *Pravda* accused the United States of "imperialist expansion under the guise of charity" and trying to "extend the Monroe Doctrine to the Old World."[77] Howard K. Smith, who was in Moscow covering the conference of the Council of Foreign Ministers for CBS, wrote that Truman's message had changed the atmosphere in Moscow and throughout Eastern Europe. In late May, the Soviets sponsored a Communist coup overthrowing the democratically elected government in Hungary. The *New York Times* opined, "The coup in Hungary is Russia's answer to our action in Greece and Turkey."[78]

The Greek civil war grew bloodier, and U.S. personnel began arriving in the war zone in June 1947. They used Greece to test tactics, some new and some old, that would later be employed in Vietnam, such as the destruction of unions, torture, napalming villages, forced mass deportations to concentration camps without trial or charges, mass imprisonment of wives and children of subversives, mass executions ordered by military court martials, and censorship of the press. Greece was thus kept in the hands of monarchists and wealthy businessmen, many of them Nazi collaborators; the victims were primarily the workers and peasants who'd resisted the Nazis.

Fighting raged on for a couple more years. Historian George Herring described it as "an especially savage conflict with atrocities on both sides in which even children became pawns."[79] In addition to sending a large contingent of "advisors," the United States armed the right-wing Greek monarchy to the teeth.

The Soviet Union temporarily assisted the left-wing forces but then cut off aid. In February 1948, Stalin ordered Yugoslavia's Marshal Josip Broz Tito to stop supporting the "guerrilla movement" in Greece, precipitating an open rift with his closest ally. When the Yugoslavs pushed back, Stalin thundered, "they have no prospect of success at all. What do you think, that Great Britain and the United States—the United States the most powerful nation in the world— will permit you to break their line of communication in the Mediterranean Sea! Nonsense. And we have no navy. The uprising in Greece must be stopped, and as quickly as possible." When Tito refused to go along with the Soviet demands, the Cominform expelled Yugoslavia.[80] The State Department reported, "For the first time in history we may now have within the international community a communist state . . . independent of Moscow. . . . A new factor of fundamental and profound significance has been introduced into the world communist movement by the demonstration that the Kremlin can be successfully defied by one of its own minions."[81] Despite providing covert support for Tito, the United States never adjusted its rhetoric to reflect the fact that international communism was not as monolithic as once believed.

Churchill later told an American journalist, "Stalin never broke his word to me. We agreed on the Balkans. I said he could have Romania and Bulgaria and he said we could have Greece. . . . He signed a slip of paper and he never broke his word. We saved Greece that way."[82]

Stalin's halting of support for the uprising spelled doom for the rebels, and Truman heralded the United States' victory. The Greek people weren't so sure. More than 100,000 people died, and 800,000 became refugees. The Greek action also had other troubling implications. Though it was a largely homegrown insurgency, Truman treated it as part of a Soviet plan for world domination, setting the stage for U.S. intervention to support right-wing governments in the name of anticommunism. The United States substituted force for diplomacy, embracing unilateralism instead of the United Nations and repression instead of treating the socioeconomic causes of popular discontent. Historian Arnold Offner concluded, "The legacy of this action was that for about three decades, successive Greek governments used the state apparatus—decrees, the police, the military, and a Central Service of Information modeled on the CIA—to systematically persecute their former enemies and deny them their basic rights and livelihood."[83]

Marshall adopted a more positive approach to the crisis in Europe: he invited European countries to come up with a plan for economic recovery and development, which the United States would finance. Seventeen European countries requested $27 billion. The United States eventually spent $13 billion between 1948 and 1952.[84] Great Britain, France, and Germany were the largest recipients, adding to the Soviet fears that the United States was recklessly restoring German power and creating a Western bloc. The Soviet Union and Eastern Europe were invited to participate but were offered terms that U.S. policy makers knew Stalin would reject. The Soviets were coming to realize that their earlier expectations that Western unity would run aground on the shoals of imperialist rivalry were mistaken.

Truman described his new doctrine and the Marshall Plan as "two halves of the same walnut."[85] Abandoning all hope for continued collaboration with the West, the Soviets offered Eastern Europe its own Molotov Plan. They also cracked down with renewed intensity. The last remaining non-Communists were soon forced out of government in Bulgaria. Early the following year, the Red Army helped overthrow the Czech government, putting an end to Czech democracy.

George Kennan provided the theoretical rationale for the new U.S. policy. His article titled "The Sources of Soviet Conduct" appeared in the July issue of

*A man labors in West Berlin on a Marshall Plan–funded project (as
indicated by the sign in the background) in June 1948. The United States
spent $13 billion on European recovery between 1948 and 1952. With
Britain, France, and Germany as its largest recipients, the plan exacerbated
Soviet fears of both a rearmed Germany and capitalist encirclement.*

Foreign Affairs under the pseudonym "X." A Soviet expert who had served in
Moscow in the 1930s and 1940s, Kennan emphasized the Soviet Union's global
appetites and laid out a plan to "contain" Soviet expansion with the goal of breaking up Soviet power and maintaining U.S. hegemony. The previous October, he
had taken a more nuanced stance, writing, "I think it is a mistake to say that the
Soviet leaders wish to establish a Communist form of government in the ring
of states surrounding the Soviet Union on the west and south. What they do
wish to do is to establish in those states governments amenable to their own
influence and authority. The main thing is that these governments should follow
Moscow's leadership.... In certain countries which are already extensively under
Soviet influence, as for example Poland, there has been as yet no effort to establish what we might call a Communist form of government."[86]

The distinction between the two interpretations of Soviet postwar intentions
is crucial. Not only did the Soviet Union not have a blueprint for postwar Sovi-
etization of Eastern Europe, it hoped to maintain friendly and collaborative relations with its wartime allies. The last thing it wanted was confrontation with the

George F. Kennan, a Soviet expert who served in the U.S. Embassy in Moscow in the 1930s and 1940s, provided the rationale for U.S. policy with his "containment" theory.

West. As Russian scholars Vladislav Zubok and Constantine Pleshakov explain, there was "no master plan in the Kremlin, and Stalin's ambitions had always been severely limited by the terrible devastation of the USSR during World War II and the existence of the American atomic monopoly."[87]

Unfortunately, Kennan's *Foreign Affairs* article offered a monochromatic analysis of a Soviet Union bent on conquest. Kennan would long regret that his words were interpreted as support for the kind of militarized response to the Soviet Union that he later abhorred. In looking back, he was appalled by even the more measured message in his telegram, which struck him as if it had been written "by the Daughters of the American Revolution" during an anti-Communist tirade.[88] Journalist Walter Lippmann criticized Kennan for resorting to military rather than peaceful settlements and for the global sweep of his containment policy, which failed to differentiate between vital interests and peripheral ones. He feared that the policy would mean "unending intervention in all the countries that are supposed to 'contain' the Soviet Union." And it would undermine the Constitution by vesting too much power in the president as commander in chief.[89]

While Truman scared the hell out of the American people about Communists abroad, the Republicans did the same regarding Communists at home. Truman decided to steal the Republicans' thunder. Just nine days after delivering his call for an international crusade against communism, he unveiled an elaborate program to root out "subversives" working for the federal government, even though, as White House aide Clark Clifford later admitted, "the President didn't attach fundamental importance to the so-called Communist scare. He thought it was a lot of baloney. But political pressures were such that he had to recognize it. . . .

We did not believe there was a real problem. A problem was being manufactured. There was a certain element of hysteria."[90] Truman mandated loyalty checks on all government employees. Those accused could neither confront their accusers nor ascertain the basis of the accusations. Having the wrong views on religion, sexual behavior, foreign policy, or race could brand one as disloyal. An Interior Department Loyalty Board chairman observed, "Of course the fact that a person believes in racial equality doesn't prove that he's a communist, but it certainly makes you look twice, doesn't it?" The FBI conducted field investigations of suspect employees. Even Truman feared that under J. Edgar Hoover, the FBI could become "an American Gestapo." Clifford believed that Hoover "was very close to being an American fascist."[91] The government organized large meetings at which employees sang "God Bless America" and took freedom pledges. Loyalty boards fired approximately three hundred government employees outright and forced ten times that number to resign between 1947 and 1951, thereby institutionalizing guilt by association and encouraging a stultifying conformity in which much of the nation equated dissent with disloyalty.

In October 1947, the House Un-American Activities Committee (HUAC) held public hearings on Communist influence in Hollywood. The committee called eleven unfriendly witnesses, including some of Hollywood's most prominent writers and directors. Invoking the First Amendment, ten refused to answer questions about whether they were members of the Communist Party, which was perfectly legal, and were cited for contempt of Congress. The eleventh, playwright Bertolt Brecht, denied being a Communist and escaped to East Germany. Brecht had earlier moved to Hollywood to escape from the Nazis. Rather than stand up for their employees, Hollywood studio executives denounced the "Hollywood Ten" and pledged not to hire anyone with suspect affiliations. Among the friendly witnesses who testified that the Communist menace in Hollywood was real was Screen Actors Guild president Ronald Reagan. Robert Taylor, Gary Cooper, and Walt Disney agreed. Far greater numbers of Hollywood celebrities publicly denounced the congressional witch hunts, including Humphrey Bogart, Gregory Peck, Gene Kelly, William Wyler, Lucille Ball, Frank Sinatra, Burt Lancaster, Edward G. Robinson, Lauren Bacall, Orson Welles, Katharine Hepburn, Pete Seeger, Henry Fonda, Ethel Barrymore, Benny Goodman, and Groucho Marx. Despite those efforts, all ten were convicted of contempt the following year and sentenced to prison.

In July 1947, following five months of hearings and heated debate, Congress passed the greatest military reform in U.S. history. The National Security Act created the National Military Establishment (later called the Department of Defense), consisting of the Departments of the Army, Navy, and Air Force, headed by a secretary of defense, and a Joint Chiefs of Staff (JCS). Truman appointed the anti-Soviet hard-liner James Forrestal as the first secretary of defense. Creating a new U.S. Air Force separate from the army confirmed the importance of atomic warfare in future military planning.

The act also created the National Security Council, a War Council, the National Security Resources Board, and the Central Intelligence Agency, all of which Marshall opposed because they gave the military too much influence over foreign policy and abridged the constitutional authority of the president and secretary of state. Truman himself feared that the CIA could turn into a "Gestapo" or "military dictatorship." [92] The Agency's clandestine nature troubled Acheson, who wrote, "I had the gravest forebodings about this organization and warned the President that as set up neither he, the National Security Council, nor anyone else would be in a position to know what it was doing or to control it." Although the act specifically authorized the Agency only to collect, analyze, and disseminate intelligence, it also empowered it to perform "other functions and duties related to intelligence affecting the national security." The Agency used that vague wording to conduct hundreds of covert operations, including eighty-one during Truman's second term alone.

In late September 1947, Kennan urged Forrestal to establish a "guerrilla warfare corps"—a suggestion Forrestal heartily endorsed—although the JCS recommended against establishing a "separate guerrilla warfare school and corps." In December, Truman approved secret annex NSC 4-A, authorizing the CIA to conduct covert operations. He had dismantled the OSS's covert paramilitary operations capabilities in September 1945, but now he brought them back in force. In the summer of 1948, he approved NSC 10/2, which called for "propaganda, economic warfare; preventive direct action, including sabotage, anti-sabotage, demolition and evacuation measures; subversion against hostile states, including assistance to underground resistance movements, guerrillas and refugee liberation groups, and support of indigenous anti-Communist elements in threatened countries of the free world." These activities were to be done in a way that would always afford the U.S. government plausible deniability. In August 1948, Truman approved NSC 20, which authorized guerrilla operations in the Soviet Union and Eastern Europe.[93]

Even the seemingly benign Marshall Plan provided a cover for subversion. Half of the 10 percent of the money allocated for administrative costs was siphoned off to fund covert actions through the CIA's Office of Policy Coordination, whose director, Frank Wisner, would actually report to the secretaries of defense and state. Tim Weiner described it as "a global money-laundering scheme." Colonel R. Allen Griffin, who headed the Marshall Plan's Far East division, confessed, "We'd look the other way and give them a little help. Tell them to stick their hand in our pocket." Kennan, the architect of this effort, described it as "the inauguration of organized political warfare." With the diverted funds, the CIA established a network of phony front organizations that recruited foreign agents as frontline warriors in the propaganda wars that ensued. Sometimes they went beyond propaganda, infiltrating unions and other existing organizations and establishing underground groups. Forrestal and the Pentagon wanted the programs to go further, including "guerrilla movements . . . underground armies . . . sabotage and assassination."[94]

Some of the diverted Marshall Aid money went to supporting a guerrilla army in Ukraine called Nightingale, which had been established by the Wehrmacht in the spring of 1941 with the help of Stephan Bandera, head of the Ukrainian National Organization's more radical wing OUN-B. The following year, Mikola Lebed founded the organization's terrorist arm, the Ukrainian Insurgent Army. It was made up of ultranationalist Ukrainians, including Nazi collaborators, who wreaked havoc in the region, assisting in or directly carrying out the murder of thousands of Jews, Soviets, and Poles, and occasionally also fighting the Germans, who opposed OUN-B's plan for a separate Ukrainian state. In 1944, Lebed helped form the Supreme Ukrainian Liberation Council (UHVR), which served as the organization's political arm.

At the end of the war, Lebed fled to Rome and contacted the Allies. The U.S. Army Counterintelligence Corps started working with him in 1947 and smuggled him to Munich, where he began collaborating with the CIA the following year. In June 1949, the CIA brought him to the United States. When the Justice Department later tried to deport him, Allen Dulles claimed he was of "inestimable value to this Agency" and was assisting in "operations of the first importance."[95]

Among those operations, Wisner's "Special Projects," was one masterminded by Munich-based CIA officer Steve Tanner, who, in late 1948, started working with the UHVR. The following year, he readied operatives to infiltrate back into Ukraine. On September 5, 1949, the CIA parachuted the first of its Ukrainian agents back into the country. The operation continued for another five years but had little success. Although the Soviets made quick work of most of the infiltrators, such operations clearly signaled the lengths to which the U.S. was willing to go to dislodge Soviet control in Eastern Europe.[96]

The Soviets tightened their grip. The last remaining non-Communists had already been driven out of the Bulgarian and Czechoslovakian administrations. Czechoslovakian Foreign Minister Jan Masaryk's manner of death—falling or being pushed out of his bathroom window—would come to haunt Forrestal. After Soviet imposition of a puppet regime in Czechoslovakia, relations between the Soviet Union and the United States froze over. The brutal Eastern European dictatorships would last another four decades.

The CIA's first covert operation involved subverting Italy's 1948 election, thus ensuring a Christian Democratic victory over the Communists. In that case, as in many throughout the post–World War II era, the U.S. commitment to "democracy" went only so far. Kennan told Marshall that a Communist victory would undermine "our whole position in the Mediterranean." He preferred to see the Italian government outlaw the Communist Party and precipitate a violent civil war, giving the United States an excuse to intervene militarily.[97]

Nor was democracy a major consideration when the CIA took over responsibility for running the Gehlen Organization in Germany from the U.S. Army. General Reinhard Gehlen, a former Nazi who had run intelligence in Eastern Europe and the Soviet Union for Hitler, recruited a network of Nazi war criminals drawn in part from the Sicherheitsdienst (SD), Gestapo, and Waffen-SS. The Gehlen Org, as it was known, provided extensive intelligence on Eastern Europe, always painting the worst possible picture of Soviet actions and threats. A retired CIA official acknowledged, "The agency loved Gehlen because he fed us what we wanted to hear. We used his stuff constantly, and we fed it to everybody else: the Pentagon; the White House; the newspapers. They loved it, too. But it was hyped up Russian boogeyman junk, and it did a lot of damage to this country."[98]

At war's end, U.S. policy makers decided not to allow their booming military industrial machine to erode. In 1948, 62 percent of all federal research and development was military-related. The air force claimed a large share. General Carl Spaatz testified before Congress that "the next war will be preponderantly an air war."[99] The United States began missile research, employing many of the hundreds of scientists it had secreted out of Germany, including almost the entirety of Wernher von Braun's rocket staff at Peenemünde. Some of the scientists had been involved in human experimentation and Nazi slave-labor programs. Equally disturbing, during the Tokyo war criminal trials, U.S. authorities secretly granted blanket immunity to Japanese officers and researchers involved with the notorious Unit 731 in exchange for sharing the results of lethal experiments conducted on three thousand prisoners in Manchuria. Meanwhile, the air force, competing with the army and the navy over funding and prestige, employed its own in-house think tank to design strategies that would promote the air force's primacy. In 1948, this division transformed itself into the independent RAND Corporation. During these years, U.S. war plans became increasingly reliant on atomic weapons and air warfare, which were determined to be far cheaper than conventional military forces. By the middle of the next decade, the air force would consume nearly as much of the defense budget as the army and navy combined.

The evolution of U.S. military strategy enhanced the strategic importance of the Middle East. By 1947, U.S. war plans called for U.S. air attacks on Soviet targets from bases in the Middle East, Okinawa, and Britain. Of particular importance was the base at Cairo-Suez, from which U.S. bombers could reach 84 percent of Soviet oil refining capacity. As part of this strategy, the United States bolstered its military capabilities in Turkey, enhancing that country's ability to impede a Soviet offensive in the region.[100]

Nineteen forty-eight was also the year that the Israeli-Palestinian issue came to a head in a way that would plague U.S. policy for the next six decades plus. The situation was complicated by the fact that despite the procrustean efforts of U.S. policy makers, Middle East issues never fit neatly into the Cold War paradigm. U.S. policy makers tried to navigate among a number of constituencies with fundamentally different interests: reactionary Arab leaders who controlled vast oil resources as well as strategic bases and routes in the region; nationalist Arab masses, often living in squalid conditions; Palestinian victims of Israeli policy; Jewish victims of the Holocaust who had been desperate for a homeland; Jewish and later conservative voters in the United States, including Christian evangelicals, who staunchly defended Israeli actions; and a united Islamic world that opposed Israeli policy and sometimes the very existence of a Jewish state in their midst. The problem had already taken form while the region was under British control.

In 1915, using their usual divide-and-conquer strategy, the British promised the Arabs an independent state in order to foment an Arab rebellion against the Ottoman Empire. Then, in 1917, Arthur Balfour, Britain's secretary of state for foreign affairs, pledged support for a Jewish homeland in Palestine, which was home to 750,000 Arabs and 65,000 Jews. Arthur Koestler described this as one nation promising another nation the land of a third nation.[101]

At Versailles, in 1919, the delegates ratified the Balfour Declaration, giving Great Britain a mandate over Palestine. In 1922, the U.S. Congress also ratified the declaration. In the early years of the century, European Jews looking to relocate typically chose the United States, not Palestine, to which only 3 percent of European Jews emigrated prior to the 1930s. Sixty-eight percent went to the United States. But Jewish emigration to the United States was sharply curtailed by the restrictive immigration acts of 1921 and 1924. During the 1930s, Jews fleeing Nazi persecution raised the number of Jewish émigrés to Palestine substantially, angering the Arab inhabitants. Arab attacks on Jewish settlers increased as the Jewish population climbed to half a million, or 30 percent of the total population. Jews retaliated in kind.

Roosevelt vacillated in his support for a Jewish homeland. Not wanting to alienate the Saudis, whom the United States was courting for their oil, and wishing to gain a foothold in the Middle East to compete with Great Britain, he made contradictory commitments to Jews and Arabs. On his way back from Yalta, he met with Saudi King Ibn Saud and was surprised by the depths of his opposition to a Jewish homeland. Saud told him to establish a Jewish homeland in Germany: "Amends should be made by the criminal, not by the innocent bystander." Roosevelt reversed his earlier commitments and promised Saud that he would "do nothing to assist the Jews against the Arabs and . . . make no move hostile to the Arab people." [102] He also did little to help Jews escape from Nazi persecution. He was hindered by a State Department that was insensitive to the tragic plight of Jewish victims, even after early 1942, when word began to filter out about the Nazi extermination policies. The United States admitted only 160,000 European Jews between 1933 and 1942, increasing the Jewish population only from 3.6 to 3.7 percent of the overall U.S. population. [103]

At war's end, the British still dominated the area, with 200,000 troops at their Suez Canal base, air bases in Iraq and Sudan and air installations at Lydda in Palestine, naval bases in Bahrain and Aden and a naval presence in Haifa, and command of the eight thousand–strong Arab League in Transjordan. Determined to do nothing that would further antagonize the Arabs and jeopardize British interests, including oil from Iraq and Iran, they continued Neville Chamberlain's 1939 policy of restricting and then halting Jewish immigration. That did not, however, staunch the flow of Holocaust survivors and other Jewish émigrés streaming "illegally" into Palestine after the war. When the British cracked down, arresting more than two thousand Jews, the Jewish terrorist organization Irgun retaliated by bombing the British secretariat and military headquarters at the King David Hotel in Jerusalem, leaving ninety-one people dead.

In mid-1946, Truman decided to back a plan that would allow 100,000 European refugees to emigrate to Palestine but, instead of creating a separate Jewish state, would establish a single state with separate Jewish and Arab provinces. Jewish leaders were adamantly opposed to the plan. Truman devoted a cabinet lunch to discussing the Palestine problem. Acheson and Forrestal urged Truman to go forward with the plan. Henry Wallace was opposed. Wallace's diary entry sheds light on the discussion and Truman's attitude: "President Truman expressed himself as being very much 'put out' with the Jews. He said that 'Jesus Christ couldn't please them when he was here on earth, so how could anyone expect that I would have any luck?' Truman said he had no use for them and didn't care what happened to them." Wallace reminded him, "You must remember that it is easy for them to get into quite a state of mind because nearly all the Jews in the country have relatives in Europe and they know that about 5 million out of the 6 million Jews have been killed and that no other people have suffered in this way." Wallace wrote, "Jim Forrestal had previously undertaken to say that the Poles had suffered more than the Jews. Forrestal brought up the question of the oil in Saudi Arabia and said if another war came along we would need the oil in Saudi Arabia. President Truman said he wanted to handle this problem not from the standpoint of bringing in oil but from the standpoint of what is right." [104]

In early 1947, Great Britain announced that along with its retrenchment in Greece and Turkey, it would terminate its mandate over Palestine and refer the problem to the United Nations without recommending a solution. In May, the Soviets surprised U.S. officials when Deputy Foreign Minister Andrei Gromyko unfurled the Soviet position before the UN General Assembly. Citing the horrors of the Holocaust, the fact that both Jews and Arabs had historical claims to the land, and the ways in which British malfeasance had exacerbated tensions between them, Gromyko said, the Soviets preferred a binational or federal state. However, if that weren't possible, they would support a two-state solution, which the Jewish militants greatly preferred and the Arabs adamantly opposed. In late 1947, the United Nations, despite fierce Arab opposition, endorsed the partition of Palestine into two independent states. The Soviets supported this solution; the British and the Arabs opposed it; and the United States equivocated but finally came on board. Arab violence flared in Palestine as soon as the partition vote was announced.

On May 14, 1948, the state of Israel proclaimed its existence. Eleven minutes later, the United States offered diplomatic recognition. Hours later, the Arab nations launched a full-scale war, hoping to eliminate the new nation before it got off the ground. Relying heavily on Soviet and Czech weapons, the badly outnumbered Israelis defeated the Arabs in the initial six-month war. In recognizing Israel, Truman defied the advice of Marshall, Forrestal, and Lovett, who feared a break with U.S. oil-producing friends in the region. They also feared losing U.S. and British access to Middle Eastern bases from which to attack the Soviet Union if war broke out. During a meeting in the Oval Office on May 12, Clifford had laid out the moral and strategic case for recognition. He envisioned Israel as an invaluable U.S. ally in a volatile region. Marshall vehemently countered Clifford's arguments and insisted that they were based on domestic political considerations: Truman's hope of winning the Jewish vote. Marshall bluntly told Truman that if Truman recognized Israel, he would not vote for him in the 1948 presidential election.

There was some truth to Marshall's contention. Truman was certainly aware of the domestic political implications of his actions. "In all of my political experience," he told a friend, "I don't ever recall the Arab vote swinging a close election." [105] And Truman was in a very close election in 1948, one in which every vote counted. But Truman, despite his frequent anti-Semitic comments and contempt for Jewish activists, was also motivated by a sincere concern for Jews' suffering in the Holocaust.

Marshall had advocated a trusteeship over Palestine under UN auspices that would keep Jews and Arabs in the same country. He and the others also worried about the close ties between Israel and the Soviet Union, whose legal recognition of Israel had followed closely behind that of the United States on May 15. U.S. intelligence reported Soviet influence with the Irgun and the Stern Gang and took note of the influx of Jewish Communists into the region. The United States and Great Britain, trying not to antagonize the Arabs completely, placed an embargo on arms shipments to both sides and the United States maneuvered to preempt UN resolutions condemning Arab aggression. U.S. policy makers, fearing Soviet military intervention either unilaterally or as part of an international peacekeeping force, pushed for a quick resolution.

Despite Ibn Saud's threats to cancel the concession to Aramco, which Texaco and Standard Oil of California had established in Saudi Arabia, the United States was not overly concerned about Arab retaliation. An early-July State Department report found that, excluding Iran, the Middle East supplied only 6 percent of Western oil supplies and that the loss could be absorbed "without substantial hardship to any group of consumers." [106]

Although Israel signed armistice agreements with Egypt, Lebanon, Jordan, and Syria in 1949, the Arabs' bitterness over the creation of a Jewish state in the Middle East persists to this day and the issues that caused the 1948 war remain unresolved. The situation was exacerbated by a massive refugee problem, as many Arabs fled from what would become Israel—some following the advice of Arab leaders and some driven out by the Israelis. The refugee problem, after more than sixty years, remains a constant source of tension in the region.

While Arabs and Israelis fought in the Middle East, the United States and the Soviet Union almost came to blows over Germany. In spring 1948, the United States and Britain took preliminary steps toward carving out a separate West German government, overcoming the reluctance of France and other Western European nations that feared a powerful, potentially remilitarized nation. Many German politicians in the western zones were also resistant to this development, fearing the severance of economic, political, and personal ties to eastern Germany.

In late June, the United States boldly and provocatively instituted currency reform in the three western sectors of occupied Berlin, which was a hundred miles inside the Soviet zone. Seeing this as not only a major step in establishing an independent, remilitarized West German state only three years after the defeat of Hitler but as a betrayal of the U.S. promise to provide desperately needed reparations from the more prosperous western zones, the Soviets cut off rail and road access to Berlin. Stalin maintained that western access had been based on wartime agreements establishing a quadripartite Allied Control Commission as the supreme authority for a unified Germany. Because the Western powers were now shattering that framework, he reasoned, they had forfeited access rights.

Western observers decried the savage cruelty of the Soviets' "Berlin blockade." The commandant of the American sector of Berlin, Fran Howley, described it as a "comprehensive criminal plan to shut off the Eastern Zone of Germany from the West and to isolate completely the three Western Sectors of Berlin." It was, Howley charged, "a wicked decision, the most barbarous in history since Genghis Khan." The Soviets, Western leaders screamed, were trying to starve West Berliners into submission. Images of Soviet cruelty would be seared into global consciousness—a perception of the crisis that still persists today.

But, contrary to this widely held view, the Soviets, for all their faults, attempted nothing of the sort. They had, in fact, gone out of their way to guarantee West Berliners' access to food and coal from the eastern zone or from direct Soviet provisions. In October 1948, U.S. military government intelligence analysts reported, the "road, rail and water blockade of Berlin by no means constitutes a complete economic blockade either by intent or in fact."[107]

What people do remember, however, is that over the next eleven months, the United States airlifted 1.6 million tons of food and fuel into West Berlin to feed 2.2 million people. Truman also sent sixty presumably atomic-capable B-29s to British and German bases. He assured Forrestal that if conditions warranted it, he would approve the use of atomic weapons. "We are very close to war," he wrote in September.[108] When Forrestal asked Kennan for his analysis of the Soviet blockade, Kennan offered the most alarming assessment: "Communist ideology and Soviet behavior clearly demonstrate that the ultimate objective of the leaders of the USSR is the domination of the world."[109] And despite knowing the risks, the United States prolonged the crisis until it achieved both a basic law outlining the West German state and the creation in April 1949 of the North Atlantic Treaty Organization (NATO), which committed the United States, for the first time in its history, to a peacetime military alliance with Western Europe. In May 1949, having won its objectives, the United States agreed to talks over the future of Germany, and it was only then that the Soviet Union lifted the blockade, ending the most dangerous postwar confrontation to date. The United States had gambled that its atomic monopoly would enable it to achieve its goals without having to go to war, and it won.

Once out of office, Henry Wallace assumed the editorship of the liberal *New Republic* and continued to criticize Truman's policies. On December 29, 1947, he announced that he was going to take his fight for peace one step farther and challenge Truman in the 1948 presidential elections. "Thousands of people all over the United States have asked me to engage in this great fight," he declared. "The people are on the march. We have assembled a Gideon's Army, small in number, powerful in conviction, ready for action . . . the people's peace will usher in the century of the common man." "The bigger the peace vote in 1948, the more definitely the world will know that the United States is not behind the bipartisan reactionary war policy which is dividing the world into two armed camps and making inevitable the day when American soldiers will be lying in their arctic suits in the Russian snow."[110]

To deal with the Wallace challenge, Clifford suggested that Truman adopt a progressive strategy on social and economic issues, ignore left-wing attacks on his foreign policy, and let others handle the job of discrediting Wallace. Clifford wrote, "Every effort must be made . . . to identify and isolate him in the public mind with the Communists. . . . [The] Administration must persuade prominent liberals and progressives—*and no one else*—to move publicly into the fray. They must point out that the core of the Wallace backing is made up of Communists and fellow-travellers" (italics in original). Red-baiting began almost immediately and was almost entirely conducted by people clearly identified with the liberal camp. They accused Wallace and the Progressive Party of being tools of Moscow. Truman could not refrain from joining the chorus: "I do not want and I will not accept the support of Henry Wallace and his Communists," he told those attending a St. Patrick's Day dinner.[111]

Wallace repeatedly denied any involvement with the Communist Party USA and warned that charges of anticommunism were being used to undermine American freedoms. This proved to be of little avail. Mobs broke up Wallace rallies. Wallace groups were banned from campuses. Universities denied Wallace the right to speak on campus, and his supporters were sometimes fired from their jobs. The *Pittsburgh Press* published the names, addresses, and places of employment of more than a thousand people in the western part of the state who had signed Wallace nominating petitions. Wallace's running mate, Senator Glen Taylor of Idaho, was arrested and beaten up by police in Birmingham, Alabama, for defying a municipal ordinance banning integrated meetings and adding insult to injury by entering the gathering of the Southern Negro Youth Congress through a door marked "Colored." Wallace wired Taylor, "This dramatizes the hypocrisy of spending billions for arms in the name of defending freedom abroad, while freedom is trampled on here at home."[112]

The Red-baiting, the dismissive treatment of Wallace by the major newspapers, Truman's move to the left on domestic issues, and a last-minute rush to Truman by Democratic voters who feared a victory by Republican Thomas Dewey resulted in an electoral disaster for the Wallace campaign. Gallup showed Wallace polling at 7 percent in early 1948. Some observers predicted that he would win more than 10 million voters. Wallace predicted 3 to 5 million. In October, he was polling at 4 percent. The final tally had him coming in fourth with 1,157,063 votes, almost 12,000 votes behind Dixiecrat Strom Thurmond. In the end, he totaled only 2.38 percent of the national vote. The *Wall Street Journal* put an interesting spin on the impact of the campaign, editorializing, "It is said by political commentators that Mr. Wallace made a bad showing because he got few votes. What they neglect is that Mr. Wallace succeeded in having his ideas adopted, except in the field of foreign affairs. From the time that Mr. Wallace announced he would run for President, Mr. Truman began to suck the wind from Mr. Wallace's sails by coming out for more and more of the Wallace domestic program." [113] But on the issues most central to the Wallace campaign, which would change the way the United States operated in the world, American voters backed the candidate who had driven the nation down the path of empire, nuclear arms race, and global confrontation. It was a sad final chapter to a storied political career by a man who never fit the mold of U.S. politicians but who espoused a moral vision of the role an enlightened United States could play in the world.

In a top secret 1948 memo, George Kennan outlined the dilemma facing U.S. policy makers, making clear why Wallace's alternatives were dismissed with such contempt:

> We have about 50 percent of the world's wealth, but only 6.3 percent of its population . . . we cannot fail to be the object of envy and resentment. Our real task in the coming period is to devise a pattern of relationships which will permit us to maintain this position of disparity. . . . To do so, we will have to dispense with all sentimentality and daydreamings. . . . We should cease to talk about vague and . . . unreal objectives such as human rights, the raising of the living standards, and democratization . . . we are going to have to deal in straight power concepts. The less we are then hampered by idealistic slogans, the better. [114]

Successful resolution of the Berlin crisis and the establishment of NATO in 1949 temporarily raised Westerners' spirits, but two colossal setbacks reversed that momentum. First, the Chinese Communist Party, under Mao Zedong, routed Jiang Jieshi's Guomindang and seized power in the world's largest and most populous nation. The *New York Times* described the Communist victory as "a vast tragedy of unforeseeable consequences for the Western World." [115] And by the end of the year the *Times* concluded, "the developments in China represent a startling defeat for the traditional Far-Eastern policy of the United States and an equally startling victory for Soviet Russia." [116]

Losing the world's most populous nation to communism represented such a reversal of fortune that some saw it as the beginning of the end for U.S. efforts in Asia. Major General Claire Chennault, the former head of the Flying Tigers, predicted a "third and more horrible world war . . . if the United States permits Communism to conquer China." "We will make a billion enemies." [117] Chinese leaders feared U.S. military action. Republicans blamed Truman for "losing" China and demanded stronger support for Jiang.

Though the American public was caught off guard, top U.S. officials had long anticipated a Communist victory due more to Jiang's incompetence and corruption than to Mao's brilliance. As Truman noted, "We picked a bad horse." Jiang's administration, he said, "was one of the most corrupt and inefficient that ever made an attempt to govern a country." [118] Jiang was sent scurrying to set up shop in Taiwan, where U.S. officials expected a Communist takeover within a year. More concerned about their own immediate security than world revolution, the Soviets had provided little assistance and less encouragement to the Chinese Communists. Even though Mao and Stalin formed an alliance in February 1950, the Soviets urged Chinese Communist leaders to maintain cordial relations with the United States, and trade between the two nations continued for several months. But China's commitment to revolutionary change and U.S. refusal to recognize the legitimacy of the new government doomed any efforts at rapprochement.

On September 23, 1949, President Truman shocked the nation: "We have evidence that within recent weeks an atomic explosion occurred in the U.S.S.R." [119] Most scientists had anticipated this and took the news in stride. In early 1946, the *Los Angeles Times* cited testimony from the chemist Harold Urey and other scientists that the Soviets would have a bomb within five years to discredit Groves's assertion that it would take the Soviets another twenty. Experts had long recognized that the challenge was an engineering, not a scientific, one. The *Times* accused Groves of "consign[ing] the American people to a fool's paradise" by promoting the fanciful notion that the United States had a "secret" worth preserving and wisely urged U.S. authorities to use "their five years of grace—not for piling up atom bombs and behaving like a dog in the manger, but for constructive statesmanship," a view widely shared by the scientists. [120] In 1948, J. Robert Oppenheimer told *Time* magazine, "Our atomic monopoly is like a cake of ice melting in the sun." [121] The air force had also just predicted that the Soviets would not test for years. Truman, who had earlier told Oppenheimer that the Soviets would never develop a bomb, initially disbelieved the reports of the Soviet test and then credited German scientists working in the Soviet Union.

Soviet scientists breathed a huge sigh of relief. Physicist Yuli Khariton commented, "In possessing such a weapon, we had removed the possibility of its being used against the USSR with impunity." The bomb, he felt, allowed "Our country . . . to defend itself from really threatening mortal danger." Physicist Igor Golovin wrote that their sleepless nights and herculean efforts had been worth it because "they had knocked the trump card from the hands of the American atomic diplomats." [122]

Americans felt more vulnerable than ever. The *Bulletin of the Atomic Scientists* moved the hands of the Doomsday Clock from seven minutes to midnight to three minutes.[123] Senate Majority Leader Scott Lucas feared that "we may be in the last stage of a great civilization, the final stage before the colossal war and the disintegration of society as we have known it in our lifetime."[124] The *New York Times* wondered if "anyone [was] rash enough today to say who is winning the cold war?"[125]

On the other hand, some people saw a silver lining. Journalist William Laurence thought it reasonable to assume that the Soviets could produce a bomb per week and would, in one year, have fifty bombs capable of destroying fifty U.S. cities containing 40 million people. But he also thought that the Soviet Union's possessing the bomb might yield the long-awaited agreement for international control because bargaining between equals was much more productive than bargaining between two decidedly unequal powers.[126] Once again, hotter heads prevailed. Additional money poured into nuclear research and expanding the U.S. arsenal. Senator Brien McMahon, chair of the Joint Committee on Atomic Energy, told David Lilienthal that the United States now had to "blow [the Soviets] off the face of the earth" and quickly.[127]

James Forrestal did not live to see what for him would have been a thoroughly nightmarish development. The details of his death are still murky. For years, Forrestal had been as fierce an anti-Communist as strode the corridors of the nation's capital. His views had helped shape the poisonous climate in Washington in which the Truman administration repeatedly attributed the most damning motives to Soviet actions. Yet he had been on the losing end of several policy battles with Truman, including recognition of Israel, military versus civilian control of atomic bombs, defense spending, strengthening the German cartels, and arming Latin American countries. In October 1948, when Truman's prospects for reelection looked bleak, newspapers reported that Forrestal had reached out to Dewey, expressing his interest in remaining in the cabinet when Dewey became president.[128]

All of that boded poorly for his relationship with Truman. On March 1, Truman asked for his resignation, leaving him "shattered." He officially retired on March 28, 1949. The following day, an aide found him sitting at his desk, staring at the wall. He was sent to Hobe Sound, Florida, to be with his wife, who was visiting recently retired Undersecretary of State Robert Lovett. "Bob, they're after me," he told Lovett upon his arrival. Whether "they" referred to the Jews and "Zionist agents" he believed were trailing him or the Communists was never specified. On April 2, the navy flew Forrestal from Florida to the District of Columbia, where he was admitted into the Bethesda Naval Hospital, reportedly suffering from a "nervous breakdown." Drew Pearson informed his radio

The first U.S. secretary of defense, James Forrestal, suffered a nervous breakdown and, tormented by his own anti-Communist paranoia, committed suicide, jumping from his sixteenth-floor room at Bethesda Naval Hospital.

audience that Forrestal was "out of his mind" after Forrestal was discovered in the street wearing his pajamas and shouting "The Russians are coming!" He believed that the Russians had invaded the United States. Pearson later reported that during his brief stay in Florida, Forrestal had attempted suicide four times by hanging, slashing his wrists, and taking sleeping pills.[129]

Communist countries milked the story of the Soviet-phobic Forrestal's mental travails for all it was worth. *Washington Post* columnist Marquis Childs described a five-column-wide May Day cartoon in *Pravda* "with the caption 'Club Aggressors.' The cartoon showed Forrestal in a strait-jacket lecturing to Winston Churchill, John Foster Dulles, and others . . . a hospital orderly restrains Forrestal who crouches on all four on a pedestal. An accompanying verse says that not the strait-jacket but the will of those who do not want war is preventing Forrestal's freedom of action." The Polish Communist paper *Tryhbuna Ludu* reported, "Insanity. Diagnosis: persecution mania. Patient: James Forrestal, Minister of War of the United States, who resigned his post two weeks ago. Symptoms: a few days ago upon hearing the siren of a fire truck passing his house, the patient rushed in to the street in his underwear shouting, 'The Russians are invading the city!' The doctors declared that the patient had long been suffering from psychic disturbances, even when he was still fulfilling his official functions." The Polish paper cited Pearson's revelation that Truman had ordered a review of all of Forrestal's recent reports, recommendations, and decisions, wanting to ascertain "whether Mr. Forrestal went mad under the pressure of cold-war propaganda, which he himself had carried on for years, or . . . whether all that propaganda was the consequence of the insanity which had seized Mr. Forrestal a long time ago."[130]

Trying to downplay the seriousness of his condition, hospital officials placed him on the sixteenth floor instead of in the first-floor mental ward to avoid suspicion. Alone in his room, he suffered constant nightmares. He thought he would suffer the same fate as Czechoslovakian Foreign Minister Jan Masaryk—to be pushed out of a window. But his condition began to improve, and on the night of May 22, 1949, he stayed up late copying Sophocles' "The Chorus from Ajax," in which the hero ponders his fate far from home. At the word "nightingale" he put his pen down and jumped.

And in a bizarre, though oddly revealing, turn of events, the man who oversaw contact with Nightingale as well as a plethora of other covert operations, Frank Wisner, would himself become infected with paranoia and psychosis. In 1965, after repeated institutionalizations and sustained electroshock therapy, Wisner blasted his own head off with a shotgun.

On January 1, 1950, the world happily bade farewell to the 1940s. For the United States, the decade ended on a bitter note with the Communist triumph in China and the first Soviet atomic bomb test. Despite the immensity of U.S. power, the United States felt besieged by enemies at home and abroad. The optimism that had reigned just years earlier with the end of the war had given way to a new sense of fear and anxiety.

Chapter 6

EISENHOWER:

A Not So Pretty Picture

On March 4, 1953, Americans woke to the news that Soviet Premier Josef Stalin had been paralyzed by a cerebral hemorrhage. The seventy-four-year-old dictator died the following day. Americans held their breath. The Soviets were in shock. Despite Stalin's extraordinary brutality, most of them revered him for having led the nation to victory over the Nazis and having turned the Soviet Union into a modern industrial state. While the public mourned, Soviet leaders secretly decided to ease tensions with the capitalist West so they could focus on improving conditions at home. Georgi Malenkov, Stalin's successor, speaking at Stalin's funeral, called for "international cooperation" and economic relations with all countries—a peace based on "prolonged coexistence and peaceful competition" between capitalism and socialism.[1] The new Soviet leaders held out an olive branch. Would the United States' newly elected president, Dwight David Eisenhower, and his secretary of state, John Foster Dulles, accept it?

Following the end of World War II, the United States slowly built its stockpile of atom bombs from thirteen in mid-1947, only one of which could have been operational within two weeks, to three hundred by mid-1950. At the same time, it enhanced its ability to deliver those bombs. The advent of the atomic age revolutionized strategic thinking. Airpower would now reign supreme. The United States Air Force (USAF) became an independent service in 1947. One of the USAF's three units, the Strategic Air Command (SAC), assumed primary responsibility for delivering the new weapons. In 1948, Lieutenant General Curtis LeMay, the mastermind of the United States' terror bombing of Japan, took charge of SAC and set out to turn it into a first-rate fighting force—one that would be ready to do battle against the Soviets at a moment's notice. "We are at war now!" he declared. When fighting began, he intended to simply overwhelm Soviet defenses, dropping

*Mourners
commemorate Stalin's
death in Dresden,
East Germany.*

133 atomic bombs on seventy cities, knocking out 40 percent of Soviet industry, and killing 2.7 million people. The SAC Emergency War Plan he designed called for delivery of the entire stockpile "in a single massive attack."[2]

The army and navy both challenged the ethics of deliberately targeting civilians in this way, finding it antithetical to U.S. moral principles. But the Joint Chiefs of Staff sided with the air force and approved the plan in late 1948. Despite some misgivings, Truman went along with this decision, motivated, in part, by budgetary concerns. Reliance on atomic weapons was less costly than maintaining the level of conventional forces needed to defend the United States and Western Europe from potential Soviet aggression.

A report commissioned by Secretary of Defense James Forrestal cast serious doubt upon U.S. prospects of defeating the Soviet Union based upon atomic warfare alone. The destruction caused would pale in comparison to the horrific levels of suffering the Soviets had sustained in the recent war. In fact, the committee warned, atomic bombardment "would validate Soviet propaganda . . . stimulate resentment against the United States, unify these people and increase their will to fight." It would also set the dangerous pattern for future use of "any weapons of mass destruction." But by the time the study arrived, Forrestal was long gone, and his successor, Louis Johnson, withheld the report from Truman.[3]

In 1948, Lieutenant General Curtis LeMay, the mastermind behind the wartime firebombing of Japanese cities, took charge of the U.S. Air Force's Strategic Air Command (SAC) and set out to turn it into a first-rate fighting force that was ready to do battle against the Soviets at a moment's notice.

In August 1949, the USSR successfully tested an atomic bomb, delivering a crushing blow to the United States' sense of military superiority and invulnerability. The stunning news caught most U.S. war planners by surprise. Truman flatly disbelieved the evidence. Once convinced, he quickly approved plans to expand U.S. inventory of atomic bombs.

The Joint Chiefs, supported by physicists Edward Teller, Ernest Lawrence, and Luis Alvarez, demanded development of a hydrogen, or "super," bomb. Atomic Energy Commission (AEC) head David Lilienthal described scientific proponents as "drooling with the prospect and 'bloodthirsty.'"[4] In secret session, General James McCormack, director of the AEC's Division of Military Application, told members of Congress that the bomb would be "infinite. You can have it any size up to the sun."[5]

Lilienthal and many of the leading scientists were appalled at the prospect. In October, the eight scientists on the General Advisory Committee to the AEC, headed by J. Robert Oppenheimer, unanimously opposed building the hydrogen bomb because its primary effect would be "exterminating civilian populations." The majority considered it to be "in a totally different category from an atomic bomb" and "might become a weapon of genocide." With its unlimited destructive capability, it would represent "a threat to the future of the human race." Committee members Enrico Fermi and I. I. Rabi declared it to be "a danger to humanity as a whole . . . an evil thing considered in any light."[6]

Among those vehemently opposed to building the hydrogen bomb was State Department Soviet expert George Kennan, who believed that the USSR might be ready for a comprehensive nuclear arms control agreement and urged Secretary of State Dean Acheson to pursue that course instead. Acheson contemptuously suggested that Kennan "resign from the Foreign Service, assume a monk's habit, carry a tin cup and stand on the street corner and say, 'The end of the world is nigh.'"[7] Disgusted by the increasingly militaristic bent of U.S. policy, Kennan resigned as State Department director of policy planning on December 31, 1949.

On January 31, 1950, Truman announced his decision to proceed with the hydrogen bomb. Two weeks later, Albert Einstein appeared on Eleanor Roosevelt's television show to warn, "If these efforts should prove successful, radioactive poisoning of the atmosphere and, hence, annihilation of all life on earth will have been brought within the range of what is technically possible."[8] Physicist Leo Szilard soon delivered more terrifying news when he told a national radio audience that the fusion of five hundred tons of deuterium in a hydrogen-cobalt bomb would be enough to "kill everybody on earth."[9]

Such warnings took a tremendous toll on the human psyche. As writer William Faulkner observed in his December 1950 Nobel Prize acceptance speech, "Our tragedy today is a general and universal physical fear so long sustained by now that we can even bear it. There are no longer problems of the spirit. There is only one question: When will I be blown up?"[10]

Kennan's replacement, Forrestal's protégé Paul Nitze, had been a vice president of the powerful Wall Street investment banking firm Dillon, Read when Forrestal was the firm's president. Nitze immediately took the lead in preparing NSC 68, a document that would fundamentally revamp the nation's defense posture. NSC 68 posited that the Soviet Union, armed with atomic bombs and "a new fanatic faith," was seeking "to impose its absolute authority over the rest of the world." Faced with an existential threat, the United States had to base its response not on what the Soviet Union was likely to do but on what, in its most malign moments, it was capable of doing: "a. To overrun Western Europe ... ; to drive toward the oil-bearing areas of the Near and Middle East; and to consolidate Communist gains in the Far East; b. To launch air attacks against the British Isles and air and sea attacks against the lines of communications of the Western Powers in the Atlantic and the Pacific; c. To attack selected targets with atomic weapons, now including ... targets in Alaska, Canada, and the U.S." No area was outside the U.S. defense perimeter because, as the document stated, "The assault on free institutions is world-wide now, and ... a defeat of free institutions anywhere is a defeat everywhere." National security and global security were now one and the same. If the Soviet Union "calculates that it has a sufficient atomic capability to make a surprise attack on us, nullifying our atomic superiority and creating a military situation decisively in its favor, the Kremlin might be tempted to strike swiftly and with stealth."[11]

Facing such a dangerous foe, Nitze concluded, U.S. survival depended on vastly increasing its nuclear and conventional arsenals, strengthening its armed

The previously little-known Wisconsin Senator Joseph McCarthy became the ugly face of midcentury anticommunism.

forces, bolstering its military alliances, and expanding its covert operations and psychological warfare capabilities. Over the next five years, military spending would have to quadruple to $50 billion, or 20 percent of GNP. Truman agreed with NSC 68's assessment of the overall strategic situation and endorsed its conclusions but blanched at the cost, having already announced plans to cut defense spending in the next fiscal year. Acheson and Nitze countered that quadrupling military spending would stimulate the economy and safeguard against another depression. The State Department's leading Soviet experts, George Kennan and Charles Bohlen, opposed such a buildup, contending that Stalin had neither the will nor the means to pursue the kind of world conquest Acheson and Nitze envisioned. Much to Acheson and Nitze's disappointment, such a stupendous increase in military spending seemed dead in the water in early 1950.

Escalating tensions abroad triggered a new onslaught of Red-baiting at home. Truman's loyalty-security program in 1947 had opened the door. Highly publicized charges of espionage and treason fed the hysteria. In January 1950, former State Department official Alger Hiss, who had been relentlessly pursued by Congressman Richard Nixon, was convicted of perjury. Later that month, physicist Klaus Fuchs was apprehended for passing nuclear secrets to the Soviet Union. Fuchs divulged the existence of a wider spy ring, which led to the arrests in July of Ethel and Julius Rosenberg.

In February 1950, little-known Wisconsin Senator Joseph McCarthy gained notoriety by telling members of the Ohio County Women's Republican Club in Wheeling, West Virginia, "I have here in my hand a list of 205—a list of names that were made known to the Secretary of State as being members of the Communist Party and who nevertheless are still working and shaping policy in the State Department."[12] The next day, in Salt Lake City, he lowered the number to 57. Though his numbers continued to fluctuate, he garnered headlines with outlandish accusations that provoked a new round of high-profile hearings. His victims included State Department Asia experts accused of assisting Mao's victory in China. Their ouster would cripple U.S. understanding of Asia for decades to come.

Though the shamelessly self-promoting Wisconsin senator, known mockingly as "tail gunner Joe" for his fabricated war exploits, became the ugly face of this repression, the real power was exercised by FBI director J. Edgar Hoover, who kept a file of incriminating evidence on members of Congress, which he trotted out when it was necessary to keep someone in line. One of Hoover's top aides described how this worked: "The other night we picked up a situation where this senator was seen drunk, in a hit-and-run accident, and some good-looking broad was with him. By noon of the next day the good senator was aware that we had the information and we never had any trouble with him on appropriations since." [13]

Officials and the media cautioned Americans that vicious, fanatical Communists bent on destroying the American way of life lurked around every corner. Truman's attorney general warned, "There are today many Communists in America. They are everywhere—in factories, offices, butcher stores, on street corners, in private business." [14] And, indeed, scientists, writers, actors, directors, artists, teachers, and people from all walks of life were persecuted for their political beliefs as a climate of fear descended upon the nation. A few hundred people served time in prison, and as many as twelve thousand may have lost their jobs. After they failed political screenings administered by the Coast Guard, almost three thousand longshoremen and seamen alone were dismissed under a port-security program allegedly implemented to defend the nation's waterfronts from saboteurs during the Korean War but actually designed to wipe out the Communist-led maritime unions. [15]

Many suspects were hauled before congressional committees, where investigators demanded they finger other Communists and fellow travelers. Writer Mary McCarthy observed that the purpose of these hearings was not to combat subversion but to convince Americans to accept "the *principle* of betrayal as a norm of good citizenship." [16] Journalist I. F. Stone condemned the "tendency to turn a whole generation of Americans into stool pigeons." [17] Many refused to testify and were blacklisted, fired, or jailed. More than a hundred college and university teachers were fired for refusing to cooperate with anti-Communist investigations. Dashiell Hammett, one of Hollywood's leading writers, was incarcerated for refusing to name contributors to the Civil Rights Congress's bail bond fund, of which he was an honorary trustee. Writer Lillian Hellman later disclosed that Hammett "did not know the name of a single contributor" but would not say so in court because he denied the government's right to demand such information. [18]

In 1947, the so-called Hollywood Ten were charged with contempt of Congress

Officials and the media cautioned Americans that dangerous Communists bent on destroying the American way of life lurked around every corner. The right-wing journal Counterattack *published* "Red Channels," *alleging Communist domination of the entertainment industry.*

and, despite a series of appeals to both the judicial system and the public, were sentenced to a year in prison. Along with another nine Hollywood radicals who had also been subpoenaed by HUAC in 1947 but never called to the stand, the ten became the first victims of a film industry blacklist. Other high-profile Hollywood progressives joined those nineteen on the blacklist. HUAC returned to investigating the film industry in 1951, and by 1954 the blacklist had increased to include 212 men and women who had refused to cooperate with the committee. No studio would hire blacklisted screen artists or studio workers. Many were left jobless. Only 10 percent of the people driven out of the film industry ever found work there again. A number of individuals, however, escaped that fate by informing on their colleagues. Fifty-eight of the 110 men and women called before HUAC in the spring of 1951 "named names." [19]

By the time all was said and done, McCarthyism had decimated the U.S. Left. The Communist movement was destroyed. The party itself endured, but many of the groups in and around it simply vanished. The Red Scare eviscerated the labor unions, political organizations, and cultural associations that had spurred the reforms of the 1930s and 1940s. With the exception of the civil rights and antinuclear movements, left-wing dissent and progressive reform would remain quiescent for more than a decade but would reemerge with new vigor and fresh approaches in the 1960s. The labor movement, however, would never recover, leaving American workers weaker and less well off in many respects than their European counterparts. [20]

The African-American civil rights movement suffered as well. Under the intense antiradical pressure of the era, organizations ousted leftist members, some of whom had long been leaders in the fight for racial justice. In 1948, the

Nine of the Hollywood Ten, who in 1947 were charged with contempt of Congress for refusing to finger fellow radicals and were subsequently blacklisted from the film industry.

NAACP went so far as to expel civil rights pioneer W. E. B. Du Bois for actively supporting Henry Wallace's presidential campaign and calling for the United Nations to address racism in the United States. Paul Robeson was similarly marginalized. Many of the left-wing organizations eliminated by McCarthyite attacks were those that had linked the issues of class-based inequality and U.S. foreign policy with domestic racism. Red baiting also dissolved alliances between civil rights organizations and labor unions, diminishing the calls for racial equality on the part of the unions and isolating the civil rights organizations from battles over wages and workplace rights. In the wake of McCarthyism, the movement's most influential leaders departed from past broad-based agendas to focus on achieving narrower legal reforms, abandoning the drive for deeper structural reforms of the economy or attacks on the ravages of imperialism abroad. It is important to remember, though, that throughout the period, African Americans played a leading role in efforts to halt the nuclear arms race and make sure that Americans never lost sight of the dangers of nuclear war.[21]

Individual radicals and movements for social, economic, and racial justice were not the only victims of the mid-twentieth-century scourge of political repression. Concomitant with the Red Scare was a "Lavender Scare," in which homosexuals were purged from the federal government. Under the guise of national security—ostensibly because "sexual perverts" were particularly susceptible to blackmail by foreign and domestic subversives—government agencies fired gays and lesbians or forced them to resign. Historian David Johnson estimates that as

Though Joseph McCarthy's name became synonymous with the Red Scare, it was FBI head J. Edgar Hoover who exercised the real power. By 1960, the FBI had begun investigations of more than 430,000 individuals and groups. Hoover also used his contacts in the media to fan the flames of anti-Communist hysteria.

many as five thousand federal employees might have lost their jobs in the early Cold War. In 1953, Undersecretary of State Donald B. Lourie told a congressional committee that in his department alone, dismissals of homosexuals were proceeding at an average rate of "about one every day." Those numbers account only for a portion of the jobs lost to the Lavender Scare. The reason for dismissals was sometimes not recorded, supposedly to save the employee from embarrassment. Others chose to resign before their sexual orientation was uncovered. Additionally, thousands of people applying for federal jobs were rejected on the basis of their sexual orientation. As with the Red Scare, the anti-homosexual purge extended to the private sector. Some businesses even hired professional investigators to ferret out "undesirables," including gays and lesbians.[22]

Throughout those years, the FBI was busy on a number of fronts. It fanned the flames of anti-Communist hysteria by leaking information to its "assets" in the press, including the likes of Walter Winchell, Drew Pearson, Westbrook Pegler, Fulton Lewis, Jr., and the Washington bureau chiefs of the United Press and *Chicago Tribune*. Its program to alert employers as to the political affiliations of their employees costs hundreds of people their jobs. People with dissenting views were subjected to surveillance on a massive scale. By 1960, the FBI had begun investigations of more than 430,000 individuals and groups. The 26,000 considered the greatest risks in 1954, predominantly members of the Communist Party, made it onto Hoover's Security Index, which designated them for detention in the event of an emergency. And in 1956, the FBI launched its Counterintelligence Program, or COINTELPRO, a panoply of dirty tricks designed to disrupt left-wing organizations engaged in completely legal and constitutionally protected activities.[23]

On June 24, 1950, North Korea invaded South Korea and the Cold War suddenly turned red hot. Nestled between Japan, China, and the Soviet Union, Korea had long been a point of contention among those three Asian powers. Japan had occupied and ruled Korea from 1910 to 1945, when it was divided into a Soviet zone north of the 38th parallel and a U.S. zone to the south. Drawn up hastily by Colonel Dean Rusk the day after Nagasaki was bombed, the arrangement was meant as a temporary one until unification and independence could be restored. In the north, the Soviets installed General Kim Il Sung, who had led guerrilla forces against the Japanese in Manchuria during the war; the Americans installed Syngman Rhee in the south. Border skirmishes occurred frequently. The Joint Chiefs had warned repeatedly against getting drawn into a war in Korea—a place of little strategic importance bordering on the Soviet Union and China— and recommended that it be excluded from the United States' defense perimeter. Acheson also excluded Korea in an important speech in January 1950, leading some critics to charge that he had deliberately invited the attack.

The Soviets watched nervously as the United States strengthened Japan economically and militarily, stationed troops on Japanese territory, and inched toward a peace treaty without Soviet participation. The chiefs cautioned that excluding the Soviets from the peace treaty might provoke a Soviet attack on Japan. The Soviets struck instead in Korea.

Rhee's repressive policies and economic blunders made him a very unpopular figure in South Korea. Under U.S. pressure, he allowed elections to proceed in 1950. His supporters received a thrashing at the polls. Despite the setback, he continued to discuss plans to militarily unify Korea under his own command in the coming months. Kim, too, spoke of reunification, but under Communist control. Rhee's electoral setback and overall unpopularity gave Kim the opening he was looking for.[24]

In spring 1950, Stalin, after repeated entreaties from the North Korean leader, gave Kim the green light to invade the South. Believing that a South Korean attack on the North was coming, Stalin decided to act first. He was feeling a new burst of confidence. He now had the atomic bomb and had just concluded a formal alliance with Mao. Kim promised a swift victory.

Truman was in Missouri when word of the North Korean invasion reached him. Immediately concluding that the attack represented a new stage of Communist aggression, he decided that the United States must respond militarily. The *New York Times* urged Truman to act decisively or risk "los[ing] half a world."[25] Acting decisively would also silence the Republicans, who blamed Truman for losing China. He quickly pushed a resolution through the UN Security Council, which the Soviets had been boycotting over its refusal to seat Communist China. Despite deploying tens of thousands of troops, Truman refused to call the intervention a "war," instead latching on to the terminology of a reporter

*(From left to right): Truman with Secretary of State Dean
Acheson, British Prime Minister Clement Attlee, and Secretary
of Defense George Marshall discussing the Korean crisis.*

who asked if it would "be possible to call this a police action under the United Nations."[26] Although it was nominally a UN effort, the United States provided half the ground forces and almost all of the naval and air power. Most of the other ground forces came from South Korea. Truman also opted to bypass congressional authorization, setting the precedent for future wars.

In a memo he wrote a month before the attack, John Foster Dulles pessimistically surveyed the declining U.S. strategic position. "The situation in Japan may become untenable," he wrote, "and possibly that in the Philippines. Indonesia, with its vast natural resources, may be lost and the oil of the Middle East will be in jeopardy. None of these places provide holding grounds once the people feel that Communism is the wave of the future." But he offered a glimmer of hope: "This series of disasters can probably be prevented if at some doubtful point we quickly take a dramatic and strong stand that shows our confidence and resolution. Probably this series of disasters cannot be prevented any other way."[27]

The United States would take that stand in Korea. Truman told congressional leaders, "If we let Korea down, the Soviet will keep right on going and swallow up one piece of Asia after another. We had to make a stand some time, or else let all of Asia go by the board. If we were to let Asia go, the Near East would collapse and no telling what would happen in Europe. Therefore, . . . [I have] ordered our forces to support Korea . . . and it . . . [is] equally necessary for us to draw the line at Indo-China, the Philippines, and Formosa." [28]

Truman particularly feared a Soviet incursion into Iran. On June 26, he called Korea "the Greece of the Far East." Spinning a globe and pointing to Iran, he told staffers, "Here is where they will start trouble if we aren't careful. . . . If we are tough enough now, if we stand up to them like we did in Greece three years ago, they won't take any next steps. But if we just stand by, they'll move into Iran and they'll take over the whole Middle East." [29]

The Communist victory in China had raised the stakes in Korea. Having lost the China market, Japan now looked to Korea and Southeast Asia, where conditions were also volatile. In Vietnam, Ho Chi Minh's Communist-led forces were challenging French rule. A powerful insurgent movement was competing for power in the Philippines. British colonial interests were under attack in Malaya. Acheson explained, "It became apparent in Washington that the U.S. [had to] adopt a very firm stance in the Far East," especially since "the governments of many Western European nations appeared to be in a state of near-panic, as they watched to see whether the United States would act or not." [30]

More than 100,000 Soviet-trained and -equipped North Korean troops overwhelmed U.S. and South Korean forces, pinning them down around Pusan. MacArthur had turned a blind eye toward CIA warnings and other evidence that the attack was coming.

Facing defeat, MacArthur requested and received permission to push past the 38th parallel and liberate the North. He staged a surprise amphibious landing of 17,000 men at Inchon in September. Truman lauded MacArthur's "brilliant maneuver" and described his Korean campaign as being rivaled by "few operations in military history." [31] Truman bent over backward to placate the prickly MacArthur. Republicans seized on any hint that Truman might hesitate to send U.S. troops across the border as a sign of "appeasement."

MacArthur assured Truman that the Chinese would not enter the fight but agreed to use only Korean troops as he moved toward the Chinese border. Acheson had also dismissed the possibility of Chinese involvement as "sheer madness." [32] MacArthur even spoke about the fighting ending by Thanksgiving and having the troops out by Christmas. He dismissed repeated warnings by Chinese Foreign Minister Zhou Enlai that the Chinese would enter the war if the United States persisted in its advance northward. The Chinese were also incensed over the U.S.-led campaign to deny them UN representation and the United States' decision to defend Formosa with the Seventh Fleet. Mao wanted to send troops, but the Chinese Politburo remained divided. Stalin sent encouragement. He assured Mao that the Soviets and Chinese were stronger than the United States, Great Britain, and their European allies, especially now, before Germany and Japan had been

General Douglas MacArthur during the U.S. surprise amphibious landing at Inchon in September 1950, which Truman lauded as a "brilliant maneuver."

rearmed. Stalin had earlier told Kim that launching the war was a way to get back at "the dishonest, perfidious, and arrogant behavior of the United States in Europe, the Balkans, the Middle East, and especially its decision to form NATO." [33]

MacArthur blithely disregarded his agreement to use only Korean troops and ordered the air force to bomb near the Chinese border. When the Joint Chiefs demanded that he not bomb within five miles of the border, he responded, "I cannot overemphasize the disastrous effect, both physical and psychological, that will result from the restrictions which you are imposing." [34]

Chinese forces attacked UN troops in Unsan on October 25. On November 8, the Joint Chiefs cabled MacArthur to suggest that his mission might need to be reconsidered. MacArthur replied that the pressure from British, French, and many Americans to stop at the 38th parallel found its "historic precedence in the action taken at Munich." "To give up any part of North Korea to the aggression of the Chinese Communists," he blustered, "would be the greatest defeat of the free world in recent times." [35]

Truman and the Joint Chiefs acceded to MacArthur's demands. On November 24, MacArthur launched the major offensive that he believed would end the war. But suddenly hundreds of thousands of Chinese troops streamed across the Yalu River, sending U.S. and Allied troops into a frantic retreat. The setback was devastating. MacArthur solemnly announced that "we face an entirely new war." [36]

Acheson told Congress that the United States was on the brink of World War III. Truman agreed. "It looks like World War III is here," he wrote in his diary. General Omar Bradley called it "the greatest military disaster in the history of the United States."[37] *Time* reported that it was the "worst defeat the U.S. had ever suffered."[38]

China's UN Security Council spokesman heralded the resurgence of liberation movements throughout the region: "Regardless of the savagery and cruelty of the American imperialist aggressors, the hard struggling people of Japan, the victoriously advancing people of Vietnam, the heroically resisting people of Korea, the people of the Philippines who have never laid down their arms, and all the oppressed nations and peoples of the East will certainly unite in close solidarity. . . . They will fight dauntlessly on to win the final victory in their struggle for national independence."[39] The British government favored ending the war as quickly as possible, believing, according to the *Chicago Tribune,* that it was "being conducted in near-hysteria and with prodigal waste."[40] But U.S. leaders decided to first lay waste to North Korea.

At the start of the war, MacArthur and others had advocated using atomic bombs in support of combat operations. "I see here a unique use for the atomic bomb—to strike a blocking blow—which would require a six months repair job. Sweeten up my B-29 force," he enthused. General Charles Bolte figured that ten to twenty atomic bombs from the U.S. arsenal could be spared. In July, Truman sent nuclear-configured bombers to Great Britain and Guam. The Joint Chiefs decided, however, that, given the small size of most Korean cities, conventional bombing would suffice. They also expressed concern about Soviet retaliation and public revulsion at such acts. But now, following the entry of the Chinese into the conflict, the United States was desperate and the Chinese offered more suitable targets.[41] Truman stunned the press corps in late November 1950 by announcing that all options, explicitly including atomic devastation, were on the table:

> If aggression is successful in Korea, we can expect it to spread throughout Asia and Europe to this hemisphere. We are fighting in Korea for our own national security and survival. . . .
>
> Q. Will that include the atomic bomb?
>
> THE PRESIDENT. That includes every weapon that we have.
>
> Q. Does that mean that there is active consideration of the use of the atomic bomb?
>
> THE PRESIDENT. There has always been active consideration of its use. . . .
>
> Q. Does that mean, Mr. President, use against military objectives, or civilian—

THE PRESIDENT. It's a matter that the military people will have to
decide. . . . The military commander in the field will have charge of the use
of the weapons, as he always has.[42]

That day, Air Force General George Stratemeyer ordered SAC commander
General Hoyt Vandenberg to dispatch atomic-capable bomb groups to the Far
East. LeMay volunteered to direct the attacks. Representative Mendel Rivers of
South Carolina declared, "If there ever was a time to use the A-bomb, it is now."[43]
Senator Owen Brewster from Maine proposed using it against the Chinese. Repre-
sentative Tom Steed of Oklahoma preferred "the Kremlin." Representative Joseph
Bryson of South Carolina just wanted to make sure it was dropped on somebody:
"The hour is at hand when every known force, including the atomic bomb, should
be promptly utilized."[44] Lloyd Bentsen of Texas, the future Democratic vice presidential candidate, proposed that the president "advise the commander of the
North Korean troops to withdraw . . . beyond the 38th parallel within one week or
use that week to evacuate civilians from a specified list of North Korean cities that
will be subjected to atomic attack by the United States Air Force."[45]

Gallup found that, by 52 to 38 percent, the public supported using atomic
bombs, reversing earlier poll results. UN delegates warned that the Asian people
would be "horrified" by such use.[46] Attlee rushed across the Atlantic to tell Truman that the Europeans shared that horror. Following Attlee's visit, Truman told
a group of congressmen that it would be wrong to hit Moscow's surrogates when
the Kremlin was the real culprit, but that using atomic bombs against the Soviet
Union would provoke retaliation against London, Berlin, and Paris.

On December 9, 1950, MacArthur requested authorization to use atomic
bombs at his discretion. On December 24, he submitted a list of twenty-six targets. He also requested four bombs to drop on invading forces and four more for
"critical concentrations of enemy air power." He calculated that dropping thirty
to fifty atomic bombs "across the neck of Manchuria" could produce "a belt of
radioactive cobalt" that would win the war in ten days. But that was just the
short-term effect. The belt of radioactive cobalt would spread "from the Sea of
Japan to the Yellow Sea." Therefore, he figured, "For at least 60 years there could
have been no land invasion of Korea from the North."[47]

While MacArthur was conjuring up visions of atomic Armageddon, others were bemoaning the tremendous setback to the United States' international
prestige caused by the debacle in Korea. *New York Times* correspondents in capitals across Europe, Asia, and the Middle East reported on the "loss of confidence
in the United States." In France, "The decline in American prestige has been little
short of disastrous." In India, where U.S. "prestige has suffered immensely," many
people were "secretly pleased to see the Westerners trounced by Asians."[48] Some

questioned U.S. ability to halt a Soviet occupation of Europe, given how poorly U.S. forces had performed against China.

With U.S. and South Korean casualties mounting rapidly, MacArthur began issuing statements from Tokyo blaming others for the military debacle and pushing for all-out war with China. On March 10, 1951, MacArthur requested a "'D' Day atomic capability" in response to the Soviet bolstering of air capabilities in Korea and Manchuria and a buildup of Chinese forces near the Korean border. "Finletter and Lovett alerted on atomic discussions. Believe everything is set," Vandenberg wrote on March 14.[49] On March 24, 1951, knowing that Truman was pressing for a cease-fire, MacArthur broadcast his own ultimatum to China. Truman bristled, "I'll show that son-of-a bitch who's boss," but let the incident slide.[50] But when Republican Congressman Joe Martin read to the entire House a letter that MacArthur had written in which he stated that "if we lose this war to Communism in Asia, the fall of Europe is inevitable,"[51] the Joint Chiefs unanimously recommended that MacArthur be relieved of his command. On April 11, the White House announced MacArthur's firing.

MacArthur's eagerness to use atomic weapons did not factor into this decision. Just the week before, the Chiefs had ordered atomic attacks on Manchurian bases if the Chinese sent in another large contingent of forces. On April 6, Truman approved that order and authorized the transfer of nine atomic weapons from AEC to military custody on Guam and Okinawa.[52]

Firing MacArthur proved calamitous for Truman, whose approval rating sank below 30 percent. "Seldom has a more unpopular man fired a more popular one," *Time* magazine noted.

Republican leaders in the House and Senate met to discuss impeachment. Senator William Jenner accused the administration of treason: "this country today is in the hands of a secret inner coterie which is directed by agents of the Soviet Union. Our only choice is to impeach President Truman."[53] Joseph McCarthy also wanted to impeach the "son of a bitch" for firing MacArthur and said that Truman must have been drunk at the time on "bourbon and benedictine." He accused Truman of signing "the death warrant of western civilization."[54]

The public sided with MacArthur. Seven and a half million spectators cheered him at a New York parade. He received a hero's welcome in Washington, Boston, San Francisco, and Chicago. MacArthur emotionally defended his conduct of the war before a joint session of Congress and bade a final farewell:

> It has been said . . . that I was a warmonger. Nothing could be further from the truth. I know war as few other men now living know it, and nothing

General Douglas MacArthur at Soldier Field in Chicago during his 1951 farewell tour after his dismissal by Truman.

to me is more revolting. I have long advocated its complete abolition, as its very destructiveness on both friend and foe has rendered it useless as a means of settling international disputes. . . . The world has turned over many times since I took the oath . . . at West Point, but I still remember the refrain of one of the most popular barrack ballads of that day which proclaimed most proudly that "old soldiers never die; they just fade away." And like the old soldier of that ballad, I now close my military career and just fade away, an old soldier who tried to do his duty as God gave him the light to see that duty. Good bye.[55]

The address was broadcast live on national radio. "We saw a great hunk of God in the flesh and we heard the voice of God," gushed Congressman Dewey Short of Missouri.[56] Truman, however, chided the "damn fool Congressmen crying like a bunch of women" over "nothing but a bunch of bullshit."[57]

MacArthur's reference to the ballad "Old Soldiers Never Die" touched off a popular music frenzy. An executive at Remick Music Corporation, which owned the copyright, described the reaction as an "earthquake" and ordered publication of fifty thousand copies of the sheet music. Gene Autry rushed off his movie set to record a version for Columbia Records, which sold twenty-five thousand copies a day. Decca Records quickly issued two versions, one by Red Foley, the other by Herb Jeffries. RCA Victor issued a version sung by Vaughn Monroe.

Capitol Records put one out by Jimmy Wakely. Bing Crosby sang it live on his radio show. Columbia and RCA Victor recordings of MacArthur's speech were selling as fast as they could be stocked.

Congressional hearings on MacArthur's firing and Asia policy went on for two months. Congressional Democrats and top military brass effectively rebutted MacArthur's arguments. General Bradley rejected MacArthur's proposed war with China as "the wrong war, at the wrong place, at the wrong time, and with the wrong enemy." After that, MacArthur's luster faded rapidly. Truman's popularity never recovered. His approval rating sank to a record low of 22 percent. Acheson said that the war "was an incalculable defeat to U.S. foreign policy and destroyed the Truman administration."[58]

MacArthur was replaced by General Matthew Ridgway, who requested thirty-eight atomic bombs in May 1951. But that spring and summer, with Stalin's help, the United States, China, and the two Koreas began negotiations, which dragged on for two years. The U.S. air war continued unabated, unleashing a firebombing campaign similar to the one the United States had visited upon Japan five years earlier. Now the weapon of choice was napalm. *New York Times* reporter George Barrett described the effect of a napalm attack on a hamlet of two hundred people north of Anyang, which he characterized as "a macabre tribute to the totality of modern war":

> The inhabitants throughout the village and in the fields were caught
> and killed and kept the exact postures they had held when the napalm
> struck—a man about to get on his bicycle, fifty boys and girls playing in
> an orphanage, a housewife strangely unmarked, holding in her hand a
> page torn from a Sears-Roebuck catalogue crayoned at mail order number
> 3,811,294 for a $2.98 "bewitching bed jacket—coral."[59]

Almost every major city in North Korea was burned to the ground. Survivors sought shelter in caves. South Koreans fared little better. The British armed forces yearbook reported for 1951, "The war was fought without regard for the South Koreans, and their unfortunate country was regarded as an arena rather than a country to be liberated. As a consequence, fighting was quite ruthless, and it is no exaggeration to state that South Korea no longer exists as a country. Its towns have been destroyed, much of its means of livelihood eradicated, and its people reduced to a sullen mass dependent upon charity. The South Korean, unfortunately, was regarded as a 'gook,' like his cousins north of the 38th parallel."[60] Casualty estimates vary widely, but approximately 3 to 4 million Koreans died, out of a total population of 30 million, as did more than a million Chinese and 37,000 Americans.

A U.S. plane releases napalm over North Korea. Even after peace negotiations began in the spring of 1951, the U.S. air war continued unabated, with napalm as the weapon of choice. Almost every major city in North Korea was burned to the ground.

Women and children search through the rubble in Seoul. During the war, 3 to 4 million Koreans died, out of a total population of 30 million, as did more than a million Chinese and 54,000 Americans.

By February 1951, only 39 percent of Americans still supported the war. It ended in a stalemate. Americans wondered how their powerful, modern military could fail to defeat an ill-equipped army of Korean and Chinese peasants.

LeMay objected to the restraints placed upon the military, recalling that when the war started,

> We slipped a note kind of under the door into the Pentagon and said,
> "Look, let us go up there . . . and burn down five of the biggest towns in
> North Korea—and they're not very big—and that ought to stop it." Well,
> the answer to that was four or five screams—"You'll kill a lot of non-
> combatants" and "It's too horrible." Yet over a period of three years or so . . .
> we burned down *every* town in North Korea and South Korea, too. . . .
> Now, over a period of three years this is palatable, but to kill a few people to
> stop this from happening—a lot of people can't stomach it.[61]

Korea was only one piece of a rapidly unraveling situation in Asia. In Indochina, the United States had decided to bolster its support for the French, making $10 million available for the French puppet Emperor Bao Dai in Vietnam. Trouble was also brewing in the Philippines, where the U.S.-backed president Manuel Roxas and his successor Elpidio Quirino had been battling the Huk peasant insurgency. After collaborating with the Japanese during the war, Roxas aligned himself with the large landowners and the Catholic Church. The United States built up the Philippine army and began a successful counterinsurgency campaign spearheaded by Major Edward Lansdale and fortified by U.S. airpower. A flamboyant advertising executive who served in the OSS and CIA and was immortalized in two famous novels, Lansdale would later lead similar counterinsurgency operations in Vietnam and Cuba but with decidedly less success. And even in the Philippines, primary credit for undercutting the Huks should go not to Lansdale but to President Ramon Magsaysay, who instituted land reform and welcomed the Huks back into the political system.

The Korean War paved the way for the dramatic remilitarization of U.S. society. Truman approved NSC 68, and the defense budget for fiscal 1951 almost quadrupled, from $13.5 billion to $48.2 billion. Within six months of the start of the war, U.S. defense spending soared to $54 billion, providing a tremendous boost to the aerospace and defense sector across the country and particularly in California. In Los Angeles County, 160,000 people worked in aircraft production, and 55 percent of county residents worked in the defense and aerospace sectors. In San Diego, the defense sector accounted for nearly 80 percent of all manufacturing.[62] NATO was transformed into a full-fledged military structure with a U.S. supreme commander and U.S. troops stationed in Europe.

U.S. decisions to rearm Germany and sign a peace treaty with Japan, regardless of Soviet participation, further hardened the enmity between the United States and the USSR, leading the newly appointed U.S. ambassador to the Soviet Union, George Kennan, to worry that "we had . . . contributed . . . by the over-militarization of our policies and statements—to a belief in Moscow that it was war we were after."[63]

Given the hypermilitarization of American life, it was only fitting that one of the nation's top military men run for president. The 1952 election pitted Illinois Governor Adlai Stevenson against General Dwight Eisenhower. Eisenhower chose anti-Communist hatchet man California Senator Richard Nixon as his running mate. During the campaign, Nixon did Ike's dirty work, denouncing "Adlai the appeaser" who "carries a Ph.D. from Dean Acheson's cowardly college of Communist containment."[64] Senator Joseph McCarthy struck a similar theme, referring to the Democratic candidate as "Alger,"[65] a reference to Alger Hiss. McCarthy had a particular vendetta against General George Marshall, whom he blamed for "losing" China during his tenure as Truman's secretary of state. Eisenhower was set to defend his friend and mentor against such scurrilous attacks while campaigning in McCarthy's home state of Wisconsin. But Eisenhower backed off from a confrontation with the anti-Communist demagogue, pusillanimously dropping a passage defending Marshall from his speech. He was apparently aware of the fact that an astounding 185 of the 221 Republican members of the House had requested appointment to the House Un-American Activities Committee.[66]

The Eisenhower campaign, which had inveighed against Democratic corruption, reached its nadir in September, when it was rocked by the news that conservative businessmen had given Nixon a secret donation of $18,000. Eisenhower's advisors echoed the public in demanding Nixon's ouster. In a last-ditch effort to rescue his candidacy, Nixon delivered his famous "Checkers speech" to 55 million television viewers.

That bit of sentimentality saved the day for Nixon. But Eisenhower let Nixon twist in the wind a bit longer. He told Nixon to meet him in West Virginia. Nixon composed a letter of resignation and barked at an aide, "What more does he want? I'm not going to crawl on my hands and knees to him." The next day Eisenhower met him at the airport and said, "Dick, you're my boy."[67] Nixon broke down and cried.

Eisenhower won the election handily, carrying thirty-nine states. U.S.-Soviet relations were extremely tense when he took office in January 1953. Eisenhower and John Foster Dulles, his new secretary of state, had done little to lower the temperature during the campaign, fanning the flames of anti-Sovietism with their calls to move beyond Democratic "containment" to Republican "liberation."

But Eisenhower had not always been such a perfervid anti-Communist. He had pushed hard for opening a second front in 1942 and later developed a friendly relationship with Soviet Marshall Georgi Zhukov. After the war, he remained confident that U.S.-Soviet friendship would endure. Stalin, who held him in high regard, told U.S. Ambassador Averell Harriman, "General Eisenhower is a very great man, not only because of his military accomplishments but because of his human, friendly, kind, and frank nature."[68] Eisenhower visited Moscow in August 1945 and received a hero's welcome from the Soviet people. Stalin accorded him the special honor of being the first foreigner to witness a parade in Red Square from the platform atop Lenin's tomb. Later, in his farewell report as army chief of staff, he rejected the facile equation of military strength and national security:

> National security does not mean militarism or any approach to it. Security cannot be measured by the size of munitions stockpiles or the number of men under arms or the monopoly of an invincible weapon. That was the German and Japanese idea of power which, in the test of war, was proved false. Even in time of peace, the index of material strength is unreliable, for arms become obsolete and worthless; vast armies decay while sapping the strength of the nations supporting them; monopoly of a weapon is soon broken.[69]

During his time in office, Eisenhower would be confronted with repeated opportunities to roll back the Cold War and arms race. Presiding over the world's most powerful nation during perhaps the tensest extended period in history, he could have taken bold action that could have put the world on a different path. Signs emanating from Moscow indicated that the Kremlin might be ready to change course. But because of ideology, political calculations, the exigencies of a militarized state, and limited imagination, he repeatedly failed to seize the opportunities that emerged. And although he deserves credit for avoiding war with the Soviet Union at a time when such a war seemed quite possible, he left the world a far more dangerous place than when he first took office.

Eisenhower didn't have to wait long for an extraordinary opportunity to reverse the course of the Cold War. On March 5, 1953, barely a month into Eisenhower's presidency, Josef Stalin died. Some of Eisenhower's close advisors urged him to take advantage of the chaotic situation in Moscow and "scare the daylights out of the enemy." The National Security Council (NSC) called for "psychological exploitation of this event," and C. D. Jackson, Eisenhower's advisor on psychological warfare, proposed "a general political warfare offensive."[70] But the new Soviet leaders moved quickly to ease tensions with the United States, instructing China and North Korea to compromise on an armistice agreement. On March 15, Georgi Malenkov publicly declared, "there is no disputed or unresolved question that cannot be settled peacefully."[71] The new CIA director, Allen Dulles, reported that Soviet leaders seriously desired to "lessen the dangers of global war."[72] They even took preliminary steps toward liberalization within the Soviet Union. Churchill, who had been reelected prime minister in 1951, had grown wary of the nuclear threat. He urged Washington to seize this unprecedented opportunity to end the Cold War conflict. He pressed for a summit with Soviet leaders.[73] Eisenhower held his tongue for six weeks while his advisors crafted a response. He finally broke his silence, offering one of the most lucid statements ever made by a U.S. president on the toll the Cold War was taking on the nation:

> Every gun that is made, every warship launched, every rocket fired signifies a theft from those who hunger and are not fed, those who are cold and are not clothed. This world . . . is spending the sweat of its laborers, the genius of its scientists, the hopes of its children. The cost of one modern heavy bomber is . . . a modern brick school in more than 30 cities. It is two electric power plants, each serving a town of 60,000 population. It is two fine, fully equipped hospitals. It is some 50 miles of concrete pavement. We pay for a single fighter plane with a half-million bushels of wheat. We pay for a single destroyer with new homes that could have housed more than 8,000 people. . . . This is not a way of life at all. . . . Under the cloud of threatening war, it is humanity hanging from a cross of iron.[74]

In what seemed a dramatic departure, Eisenhower called for peace, disarmament, and third-world development. But in equally fundamental ways, he remained an orthodox Cold Warrior, blaming the Soviets for the troubled state of the world.

The *New York Times* called the speech "magnificent and deeply moving."[75] The *Washington Post* hoped that it signaled a rejection of Truman's "provocative words," "belligerent gesturings," "militarization of policy," and "aid . . . to everybody who would turn anti-Communist." Eisenhower, the *Post* felt, still needed to repudiate "the theory that a crack of the whip from Moscow produces automatic obedience in the far corners of the satellite states and throughout Red China and Communist-infected Asia."[76]

The Soviets reprinted the speech widely and offered some hopeful measures of their own. But the optimism proved short-lived. Two days later, Dulles dismissed Malenkov's "peace offensive" as a "peace defensive" taken in response to U.S. strength. He accused the Communists of "endlessly conspir[ing] to overthrow from within, every genuinely free government in the world."[77]

Perplexed, the Soviets wondered whether Eisenhower or Dulles spoke for the administration. They applauded Eisenhower for detailing the costs of U.S. militarism but chided him for leaving out the astronomical cost of accumulating a vast nuclear arsenal and constructing hundreds of military bases around the world.

Nor did the steps taken to end the fighting in Korea necessarily augur well for future relations. Despite making progress in the negotiations, Eisenhower threatened to widen the war and considered using tactical atomic weapons, which the United States first tested in January. At an NSC meeting in February, Eisenhower identified the Kaesong area in North Korea as a good place to use the new weapon. In May, when Army Chief of Staff General J. Lawton Collins said that he was "very skeptical about the value of using atomic weapons tactically in Korea," Eisenhower callously replied, "it might be cheaper, dollar-wise, to use atomic weapons in Korea than to continue to use conventional weapons." [78] That month, the Joint Chiefs recommended and the NSC endorsed atomic attacks on China. Eisenhower and Dulles made sure the Communist leaders knew of those threats.

The United States also began bombing the dams near Pyongyang, causing enormous floods and destroying the rice crop. The Nuremberg tribunal had condemned similar Nazi actions in Holland in 1944 as a war crime. Finally, in June, the two sides signed agreements settling the POW issue and agreeing on a truce demarcation line, but fighting intensified and casualties skyrocketed on both sides. The morale of the UN forces plummeted. Desertions increased. Self-inflicted wounds reached epidemic proportions. On July 27, 1953, an armistice was finally signed by North Korea, China, and the United States, two years and seventeen days after talks began. South Korea has still not signed. In August, Eisenhower kept up pressure, instructing LeMay to dispatch twenty nuclear-armed B-36 bombers to Kadena Air Base in Okinawa as part of Operation "Big Stick." LeMay invited the press to observe their arrival.

Eisenhower used atomic bombs repeatedly throughout his presidency in the same sense, as Daniel Ellsberg has argued, that a robber holding a gun to someone's head uses the gun without pulling the trigger. Among those who learned the lesson that nuclear threats could frighten an enemy into capitulating was Richard Nixon. In 1968, Nixon explained his strategy for dealing with North Vietnam to Bob Haldeman: "I call it the madman theory, Bob. I want the North Vietnamese to believe I've reached the point where I might do anything to stop the war. We'll just slip the word to them that, 'for God's sake, you know Nixon is obsessed about Communists. We can't restrain him when he's angry—and he has his hand on the nuclear button'—and Ho Chi Minh himself will be in Paris in two days begging for peace."

Haldeman explained that Nixon "saw a parallel in the action President Eisenhower had taken. . . . When Eisenhower arrived in the White House, the Korean War was stalemated. . . . He secretly got word to the Chinese that he would drop nuclear bombs. . . . In a few weeks, the Chinese called for a truce and the Korean War ended."

"It worked," Nixon insisted. "It was the bomb that did it." He credited

Eisenhower with teaching him the value of unpredictability. "If the adversary feels that you are unpredictable, even rash," he wrote, "he will be deterred from pressing you too far. The odds that he will fold increase greatly and the unpredictable president will win another hand." [79] Eisenhower was certainly not a "madman," but he paid little heed to how someone like Nixon might mimic his actions.

The Korean War had its winners and its losers. Rhee's and Jiang's shaky regimes survived. Japan profited. China had stood up to the Americans, enhancing its international prestige, but the Soviets had not, accelerating the Sino-Soviet split. And Churchill grasped the real meaning for the United States: "Korea does not really matter now. I'd never heard of the bloody place until I was 74. Its importance lies in the fact that it has led to the re-arming of America." [80]

Among the war's victims were the accused atomic spies Ethel and Julius Rosenberg. Upon sentencing them to death in a highly controversial ruling, the judge charged, "your conduct has already caused the communist aggression in Korea with the resultant casualties exceeding 50,000 Americans." [81]

A casualty of a different sort was Henry Wallace. The Progressive Party's ranks had dwindled sharply after the 1948 election debacle, leaving it largely in the hands of Communists who, for the most part, remained uncritical of the Soviet Union. Wallace had seen enough of Stalinism to know how abhorrent it was. He told delegates to the Progressive Party convention in late February 1950, "The United States and Russia stand out today as the two big brutes of the world. Each in its own eyes rests on high moral principles, but each in the eyes of other nations is guided by force and force alone."

The North Korean invasion of South Korea proved the final straw for Wallace. When Progressive Party leaders opposed UN action, he issued his own "statement of conscience." Insisting that the Soviets could have blocked the North Korean invasion in the first place if they'd wanted and could stop it now, he declared, "I hold no brief for the past actions of either the United States or Russia but when my country is at war and the United Nations sanctions that war, I am on the side of my country and the United Nations." But he urged U.S. leaders to break with recent policies, which he continued to deplore: "The United States will fight a losing battle in Asia as long as she stands behind feudal regimes based on exorbitant charges of land lords and money lords. Russia is using a mightier power than the atom bomb as long as she helps the people get out from under their ancient aggressors. But we in the United States have a still mightier power if we will only use it for the people." Three weeks later, he resigned from the Progressive Party. After years of waging an often lonely, though courageous, struggle against overwhelming odds, the indomitable visionary leader had finally had enough. Stalin's betrayals, when combined with the growing influence of domestic Cold Warriors, had sapped him of the strength needed to continue the fight. He retreated to his farm in upstate New York and spent his remaining years largely tending to his corn and chickens, which were then feeding much of the world.

The final casualty of the war, some feared, was American manhood. One postwar study found that 70 percent of U.S. POWs had "collapsed" and collaborated with their captors. Some attributed the phenomenon to Communist brainwashing. Others pointed to something more troubling. One army doctor who traveled about the camps to treat U.S. prisoners reported, "the strong regularly took food from the weak. . . . Many men were sick, and these men, instead of being helped and nursed by the others, were ignored, or worse. . . . On winter nights, helpless men with dysentery were rolled outside the huts by their comrades and left to die in the cold." An astounding 38 percent of U.S. prisoners died. Most withdrew into themselves and made little effort to find food or keep clean. The doctor attributed this to "some new failure in the childhood and adolescent training of our young men—a new softness."[82]

If American men were getting soft, American technology would compensate. Just three days before Eisenhower's election, the United States tested its first prototype hydrogen bomb on the island of Elugelab in the Enewetak Atoll in the Marshall Islands. The island burned for six hours under a mushroom cloud a hundred miles across and then disappeared. The more-than-10-megaton blast exceeded all expectations. A sailor commented, "You would swear the whole world was on fire."[83] Physicist Harold Agnew was aboard ship twenty-five miles away. He observed, "something I'll never forget was the heat. Not the blast . . . the heat just kept coming on and on and on. And it was really scary."[84] Eisenhower acknowledged the new reality in his inaugural address. "Science," he warned, "seems ready to confer upon us . . . the power to erase human life from this planet."[85] Yet his policies over the next eight years propelled us ever more disastrously toward realizing that threat. It was as if Lewis Mumford's brilliant 1946 essay about the madness of American leaders had been written with the future Eisenhower in mind.

As with his anticommunism, Eisenhower's embrace of nuclearism came later in life. He had opposed the atomic bombing of Japan on both military and moral grounds. He was actually in Moscow when he learned about Hiroshima. He told a journalist, "Before the atom bomb was used, . . . I was sure we could keep the peace with Russia. Now, I don't know. I had hoped the bomb wouldn't figure in this war. Until now I would have said that we three, Britain . . . , America . . . , and Russia . . . could have guaranteed the peace of the world for a long time to come. But now, I don't know. People are frightened and disturbed all over. Everyone feels insecure again."[86]

After the war, he supported efforts at international control, wanting atomic bombs to be turned over to the United Nations and destroyed. He spoke out consistently for civilian rather than military control of the bomb. And he continued to raise moral concerns about the use of such a weapon. In 1947, he told a luncheon, "I decry loose and sometimes gloating talk about the degree of security implicit in a weapon that might destroy millions overnight."[87]

As David Rosenberg notes, "Dwight D. Eisenhower entered the presidency in January 1953 with a more thorough knowledge of nuclear weapons than any President before or since." As army chief of staff, temporary chairman of the Joint Chiefs of Staff, and NATO supreme commander, he had been intimately involved in early nuclear-war planning. During those years, his abhorrence of nuclear weapons had abated considerably, but it had not disappeared. In March 1953, he warned his cabinet not to think of the bomb as "a cheap way to solve things." He reminded them, "It is cold comfort for any citizen of Western Europe to be assured that—after his country is overrun and he is pushing up daisies—someone still alive will drop a bomb on the Kremlin."[88]

He was determined to build on the United States' lead in the nuclear arms race. In summer 1953, the CIA reported reassuringly that there was no evidence that the Soviets were working on a hydrogen bomb. On August 12, 1953, much to the CIA's chagrin, the Soviets exploded what was believed to have been a 400-kiloton hydrogen bomb in Kazakhstan. Though far less powerful than the U.S. model, the Soviet bomb was not only deliverable, it was "dry," needing no refrigeration. The *Bulletin of the Atomic Scientists* moved the hands of the Doomsday Clock to two minutes before midnight. It had stood at three since the Soviet atomic bomb test in 1949.[89] The Soviets were closing the gap at a stunning pace.

The *New York Times* took "comfort in the fact that" the United States still possessed a lead in atomic and hydrogen bomb production but recognized that "these advantages are bound to diminish with time." The *Times* noted that even Secretary of State Dulles had declared that "the central problem now is to save the human race from extinction."[90]

Dulles and his relatives had helped design the American Empire. John Foster Dulles's maternal grandfather, John W. Foster, and his uncle Robert Lansing had both served as secretary of state. John W. painstakingly tutored his eldest grandson throughout his childhood, instilling a firm belief in the United States' global role. John Foster Dulles's paternal grandfather and his father had both been Presbyterian ministers, his grandfather serving as a missionary in India. His younger brother, Allen, became director of the CIA. When his uncle Lansing served as Wilson's secretary of state during and after the First World War, Dulles was secretary-treasurer of the government's new Russian Bureau, whose main function was to assist anti-Bolshevik forces challenging the Russian Revolution. Financier Bernard Baruch, an old family friend, next tapped the young lawyer to serve as legal advisor to the U.S. delegation to the Inter-Allied Reparations Commission at Versailles, after which he returned to practice law at

Sullivan and Cromwell, overseeing the accounts of some of the pillars of the emerging empire: J. P. Morgan & Company; Brown Brothers Harriman; Dillon, Read; Goldman Sachs; United Fruit Company; International Nickel Company; United Railways of Central America; and the Overseas Securities Corporation.[91]

Though journalistic accounts of Dulles's unabashed affection for Hitler in the early years of the Nazi dictatorship are hard to verify, there is no doubt that he maintained some involvement in German business activities. He participated actively in the vast interwar cartelization, which afforded a means to stabilize the shaky U.S. economy, reduce competition, and guarantee profits. Dulles dealt extensively with I. G. Farben through the nickel and chemical cartels. Despite his later vehement denials of any dealings with the Nazi regime, he is known to have visited Berlin in 1934, 1935, 1936, 1937, and 1939.[92] In assessing Dulles's involvement, award-winning *New York Times* and *Boston Globe* foreign correspondent Steven Kinzer, citing Nancy Lisagor and Frank Lipsius's "exhaustive study" of Sullivan & Cromwell, writes that "the firm 'thrived on its cartels and collusion with the new Nazi regime,' and Dulles spent much of 1934 'publicly supporting Hitler,' leaving his partners 'shocked that he could so easily disregard law and international treaties to justify Nazi repression.'"[93]

Dulles never wavered in his commitment to maintaining U.S. hegemony and protecting U.S. business interests or in his hatred of communism. Despite outward appearances, the rigid, sometimes belligerent secretary of state and the affable president differed little on substantive policy issues. Eisenhower understood that even with income tax rates topping 90 percent for the wealthiest Americans, the nation's bloated military budget would prove impossible to sustain, ultimately bankrupting the country. He worried, "This country can choke itself to death piling up military expenditures."[94] He decided to curb ballooning defense spending by relying on nuclear arms, which were cheaper than maintaining a large standing army. In late October 1953, he approved a new Basic National Security Policy, NSC 162/2, the core of his "New Look" defense policy, which stated, "in the event of hostilities, the United States will consider nuclear weapons to be as available for use as other munitions."[95] Based on the assumption that any war with the Soviet Union would quickly evolve into a full-scale nuclear war, the New Look downplayed conventional military capabilities and relied upon massive nuclear retaliation by the fortified Strategic Air Command. Thus the savings made by reducing the size of the army were offset, in large part, by increased spending on the air force and navy. Eisenhower ended up cutting Truman's 1954 defense budget from $41.3 billion to $36 billion.

Eisenhower felt constrained by the fact that neither the U.S. public nor his British allies were as sanguine as he and Dulles about the use of nuclear weapons. He set about to erase the line between conventional and nuclear weapons.

According to the minutes of a late March 1953 NSC discussion of using nuclear weapons in Korea, "the President and Secretary Dulles were in complete agreement that somehow or other the tabu which surrounds the use of atomic weapons would have to be destroyed."[96]

Dulles called for breaking "down this false distinction" between conventional and nuclear weapons, which he attributed to a Soviet propaganda campaign.[97] Joint Chiefs Chairman Admiral Arthur Radford explained to listeners at the Naval War College in May 1954 that "atomic forces are now our primary forces . . . actions by forces, on land, sea or air are relegated to a secondary role . . . nuclear weapons, fission and fusion, will be used in the next major war."[98]

In meetings in Bermuda with Britain's Churchill and French Premier Joseph Laniel in December 1953, Eisenhower sought his allies' support for using atomic bombs if fighting started in Korea again. Churchill sent his private secretary Jock Colville to Eisenhower to express his concerns. Colville was taken aback by Eisenhower's response: "whereas Winston looked on the atomic bomb as something entirely new and terrible, he looked upon it as just the latest improvement in military weapons. He implied that there was no distinction between 'conventional' weapons and atomic weapons: all weapons in due course become conventional."[99] Colville later wrote, "I could hardly believe my ears." Eisenhower similarly told Anthony Eden, "The development of smaller atomic weapons and the use of atomic artillery makes the distinction [between atomic and conventional weapons] impossible to sustain."[100]

In 1955, Eisenhower responded to a reporter's question about using tactical atomic weapons: "Yes of course they would be used. In any combat where these things can be used on strictly military targets and for strictly military purposes, I see no reason why they shouldn't be used just exactly as you would use a bullet or anything else."[101]

The very next day, Nixon reinforced the point: "tactical atomic explosives are now conventional and will be used against the targets of any aggressive force."[102] A few weeks later, Ike told Congress that "a wide variety" of tactical atomic weapons "have today achieved conventional status in the arsenals of our armed forces."[103]

Eisenhower prepared for their use by transferring control of the atomic stockpile from the AEC to the military. Truman had transferred nine weapons to Guam in 1951 but had otherwise insisted on retaining civilian control. He said he did not want "to have some dashing lieutenant colonel decide when would be the proper time to drop one."[104] Eisenhower had no such compunctions. In June 1953, he began transferring atomic bombs from the AEC to the Defense Department to enhance operational readiness and protect them from surprise Soviet attack. In December 1954, he ordered 42 percent of atomic bombs and 36 percent of hydrogen bombs deployed overseas, many menacingly close to the Soviet Union. By

1959, the military had custody of more than 80 percent of U.S. nuclear weapons.

The United States' European allies were terrified that the United States would start a nuclear war, and they pressured Eisenhower to lower the tensions. He responded on December 8, 1953, mesmerizing the 3,500 delegates at the United Nations with his "Atoms for Peace" speech declaring that the United States would devote "its entire heart and mind to find the way by which the miraculous inventiveness of man shall not be dedicated to his death, but consecrated to his life" by spreading the benefits of peaceful atomic power at home and abroad.[105]

The U.S. media rang out with praise. *New York Times* military correspondent Hanson Baldwin wrote that Eisenhower's "eloquent" and "moving argument for peace . . . represented an earnest attempt to halt the atomic arms race." However, Baldwin regretted that the prospects for success remained bleak because "the Soviet Union's whole concept is built upon world struggle and ultimate world domination."[106]

Eisenhower was so desperate to put a smiling face on the atom that he ignored numerous warnings about the danger of proliferation. The AEC's only nuclear physicist, Henry Smyth, dismissed Atoms for Peace as a "thoroughly dishonest proposal" that ignored proliferation risks and exaggerated the prospects of nuclear power.[107] Others echoed his dissent.

Soviet leaders were particularly irked by the dangers of proliferation. Five top scientists, including nuclear physicist Igor Kurchatov, asserted that "the development of the industrial use of atomic energy by itself does not only not exclude, but leads directly, to an increase of military atomic potential." Foreign Minister Molotov reiterated this point in meetings with Dulles and in a note stating that it was "possible for the very application of atomic energy for peaceful purposes to be utilized for increasing the production of atomic weapons." When Molotov again raised the proliferation risk at their May 1 meeting, Dulles couldn't grasp the concept and replied that he "would seek out a scientist to educate him more fully."[108]

If Eisenhower's UN address raised hopes for an easing of international tensions, Dulles's January 12 speech to the Council on Foreign Relations dashed them thoroughly. He warned that local defenses against communism would be backed by "massive retaliatory power" deployed "at places and with means of [our] own choosing."[109]

Reliance on nuclear weapons represented a fundamental departure from previous policy. Whereas Truman, after Hiroshima and Nagasaki, had viewed atomic bombs as weapons that would be used only in the most desperate circumstances, Eisenhower made them the foundation of U.S. defense strategy. The *Wall Street Journal* reported, "There was a wide assumption that here was a reckless policy of turning every minor clash into an atomic Armageddon."[110] The *New York Times'* James Reston was stunned that Eisenhower and Dulles were enacting a " 'new strategy,' potentially graver than anything ever proposed by any United States Government," and not a single congressman even questioned this commitment to "sudden atomic retaliation." He worried about the constitutional implications of such expanded presidential powers. If the Chinese moved into Indochina or the Soviets into Iran, who, he asked, would give the order to deploy "massive retaliatory power" against Beijing or Moscow? How, he wondered, could the president "seek the consent of the Congress without alerting the Kremlin and risking a sudden atomic blow upon the United States?"[111]

RAND analyst Joseph Loftus became concerned that the new SAC Emergency War Plan was targeting Soviet cities and civilian populations. While Loftus was visiting SAC headquarters in Omaha, General James Walsh, the director of SAC intelligence, invited him over to his house for cocktails and began lecturing him on the need to maximize destruction. Walsh suddenly exploded. "Goddammit, Loftus, there's only one way to attack the Russians, and that's to hit them hard with everything we have and"—he shouted, pounding his fist on the enormous Bible on the table—"knock their balls off!"[112]

By the spring of 1954, SAC's war plan called for attacking the Soviet Union with 600 to 750 bombs and turning it into "a smoking, radiating ruin at the end of two hours."[113] The plan involved killing 80 percent of the population in 118 major cities, or 60 million people. Later that year, the United States began deploying nuclear weapons on the soil of its European allies. By 1958, almost three thousand had been placed in Western Europe.

Meanwhile, the U.S. arsenal continued to grow at a dizzying pace, expanding from slightly over 1,000 when Eisenhower took office to over 22,000 bombs when he left office eight years later.

Massive retaliation might frighten the Soviets, but it would do little to thwart the revolutionary upsurge in the developing world, where the Soviet Union was poised to take advantage of widespread discontent. The most important third-world leaders—Gamal Abdel Nasser of Egypt, Josip Broz Tito of Yugoslavia, and Jawaharlal Nehru of India—steered a neutral course between the capitalist and socialist blocs and thought it obscene to spend billions of dollars and rubles on arms when money for economic development was in short supply. On his first trip abroad, in May 1953, Dulles learned of hostility toward the United States in Asia, where the Soviet system had real appeal, and the Middle East. During his trip, he wrote to Eisenhower about "bitterness" in the Arab world, where "the United States suffered from being linked with British and French imperialism"[114] and from its blind support for Israel.

Dulles wasn't sure that the United States could ever win the allegiance of third-world peoples. He noted that asking underdeveloped countries to embrace capitalism was like asking people who were undernourished and suffering from rickets to play rugby: "You say to them, 'Have a free competitive system.' And they say, 'Good god, there must be a better way of doing things!'"[115] Eisenhower was also troubled by the depth of animosity toward the United States among the world's impoverished masses. He raised the issue at a March 1953 NSC meeting, wondering why it wasn't possible "to get some of the people in these downtrodden countries to like us instead of hating us."[116]

The United States' role in the Iranian conflict should have provided all the answer Eisenhower needed. Upon taking office, Eisenhower confronted a crisis in Iran, where the government of Mohammad Mossadeq was challenging the monopoly held by Britain's Anglo-Iranian Oil Company, the forerunner of British Petroleum (BP) and the world's third largest crude-oil producer. The company, which was 51 percent owned by the British government, had developed cozy relations with Reza Shah Pahlavi, who had seized power after World War I and become shah in 1925, and with his son Mohammad Reza Shah Pahlavi, who replaced his father in 1941, when the elder's Nazi sympathies had provoked a joint occupation of Iran by Britain and the Soviet Union.

Anglo-Iranian kept 84 percent of the revenue for itself, leaving at most a paltry 16 percent for the Iranians. It paid taxes in Britain rather than Iran. In fact, its British taxes were more than double the amount that the Iranians received in royalties.[117] While the British got rich off Iranian oil, the Iranians lived in poverty. Oil-field workers earned less than 50 cents per day and received no benefits or vacations. The Iranians' outrage was ignited in 1950 when the U.S. oil company ARAMCO signed a contract giving Saudi Arabia 50 percent of the profits from Saudi oil. Under pressure, Anglo-Iranian offered improved terms. But Mossadeq so hated British colonialism that he refused to consider the company's offer. The Iranian parliament, reflecting Iranians' near-universal antipathy toward Anglo-Iranian, voted unanimously to nationalize the oil industry and compensate the British for their investment. Britain's Labour government seemed hardly in a position to object, having nationalized Britain's coal and electricity companies and railroads.

A former finance and foreign minister, Mossadeq, despite his legendary eccentricities, was an enormously popular figure inside Iran and a well-respected one internationally. He was the first Iranian to earn a doctor of law degree from a European university. He had attended the Versailles Conference in a futile attempt to block the assertion of British control and had led the decolonization fight in succeeding decades. *Time* magazine named him Man of the Year for 1951. The U.S. ambassador reported that Mossadeq "has the backing of 95 to 98 percent of the people of this country."[118] His defiance of the colonial masters thrilled the Arab masses throughout the region.

With Iran producing 40 percent of Middle Eastern oil, the United States understood the importance of easing the tension. It had been pushing the British to improve their offer and avoid the crisis since 1948. Truman derided Sir William Fraser, the head of Anglo-Iranian, as a "typical nineteenth century colonial exploiter."[119]

Members of the British cabinet responded in the fashion typical of twentieth-century colonial exploiters and debated the pros and cons of invading. It became clear that such an invasion would prove costly and might not succeed. But capitulating to the Iranians, some felt, could put the final nail in the empire's coffin. "If Persia were allowed to get away with it, Egypt and other Middle Eastern countries would be encouraged to think they could try things on," Defense Minister Emanuel Shinwell feared. "The next thing might be an attempt to nationalize the Suez Canal." Opposition leader Winston Churchill told Prime Minister Clement Attlee that he was "rather shocked at the attitude of the United States, who did not seem to appreciate fully the importance of the great area extending from the Caspian to the Persian Gulf: it was more important than Korea." Foreign Secretary Herbert Morrison also deplored the policy of "scuttle and surrender."[120]

Acheson attempted to mediate, fearing that military action by Great Britain in the south might provoke a Soviet incursion in the north. Though frustrated by Mossadeq's intransigence, Acheson sympathized with the Iranians' position. He convinced Averell Harriman to go to Tehran to defuse the situation. Harriman reported that the "situation that has developed here is a tragic example of absentee management combined with world-wide growth of nationalism in underdeveloped countries."[121] The British put the invasion on hold, initiating economic warfare in its stead. They embargoed oil coming out of Iran and goods going in. With U.S. approval, the Bank of England halted the finance of and trade with Iran. The Iranian economy slowly ground to a halt.

Winston Churchill and his Conservative Party returned to power in October 1951, increasing the pressure for military intervention. Churchill had earlier written to Truman that "Mussy Duck" was "an elderly lunatic bent on wrecking his country and handing it over to communism."[122] When Mossadeq got wind of British plans to launch a coup, he shut the British Embassy and expelled its employees.

When Eisenhower took office, the Dulles brothers met with Kermit "Kim" Roosevelt, Theodore Roosevelt's grandson and the CIA's top Middle East expert, to discuss eliminating "that madman Mossadeq."[123] John Foster Dulles acknowledged that Mossadeq wasn't a Communist, but he feared a takeover by the Communist Tudeh party that would deliver Iran's oil to Moscow. Soon, he argued, the rest of Middle Eastern oil would come under Soviet control. Mossadeq had moved closer to Tudeh as the crisis unfolded. The new administration portrayed Mossadeq as an unstable extremist—"not quite sane," according to U.S. Ambassador Loy Henderson.[124]

Behind the scenes, the CIA went to work, launching "Operation Ajax" headed by Roosevelt. British intelligence, MI6, provided support. But things did not go as planned. When the CIA's Tehran station chief opposed this tawdry operation as being inimical to the United States' long-term interests, Allen Dulles fired him. Mossadeq uncovered the shah's collaboration with the coup attempt, forcing the shah to flee the country.

The CIA, meanwhile, had been buying up Iranian journalists, preachers, army and police officers, and members of parliament, who were instructed to foment opposition to the government. The CIA also purchased the services of the extremist Warriors of Islam, a "terrorist gang," according to a CIA history of the coup.[125] In August, Roosevelt began setting mobs loose to create chaos in the capital, Tehran. He spread rumors that Mossadeq was a Communist and a Jew. His street thugs, pretending to be members of the Tudeh party, attacked mullahs and destroyed a mosque. Among the rioters was Ayatollah Ruhollah Musavi Khomeini, Iran's future leader. On August 19, 1953, in the midst of the anarchy, Roosevelt brought General Fazlollah Zahedi out of his CIA hiding place. Zahedi announced that the shah, then in Italy, had appointed him the new prime minister. After an armed battle, coup plotters arrested Mossadeq and thousands of his supporters. Some were executed. Mossadeq was convicted of treason and imprisoned. The shah returned to Tehran. At a final meeting with Roosevelt, the shah offered a toast: "I owe my throne to God, my people, my army—and to you."[126]

The American oil companies were also grateful. Previously frozen out of Iranian oil production, five U.S. oil companies now received 40 percent ownership of the new consortium established to develop Iranian oil. And the United States opened its coffers to the shah. Within two weeks of the coup, the United States granted Iran $68 million in emergency aid, with more than $100 million more soon to follow. The United States had gained an ally and access to an enormous supply of oil but in the process had outraged the citizens of a proud nation whose resentment at the overthrow of their popular prime minister and imposition of a repressive regime would later come back to haunt it. The shah continued to rule for more than twenty-five years, with strong U.S. backing, by fixing elections and relying on the repressive power of SAVAK, his newly created intelligence service.

The CIA, having toppled its first government, now saw itself as capable of replicating the feat elsewhere and would attempt to do so repeatedly in succeeding years. The Soviets, therefore, instead of seeing a softening of U.S. policy in the aftermath of Stalin's death, saw the United States impose another puppet government in a nation with which the Soviet Union shared a thousand-kilometer border as part of an ongoing strategy of encirclement.

On the heels of this "success" in Iran, the Eisenhower administration targeted the small, impoverished Central American nation of Guatemala. Guatemalans had suffered under a brutal U.S.-backed dictator, Jorge Ubico, whom

A pro-Mossadeq demonstration in Iran in February 1953.
Enormously popular inside his country and well-respected
internationally, Mossadeq was overthrown by the CIA in 1953.

they overthrew in 1944. Before the reform government took power, 2 percent of the population owned 60 percent of the land, while 50 percent of the people eked out a living on only 3 percent of the land. The Indian half of Guatemala's population barely survived on less than 50 cents per day. In 1950, Guatemalans elected the handsome, charismatic thirty-eight-year-old Colonel Jacobo Árbenz Guzmán president in an election remarkable for its fairness. At his March 1951 inauguration, he declared his commitment to social justice and reform.

> All the riches of Guatemala are not as important as the life, the freedom, the dignity, the health and the happiness of the most humble of its people . . . we must distribute these riches so that those who have less— and they are the immense majority—benefit more, while those who have more—and they are so few—also benefit, but to a lesser extent. How could it be otherwise, given the poverty, the poor health, and the lack of education of our people?[127]

The U.S. media wasted little time in denouncing Guatemala's Communist "tyranny," beginning its assault long before Árbenz had time to start implementing his reform agenda. In June, the *New York Times* decried "The Guatemalan

Cancer," registering "a sense of deep disappointment and disillusionment over the trend of Guatemalan politics in the two months since Colonel Árbenz became President." The editors took particular umbrage at the growth of Communist influence, complaining that "the Government's policy is either running parallel to, or is a front for, Russian imperialism in Central America."[128] The *Washington Post* carried an editorial a few months later titled "Red Cell in Guatemala" that branded the new president of Guatemala's Congress a "straight party liner" and dismissed Árbenz as little more than a tool.[129]

Ignoring his critics, Árbenz set out to modernize Guatemala's industry and agriculture and develop its mineral resources. To do so meant challenging the power of United Fruit Company, which dominated the Guatemalan economy. Called "the octopus" by Guatemalans, United Fruit reached its tentaclelike arms deep into railroads, ports, shipping, and especially banana plantations. Árbenz announced plans for a massive land reform program beginning with the nationalization of 234,000 acres of United Fruit Company land, more than 90 percent of which the company was not using. In all, the company's 550,000 acres represented approximately one-fifth of Guatemala's arable land. Árbenz offered to compensate United Fruit in the amount of $600,000, based on the company's own greatly underpriced assessment of the land's value in previous tax returns. The company demanded more. Árbenz took steps to appropriate another 173,000 acres. The public relations pioneer and master propagandist Edward Bernays, Sigmund Freud's nephew, had already launched a campaign to brand Árbenz a Communist. He found willing allies at the *New York Times*. Bernays paid a visit to *Times* publisher Arthur Hays Sulzberger. Dutifully, the *Times* soon began publishing articles about the Communist threat in Guatemala. Leading congressmen, including Senator Henry Cabot Lodge, whose family had gorged on United Fruit for decades, decried this growing Communist menace.[130]

Truman took heed of the alleged Communist threat emanating from Guatemala. In April 1952, he hosted a state dinner for Nicaraguan dictator Anastasio Somoza, who had long been persona non grata in Washington. Somoza assured State Department officials that if the United States would provide arms, he and exiled Guatemalan colonel Carlos Castillo Armas would get rid of Árbenz. The Truman administration decided to overthrow Árbenz in September 1952 but reversed course when U.S. involvement was exposed.[131]

Eisenhower had no such compunctions. He appointed Jack Peurifoy as his ambassador to Guatemala. Peurifoy, who spoke no Spanish, had been serving in Greece, where his role in helping restore the monarchy to power had earned him the sobriquet "the butcher of Athens." A photo of the Greek royal family still adorned his desk. His penchant for wearing a gun in his belt led his wife to nickname him "pistol packing Peurifoy."[132] Before Greece, he had helped purge the State Department of liberals and leftists. Árbenz invited the new U.S. ambassador and his wife to dinner. They clashed for six hours over Communist influence in the Guatemalan government, land reform, and treatment of United Fruit. Peurifoy sent Secretary of State Dulles a long cable detailing their discussion that concluded, "I am definitely convinced that if the President is not a communist, he will certainly do until one comes along." [133]

In Peurifoy's mind, that equated to being a tool of Moscow: "Communism is directed by the Kremlin all over the world, and anyone who thinks differently doesn't know what he is talking about." [134] In reality, Guatemalan communism was indigenous and the Partido Guatemalteco del Trabajo was independent of the Soviet Union. The Communists held only four of the fifty-six seats in Congress and no cabinet posts. The party had approximately 4,000 members in a population of 3.5 million.

To suggest that United Fruit had friends among the high and mighty in the Eisenhower administration would be an understatement. The Dulles brothers' law firm, Sullivan and Cromwell, had written United Fruit's 1930 and 1936 agreements with Guatemala. Allen Dulles's predecessor at the CIA, Undersecretary of State Walter Bedell Smith, would become a vice president of the company in 1955. Assistant Secretary of State for Inter-American Affairs John Moors Cabot was a major shareholder. His brother Thomas Dudley Cabot, the director of international security affairs in the State Department, had been president of United Fruit. NSC head General Robert Cutler had been chairman of the board. John J. McCloy was a former board member. And U.S. Ambassador to Costa Rica Robert Hill would later join the board.

Concerns about United Fruit interests reinforced the Eisenhower administration's deep-seated anticommunism. In August 1953, administration officials decided to take Árbenz down through covert action. One U.S. official cautioned, "Were it to become known that the United States had tried a Czechoslovakia in Guatemala, the effect on our relations in this hemisphere, and probably in the world . . . could be . . . disastrous." [135] Undeterred, Allen Dulles asked Iran coup instigator Kim Roosevelt to lead "Operation Success," but Roosevelt declined, not trusting that the operation's title reflected the prospects on the ground. Dulles then chose Colonel Albert Haney, a former South Korea station chief, as field commander with Tracy Barnes as chief of political warfare. As Tim Weiner points out in his history of the CIA, Barnes had the classic CIA résumé of that era. Raised on Long Island's Whitney estate, replete with its own private golf course, he matriculated at Groton, Yale, and Harvard Law. Serving with the OSS in World War II, he captured a German garrison, earning him a Silver Star. But because Barnes had a reputation as a bumbler, former CIA director Walter Bedell Smith, a Dulles protégé, was tasked with overseeing the operation. [136]

Guatemalan president Jacobo Árbenz Guzmán speaking to supporters in 1954. After his reform efforts upset the United Fruit Company, he was branded a Communist and overthrown by a military junta in a 1954 coup engineered by the CIA.

In late January 1954, word leaked out that the United States was collaborating with Colonel Castillo Armas to train the invading force. The Guatemalan government then turned to Czechoslavakia for a shipload of arms. The United States loudly decried Soviet penetration of the hemisphere. The chairman of the Senate Foreign Relations Committee, Alexander Wiley, described the allegedly "massive" shipment as "part of the master plan of world communism."[137] The Speaker of the House deemed it an atom bomb in America's backyard.[138]

In a surprising reversal, *New York Times* correspondent Sydney Gruson began providing coverage of the unfolding Guatemalan crisis that accurately captured that nation's outrage over U.S. bullying and accusations. Gruson had just been allowed back into the country after having been expelled by the government as "undesirable" in February.[139] On May 21, he wrote that U.S. pressure had "boomeranged," inspiring "a greater degree of national unity than [Guatemala] has experienced in a long time." Even Guatemalan newspapers "that normally are in constant opposition," he reported, "have rallied to defend the Government's action." "Both newspapers," he noted, had "assailed what they termed the United States willingness to provide arms to right-wing dictators in the hemisphere while refusing to fulfill Guatemala's legitimate needs."[140] In another front-page article the following day, Gruson recounted the Guatemalan foreign minister's charge that the U.S. State Department was aiding exiles abroad and domestic dissidents who were trying to overthrow the government. He reported that the State Department had pressured Guatemala to raise its compensation to United Fruit to $16 million and quoted the foreign minister's assertion that "Guatemala is not a colony of the United States nor an associated state that requires permission of the United States Government to acquire the things indispensable for its defense and security, and it repudiates the pretension of [the United States] to supervise the legitimate acts of a sovereign government."[141] On the twenty-fourth, Gruson insisted that the United States had chosen the wrong issue to make a stand on and had only sparked a "great upsurge of nationalism" and anti-Americanism.[142] Gruson's days as a *Times* reporter in Guatemala were numbered. Over dinner, Allen Dulles spoke to his friend *Times* business manager Julius Adler, who conveyed the administration's complaints to publisher Sulzberger. Gruson was sent packing to Mexico City.[143]

Meanwhile, Peurifoy and other U.S. officials waged a vigorous propaganda and disinformation campaign both inside Guatemala and in neighboring states to discredit the Árbenz government and weaken its hold on power. In June 1954, CIA-trained mercenaries attacked from bases in Honduras and Nicaragua, backed by U.S. air support. When the initial attack stalled, Eisenhower provided Castillo Armas with additional planes. Even British and French officials balked at the thought of supporting such naked aggression. Henry Cabot Lodge, U.S. ambassador to the United Nations, confronted his British and French counterparts and threatened to withdraw U.S. support to Great Britain on Egypt and Cyprus and to France on Tunisia and Morocco if they failed to back the United States on Guatemala.[144]

On June 27, Árbenz, assuming that resistance was futile, handed power to a military junta headed by the army chief of staff. That night, he delivered a final radio address in which he charged, "The United Fruit Company, in collaboration with the governing circles of the United States, is responsible for what is happening to us." He warned about "twenty years of fascist bloody tyranny."[145] That night the CIA station chief and another agent visited the new head of the junta and told him, "You're just not convenient for the requirements of American foreign policy."[146] When he refused to step down, the CIA bombed the parade ground of the main military base and the government radio station. Castillo Armas, who had been trained at Fort Leavenworth, Kansas, returned in a U.S. Embassy plane to head the new government. Dulles addressed the American public on June 30 and applauded the victory of "democracy" over "Soviet communism." He announced that the situation was "being cured by the Guatemalans themselves."[147] One British official, gagging on Dulles's mendacity, observed of the speech that "in places it might almost be Molotov speaking about . . . Czechoslovakia—or Hitler about Austria."[148]

Shortly thereafter, Castillo Armas visited Washington and assured Nixon of his fealty. "Tell me what you want me to do and I will do it," he promised the vice president.[149] He received $90 million in U.S. aid in the next two years, 150 times as much as the reform government had received in a decade. He set up a brutal military dictatorship and was assassinated three years later. United Fruit got its land back.

Dulles said that the country had been saved from "Communist imperialism" and declared the addition of "a new and glorious chapter to the already great tradition of the American States." [150] One retired Marine Corps colonel who participated in the overthrow wrote later that "our 'success' led to 31 years of repressive military rule and the deaths of more than 100,000 Guatemalans." [151] The actual death toll might have been twice that number. Árbenz proved to have been optimistic when he predicted "twenty years of fascist bloody tyranny." The fascist bloody tyranny in Guatemala actually lasted forty years.

While Eisenhower administration officials celebrated their victory, having fortified their belief that covert operations could be used to topple popular reform governments, others drew very different lessons. Among the witnesses to Guatemalan "regime change" was a young Argentinian doctor named Ernesto "Che" Guevara, who was in Guatemala City to observe Árbenz's reform efforts. He wrote to his mother from the Argentinean Embassy, where he had taken refuge during the subsequent slaughter. Árbenz made one major mistake, he contended: "He could have given arms to the people, but he did not want to—and now we see the result." Che would not make that mistake when the time came to protect the Cuban Revolution a few years later. [152] The revolution faced its main counterrevolutionary challenge when an invading force of U.S.-backed exiles was smashed in 1961 at the Bay of Pigs. Several of those who played leading roles in the Guatemalan overthrow of 1954 would also figure prominently in the 1961 fiasco, including Ambassador William Pawley, CIA operatives E. Howard Hunt and Richard Bissell, Tracy Barnes, and Allen Dulles.

Events of even greater significance were unfolding simultaneously in Vietnam. In April 1954, Ho Chi Minh's peasant liberation army, commanded by General Vo Nguyen Giap, and peasant supporters hauled extremely heavy antiaircraft guns, mortars, and howitzers through seemingly impassable jungle and mountain terrain to lay siege to desperate French forces at Dien Bien Phu. Incredibly, the United States was then paying 80 percent of the French costs to keep the colonialists in power. Eisenhower explained in August 1953, "when the United States votes $400,000,000 to help that war, we are not voting a giveaway program. We are voting for the cheapest way that we can to prevent the occurrence of something that would be of a most terrible significance to the United States of America, our security, our power and ability to get certain things we need from the riches of the Indonesia territory and from Southeast Asia." [153] He envisioned countries in the region falling like dominoes, ultimately leading to the loss of Japan. Nixon agreed: "If Indochina falls, Thailand is put in an almost impossible position. The same is true of Malaya with its rubber and tin. The same is true of Indonesia. If this whole part of Southeast Asia goes under Communist domination or Communist influence, Japan, who trades and must trade with this area in order to exist, must inevitably be oriented towards the Communist regime." [154] And *U.S. News & World Report* cut entirely through any rhetoric about fighting for the freedom of oppressed peoples and admitted, "One of the world's richest areas is open to the winner in Indochina. That's behind growing U.S. concern . . . tin, rubber, rice, key strategic raw materials are what the war is really about. The U.S. sees it as a place to hold—at any cost." [155]

The French asked for help. Though Eisenhower ruled out sending U.S. ground forces, he and Dulles considered various options to stave off an imminent French defeat. Pentagon officials drew up plans for Operation Vulture, an air campaign against Viet Minh positions. They also discussed the possibility of using two or three atomic bombs. Air Force Chief of Staff General Nathan Twining later commented,

> what [Radford and I] thought would be—and I still think it would have been a good idea—was to take three small tactical A-bombs—it's a fairly isolated area. . . . You could take all day to drop a bomb, make sure you put it in the right place. No opposition. And clean those Commies out of there and the band could play the 'Marseillaise' and the French would come marching out of Dien Bien Phu in fine shape. And those Commies would say, 'Well, those guys may do this again to us. We'd better be careful.' [156]

Eisenhower discussed the use of atomic bombs with Nixon and Robert Cutler of the NSC on April 30, 1954. Foreign Minister Georges Bidault and other French officials reported that Dulles had offered them two atomic bombs one week earlier. Eisenhower and Dulles later disputed such reports, but the use of atomic bombs would certainly have been consistent with U.S. policy at the time. Neither the British nor the French thought this wise or feasible. Evidence also suggests that the "new weapons" were vetoed because the Viet Minh at Dien Bien Phu were too close to French soldiers, who would be put into harm's way. As Eisenhower told Walter Cronkite in 1961, "we were not willing to use weapons that could have destroyed the area for miles and that probably would have destroyed Dien Bien Phu." [157]

Many scholars believe Eisenhower's and Dulles's disclaimers, but the United States' offer is mentioned in diaries and memoirs of French General Paul Ely, Foreign Minister Bidault, and Foreign Ministry Secretary General Jean Chauvel. France's interior minister had asked Premier Laniel to request the bombs. [158] McGeorge Bundy also thinks it likely that Dulles raised the possibility with Bidault, as Bidault claimed, in part because the alleged offer coincided precisely with Dulles's comments to NATO about the necessity of making nuclear weapons conventional. In late April, the Policy Planning Staff of the NSC again discussed the prospect of using nuclear weapons. When Robert Cutler broached the subject with Eisenhower and Nixon, the record indicates that they again considered giving a few of the "new weapons" to the French. Years later, Eisenhower's recollection was quite different. He told his biographer Stephen Ambrose that he had replied to Cutler, "You boys must be crazy. We can't use those awful things against Asians for the second time in less than ten years. My God." [159]

Although no nuclear weapons were used at the time, Eisenhower did approve the Joint Chiefs' recommendation that should the Chinese intervene, the United States would respond with atomic bombs, not ground troops. [160]

The day before Eisenhower's "falling domino" press conference, Massachusetts Senator John F. Kennedy had taken the floor of the Senate to oppose the proposed U.S. military intervention. He dismissed the optimistic blather with which U.S. and French officials had been regaling the public for the past three years, including recent assurances of French victory by Arthur Radford and Secretary Dulles: "No amount of American military assistance in Indochina can conquer an enemy which is everywhere and at the same time nowhere, 'an enemy of the people' which has the sympathy and covert support of the people." [161] Senator Lyndon Johnson had recently said that he was "against sending American GIs into the mud and muck of Indochina on a blood-letting spree to perpetuate colonialism and white man's exploitation in Asia." [162]

On May 7, after fifty-six days, the French garrison fell. Representatives of the United States, France, Great Britain, the Soviet Union, and China met in Geneva. Dulles attended just long enough to make his displeasure apparent. He refused to shake hands with Chinese Foreign Minister Zhou Enlai or to sit near any Communist delegates, and he objected to everything that was proposed, causing British Foreign Minister Anthony Eden's secretary to describe his "almost pathological rage and gloom." [163] Despite the fact that the Viet Minh controlled most of the country and believed it deserved to govern it all, Viet Minh negotiators succumbed to Soviet and Chinese pressure and accepted a proposal that would briefly defer their nationwide takeover and allow France to save face. The two sides agreed to temporarily divide Vietnam at the 17th parallel, with Ho's forces withdrawing to the north and French-backed forces retreating to the south. The final declaration clearly stated, "the military demarcation line is provisional and should not in any way be interpreted as constituting a political or territorial boundary." [164] The agreement also stipulated that neither side allow foreign bases on its soil or join a military alliance.

The Viet Minh accepted this, in large part, because a national election was scheduled for July 1956 to unify the country. The United States refused to sign the accords but promised not to interfere with their implementation. But in fact it was betraying that promise as the words were coming out of U.S. representative General Walter Bedell Smith's mouth.

So long as Bao Dai remained in charge in the South, the United States' prospects of holding Vietnam were virtually nonexistent. Bao Dai was unknown by the

Eisenhower and Dulles greet South Vietnamese president Ngo Dinh Diem at Washington National Airport. American leaders had maneuvered to replace the French puppet Bao Dai with Diem, who wasted no time in crushing his rivals and unleashing a wave of repression against former Viet Minh members in the south, thousands of whom were executed.

peasants and scorned as a French puppet and despised by the intellectuals, while Ho was heralded as a nationalist leader and adulated as the country's savior.[165] As French troops prepared to leave the country, Americans maneuvered to replace Bao Dai with Ngo Dinh Diem, a conservative Catholic fresh from four years in exile, whom Bao had named prime minister. With the aid of Edward Lansdale, Diem wasted no time in crushing rivals and unleashing a wave of repression against former Viet Minh members in the south, thousands of whom were executed.

In 1955, Diem called a referendum asking the South Vietnamese to choose between Bao Dai and himself. With the assistance of Lansdale, Diem "won" 98 percent of the vote. Diem's U.S. backers formed the American Friends of Vietnam. Diem enthusiasts included Cardinal Francis Spellman and Joseph Kennedy, as well as Senators Mike Mansfield, Hubert Humphrey, and John F. Kennedy. Blinded by their anticommunism and their faith that this ascetic Catholic nationalist could turn the tide against overwhelming odds, they ignored what was obvious to independent observers like University of Chicago political theorist and foreign policy expert Hans Morgenthau. After visiting Vietnam in early 1956, Morgenthau described Diem as "a man . . . who acts with a craftiness and ruthlessness worthy of an Oriental despot . . . who as statesman lives by his opposition to Commu-nism, but who is building, down to small details, a faithful replica of the totalitarian regime which he opposes." Morgenthau outlined a situation in which nine of the eleven opposition parties dared not operate openly: "Freedom of the press does not exist," and "nobody knows how many people are shot every day by the armed forces of the regime and under what circumstances." [166]

With the United States' backing, Diem subverted the most important pro-vision of the Geneva agreement, canceling the 1956 election that would have turned control of the nation over to the Communists. Eisenhower later com-mented, "I have never talked or corresponded with a person knowledgeable in Indo-Chinese affairs who did not agree that had elections been held as of the time of the fighting, possibly 80 percent of the population would have voted for the Communist Ho Chi Minh as their leader rather than Chief of State Bao Dai." [167] The insurgency was soon rekindled.

Growing U.S. involvement in Vietnam was taking place against a backdrop of heightened nuclear tensions. In late February 1954, U.S. authorities evacuated islanders and cleared all vessels from a large area of the Pacific in preparation for a new series of hydrogen bomb tests. Even though the wind shifted, they decided to proceed as planned with the March 1 Bravo test, knowing that this would put many people in harm's way. To make matters worse, the bomb exploded with twice the force predicted. At 15 megatons, it was a thousand times more pow-erful than the bomb that destroyed Hiroshima. The cloud of radioactive coral drifted toward the Marshall Islands of Rongelap, Rongerik, and Utrik, contami-nating 236 islanders and 28 Americans. Unaware of the danger, children played in the radioactive fallout. Many of the islanders were not evacuated for three days, by which time they were showing signs of radiation poisoning. Twenty-three fishermen aboard a Japanese trawler, *Daigo Fukuryu Maru* (*Lucky Dragon No. 5*), suffered a similar fate as they were blanketed by the deadly white ash that fell from the skies for three hours. When they pulled into port thirteen days later with their contaminated tuna, crew members were showing signs of advanced poisoning. The first died several months later.

The world was shocked by the United States' negligence and by the incred-ible power of the latest generation of nuclear weapons. Panic set in when people realized that the Japanese ship's contaminated tuna had been sold in four major cities and eaten by scores of people. Many people stopped eating fish entirely. Four hundred fifty-seven tons of tuna were eventually destroyed. AEC Chair-man Lewis Strauss told the White House press secretary that the boat had really been a "red spy outfit" conducting espionage for the Soviet Union, a blatant false-hood that the CIA quickly dispelled. [168] Speaking at Eisenhower's press confer-ence, Strauss emphasized the test's contribution to the United States' "military posture," blamed the fishermen for ignoring AEC warnings, and downplayed the damage to their health.[169] The inhabitants of Utrik were allowed to return within two months. The Rongalapese did not return home until 1957. They remained in Rongelap until 1985, when scientific findings confirmed their suspicions that the island was still contaminated.

The international community was appalled. Belgian diplomat Paul-Henri Spaak warned, "If something is not done to revive the idea of the President's speech—the idea that America wants to use atomic energy for peaceful purposes—America is going to be synonymous in Europe with barbarism and horror." Indian Prime Minister Jawaharlal Nehru said publicly that U.S. leaders were "dangerous self-centered lunatics" who would "blow up any people or country who came in the way of their policy."[170]

Eisenhower told the NSC in May 1954, "Everybody seems to think that we are skunks, saber-rattlers, and warmongers."[171] Dulles added, "We are losing ground every day in England and in other allied nations because they are all insisting we are so militaristic. Comparisons are now being made between ours and Hitler's military machine."[172]

The bomb test had other unforeseen consequences. The terrifying power of hydrogen bombs and the slightly veiled threat of nuclear war now figured much more prominently in international diplomacy. The nuclear threat influenced the behavior of the major players at the Geneva Conference more than most people realized. Shortly after the test, Churchill told Parliament that the topic occupied his thinking "out of all comparison with anything else." Dulles met with him in early May, afterward telling Eisenhower that he "found the British, and particularly Churchill, scared to death by the specter of nuclear bombs in the hands of the Russians." Anthony Eden connected this fear to the proceedings at the conference. "This was the first international meeting," he noted, "at which I was sharply conscious of the deterrent power of the hydrogen bomb. I was grateful for it. I do not believe that we should have got through the Geneva Conference and avoided a major war without it."[173]

The *Lucky Dragon* incident also catalyzed a worldwide movement against nuclear testing and popularized the previously obscure term "fallout." It sparked renewed questioning of Eisenhower's New Look.

Nowhere was the reaction stronger than in Japan, where postwar U.S. efforts to censor discussion of the atomic bombings had not succeeded in extinguishing the memory of what the United States had done to Hiroshima and Nagasaki. A petition circulated by Tokyo housewives calling for banning hydrogen bombs gathered 32 million signatures, an extraordinary total representing one-third of the entire Japanese population.

To counter this pervasive anti-nuclear sentiment, the NSC's Operations

Coordinating Board proposed that the United States launch a "vigorous offensive on the non-war uses of atomic energy" and offer to build Japan an experimental nuclear reactor.[174] AEC Commissioner Thomas Murray applauded this "dramatic and Christian gesture," believing it "could lift all of us far above the recollection of the carnage" of Hiroshima and Nagasaki.[175] The *Washington Post* offered its own hearty endorsement, seeing the project as a way to "divert the mind of man from his present obsession with the armaments race" and added, in an extraordinary admission, "Many Americans are now aware . . . that the dropping of the atomic bombs on Japan was not necessary. . . . How better to make a contribution to amends than by offering Japan the means for the peaceful utilization of atomic energy. How better, indeed, to dispel the impression in Asia that the United States regards Orientals merely as cannon fodder!"

In what would seem the cruelest irony yet, Murray and Illinois Representative Sidney Yates proposed building the first nuclear power plant in Hiroshima. In early 1955, Yates introduced legislation to build a 60,000 kilowatt generating plant in the city that less than a decade earlier had been the first target of the atomic bomb.

Over the next few years, the U.S. Embassy, the CIA, and the United States Information Agency waged a large-scale propaganda and educational campaign to reverse the Japanese people's deep-seated hostility to nuclear power. The *Mainichi* newspaper denounced the campaign: "First, baptism with radioactive rain, then a surge of shrewd commercialism in the guise of 'atoms for peace' from abroad."[176]

A month after the powerful Bravo test, the *New York Times* reported that the recent tests confirmed Szilard and Einstein's fear that the cobalt bomb could be built, leading to widespread discussion of Szilard's revised estimate that four hundred one-ton deuterium-cobalt bombs would release enough radioactivity to end all life on the planet.[177]

A front-page article in the *Los Angeles Times* two days later offered the sobering news that Japanese scientist Tsunesaburo Asada had informed the Japan Pharmacological Society that the Soviets were producing a nitrogen bomb—a hydrogen bomb enclosed with nitrogen and helium—so dangerous that "if 30 such bombs are detonated simultaneously all mankind will perish in several years' time."[178] As if that weren't frightening enough, the following February, German Nobel Laureate Otto Hahn, the physicist who had first split the uranium atom, lowered the requisite number from four hundred cobalt bombs to ten in a radio address that could be heard throughout most of Europe.[179]

Although a cobalt bomb has never been built, the possibility that it could be gave shape to the decade's darkest nightmares. The *Lucky Dragon* crew members remained hospitalized for more than a year. While recuperating in the hospital, one issued a poignant warning: "Our fate menaces all mankind. Tell that to those who are responsible. God grant that they may listen."[180]

Chapter 7

JFK:

"The Most Dangerous Moment in Human History"

In October 1962, the United States and the Soviet Union girded for war with nuclear missiles pointed at each other's military installations and population centers. The world would come closer to nuclear obliteration than most people realize. For decades, the public has been told that John F. Kennedy's statesmanship and resolve, abetted by Nikita Khrushchev's sober realism, averted a holocaust. The leaders of the planet's two most powerful nations endeavored to resolve the Cuban missile crisis peacefully, but their power to control events was severely limited as the world careened toward disaster. The lessons the two leaders drew from this harrowing encounter convinced them that life on earth might not survive a continuing Cold War. Their efforts to end that dangerous and wasteful conflict may have spelled doom for both of them, but it may also, in the process, have opened up some breathing space for the rest of a threatened humanity.

Nikita Khrushchev actually had a lot in common with Kennedy's predecessor, Dwight Eisenhower. Both had humble upbringings. Ike's fifth-grade class photo in Abilene, Kansas, shows him wearing overalls while everyone else wore Sunday clothes. Khrushchev, the grandson of serfs and son of peasants, worked in his youth as a shepherd, coal miner, and machinist. Though brutal as party czar in Ukraine during the 1930s and 1940s and in his harsh suppression of the Hungarian uprising of 1956, he could also be funny, charming, earthy, and ingratiating. He yearned to set a new course for the Soviet Union. At the Twentieth Party Congress in February 1956, he accused Stalin of having conducted a dictatorial reign of "suspicion, fear, and terror." [1] He decried Stalin's cult of personality and began a desperately needed process of de-Stalinization. Like Eisenhower, he had seen World War II up close and developed a deep abhorrence of war. But

*Dwight Eisenhower and
Nikita Khrushchev had
much in common. Each
came from humble origins,
and each believed deeply
in the superiority of his
own political system.*

he believed as deeply in the superiority of the Soviet system as Eisenhower did
in the capitalist system. To prove socialism's superiority over capitalism, he set
out to sharply reduce military spending so he could devote greater resources to
improving the Soviet people's standard of living, which had long been sacrificed
to the exigencies of national defense and self-preservation against seemingly
implacable foes.

In August 1957, the Soviet Union successfully tested the world's first intercontinental ballistic missile, or ICBM. For the Soviet Union, ICBMs could
potentially offset the enormous military advantage the United States derived
from bombers housed at NATO bases in Europe. Less than two months later, on
October 4, 1957, while the school desegregation crisis in Little Rock, Arkansas,
dominated American news and *Leave It to Beaver* made its television debut, a
Soviet R-7 ICBM launched the first artificial satellite into orbit around the earth.
Sputnik Zemlya, meaning "companion of Earth" or "fellow traveler," weighed
184 pounds and was 22.8 inches in diameter. It orbited the earth once every
ninety-six minutes and seventeen seconds, transmitting a series of beeps to listeners below. Soviet officials crowed about the triumph of Soviet science and
technology, which, they claimed, proved the overall superiority of the Soviet
Union's new socialist society.

The Soviets had indeed punctured the belief that the United States' technological sophistication and the Soviet Union's backwardness would guarantee

In August 1957, the Soviet Union successfully tested the world's first intercontinental ballistic missile (ICBM). For the USSR, ICBMs could potentially offset the enormous military advantage the United States derived from bombers housed at NATO bases in Europe. When the Soviets used an ICBM to launch Sputnik in October, some Americans panicked.

U.S. victory in the Cold War. Writer John Gunther noted, "for a generation it had been part of the American folklore that the Russians were hardly capable of operating a tractor." Radio Cairo declared that Sputnik would "make countries think twice before tying themselves to the imperialist policy led by the United States." Khrushchev taunted, "any idiot can see . . . they might as well put bombers and fighters in the museum."[2] Drawing attention to both the Soviet achievement and U.S. racial problems, Radio Moscow pointedly announced every time Sputnik passed over Little Rock.

Some Americans panicked, speculating that the Soviet Union must now have ICBMs with nuclear warheads poised to attack U.S. targets. That fear was fueled by the Soviet Union's announcement, three days after Sputnik's launch, that it had successfully tested a new ballistic-missile-compatible thermonuclear warhead. Senate Majority Leader Lyndon Johnson warned that the Soviets would soon "be dropping bombs on us from space like kids dropping rocks onto cars from freeway overpasses."[3] Edward Teller bemoaned the fact that the United States had lost "a battle more important and greater than Pearl Harbor."[4] One satirist cracked, "General LeMay is planning to send a fleet of bombers around the world to impress the Russians; I'm sure it will—if they bother to look down."[5]

The Soviets beating the United States into space tore deep cracks in the fragile façade of American confidence—a confidence that had already been shaken by the Korean War and the domestic and foreign policy crises of the first half of the 1950s. Critics decried the shallow materialism and purposelessness of American life and enumerated the shortcomings of the educational system. Republican Senator Styles Bridges urged Americans to "be less concerned with the depth of the pile on the new broadloom rug or the height of the tailfin on the new car and to be more prepared to shed blood, sweat, and tears if this country and the free world are to survive."[6] Esteemed Soviet space scientist Leonid Sedov commented to a German-American counterpart, "You Americans have a better standard of living than we have. But the American loves his car, his refrigerator, his house. He does not, as we Russians do, love his country."[7] Congresswoman Clare Boothe Luce described Sputnik's beep from space as "an intercontinental outer-space raspberry to a decade of American pretensions that the American way of life was a gilt-edged guarantee of our national superiority."[8]

The administration deliberately downplayed the threat posed by the Soviet achievement in an effort to reassure the public. "The satellite . . . does not rouse my apprehensions," Eisenhower said, "not one iota. I can see nothing . . . that is significant . . . they have put one small ball into the air."[9] To drive the point home, Ike played five rounds of golf that week. He could not disclose the reason for his lack of concern. Highly secret U-2 reconnaissance planes, flying above 70,000 feet, had been crossing Soviet airspace for more than a year and taking photos revealing that the Soviets were lagging behind in the arms race. The American people were kept in the dark about those illegal and provocative missions, but the Soviet Union launched a formal protest in July 1957. Allen Dulles later chortled, "I was able to get a look at every blade of grass in the Soviet Union,"[10] but it would still be a few years before this was true.

On November 3, the Soviets launched Sputnik II—a massive six-ton satellite carrying a live dog named Laika. The Soviets reveled in their victory. But Khrushchev used the occasion to reach out to U.S. leaders by calling for peaceful space competition and an end to the Cold War:

> Our satellites are . . . waiting for the American and other satellites to join
> them and to form a commonwealth of satellites. A commonwealth of this
> kind . . . would be much better than competition in the race to manufacture
> lethal weapons. . . . We would like a high-level meeting of representatives
> of capitalist and Socialist countries . . . so as to reach an agreement based
> on . . . the exclusion of war as a method of settling international problems,
> to stop the cold war and the armaments race and to establish relations
> among states on the basis of coexistence, to settle disputes . . . by means of
> peaceful competition in the culture and in the best satisfaction of human
> requirements and needs.[11]

Now on the defensive, Eisenhower ignored Khrushchev's overture, instead highlighting the United States' vast military superiority and its intention to stay far ahead in the arms race:

> Our nation has . . . enough power in its strategic retaliatory forces to bring near annihilation to the war-making capabilities of any other country. Atomic submarines have been developed. . . . A number of huge naval carriers are in operation, supplied with the most powerful nuclear weapons and bombers of great range to deliver them. Construction has started which will produce a carrier to be driven by atomic power. . . . In numbers, our stock of nuclear weapons is so large and so rapidly growing that . . . we are well ahead of the Soviets . . . both in quantity and in quality. We intend to stay ahead.[12]

Eisenhower knew that words would not suffice. Determined to beat the Soviets at their own game on December 6, the United States attempted to launch a satellite with a Vanguard rocket. It stayed aloft for only two seconds, reaching a height of four feet. Newspapers scornfully dubbed the grapefruit-sized sphere "Kaputnik," "Flopnik," and "Stayputnik." Eisenhower finally unleashed the former Nazi rocketeer Wernher von Braun and his army Redstone team to put something up in the air. By January 31, they successfully orbited a thirty-one-pound Explorer satellite.

The United States even contemplated detonating a Hiroshima-sized atomic bomb on the moon to restore its prestige. The resulting dust cloud would have been widely visible from Earth. The study was conducted from May 1958 to January 1959 by a ten-person staff that included the young astronomer Carl Sagan, who worked for the Air Force Special Weapons Center in Albuquerque. Finally, the scientists joined with others in convincing authorities that "there was no point in ruining the pristine environment of the moon."[13]

Later in the decade, the air force devised even more grandiose schemes. Testifying before the House Armed Services Committee in February 1958, Lieutenant General Donald Putt disclosed plans for missile bases on the moon. Putt explained, "Warheads could be catapulted from shafts sunk deep into the moon's surface," providing "a retaliation base of considerable advantage over earthbound nations" if the United States were militarily destroyed. An enemy wanting to take out those bases prior to attacking on earth would "have to launch an overwhelming nuclear attack against those bases one to two days prior to attacking the continental United States," clearly signaling that such an attack was coming. Air Force Assistant Secretary Richard Horner later testified that such bases could break a nuclear stalemate on earth and restore the United States' first-strike capability. Putt added that if the Soviets established their own moon bases to neutralize the United States' advantage, the United States could erect bases on more distant planets from which it could retaliate against both the Soviet Union and its moon bases. In assessing those plans, the independent journalist I. F. Stone astutely noted that the Latin word for "moon" is *luna* and suggested that the military establish a fourth branch for space warfare and call it the Department of Lunacy.[14]

Propelled by irrational fear of being overtaken by the Soviets, intelligence officials advanced preposterous estimates of Soviet military strength. In December 1957, a National Intelligence Estimate projected a potential Soviet arsenal of a hundred operational ICBMs in the next two years and projected a worst-case scenario of five hundred Soviet ICBMs in 1960.[15]

Eisenhower commissioned a top secret security review headed by H. Rowan Gaither of the Ford Foundation. The report predicted that by 1959 the "USSR may be able to launch an attack with ICBMs carrying megaton warheads, against which SAC will be almost completely vulnerable under present programs."[16] It recommended commencing a massive U.S. military buildup to counter the growing missile gap, increasing the number of Titan and Atlas ICBMs to be deployed in 1959 from 80 to 600, and increasing the number of Thor and Jupiter intermediate-range ballistic missiles to be placed in Europe from 60 to 240. It also called for a $25 billion national fallout shelter program. When the report was leaked to the press, the *Washington Post* painted a dire picture:

> The still top-secret Gaither Report portrays a United States in the gravest
> danger in its history. It pictures the Nation moving in frightening course
> to the status of a second-class power. It shows an America exposed to
> an almost immediate threat from the missile-bristling Soviet Union. It
> finds America's long-term prospect one of cataclysmic peril in the face
> of rocketing Soviet military might and of a powerful, growing Soviet
> economy and technology.... To prevent what otherwise appears to be an
> inevitable catastrophe, the Gaither Report urgently calls for an enormous
> increase in military spending—from now through 1970.[17]

Sputnik provided Democrats a tremendous political opening. A legislative aide informed Lyndon Johnson that "the issue . . . if properly handled, would blast the Republicans out of the water, . . . and elect you President."[18] Taking the cue, the Senate launched an inquiry into Eisenhower's defense programs.

Among those who jumped enthusiastically on this "missile gap" bandwagon was the junior senator from Massachusetts, John F. Kennedy. By late 1957, Kennedy was warning that the United States might be several years behind the

Soviets in intermediate- and long-range ballistic missiles. Egged on by his friend the columnist Joseph Alsop, he adopted an even more alarmist tone the following year. Alsop had accused the Eisenhower administration of "gross untruth" regarding U.S. national defense. He detailed the scope of the projected missile gap. In 1959, the United States would have 0 ICBMs, the Soviets 100. In succeeding years the ratio would be 30 U.S. to 500 Soviet in 1960, 70 to 1,000 in 1961, 130 to 1,500 in 1962, and 130 to 2,000 in 1963.[19]

Relying largely on Alsop's information, Kennedy rose up in the Senate to decry the U.S. "missile-lag," which would soon produce "a peril more deadly than any wartime danger we have ever known," increasing the possibility of a Soviet attack and making nuclear disarmament more urgent than ever.[20] Eisenhower, whose U-2 surveillance planes had failed to identify a single deployed ICBM, had little patience for Washington insiders who tried to exploit the missile gap to advance their own careers. He dismissed them as "sanctimonious hypocritical bastards."[21]

U.S. interests and prestige were dealt another devastating blow when revolutionaries, led by Fidel Castro and Che Guevara, toppled Cuba's U.S.-friendly dictator, Fulgencio Batista, on New Year's Day 1959. American corporations had dominated the island since 1898. In 1959, they controlled more than 80 percent of Cuba's mines, cattle ranches, utilities, and oil refineries, 50 percent of the railroads, and 40 percent of the sugar industry. The United States still retained its naval base at Guantánamo Bay. Castro quickly set about reforming the education system and redistributing land. The government seized more than a million acres from United Fruit and two other American companies. When the United States tried to strangle the new regime economically, Castro turned to the Soviet Union for aid. On March 17, 1960, Eisenhower instructed the CIA to organize a "paramilitary force" of Cuban exiles to overthrow Castro.

During the coming months, the United States, with Eisenhower's authorization, would also be involved in an effort to assassinate Patrice Lumumba, the democratically elected prime minister of the resource-rich Congo, whom Allen Dulles characterized as an African Fidel Castro. Lumumba was indeed assassinated the following January, but the Congo's former colonial rulers—the Belgians—deserve the lion's share of the blame. The CIA backed Joseph Mobutu to succeed Lumumba. After several years of struggle, Mobutu managed to consolidate his control. In his Pulitzer Prize–winning history of the CIA, *Legacy of Ashes*, Tim Weiner assessed Mobutu's reign: "He ruled for three decades as one of the world's most brutal and corrupt dictators, stealing billions of dollars in revenues from the nation's enormous deposits of diamonds, minerals, and strategic metals, slaughtering multitudes to preserve his power." During that time, he was the CIA's most trusted ally in Africa.[22]

Eisenhower's embrace of third-world dictators, indefensible as it was, paled

Fidel Castro at a meeting of the UN General Assembly in September 1960. Castro led the revolution that overthrew Fulgencio Batista's U.S.-friendly dictatorship on New Year's Day 1959. When the United States tried to strangle the new regime economically, Castro turned to the Soviet Union for aid.

in comparison to the most disturbing and potentially lethal aspect of his presidency, his buildup of nuclear weapons and dangerous reliance upon nuclear blackmail to gain advantage in the Cold War. He had deliberately blurred the line between conventional and nuclear weapons and was in the process of adding terrifyingly powerful thermonuclear weapons to the arsenal.

No document condemned this policy more powerfully than the Russell-Einstein Manifesto of 1955. Initiated by philosopher-mathematician Bertrand Russell and enthusiastically supported by Albert Einstein, whose signature arrived in the last letter he wrote before his death, the manifesto was signed by eleven of the world's most prominent scientists, nine of whom were Nobel laureates. Drafted by future Nobel Peace Prize winner Joseph Rotblat, it pleaded with passion and urgency, "We are speaking on this occasion, not as members of this or that nation, continent or creed but as human beings, members of the species man, whose continued existence is in doubt." The signers urged readers to think of themselves "only as members of a biological species which has had a remarkable history, and whose disappearance none of us can desire." They explained, "All, equally, are in peril, and, if the peril is understood, there is hope that they may collectively avert it." They expressed concern that most people still thought in terms of the "obliteration of cities." Demolition of cities in an H-bomb war, they warned, "is one of the minor disasters that would have to be faced. If everybody in London, New York, and Moscow were exterminated the world might, in the course of a few centuries, recover from the blow." But now, with the capability of building bombs 2,500 times as powerful as the one used on Hiroshima and the new knowledge of the widespread dispersal of "lethal radioactive particles," "the best authorities are unanimous in saying that a war with H-bombs might quite possibly put an end to the human race. It is feared that if many H-bombs are used there will be universal death—sudden only for a minority, but for the majority a slow torture of disease and disintegration." The signers asked, "Shall we put an end to the human race; or shall mankind renounce war?" They concluded with the words "We appeal, as human beings, to human beings: remember your humanity, and forget the rest. If you can do so, the way lies open to a new paradise; if you cannot, there lies before you the risk of universal death." [23]

Less than one week later, scientists meeting in Lindau, Germany, released the Mainau Declaration, signed by eighteen Nobel laureates. Reaching out once again to "all men everywhere," the declaration warned that "in an all-out war the earth can be made so radioactive that whole nations will be destroyed." Nations would either have to "renounce force" or "they will cease to exist." [24]

Eisenhower and Secretary of State John Foster Dulles begged to differ, defying the opinion of most of humanity and insisting that recklessly brandishing nuclear threats was not only defensible, it worked. An early–January 1956 interview in *Life* magazine quoted Dulles as saying that the Eisenhower administration had "walked to the brink" of nuclear war on three recent occasions and forced the Communists to back down. U.S. resolve, he argued, had thwarted Communist aggression in Korea, Indochina, and the Formosa Strait. [25]

Dulles's penchant for playing nuclear "chicken" produced a firestorm of controversy. Democratic Speaker of the House Sam Rayburn deplored Dulles's "pitiful performance." [26] Adlai Stevenson accused Dulles of playing "Russian roulette with the life of our Nation." [27] India's *Hindustan Standard* newspaper charged that Dulles's brinksmanship "condemns millions of men to live in a state of perpetual fear and misery." [28] Twelve leading Protestant clergymen and editors of important religious journals wrote to Eisenhower, complaining that they were "deeply shocked" by Dulles's "reckless and irresponsible policies." "It remained for Mr. Dulles to tell a world aghast that the United States government three times came near the 'brink' of annihilating the human race in an atomic Armageddon." [29]

As historian Richard Immerman has shown, Dulles's private views were more complicated. He understood the dangers posed by the increasing destructiveness of nuclear weapons, the challenges of Soviet nuclear parity, the growing international outcry against a policy that threatened human annihilation, and, as he told Eisenhower in April 1958, reliance on a strategy of massive retaliation that "invoked massive nuclear attack in the event of any clash anywhere of U.S. with Soviet forces." [30] But that did not stop the administration from again threatening China with nuclear attack in the second conflict over the disputed islands

Quemoy and Matsu in 1958, as it had in the 1955 conflict, or from threatening the Soviet Union with nuclear retaliation during the Suez Crisis in 1956, when Israel, Britain, and France invaded Egypt following Nasser's nationalization of the Suez Canal. Vice President Richard Nixon drew dangerous lessons from the success of that strategy against the Soviets over Suez: "In 1956 we considered using the Bomb in Suez, and we did use it diplomatically. . . . Eisenhower . . . got Al Gruenther, the NATO commander, to hold a press conference, and Gruenther said that if Khrushchev carried out his threat to use rockets against the British Isles, Moscow would be destroyed 'as surely as day follows night.' From that time on, the U.S. has played the dominant role in the Mideast."[31] Nixon tried to repeat that performance during the 1970 Jordanian civil war, in which U.S.-allied King Hussein drove the Palestinian Liberation Organization out of Jordan.

Democratic presidential candidate Adlai Stevenson emphasized the growing nuclear threat in his 1956 presidential campaign, insisting that he could not "accept the apparent Administration position that we are powerless to do anything to stop this headlong race for extinction" and calling Eisenhower's nuclear buildup "madness."[32] He pledged to push for an agreement to stop testing as his "first order of business if elected."[33] British, U.S., and Soviet tests in spring 1957 aroused international ire. Indian Prime Minister Nehru demanded an end to all nuclear tests, fearing that they "might put an end to human life as we see it."[34] The *New York Times* reported a "world-wide concern that the continuation of tests poses a threat to the future existence of all living things on earth."[35]

In November 1957, following a new round of tests, the National Committee for a Sane Nuclear Policy placed an ad, written largely by Norman Cousins, in the *New York Times*. Signed by forty-eight prominent citizens, it called for an end to nuclear testing as the first step toward arms control. The unexpected public response to the ad sparked the formation of a major national antinuclear organization, popularly known as SANE.[36]

SANE was only one of several initiatives launched in 1957. The first Pugwash Conference was held in Nova Scotia in July. Participating scientists from all over the world, including five from the United States and three from the USSR, called for abolishing war, ending the arms race, and halting nuclear testing.[37]

Reacting to the public outcry, Eisenhower began a campaign at home and abroad to promote what he called "the peaceful atom," building on the momentum generated by his December 1953 UN address. The Atomic Energy Commission (AEC) marketed nuclear power not only as a protector against godless communism but as a magic elixir that would power transportation vehicles, feed the hungry, light the cities, heal the sick, and excavate the planet. The U.S. Postal Service issued a stamp celebrating "Atoms for Peace: To Find the Way by Which the Inventiveness of Man Shall Be Consecrated to New Life."

In late April 1955, Eisenhower unveiled plans for an atomic-powered merchant ship that would visit ports all over the world to show the United States' commitment to a "just and lasting peace." In July, the United States generated its first commercial nuclear power. In October 1956, Eisenhower announced that Atoms for Peace was succeeding. The United States had agreements with Japan and thirty-six other nations to build atomic reactors and was negotiating with fourteen more. Meanwhile, the United States was proceeding with the development of an atomic plane, but a proposed $60 million atomic-powered Coast Guard icebreaker proved too costly and Eisenhower vetoed it.

By 1958, the United States was becoming almost giddy with the prospect of something even more ambitious, grandiose, and absurd: planetary excavation under the AEC's Project Plowshare. In September 1957, the AEC detonated a 2-kiloton bomb inside a mountain in Nevada. Willard Libby, who had replaced the independent-minded Henry Smyth as the only scientist on the AEC in 1954, reported in December that radioactive fallout from the Rainier test had been entirely contained within the mountain, making possible a broad range of peace-ful uses for atomic explosions. Libby exulted, "I've not seen anything in years so exciting." [38] AEC chairman Lewis Strauss understood the real purpose of the program. In February, he admitted that Plowshare had been intended to "highlight the peaceful applications of nuclear explosive devices and thereby create a climate of world opinion that is more favorable to weapons development and tests." [39]

The New York Times reported on its front page on March 14 that "atomic explosions up to ten times the power of the World War II Hiroshima bomb may be within a couple years an every-day occurrence almost anywhere in the country under a program being pressed by scientists of the Atomic Energy Commission." [40] In June, the AEC announced Project Chariot, a plan to create a three-hundred-foot harbor in Alaska north of the Arctic Circle with four hydrogen bombs. Officials anticipated that the bombs would be used to free inaccessible oil deposits trapped in both tar sand and shale formations. Similar explosions could also create huge underground reservoirs, produce steam, desalinize water, crack copper and other impenetrable ores, and produce radioactive isotopes for use in medicine, biology, agriculture, and industry.

Experts wanted to blast a new, bigger, and better Panama Canal. Some wanted to alter weather patterns. Jack Reed of the Sandia Laboratory in Albuquerque proposed exploding a 20-megaton bomb alongside the eye of a hurricane to reverse its course. He was confident that any resulting radioactivity would fall harmlessly. A U.S. Weather Bureau scientist, Harry Wexler, proposed a plan to accelerate melting of the polar icecaps by detonating ten 10-megaton bombs near the Arctic Circle, which he calculated would warm the polar area by approximately 10°F.

The AEC doubled the Plowshare budget for 1960. Almost a hundred staff members at the Lawrence Livermore National Laboratory were slated to work on the project. Physicist Edward Teller, who directed the lab, was extremely enthusiastic about the prospects. But the project hit a snag. In September 1958, Eisenhower had yielded to domestic and international pressure and announced that the United States would go along with a Soviet-initiated nuclear test moratorium. To continue the project, Eisenhower would have had to defy the moratorium. He pressed the Soviets for an agreement allowing peaceful tests. When it looked as though the Soviets might be yielding, he approved plans for a 10-kiloton explosion deep in a salt bed near Carlsbad, New Mexico, in summer 1959. Project Gnome, as it was called, would explore the feasibility of creating an underground reservoir of heat that would remain trapped in melted salt and could be used to produce electricity. The blast would also yield valuable radio-isotopes that the United States would attempt to recover for medical purposes. A spokesman for the Interior Department, whose National Park Service ran the nearby Carlsbad Cavern National Park, reported that the department was "completely flabbergasted" by the announcement.[41]

Project Chariot was to follow in summer 1960. Some citizens even came up with their own suggestions for worthy projects as part of Plowshare. One woman suggested that the AEC use hydrogen bombs to kill all the snakes in Africa.[42]

Despite the administration's aggressive effort to promote the peaceful atom, public awareness of the dangers of nuclear testing was increasing rapidly. In April 1957, Nobel Peace Prize winner Albert Schweitzer added his voice to the growing international chorus of people demanding the cessation of nuclear testing. Schweitzer broadcast his "Declaration of Conscience" to approximately fifty countries.[43] The *New York Times* reported "world-wide concern that the continuation of tests poses a threat to the future existence of all living things on earth."[44] A May Gallup Poll showed that 63 percent of Americans favored an international halt to bomb tests, more than double the 27 percent who opposed such a move. Just the previous fall, only 24 percent had supported Stevenson's call for a test ban.[45]

The publication, a few months later, of Nevil Shute's riveting novel *On the Beach*, which was serialized in the *Washington Post*, the *Los Angeles Times*, and other papers, added fuel to the fire. The novel described the aftermath of a thirty-seven-day nuclear war in which four thousand cobalt bombs were exploded, tracing the final days of the last surviving pocket of humans in Melbourne, Australia, as the radioactive cloud was descending on them. Earle Brown's review in the *Washington Post*, titled "The Facing of Certain Death," with a heading above it, "Atomic Armageddon of 1960s," began, "Nevil Shute has written the most important and dramatic novel of the atomic age, and if you read only one book a year this should be the one." Brown concluded, "I hope Nevil Shute's book will go into a few cornerstones or time capsules, so that if an atomic Armageddon ever comes, future civilizations may realize that this generation went down the road to destruction with its eyes wide open. It should be required reading—on both sides of the curtain."[46]

Winston Churchill was attending a party at Lord Beaverbrook's villa in Cap d'Ail, France, in September 1957 when guests began discussing Shute's chilling novel. Churchill announced plans to send a copy to Khrushchev. Someone asked if he was also planning to send one to Eisenhower, to which Churchill replied, "It would be a waste of money. He is so muddle-headed now. . . . I think the earth will soon be destroyed. . . . And if I were the Almighty I would not recreate it in case they destroyed him too the next time."[47]

Stanley Kramer's film version premiered simultaneously in all the major capitals of the world in December 1959 to unprecedented international fanfare. *New York Times* reviewer Bosley Crowther concluded his glowing assessment of the film with the observation: "The great merit of this picture, aside from its entertainment qualities, is the fact that it carries a passionate conviction that man is worth saving, after all."[48] Eisenhower's cabinet discussed ways to counter the film's powerful nuclear abolitionist message. Officials in the cabinet, AEC, and State Department attempted to discredit the film by alleging that it contained serious errors that invalidated its central premises.[49] The U.S. Information Agency created a file titled "Possible Questions and Suggested Answers on the Film 'On the Beach.'"[50] But the numerous filmgoers, many of whom left the theaters in tears, were probably more impressed with the simple, straightforward repudiation of deterrence theory offered by Julian, the scientist ably played by Fred Astaire, who was asked who he thought started the war. He responded, "Who would ever have believed that human beings would be stupid enough to blow themselves off the face of [the] earth?" When his questioner persisted, Julian explained:

> The war started when people accepted the idiotic principle that peace could be maintained by arranging to defend themselves with weapons they couldn't possibly use without committing suicide. Everybody had an atomic bomb. And counter bombs. And counter-counter bombs. The devices outgrew us. We couldn't control them. I know. I helped build them. God help me. Somewhere some poor bloke probably looked at a radar screen and thought he saw something. Knew that if he hesitated 1/1000th of a second his own country would be wiped off the map so. . . . So he pushed a button and the world went crazy. And and . . .

The film's details might have been wrong, but its understanding of the world Eisenhower had helped create was not. One could certainly paint a more benign portrait of Eisenhower's nuclear policies. After all, he resisted the Joint Chiefs' pressure to use nuclear weapons. He limited civil defense expenditures and restrained the growth of overall defense spending. He worked to enact a test ban. He resisted pressure for a massive buildup after Sputnik. He confronted the powerful and sometimes hostile Soviet Union while trying to hold the NATO alliance together. And he was often a voice of moderation in the midst of far more hawkish and extreme advisors.

Yet under Eisenhower the United States went from having a little more than 1,000 nuclear weapons to approximately 22,000, aimed at 2,500 targets in the Soviet Union. But even the 22,000 figure is misleading. Procurements authorized by Eisenhower continued into the 1960s, making Eisenhower responsible for more than 30,000 nuclear weapons during the Kennedy administration. Between 1959 and 1961, the United States added 19,500 nuclear weapons to its arsenal. The United States was producing new weapons at the rate of 75 per day and doing so at bargain-basement prices. As Pulitzer Prize–winning author Richard Rhodes notes, "Nuclear warheads cost the United States about $250,000 each: less than a fighter-bomber, less than a missile, less than a patrol boat, less than a tank." [51] Total megatonnage increased sixty-five-fold in five years, reaching 20,491 megatons in 1960. In pure megatonnage, that was the equivalent of 1,360,000 Hiroshima bombs. Although the total megatonnage began to drop in 1961, as 950 10-megaton B36 bombs were retired, the bombs' destructive capability actually increased as the introduction of ballistic missiles made targeting more accurate. Doubling the accuracy of delivery allows for an eightfold reduction in yield without sacrificing the bombs' destructive capability. [52]

What is little known is that Eisenhower had delegated to theater commanders and other specified commanders, including the Strategic Air Command and NORAD, the authority to launch a nuclear attack if they believed it was mandated by circumstances and were out of communication with the president, or if the president had been incapacitated. With Eisenhower's approval, some of the theater commanders had in turn delegated this authority to lower commanders under similar circumstances. This subdelegation included commanders of numbered air forces, fleets, and navies. Thus there were dozens of fingers on the triggers, if not more. According to RAND analyst Daniel Ellsberg, who had discovered the dangerous circumstances surrounding delegation and subdelegation during his studies of nuclear command and control for the Pentagon, "It was a doomsday machine on a hair trigger with delegation." [53] And given the fact that there were then no locks on nuclear weapons, many more people had the actual power, if not the authority, to launch a nuclear attack, including pilots, squadron leaders, base commanders, and carrier commanders. During the next decade, locks were put on nuclear weapons in Europe and then on tactical nuclear weapons. Locks on SAC bombers came much later. No locks were put on submarine missiles until the 1980s, meaning that any submarine commander still had the power to wipe out the USSR.

In August 1960, President Eisenhower approved the preparation of a National Strategic Target List and Single Integrated Operational Plan (SIOP). The country's first SIOP detailed a plan to deploy the country's strategic nuclear forces in a simultaneous strike against the Sino-Soviet bloc within the first twenty-four hours of a war. Its goal was maximum destruction. The targets included Soviet nuclear forces, government control centers, and the urban-industrial base. When briefed on the magnitude and redundancy of destruction, Eisenhower admitted to his naval aide, Captain E. P. Aurand, that it "frighten[ed] the devil out of me." [54] As well it should have. The Joint Chiefs of Staff were subsequently asked to estimate the death toll from such an attack. The numbers were shocking: 325 million dead in the Soviet Union and China, another 100 million in Eastern Europe, a similar number in Western Europe from fallout, and up to another 100 million from fallout in bordering countries including Finland, Sweden, Austria, Afghanistan, Pakistan, and Japan. Those figures did not include the deaths caused by Soviet nuclear weapons or by U.S. tactical weapons. [55] Nor did they include the then-unknown fact that an attack of this magnitude would almost certainly have triggered a nuclear winter, raising the possibility of extinction. Though horrified by the prospect of millions dying if the SIOP were enacted, Eisenhower passed the plan, unaltered, on to the new administration.

Having justified this precarious—one might say insane—nuclear buildup as the price of keeping defense spending down, Eisenhower's FY 1960 federal budget had increased by only 20 percent over his first budget despite a nearly 25 percent rise in GNP over that time period.

The Eisenhower years were relatively peaceful and prosperous, but many Americans feared that the country was stagnating and hungered for a new dynamism. Democrats turned to the youthful Bostonian John F. Kennedy. Kennedy hailed from a prominent and politically ambitious family. His father, the controversial Joseph Kennedy, was a successful Wall Street speculator and major financial backer of Franklin Roosevelt. His stint as ambassador to Great Britain was cut short because of his appeasement policy toward Hitler and his open pessimism about Great Britain's prospects in the war.

Elected to the Senate in 1952, John Kennedy's congressional career offered little indication of the heights to which he would later rise. A Cold War liberal, he supported Richard Nixon's Red-baiting congressional campaign against the progressive Democrat Helen Gahagan Douglas. Illness enabled him to miss the December 1954 Senate vote of censure against Joseph McCarthy, an old family friend, whom he had avoided criticizing. Alluding to the title of Kennedy's Pulitzer Prize–winning book, *Profiles in Courage*, Eleanor Roosevelt said she wished

that Kennedy "had a little less profile and a little more courage."[56] His brother
Robert had even served on McCarthy's staff. Kennedy tried to win the support
of the Eleanor Roosevelt–Adlai Stevenson liberal wing of the party but never
gained its trust. His opportunistic, though politically astute, choice of Lyndon
Johnson as running mate confirmed the liberals' mistrust of him.

Kennedy defeated Nixon by the narrowest of margins in 1960. Nixon had
touted his vice presidential experience and strong contribution to the Eisenhower administration. But when a reporter asked Eisenhower to name an important decision Nixon had participated in, Eisenhower said that if you gave him a
week he might think of one.[57]

Kennedy positioned himself as the candidate of change. But not all the
changes he promised were positive ones. Running as a hawk, he criticized the
Eisenhower-Nixon administration for tolerating Castro's takeover in Cuba and
for allowing a dangerous missile gap to develop.

On some level, Eisenhower understood the potentially cataclysmic situation
he had created and regretted the virtual doomsday machine he had bequeathed
to his successor. He was deeply disappointed that pressure from hawkish scientists and military advisors had thwarted his efforts to conclude a test ban treaty
before leaving office. With that in mind, he delivered an extraordinary farewell
address whose warning about the rise of an increasingly powerful and threatening "military-industrial complex" not only flew in the face of his actual track
record as president but described a phenomenon whose growth Eisenhower had
personally masterminded.

This speech, the best remembered of Eisenhower's presidency, originated in
conversations between the president's chief speechwriter, Malcolm Moos, a Johns
Hopkins political scientist, and Ralph Williams, a retired navy captain who was
also on the speechwriting staff. Moos and Williams met on October 31, 1960, to
discuss ideas for the farewell address and agreed that it was necessary to expose the
"problem of militarism." Williams's memo spelled out their concern very clearly:

> ... for the first time in its history, the United States has a permanent war-
> based industry. . . . Not only that, but flag and general officers retiring at
> an early age take positions in /a/ war based industrial complex shaping its
> decisions and guiding the direction of its tremendous thrust. This creates a
> danger that what the Communists have always said about us may become
> true. We must be careful to ensure that the "merchants of death do not
> come to dictate national policy."[58]

The specific phrase "military-industrial complex," which the speech immor-
talized, was apparently suggested by physicist Herbert York, the former director

of the Lawrence Livermore National Laboratory. In 1971, while working for the summer at the Stockholm International Peace Research Institute (SIPRI), York told a younger American colleague that he had been the one to suggest the precise wording to President Eisenhower for insertion into the speech.[59] Eisenhower agreed and sounded the tocsin:

> This conjunction of an immense military establishment and a large arms industry is new in the American experience. The total influence— economic, political, even spiritual—is felt in every city, every state house, every office of the Federal Government. . . . we must not fail to comprehend its grave implications. Our toil, resources and livelihood are all involved; so is the very structure of our society. In the councils of government, we must guard against the acquisition of unwarranted influence, whether sought or unsought, by the military-industrial complex. . . . We must never let the weight of this combination endanger our liberties or democratic processes. . . . Only an alert and knowledgeable citizenry can compel the proper meshing of the huge industrial and military machinery of defense with our peaceful methods and goals, so that security and liberty may prosper together.[60]

For most Americans, the significance would not be understood for a long time. But there were some notable exceptions. Walter Lippmann astutely compared Eisenhower's farewell address to George Washington's. As Washington had warned about the foreign "menace to civilian power," Eisenhower warned about the domestic military menace.[61] Eisenhower considered Washington his "hero." In *At Ease*, Eisenhower shared the fact that Washington's "farewell address . . . exemplified the human qualities I frankly idolized."[62]

The *New York Times*' Jack Raymond provided a full-page analysis of the military-industrial complex, replete with graphs detailing the exorbitance of U.S. defense spending, which accounted for 59 percent of the nearly $81 billion national budget. In addition to spending half the federal budget, he noted, the Pentagon also controlled $32 billion worth of real estate, including air bases and weapons arsenals. Raymond explained how the military and industry worked hand in glove to achieve this. The United States' excessive militarism, he added, was hurting the nation's image abroad: "in carrying a big stick, the United States appears to have forgotten the other part of Theodore Roosevelt's dictum to 'speak softly.'"[63]

Kennedy's close advisor and biographer Theodore Sorensen later mused, "I think that the principal reason Kennedy ran for the presidency was he thought the Eisenhower-Dulles policy of massive retaliation and all of that was heading the country toward nuclear war. He felt the policy of massive retaliation—in which we supposedly kept the peace by saying if you step one foot over the line in West Berlin or somewhere else, we will respond by annihilating you with nuclear weapons—he felt that was mad."[64] But little in the 1960 presidential campaign would have led observers to believe that Kennedy was going to reduce the risk of nuclear war or that the new administration would do anything other than fuel U.S. militarism. Kennedy attacked Eisenhower's "willingness to place fiscal security ahead of national security," especially at a time when the Soviets would soon be able to outproduce the United States "two to three to one" in missiles.[65] During the campaign, Kennedy acknowledged that he didn't expect the Soviets to "use that lead to threaten or launch an attack upon the United States," but he wouldn't take any chances. Calling for increased defense spending, he declared that "those who oppose these expenditures are taking a chance on our very survival as a nation."[66]

Kennedy's inauguration was resplendent with symbolism. Eighty-six-year-old Robert Frost became the first poet ever to participate in a presidential inauguration. Marian Anderson, the talented singer whom the Daughters of the American Revolution had once barred from Constitution Hall because of her race, sang the National Anthem. And Kennedy delivered a ringing inaugural address that both reached out to the Soviet Union in hopes of building friendship "before the dark powers of destruction unleashed by science engulf all humanity" and welcomed the fact that his generation had been granted the opportunity "to defend freedom in its hour of maximum danger" and would "pay any price, bear any burden, meet any hardship" in order to do so.[67]

The new administration recruited establishment insiders from the leading foundations, corporations, and Wall Street firms and leavened them with a sprinkling of progressives in secondary positions. David Halberstam labeled them "the best and the brightest," chronicling how their intelligence, achievements, and can-do spirit combined with hubris and profound moral blindness to land the United States in Vietnam. They were typified by National Security Advisor McGeorge Bundy, the dean of the faculty of arts and sciences at Harvard, who had been the first applicant to get perfect scores on all three Yale entrance exams, and Defense Secretary Robert McNamara, who was renowned for his computerlike mind and managerial brilliance. During a CINCPAC meeting on materials in the pipeline to Vietnam, McNamara stopped the projector and accurately complained that the data in slide 869 contradicted what had been presented seven hours earlier in slide 11. The intelligence of Kennedy's advisors was never in question. Their judgment, however, was. John Kenneth Galbraith, who served as Kennedy's ambassador to India, regretted that "foreign policy was still with the Council on Foreign Relations people. We knew their expertise was nothing. . . . All they knew was the difference between a Communist and an anti-Communist . . . they had this mystique and it still worked and those of us who

John F. Kennedy delivered a ringing inaugural address that both reached out to the Soviet Union in hopes of building friendship and reaffirmed his generation's willingness "to defend freedom in its hour of maximum danger" and "pay any price, bear any burden, meet any hardship" in order to do so.

doubted it . . . were like Indians firing occasional arrows into the campsite from the outside."[68] As a result of this odd mix of arrogance and ignorance, the new administration blundered badly in foreign policy right from the start.

Kennedy proceeded with Eisenhower's plan to have the CIA secretly train an invading force of 1,500 Cuban exiles in Guatemala. When he initially expressed doubts about the wisdom of such a scheme, Allen Dulles assured him that an invasion would inspire anti-Castro Cubans to rise up and overthrow the government. Administration officials Chester Bowles, Arthur Schlesinger, Jr., and Richard Goodwin took sharp issue with the plan, and Senate Foreign Relations Committee Chair J. William Fulbright urged Kennedy to abandon it entirely. But the new and inexperienced president feared blocking an operation backed by Eisenhower and the Joint Chiefs. Three days before the operation was set to begin, eight U.S. B-26 bombers destroyed or incapacitated half of Castro's air force. The invading force arrived at the Bay of Pigs in seven ships, two of which belonged to the United Fruit Company. The Cuban army easily subdued the invaders, who begged for direct U.S. military assistance.

The promised popular uprising never materialized. Bundy, Rusk, and Kennedy himself had repeatedly made it clear to CIA officials that no air support

Kennedy's new administration recruited ambitious, highly intelligent establishment insiders, whom David Halberstam would later label, somewhat ironically, "the best and the brightest." They were typified by National Security Advisor McGeorge Bundy (with Kennedy, left), the dean of the Faculty of Arts and Sciences at Harvard, and Defense Secretary Robert McNamara (right), renowned for his computerlike mind and managerial brilliance.

would be forthcoming. They knew that such action would damage the United States' image abroad and invite a Soviet move against West Berlin. Shortly before midnight on April 18, Kennedy, Johnson, McNamara, and Secretary of State Dean Rusk met in the White House with General Lyman Lemnitzer, the chairman of the Joint Chiefs, Navy Chief Admiral Arleigh Burke, and the CIA's chief of clandestine services, Richard Bissell. Burke and Bissell spent three hours trying to persuade Kennedy to send ground and air support. They had known all along that that was their only hope of success and fully expected that Kennedy would cave in to their pressure. Kennedy said, "They were sure I'd give in to them and send the go-ahead order."[69] "It was inconceivable to them," Kennedy's advisor Walt Rostow later wrote, "that the president would let it openly fail when he had all this American power."[70] Lemnitzer charged that "pulling out the rug" was "unbelievable . . . absolutely reprehensible, almost criminal." But Kennedy stood strong. As he explained to an old friend, "We're not going to plunge into an irresponsible action just because a fanatical fringe in this country puts so-called national pride above national reason."[71] One hundred fourteen men were killed, 1,189 captured. Among the casualties were four U.S. pilots under contract to the CIA from the Alabama National Guard.

*Cuban counterrevolutionaries after their capture in the Bay of Pigs.
Encouraged to believe that an invasion would inspire anti-Castro
Cubans to rise up and overthrow the government, Kennedy proceeded
with Eisenhower's plan to have the CIA secretly train an invading
force of 1,500 Cuban exiles in Guatemala. The Cuban army easily
subdued the invaders, who begged for direct U.S. military assistance.
Kennedy refused, and the promised popular uprising never materialized.
One hundred fourteen men were killed and 1,189 captured.*

The postmortems started quickly. The *Chicago Tribune* put it succinctly:
"The main results of the supposed Cuban 'invasion' are that the Castro dictatorship is more firmly installed than ever, the communists have made hay all over
the world, and the United States has taken a dreadful kick in the teeth."[72] The
Wall Street Journal declared that "the U.S. finds itself in a sorry mess. . . . This
country is reviled around the world. . . . But we suspect that the deeper feeling,
especially in the capitals of international Communism, is one of astonishment
at U.S. weakness."[73] The *New York Times* fretted that U.S. "hegemony . . . in the
Western Hemisphere is threatened for the first time in a century" as the Cuban
Revolution offered a "model" for the rest of Latin America.[74]

The world was indeed shocked by the United States' ineptitude and mis-
judgment. Dean Acheson reported from Europe that the fiasco "shattered the
Europeans," who saw it as "a completely unthought out, irresponsible thing
to do. They had tremendously high expectations of the new administration,
and . . . they just fell miles down with a crash."[75] Bowles wrote in his diary, "The
Cuban fiasco demonstrates how far astray a man as brilliant and well intentioned

as Kennedy can go who lacks a basic moral reference point."[76] Bowles would soon be unceremoniously ushered out of the State Department. Kennedy took responsibility for the botched invasion but vowed to redouble his efforts to combat Communism:

> We dare not fail to see the insidious nature of this new and deeper struggle.
> We dare not fail to grasp the new concepts, the new tools, the new sense of
> urgency we will need to combat it, whether in Cuba or South Vietnam. . . .
> The message of Cuba, of Laos, of the rising din of Communist voices in
> Asia and Latin America—these messages are all the same. The complacent,
> the self-indulgent, the soft societies are to be swept away with the debris of
> history. . . . Let me then make clear as President of the United States that
> I am determined upon our system's survival and success regardless of the
> cost and regardless of the peril.[77]

Democratic Senator Al Gore, Sr., who was a member of the Senate Foreign Relations Committee, called for "a shake-up of the Joint Chiefs of Staff. All the members should be replaced by new, wiser and abler men." The *New York Times* placed the lion's share of blame on the CIA and called for the agency's "thorough reorganization."[78]

Cuban exiles blamed the mission's failure on Kennedy's refusal to provide air support. Most of them would never forgive him. But despite the broad-based criticism of his handling of this affair, Kennedy's overall approval ratings jumped to the highest level of his presidency, leading him to comment, "It's just like Eisenhower. The worse I do the more popular I get."[79]

The entire sordid affair had a profound effect on the inexperienced president. Kennedy developed a healthy skepticism toward military advisors and intelligence officials. He explained to Schlesinger, "If someone comes to tell me this or that about the minimum wage bill, I have no hesitation in overruling them. But you always assume that the military and the intelligence people have some secret skill not available to ordinary mortals."[80] Kennedy told journalist Ben Bradlee, "The first advice I'm going to give my successor is to watch the generals and to avoid feeling that just because they were military men their opinions on military matters were worth a damn."[81] Kennedy's post-invasion remarks seemed to reveal the first flickering of understanding of Eisenhower's poignant warning. But his learning curve would need to be a steep one for him to escape the steel trap of Cold War thinking.

Following the botched invasion, Kennedy decided to shake up the Joint Chiefs "sons of bitches" and "those CIA bastards." He threatened to "shatter the CIA into a thousand pieces, and scatter it to the winds."[82] He named General

Maxwell Taylor to replace Lemnitzer as chairman of the Joint Chiefs but, hoping to placate hawkish critics, chose Curtis LeMay as air force chief of staff—a decision he would come to regret. At the CIA, he replaced Dulles with conservative Republican businessman John McCone. He also forced the resignation of Deputy Director Richard Bissell, and Deputy Director General Charles Cabell. He placed all CIA agents and other overseas U.S. personnel under the local ambassador and took steps to cut the CIA budget, shooting for a 20 percent reduction by 1966.

Kennedy put his brother Robert in charge of a significant portion of covert operations. The new responsibility kept the youthful attorney general very busy. Under his watch, the CIA launched 163 major covert operations in three years, only seven fewer than had been conducted under Eisenhower in eight years.[83]

Before assuming his new position, General Taylor conducted an inquiry into what went wrong in the Cuban operation. General Walter Bedell Smith testified, "A democracy cannot wage war. When you go to war, you pass a law giving extraordinary powers to the President. The people of the country assume when the emergency is over, the rights and powers that were temporarily delegated to the Chief Executive will be returned to the states, counties and to the people." Smith thought that the CIA's usefulness might have come to an end and a new covert agency was needed. He remarked, "It's time we take the bucket of slop and put another cover over it."[84]

Kennedy's growing mistrust of his military and intelligence advisors made it easier to rebuff their pressure to send troops to Laos, something that Eisenhower had warned him might be necessary to defeat the Communist Pathet Lao. If not for the Bay of Pigs, Kennedy told Ted Sorensen and Arthur Schlesinger, Jr., it would probably have happened. The Joint Chiefs insisted that Kennedy give prior commitment to a large-scale invading force and approval for taking the war to China if necessary, even if it meant using nuclear weapons. Kennedy resisted such demands and angered the generals by opting for a neutralist solution. "After the Bay of Pigs," Schlesinger told David Talbot, "Kennedy had contempt for the Joint Chiefs. . . . He dismissed them as a bunch of old men. He thought Lemnitzer was a dope."[85]

Still reeling from the Bay of Pigs, Kennedy prepared meticulously for his June meeting with Khrushchev in Vienna. Khrushchev had earlier reached out to the new president, hoping to ease tensions and reach an accord on nuclear testing, Laos, and Berlin. But now the mood had darkened. During the summit, the Soviet premier bristled with accusations. Khrushchev berated the young president for the United States' global imperialism. He declared that U.S.-Soviet relations hinged on resolution of the German question and deplored Germany's remilitarization and prominence in NATO. He demanded a treaty recognizing two separate Germanys by the end of the year. Berlin would function as a "free demilitarized city" under East Germany's jurisdiction, with guaranteed access from the west. Kennedy's parting comment to Khrushchev was "I see it's going to be a very cold winter."[86] He told one reporter, "If Khrushchev wants to rub my nose in the dirt, it's all over."[87] George Kennan thought that Kennedy was "strangely tongue-tied" during the summit.[88] The browbeaten president sat down afterward with James Reston, who asked, "Pretty rough?" Kennedy responded, "Roughest thing in my life." He explained:

> I've got two problems. First, to figure out why he did it, and in such a
> hostile way. And second, to figure out what we can do about it. I think . . .
> he did it because of the Bay of Pigs . . . he thought that anyone who was
> so young and inexperienced as to get into that mess could be taken, and
> anyone who got into it, and didn't see it through, had no guts. So he just
> beat hell out of me. So I've got a terrible problem . . . in trying to make our
> power credible, and Vietnam looks like the place.[89]

It would have been easier for Kennedy to comprehend Khrushchev's belligerence if he had understood the depth of Soviet concerns about Germany. These went well beyond the placement of U.S.-controlled intermediate-range ballistic missiles (IRBMs) on German soil and beyond the flood of East Germans escaping through West Berlin. What really terrified Khrushchev was the prospect of Germany getting control over its own nuclear weapons. He threatened to sign a separate peace treaty with East Germany and cut off British, French, and U.S. access to West Berlin.

Khrushchev explained to an American journalist:

> I can understand how Americans look at Germany somewhat differently
> than the way we do. . . . We have a much longer history with Germany. We
> have seen how quickly governments in Germany can change and how easy
> it is for Germany to become an instrument of mass murder. It is hard for
> us even to count the number of our people who were killed by Germany
> in the last war. . . . We have a saying here: "Give a German a gun; sooner or
> later he will point it at Russians." This is not just my feeling. I don't think
> there's anything the Russian people feel more strongly about than the
> question of the rearmament of Germany. You like to think in the United
> States that we have no public opinion. Don't be too sure about this. On
> the matter of Germany our people have very strong ideas. I don't think
> that any government here could survive if it tried to go against it. I told this
> to one of your American governors and he said he was surprised that the

During their June 1961 summit in Vienna, Khrushchev berated Kennedy about the United States' global imperialism. He declared that U.S.-Soviet relations hinged on resolution of the German question. Kennedy left frustrated, telling Khrushchev, "I see it's going to be a very cold winter."

Soviet Union, with all its atomic bombs and missiles, would fear Germany. I told your governor that he missed the point. Of course we could crush Germany. We could crush Germany in a few minutes. But what we fear is the ability of an armed Germany to commit the United States by its own actions. We fear the ability of Germany to start a world atomic war. What puzzles me more than anything else is that the Americans don't realize that there's a large group in Germany that is eager to destroy the Soviet Union. How many times do you have to be burned before you respect fire?[90]

The failure to bridge differences over key matters in Vienna made for one of the tensest summers in the Cold War. Dean Acheson, who prepared the background papers on Germany for the summit, advised Kennedy to take a strong, uncompromising stand on Berlin and avoid negotiations. He felt that nuclear war was worth risking. In the event of a confrontation, the United States planned to send a few brigades to Berlin. If the Warsaw Pact resisted militarily, the United States was ready to launch an all-out nuclear attack. As Bundy explained to Kennedy, "The current plan calls for shooting off everything we have in one shot, and it is so constructed as to make any more flexible course very difficult."[91]

At a special meeting on July 20, Lemnitzer and other military officials briefed Kennedy on plans for and consequences of nuclear war. Lemnitzer reviewed a report detailing a "surprise attack" on the Soviet Union for late 1963. Kennedy asked what would happen if the attack were launched in late 1962. Allen Dulles responded that the United States would not have enough missiles available until December 1963. Kennedy asked how long, if war occurred, would U.S. citizens have to remain in fallout shelters. Two weeks, he was told. He ordered that no one present even disclose the subject of the meeting. Deputy Secretary of Defense Roswell Gilpatric reported that Lemnitzer gave the briefing "as though it were for a kindergarten class. . . . Finally Kennedy got up and walked right out in the middle of it, and that was the end of it." [92]

In his 1990 memoirs, Dean Rusk described Kennedy's reaction: "President Kennedy clearly understood what nuclear war meant and was appalled by it. In our many talks together, he never worried about the threat of assassination, but he occasionally brooded over whether it would be his fate to push the nuclear button." [93] In September, Lemnitzer briefed Kennedy, McNamara, and Rusk on SIOP-62, including the option for a full-scale preemptive attack against the Soviet Union. Afterward, Kennedy disgustedly said to Rusk, "And we call ourselves the human race." [94]

Despite his reservations, Kennedy intensified the crisis. On July 25, he addressed the nation:

> The immediate threat to free men is in West Berlin. But that isolated outpost is not an isolated problem. The threat is world-wide. . . . We do not want to fight—but we have fought before. And others in earlier times have made the same dangerous mistake of assuming that the West was too selfish and too soft and too divided. . . . The source of world trouble and tension is Moscow, not Berlin. And if war begins, it will have begun in Moscow and not Berlin.

Kennedy announced an additional $3.45 billion for defense, an increase in draft calls to make possible a 25 percent expansion in the size of the army, activation of select reserve and National Guard units, and a national program to construct fallout shelters, both public and private. He emphasized the need to be prepared for nuclear war and reminded citizens, "Now in the thermonuclear age any misjudgments on either side about the intentions of the other could rain more devastation in several hours than has been wrought in all the wars of human history." [95]

The Warsaw Pact nations responded in dramatic fashion, implementing changes that had been under discussion for months. On August 13, East German troops began erecting barbed-wire barricades and roadblocks to shut off the stream of escaping East German citizens. Construction workers soon replaced the barbed wire with concrete. Kennedy sent 1,500 U.S. troops by road from West Germany to West Berlin, where they were met by Vice President Johnson. The world teetered nervously on the brink of war. Eighteen-year-old James Carroll waited at the Pentagon to pick up his father, Joseph Carroll, who had just been appointed the director of the newly created Defense Intelligence Agency. Carroll, who would later win the National Book Award for his powerful memoir *An American Requiem: God, My Father, and the War That Came Between Us,* vividly recalled his father's unsettling words. "Tonight Dad is in a somber mood," he wrote.

> . . . He is smoking, flicking ashes out the window. He has said nothing. Finally crushes the cigarette in the dashboard ashtray and turns to me. "Son, I want to say something to you. I'm only going to say it once, and I don't want you asking me any questions. Okay? You read the papers. You know what's going on. Berlin. The bomber they shot down last week. I may not come home one of these nights. I might have to go somewhere else. The whole Air Staff would go. If that happens, I'm going to depend on you to take my place with Mom and the boys." "What do you mean?" "Mom will know. But you should know too. I'll want you to get everybody in the car. I'll want you to drive south. Get on Route One. Head to Richmond. Go past it. Go as far as you can before you stop." He didn't say anything else . . . neither did I. We must have driven the rest of the way home in silence. I do remember very distinctly . . . what I felt . . . fear. . . . Despite all the talk of war, I had believed that my father and the others like him—Curtis LeMay, Tommy White, Pearre Cabell, Butch Blanchard, our neighbors on Generals' Row—would protect us from it. Now I saw that Dad himself no longer thought they could. I felt my father's fear, which until then I'd thought impossible. I began to be afraid that night and I stayed afraid for many years, first of what our enemy would do, later of what we would do.[96]

When recounting the story more than four decades later at a conference on the nuclear threat in Washington, D.C., Carroll concluded with the words, "And I have been driving south ever since."

The Berlin Wall defused the immediate danger, enabling Khrushchev to back off his threat to sign the provocative treaty with East Germany. Kennedy confided to aides, "It's not a very nice solution, but a wall is a hell of a lot better than a war."[97] Khrushchev understood the West's vulnerability in Berlin, which he viewed as "the testicles of the West. Every time I want to make the West scream," he said, "I squeeze on Berlin."[98]

Khrushchev found another way to make Kennedy scream in August 1961: he resumed nuclear testing. When Kennedy learned it would soon happen, he erupted, "Fucked again!" His advisors urged him to hold off responding in kind so that they could score a propaganda victory, but Kennedy brushed them off, exclaiming, "What are you? Peaceniks? They just kicked me in the nuts. I'm supposed to say that's okay?"[99]

Kennedy's warnings during the Berlin crisis infused the debate over fallout shelters with a new sense of urgency. Recommendations to build shelters during the 1950s had largely fallen on deaf ears. In March 1960, Representative Chet Holifield, who chaired the Government Operations Subcommittee, declared civil defense to be in "deplorable shape" with only 1,565 home fallout shelters having been built in thirty-five states.[100] Few people could afford or were willing to spend the several thousand dollars it cost to have the shelters installed in their homes. Nobel Prize–winning UCLA nuclear expert Willard Libby, a former member of the Atomic Energy Commision, proposed a solution. To much fanfare, he built a shelter at his Bel Air, California, home for $30 and lectured, "If your life is worth $30, then you can afford a fallout shelter such as this." Libby dug a five-foot-wide, five-foot-deep, seven-foot-long hole into the side of a hill. He lined the sides, top, and entrance with a hundred dirt-filled burlap bags. He made the roof from sixteen eight-foot-long railroad ties. Unfortunately for the Libbys, a fire swept through the Santa Monica mountains in February 1961, destroying their home. Mrs. Libby had time to salvage only two items: her husband's Nobel Prize and a mink coat. After initial reports that the fallout shelter had survived intact, the *Washington Post* sadly reported, "Fire Wrecks Libby's Bel Air Fallout Shelter."[101] The timing was regrettable. Newspapers were currently running Libby's multipart series titled "You Can Survive Atomic Attack." Physicist Leo Szilard commented that this "proves not only that there is a God but that he has a sense of humor."[102]

To an outside observer, it might have seemed that Americans had taken leave of their senses in the summer and fall of 1961 as the nation conducted an extended conversation about the ethics of killing friends and neighbors in order to protect the sanctity, security, and limited resources in one's home fallout shelter. In August, *Time* magazine published an article titled "Gun Thy Neighbor," which quoted one Chicago suburbanite as saying, "When I get my shelter finished, I'm going to mount a machine gun at the hatch to keep the neighbors out if the bomb falls. I'm deadly serious about this. If the stupid American public will not do what they have to do to save themselves, I'm not going to run the risk of not being able to use the shelter I've taken the trouble to provide to save my own family."[103]

At public meetings, neighbors with shelters told next-door neighbors and best friends that they would shoot them if necessary. Clergy weighed in on both sides of the issue. Rev. L. C. McHugh, a former professor of ethics at Georgetown, fueled the controversy when he wrote in the Jesuit magazine *America:*

A model home fallout shelter designed by the U.S. Office of Civil and Defense Mobilization. The 1961 Berlin crisis infused the fallout shelter debate with a new sense of urgency.

"Think twice before you rashly give your family shelter space to friends and neighbors or to the passing stranger . . . others try[ing] to break in . . . may be . . . repelled with whatever means will effectively deter their assault. . . . Does prudence also dictate that you have some 'protective devices' in your survival kit, e.g. a revolver for breaking up traffic jams at your shelter door? That's for you to decide, in the light of your personal circumstances."[104]

Right Reverend Angus Dun, the Episcopal bishop of Washington, D.C., denounced the every-family-for-itself approach as "immoral, unjust and contrary to the national interest." He averred that the kind of person who would be "most desperately needed in a post-attack world is least likely to dig himself a private molehole that has no room for his neighbor."[105]

Many people took sad note of the ways that the Cold War and threat of annihilation had warped the American conscience. *Bulletin of the Atomic Scientists* editor Eugene Rabinowitch called home fallout shelters "pathetic" and viewed discussions of killing one's neighbors as "demonstrations of human depravity." Historian Gabriel Kolko said that government neutrality on the gun-thy-neighbor debate suggested that it would "not complain when shelter-less neighbors remove their armed neighbors' shelter filters, or slip a plastic bag over the air intake."[106] The *New York Times* reported on one satirical cabaret skit in which shelter owners were encouraged to shoot their neighbors now rather than wait until they tried to break into their shelters. Bob Dylan recorded a song intended for his *The Freewheelin' Bob Dylan* album titled "Let Me Die in My Foot-steps." The unreleased song began, "I will not go down under the ground/'Cause somebody tells me that death's coming 'round./And I will not carry myself down to die/When I go to my grave my head will be high." For the chorus, Dylan sang, "Let me die in my footsteps/Before I go down under the ground." In perhaps the most creative response, one protester showed up at the Jesuit publication's office with an umbrella labeled "Portable Fallout Shelter." An arrow pointing to the end opposite the handle read, "For stabbing shelterless neighbors."[107] Despite government pressure, surprisingly few Americans actually built fallout shelters, apparently recognizing that shelters would offer scant protection in the event of nuclear war or that such a war might not be worth surviving.

Still, the chilling specter of nuclear war hung over the first two years of the Kennedy presidency. Having won the election in part by exploiting the fear of a missile gap, once in office Kennedy asked McNamara to quickly ascertain just how big the gap was. It took only three weeks to confirm that a gap did exist, but it was in the United States' favor.

Kennedy wanted to keep that information from the public. He intended to exploit the apocryphal missile gap to justify a robust increase in defense spending. But on February 6, his politically inexperienced secretary of defense shocked reporters by announcing "There's no missile gap." McNamara offered to resign over this faux pas. Kennedy explained that all such judgments were "premature," and the issue faded quickly.

But in October 1961, Kennedy decided to come clean on the striking disparity between U.S. and Soviet military strength. He authorized Gilpatric to publicly flaunt the United States' superiority in a speech to the Business Council in Hot Springs, Virginia. The speech was carefully crafted by young RAND consultant Daniel Ellsberg. Gilpatric announced that the United States "has a nuclear retaliatory force of such lethal power that an enemy move which brought it into play would be an act of self-destruction. . . . The total number of our nuclear delivery vehicles, tactical as well as strategic, is in the tens of thousands." McNamara publicly confirmed that the United States possessed "nuclear power several times that of the Soviet Union."[108] Several times was an understatement. The United States had approximately forty-five ICBMs.[109] The Soviets had only four, and those were very vulnerable to a U.S. attack. The United States had more than 3,400 deliverable nuclear warheads on submarines and bombers. The United States had more then 1,500 heavy bombers to the Soviets' 192. The United States also had some 120 IRBMs stationed in Turkey, Britain, and Italy, 1,000 tactical fighter bombers within range of the USSR, and nuclear missiles on Polaris subs.

Overall, the United States had approximately 25,000 nuclear weapons; the Soviets had one-tenth that number.[110]

SAC Commander General Thomas Power was not pleased by this revelation, having based his enormous funding requests on the contention that the United States faced a dire crisis. Refusing to go quietly, he began spotting Soviet missile sites everywhere, disguised as grain silos, monastery towers, and even a Crimean War Memorial. Power, a LeMay protégé who led the firebombing attack on Tokyo in World War II, opposed all efforts to constrain SAC. In December 1960, when briefed by RAND's William Kaufmann on the need to avoid targeting civilians, Power exploded, "Why do you want us to restrain ourselves? Restraint! Why are you so concerned with saving their lives? The whole idea is to kill the bastards!" He added, "Look. At the end of the war, if there are two Americans and one Russian, we win!" Exasperated, Kaufmann responded, "Well, you better make sure that they're a man and a woman."[111]

Despite the fact that the United States' nuclear superiority was vast and growing, the air force wanted to increase the number of missiles to 3,000. SAC wanted 10,000. McNamara's studies showed that the United States did not need more than 400 but settled on 1,000 as the lowest number he could get away with under the circumstances.[112]

Soviet Defense Minister Rodion Malinovsky interpreted Gilpatric's October statement to mean that "the imperialists are planning ... a surprise nuclear attack on the USSR and the socialist countries."[113] The Soviets, who had chosen not to exploit their advantage in the one area in which they were ahead of the United States—missile technology—responded by detonating a 30-megaton bomb, the biggest yet exploded, two days later. The next week they tested a 50-plus-megaton bomb, which they could have made 100 megatons, but they decided to leave off the third stage. McNamara later acknowledged that a surprise first strike was indeed one of the options under the SIOP—an option General LeMay was openly discussing.[114] LeMay had reportedly advocated building a single bomb big enough to destroy the entire Soviet Union.[115]

War seemed terrifyingly close in the fall of 1961. Robert Lowell wrote, "All autumn, the chafe and jar/of nuclear war; we have talked our extinction to death."[116]

Kennedy's unwavering commitment to overthrowing the revolutionary Cuban government further inflamed tensions with the Soviet Union. Robert Kennedy told CIA head John McCone in January 1962 that overthrowing Castro was "the top priority of the United States Government." Two months earlier, the Kennedys had unleashed Operation Mongoose, a terror campaign against Cuba under CIA auspices. Robert Kennedy outlined the policy: "My idea is to stir things up ... with espionage, sabotage, general disorder, run and operated by Cubans themselves."[117] The objective was to wreck the Cuban economy and assassinate Castro. Kennedy put master counterinsurgent and dirty-tricks expert Edward Lansdale in charge. The CIA assembled an enormous intelligence operation that included 600 CIA officers in South Florida, nearly five thousand CIA contractors, and the third largest navy in the Caribbean.[118] In March, Lansdale asked the Joint Chiefs for a "description of pretexts" to justify "US military intervention in Cuba." Brigadier General William Craig, the Operation Mongoose Program Officer, quickly produced an astounding list, which was approved by the Joint Chiefs and actively promoted by Chairman Lemnitzer.

Craig had recently suggested that if John Glenn's upcoming Mercury orbital flight failed, the United States should manufacture evidence blaming Cuban electronic interference. He appropriately named this Operation Dirty Trick. His new suggestions for Lansdale were code-named Operation Northwoods. They included a "Remember the *Maine*" incident modeled on the ship sinking that had triggered the Spanish-American war; a "terror campaign" against Cuban refugees, including sinking a boatload of Cubans escaping to Florida; hijacking attempts against U.S. aircraft that would be pinned on the Cuban government; staging a Cuban government shootdown of a civilian airliner ("the passengers could be a group of college students off on a holiday"); "an incident which will make it appear that Communist Cuban MIGs have destroyed a USAF aircraft over international waters in an unprovoked attack"; and "a series of well coordinated incidents . . . in and around Guantanamo to give genuine appearance of being done by hostile Cuban forces." These would include blowing up ammunition inside the base, starting fires, burning aircraft on the base, lobbing mortar shells, inciting riots, and sabotaging ships.[119]

U.S. actions throughout 1962 convinced the Soviets that an invasion was imminent. In January, the United States coerced Latin American countries to suspend Cuba's membership in the OAS. In April, 40,000 U.S. troops engaged in a two-week exercise culminating in an invasion of a Caribbean island. Two smaller exercises followed in May. During the summer and fall, the United States intensified its contingency planning for an invasion. In October 1962, the U.S. announced Operation Ortsac, a large exercise including a mock invasion by 7,500 marines of a Caribbean island replete with the overthrow of its government. The message was clear; Ortsac was Castro spelled backward. Scheduled to begin on October 15, the unfolding crisis would force Ortsac's cancellation.

Kennedy was also intent upon standing up to the Communists in Vietnam, despite understanding the difficulties the United States faced there. After visiting Vietnam in 1951, he had advised against aiding the French colonialists and later spoke more broadly of needing to win the support of Arabs, Africans, and Asians who "hated . . . the white man who bled them, beat them, exploited them, and ruled them."[120] He pointed out the contradiction in opposing the Soviets in Hungary and Poland while supporting the French in Vietnam, Algeria, Morocco, and Tunisia. But he was soon defending Diem's cancellation of elections and urging U.S. support for the South Vietnamese government. The United States' "prestige in Asia" was at stake. "Vietnam," he now insisted, "represents the cornerstone of the Free World in Southeast Asia, the keystone in the arch, the finger in the dike. Burma, Thailand, India, Japan, the Philippines and obviously Laos and Cambodia are among those whose security would be threatened if the red tide of Communism overflowed into Vietnam." [121]

In the late 1950s, Diem's repressive rule had sparked armed resistance in the South. In December 1960, with Hanoi's blessing, the National Front for the Liberation of South Vietnam (NLF) came into being as a broad coalition united around opposition to Diem. Its ten-point program called for the ouster of U.S. advisors, steps toward peaceful reunification of the country, and radical social reforms. Diem ignored U.S. pressure to democratize, choosing instead to ban public assembly, public dancing, and political parties. Instead of using this as an excuse to reduce U.S. involvement, Kennedy increased the number of U.S. military personnel in the country in a conscious contravention of the Geneva Accords and vastly expanded U.S. support for counterinsurgency programs.

In May 1961, Kennedy sent Vice President Johnson to Vietnam to demonstrate the United States' resolve. Johnson anointed Diem the "Winston Churchill of Southeast Asia" [122] and urged Americans to dig in their heels. In October, Kennedy sent Maxwell Taylor, who was then his personal military advisor, and Walt Rostow, the deputy assistant for National Security Affairs. They painted a bleak picture and pressed for a much larger U.S. involvement. Taylor was part of a growing chorus of Kennedy advisors who pushed for deployment of U.S. combat troops. McNamara and the Joint Chiefs agreed with Taylor's assessment that only U.S. combat troops could possibly forestall a Communist victory. Like Taylor, they acknowledged that an initial troop deployment would increase the pressure to send more troops, possibly vast numbers of them. Kennedy understood this dynamic all too well and resisted. He explained to Schlesinger, "The troops will march in; the bands will play; the crowds will cheer; and in four days everyone will have forgotten. Then we will be told we have to send in more troops. It's like taking a drink. The effect wears off, and you have to take another." [123]

Kennedy did approve Taylor's other recommendations and expanded U.S. involvement. The number of U.S. military personnel in Vietnam jumped from 800 when Kennedy took office to over 16,000 in 1963. The United States began resettling villagers at gunpoint behind barbed-wire-enclosed compounds guarded by government troops and using herbicides to defoliate areas where guerrillas operated. The long-term environmental and health effects would prove disastrous for Vietnamese and Americans alike.

But it was the Cuban Missile Crisis in October 1962 that really impressed

A U.S. aircraft sprays herbicide over a South Vietnamese forest to defoliate a guerrilla-infested area. The long-term environmental and health effects would prove disastrous for Vietnamese and Americans alike.

upon Kennedy the potentially disastrous repercussions of his hard-line Cold War policies. On Sunday, October 14, a U-2 surveillance plane brought back startling photos from Cuba. The next day, photoanalysts determined that the Soviets had placed SS-4 medium range ballistic missiles (MRBMs) on the island that were capable of delivering 1-megaton warheads to the continental United States.

Kennedy was in a bind. Leading Republicans and his own CIA director had warned that the Soviets would one day put offensive weapons on Cuba. Kennedy had repeatedly assured critics that if the Soviets did so, he would act decisively.

The last thing the Soviets wanted in 1962 was a direct military confrontation with the United States. With little more than ten ICBMs that could reliably reach U.S. soil and fewer than 300 nuclear warheads, they stood no chance against the United States' 5,000 nuclear bombs and nearly 2,000 ICBMs and bombers.[124] Fearing a U.S. first strike, the Soviets gambled that placing missiles in Cuba could both deter an attack on themselves and protect Cuba against an anticipated U.S. invasion. Khrushchev also saw this as an inexpensive way to placate Kremlin hawks. Having deliberately misled Kennedy with promises that no offensive weapons would be placed in Cuba, he said he wanted to give the Americans "a little bit of their own medicine" and show them that "it's been a long time since you could spank us like a little boy—now we can swat your ass."[125] Khrushchev equated Soviet missiles in Cuba with U.S. missiles on the Soviet Union's border

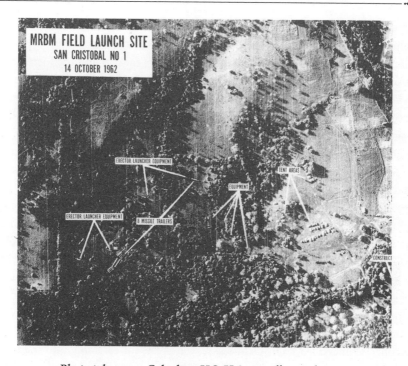

MRBM FIELD LAUNCH SITE
SAN CRISTOBAL NO 1
14 OCTOBER 1962

ERECTOR LAUNCHER EQUIPMENT

EQUIPMENT

TENT AREAS

ERECTOR LAUNCHER EQUIPMENT

8 MISSILE TRAILERS

CONSTRUCT

*Photo taken over Cuba by a U.S. U-2 surveillance plane on
October 14, 1962. The photo revealed that the Soviets had placed
medium-range ballistic missiles (MRBMs) on the island that
were capable of delivering 1-megaton warheads to the continental
U.S. This revelation sparked the Cuban Missile Crisis.*

in Turkey and in Western Europe. He had intended to announce their presence on November 7 at the forty-fifth anniversary of the Bolshevik Revolution.[126]

On October 16, Kennedy pondered Soviet motives. "What is the advantage of" putting ballistic missiles in Cuba, he asked his advisors. "It's just as if we suddenly began to put a major number of MRBMs in Turkey. Now that'd be goddamn dangerous, I would think." The room fell silent until Bundy replied, "Well, we did it, Mr. President."[127]

Kennedy hoped to stop the Soviets before the missiles had been fully installed. He conferred with his advisors to determine his options. On October 19, he met with the Joint Chiefs of Staff. The majority, led by LeMay, favored an air strike to destroy the missiles. LeMay advised, "The Russian bear has always been eager to stick his paw in Latin American waters. Now we've got him in a trap, let's take his leg off right up to his testicles. On second thought, let's take off his testicles, too."[128] LeMay assured Kennedy that the Soviets would not respond to an attack on the missiles in Cuba. Kennedy replied that they would have to respond—if not in Cuba, then in Berlin. LeMay welcomed that scenario, believing that the time was ripe not only to overthrow Castro but to wipe out the Soviet Union. Kennedy was shaken by LeMay's cavalier attitude toward the possibility of nuclear war. After the meeting he remarked to his aide Kenneth O'Donnell, "Can you imagine LeMay saying a thing like that? These brass hats have one great advantage in their favor. If we listen to them, and do what they want us to do, none of us will be alive later to tell them that they were wrong." [129]

Most of the chiefs and several of the other advisors wanted the strike to be followed by an invasion. Those less ready to risk war preferred a blockade. McNamara contended that the presence of Soviet missiles did not change the strategic balance. Kennedy agreed but believed that allowing the missiles to stay would have devastating political consequences abroad, especially in Latin America. Kennedy also confided to his brother Robert that if he didn't take strong action, he would be impeached. But in the coming days, he rejected the advice of his military leaders, of the civilian hard-liners Acheson and Nitze, and of former President Eisenhower, and opted for the blockade, which he referred to as a "quarantine" to downplay the fact that this too was an act of war. LeMay was furious. "This is almost as bad as the appeasement at Munich," he charged at the October 19 meeting. [130] On October 22, the president solemnly informed the American people of what had transpired. "The purpose of these bases," he noted, "can be none other than to provide a nuclear strike capability against the Western Hemisphere." In words that could hardly have been comforting, he declared, "We will not prematurely or unnecessarily risk the course of worldwide nuclear war in which even the fruits of victory would be ashes in our mouth, but neither will we shrink from that risk at any time it must be faced." [131]

Tensions heightened daily as the crisis dragged on. On October 25, Soviet leaders decided they would have to remove the missiles, but they wanted to secure the best terms they could before doing so. They hoped to trade Soviet missiles in Cuba for U.S. Jupiters in Turkey. But before they could act on that decision, Khrushchev received word that the U.S. invasion was about to begin. He sent Kennedy what McNamara described as "the most extraordinary diplomatic message I have ever seen." Khrushchev warned that the United States and USSR were heading inexorably toward war: "if war should indeed break out, then it would not be in our power to stop it . . . war ends when it has rolled through cities and villages, everywhere sowing death and destruction." [132]

In that letter, Khrushchev asked simply for a promise not to invade Cuba. Even ignoring the faulty information about the invasion beginning, Khrushchev had abundant reason to worry. A series of "incidents" occurred, any one of which could have triggered the nuclear holocaust that he and Kennedy desperately sought to avoid. A SAC test missile was launched from Vandenburg Air

Force Base toward the Marshall Islands, and U.S. officials mistakenly reported that Tampa and Minnesota were under attack.

On October 22, SAC went to DEFCON 3. At 10:30 A.M. on October 24, for the first time in history, SAC was placed on DEFCON 2 and prepared to strike targets in the Soviet Union. The decision to go to the precipice of nuclear war was made by General Power on his own authority without consulting the president. To make matters worse, instead of putting out this order in code, as would be expected, he sent it out in the clear to make sure that the Soviets would pick it up. Thereafter, the SAC fleet remained airborne, refueled by aerial tankers and getting ready to attack with close to three thousand nuclear weapons, expected to kill hundreds of millions of people.

Tensions continued to ratchet up. On October 27, an incident occurred that Schlesinger accurately described as "not only the most dangerous moment of the Cold War. It was the most dangerous moment in human history." [133] A navy group led by the carrier USS *Randolph* began dropping depth charges near a Soviet B-59 submarine sent to protect the other Soviet ships approaching Cuba. Those inside the U.S. destroyers were unaware that the Soviet sub was carrying nuclear weapons. Soviet signals officer Vadim Orlov described the scene: "The [depth charges] exploded right next to the hull. It felt like you were sitting in a metal barrel, which somebody is constantly blasting with a sledgehammer. The situation was quite unusual, if not to say shocking—for the crew."

The temperature rose sharply, especially inside the submarine's engine room. The ship went dark, with only emergency lights continuing to function. Carbon dioxide in the air reached near-lethal levels. People could barely breathe. "One of the duty officers fainted and fell down. Then another one followed, then the third one. . . . They were falling like dominoes. But we were still holding on, trying to escape. We were suffering like this for about four hours." Then "the Americans hit us with something stronger. . . . We thought—that's it—the end."

Panic ensued. Commander Valentin Savitsky tried unsuccessfully to reach the general staff. He then ordered the officer in charge of the nuclear torpedo to prepare it for battle and shouted, "Maybe the war has already started up there, while we are doing somersaults here. We're going to blast them now! We will die, but we will sink them all—we will not disgrace our Navy." Captain Valentin Savitsky turned to the other two officers aboard. Commander Vasili Arkhipov was able to calm him down and convince him not to launch, single-handedly preventing nuclear war and single-handedly saving humanity. [134]

In the midst of this harrowing confrontation, the Executive Committee of the National Security Council received word that a U-2 plane had been shot down over Cuba. The Joint Chiefs, believing that the Soviets were trying to blind the United States, demanded that Kennedy authorize an air strike and invasion. With reconnaissance missions also drawing fire, reports came in that Soviet missiles were being placed on launchers. Kennedy acknowledged that "time was running out."[135] The United States completed its preparations. Two hundred fifty thousand troops were mobilized and ready to invade. Plans were in place to install a new Cuban government. Two thousand bombing sorties were readied. The invasion seemed imminent.

Predicting a U.S. strike in twenty-four to seventy-two hours, Castro urged Khrushchev to respond by launching a nuclear attack against the U.S. imperialists before the United States attacked the Soviet Union. Kennedy, meanwhile, received a second letter from Khrushchev that further complicated the situation. Unlike the first, which had been highly personal, this one sounded as though it had been written by a committee. Some suspected that a military coup had taken place and Khrushchev had been ousted. The letter demanded both the pledge not to invade Cuba and the removal of NATO missiles in Turkey. Undersecretary of State George Ball and Adlai Stevenson had already suggested swapping Turkish missiles for Cuban ones, and Kennedy, prior to the current crisis, had himself twice endorsed U.S. removal of the obsolete Jupiters from Turkey. Now, however, Kennedy rejected a missile swap, fearing that yielding to Soviet demands under those circumstances could alienate Turkey and destroy NATO.

Kennedy decided to respond only to the first letter, offering a pledge not to invade Cuba. At the height of the crisis, a U-2 plane "accidentally" strayed over Soviet territory protected by jets armed with nuclear air-to-air missiles, and, unbeknown to the Americans, a Soviet nuclear missile battery was moved to fifteen miles from the U.S. base at Guantánamo, ready to blow it to smithereens. War drew closer by the second. In a last-ditch effort, Robert Kennedy met with Ambassador Anatoly Dobrynin on Saturday, October 27, and told him the United States was about to attack unless it received an immediate Soviet commitment to remove its bases from Cuba. He promised to withdraw the Jupiter missiles from Turkey within four to five months but only if Soviet leaders never publicly disclosed this secret agreement. While waiting anxiously for the Soviet response, a distraught President Kennedy admitted revealingly to a young female companion, "I'd rather my children be red than dead." Fortunately for all, such heresy departed profoundly from the then more conventional views of Eisenhower, who once told the British Ambassador that he "would rather be atomized than communized." Going to bed, McNamara thought that he might not live to see another Saturday night.[136] Fortunately for everyone, Khrushchev, who had been unable to sleep for several days when he was first briefed on nuclear weapons in 1953,[137] decided that it was not worth the slaughter of hundreds of millions of people or more to save face. The next morning, the Soviets announced that they

*Kennedy meets with the Executive Committee (EXCOMM)
of the National Security Council during the crisis.*

would withdraw the missiles. In his 1970 memoirs, Khrushchev claimed that Robert Kennedy's message was even more desperate. "Even though the President himself is very much against starting a war over Cuba, an irreversible chain of events could occur against his will," he warned. ". . . If the situation continues much longer, the President is not sure that the military will not overthrow him and seize power. The American army could get out of control." [138]

The crisis was over. Or was it? Although people everywhere breathed a huge sigh of relief, the crisis actually continued for three more weeks. Kennedy also demanded that the Soviets remove their Il-28 bombers from Cuba on the grounds that they could potentially carry nuclear weapons and that they cut the number of their military personnel on the island down to 3,000. For Khrushchev, acceding to this demand was complicated by the fact that the planes now belonged to Cuba. On November 11, Khrushchev made an offer similar to the one Robert Kennedy made to Dobrynin: he offered his "gentlemen's word" that he would remove the Il-28s at some later date. [139] Kennedy turned him down flat, demanding that he publicly announce their immediate withdrawal. The United States remained on DEFCON 2 throughout this ordeal, rubbing the Soviet Union's vulnerability in its face. The crisis finally ended on November 20, when the Soviets complied with U.S. demands.

The United States had come within a hairsbreadth of invading Cuba. U.S. officials, it turned out, had little idea of what they were about to encounter had they done so. Reconnaissance flights had succeeded in photographing only thirty-three of the forty-two SS-4 medium-range ballistic missiles and never found the nuclear warheads that were also present. SS-5 intermediate-range ballistic missiles, which could travel 2,200 miles and hit most of the continental United States, had also been shipped. The United States remained completely ignorant of the fact that the Soviets had also placed approximately a hundred battlefield nuclear weapons in Cuba to repel a U.S. invading force.[140] They included eighty FKR cruise missiles armed with 12-kiloton warheads, twelve Luna ground-to-ground rockets with 2-kiloton warheads, and six 12-kiloton bombs for Il-28 bombers with a range of 750 miles. Anticipating that U.S. forces would confront 10,000 Soviet military personnel and 100,000 armed Cubans, the United States expected to suffer 18,000 total casualties and 4,500 dead in an invasion. When McNamara later learned that there were actually 43,000 Soviet military personnel and 270,000 armed Cubans, he raised the estimate of U.S. deaths to 25,000. Thirty years after the crisis, in 1992, McNamara discovered that the battlefield nuclear weapons were in place and would likely have been used against U.S. invaders. He blanched and responded that in that case, 100,000 Americans would have died and the United States would have responded by wiping out Cuba with a "high risk" of nuclear war between the United States and Soviet Union. Hundreds of millions of people might have perished—possibly all mankind. It has also recently been discovered that on the island of Okinawa, a large force of Mace missiles with 1.1 megaton nuclear warheads and F-100 fighter bombers armed with hydrogen bombs was preparing for action. Their likely target was not the Soviet Union but China.[141]

As Daniel Ellsberg has astutely pointed out, Khrushchev made a blunder of epic proportions by not divulging the fact that the warheads had arrived before the blockade went into effect and then, even more bafflingly, not announcing that he had delivered tactical cruise and ballistic missiles along with their nuclear warheads. By keeping these facts secret, he had undercut the missiles' deterrent effect. Had U.S. policymakers known for sure of the warheads' arrival for the MRBMs, they would have hesitated to strike and risk a retaliatory launching. Similarly, had they known that tactical missiles with nuclear warheads might be fired at U.S. troops, they would likely have forsworn an invasion. In fact, the Kremlin had initially given local Soviet commanders authority to launch the tactical missiles at their own discretion if the U.S. invaded. Such authorization was later withdrawn, but that did not preclude the possibility of an unauthorized launching. Although the details were different, this frightening scenario of deterrence gone awry with cataclysmic consequences was hauntingly similar to the one that Stanley Kubrick presented little more than a year later in his satirical masterpiece *Dr. Strangelove.*

U.S. military leaders were furious when the crisis ended without an attack on Cuba. On several occasions, they had as much as accused Kennedy of cowardice for resisting their recommendations. McNamara recalled their bitterness at a meeting with Kennedy the day after the Soviets agreed to remove their missiles: "The President invited the chiefs in to thank them for their support during the crisis, and there was one hell of a scene. Curtis LeMay came out saying, 'We lost. We ought to just go in there today and knock 'em off!'"[142] Kennedy viewed the outcome differently. He privately boasted that he had "cut [Khrushchev's] balls off."[143] Khrushchev was vilified for his restraint. The Chinese charged him with cowardice for caving in to U.S. demands. Some Soviet officials agreed and spread the word that Khrushchev had "shitted his pants."[144] Many U.S. officials, believing that the United States' willingness to go to war had forced the Soviets to back down, decided that superior force would also work elsewhere, including in Vietnam. The Soviets drew the opposite lesson: determined to never again be so humiliated and forced to capitulate from weakness, they began a massive buildup of nuclear weapons to achieve parity with the United States. Weakened by the crisis, Khrushchev would be forced out of power the following year.

Shaken by how close the world had come to a nuclear holocaust, Khrushchev wrote Kennedy another long letter on October 30. "Evil has brought some good," he reflected. "The good is that now people have felt more tangibly the breathing of the burning flames of thermonuclear war and have a more clear realization of the threat looming over them if the arms race is not stopped." He guessed that Americans "felt as much anxiety as all other peoples expecting that thermonuclear war would break out any moment." In light of this, he made a series of bold proposals for eliminating "everything in our relations capable of generating a new crisis." He suggested a nonaggression treaty between NATO and the Warsaw Pact nations. Even better, he said, why not "disband all military blocs?" He wanted to move quickly to finalize a treaty for cessation of all nuclear weapons testing—in the atmosphere, in outer space, under water, and also underground, seeing it as transitional to complete disarmament. He proposed a formula for resolving the ever-dangerous German question: formal acceptance of two Germanys based on the existing borders. He urged the United States to recognize China and let it assume its legitimate place in the United Nations. He encouraged Kennedy to offer his own counterproposals so that together they could move toward peaceful resolution of the problems threatening mankind.[145] But Kennedy's tepid response and insistence on additional on-site inspections before signing a comprehensive test ban treaty frustrated Khrushchev.

Saturday Review editor and antinuclear activist Norman Cousins helped to break the impasse. Khrushchev had invited Cousins, who often attended Soviet-American conferences, to visit him in early December 1962. Prior to leaving, Kennedy asked Cousins to do what he could to convince Khrushchev that Kennedy was sincere about wanting to improve relations and conclude a test ban treaty. In a meeting that lasted more than three hours, Khrushchev told Cousins,

"Peace is the most important goal in the world. If we don't have peace and the nuclear bombs start to fall, what difference will it make whether we are Communists or Catholics or capitalists or Chinese or Russians or Americans? Who could tell us apart? Who will be left to tell us apart?"[146]

Khrushchev confirmed his eagerness to conclude a test ban treaty quickly and was confident that it was possible "for both our countries to agree on the kind of inspection that will satisfy you that we're not cheating and that will satisfy us you're not spying."[147] The prospects for a treaty looked good until negotiations hit a snag when Kennedy, under pressure from U.S. hawks, more than doubled the number of on-site inspections the United States would require. Hoping to salvage an agreement, Cousins returned to the Soviet Union in April 1963 and met with the Soviet premier for six hours. Khrushchev described the pressure he was under from Kremlin hawks. When Cousins briefed Kennedy on Khrushchev's predicament, the president observed, "One of the ironic things about this entire situation is that Mr. Khrushchev and I occupy approximately the same political positions inside our governments. He would like to prevent a nuclear war but is under severe pressure from his hard-line crowd, which interprets every move in that direction as appeasement. I've got similar problems."[148] That April, Undersecretary of State Averell Harriman, the former ambassador, also spoke with Khrushchev and cabled to Kennedy that Khrushchev "meant what he was saying about peaceful coexistence."[149] Harriman and Khrushchev interrupted their meetings to attend a track meet at Lenin Stadium between an Amateur Athletic Union team from the United States and a Soviet team. When the runners from the two nations that had so recently been on the brink of nuclear war marched onto the field arm in arm, the crowd went wild. Harriman and Khrushchev rose to a huge ovation. Harriman said he saw tears in Khrushchev's eyes.[150]

After his two visits with Khrushchev, Cousins reported to Kennedy that the Soviet leader sincerely sought a new relationship with the United States but felt bitter at Kennedy's unresponsiveness. Kennedy asked Cousins what he could do to break the stalemate. Cousins suggested a presidential address offering "a breathtaking new approach toward the Russian people, calling for an end to the cold war and a fresh start in American-Russian relations." Cousins even submitted a draft of the speech, much of which Ted Sorensen incorporated into the final version of Kennedy's historic American University commencement address.[151] Albeit a little more hesitantly at first than his Soviet counterpart, Kennedy began demonstrating that he too was ready for a fundamental restructuring of relations between the capitalist and Communist worlds.

Kennedy saw Vietnam as one place to step back from confrontation, but he knew it would not be easy. Among the earliest administration officials to question U.S. involvement in Vietnam was Ambassador to India John Kenneth Galbraith.

After reading Galbraith's report in early 1962, Kennedy instructed Harriman and NSC staffer Michael Forrestal to "seize upon any favorable moment to reduce our commitment." The Joint Chiefs emphatically rejected Galbraith's suggestions. McNamara asked General Paul Harkins for a plan to complete training South Vietnamese troops and withdraw U.S. forces by the end of 1965. It is important to note that in McNamara's mind, the withdrawal should occur whether victory was attained or not. He stated in his oral history for the Office of the Secretary of Defense, "I believed that to the extent we could train those forces, we should do so, and having done it, we should get out. To the extent those trained forces could not handle the problem—the subversion by North Vietnam—I believed we should not introduce our military forces in support of the South Vietnamese, even if they were going to be 'defeated.'"[152]

Kennedy started voicing doubts a little bit later. In late 1962, he asked Senator Mike Mansfield to visit Vietnam and evaluate the situation. Mansfield returned with a very pessimistic assessment and recommended that the United States withdraw its forces. O'Donnell described Kennedy's reaction: "The president was too disturbed by the senator's unexpected argument to reply to it. He said to me later when we talked about the discussion, 'I got angry with Mike for disagreeing with our policy so completely, and I got angry with myself because I found myself agreeing with him.'"[153] In April 1963, Kennedy told journalist Charles Bartlett, "We don't have a prayer of staying in Vietnam. We don't have a prayer of prevailing there. Those people hate us. They are going to throw our tails out of there at almost any point. But I can't give up a piece of territory like that to the Communists and then get the American people to reelect me."[154]

McNamara, meanwhile, began pressing the resistant Joint Chiefs for a plan for phased withdrawal. Kennedy approved the plan in May 1963. The first 1,000 men were set to depart at the end of that year. In September, Kennedy sent McNamara and Taylor on a ten-day fact-finding expedition to Vietnam. They gave the president their report on October 2. It called for beginning withdrawal before the end of 1963 and completing it by the end of 1965. Kennedy insisted that the withdrawal dates be included in the statement released to the press. He formalized this commitment in NSAM 263, which he signed on October 11, 1963.[155]

The debate over Kennedy's true intentions in Vietnam has at times been quite acrimonious. Kennedy's own contradictory statements and mixed signals have added to the confusion. Clearly, Kennedy was under enormous pressure to stay the course in Vietnam. The Joint Chiefs issued shrill warnings that the loss of South Vietnam would bring Communist domination of all Southeast Asia and beyond and pushed for the introduction of ground forces. Kennedy went out of his way to convince the American people that he believed it essential for the United States to prevail. In July 1963, he told a news conference that "for us to withdraw from that effort would mean a collapse not only of South Vietnam but Southeast Asia."[156] The fact that when he did discuss withdrawal, he made it contingent upon being able to depart victoriously, also fed the belief that he had no intention of changing course.

Kennedy's determination to pull out U.S. forces was made clear in private conversations with several of his closest advisors and confidants. But political considerations drove his decision to postpone action until after the 1964 elections. In several cases, such considerations also convinced his friends to sit on that knowledge long past the time when having divulged it might have helped prevent the nightmare that was to ensue. Kennedy explained the political calculations behind his regrettable delaying tactics to O'Donnell: "If I tried to pull out completely now from Vietnam, we would have another Joe McCarthy scare on our hands, but I can do it after I'm re-elected."[157]

Among those who later came forward with confirmation of Kennedy's intention to withdraw were Robert Kennedy, Robert McNamara, Arthur Schlesinger, Jr., Ted Sorensen, Mike Mansfield, Tip O'Neill, and Assistant Secretary of State Roger Hilsman. When Daniel Ellsberg interviewed Robert Kennedy in 1967, prior to the Tet Offensive and the shift in public opinion on the war, Kennedy explained that his brother had been "absolutely determined not to send ground units." Ellsberg asked if the president would have been willing, as a result, to accept defeat at the hands of the Communists, and Kennedy replied, "We would have fuzzed it up. We would have gotten a government in that asked us out or that would have negotiated with the other side. We would have handled it like Laos." In response to Ellsberg's question as to why the president was so smart when most of his senior advisors were still committed to prevailing, Kennedy responded so sharply that Ellsberg jumped in his chair, "Because we were there! We were there, in 1951. We saw what was happening to the French. We saw it. My brother determined, determined, never to let that happen to us."[158] President Kennedy even told Wayne Morse, the most outspoken war critic in Congress, that Morse was "absolutely right" in his criticism of Kennedy's Vietnam policy. "I've decided to get out. Definitely!" he assured him.[159]

Kennedy's most emphatic response to Khrushchev's peace overtures came in his June 1963 American University address. He and his closest advisors had drafted the speech without input from the Joint Chiefs, the CIA, or the State Department. It may be the most enlightened speech made by any president in the twentieth century.

> I have ... chosen this time and this place to discuss a topic on which
> ignorance too often abounds and the truth is too rarely perceived—yet it
> is the most important topic on earth: world peace. What kind of peace do I

Kennedy's most emphatic response to Khrushchev's overtures for peace during the previous year came in his extraordinary 1963 commencement address at American University. He and his closest advisors had drafted the speech without input from the Joint Chiefs, the CIA, or the State Department.

mean? What kind of peace do we seek? Not a Pax Americana enforced on the world by American weapons of war.... I am talking about genuine peace—the kind of peace that makes life on earth worth living—the kind that enables men and nations to grow and to hope and to build a better life for their children—not merely peace for Americans but peace for all men and women—not merely peace in our time but peace for all time. I speak of peace because of the new face of war. Total war makes no sense in an age when great powers can maintain large and relatively invulnerable nuclear forces and refuse to surrender without resort to those forces. It makes no sense in an age when a single nuclear weapon contains almost ten times the explosive force delivered by all of the allied air forces in the Second World War. It makes no sense in an age when the deadly poisons produced by a nuclear exchange would be carried by the wind and water and soil and seed to the far corners of the globe and to generations unborn.... Second: Let us re-examine our attitude toward the Soviet Union ... it is sad to ... realize the extent of the gulf between us. But it is also ... a warning to the American people not to ... see only a distorted and desperate view of the other side, not to see conflict as inevitable, accommodations as impossible and communication as nothing more than an exchange of threats.... Today, should total war ever break out again.... All we have built, all we have worked for, would be destroyed in the

first 24 hours. . . . In short, both the United States and its allies, and the Soviet Union and its allies, have a mutually deep interest in a just and genuine peace and in halting the arms race. . . . And if we cannot end now our differences, at least we can help make the world safe for diversity. For, in the final analysis, our most basic common link is that we all inhabit this planet. We all breathe the same air. We all cherish our children's future. And we are all mortal.
Third: Let us re-examine our attitude toward the Cold War . . . we shall also do our part to build a world of peace where the weak are safe and the strong are just. We are not helpless before that task or hopeless of its success. Confident and unafraid, we labor on—not toward a strategy of annihilation but toward a strategy of peace.[160]

McNamara was convinced that Kennedy was about to change the course of history. The secretary of defense told an interviewer, "The American University speech laid out exactly what Kennedy's intentions were. If he had lived, the world would have been different. I feel quite confident of that."[161]

Nowhere was Kennedy's speech more appreciated or more widely circulated than in the Soviet Union. Khrushchev considered it the best speech by a U.S. president since Roosevelt. Encouraged by what he heard, he publicly supported an atmospheric test ban treaty for the first time.[162] On July 25, U.S., Soviet, and British representatives initialed the historic treaty. It was the first nuclear arms control agreement in history.

Passage by the U.S. Senate, however, was far from certain. The Joint Chiefs argued in April 1963 that "only through an energetic test program in all environments can the United States achieve or maintain superiority in all areas of nuclear weapons technology."[163] The public seemed to concur. Congressional mail was running fifteen to one against the treaty.

Kennedy feared a future in which nuclear weapons might proliferate widely. He foresaw "the possibility in the 1970's . . . of the United States having to face a world in which 15 or 20 or 25 nations may have these weapons. I regard that," he told reporters at a March press conference, "as the greatest possible danger and hazard."[164] In order to avert that, he fought doggedly for passage, assuring aides that he would "gladly" forfeit reelection if that were the cost of passing the treaty.[165]

His efforts were rewarded. The Senate passed the Partial Nuclear Test Ban Treaty on September 24 by a vote of 80–19. Ted Sorensen believed that "no other accomplishment in the White House ever gave Kennedy greater satisfaction."[166] The treaty was ratified on October 7, 1963—Henry Wallace's seventy-fifth birthday. In recognition of this monumental achievement, the editors of the *Bulletin of the Atomic Scientists* moved the hands of the Doomsday Clock back to twelve minutes before midnight.

Kennedy wanted to eradicate all the long-standing sources of tension between the two nations. Foreign Minister Andrei Gromyko visited New York for the General Assembly meetings in September 1963, and Dean Rusk went to see him. As Gromyko recalled:

> He said, "The President wants to find ways of improving relations with the Soviet Union and reducing tension." He went on: "Could we go for a ride out of town and carry on our conversation."
>
> I realised something serious was afoot, and of course accepted.
>
> We drove beyond the city limits, where Rusk reported the President's message: "Kennedy is thinking of reducing the number of US forces in Europe."
>
> We discussed this walking along the side of the road.
>
> It seemed to me that common sense about this issue had at last gained the upper hand in Washington. The question had been present, visibly or invisibly, at almost every Soviet-US meeting since the war, whenever NATO policy and the remilitarisation of West Germany were discussed. The Soviet view was that US forces and bases in western Europe represented an obstacle to peace. Kennedy's idea therefore seized our attention.
>
> I reported what Rusk had told me to Khrushchev, and said: "If the President has the political strength to carry out his idea, he'll be doing a great thing for Europe, for the world and for the USA. Well, we'll just have to wait and see."
>
> Sadly, however, the President's days were numbered.[167]

Believing that he and Khrushchev could actually end the Cold War, he confided in two friends that he planned to conclude another arms control agreement and then become the first sitting U.S. president to visit the Soviet Union. The Soviet people, he was sure, would give him a hero's welcome.

Kennedy even announced that he was ready to call off the space race with the Soviet Union and replace competition with cooperation. That was another stunning reversal. During the 1960 campaign, he had emphasized how badly Soviet space triumphs had diminished the United States' stature abroad:

> The people of the world respect achievement. For most of the 20th century they admired American science and American education, which was second to none. But they are not at all certain about which way the future lies.
>
> The first vehicle in outer space was called Sputnik, not Vanguard. The first country to place its national emblem on the moon was the Soviet Union, not the United States. The first canine passengers in space who safely returned were named Strelka and Belka, not Rover or Fido, or even Checkers.[168]

The Soviets had reaped a political windfall from those triumphs. On April 12, 1961, five days before the Bay of Pigs invasion, Soviet cosmonaut Yuri Gagarin became the first human to orbit the earth. Flying over Africa, he sent greetings to Africans below who were struggling against colonialism. Alan Shepard's suborbital flight three weeks later paled by comparison. After that flight, 40 percent of Western Europeans believed that the Soviets were ahead in total military strength and overall scientific achievement. Worried that U.S. prestige was at stake, Kennedy called a rare joint session of Congress and announced that "if we are to win the battle . . . between freedom and tyranny, . . . this nation should commit itself to achieving the goal, before this decade is out, of landing a man on the moon and returning him safely to earth." [169] Almost a year later, in February 1962, John Glenn became the first American to orbit the earth. Though his three-orbit flight almost ended in disaster, it boosted Americans' spirits. But in August, the Soviets launched Vostok III, which circled the earth seventeen times and was joined the next day by Vostok IV. The following June, they captured the world's attention with a weeklong mission that included Valentina Tereshkova, the first woman in space.

Kennedy had gambled so much of his own and the country's prestige on winning the race to the moon that his sudden about-face in September 1963 came as a complete surprise. He stated:

> Finally, in a field where the United States and the Soviet Union have a special capacity—in the field of space—there is room for new cooperation, for further joint efforts in the regulation and exploration of space. I include among these possibilities a joint expedition to the moon. Space offers no problems of sovereignty; by resolution of this Assembly, the members of the United Nations have foresworn any claim to territorial rights in outer space or on celestial bodies, and declared that international law and the United Nations Charter will apply. Why, therefore, should man's first flight to the moon be a matter of national competition? Why should the United States and the Soviet Union, in preparing for such expeditions, become involved in immense duplications of research, construction, and expenditure? Surely we should explore whether the scientists and astronauts of our two countries— indeed of all the world—cannot work together in the conquest of space, sending someday in this decade to the moon not the representatives of a single nation, but the representatives of all of our countries.[170]

During the remarkable last few months of his life, Kennedy even contemplated a course reversal when it came to relations with Castro's Cuba—a relationship in which he was personally deeply invested and in which his policies were consistently wrongheaded. But just as he clung to the hope of victory in Vietnam while taking steps toward withdrawal, he endorsed a new round of CIA sabotage in Cuba while holding out hope for friendship and reconciliation with Fidel Castro. His ambivalence toward Castro represented, in microcosm, his lingering ambivalence in dealing with all of Latin America, where he spoke of democracy and reform yet continued aiding repressive dictators and supported a military coup in Guatemala as late as March 1963.

But even in Latin America, he began showing signs of rethinking U.S. policy. ABC News correspondent Lisa Howard interviewed Castro in April 1963 and reported that he had expressed his willingness to normalize relations if the United States was interested in doing so. U.S. intelligence officials were fully aware that Castro had become disillusioned with the Soviet Union after its capitulation during the missile crisis and was seeking to reduce dependence on his erstwhile ally. In September 1963, Kennedy asked journalist and diplomat William Attwood to explore with Cuban leaders the possibility of a rapprochement. Although UN Ambassador Adlai Stevenson authorized Attwood "to make discreet contact" with Cuba's UN ambassador, Carlos Lechuga, to determine whether dialogue with Castro was possible, Stevenson added regretfully that "the CIA is still in charge of Cuba" so not much was expected of this overture.[171]

Attwood and Lechuga had several productive discussions, but Attwood's request for a meeting with Castro was rejected on the grounds that such talks would not be "useful at this time." Kennedy decided to try another avenue of approach. French journalist Jean Daniel, an old friend of Attwood's, was about to go to Cuba to interview Castro. Attwood arranged for him to interview Kennedy before meeting with Castro. In that interview, Kennedy offered an extraordinarily sympathetic portrait of the Cuban Revolution:

> I believe that there is no country in the world, including all the African regions, including any and all the countries under colonial domination, where economic colonization, humiliation and exploitation were worse than in Cuba, in part owing to my country's policies during the Batista regime.... I approved the proclamation which Fidel Castro made in the Sierra Maestra, when he justifiably called for justice and especially yearned to rid Cuba of corruption. I will go even further: to some extent it is as though Batista was the incarnation of a number of sins on the part of the United States. Now we shall have to pay for those sins. In the matter of the Batista regime, I am in agreement with the first Cuban revolutionaries. That is perfectly clear.[172]

Daniel spent three weeks touring Cuba but made no headway in his efforts to interview Castro. As Daniel's departure from Cuba drew near, Castro showed up unexpectedly at Daniel's hotel. During the six-hour conversation, he wanted to hear every detail of Daniel's interview with Kennedy. Although Castro expressed as much criticism of Kennedy's behavior as Kennedy had of his, he, too, held out hope for a new departure, stating, just two days before Kennedy's assassination:

> I cannot help hoping that a leader will come to the fore in North America (why not Kennedy, there are things in his favor!), who will be willing to brace unpopularity, fight the trusts, tell the truth and, most important, let the various nations act as they see fit. Kennedy could still be this man. He still has the possibility of becoming, in the eyes of history, the greatest President of the United States, the leader who may at last understand that there can be coexistence between capitalists and socialists, even in the Americas. He would then be an even greater President than Lincoln.[173]

In little more than a year since the end of the Cuban Missile Crisis, Jack Kennedy, the erstwhile Cold Warrior, had undergone a remarkable transformation. He and Nikita Khrushchev had taken steps to ease Cold War tensions that in October 1962 or at any point in the previous sixteen years would have seemed unimaginable. Both had made enemies who were ready to pounce. On November 7, New York Governor Nelson Rockefeller launched his bid for the Republican presidential nomination. For the next two weeks, he kept up a steady assault on Kennedy's policies. Kennedy, he charged, was soft on communism. He naively believed that Soviet leaders were "reasonable, amenable to compromise, and desirous of reaching a fundamental settlement with the west." As a result, "the foundations of our safety are being sapped." He hadn't stopped Communist aggression in Laos. He had failed to provide air support during the Bay of Pigs invasion and stood "idly by while the wall was being built in Berlin." And the Partial Nuclear Test Ban Treaty had caused "profound shock" among the United States' European allies.[174]

But Rockefeller's wrath was nothing compared to that of the CIA and Joint Chiefs of Staff, which Kennedy had repeatedly provoked since the start of his presidency. In the summer of 1962, Kennedy read an advance copy of the soon-to-be-best-selling novel *Seven Days in May* by Fletcher Knebel and Charles Bailey, in which a military coup occurs in the United States. Knebel had gotten the idea when interviewing General Curtis LeMay. Kennedy told a friend:

> It's possible. It could happen in this country. . . . If, for example, the country had a young president, and he had a Bay of Pigs, there would be a certain uneasiness. Maybe the military would do a little criticizing behind his back, but this would be written off as the usual military dissatisfaction with

civilian control. Then if there were another Bay of Pigs, the reaction of the country would be, "Is he too young and inexperienced?" The military would almost feel that it was their patriotic obligation to stand ready to preserve the integrity of the nation, and only God knows just what segment of democracy they would be defending if they overthrew the elected establishment. Then, if there were a third Bay of Pigs, it could happen.[175]

In the minds of some leaders in the military and intelligence community, Kennedy was guilty of far more than three betrayals: he was guilty of not following through in the Bay of Pigs, disempowering the CIA and firing its leaders, resisting involvement and opting for a neutralist solution in Laos, concluding the atmospheric test ban treaty, planning to disengage from Vietnam, flirting with ending the Cold War, abandoning the space race, encouraging third-world nationalism, and, perhaps most damningly, accepting a negotiated settlement in the Cuban Missile Crisis.

On November 22, 1963, before the young president had a chance to realize the dreams he and Khrushchev shared for refashioning the world, bullets from one or more assassins cut Kennedy down on the streets of Dallas. We may never know who was responsible or what the motive was. The Warren Commission concluded that Lee Harvey Oswald was the lone assassin. Commission member John McCloy insisted that the report be unanimous even though four of the seven members—Richard Russell, Hale Boggs, John Sherman Cooper, and McCloy himself—harbored serious doubts about the lone-gunman and magic-bullet theories. Lyndon Johnson, Governor John Connally, who had also been wounded, and Robert Kennedy also questioned the findings. The public found the report unconvincing.

We do know that Kennedy had many enemies who deplored progressive change just as fervently as did those who had blocked Henry Wallace in 1944 when he was trying to lead the United States and the world down a similar path of peace and prosperity. Kennedy bravely defied the powerful forces who would have pushed the United States into a war with the Soviet Union. His courage was more than matched by Khrushchev's. Future generations owe an enormous debt and possibly their very existence to the fact that those two men stared into the abyss and recoiled from what they saw. And they owe a special debt to an obscure Soviet submarine commander who single-handedly blocked the start of nuclear war. In his inaugural address, Kennedy said that the torch had been passed to a new generation. With Kennedy's death, the torch was passed back to an old generation—the generation of Johnson, Nixon, Ford, and Reagan—leaders who, though not much older, would systematically destroy the promise of the Kennedy years as they returned the country to war and repression.

Chapter 8

LBJ:

Empire Derailed

Castro was dining with French journalist Jean Daniel when he learned of Kennedy's assassination. Three times he exclaimed, "This is bad news!" The previous day he had told Daniel that Kennedy might prove to be the United States' greatest president. Now everything had changed. He predicted, "You watch and see. I know them, they will try to put the blame on us for this thing." Learning that news reports were labeling Oswald a "pro-Castro Marxist" heightened his concerns. He asked Daniel what Johnson thought of the Bay of Pigs and "What authority does he exercise over the CIA?"[1]

When Khrushchev heard the news, he broke down and cried. It was days before he could resume his duties. An embassy official told White House Press Secretary Pierre Salinger, "He just wandered around his office for several days, like he was in a daze."[2] He visited the U.S. Embassy to sign the condolence book and sent Deputy Soviet Premier Anastas Mikoyan to personally represent him at the funeral. Trembling badly, Mikoyan approached Jacqueline Kennedy on the receiving line. Deeply moved, she took his hands in hers. There are two accounts of what she said. She remembered saying, "Please tell Mr. Chairman President that I know he and my husband worked together for a peaceful world, and now he and you must carry on my husband's work." Dean Rusk reported hearing her say, "My husband's dead. Now peace is up to you."[3] Jacqueline Kennedy wrote to Khrushchev that though he and her husband were "adversaries," they "were allied in a determination that the world should not be blown up."[4]

Lyndon Johnson was worlds apart from his fallen predecessor in every imaginable way. He was born in Stonewall, Texas, in 1908; his parents were teachers. His father also served five terms in the Texas House of Representatives. After graduating from Southwest Texas State Teachers College, Lyndon worked his

*Lyndon Johnson
taking the oath
of office following
Kennedy's
assassination on
November 22, 1963.
The new president
was worlds apart
from his fallen
predecessor.*

way up in Texas politics and won election to the U.S. House of Representatives in 1937 and the Senate in 1948. He thrived as Senate majority leader, where the "Johnson treatment" became the stuff of legends. Columnists Rowland Evans and Robert Novak noted that it "could last ten minutes or four hours . . . whenever Johnson might find a fellow Senator within his reach. Its tone could be supplication, accusation, cajolery, exuberance, scorn, tears, complaint, the hint of threat. . . . It ran the gamut of human emotions. . . . Interjections from the target were rare. Johnson anticipated them before they could be spoken."[5] He was egotistical, overbearing, insecure, and extremely coarse, taking pleasure in inviting associates into the bathroom so he could conduct conversations while sitting on the toilet. Not a deep foreign policy thinker, he was a dedicated anti-Communist. He liked to say, "If you let a bully come in your front yard, he'll be on your porch the next day and the day after that he'll rape your wife in your own bed."[6]

Johnson wasted no time affirming that he was "not going to lose Vietnam."[7] Yet his real commitment was not to fighting faraway wars but to carrying out social reforms at home. "I do not want to be the President who built empires, or sought grandeur, or extended dominion. I want to be the President who educated young children . . . who helped to feed the hungry . . . who helped the poor to find their own way and who protected the right of every citizen to vote in every election." Averell Harriman believed that if it hadn't been for Vietnam, "he'd have been the greatest president ever." Sadly, he never came close.[8]

On his second day in office, Johnson assured his advisors of his resolve to aggressively defend U.S. interests in Vietnam. CIA Director John McCone immediately realized that Johnson was rejecting Kennedy's "emphasis on social reforms [in Vietnam]; he has very little tolerance with our spending so much time being 'do-gooders.'"[9] Nor did Johnson support Kennedy's plan to have

*Johnson gives Senator Richard Russell the infamous
"treatment." Egotistical, overbearing, insecure, and extremely
coarse, Johnson was not a deep foreign policy thinker.*

the troops out of Vietnam by 1965. Yet he initially had no intention of sending in U.S. combat troops or bombing North Vietnam in an election year. But the unpopular, repressive, and corrupt U.S.-backed government continued to lose more ground to the National Liberation Front.

Four days after Kennedy's death, Johnson issued National Security Action Memorandum (NSAM) 273, signaling that the United States would be taking a more hands-on approach to Vietnam. Earlier drafts of NSAM 273 had clearly limited covert actions against the North to South Vietnamese forces. NSAM 273 left the door open to covert action by U.S. forces as well.[10]

From the start, Johnson made the fatal mistake of believing fanciful assessments of how well the war was going instead of sober accounts of the faltering military and political campaigns. When CIA Director McCone tried to warn Johnson that conditions in South Vietnam were much worse than Johnson realized, Johnson slammed the door in his face. McCone was no longer welcome in the Oval Office and was reduced to communicating via written reports that the president might or might not read.[11]

Johnson initially questioned the importance of persevering in Vietnam. He confronted McGeorge Bundy in May 1964, asking, "What in the hell is Vietnam worth to me?"[12] Johnson himself had offered one answer in a 1954 newsletter, telling constituents that "Indochina is a rich prize" with its tin and manganese deposits.[13] Ambassador Henry Cabot Lodge had a more capacious view: "He who holds or has influence in Vietnam can affect the future of the Philippines and Formosa to the east, Thailand and Burma with their huge rice surpluses to the west, and Malaysia and Indonesia with their rubber, ore, and tin to the south. Vietnam thus does not exist in a geographical vacuum—from it large storehouses of wealth and population can be influenced and undermined."[14] Arthur Tunnell of the Saigon office of Investors Overseas Service predicted, "After the war, there is going to be a big future for American businessmen here."[15] Charles Murphy wrote in *Fortune*, "Acre for acre the region in which Vietnam currently forms the dramatic foreground is as rich as any land on the face of the earth." Senator Gale McGee described Southeast Asia as "the last major resource area outside the control of any of the major powers on the globe." He admitted that "the conditions of the Vietnamese people" were "secondary."[16]

Johnson also feared the political consequences of losing the war. He had a recurring nightmare about what would happened if he vacillated or lost:

> There would be Robert Kennedy . . . telling everyone that I had betrayed
> John Kennedy's commitment to South Vietnam. . . . That I was a coward.
> An unmanly man. A man without a spine. . . . Every night when I fell asleep
> I would see myself tied to the ground in the middle of a long, open space.
> In the distance, I could hear the voices of thousands of people. They were
> all shouting and running toward me: "Coward! Traitor! Weakling!"[17]

Johnson endorsed McNamara's strategy of graduated pressure on the North. The Joint Chiefs bristled under the constraints.

In August 1964, Johnson and McNamara used a fabricated incident in the Gulf of Tonkin as an excuse to escalate the war. McNamara and other administration officials testified that the alleged attacks on U.S. destroyers had been "deliberate and unprovoked."[18] The American press parroted that line.

Johnson still ran as the peace candidate in 1964, thoroughly thrashing the even more hawkish Arizona Senator Barry Goldwater, who threatened to use nuclear weapons in Vietnam. During the campaign, Johnson assured voters, "We are not about to send American boys nine or ten thousand miles away from home to do what Asian boys ought to be doing for themselves." The public overwhelmingly agreed. In a January 1965 survey of eighty-three senators, only seven favored bombing the North or deploying combat troops to the South. Vice President Hubert Humphrey urged Johnson not to escalate the war. Johnson responded by freezing Humphrey out of subsequent policy-making sessions, excluding him from National Security Council meetings for a year despite the fact that the vice president was, by law, a member of the NSC.[19]

Following the election, Johnson began a steady process of escalation. In December 1964, UN Secretary-General U Thant alerted Dean Rusk to Hanoi's willingness to begin secret negotiations. But the United States ignored his entreaty, prompting Thant to declare in late February:

> I am sure the great American people, if only they knew the true facts and background to the developments in South Viet-Nam, will agree with me that further bloodshed is unnecessary. And that the political and diplomatic methods of discussions and negotiations alone can create conditions which will enable the United States to withdraw gracefully from that part of the world. As you know, in times of war and of hostilities the first casualty is truth.[20]

Johnson wasn't interested in peaceful solutions. In March, he told George Ball that he would "get sick and leave town" before he listened to any more peace proposals from Thant and British Prime Minister Harold Wilson.[21]

Meanwhile, the United States sharply expanded the "free-fire zones," in which anything that moved was considered a legitimate target. The U.S. arsenal of acceptable weapons included napalm, cluster bombs, and white phosphorus, which burned from the skin straight through to the bone, causing horrific and painful deaths.

That such tactics had failed to slow the NLF's steady gains in the countryside was becoming more obvious by the day. Johnson, who had been resisting pressure to bomb the North, finally relented. But first the United States needed a pretext for escalation. It decided to manufacture one. The CIA did what it could to "prove" that North Vietnam was instigating the southern insurgency. Twenty-five-year CIA agent Ralph McGehee exposed the effort to mislead the public: "The agency took tons of Communist-made weapons out of its warehouses, loaded them on a Vietnamese coastal vessel, faked a firefight, and then called in Western reporters . . . to 'prove' North Vietnamese aid to the Viet Cong."[22] The State Department followed up with a white paper devoting seven pages to this phony "evidence." On February 7, 1965, the NLF attacked a U.S. helicopter base at Pleiku, killing eight and wounding a hundred U.S. troops. From Saigon, Bundy told Johnson and his advisors that Hanoi had "thrown down the gauntlet."[23] But Bundy admitted to David Halberstam that Pleiku was really no different from other episodes. "Pleikus are like streetcars," as he put it.[24]

Johnson initiated a new, and more brutal, phase of the war. He began Rolling Thunder, an ongoing bombing campaign against the North.

Despite the intensification of violence, U.S. prospects remained bleak. In early April, as McCone stepped down as head of the CIA, he told Johnson that the road he was heading down was one of pure folly: "We will find ourselves mired down in combat in the jungle in a military effort that we cannot win, and from which we will have extreme difficulty in extracting ourselves."[25]

But Johnson dismissed intelligence reports that didn't conform to what he wanted to hear. He later commented, "Let me tell you about these intelligence guys. When I was growing up in Texas, we had a cow named Bessie. I'd get her in the stanchion, seat myself and squeeze out a pail of fresh milk. One day, I'd worked hard and gotten a full pail of milk, but I wasn't paying attention and old Bessie swung her shit-smeared tail through that bucket of milk. Now, you know, that's what these intelligence guys do. You work hard and get a good program or policy going, and they swing a shit-smeared tail through it."[26]

The Joint Chiefs continued to pressure Johnson for a very large troop commitment and an expanded bombing campaign. In April, Johnson sent another 40,000 troops, bringing the total to 75,000. He understood full well that once the United States committed to sending combat troops, the initial deployment would be just the tip of the iceberg. In June, he asked General Earle Wheeler, the chairman of the Joint Chiefs of Staff, how many troops would be required to win. Wheeler replied, "If you intend to drive the last Vietcong out of Vietnam it will take seven hundred, eight hundred thousand, a million men and about seven years."[27]

McNamara began signaling Hanoi that the United States would even consider using nuclear weapons. An international uproar ensued, forcing McNamara to qualify his statements. Soviet UN Ambassador Nikolai Fedorenko wasn't satisfied. As he put it:

> The American militarists do not preclude the possible use of nuclear
> weapons in South Viet-Nam. See the statement made today by Mr.
> McNamara . . . when he said that only in the present situation there is no
> military need for the use of nuclear weapons. This means that the United
> States means that situations may arise in Viet-Nam where provision
> has been made for resorting to these weapons of mass destruction. The
> United States has gone so far in its desire to stifle the National Liberation
> Movement that it is ready to threaten mankind with nuclear war.

He reminded delegates to the U.N. Disarmament Commission that this would not be the first time the United States had resorted to such measures: "The United States is not adverse to utilizing . . . nuclear warheads against the people of an Asian country as they have done once before, covering themselves with indelible shame for centuries to come."[28] He also condemned U.S. use of chemical warfare against the Viet Cong, warning that future generations would

*Napalm (**TOP**) and white phosphorus (**ABOVE**) bombs being dropped over Vietnam. Under Johnson, the U.S. arsenal of acceptable weapons in Vietnam grew to include napalm, cluster bombs, and white phosphorous, which burned straight to the bone, causing horrific and painful deaths.*

"shudder on remembering" this "crime, an act of lawlessness, a most cruel violation of the laws of international policy and a trampling of elementary moral principles."[29]

In May 1965, a new government—the fifth since the overthrow of Diem a year and a half earlier—seized power, headed by Air Marshal Nguyen Cao Ky and General Nguyen Van Thieu. Assistant Secretary of State William Bundy later commented that the new regime "seemed to all of us the bottom of the barrel, absolutely the bottom of the barrel." Ky's commitment to democratic ideals was tenuous at best. He commented, "People ask me who my heroes are. I have only one: Hitler." He displayed his understanding of democracy when commenting prior to the 1967 elections that if the person elected "is a Communist or if he is a Neutralist, I am going to fight him militarily. In any democratic country you have the right to disagree with the views of others." But even Ky admitted to the *New York Times'* James Reston in 1965 that the Communists were "closer to the people's yearning for social justice and an independent life," as Reston put it, than his own government was.[30] Former military advisor John Paul Vann, who had returned to work on the pacification program, concurred:

> There is a revolution going on in this country—and the principles, goals, and desires of the other side are much closer to what Americans believe in than those of GVN. . . . I am convinced that, even though the NLF is Communist-dominated, . . . the great majority of the people supporting it are doing so because it is their only hope to change and improve their living conditions and opportunities. If I were a lad of eighteen faced with the same choice—whether to support the GVN or the NLF—and a member of a rural community, I would surely choose the NLF.[31]

Faced with a crumbling political situation, Johnson and his advisors again decided to increase the number of troops. Meeting on July 22, they estimated long-term troop requirements at between 500,000 and 600,000, assuming the Chinese did not become involved. If the Chinese entered the conflict, an additional 300,000 would be required. In the short run, they agreed, 100,000 would be needed by the end of the year and another 100,000 in January 1966 just to halt the slide and prevent defeat. They were relieved that the president would finally have to level with the American people about the country's commitment to a major war. Johnson addressed the nation on July 28. He announced an immediate troop increase of 50,000, raising the total in the country to 125,000. Because an unspecified number of additional forces would be needed later, he was raising the monthly draft call from 17,000 to 35,000 per month, but he had decided against calling up the reserves.

*General Nguyen Van Thieu with Johnson (background) and Air Marshall
Nguyen Cao Ky with McNamara (foreground). Ky and Thieu headed
the South Vietnamese government that seized power in May 1965.
William Bundy later commented that the new regime "seemed to all
of us the bottom of the barrel, absolutely the bottom of the barrel."*

Congress applauded Johnson's restraint, taking comfort in the moderate
troop commitment. At the Pentagon, however, both civilians and military advisors were shocked by Johnson's decision to deliberately mislead the American
people about the reality of the situation in Vietnam and the commitment the
United States was making to a major war destined to last for years. Joint Chiefs
Chairman Wheeler later explained, "We felt that it would be desirable to have
a reserve call-up in order to make sure that the people of the U.S. knew that we
were in a war and not engaged at some two-penny military adventure."[32]

No one was angrier than Army Chief of Staff General Harold Johnson. Johnson put on his best dress uniform and set off to see the president. In the car ride
over, he unpinned the stars from his shoulders. But before seeing the president
he had a change of heart and pinned them back on—a decision he later regretted.
He told one colleague, "I should have gone to see the president. I should have
taken off my stars. I should have resigned. It was the worst, the most immoral
decision I've ever made."[33]

From there on, troop deployments steadily escalated. Meanwhile, the NLF
continued to make gains throughout the country.

Not everyone supported sending combat troops. Clark Clifford tried repeatedly to convince Johnson and McNamara not to commit more troops, a position shared, at least privately, by Hubert Humphrey, Chester Bowles, William Bundy, George Ball, John Kenneth Galbraith, Assistant Secretary of Defense John McNaughton, NSC official Chester Cooper, White House Press Secretary Bill Moyers, and Deputy Assistant Secretary of Defense Adam Yarmolinsky.

Johnson chose catastrophe over capitulation. But he did so gradually instead of all-out, as the Joint Chiefs wanted. Major Charles Cooper, an aide to Admiral David McDonald, the chief of naval operations, accompanied McDonald to a meeting of the Joint Chiefs in November 1965 at which General Wheeler expressed "serious misgivings" about the direction of the war and urged the use of "overwhelming naval and air power," including mining Haiphong harbor, blockading the North Vietnamese coastline, and bombing the North, including Hanoi. The other chiefs assured Johnson that they endorsed Chairman Wheeler's proposal. Cooper recalled Johnson's response:

> Johnson exploded.... He just started screaming these obscenities....
> It was something like: "You goddamn fucking assholes. You're trying to
> get me to start World War III with your idiotic bullshit—your 'military
> wisdom.'" He insulted each of them individually. "You dumb shit. Do
> you expect me to believe that kind of crap? I've got the weight of the Free
> World on my shoulders and you want me to start World War III?"
> He called them shitheads and pompous assholes and used the f-word more
> freely than a marine in boot camp. He really degraded them and cursed
> at them. Then he stopped and went back to a calm voice.... "Imagine
> that you're me—that you're the president of the United States—and five
> incompetents come into your office and try to talk you into starting World
> War III.... What would you do?" General Wheeler said: I can't do it, Mr.
> President.... It's got to be your decision and yours alone." ...Johnson
> erupted again. "The risk is just too high. How can you fucking assholes
> ignore what China might do? You have just contaminated my office, you
> filthy shitheads. Get the hell out of here right now."

"I know memories are usually dimmed by time," Cooper assured his interviewer, "but not this one. My memory of Lyndon Johnson on that day is crystal clear."[34]

The United States gradually increased its bombing of the North, expanding the list of targets to heighten pressure on Hanoi. Responding to his advisors' concerns about provoking China, Johnson believed this gradual approach would limit the possibility of Chinese entry into the war. He reasoned that the slow escalation of the air war in the North and the increasing pressure on Ho Chi Minh was seduction, not rape. If China should suddenly react to slow escalation, as a woman might react to attempted seduction, by threatening to retaliate (a slap in the face, to continue the metaphor), the United States would have plenty of time to ease off the bombing. On the other hand, if the United States were to unleash an all-out, total assault on the North—rape rather than seduction—there could be no turning back, and Chinese reaction might be instant and total.[35]

When Senator George McGovern warned that the bombing might provoke strong responses by both the Chinese and North Vietnamese, Johnson responded, "I'm watching that very closely. I'm going up her leg an inch at a time. . . . I'll get to the snatch before they know what's happening."[36]

U.S. bombing sparked protests around the world. In March 1965, students and faculty held an all-night teach-in at the University of Michigan. The following month, Students for a Democratic Society (SDS) held an antiwar demonstration in Washington, D.C., at which an astounding 25,000 people showed up.

Convinced that Communist governments were behind the nascent antiwar movement, the CIA began a massive surveillance and information-gathering effort against antiwar activists. Johnson demanded the CIA uncover proof of Communist involvement. The CIA's illegal domestic surveillance operation, code-named Chaos, was run by a newly created Special Operations Group. It lasted almost seven years, compiling a computer index of 300,000 citizens and organizations and extensive files on 7,200 individuals.[37] Johnson nevertheless berated CIA Director Richard Helms for failing to prove Communist involvement.

Among the FBI's principal targets was Nobel Peace Prize winner Dr. Martin Luther King, Jr., who labeled the U.S. government "the greatest purveyor of violence in the world today."[38]

Top administration officials, including McNamara, began voicing their own doubts. In August 1966, McNamara asked the CIA for an estimate of the enemy forces and had his aide Leslie Gelb oversee the compiling of the top secret history of the war since 1954 that came to be known as the Pentagon Papers. When McNamara later began reading the report, he told a friend, "You know they could hang people for what's in there."[39] He conveyed his growing doubts to the president and, in August 1967, provoked Johnson's ire by telling a Senate committee that bombing the North would not bring Hanoi to the negotiating table. Johnson would not stand insubordination. "I don't want loyalty. I want *loyalty*," he said of one aide. "I want him to kiss my ass in Macy's window at high noon and tell me it smells like roses. I want his pecker in my pocket."[40] In November, Johnson announced that

LEFT: *Peter Kuznick speaking at an antiwar rally on the campus of Rutgers University in New Brunswick, New Jersey. As stories of atrocities in Vietnam reached the United States, the antiwar movement continued to grow.*

BELOW: *In 1967, Oliver Stone (center) enlisted in the U.S. Army and volunteered for combat duty in Vietnam, where he served for fifteen months and was wounded twice. He was awarded a Bronze Star for combat gallantry and a Purple Heart with an Oak Leaf Cluster.*

*A visibly upset Johnson with McNamara during a Cabinet Room
meeting in February 1968. After McNamara drew the president's
ire by expressing doubts about the war, Johnson surprised
McNamara by appointing him to head the World Bank.*

McNamara had been appointed to head the World Bank. The news came as a surprise to the now former secretary of defense.

By that point, most of the old Kennedy team was gone, as Johnson's foreign policy had moved sharply to the right. Robert Kennedy had left long before. McGeorge Bundy departed in 1966 to head the Ford Foundation. The comparatively colorless Dean Rusk, however, persevered. Johnson let Rusk play a much bigger role than he had under Kennedy, but Johnson had low regard for the State Department bureaucracy. He told J. Edgar Hoover that State officials were "a bunch of sissy fellows" who were "not worth a damn."[41] Rusk regularly offered his resignation, including in the summer of 1967, when he informed Johnson that his daughter was marrying a black man. But he stuck with Johnson to the bitter end, never wavering in his support for the war.

Although Rusk may have met Johnson's standards of loyalty, growing numbers of Americans had had enough of his vicious war and its distorting impact on American society. Black America was in a state of near rebellion. Rioting, which had rocked U.S. cities for several years, shattered Americans' quiescence in the summer of 1967. Twenty-five major riots, lasting two days or more, and thirty minor ones erupted. Fires burned and blood flowed in the streets. Police and national guard troops killed twenty-six African Americans in Newark and forty-three in Detroit.[42]

The campuses were also abuzz with activism. Incipient student radicalism was enflamed by the February 1967 exposé of rampant and illegal CIA infiltration and financing of seemingly liberal organizations at home as well as abroad. *Ramparts* magazine set things into motion by revealing that the CIA had been funding the National Student Association. The *New York Times* and the *Washington Post* exposed other groups as Agency fronts. These and other publications disclosed that the CIA had been funneling money to anti-Communist professors, journalists, aid workers, missionaries, labor leaders, and civil rights activists who did the Agency's dirty work. Among the discredited organizations were the Congress for Cultural Freedom, the Ford Foundation, Radio Free Europe, and Radio Liberty.

The public outcry was intense. Walter Lippmann noted that to the American people the CIA's covert activities had "begun to smell like a backed up cesspool."[43]

The *Ramparts* exposé sent shivers down the spine of intelligence officials, who feared that other CIA operations would be blown. Under the leadership of James Angleton, who headed the agency's counterintelligence operations from 1954 to 1974, the CIA had been actively involved in creating and using foreign police forces, security forces, and counterterrorism units in numerous countries. Angleton's obsession with a menacing Soviet Union bent upon domination, conquest, and infiltration was revealed in an internal CIA history that was declassified in 2007. The Overseas Internal Security Program, as it was called, had trained 771,217 military and police officers in twenty-five countries and helped create the secret police in Cambodia, Colombia, Ecuador, El Salvador, Guatemala, Iran, Iraq, Laos, Peru, the Philippines, South Korea, South Vietnam, and Thailand. Many had received training at the School of the Americas in Panama, including future death squad leaders in Honduras and El Salvador. Robert Amory, the CIA intelligence chief under Eisenhower and Kennedy, worried that the operations and their "Gestapo-type tactics put the agency on dangerous ground."[44]

In April 1967, hundreds of thousands rallied against the war in New York City, as U.S. troop levels approached 525,000. The Vietnamese assault on Khe Sanh began in late January 1968, with an enormous rocket and missile attack. The United States responded with the heaviest air raids in the history of warfare. B-52s dropped 100,000 tons of bombs, rockets, and explosives on enemy positions. One NLF leader described the terror of a B-52 attack:

Secretary of State Dean Rusk advises Johnson. As Johnson's foreign policy moved to the right, most of Kennedy's old team left the administration. But Rusk remained, playing a much larger role than he had under Kennedy. Although he regularly offered to resign, Rusk stuck with Johnson to the bitter end, never wavering in his support for the war in Vietnam.

From a kilometer away, the sonic roar of the B-52 explosions tore eardrums, leaving many of the jungle dwellers permanently deaf. From a kilometer, the shock waves knocked their victims senseless. Any hit within half a kilometer would collapse the walls of an unreinforced bunker, burying alive the people cowering inside. Seen up close, the bomb craters were gigantic—thirty feet across and nearly as deep. . . . The first few times I experienced a B-52 attack it seemed . . . that I had been caught in the Apocalypse. The terror was complete. One lost control of bodily functions as the mind screamed incomprehensible orders to get out.[45]

While the seventy-seven-day siege was just getting under way and all eyes were fixed on Khe Sanh, the NLF unleashed the Tet Offensive, catching the United States completely off guard. The NLF suffered huge losses. Though a military defeat for the North Vietnamese and NLF, the Tet Offensive was a political victory for Hanoi and its southern allies. The mood in Washington and Saigon changed from optimism to despair. The falsely propagated belief that victory was

*Johnson and National Security Advisor Walt Rostow review a
map of the South Vietnamese village of Khe Sanh. The United
States responded to the NLF's invasion of the village with the
heaviest air raids in the history of warfare. B-52s dropped 100,000
tons of bombs, rockets, and explosives on enemy positions.*

at hand was dealt a severe blow as Americans saw that the war was far from over
and perhaps not winnable under any circumstances.

Controversy erupted again over the United States' consideration of using
nuclear weapons at Khe Sanh. British Prime Minister Harold Wilson used his
toast at a White House dinner to inveigh against such an imprudent policy. He
was blunter in his appearance on *Face the Nation:* "Any attempt to escalate this
war will be most dangerous. . . . As for the proposal to use tactical nuclear weapons, this would be sheer lunacy. It would not only be disastrous to America's
position, it would run a very, very great risk of escalation for the world." [46]

Johnson succeeded in curbing the speculation. General William Westmoreland, commander of U.S. forces in Vietnam from 1964 to 1968, later regretted
that nuclear weapons had not been used. He wrote in his memoirs, "If Washington officials were so intent on 'sending a message' to Hanoi, surely small tactical
nuclear weapons would be a way to tell Hanoi something." [47]

Meanwhile, as popular opposition to the war exploded, Hoover's FBI did
everything it could to disrupt the antiwar movement, as it had been doing to the
civil rights movement for years. Hundreds of FBI agents infiltrated antiwar and
New Left organizations. In 1968, FBI activities escalated with the deliberate inclusion of New Left groups in the FBI's ongoing COINTELPRO program. The

*Antiwar protestors
at the October 1967
march on the Pentagon.
As popular opposition
to the war exploded,
the FBI tried to disrupt
the antiwar movement.*

Church Committee reported on the FBI's use of friendly news sources throughout the media.[48] In 1965, the FBI had twenty-five media assets in the Chicago area and twenty-eight in New Haven.[49] The CIA maintained its own stable of media assets. FBI and CIA flacks went to great lengths to mobilize support for the war while marginalizing the war's critics and impugning their patriotism.

Following Tet, Westmoreland requested another 206,000 troops. Johnson asked Clark Clifford, who was about to replace McNamara as secretary of defense on March 1, to chair a task force reviewing the situation. He assumed that the reliably hawkish senior advisor would support further escalation, but Clifford balked and called together a bipartisan group of "Wise Men." Following two days of meetings by those elder statesmen, Dean Acheson summed up the consensus view that the country could "no longer do the job we set out to do in the time we have left and we must begin to disengage."[50] Taken by surprise, Johnson was furious. "Everybody is recommending surrender," he complained.[51]

In the aftermath of Tet, Johnson's popularity plummeted. On March 31, he announced that he was not running for reelection. The war had taken another casualty. Johnson would be far from its last.

Vietnam was not the only place where U.S. policy in the 1960s was a disaster. Former *Time* magazine correspondent and *Newsweek* editor John Gerassi described the crushing poverty in Peru, which typified conditions throughout Latin America:

> more than half the people live outside the money economy altogether. . . .
> Of the other half, 80 percent earn $53 a year, while 100 families own 90

A Cabinet Room meeting during a summit of "Wise Men." In March 1967,
following two days of meetings by these elder statesmen, Dean Acheson
summed up the consensus view that they could "no longer do the job we
set out to do in the time we have left and we must begin to disengage."

Johnson's March 31, 1968, press conference announcing
that he would not run for reelection. Johnson's presidency
would be far from Vietnam's last casualty.

percent of the native . . . wealth. . . . Of this total, 80 percent is in the hands of just 30 families. Meanwhile, 65 percent of the population is illiterate and 45 percent has never seen a doctor. In Lima, the capital, whose colonial mansions enveloped by ornate wooden balconies help make it one of the most beautiful cities in the world, half of the 1.3 million inhabitants live in rat-infested slums. One, called El Montón, is built around, over, and in the city dump. There, when I visited it, naked children, some too young to know how to walk, competed with pigs for a few bits of food scraps accidentally discarded by the garbage men. . . . Peruvians . . . outside the money economy . . . chew . . . coca leaves to still hunger pains, and average 500 calories a day. Where there is grass, the Peruvian Andes Indian eats it—and also the sheep he kills when it gets so hungry that it begins tearing another sheep's wool off for its food. The peons who work the land of the whites average one sol (4 cents) a day, and not only labor from sunup to sundown but must also furnish servants for the master's hacienda or Lima house.[52]

As unrest surfaced throughout the continent, policy makers in the United States feared the prospect of more Castro-style revolutions and called for increased training for Latin American militaries and police forces. Brazil was one such case. A longtime U.S. ally, Brazil was perhaps the most strategically significant country in Latin America. It was the fifth largest country in the world—its 75 million people occupied an area larger than the continental United States— and it was rich in resources. In August 1961, Brazil's president stepped down, handing the reins of power to democratically elected Vice President João Goulart. Goulart pushed for economic and land reform, extension of democratic rights, and legalization of the Communist Party. The United States began planning for his ouster.

The United States implemented a series of measures designed to destabilize the government and precipitate a right-wing military takeover. The *Wall Street Journal* greased the skids, calling Goulart a "desperately devious, totally ambitious figure whose aim is to seize permanent power and run a fascist state." In June 1963, the United States cut off all aid to the central government, but increased aid to the military. The Alliance for Progress offered funds to individual states whose governors opposed Goulart. A National Intelligence Estimate the following month reported that "under Goulart, Communists and their sympathizers have achieved . . . influence over Brazilian policy. . . . This could lead ultimately to the establishment of an extreme leftist regime with a strongly anti-US character."[53]

Johnson met with CIA Director McCone on November 25, 1963, and made it clear that his Latin American policy, much like his Vietnam policy, would differ sharply from Kennedy's. In December, he appointed Assistant Secretary of

State for Inter-American Affairs Thomas Mann as coordinator for Latin America. Under Mann, the United States abandoned all pretense of promoting reform. Mann thought that Latin America's military leaders were "a pretty decent group of people."[54] He considered military aid a wiser investment than economic aid, and U.S. policy reflected his priorities. On March 18, at a closed session at the State Department, he unveiled the "Mann Doctrine" to all U.S. ambassadors and chiefs of aid missions in Latin America. He announced that Latin American countries would now be judged on how they promoted U.S. interests, not those of their own people. And the United States would no longer discriminate against right-wing dictators or governments that came to power through military coups. The United States would aggressively protect the $9 billion in U.S. investments in Latin America. Whereas Kennedy had claimed to promote democracy, Johnson would simply support anticommunism.

In 1964, the United States demanded that Goulart impose austerity on his suffering citizens. Goulart instead offered a program of land reform and control of foreign capital. He also recognized Cuba. The United States cut off aid in an attempt to destabilize the economy. Inflation skyrocketed. Goulart seized U.S. properties. U.S. Embassy officials prodded right-wing Brazilian officers to overthrow Goulart. On March 27, Ambassador Lincoln Gordon urged top officials, including McCone, Rusk, and McNamara, to back Army Chief of Staff General Humberto Castelo Branco and "help avert a major disaster . . . which might make Brazil the China of the 1960s."[55] The CIA went to work behind the scenes.

When the government fell, Gordon cabled Washington reporting that the generals had carried out a "democratic rebellion,"[56] which was "a great victory for the free world."[57] It had prevented a "total loss . . . of all South American Republics" and improved the climate for "private investments." Johnson wired his "warmest good wishes" to the new head of state and applauded him for solving the problem "within a framework of constitutional democracy and without civil strife." Mann said to Johnson, "I hope you're as happy about Brazil as I am." "I am," Johnson assured him.[58] Later that day, Rusk told the NSC and congressional leaders that the "United States did not engineer the revolt. It was an entirely indigenous effort."[59]

Within days, the new government declared a state of siege, limited the National Congress's powers, and empowered the president to deny citizenship rights to anyone deemed a national security threat. This was quickly applied to three presidents, two Supreme Federal Court justices, six state governors, fifty-five members of the National Congress, and three hundred other politically active individuals. On April 11, General Castelo Branco took power. Johnson told Bundy that he wanted to send Castelo Branco a warm message on his inauguration. Bundy cautioned him about the repressive measures already being implemented. Johnson replied,

Brazilian president João Goulart in New York in April 1962. After refusing to impose austerity measures on his people and instead instituting a program of land reform and control of foreign capital and recognizing Cuba, Goulart was overthrown in a coup backed by the United States.

"I know it. But I don't give a damn. I think that . . . some people . . . need to be locked up here and there too."[60] The new regime arrested more than 50,000 people the first month alone. Over the next few years, enormous sums flowed into Brazil from USAID, the World Bank, the Inter-American Development Bank (IDB), and U.S. corporations. From 1964 to 1966, Brazil received almost half of all USAID funds. A repressive military regime would rule for the next twenty years, backed by U.S. dollars. Brazil would have the largest gap between rich and poor on the earth. But the Brazilian dictators would again be counted among the closest U.S. allies, ever ready to intervene militarily to quash progressive movements in other Latin American nations.

The reverse situation existed in Peru, where the civilian government, wanting to improve the living conditions of that country's impoverished citizens, attempted to take control of Peru's biggest oil company, a subsidiary of Standard Oil of New Jersey. The United States cut aid to the government but continued funding the military. Comparing Brazil and Peru, New York Senator Robert Kennedy noted, "What the Alliance for Progress has come down to then is that you can close down newspapers, abolish congress, jail religious opposition . . . and you'll get lots of help, but if you fool around with a U.S. oil company, we'll cut you off without a penny."[61]

The Dominican Republic posed a different kind of challenge. Upon assuming office, Johnson recognized the military regime that had recently ousted Juan

Bosch, who had come to power in a democratic election in December 1962. In 1965, a popular uprising supported by midlevel officers, liberals, and leftists attempted to restore the constitutional order and return Bosch to power. The uprising began on new CIA Director William "Red" Raborn's first day on the job. Johnson had handpicked the retired admiral, a fellow Texan, over the objections of his advisors. A former colleague described the swearing-in ceremony: "After the President had said some kind things about him, about how he'd searched the country over and the only man he could find really capable of running it was 'Red' Raborn, there he was with tears trickling down his cheeks and coming off his chin in steady little drops." [62]

Raborn would last barely a year in the job, but that would be long enough to crush Dominican democracy. He told Johnson, "There is no question in my mind that this is the start of Castro's expansion." Johnson asked, "How many Castro terrorists are there?" Eight, Raborn replied, neglecting to mention that the CIA memo reporting that number also stated, "There is no evidence that the Castro regime is directly involved in the current insurrection." "There ain't no doubt about this being Castro now," Johnson told his lawyer Abe Fortas, "... They are moving other places in the hemisphere. It may be part of a whole Communistic pattern tied in with Vietnam." [63]

McNamara doubted the report's veracity, but Johnson's special assistant, Jack Valenti, warned him, "If the Castro-types take over the Dominican Republic, it will be the worst domestic political disaster any Administration could suffer." [64] Johnson sent in 23,000 U.S. troops, keeping another 10,000 offshore. He addressed the nation: "Communist leaders, many of them trained in Cuba, seeing a chance to increase disorder, to gain a foothold, joined the revolution. They took increasing control, and what began as a popular democratic revolution, committed to democracy and social justice, very shortly ... was taken over and really seized and placed into the hands of a band of communist conspirators. ... The American nations cannot, must not, and will not permit the establishment of another communist government in the western hemisphere." [65]

Before the UN Security Council, the Soviet representative assailed the intervention as a "gross violation" of the UN Charter. He deplored the "dirty and shameless" excuse, which "excels the work of Goebbels and his ilk," and wondered why the United States sends troops to the Dominican Republic "far more freely" than to Alabama, where "the racists hold sway." [66] One Latin American diplomat charged the United States with reverting to "gunboat diplomacy." [67]

Bosch decried the United States' "dirty propaganda" and declared the intervention as immoral as the Soviet invasion of Hungary. "A democratic revolution," he said, had been "smashed by the leading democracy of the world." [68] Even after the U.S. military took control of the country, the reformers refused

*Honduran troops en route to the Dominican Republic to support
the U.S. invasion of the country in 1965. The United States
crushed a popular uprising intended to restore constitutional
order and return to power the democratically elected president
Juan Bosch, who had recently been ousted by the military.*

to accept the restoration of the repressive regime. After Bundy's effort to broker an agreement failed, Johnson sent Fortas to Puerto Rico to pressure Bosch into stepping down. Fortas, a future U.S. Supreme Court justice, complained, "This fellow Bosch is a complete Latin poet-hero type and he's completely devoted to this damn constitution."[69] It later turned out that among the rebels, fewer than fifty were Communists.

Few nations were more strategically significant than Indonesia. Consisting of a vast archipelago of a half-dozen large and several thousand small islands, it was the most populous Muslim nation and the fifth most populous nation in the world. It also sat astride Southeast Asia's principal shipping lanes, exporting oil, rubber, tin, and other critical resources. In 1948, George Kennan wrote that "the problem of Indonesia" is "the most crucial issue of the moment in our struggle with the Kremlin. Indonesia is the anchor in that chain of islands stretching from Hokkaido to Sumatra which we should develop as a politico-economic counter-force to communism." In 1949, Indonesia finally ousted the Dutch colonizers, ending four centuries of Dutch rule, interrupted by Japan's wartime occupation. Sukarno, a leader of the decolonization movement, assumed the presidency and quickly became a thorn in the United States' side.[70]

In 1955, Sukarno hosted the leaders of twenty-nine Asian, African, and

Middle Eastern nations in Bandung at a conference that launched the non-aligned movement. The movement called for neutrality between the two Cold War behemoths, supported decolonization efforts, and encouraged third-world nations to assert greater control over their resources.

Secretary of State John Foster Dulles felt particular rancor toward Sukarno for spearheading this effort. In 1955, the CIA's appropriately nicknamed Health Alteration Committee contemplated assassinating him. "There was planning of such a possibility," CIA Deputy Director Richard Bissell acknowledged. After the conference, Sukarno inched toward the Communist bloc, visiting the Soviet Union and China and purchasing arms from Eastern Europe. The Indonesian Communist Party (PKI) had begun to play a prominent role in Sukarno's coalition government. The CIA attempted to weaken Sukarno by spreading rumors that he was involved with a beautiful Russian blonde who had him under her control. The CIA planned to release a pornographic film with a couple resembling Sukarno and his seductress. Failing to find a suitable facsimile, it sent a Sukarno mask to be worn by a porn actor, but the film, if made, was never actually released.[71]

With Eisenhower's approval, the CIA actively supported a coup hatched in late 1957 by rebel officers. CIA pilots supplied the rebels and bombed military and civilian targets. The United States was badly embarrassed in late May when a CIA pilot, Allen Pope, who had been shot down, was presented at a news conference. Years later, Pope remarked, "I enjoyed killing Communists. I liked to kill Communists any way I could get them."[72] Eisenhower had publicly denied U.S. involvement in the coup attempt, an assurance dutifully echoed by the *New York Times*.[73]

The coup proved to be as successful as the porn-movie venture. The CIA put out cover stories that its training teams in Indonesia were big-game hunters caught in the uprising and scientists searching for exotic butterflies. Among the casualties of this bungled operation was Frank Wisner, chief of the clandestine service, the Directorate of Plans, at the CIA, who, having already started to become unglued, went completely crazy. Diagnosed with "psychotic mania," he underwent six months of electroshock therapy and was later reassigned to head the agency's London office. Sukarno responded to the coup by eliminating most of the opposition political parties and speaking out more forcefully against U.S. foreign policy, especially in Vietnam.[74]

Following the failed coup, PKI membership and influence grew by leaps and bounds. Partly in response, Sukarno strengthened Indonesia's ties to Communist China. The CIA remained committed to overthrowing the Indonesian leader. Bissell lumped Sukarno together with Patrice Lumumba as "two of the worst people in public life . . . mad dogs . . . dangerous to the United States."[75] But President Kennedy forced a reversal of policy. Sukarno visited the White House in 1961, and Robert Kennedy returned the favor with a visit to Indonesia the following year. Meanwhile, President Kennedy helped broker an agreement between Indonesia and the Netherlands—Indonesia's former colonizer—that averted a war between the two countries. Prior to Sukarno's 1961 visit, Kennedy had remarked, according to Roger Hilsman, "when you consider things like the CIA's support to the 1958 rebellion, Sukarno's frequently anti-American attitude is understandable." Sukarno had gotten wind of that comment and appreciated it greatly. He urged the president to visit him in Indonesia, promising him "the grandest reception anyone ever received here." On November 19, three days before the assassination, Kennedy decided he would visit early the next year.[76]

Johnson again reversed course. But when he threatened to cut off economic aid to Indonesia, Sukarno chided him, "Don't publicly treat Sukarno like a spoiled child by refusing him any more candy unless he's a good boy because Sukarno has no choice but to say 'to hell with your aid.'"[77] Johnson backed down, fearing that curtailing aid would drive Indonesia into the Communist camp and jeopardize substantial U.S. investments. He decided to wait for a more propitious moment.

In October 1964, two major global developments occurred in rapid-fire succession. On October 16, the world awoke to the news that Nikita Khrushchev had been ousted. His duties were divided between two of his top lieutenants: Leonid Brezhnev would serve as Communist Party chief, and Alexei Kosygin would be premier. The news caught Washington completely off guard. The ouster was a response to the slowing economy and a series of foreign policy failures, including Khrushchev's recklessness in placing missiles into Cuba and then the humiliation of withdrawing them. He was faulted for putting too much stock in peaceful coexistence with the United States. His ouster was also seen as a concession to the Chinese, who had been demanding his removal as the first step toward repairing relations between the two countries.

The very day the news from Moscow was breaking, the Chinese exploded an atomic bomb at their Lop Nor test site. The test had long been anticipated by U.S. authorities. In fact, Kennedy had several times sounded out the Soviet Union's willingness to join the United States in a preemptive strike against the Chinese nuclear site. Johnson, too, had resisted the Pentagon's pressure to act unilaterally, instead sounding out Soviet willingness to launch a joint attack. Rusk had alerted the public to the possibility of a Chinese test just two weeks earlier. But that didn't cushion the blow when it actually occurred. Experts estimated a yield of 10 to 20 kilotons. Johnson insisted that it would be many years before the Chinese possessed "a stockpile of reliable weapons with effective delivery systems."[78] But U.S. officials feared that the successful test would enhance Chinese prestige and encourage a more aggressive stance in Southeast Asia.

China's gains raised the stakes in Indonesia. By 1965, the 3.5 million–member

PKI had become the third largest Communist Party in the world behind the Soviet Union's and China's. Thus emboldened, Sukarno repeatedly declared that Indonesia would soon test an atomic bomb, presumably with Chinese assistance. Meanwhile, within Indonesia, activists seized a US Information Agency library, ransacked the U.S. Consulate, and expropriated 160,000 acres of United States Rubber Company plantations and of Caltex, which was owned by the Texas Company and Standard Oil of California. U.S. officials contemplated provoking an incident that would turn the army against the PKI. Ambassador Howard Jones believed that an unsuccessful PKI coup attempt might prove the most effective catalyst. His successor, Marshall Green, arrived in Jakarta in July. His first report to Washington warned, "Sukarno is deliberately promoting Communism's cause in Indonesia."

On October 1, 1965, a group of junior military officers, led by the commander of Sukarno's palace guard, killed six generals whom they accused of plotting a CIA-backed overthrow of Sukarno. But mysteriously, both General Abdul Haris Nasution, the defense minister, and General Suharto, the head of the Army Strategic Reserve, managed to escape. Before the day was out, Suharto led the army in crushing Sukarno's supporters. Suharto accused the PKI of masterminding the affair. Undersecretary of State George Ball expressed hope that the army might "keep going and clean up the PKI." Ambassador Green urged military leaders to act forcefully. The United States added as much fuel to the fire as it could, even though it had no evidence that PKI leaders were actually involved.[79]

The new military rulers circulated photos of the slain generals, claiming that Communists, particularly Communist women, had tortured and castrated them and gouged out their eyes. The United States helped circulate such charges. Later autopsies showed the claims to be complete fabrications. But by then the damage had been done.

Egged on by the new rulers, mobs began attacking PKI members and sympathizers in what the New York Times called "one of the most savage mass slaughters of modern political history." Islamic extremists functioned as death squads, often parading victims' heads around on spikes. The Times described one incident: "Nearly 100 Communists, or suspected Communists, were herded into the town's botanical garden and mowed down with a machine gun . . . the head that had belonged to the school principal . . . was stuck on a pole and paraded among the former pupils." U.S. diplomats later acknowledged providing thousands of names of Communists to the Indonesian army for elimination. The Brits and Aussies added more names. Embassy staffer Robert Martens admitted unrepentantly, "It really was a big help to the army. They probably killed a lot of people, and I probably have a lot of blood on my hands, but that's not all bad. There's a time when you have to strike hard at a decisive moment." Ambassador Green confessed that the United States had much better intelligence as to PKI

TOP: *President Sukarno during a 1956 visit to the United States.*

ABOVE: *President Nixon greets President Suharto, who seized power in Indonesia after the U.S.-aided massacre of between a half million and a million Communists and other leftists in what the CIA later called "one of the worst mass murders of the 20th century."*

membership than did the Indonesian army, which relied on U.S. information. Howard Federspiel, the State Department's Indonesia expert, stated, "No one cared, as long as they were Communists, that they were butchered. No one was getting very worked up about it." U.S. efforts to cultivate close relationships with the Indonesian military were paying off. Perhaps one-third of the Indonesian general staff and almost half of the officer corps had received some training from Americans. McNamara defended U.S. involvement during the ensuing Senate inquiry, assuring listeners that U.S. "aid was well justified," paying handsome dividends.[80]

The following months saw the massacre of between a half million and a million Communists and other leftists, many by means of U.S. arms. Perhaps a million people were imprisoned, some for decades. McGeorge Bundy told Johnson that the events following October 1 were "a striking vindication of U.S. policy."[81]

His base decimated, Sukarno was forced out in 1967, replaced by Suharto. American businessmen felt great relief. The U.S. Embassy in Jakarta telegrammed Washington in December 1965, "Pressure for removing foreigners from direct control of extractive raw material production has been building for years." Without the uprising, "removal of foreign oil companies would have been certainty."[82] Among the foreigners looking for concessions in the aftermath of the slaughter was the right-wing oilman H. L. Hunt. Hunt proclaimed Indonesia the sole bright spot for the United States in the Cold War and called the ouster of Sukarno the "greatest victory for Freedom since the last decisive battle of World War II." In late 1968, the National Intelligence Estimate for Indonesia reported:

> An essential part of the Suharto government's economic program ... has been to welcome foreign capital back to Indonesia. Already about 25 American and European firms have recovered control of mines, estates, and other enterprises nationalized under Sukarno. In addition, liberal legislation has been enacted to attract new private foreign investment. Tax incentives are offered and the rights of managerial control, repatriation of profits, and compensation in the event of expropriation are, in large measure, guaranteed. The prospects for private foreign investment in extractive industries are fairly good ... there is substantial foreign investment in relatively untapped resources of nickel, copper, bauxite, and timber. The most promising industry, from the standpoint of both foreign capital and Indonesian economic growth, is oil. Crude production, chiefly from the fields of Caltex 5 in Central Sumatra, now averages 600,000 barrels per day, and daily output will probably exceed one million barrels within the next three years.[83]

In 1968, the CIA acknowledged that "in terms of the numbers killed, the anti-PKI massacres in Indonesia rank as one of the worst mass murders of the 20th century."[84] Ambassador Green told a secret session of the Senate Foreign Relations Committee that nobody knew the actual death toll: "We merely judge it by whole villages that have been depopulated."[85]

Suharto and other military dictators remained in power for decades. Despite the country's tremendous natural wealth, the average Indonesian stayed mired in poverty. As the *New York Times*, which had been effusive in its praise for Suharto

A distraught Johnson listens to a tape sent from Vietnam in July 1968. To the detriment of both his presidency and the nation, Johnson chose Vietnam over the Great Society.

over the years, reported in 1993, "the average Indonesian earns the equivalent only of $2 or $3 a day and thinks of regular electricity or indoor plumbing as unimaginable luxuries."[86] U.S. corporations, however, thrived in the post-1965 business-friendly climate that was shaped with the help of U.S. economic advisors and safeguarded by a brutal military that violently repressed the least signs of opposition.

Johnson, stubborn, vain, coarse, and narrow-sighted, sacrificed his dreams of being a great domestic reformer in order to pursue his anti-Communist obsessions in Vietnam, Indonesia, and elsewhere around the globe. Looking back in 1970, he told historian Doris Kearns that he had faced an impossible choice and ended up sacrificing "the woman I really loved—the Great Society—in order to get involved with that bitch of a war on the other side of the world." But, if he hadn't done so, he explained, he would have been seen as a "coward" and the United States as an "appeaser."[87] Johnson claimed that he made the choice knowing full well what it meant for him and understanding clearly how previous wars had destroyed the hopes and dreams of prior generations:

> Oh, I could see it coming all right. History provided too many cases where the sound of the bugle put an immediate end to the hopes and dreams

of the best reformers: the Spanish-American War drowned the populist spirit; World War I ended Woodrow Wilson's New Freedom; World War II brought the New Deal to a close. Once the war began, then all those conservatives in Congress would use it as a weapon against the Great Society . . . they'd use it so say they were against my programs, not because they were against the poor . . . but because the war had to come first. First, we had to beat those Godless Communists and then we could worry about the homeless Americans. And the generals. Oh, they'd love the war, too. It's hard to be a military hero without a war. Heroes need battles and bombs and bullets in order to be heroic. That's why I am suspicious of the military. They're always so narrow in their appraisal of everything. They see everything in military terms.

When it finally came down to it, Johnson made his choice—a choice whose consequences will always define his legacy and besmirch that of the nation whose forces he commanded. "Losing the Great Society," he lamented, "was a terrible thought, but not so terrible as the thought of being responsible for America's losing a war to the Communists. Nothing could possibly be worse than that."[88]

Some would say that the United States lost its soul in the jungles of Vietnam. And it would pay a double price in doing so. The war, which the United States would lose ignominiously despite Johnson's efforts, would also spell the end of the last significant period of social and political reform the United States has seen. Promising both guns and butter, the United States would only deliver on the former. Postwar prosperity would at first slow and then come crashing to a halt.

Chapter 9

NIXON AND KISSINGER:

The "Madman" and the "Psychopath"

Richard Nixon and Henry Kissinger dominated their era as few other men have. Their bold moves brought the world closer to peace. But they also ushered in cruel and vindictive policies that more than offset their achievements. They were as unlikely a pair as ever held high office. Kissinger found Nixon "a very odd man . . . a very unpleasant man . . . so nervous . . . an artificial man . . . [who] hated to meet new people." He found it strange that such a loner "became a politician. He really dislikes people."[1] White House Chief of Staff Bob Haldeman spent a great deal of time with Nixon but said he "didn't see me as a person, or even . . . as a human being. . . . To this day he doesn't know how many children I have nor anything else about my private life."[2]

Kissinger and Nixon were privately contemptuous of each other, fighting incessantly over who would get credit for their achievements. Kissinger disparaged Nixon as "that madman," "our drunken friend," and "the meatball mind," while fawning all over him in his presence. Nixon referred to Kissinger as his "Jew boy" and called him "psychopathic."[3] But the madman and the psychopath shared a vision of the United States as global hegemon. Nixon considered Woodrow Wilson the "greatest President of this century" because he had "the greatest vision of America's world role." Wilson had proclaimed the United States to be the world's savior. Kissinger similarly observed, "Our experience led us to look upon ourselves and what we did as having universal meaning, a relevance that extended beyond national boundaries to encompass the well-being of all mankind. America was not itself unless it had a meaning beyond itself. This is why Americans have always seen their role in the world as the outward manifestation of an inward state of grace."[4] But neither Kissinger nor Nixon understood the basic decency that should have guided the United States' exercise of power.

Lawrence Eagleburger, who had worked closely with Kissinger over many years, observed, "Henry is a balance-of-power thinker. He deeply believes in stability. These kind of objectives are antithetical to the American experience. Americans . . . want to pursue a set of moral principles. Henry does not have an intrinsic feel for the American political system, and he does not start with the same basic values and assumptions."[5] Nixon and Kissinger would suffer different fates. Nixon would be brought low by pettiness, venality, suspicion, and ambition. Kissinger, though equally flawed, would win the Nobel Peace Prize. But ugly accusations and the threat of indictment for war crimes would haunt him the remainder of his days.

Nineteen sixty-eight was one of the most extraordinary years of the century. Both the United States and the world crackled with energy. Change was in the air. A critical presidential election pitted Republican Richard Nixon against Democrat Hubert Humphrey, whose image was tarnished by years of obsequiously defending Johnson's Vietnam policies as vice president. Stunningly, the segregationist Alabama Governor George Wallace, running as a right-wing populist with retired General Curtis LeMay as his running mate, was polling 21 percent with barely a month to go before the election. His law-and-order message resonated with white voters concerned about ghetto rebellions, campus disruptions, and rising crime.

Postwar baby boomers had begun flooding college campuses in 1964. Imbued with youthful idealism inspired by the civil rights movement and dismissive of Cold War shibboleths, their protests swept the country. In April 1968, Columbia University students occupied several campus buildings to challenge the university's treatment of the surrounding black community and its support for military research. Columbia President Grayson Kirk charged, "Our young people, in disturbing numbers, appear to reject all forms of authority . . . and they have taken refuge in a turbulent and inchoate nihilism whose sole objectives are destructive. I know of no time in our history when the gap between the generations has been wider or more potentially dangerous."[6]

Kirk was right about the generation gap, but his charge of nihilism couldn't have been farther from the truth. After eight days, New York police violently dragged the protesters from the buildings. Eight hundred were arrested and more than a hundred injured. Nixon called the protests "the first major skirmish in a revolutionary struggle to seize the universities of this country and transform them into sanctuaries for radicals and vehicles for revolutionary political and social goals."[7] The viciousness of the attack seemed to confirm radical students' contention that when push came to shove, U.S. officials would employ violence against their own citizens as they did to defend U.S. corporate and geopolitical interests overseas in Vietnam and Indonesia.

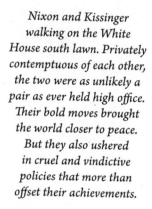

Nixon and Kissinger walking on the White House south lawn. Privately contemptuous of each other, the two were as unlikely a pair as ever held high office. Their bold moves brought the world closer to peace. But they also ushered in cruel and vindictive policies that more than offset their achievements.

Uprisings of students and young workers convulsed industrial nations around the globe. Massive demonstrations rocked Prague, Paris, Tokyo, West Berlin, Turin, Madrid, Rome, and Mexico City, where U.S.-equipped police and soldiers massacred hundreds of protesting students.

In the United States, antiwar forces mounted a challenge to the Democratic Party establishment, throwing their support to Robert Kennedy and Eugene McCarthy. In June, Kennedy was assassinated minutes after his victory in the California primary, dashing hopes for a progressive alternative to Humphrey and his insipid "politics of joy." In August, antiwar delegates and 10,000 protesters converged on the Democratic National Convention in Chicago. They were met by 12,000 Chicago police, 6,000 National Guardsmen, and 1,000 FBI agents. An additional 7,500 U.S. Army troops were deployed to patrol the black community. Television cameras showed club-wielding police indiscriminately attacking not only the protesters but also bystanders and the media in what a blue-ribbon commission later called a "police riot."

By a stunning two-to-one margin, the public supported the police over the protesters. Nixon identified those Americans as the "silent majority" and rode their resentments into the White House, narrowly defeating Humphrey. The riot

In what a blue-ribbon commission later called a "police riot," police indiscriminately clubbed antiwar demonstrators, bystanders, and the media outside the Democratic National Convention in Chicago in August 1968.

dashed Johnson's hope that a deadlocked convention would turn to him at the last minute. He still kept a tight grip over convention proceedings, even blocking the moderate platform plank on Vietnam that Humphrey desperately needed. Clark Clifford called the platform defeat "a disaster for Humphrey."[8] Humphrey didn't help his cause by waiting until late September to distance himself slightly from Johnson's unpopular Vietnam policies. Nixon, on the other hand, insisted that he had a secret plan to end the war, refusing to divulge the details. In reality, this "plan," as Secretary of Defense Melvin Laird admitted, amounted to little more than a strategy to pummel North Vietnam into submission.[9]

In the final weeks of the campaign, Johnson jump-started the stalled peace talks, ordering a bombing halt to bring Hanoi back to the table. Fearing such an "October surprise," Nixon employed Anna Chennault, widow of famed World War II general Claire Chennault, as his liaison with the South Vietnamese government. Johnson put her under surveillance and determined in late October that she was telling South Vietnamese president Nguyen Van Thieu to withdraw from the talks because he would receive better terms from Nixon. Johnson considered Nixon's behavior treasonous. But lacking ironclad proof, Humphrey foolishly declined to expose Nixon's machinations. "Johnson was furious," White House aide Joseph Califano reported. Not exposing Nixon's "treason," Johnson believed, had been "the dumbest thing in the world," proving

*Nixon during the 1968 campaign. Riding the resentment of
antiwar protesters by what he called the "silent majority"
and claiming that he had a secret plan to end the war in
Vietnam, Nixon narrowly defeated Hubert Humphrey.*

that "Hubert had no balls, no spine, no toughness," and it cost Humphrey the presidency.[10]

With less than a week to go in the campaign, Thieu and Vice President Ky did indeed pull out of the talks, sealing Humphrey's fate. Years later, Chennault, who cochaired Republican Women for Nixon, confessed her role. Until that discovery, just days before the election, Johnson provided little assistance to Humphrey, believing that Nixon would more likely continue his Vietnam policies. Humphrey, he feared, would seek peace at any price. Johnson even had the FBI tap Humphrey's phones so he would get advance notice if Humphrey planned to openly oppose the war.

Nixon had another source of information. Harvard Professor Henry Kissinger had been a close advisor to New York Governor Nelson Rockefeller, Nixon's foe in the Republican primary. When Nixon won the nomination, Kissinger sneered, "The man is . . . a disaster . . . he can't be elected—or the whole country would be a disaster." He told others, "That man is unfit to be president."[11] That, however, didn't deter him from offering Nixon secret information about the Paris peace talks that Nixon used to sabotage the negotiations. He alerted Nixon to a major breakthrough in early October that made a bombing halt imminent. The U.S. delegation in Paris, he reported, had "broken open the champagne."[12]

Kissinger simultaneously ingratiated himself with the Humphrey camp. He told Zbigniew Brzezinski, "Look, I've hated Nixon for years," and offered to give Humphrey access to Rockefeller's Nixon "shit files."[13] Humphrey naively believed that Kissinger was working for him and later said that he had planned to name him as national security advisor.

Nixon had little interest in domestic policy, which he once dismissed as "building outhouses in Peoria."[14] His domestic programs catered to moderates, alienating hard-core conservatives. It was foreign policy where he hoped to make his mark. He and Kissinger decided to bypass the "impossible fags"[15] in the State Department and run foreign policy out of the White House. Nixon chose his secretary of state accordingly: he selected an attorney, William Rogers, who told Nixon that he knew little about foreign policy. Nixon confessed, "It was that ignorance that made the job his."[16] Kissinger cracked, "Few Secretaries of State can have been selected because of their President's confidence in their ignorance of foreign policy."[17] Kissinger made sure that Rogers was kept out of the loop on critical intelligence and decision making. The Nixon/Kissinger policies proved less ideological than many expected. "American-style democracy," Nixon declared in 1967, "is not necessarily the best form of government for people in Asia, Africa, and Latin America with entirely different backgrounds."[18] He advised Kissinger to disregard Africa. "Henry," he said, "let's leave the niggers to Bill [Rogers] and we'll take care of the rest of the world."[19]

During the transition period, Kissinger commissioned the RAND corporation to come up with a set of policy options on Vietnam. RAND assigned Daniel Ellsberg, who had just completed work for Robert McNamara on a secret study of U.S. involvement in the war that would later gain fame as the Pentagon Papers. In drafting his options, Ellsberg refused to include a nuclear option, on principle, or a win option, because he thought victory impossible.

Ellsberg's second report, NSSM 1, posed a series of questions. In response, the Joint Chiefs of Staff stated that the absolute best the United States could hope for was to control South Vietnam in eight to thirteen years, but at a tremendous cost in dollars and lives. Facing that prospect, Nixon decided to quickly end U.S. involvement, but he insisted on ending it on his terms—"with honor"—even if that meant laying waste to much of Southeast Asia in the process.[20]

Nixon gradually shifted the burden of fighting from U.S. troops, whose numbers had peaked at 543,000, to U.S.-trained and equipped Vietnamese, but he made it clear to Hanoi that this did not indicate a lessening of resolve. He first intensified the bombing in South Vietnam and Laos and then, in March 1969, began bombing North Vietnamese sanctuaries in Cambodia.

Nixon wanted to make it clear that he refused to be constrained by previous limits and might act irrationally if provoked. In explaining his "madman theory" to Bob Haldeman in 1968, he highlighted the value of nuclear threats.[21]

South Vietnamese soldiers undergo U.S. training in 1970. In April 1969, Nixon approved plans to withdraw U.S. forces and replace them with U.S.-trained and -equipped Vietnamese. If this approach didn't work, Nixon felt he could always play his "madman" card: threaten North Vietnam with nuclear attack.

Nor was it always clear that he was just bluffing. After briefing then Vice President Nixon about nuclear weapons, J. Robert Oppenheimer told a friend that he had "just come from a meeting with the most dangerous man I have ever met."[22] Nixon had, in fact, supported using atomic bombs to bail out the French at Dien Bien Phu.

Fearing a massive public outcry over the bombing of Cambodia, the administration devised an elaborate system of dual target reporting to erase the evidence. Each afternoon, Major Hal Knight, who commanded the radar site at Bien Hoa Air Base, was given alternate targets to pass on to his pilots, who were sworn to secrecy. Neither the radio operator who called in the strike reports nor the intelligence officers who logged in the reports knew that the original targets in Vietnam had not been bombed. Knight, knowing that his actions were in violation of the Military Code of Justice, finally informed Congress in 1973.[23]

When the *New York Times* exposed the bombing of sanctuaries in Cambodia in April 1969, Kissinger called Laird a "son of a bitch" and accused him of leaking the story. Nixon, equally furious, ordered J. Edgar Hoover to wiretap three of Kissinger's top aides, one defense official, and four journalists. Others would later be added to the list.[24]

In case Nixon's bombing and threats failed to bring the National Liberation

Front (NLF) and the North to heel, he and Kissinger prepared to deliver a crippling blow. Nixon had Admiral Thomas Moorer, the chief of naval operations, secretly draft the plan for Operation Duck Hook without Laird's knowledge.[25] Kissinger instructed the special NSC committee charged with evaluating the plan, "I refuse to believe that a little fourth-rate power like North Vietnam does not have a breaking point. . . . It shall be the assignment of this group to examine the option of a savage, decisive blow against North Vietnam. You start without any preconceptions at all."[26]

Roger Morris, research coordinator for the planning group, saw plans targeting two sites in the North for nuclear airbursts. He noted, "Savage was a word that was used again and again . . . a savage unremitting blow on North Vietnam to bring them around."[27] Haldeman told Special Counsel to the President Charles Colson that "Kissinger had lobbied for nuclear options in the spring and fall of 1969." Laird said the nuclear threat had been "always . . . an option" for Kissinger.[28] Even without nuclear weapons, Duck Hook would be brutal beyond comparison. Options included invading North Vietnam, saturation bombing of Hanoi and Haiphong, mining Haiphong harbor, and bombing North Vietnam's dikes to destroy its food supply. Kissinger met secretly with the Vietnamese in Paris in early August and conveyed the planned ultimatum: "If by November 1 no major progress has been made toward a solution, we will be compelled—with great reluctance—to take measures of the greatest consequences."[29] On October 2, Kissinger sent Nixon a top secret memo stating, "we must be prepared to play out whatever string necessary. . . . To achieve its full effect on Hanoi's thinking, the action must be brutal."[30]

Kissinger's late-September meeting with Soviet Ambassador Anatoly Dobrynin was interrupted by a prearranged phone call from Nixon, after which Kissinger alerted Dobrynin, "It was a pity that all our efforts to negotiate had failed. The President had told me in his call that the train had just left the station and was now headed down the track."[31]

Fortunately, the train pulled back into the station. For a number of reasons, including opposition by Laird and Rogers, concerns about effectiveness, growing antiwar sentiment, and major upcoming antiwar protests, Nixon called Duck Hook off. "The only chance for my ultimatum to succeed," he reasoned, "was to convince the Communists that I could depend on solid support at home if they decided to call my bluff. However the chances I would actually have that support were becoming increasingly slim [given] signs of a new level of intensity in the antiwar movement."[32] He opted to convey his toughness another way.

On October 13, 1969, Nixon put the U.S. military on secret nuclear alert. Nuclear-armed SAC bombers were dispersed to military bases, awaiting the order to attack. Thirty-two B-58s, 144 B-52s, and 189 KC-135 refueling tankers were readied. Nixon was signaling the Soviets that they had better dramatically increase

*A bomb explodes in O Dar, Cambodia, in November 1970. Nixon and
Kissinger began secretly bombing Cambodia in March 1969. As Nixon put
it, they would "bomb the bejesus out of Cambodia, send in ground troops,
and keep the whole operation secret" from Congress and the "peaceniks."*

pressure on Hanoi to negotiate.[33] Laird thought it a futile gesture vis-à-vis Vietnam and a potentially reckless one if the Soviets misread U.S. intentions. Undeterred, the United States escalated further on October 25, loading more aircraft with nuclear weapons and placing them on SAC runways. The following day, SAC began flying nuclear-armed B-52s over the polar icecap, taking them ominously close to the Soviet Union. Largely unknown to U.S. leaders, at the same moment the Soviet Union and China were on the verge of war over a border dispute. The Soviets had even sounded out the United States' willingness to collaborate on a preemptive strike against Chinese nuclear facilities, much as Kennedy and Johnson had sounded out Soviet willingness a decade earlier. China had mobilized nearly a million soldiers and was prepared to respond with nuclear weapons to a Soviet attack. The Soviets might have interpreted Nixon's provocation not as a signal regarding Vietnam but as a real attack in coordination with China.

Morris later acknowledged that Duck Hook had been a harebrained scheme: "The Chiefs had been trotting this crap out for years. It was one more quick fix in a war which had no quick fixes. . . . It was a military and political fiasco which had taken on reality in . . . the Pentagon, where, to put it kindly, some not-very-gifted minds were applying military solutions to these problems."[34] Even hawkish Edward Teller found the nuclear option "irrational." He later told an interviewer, "Only a few idiots—and they really were idiots—suggested the use of nuclear weapons in Vietnam."[35]

Nixon went out of his way to suppress attendance at the October and November antiwar marches. The White House spread rumors of Communist involvement. Prowar groups orchestrated by the White House suddenly popped up, condemning the planned rallies. Infiltration of antiwar groups intensified. Antiwar members of Congress were targeted. The beleaguered president even tried to placate the antiwar movement by announcing further troop withdrawals, temporarily suspending draft calls, and firing Lewis Hershey, the despised head of the Selective Service Board, whose announcement that draft boards would review protesters' records had made him a target of activists' wrath.

Despite this unprecedented effort to suppress attendance, some 2 million protesters gathered in cities and towns across the nation on October 15. Nixon recalled, "Although publicly I continued to ignore the raging antiwar controversy, I had to face the fact that it had probably destroyed the credibility of my ultimatum to Hanoi."[36]

American society became so polarized around the war and other issues that some people began speaking of a civil war. College campuses were the front lines in the battle. Demonstrations, rallies, and strikes erupted on hundreds of campuses. Government and industry spokespersons set foot on campuses at their own peril.

Activists condemned the unethical use of science to further the country's military agenda. Scientists, having helped spark the antiwar movement, were often in the forefront of such protests. The American Association for the Advancement of Science (AAAS), the nation's largest scientific body, with more than 100,000 members, was the first professional organization to pass an antiwar resolution in December 1965. The resolution stated:

> Prolongation of the Vietnamese war, with its increasing danger of universal
> catastrophe, threatens not only the lives of millions, but the humanitarian
> values and goals which we are striving to maintain. . . . Beside this concern
> which we share with all citizens, we bear a special responsibility as
> scientists to point out the large costs of war for the continued vigor of
> scientific research. Like all scholarship, the sciences cannot fully flourish,
> and may be badly damaged, in a society which gives an increasing share of
> its resources to military purposes.[37]

Scientists' opposition only intensified in subsequent years. In January 1966, twenty-nine scientists from Harvard, MIT, and other nearby institutions condemned the United States' use of chemical agents to destroy crops. The statement, presented by Harvard biochemist John Edsall, decried the "barbarous" use of such an indiscriminate weapon. "The fact that we are now resorting to such methods," the scientists charged, "shows a shocking deterioration of our moral standards. These attacks are also abhorrent to the general standards of civilized mankind, and their use will earn us hatred throughout Asia and elsewhere."[38] The AAAS urged McNamara to stop the spraying, and Johnson received a petition from some five thousand scientists, including many Nobel laureates, demanding that he do the same.

In April 1967, the AAAS magazine, *Science,* reported that Defense Department officials were having trouble recruiting scientists to perform military research. Former Stanford defense researcher Harold Adams explained, "There is a fundamental revulsion on Vietnam in the egghead community. Academics would rather support the forces of life than those of death."[39] Over the next few years, scientists would increasingly employ the metaphor of choosing "forces of life" over "forces of death" to explain their antipathy toward military research.

In April 1968, when Johnson announced that he would not seek reelection, scientists flocked to support antiwar candidate Eugene McCarthy. In May, Scientists and Engineers for McCarthy was formed, with five thousand dues-paying members, including more than 115 members of the prestigious National Academy of Sciences and 12 Nobel Prize winners. Frustrated Humphrey supporters confessed that they had abandoned attempts to organize a scientists' support group. On the Republican side, neither Richard Nixon nor Nelson Rockefeller had even made the effort.

In January 1969, MIT graduate students and faculty members called for a national research stoppage on March 4 to alert the public to how the "misuse of scientific and technical knowledge presents a major threat to the existence of mankind."[40] Approximately thirty universities participated. The events at MIT proved to be the high point of the national effort. Speaker after speaker emphasized the need for scientists to assume responsibility for the social consequences of their work. In the most passionate address, which the *Boston Globe* called perhaps "the most important speech given in our time," Harvard biologist George Wald asserted that the real purpose of government was to preserve life, but "our government has become preoccupied with death and the preparation for death." He said, "We scientists, we opt for life."[41]

Events that spring exacerbated the public's mistrust of science; they were highlighted by a nine-day takeover of Stanford's Applied Electronics Laboratory and the growing furor over the use of chemical and biological weapons, which forced the Nixon administration to announce a partial cessation of their use in Vietnam.

Meanwhile, Nixon's threats continued. Neither Moscow nor Hanoi took them seriously. Nguyen Co Thach, North Vietnam's foreign minister, said that he had read Kissinger's books. "It is Kissinger's idea that it is a good thing to make a false threat the enemy believes is a true threat. It is a bad thing if we are threatening an enemy with a true threat and the enemy believes it is a false threat. I told Kissinger that 'False or true, we Vietnamese don't mind. There must be a third category—for those who don't care whether the threat is true or false.'" Thach even disputed Kissinger's claim to having issued an ultimatum in August: "Never has Kissinger threatened us in the secret talks. Because if he threatens us, we would turn our backs. We would stop the talks. They could not threaten us for we knew that they could not stay in Vietnam forever, but Vietnam must stay in Vietnam forever." [42]

Thach understood a basic truth that U.S. leaders never grasped: the Vietnam War was about time, not territory or body counts. The United States wreaked unconscionable destruction; it won every major battle. But it could not win the war. Time was on the side of the Vietnamese, who didn't have to defeat the Americans but simply to outlast them. They would pay a terrible price for independence and freedom. But they would ultimately triumph. North Vietnamese military leader Vo Nguyen Giap explained, looking back:

> We won the war because we would rather die than live in slavery.
> Our history proves this. Our deepest aspiration has always been self-
> determination. That spirit provided us with stamina, courage, and creativity
> in the face of a powerful enemy.
>   Militarily, the Americans were much more powerful than we were.
> But they made the same mistake as the French—they underestimated
> Vietnamese forces of resistance. When the Americans started their air
> raids, Uncle Ho said, "The Americans can send hundreds of thousands,
> even millions of soldiers; the war can last ten years, twenty years, maybe
> more, but our people will keep fighting until they win. Houses, villages,
> cities may be destroyed, but we won't be intimidated. And after we've
> regained our independence, we will rebuild our country from the ground
> up even more beautifully." [43]

Policy makers arrogantly assumed that the United States' superior wealth, technology, and firepower would prevail by inflicting such suffering that the Vietnamese would rationally calculate that the price of victory exceeded the benefits. Nixon, in fact, bore some responsibility for Americans' ignorance of Vietnamese history and culture. As a charter member of Washington's China lobby—anti-Communist zealots in the Congress, military, media, and business who blamed the State Department for the "loss" of China in 1949—Nixon had hounded the most knowledgeable China and East Asia experts out of the State Department in the 1950s. In explaining the U.S. blunders in Vietnam, McNamara later admitted:

I had never visited Indochina, nor did I understand or appreciate its history, language, culture, or values. The same must be said, to varying degrees, about . . . Kennedy . . . Rusk, . . . Bundy, . . . Taylor, and many others. . . . When it came to Vietnam, we found ourselves setting policy for a region that was terra incognita.

Worse, our government lacked experts for us to consult to compensate for our ignorance. . . . The irony of this gap was that it existed largely because the top East Asia and China experts in the State Department—John Patton Davies, Jr., John Stewart Service, and John Carter Vincent—had been purged during the McCarthy hysteria of the 1950s . . . we—certainly I—badly misread China's objectives and mistook its bellicose rhetoric to imply a drive for regional hegemony. We also totally underestimated the nationalist aspect of Ho Chi Minh's movement.[44]

Ignorance of the enemy filtered down through the ranks. The Vietnamese, on the other hand, strove mightily to understand the Americans. U.S. infantryman Larry Heinemann, who later won the National Book Award for his novel *Paco's Story,* attended a literary conference in Hanoi in 1990, where he met Hanoi University Professor of American Literature Nguyen Lien. Heinemann recounted their conversation:

I asked him what he did during the war. . . . He said that his job was to go to Beijing and learn English and then go to Moscow University to read and study American literature. Then he went back to Hanoi and out to the Ho Chi Minh Trail and gave lectures on American literature to the troops traveling south . . . he talked to them about Whitman, Jack London, Hemingway, Faulkner, Fitzgerald.

A lot of Vietnamese soldiers carried translations of American literature in their packs. Le Minh Khue—a young woman who worked on the Ho Chi Minh Trail disarming bombs—carried Ernest Hemingway. Professor Lien asked me this question, "Now what Vietnamese literature did the American military teach to you?" I laughed so hard I almost squirted beer up my nose.[45]

While U.S. leaders and the troops they deployed remained in the dark about the country they were invading, the American people were discovering the ugliness of the war their tax dollars were financing. As the November 15 mobilization neared, freelance journalist Seymour Hersh reported that U.S. forces had massacred up to five hundred civilians in the South Vietnamese village of My Lai, which the GIs had nicknamed "Pinkville" for its strong Viet Cong sympathies. Many of the women had been raped. The slaughter had gone on so long that the soldiers interrupted the killing and raping to take lunch and cigarette breaks. Not a single round had been fired at the U.S. infantrymen in return.

U.S. troops were on a typical search-and-destroy mission that day in the Son My hamlet. They arrived to find, with few exceptions, a village of women, children, and old men. Much of the killing was carried out by members of the 1st Platoon, commanded by Lieutenant William Calley. The slaughter was finally halted when Hugh Thompson landed his helicopter between rampaging soldiers and fleeing Vietnamese who were about to be slaughtered. Thompson ordered his crewmates Larry Colburn and Glenn Andreotta to open fire on U.S. troops if they tried to harm the Vietnamese he was rescuing from the bunker. Colburn recalled, "These were elders, mothers, children, and babies. . . . They come into a town and rape the women, kill the babies, kill everyone. . . . And it wasn't just murdering civilians. They were butchering people. The only thing they didn't do is cook 'em and eat 'em. How do you get that far over the edge?" [46]

The appalling incident had been covered up for more than a year. The truth might never have surfaced if it hadn't been for the persistence of Vietnam veteran Ron Ridenhour, who was so troubled by what he had heard about the massacre that when he returned to the United States, he wrote a two-thousand-word letter, which he sent to thirty members of Congress and executive branch and military officials.

Before Ridenhour sent his letter, the army had managed to suppress the story despite the fact that at least fifty officers, including generals, had knowledge of the massacre and the cover-up. The mainstream media ignored the story until it was finally broken by Hersh through the alternative Dispatch News Service, after the major publications rejected his stories.

Americans were shocked by the news and outraged by the grotesque and increasingly undeniable inhumanity of the war. The mother of one of the My Lai participants, an Indiana farmworker, told a reporter, "I gave them a good boy and they sent me back a murderer." [47]

Nixon complained about the negative publicity resulting from the news of the massacre, repeatedly saying to his deputy assistant, Alexander Butterfield, "It's those dirty rotten Jews from New York who are behind it." [48]

My Lai was extreme, but indiscriminate killing of civilians was an everyday occurrence. Specialist Fourth Class Tom Glen, who had served in a mortar platoon, described the routine brutality in a letter to General Creighton Abrams, the commander of all U.S. forces in Vietnam:

> The average GI's attitude toward and treatment of the Vietnamese people
> all too often is a complete denial of all our country is attempting to
> accomplish . . . [and] discount[s] their very humanity. . . .

The bodies of dead Vietnamese in the aftermath of the U.S. massacre at My Lai. In November 1969, Americans learned from the journalist Seymour Hersh that U.S. forces had, the previous November, slaughtered some five hundred civilians in a village of mostly women, children, and old men.

[Americans,] for mere pleasure, fire indiscriminately into Vietnamese homes and without provocation or justification shoot at the people themselves. . . . Fired with an emotionalism that belies unconscionable hatred, and armed with a vocabulary consisting of "You VC," soldiers commonly "interrogate" by means of . . . [s]evere beatings and torture at knife point.

Glen's letter was forwarded to Major Colin Powell in Chu Lai, who discounted Glen's complaints. "In direct refutation of this portrayal," Powell concluded, "is the fact that relations between American [Division] soldiers and the Vietnamese people are excellent." [49]

The antiwar movement continued to grow. As many as three quarters of a million protesters flocked to Washington, D.C., for the November 1969 march; 150,000 more demonstrated in San Francisco. Despite the size of the protests, the war's dehumanizing effects spread beyond the battlefield, hardening the hearts of the populace as a whole. Sixty-five percent of Americans told pollsters that they weren't bothered by the My Lai massacre. The steady inuring against human sympathy that Dwight Macdonald had so eloquently described as resulting from the terror bombing of Japanese cities had again infected much of the nation.

News of My Lai opened the door to a steady spate of horror stories. The public learned of "free-fire zones," where anything that moved would be shot. It learned of the tens of thousands killed by the CIA as part of the "Phoenix Program" and the "tiger cages" in which political prisoners were incarcerated and brutalized. It learned of the displacement of more than 5 million Vietnamese peasants, who were relocated to wire-enclosed refugee camps. It learned of widespread and wanton torture and many other crimes that outraged the sensibilities of at least some Americans and brought forth calls for war-crimes trials.

Exploding antiwar sentiment may have forced Nixon to cancel Duck Hook, but on April 30, 1970, he announced a joint U.S.–South Vietnamese ground invasion of Cambodia to destroy North Vietnamese bases along the border, insisting that the United States would not act "like a pitiful, helpless giant." [50]

Nixon steeled himself for the decision by drinking heavily and watching the movie *Patton* over and over again. He seemed particularly agitated when he went to the Pentagon the next morning for a briefing. First he called protesting students "bums . . . blowing up the campuses . . . burning up the books." [51] Then he cut short the briefing by the Joint Chiefs and repeatedly declared he was going to "take out all those sanctuaries." He proclaimed, "You have to electrify people with bold decisions. Bold decisions make history. Like Teddy Roosevelt charging up San Juan Hill—a small event but traumatic, and people took notice." He concluded his expletive-laden diatribe with "Let's go blow the hell out of them," as the Joint Chiefs, Laird, and Kissinger looked on in stunned disbelief. [52]

The campuses erupted. Students and professors went on strike. More than one-third of colleges and universities suspended classes. Violence flared. Ohio National Guardsmen opened fire on protesters at Kent State University, killing four and wounding nine. Mississippi state police shot into a crowd of protesters at Jackson State College, killing two and wounding twelve.

Protests and violent confrontations spread to more than seven hundred campuses. The *Washington Post* reported, "The overflow of emotion seemed barely containable. The nation was witnessing what amounted to a virtual general and uncoordinated strike by its college youth." [53] Scores of thousands of protesters descended on Washington. Kissinger described the capital as "a besieged city" with the "very fabric of government . . . falling apart." [54] Secretary of the Interior Warren Hickel urged Nixon to heed the protesters. When his letter leaked to the press, Nixon fired him.

More than two hundred Foreign Service officers signed a petition protesting the invasion of Cambodia. Nixon ordered an undersecretary to "Fire them all!" Four of Kissinger's top aides resigned in protest, as did NSC consultant Morton Halperin. Morris regretted not having gone to the press with documents because he believed that Kissinger was a restraining influence. He told Daniel

Nixon during his April 30, 1970, press conference, announcing the invasion of Cambodia. The president's decision prompted outrage on campuses across the country and ignited a dramatic wave of protests.

Ellsberg, "We should have thrown open the safes and screamed bloody murder, because that's exactly what it was." [55] He later concluded that there were no limits to Kissinger's ruthlessness.

A delegation of Kissinger's Harvard friends informed him that they would no longer serve as advisors. Thomas Schelling explained, "As we see it there are two possibilities. Either, one, the President didn't understand when he went into Cambodia that he was invading another country; or, two, he did understand. We just don't know which one is scarier." [56]

Nixon's behavior became increasingly erratic. He and his valet visited the Lincoln Memorial at 5 A.M. for an awkward exchange with student protesters. Kissinger feared that Nixon might have a nervous breakdown. Under mounting pressure, Nixon announced that all combat troops would be out of Cambodia by the end of June. As Joint Chiefs Chairman Moorer acknowledged, "The reaction of noisy radical groups was considered all the time. And it served to inhibit and restrain the decision makers." [57] But the bombing campaign intensified, devastating much of Cambodia.

The White House made broad claims about its authority to break the law in order to curb dissent. Testifying before the Senate, Tom Huston, who was in charge of White House internal security, explained, "It was my opinion at the time that simply the Fourth Amendment did not apply to the president in the exercise of matters relating to the internal security or national security." [58] When David Frost later confronted Nixon with his lawbreaking, Nixon replied simply, "when the President does it, that means that it is not illegal." [59] That argument was very similar to the one the George W. Bush White House would make years later to justify its own illegal measures.

Nixon also justified overthrowing a popular government in Chile. A rarity in Latin America, Chile had been a democracy since 1932. Nixon and Kissinger would soon change that. Chile's importance was magnified by the fact that it was the world's leading copper producer, with production dominated by two American-owned firms, Kennecott and Anaconda. In 1964, the CIA, which had been meddling in Chilean affairs since 1958, helped moderate Eduardo Frei defeat Socialist Salvador Allende for the presidency. Over the next few years, the United States spent millions more supporting anti-Communist groups and provided $163 million in military aid, placing Chile, among the Latin American states, second only to Brazil, whose reform government the United States had helped overthrow in 1964. Meanwhile, the United States trained some four thousand Chilean military officers in counterinsurgency methods at the U.S. Army School of the Americas in the Panama Canal Zone and on U.S. military bases. [60]

Whereas Kennedy and, to some extent, Johnson had tried to work with democratic elements in the region, Nixon and Kissinger opted for the naked use of force. Nixon informed the NSC, "I will never agree with the policy of downgrading the military in Latin America. They are power centers subject to our influence. The others, the intellectuals, are not subject to our influence." [61]

Allende ran again in 1970, promising to redistribute wealth and nationalize U.S. companies that controlled Chile's economy, such as ITT. Prodded by Chase Manhattan Bank's David Rockefeller and former CIA director and ITT board member John McCone, Kissinger instructed U.S. Ambassador Edward Korry and CIA station chief Henry Hecksher to stop Allende. Hecksher enlisted the help of Chilean power broker Agustín Edwards, who owned copper mines, the Pepsi-Cola bottling plant, and *El Mercurio,* Chile's biggest newspaper. The CIA conducted a massive propaganda campaign to convince the Chilean people that Allende would destroy democracy. Korry later deplored the CIA's incompetence: "I had never seen such dreadful propaganda in a campaign anywhere in the world. I said that the idiots in the CIA who had helped create the 'campaign of terror' . . . should have been sacked immediately for not understanding Chile and Chileans." [62] Despite U.S. efforts, Allende narrowly outpolled his two rivals. When Kissinger told Nixon that Rogers wanted to "see what we can work out [with Allende]," Nixon shot back, "Don't let them do it." [63]

At a September 15 meeting with Attorney General John Mitchell and Kissinger, Nixon instructed Helms "to prevent Allende from coming to power or to unseat him." He told him to use his "best men" and gave assurances that he was "not concerned [about the] risks involved." "Make the economy scream," he ordered. He told Helms to run the coup planning without notifying Rogers, Laird, or the "40 Committee," the five-member Kissinger-chaired review panel that authorized and oversaw all CIA clandestine activity. McCone informed Kissinger that ITT's chief executive officer, Harold Geneen, had offered $1 million to support the effort.[64]

Nixon instructed the CIA to pursue a two-track operation. Track one had two components: spreading propaganda to terrify the Chilean public about the consequences of an Allende presidency and bribing elected officials to block Allende's confirmation by the Chilean Congress. Track two called for a military coup. Assistant Secretary of State for Inter-American Affairs Charles Meyer, Hecksher, and Viron Vaky, Kissinger's chief advisor on Latin America, all opposed the coup option. Trying to reason with Kissinger, Vaky wrote, "What we propose is patently a violation of our own principles and policy tenets.... If these principles have any meaning, we normally depart from them only to meet the gravest threat to us., e.g. to our survival. Is Allende a mortal threat to the U.S.? It is hard to argue this."[65]

Clearly, Allende posed no "mortal threat" to the American people. A National Security Study Memo commissioned by Kissinger concluded that "the U.S. has no vital national interests within Chile" and an Allende government would not significantly change the balance of power.[66] Kissinger himself had earlier disparaged Chile as "a dagger pointed at the heart of Antarctica."[67] But he now feared that a successful democratic socialist government in Chile could inspire similar uprisings elsewhere. "What happens in Chile," he figured, would have an effect "on what happens in the rest of Latin America and the developing world . . . and on the larger world picture, including . . . relations with the USSR."[68]

For Kissinger, Chile's democratic traditions and the freely expressed will of the Chilean people were of little, if any, concern. While chairing a meeting of the "40 Committee," Kissinger remarked, "I don't see why we need to stand by and watch a country go Communist due to the irresponsibility of its own people."[69]

Helms chose Brazil station chief David Atlee Phillips to head the Chile task force. Phillips was well suited to the job, having helped overthrow a democratic government in Guatemala, and suppress a democratic uprising in the Dominican Republic. Despite having twenty-three foreign correspondents on his payroll, he doubted that track one would succeed. Chilean elected officials were simply too honest to bribe. He also doubted the efficacy of track two. Chile's military, under General René Schneider, a strong supporter of the Constitution, was staying out of politics.

CIA propaganda was having more of an impact in the United States than it was in Chile. *Time* magazine's October 19 issue had a bright red cover featuring

Allende titled "Marxist Threat in the Americas—Chile's Salvador Allende." *Time* trumpeted the CIA line, warning that if Allende "is acknowledged the winner, as seemed virtually certain last week, Chile may not have another free election for a long, long time." Even worse, it opined, a Communist takeover would inevitably follow.[70]

In a subsequent issue, however, one astute reader, Michael Dodge of St. Paul, Minnesota, challenged *Time*'s biased coverage:

> Sir: Intrigued by your marvelous cold war headline, MARXIST THREAT IN THE AMERICAS, I read on to see who is being threatened. Apparently it's some U.S. copper firms, the telephone company, and assorted juntas. Somehow, I'm not alarmed. I am, however, irritated by your persistent assumption that any form of Marxism enjoying any form of success in any part of the world is, *ipso facto*, a threat. This kind of thinking gave us Viet Nam. And it ignores the obvious: non-Marxist politicians have generally failed to meet the needs of the masses. I suggest we let our humanity transcend our cold war reflexes and hope that the people of Latin America are finding some kind of solution to their problems. We haven't been much help.[71]

As the futility of track one became apparent, the focus shifted to track two. With the assistance of allies like Edwards, the United States proceeded to destabilize Chile politically and economically. "You have asked us to provoke chaos in Chile," Hecksher acknowledged in a cable to Langley. Ambassador Korry warned Chilean Defense Minister Sergio Ossa, "We shall do all within our power to condemn Chile and the Chilean people to utmost deprivation and poverty." But even Korry later cabled Kissinger that he was "appalled" by the coup. Undeterred, Kissinger had Helms cable the CIA station in Santiago: "Contact the military and let them know USG [U.S. Government] wants a military solution, and that we will support them now and later. . . . Create at least some sort of coup climate. . . . Sponsor a military move."[72]

On October 13, after a meeting with Kissinger, Thomas Hercules Karamessines, director of the CIA's clandestine services, cabled Hecksher, "It is firm and continuing policy that Allende be overthrown by a coup." Karamessines instructed the Santiago station chief to encourage General Roberto Viaux to join forces with General Camilo Valenzuela and other coup planners in the military. The CIA provided guns and money to two of Valenzuela's henchmen as part of a plan to kidnap General Schneider—the first step in initiating the coup. But on October 22, Viaux's men apparently got to Schneider first and assassinated him. Exactly one week earlier, Nixon had assured Korry that he was going to "smash" that "son of a bitch Allende."[73]

*Salvador Allende outside his home on October 24, 1970, after learning
he'd been elected president of Chile. The new president took office
on November 3. Two days later, Nixon called for his ouster.*

Allende took office on November 3, 1970, having been certified by a vote
of 153–24. Two days later, Nixon instructed the National Security Council to
topple Allende: "If we let . . . potential leaders in South America think they can
move like Chile . . . we will be in trouble. . . . No impression should be permitted
in Latin America that they can get away with this, that it's safe to go this way."[74]

Infuriated by the CIA's failure to block Allende's election and its tepid
response to his coup plans, Nixon decided to clean house. Egged on by Kissinger's deputy Alexander Haig, who urged him to eliminate "the key left-wing
slots under Helms" and revamp the entire covert operations, Nixon threatened
to slash the agency budget and fire Helms if he didn't conduct a thorough purge.
Haig knew that it would be "the most controversial gutfight" in memory. Helms
axed four of his six deputies. Nixon ordered him to turn control of the agency
over to his deputy, General Robert Cushman, and stay on as figurehead. Helms
refused to go along. He also refused to have the CIA take the fall for the Watergate break-in. Nixon ended up firing him.[75]

The Export-Import Bank, the Agency for International Development, the
Inter-American Development Bank, and the McNamara-led World Bank cut off
economic assistance and loans to Chile. U.S. business interests in Chile helped
Washington destabilize the government. The CIA jumped in, funding opposition
parties and organizations, running propaganda and disinformation campaigns, and
initiating demonstrations and violent actions against the government. The Chilean

National Congress responded in July 1971 by nationalizing Kennecott, Anaconda, and Cerro Mining and assuming management control of ITT. Chilean authorities calculated that in light of the exorbitant profits that Kennecott and Anaconda had accrued over the years, they were entitled to no compensation. One of Anaconda's lawyers complained, "We used to be the fucker. Now we're the fuckee."[76] Nor was ITT in line for compensation after columnist Jack Anderson exposed the company's efforts to block Allende's election and destabilize Chile afterward.

On December 4, 1972, Allende took his case against the United States and the multinational corporations to the United Nations. In a powerful ninety-minute indictment that left listeners in the packed General Assembly hall cheering wildly and yelling "Viva Allende!" the Chilean president detailed the concerted attempt "to prevent the inauguration of a Government freely elected by the people and . . . to bring it down ever since." "It is action," he charged, "that has tried to cut us off from the world, to strangle our economy and to paralyze trade in our principal export, copper, and to deprive us of access to sources of international financing." He spoke of the plight of all underdeveloped countries being ruthlessly exploited by multinational corporations when he said:

> Our economy could no longer tolerate the subordination implied by
> having more than eighty percent of its exports in the hands of a small
> group of large foreign companies that have always put their interests ahead
> of those of the countries where they make their profits. . . . These same
> firms exploited Chilean copper for many years, made more than four
> billion dollars in profit in the last forty-two years alone, while their initial
> investments were less than thirty million. . . . We find ourselves opposed by
> forces that operate in the shadows, without a flag, with powerful weapons,
> from positions of great influence. . . . We are potentially rich countries,
> yet we live in poverty. We go here and there, begging for credits and aid,
> yet we are great exporters of capital. It is a classic paradox of the capitalist
> economic system.[77]

Because of Chile's "decision to recover its own basic resources," Allende contended, international banks had colluded to cut off its access to credit. "In a word," he declared, "it is what we call imperialist insolence." He singled out the outrageous behavior of ITT, "whose capital is larger than the national budgets of several Latin American countries put together," and Kennecott Copper, which, he alleged, had averaged 52.8 percent annual profit on its investment between 1955 and 1970. He decried the fact that huge, totally unaccountable "transnational" corporations were waging war against sovereign nations. "The entire political structure of the world," he warned, "is being undermined."[78]

Allende spoke on behalf of millions of Latin Americans who had been ruthlessly exploited for decades by U.S. corporations backed by U.S. diplomatic, military, and intelligence forces. It was the same indictment that General Smedley Butler and Henry Wallace had made so eloquently decades earlier.

U.S. UN Ambassador George H. W. Bush, who, according to the *Chicago Tribune*, had joined in the standing ovation, feebly replied, "We don't think of ourselves as imperialists." "The charge that private enterprise abroad is imperialistic bothers me. It's one of the things that makes us great and strong." Nor, he claimed, was the United States participating in any boycott of Chile. All the United States wanted to see was that the nationalized firms received just compensation.

ITT's response was equally disingenuous. A company spokesman said, "I.T.T. never intervened or interfered in the internal affairs of Chile in any way. . . . I.T.T. has always respected a host's [*sic*] country's desire to nationalize an I.T.T. property." [79]

In delivering his courageous speech to the United Nations, Allende may have been signing his own death warrant. In early 1973, the CIA urged its Chilean agents to "induce as much of the military as possible, if not all, to take over and displace the Allende govt." [80] Strikes and antigovernment protests escalated. Chilean military leaders, directed by General Augusto Pinochet, the army commander, set the coup for September 11, 1973. When Allende heard that military uprisings had begun across the country, he made a final radio address from the presidential palace: "I will not resign. . . . Foreign capital—imperialism united with reaction—created the climate for the army to break with their tradition. . . . Long live Chile! Long live the people! These are my last words. I am sure that my sacrifice will not be in vain. I am sure it will be at least a moral lesson, and a rebuke to crime, cowardice and treason." [81] Allende took his own life with a rifle he had been given as a gift. A gold-medal plate embedded in the stock was inscribed, "To my good friend Salvador Allende from Fidel Castro." [82]

Pinochet seized power. After the coup, Nixon and Kissinger assessed the possible damage. Speaking by phone, Kissinger, who was getting ready to attend the Redskins' season opener, complained that the newspapers were "bleeding because a pro-Communist government has been overthrown." Nixon muttered, "Isn't that something. Isn't that something." Kissinger replied, "I mean instead of celebrating—in the Eisenhower period we would have been heroes." Nixon said, "Well we didn't—as you know—our hand doesn't show on this one though." Kissinger amended that statement: "We didn't do it. I mean we helped them. _____ created the conditions as great as possible." To which Nixon responded, "That is right . . . as far as people are concerned . . . they aren't going to buy this crap from the Liberals on this one. . . . it is a pro-Communist government and that is the way it is." "Exactly. And pro-Castro," Kissinger agreed. "Well the main thing was. Let's forget the pro-Communist. It was an anti-American government all the way," Nixon added. "Oh wildly," Kissinger concurred. He assured Nixon that he was just reporting the criticism. But it wasn't bothering him. Nixon reflected, "Yes, you are reporting it because it is just typical of the crap we are up against." "And the unbelievable filthy hypocrisy," Kissinger averred.[83]

Pinochet murdered more than 3,200 of his opponents and jailed and tortured tens of thousands more in a reign of terror that began with the actions of the Chilean Army death squad known as Caravan of Death. Kissinger saw to it that the United States quickly recognized and provided aid to the murderous regime. In June 1976, he visited the Chilean dictator and assured him, "We are sympathetic to what you are trying to do here."[84]

Pinochet didn't limit his killing to Chile. Three months after Kissinger's visit, Pinochet's assassins killed Orlando Letelier, Allende's ambassador to the United States, and Ronni Moffitt, Letelier's colleague at the Institute for Policy Studies. The car bombing, which occurred fourteen blocks from the White House, had been carried out under Operation Condor, an assassination ring run by a network of Latin American intelligence agencies based in Chile. Members included the right-wing governments of Chile, Argentina, Uruguay, Bolivia, Paraguay, and Brazil. At a minimum, the United States facilitated communications among the intelligence chiefs. The operation was masterminded by Colonel Manuel Contreras, the head of Chilean intelligence, who served as a CIA asset and received at least one payment for his services. Many of those assassinated were left-wing guerrilla leaders. But Assistant Secretary of State for Inter-American Affairs Harry Shlaudeman informed Kissinger that the targets actually included "nearly anyone who opposes government policy."[85]

Kissinger could have disrupted the Condor operations, including the Letelier-Moffitt assassinations. On August 30, 1976, Shlaudeman sent him a memo, stating, "what we are trying to head off is a series of international murders that could do serious damage to the international status and reputation of the countries involved."[86] Kissinger had already approved sending a diplomatic protest to the heads of state of Chile, Argentina, and Uruguay, expressing "our deep concern" over "plans for the assassination of subversives, politicians, and prominent figures both within the national borders of certain Southern Cone countries and abroad." But the démarche was never delivered because, on September 16, Kissinger canceled the warning, cabling Shlaudeman that he had "instructed that no further action be taken on this matter."[87]

Under Condor, assassination squads tracked down and killed more than 13,000 dissidents outside their home countries. Hundreds of thousands more were thrown into concentration camps.[88]

Although Nixon and Kissinger have been rightly condemned for the vicious-

*Augusto Pinochet greeting Kissinger, June 1976. After overthrowing
Allende in a CIA-aided coup ordered by Nixon himself, Pinochet seized
power and proceeded to murder more than 3,200 opponents and jail
and torture tens of thousands more. Kissinger saw to it that the United
States quickly recognized and provided aid to the murderous regime.*

ness of their policies in Vietnam, Laos, Cambodia, and Chile, they have also garnered praise for easing tensions in other areas. Normalizing relations with China
was the most obvious case in point.

Nixon followed up his triumphal February 1972 visit to China with a May
visit to the Soviet Union. Wary of the United States' new friendship with China,
the Soviets greeted him warmly. In Moscow, Nixon and General Secretary Leonid Brezhnev signed the Strategic Arms Limitation Treaty (SALT), the first strategic arms agreement, which restricted each side to two defensive antiballistic
missile systems and placed limits on the number of offensive ICBMs and sub-
marine-launched ballistic missiles (SLBMs). The treaty failed to slow the growth
of nuclear warheads because it placed no restraints on multiple independently
targetable reentry vehicles (MIRVs)—missiles that could carry several bombs
aimed at separate targets. Nor did it do anything to roll back the massive existing
arsenals that gave each side the ability to destroy the other several times over.
But as a first step, the agreement was of great symbolic importance. Brezhnev
and Nixon also initiated the process that resulted in recognition of Eastern
Europe's borders in return for pledges to respect human rights in the Helsinki
Accords of 1975. They issued a joint communiqué and a statement of "Basic

Principles." The first of those principles stated that both countries "will proceed from the common determination that in the nuclear age there is no alternative to conducting their mutual relations on the basis of peaceful coexistence."[89] Nixon addressed a joint session of Congress upon his return, saying:

> Everywhere new hopes are rising for a world no longer shadowed by fear and want and war. . . . To millions of Americans for the past quarter century the Kremlin has stood for implacable hostility toward all we cherish, and to millions of Russians the American flag has long been held up as a symbol of evil. No one would have believed even a short time ago that these two apparently irreconcilable symbols would be seen together as we saw them for those few days. . . . Three-fifths of all the people alive in the world today have spent their whole lifetimes under the shadow of a nuclear war. . . . Last Friday in Moscow we witnessed the beginning of the end of that era.[90]

Nikita Khrushchev, who had helped pave the way for this monumental change, was not around to see it; he had died of heart failure the previous September. Living in a log cabin, he had become a critic of the Soviet government and its heavy-handed suppression of dissent. He infuriated Soviet leaders by smuggling his memoirs out of the country. Published in the West under the title *Khrushchev Remembers,* it became a best seller. In it, he mused sadly about the peaceful world he and Kennedy had wanted to achieve. The Soviet Central Committee decided to downplay his funeral, burying him in a corner of a Moscow cemetery. No monument was erected for four years.

On June 17, 1971, the United States and Japan signed a treaty that allowed Okinawa to revert to Japan in May 1972. The Japanese had recoiled at the United States' use of Okinawa as a base for operations in Vietnam and a storage site for nuclear weapons. Okinawans concurred. According to the new treaty, the United States would sell Okinawa back to Japan but would retain its bases on the island and use them for combat in the region. Japan not only paid the United States an exorbitant sum to "buy back" the island, it agreed to make large annual payments toward the costs of retaining the bases. Elsewhere, the United States paid host countries for the privilege of putting bases on their land or at least shared the cost. To make matters worse, Prime Minister Eisaku Sato subverted the agreement by secretly allowing the United States to reintroduce nuclear weapons into Okinawa.

The conflict over Okinawa went back more than a decade. In 1960, the United States and Japan had concluded the Treaty of Mutual Cooperation and Security, widely known by the Japanese abbreviation AMPO, which sanctioned continued U.S. occupation of Okinawa and retention of U.S. military bases elsewhere in Japan. Opposition had been so widespread and protests so massive

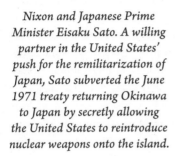

Nixon and Japanese Prime Minister Eisaku Sato. A willing partner in the United States' push for the remilitarization of Japan, Sato subverted the June 1971 treaty returning Okinawa to Japan by secretly allowing the United States to reintroduce nuclear weapons onto the island.

that the government of Prime Minister Nobusuke Kishi, Sato's older brother, had been forced to resign. Kishi had also blundered by telling the Diet that the Japanese Constitution did not ban the development of nuclear weapons, a view that was anathema to most Japanese. U.S. Ambassador Douglas MacArthur had complained that "latent neutralism is fed on anti-militarist sentiments, pacifism, fuzzy-mindedness, nuclear neuroses and Marxist bent of intellectuals and educators." The previous year, MacArthur had pressured the chief justice of the Japanese Supreme Court to overturn a Tokyo District Court ruling that U.S. forces in Japan represented "war potential" and therefore infringed upon the antimilitarist Article 9 of the Japanese Peace Constitution that General Douglas MacArthur, the ambassador's uncle, had helped fashion during the occupation. Article 9 states, "the Japanese people forever renounce war as a sovereign right of the nation" and that "land, sea, and air forces, as well as other war potential, will never be maintained." During that time the Japanese government had also concluded the first of a series of "secret agreements" with the United States in which the government supported U.S. nuclear strategy and military preparations. The most egregious offense had come in the "tacit agreement" that "no prior consultation is required for US military vessels carrying nuclear weapons to enter Japanese ports or sail in Japanese territorial waters." [91]

But the smoldering tension between the United States and Japan flared under Nixon. Japan's consternation and surprise over the United States' opening to China only exacerbated the two countries' long-standing military and economic differences. U.S. leaders had continuously pressured Japan to revoke Article 9 and play a greater role in regional defense. The United States also threatened to impose import quotas against Japanese textiles, forcing Japan to cut its textile exports, allow in more U.S. imports, and open its markets to U.S. investors. Nixon privately complained about the "Jap betrayal" and expressed his eagerness to "stick it to Japan."[92]

Sato had been a willing partner in the United States' push for the remilitarization of Japan—perhaps too willing. He had taken office in November 1964, just one month after the Chinese atomic bomb test. He had met with President Johnson in January 1965 and declared that "if Chicoms [Chinese Communists] had nuclear weapons, the Japanese also should have them." He had added that "Japanese public opinion will not permit this at present, but I believe that the public, especially the younger generation, can be 'educated.'" Such a view had widespread support among Japanese leaders in the ruling Liberal Democratic Party. Yasuhiro Nakasone, the director of the Japanese Defense Agency and a future prime minister, commissioned a report by the agency that concluded, "it would be possible in a legal sense to possess small-yield, tactical, purely defensive nuclear weapons without violating the Constitution." But the agency recommended against doing so at that point, a stance that Johnson welcomed.[93]

It was Sato who tried to hoodwink the Japanese people into believing the sincerity of his antinuclear statements when he articulated the "Three Non-Nuclear Principles" before the Diet in December 1967. According to those principles, Japan would not manufacture, possess, or permit the introduction of nuclear weapons into Japan, a commitment that Sato was regularly breaking and that he described to U.S. Ambassador U. Alexis Johnson as "nonsense." When Japan had signed the Non-Proliferation Treaty in 1970, it had extracted a promise from the United States that it would not "interfere with Tokyo's pursuit of independent reprocessing capabilities in its civilian nuclear power program."[94] Given Japan's technological capability and stockpile of spent fuel, it would always remain one "screwdriver twist" away from having nuclear bombs.

Not everyone applauded Nixon's rapprochement with China and the Soviet Union. The North Vietnamese feared that they were being hung out to dry. As a *New York Times* editorial noted, "Chairman Mao received President Nixon shortly after heavy bombing of North Vietnam had resumed; Secretary General Brezhnev received the President shortly after North Vietnam's harbors were mined. No words are needed for Hanoi to understand that the Chinese and Soviet leaders put their own interests first."[95]

Though most Americans applauded his bold initiatives, Nixon braced for a "revolt" by former allies on the right who thought he had betrayed them by visiting China, concluding arms control treaties that allowed the Soviet Union to gain nuclear parity, pulling most U.S. troops out of Vietnam, taking the United

States off the gold standard, imposing wage and price controls, and embracing Keynesian economics. They were also upset that he had established the Occupational Safety and Health Administration (OSHA) and the Environmental Protection Agency (EPA), endorsed a guaranteed annual income for all families, supported the Equal Rights Amendment and Endangered Species Act, and strengthened the Voting Rights Act.

Opponents of détente and arms control struck back, spurred by former RAND nuclear expert Albert Wohlstetter. Applying game theory and systems analysis to defense policy, Wohlstetter based his projections not on what the Soviets were likely to do but on what they were capable of doing—no matter how irrational or self-destructive. He worried that SAC bombers and ICBMs might be vulnerable to a surprise Soviet nuclear attack and supported the deployment of an anti-ballistic missile (ABM) system to defend them. McNamara had dropped plans to build a large-scale ABM system when he learned that defensive weapons cost five times as much as the missiles they protected against and could be easily overwhelmed by sending more ICBMs. Scientists throughout the country mobilized in opposition to ABM, which they believed expensive, unnecessary, unworkable, and likely to further propel the arms race. McNamara knew that the U.S. deterrent was more than adequate. When he declared in 1964 that a 400-megaton nuclear force would be enough to destroy the Soviet Union, the U.S. stockpile was already 42.5 times that size and growing rapidly.

Wohlstetter and veteran hawk Paul Nitze formed the Committee to Maintain a Prudent Defense Policy and set out to defeat the ABM treaty. They recruited Richard Perle, Edward Luttwak, Peter Wilson, and Paul Wolfowitz. One committee enthusiast, Dean Acheson, anointed them "our four musketeers."[96] Wilson and Wolfowitz had studied with Wohlstetter at the University of Chicago, where he taught political science. Perle had become a disciple while still in high school.

Following the unsuccessful effort to stop the ABM treaty, Perle took a job with Democratic Senator Henry "Scoop" Jackson's powerful Permanent Subcommittee on Investigations. Operating from what was known as "the Bunker," Jackson's foreign policy team would eventually include a gaggle of leading neoconservatives. Jackson and his acolytes bristled at the fact that the SALT treaty allowed the Soviets a temporary advantage in the number of missiles and in missile throw weight. They ignored the fact that the United States had significant advantages in terms of both numbers of nuclear warheads and technology. The United States also had a three-to-one advantage in bombers. Jackson charged U.S. negotiators with having "caved in" to their Soviet counterparts. He attached an amendment to the SALT treaty stipulating that no future treaty could permit the United States anything less than numerical parity in any category of weapons. Jackson pressured the White House into firing a quarter of the Arms Control and Disarmament Agency (ACDA) staff, including a dozen people involved in SALT negotiations. The new, more conservative head of the ACDA, Fred Ikle, recruited Wolfowitz to fill one of the vacancies. In 1974, Jackson's allies passed the Jackson-Vanik Amendment, which denied trade benefits to any Communist nation that restricted citizens' rights to emigrate freely. Kissinger was furious, claiming that the amendment had "blighted U.S.-Soviet relations ever after," which was just what Jackson, Perle, and company wanted.[97]

In June 1971, the *New York Times* began publishing the Pentagon Papers, the Defense Department's secret history of the Vietnam War, showing that the government had systematically lied to the public about Vietnam for years. RAND analyst Daniel Ellsberg was one of the few people to have had access to the study in the summer of 1969. The more he read of the history of the French and then U.S. invasions, the more he understood the moral indefensibility of U.S. policy. By September 1969, he had drawn several key conclusions: The war had been "an American war almost from the beginning." It was a "struggle of Vietnamese . . . against American policy and American financing, proxies, technicians, firepower, and finally, troops and pilots." It was only U.S. money, weapons, and manpower that had kept the political violence at the scale of a "war" since 1954. And, most significantly, he understood that

> It was no more a "civil war" after 1955 or 1960 than it had been during the U.S.-supported French attempt at colonial reconquest. A war in which one side was *entirely* equipped and paid by a foreign power—which dictated the nature of the local regime in its own interest—was not a civil war. To say that we had "interfered" in what is "really a civil war," as most American academic writers and even liberal critics of the war do to this day, simply screened a more painful reality and was as much a myth as the earlier official one of "aggression from the North." In terms of the UN Charter and of our own avowed ideals, it was a war of foreign aggression, American aggression.

Ellsberg recalled his former Pentagon boss John McNaughton telling RAND researchers that "if what you say is true, we're fighting on the wrong side." Ellsberg realized that stating it that way had "missed the reality since 1954. We *were* the wrong side." Therefore, in his mind, the war was a "crime," an "evil," "mass murder." And he knew that Nixon was lying about ending it. In fact, through his bombing policy, Nixon was showing the North that there were no limits to what he was willing to do to achieve "victory."[98]

Inspired by the example of young activists who chose to go to prison to protest the war and increasingly desperate to end the bloodshed, Ellsberg photocopied the forty-seven-volume McNamara study. He then tried to convince several senators to enter the study into the public record. When that failed, he went to Neil Sheehan of the *New York Times*. On Sunday, June 13, 1971, the *Times* published the first installment of the Pentagon Papers. On June 15, the Justice Department filed for an injunction in Federal District Court in New York. The judge issued a temporary restraining order against the *Times*. Such an action was unprecedented. An injunction had never before been used to stop the presses in the United States.

To circumvent the injunction, Ellsberg then gave the documents to the *Washington Post*, which took up where the *Times* left off until it too was blocked. But, anticipating that, Ellsberg had gotten copies to seventeen other newspapers. After the *Post* was enjoined, excerpts appeared in the *Boston Globe* and then the *St. Louis Post-Dispatch*. In all, nineteen newspapers printed sections of the papers. Meanwhile, the FBI conducted a thirteen-day manhunt to try to find Ellsberg, who had gone into hiding. The *Detroit News* interviewed Ellsberg's father, a Republican who had twice voted for Nixon. The elder Ellsberg proudly defended his son's actions: "Daniel gave up everything to devote himself to ending that foolish slaughter. . . . If he did give them that report, and if the government accuses him of some crime . . . well, he might be saving some boys they'd have sent there otherwise." [99]

On June 28, Ellsberg surrendered to the authorities. As he walked toward the federal building, a reporter asked, "How do you feel about going to prison?" Ellsberg replied, "Wouldn't you go to jail to help end the war?" [100] On June 29, Alaska Democratic Senator Mike Gravel tried unsuccessfully to read the papers on the floor of Congress, but he later managed to read them into the record in a hastily called evening subcommittee session. He also distributed a large number of unpublished top secret documents to reporters. The following day, the Supreme Court ruled in favor of the *Times*, releasing the *Times* and *Post* to resume publication. Ellsberg, however, was indicted on criminal felony charges and faced 115 years in prison.

Nixon actually welcomed the leaks showing years of lies about Vietnam by Democratic administrations. He salivated at the thought of leaking more documents exposing Kennedy's involvement in the Diem assassination. Kissinger called it a "gold mine," but when he hesitated to undertake the leaking himself, Nixon instructed Charles Colson to do so.

Nixon and Kissinger decided to destroy Ellsberg. Kissinger told Nixon, "Daniel Ellsberg is the most dangerous man in America today. He must be stopped at all costs." In late July, Kissinger railed against Ellsberg to Nixon: "that son of a bitch—First of all, I would expect—I know him well. . . . I am sure he has some more information. . . . I would bet that he has more information that he's saving for the trial. Examples of U.S. war crimes that triggered him into it." [101]

Having come to understand the moral indefensibility of the Vietnam War and infuriated by the profusion of official lies, RAND analyst Daniel Ellsberg photocopied the forty-seven-volume Pentagon Papers and released them to the New York Times *and eighteen other newspapers. Indicted on criminal felony charges, Ellsberg faced 115 years in prison.*

In July, Nixon approved establishing a White House Special Investigations Unit. Former FBI agent G. Gordon Liddy and former CIA agent E. Howard Hunt were brought in to help run things. They hung a "Plumbers" sign on their door and set out to plug the leaks. In September, they broke into Ellsberg's psychiatrist's office in hopes of finding something to use to silence him before he could release documents Nixon thought he had revealing Nixon's threats to use nuclear weapons in Vietnam. Coming up empty with that break-in, they made further plans to silence Ellsberg, unleashing a wave of dirty tricks and criminal activities that would eventually bring multiple indictments and Nixon's ignominious resignation.

Hanoi's spring 1972 offensive pulverized the South Vietnamese army. Desperate to avoid defeat before the election, Nixon contemplated measures so extreme that even Kissinger objected. "... power plants ... the docks ... And, I still think we ought to take the dikes out now. Will that drown people?" Nixon asked. "About two hundred thousand people," Kissinger informed him. "No, no, no ... I'd rather use the nuclear bomb," Nixon asserted. Kissinger hesitated, "That, I think, would just be too much." "The nuclear bomb, does that bother you?" Nixon asked, "I just want you to think big, Henry, for Christsakes." [102]

Nixon bombed North Vietnamese cities for the first time since 1968 as well as sites throughout the South and mined Haiphong. He wanted Hanoi to be "bombed to smithereens," declaring that the "bastards have never been bombed like they're going to be bombed this time." [103] Civilian casualties soared. Nixon felt no remorse, telling Kissinger, "The only place where you and I disagree . . . is with regard to the bombing. You're so goddamned concerned about the civilians and I don't give a damn. I don't care." Kissinger assured Nixon that his restraint was based on political calculations, not humanitarian ones: "I'm concerned about the civilians because I don't want the world to be mobilized against you as a butcher."[104]

In October, the stalled Paris talks suddenly revived. Kissinger announced, "Peace is at hand."[105] But after winning reelection, Nixon unleashed a massive twelve-day "Christmas bombing" campaign against Hanoi and Haiphong—the heaviest bombing of the war. The international outcry was deafening. Peace talks resumed. On January 23, Nixon announced an agreement that would "end the war and bring peace with honor."[106] The Paris Peace Accords were signed on January 27. The United States ceased military activities, and the last U.S. troops departed on March 29, 1973. Approximately 150,000 North Vietnamese soldiers remained in the South, though they were to respect the cease-fire. Thieu would retain power pending the results of elections in which all would participate. But in fact he made no effort to hold such elections. Nixon assuaged Thieu by increasing the already massive military support and promising to restart the bombing if the Communists attempted a new offensive.

In April, within weeks of the U.S. troops' departure, Nixon and Kissinger ordered a resumption of bombing in both the North and the South—bombing more intense than at any previous point in the war. The order was rescinded, *Time* magazine reported, when Nixon learned of John Dean's damning revelations to Watergate prosecutors. Nixon decided not to inflame public opinion by bombing at the same time he was preparing to battle Congress, a determination he would make for the rest of his time in office.

The war dragged on for two more years. On April 30, 1975, the North Vietnamese seized Saigon. The war was finally over. By its end, the United States had dropped more bombs on tiny Vietnam than had been dropped by all sides in all previous wars throughout history—three times as many explosives as were dropped by all sides in World War II. Unexploded ordnance blanketed the countryside. Nineteen million gallons of herbicide poisoned the environment. In the South, the United States had destroyed 9,000 of the 15,000 hamlets. In the North, it had rained destruction on all six industrial cities, leveling 28 of 30 provincial towns and 96 of 116 district towns. Le Duan, who took over the leadership of North Vietnam when Ho died in 1969, told a visiting journalist that the United States had threatened to use nuclear weapons on thirteen different occasions. The war's human toll was staggering. More than 58,000 Americans had died in the fighting. But that paled in comparison to the number of Vietnamese killed and wounded. Robert McNamara would later tell students at American University that 3.8 million Vietnamese had died.[107]

The horrors of Cambodia exceeded those of Vietnam. In December 1972, Nixon instructed Kissinger, "I want everything that can fly to go in there and crack the hell out of them. There is no limitation on mileage and there is no limitation on budget. Is that clear?" [108]

Kissinger conveyed the orders to his assistant General Alexander Haig: "He wants a massive bombing campaign in Cambodia. He doesn't want to hear anything. It's an order, it's to be done. Anything that flies, on anything that moves. You got that?" [109]

The bombing continued until August 15, 1973, when Congress cut funding for the war. More than 100,000 sites were hit with more than 3 million tons of ordnance. The attacks left hundreds of thousands of civilians dead. The Cambodian economy lay in tatters. Inflation skyrocketed, especially food prices. Production dwindled. Rice production was barely one-sixth of prewar levels. Starvation was rampant. Not everyone suffered, though; the elite frolicked in opulence and splendor. Refugees flooded into Phnom Penh, creating a humanitarian crisis. Approximately 95 percent of all income came from the United States. By early 1974, U.S. humanitarian aid totaled $2.5 million compared with $516.5 million in military aid.

The Khmer Rouge, which had been a weak force prior to the bombing, used those atrocities to recruit in the same way that others would later use U.S. atrocities to recruit in Iraq and Afghanistan. According to Khmer Rouge officer Chhit Do:

> Every time after there had been bombing, they would take the people
> to see the craters, to see how big and deep the craters were, to see how
> the earth had been gouged out and scorched. . . . The ordinary people
> sometimes literally shit in their pants when the big bombs and shells came.
> Their minds just froze up and they would wander around mute for three or
> four days. Terrified and half crazy, the people were ready to believe what
> they were told. It was because of their dissatisfaction with the bombing
> that they kept on co-operating with the Khmer Rouge, joining up with the
> Khmer Rouge, sending their children off to go with them. . . . Sometimes
> the bombs fell and hit little children, and their fathers would be all for the
> Khmer Rouge. [110]

The Khmer Rouge grew exponentially. Terrifying reports circulated of the fanaticism of its young cadre. In 1975, it seized power. It wasted little time in unleashing new horrors against its own people, leading to a genocide in which more than 1.5 million people perished on top of the half million or so who had been killed in the U.S. phase of the war. The United States, given its new alliance with China, Cambodia's principal ally, maintained friendly relations with the brutal Pol Pot regime. In late 1975, Kissinger told the Thai foreign minister, "You should . . . tell the Cambodians that we will be friends with them. They are murderous thugs, but we won't let that stand in our way."[111]

Fortunately, Hanoi did not turn a blind eye. In 1978, it tried to spark the Cambodians to rise up against a government Vietnamese leaders described as "the most disgusting murderers in the latter half of this century." Vietnam invaded that year, eventually toppling Pol Pot's heinous regime. The Vietnamese reported, "In Cambodia, a former island of peace . . . no one smiles today. Now the land is soaked with blood and tears. . . . Cambodia is hell on earth."[112] Perhaps a quarter of Cambodia's population died during the Khmer Rouge's brief rule.

If the United States did not wreak similar devastation on Laos, it was not for lack of trying. The United States had been "secretly" bombing Laos since 1964. It was no secret to the Laotians. Starting in 1967, the pace of the bombing picked up. Civilian suffering increased. When Nixon took over, all restraints were removed. Belgian UN advisor Georges Chapelier detailed the situation on the basis of interviews with survivors:

> Prior to 1967, bombing was light and far from populated centers. By 1968 the intensity of the bombings was such that no organized life was possible in the villages. The villages moved to the outskirts and then deeper and deeper into the forest as the bombing climax reached its peak in 1969 when jet planes came daily and destroyed all stationary structures. Nothing was left standing. The villagers lived in trenches and holes or in caves. They only farmed at night. All of the interlocutors, without any exception, had his village completely destroyed. In the last phase, bombings were aimed at the systematic destruction of the material basis of the civilian society. Harvest burned down and rice became scarce.[113]

Between 1965 and 1973, the United States dropped 2,756,941 tons of ordnance in 230,516 sorties on 113,716 sites.

The Pathet Lao–controlled Plain of Jars region was one of the areas that took the brunt of the U.S. offensive. Most of the young left to join the Pathet Lao. U.S.-allied Meo soldiers evacuated the remaining villagers. By September 1969, the area was largely deserted. Fred Branfman, who interviewed more than a thousand refugees, wrote, "after a recorded history of seven hundred years, the Plain of Jars disappeared." Much of Laos suffered a similar fate.[114]

Nixon barely had time to savor his 1972 electoral victory before the Watergate scandal engulfed his administration. Congressional investigations revealed the depths of corruption and abuses of power. The floodgates opened when Alexander Butterfield disclosed the White House tapes, without which Nixon would have avoided impeachment. At the time, Butterfield said he hoped he wouldn't be asked about the tapes and, when asked, did not want to perjure himself. He later admitted privately that he hoped committee members would ask that question. He said that while sitting in on Nixon, Ehrlichman, and Haldeman's discussions of who they were going to pin Watergate on, he had concluded that they were despicable, ruthless human beings and had decided not to protect them.[115] The public soon discovered what John Mitchell referred to as the "White House horrors."[116]

In October, Vice President Spiro Agnew was forced out of office over bribes and kickbacks he had received when governor of Maryland. Nixon appointed the likable but undistinguished House Minority Leader Gerald Ford to replace Agnew. One observer noted, "few men are better qualified than Ford for a job that demands practically nothing of the man who holds it."[117]

The House Judiciary Committee drafted three articles of impeachment for obstructing justice, misusing the powers of the presidency, and refusing to comply with the committee's requests for information. Pressure to resign came from all sides. Many observers felt that Nixon was becoming dangerously paranoid. Wary of what Nixon might do, Secretary of Defense James Schlesinger met with the chairman of the Joint Chiefs of Staff and instructed that no military units respond to orders from the White House without first getting his approval. By early August, Nixon's support in Congress had evaporated. Having run out of time and options, he resigned on August 9, 1974.

Gerald Ford announced: "Our long national nightmare is over" and later gave the "madman" Nixon a controversial pardon. But forty government officials and members of Nixon's reelection committee were convicted of felonies. Among those sentenced to prison terms were Dean, Mitchell, Haldeman, Ehrlichman, political assistants Charles Colson, Egil Krogh, and Jeb Stuart Magruder, and the president's lawyer, Herbert Kalmbach. Nixon impersonator David Frye quipped, "There's a bright side to Watergate. My administration has taken crime out of the streets and put it in the White House where I can keep an eye on it."[118]

"Psychopathic" Kissinger came through unscathed. In October 1973, he and North Vietnam's Le Duc Tho were awarded the Nobel Peace Prize. Tom Lehrer, America's most brilliant political satirist, announced that Kissinger's winning the Nobel Peace Prize made political satire obsolete and refused ever to perform again. Unlike Kissinger, Le Duc Tho, knowing that peace had not yet been achieved, had the decency to turn the prize down.

Historian Carolyn Eisenberg aptly pointed out, "Richard Nixon was the only President in American history to engage in sustained military action against three nations without a mandate from the public, the press, the government bureaucracies or the foreign elite."[119]

Chapter 10

COLLAPSE OF DETENTE:

Darkness at Noon

Jimmy Carter has been a marvelous ex-president—perhaps, as he has claimed, the best in U.S. history. Although John Quincy Adams, who returned to Congress to wage an impassioned struggle against slavery, could have given him a run for his money, Carter can make a very strong case. In 1982, he founded the Carter Center, through which he has promoted democracy, improved health care in underdeveloped countries, secured the release of prisoners, helped restore Haiti's democratically elected President Jean-Bertrand Aristide to power, and spoken on Cuban TV urging the United States to end its embargo and imploring Castro to improve civil liberties. In 1994, he negotiated a nuclear deal with Kim Il Sung that significantly slowed the growth of North Korea's nuclear arsenal. In his work monitoring elections around the world, he dismissed the opposition's claims of fraud in sanctioning the 2004 recall election victory of Venezuelan President Hugo Chávez. He has tried to inject reason into the long-festering Arab-Israeli conflict, issuing highly controversial criticisms of all the antagonists, including the Israelis. He decried George W. Bush's invasion of Iraq, called for the shuttering of the prison at Guantánamo Bay, and labeled the Bush-Cheney administration "the worst in history."[1] He has called for the abolition of nuclear weapons and remains the only U.S. president ever to have visited the city of Hiroshima. For his courageous stands and global leadership, he was awarded the Nobel Peace Prize in 2002.

Yet Carter, who has performed in such exemplary fashion out of office, was inept in office, disappointing his supporters, betraying his convictions, and leaving with an approval rating of 34 percent. Carter's most enduring legacy as president was not his hypocrisy-stained campaign for human rights; it was his opening the door to the dark side, legitimizing the often brutal policies of his successor, Ronald Reagan—policies that rekindled the Cold War and left a trail of innocent victims stretching from Guatemala to Afghanistan and back again to the World Trade Center. How did that happen? Were the same forces at work during the Carter years that had undermined the administrations of other Democratic presidents, including Wilson, Truman, Johnson, Bill Clinton, and Barack Obama?

Nixon's resignation in August 1974 and the withdrawal of U.S. forces from Vietnam paved the way for a serious assessment of what had gone wrong and a reversal of the policies that had led the nation astray, both domestically and globally. But that rarely occurred—certainly not during the presidency of the amiable and well-meaning but extremely limited Gerald Ford, a man who, Lyndon Johnson said, could not walk and chew gum at the same time. From the start, Ford sent all the wrong signals.

First he announced that Henry Kissinger would stay on as both secretary of state and national security advisor. Kissinger understood that the United States was facing severe economic and political challenges. After seventy years of trade surpluses, it had run its first deficit in 1971. Now that deficit was widening. The oil-exporting countries in the Middle East, which had joined together to form OPEC, decided to punish the United States, Western Europe, and Japan for supporting Israel in the 1973 Arab-Israeli War. The price of oil quadrupled in the next year. The United States, which in the 1950s had produced all the oil it needed, was now importing more than one-third of its supply, making it very vulnerable to this kind of economic pressure. With wealth and power shifting to the Middle East, several U.S. allies adopted more Arab-friendly policies, which Kissinger denounced as "contemptible."[2] Kissinger and other top officials contemplated a different kind of response, even floating the idea of invading Saudi Arabia.

Did the United States really want another war? The country was still reeling from its humiliating defeat by Vietnam, which Kissinger had denigrated as "a little fourth-rate power."[3] No wonder he was feeling despondent over the future of the American Empire. Two months into the Ford administration, he told the *New York Times'* James Reston, "As a historian, you have to be conscious of the fact that every civilization that has ever existed has ultimately collapsed. History is a tale of efforts that failed, of aspirations that weren't realized, of wishes that were fulfilled and then turned out to be different from what one expected. So, as a historian, one has to live with a sense of the inevitability of tragedy."[4]

North Vietnam began its final offensive in March 1975. The South offered little resistance. Without U.S. forces there to fight its battles and bolster its resolve, the South Vietnamese army simply collapsed. One South Vietnamese officer called it a rout "unique in the annals of military history." With the South Vietnamese troops in full flight, chaos engulfed much of the country. Soldiers murdered

(**top**) *Gerald Ford being sworn in as president upon Nixon's resignation in August 1974.* (**above**) *Ford with Henry Kissinger. From the start, Ford sent all the wrong signals. Among them was announcing that Kissinger would stay on as both secretary of state and national security advisor.*

officers, fellow soldiers, and civilians. Defense Secretary James Schlesinger told Ford that only tactical nuclear weapons could prevent defeat. Ford resisted the temptation to use them. Journalist Jonathan Schell realized that this final collapse revealed "the true nature of the war." He wrote of South Vietnam, "It was a society entirely without inner cohesion, held together only by foreign arms, foreign money, foreign political will. When deprived of that support, it faced its foe alone and the mirage evaporated."[5]

Under pressure from the United States, Nguyen Van Thieu resigned on April

Henry Kissinger speaking on the phone in Deputy National Security Advisor Brent Scowcroft's office during the fall of South Vietnam. By the beginning of Ford's administration, Kissinger was feeling despondent over the future of the American Empire. He told the New York Times' *James Reston, "As a historian, you have to be conscious of the fact that every civilization that has ever existed has ultimately collapsed. History is a tale of efforts that failed, of aspirations that weren't realized, of wishes that were fulfilled and then turned out to be different from what one expected. So as a historian, one has to live with a sense of the inevitability of tragedy."*

21. On April 30, General Duong Van Minh surrendered to North Vietnamese Colonel Bui Tin. Minh said, "I have been waiting since early this morning to transfer power to you." Bui Tin responded, "You cannot give up what you do not have."[6] Images of South Vietnamese soldiers shooting their way onto planes and U.S. marines beating down desperate Vietnamese trying to escape on the last U.S. helicopters lifting off the embassy roof would remain indelibly imprinted in the American psyche for decades to come. Two years earlier, at the Paris Peace Conference, Nixon had signed a secret protocol promising between $4.25 and $4.75 billion in postwar aid "without any political conditions." Nixon and Secretary of State William Rogers denied the protocol's existence. "We have not made any commitment for any reconstruction or rehabilitation effort," Rogers insisted.[7] Ford cited the North Vietnamese victory as proof that Hanoi had reneged on the Paris Agreements and blocked the promised aid. He also imposed an embargo on all of Indochina, froze Vietnamese assets in the United States, and vetoed Vietnamese membership in the United Nations.

The Vietnamese, who had suffered so deeply during the U.S. invasion, would be left to rebuild their war-ravaged land on their own. Nearly 4 million of their citizens had been killed. The landscape had been shattered. The beautiful

North Vietnam began its final offensive in March 1975. Without the aid of U.S. forces, the South Vietnamese army simply collapsed. Images of South Vietnamese soldiers shooting their way onto planes and U.S. marines beating down desperate Vietnamese trying to escape on the last U.S. helicopters lifting off the U.S. Embassy roof would remain indelibly imprinted in the American psyche for decades to come.

triple-canopy forests were largely gone. In 2009, land mines and unexploded bombs still contaminated over a third of the land in six central Vietnamese provinces. Efforts by the Vietnamese government, the Vietnam Veterans of America Foundation, and the Vietnam Veterans of America, sometimes led by dedicated U.S. veterans like Chuck Searcy in Quang Tri Province, had cleared over 3,000 acres. But over 16 million acres remained to be cleared. Beyond the terrible toll of the war itself, 42,000 more Vietnamese, including many children, were killed by leftover explosives in the years after the war ended. U.S. veterans would suffer too.[8] By some estimates, the number of Vietnam vets who have committed suicide has exceeded the 58,000-plus who died in combat.

Instead of helping the American people learn from this execrable episode in U.S. history, Ford encouraged Americans to "regain the sense of pride that existed before Vietnam."[9] The fact that the United States had not learned the lesson that it should never again support a corrupt dictatorship determined to silence the cries for justice from an oppressed people would come back to haunt it repeatedly in future years.

Reeling from defeat in Vietnam, the United States went out of its way to cultivate anti-Communist allies in the region. Ford and Kissinger visited General

Suharto, Indonesia's right-wing dictator, in early December. The day they left, Suharto's military invaded the newly independent nation of East Timor, a former Portuguese colony. Suharto had asked his guests for "understanding if we deem it necessary to take rapid or drastic action" in toppling East Timor's left-wing government. Ford assured him, "We will understand and not press you on the issue." Kissinger urged Suharto to postpone the invasion until he and Ford had returned to the United States and to finish the job quickly. The invasion proved to be bloody and the occupation prolonged. The estimated death toll from the invasion plus starvation and disease ranges from 100,000 to 200,000 and more. Three hundred thousand people, over half the population, were relocated to camps run by the Indonesian military. The United States continued providing military aid to Indonesia until 1999. East Timor did not regain full independence until 2002.[10]

Following Nixon's ouster, conservatives set out to purge the intelligence community of CIA analysts who didn't believe the Soviets were out to conquer the world. Led by Air Force Intelligence Chief Major General George Keegan, they convinced CIA Director George H. W. Bush to give a group of anti-Soviet hardliners, labeled Team B, unprecedented access to the country's most sensitive intelligence so that they could challenge the CIA's findings about the Soviet Union. In the eyes of CIA analysts, Keegan had already discredited himself with fanciful reports of a Soviet-directed energy weapons program that would give the Soviet Union an enormous advantage over the United States. Rebuffed by military and intelligence experts, he went public with his outlandish theories when he retired. He convinced the editors of *Aviation Week & Space Technology* to write in May 1977, "The Soviet Union has achieved a technical breakthrough in high-energy physics applications that may soon provide it with a directed-energy beam weapon capable of neutralizing the entire United States ballistic missile force and checkmating this country's strategic doctrine. . . . The race to perfect directed-energy weapons is a reality."[11] Despite the fact that no such Soviet project existed, the United States began its own space-based laser weapons program in 1978 under the Defense Advanced Research Projects Agency (DARPA). This eventually led to the much-ballyhooed and incredibly wasteful Strategic Defense Initiative (SDI). Keegan also incorrectly insisted that the Soviets were building a large-scale civil defense system designed to safeguard much of the Soviet population in the event of a nuclear war. Howard Stoertz, who oversaw the production of National Intelligence Estimates on the Soviet Union, explained why he and others at the CIA objected to this type of outside scrutiny: "Most of us were opposed to it because we saw it as an ideological, political foray, not an intellectual exercise. We knew the people who were pleading for it."[12]

Harvard Russia historian Richard Pipes, a virulently anti-Soviet Polish immigrant, was put in charge of Team B. Pipes quickly recruited Paul Nitze and

Paul Wolfowitz. According to Anne Cahn, who worked at the Arms Control and Disarmament Agency under President Carter, Team B members shared an "apoplectic animosity toward the Soviet Union."[13] They greatly overestimated the USSR's military spending and capabilities, predicting that the Soviets would have around five hundred Backfire bombers by early 1984, more than double the actual number. They put the most malign interpretation on the Soviets' intentions, accusing them of using détente as a ruse to gain hegemony. They rejected the CIA assessment that Soviet nuclear capabilities were primarily defensive in nature, designed to deter and retaliate, not attack.

Pipes complained that the CIA assessments "happened to favor détente and to place the main burden for its success on the United States." He attributed this to the fact that the CIA's "analytic staff . . . shared the outlook of U.S. academe, with its penchant for philosophical positivism, cultural agnosticism, and political liberalism." Actual Soviet behavior, Pipes argued, "indicated beyond reasonable doubt that the Soviet leadership . . . regarded nuclear weapons as tools of war whose proper employment . . . promised victory."[14]

Pipes's report found the Soviets far ahead in every strategic category. The CIA dismissed it as "complete fiction." Cahn concluded, "if you go through most of Team B's specific allegations about weapons systems, . . . they were all wrong."[15]

On November 5, Team B members debated the CIA Soviet analysts, most of whom were younger and less experienced. One of the CIA participants recalled, "We were overmatched. People like Nitze ate us for lunch." A CIA official reported, "It was like putting Walt Whitman High versus the Redskins." The Agency had blundered, Pipes gloated, by pitting "a troop of young analysts, some of them barely out of graduate school" against "senior government officials, general officers, and university professors." Pipes reported that when Team A's "champion," the young analyst Ted Cherry, began his criticism of Team B's findings, Nitze "fired a question that reduced him to a state of catatonic immobility: we stared in embarrassment as he sat for what seemed an interminable time with an open mouth, unable to utter a sound."[16]

Though Bush and his successor, Stansfield Turner, both joined Kissinger in dismissing Team B's findings, Bush made sure that this harsher assessment of Soviet capabilities and intentions was incorporated into intelligence reports.

This ill-fated intervention in CIA affairs turned more ominous in September 1978 when a former high-level CIA official, John Paisley, went missing after sailing in the Chesapeake Bay. Paisley, who had been deputy director of strategic research, was an expert on Soviet nuclear and other weapons programs, with authority to request launching of spy satellites. He had been the CIA liaison with Team B. His son claimed that he had been responsible for leaking the story of Team B's existence to the press.[17]

A week later a badly decomposed body was pulled from the bay and identi-fied as Paisley's by Maryland police. It had a gunshot wound in the head. The police quickly concluded that it was a case of suicide. But if so, it was a bizarre suicide indeed. The body found had two nineteen-pound diver's belts strapped across its midsection. It was four inches shorter than the five-foot, eleven-inch Paisley. And, according to writer Nicholas Thompson, "If the body was his, and if he had done himself in, he had chosen an awkward method. Paisley was right-handed, but he would have had to have attached the weights, leaned over the side, and shot himself, execution style, through the left temple."[18]

In addition to the investigation by the Maryland State Police, investigations were conducted by the CIA, the FBI, and the Senate Intelligence Committee. Meanwhile, the CIA put out various cover stories, which were quickly discred-ited. The CIA described Paisley, who had supposedly left the Agency in 1974, as a "part-time consultant with a very limited access to classified information," a description that a former high-level staffer on the President's Foreign Intel-ligence Advisory Board (PFIAB) found "shocking." "There is no question that Paisley, at the time of his death, had access to highly classified intelligence infor-mation," he informed the *Baltimore Sun*, which conducted its own three-month investigation.

One former PFIAB White House staffer revealed, "It was Paisley who devel-oped the list of people who would serve on the B Team. It was his job to get these guys clearances ... to discuss their backgrounds with us. Then, after the team had been selected, he would schedule the briefings. He shaped the entire process." The *Sun* reported that at the time of his death, Paisley was writing a "retrospec-tive analysis" of Team B for an in-house agency publication. Among the papers found on the boat were Paisley's notes on the history of the project. Other highly classified documents relating to Soviet defense spending and the state of Soviet military readiness were also in his possession.[19]

Speculation abounded that something more nefarious had occurred. Some CIA insiders told reporters that they believed the KGB had murdered Pais-ley. Others contended that he was a KGB "mole," who had been whacked by the CIA.[20] Paisley's wife charged that the body didn't belong to her estranged husband and hired an attorney and investigator. "My feeling is that something very sinister is happening," she said, accusing the CIA of telling "lies" about her husband. Two prominent insurance companies initially refused to pay benefits to Mrs. Paisley because of doubts that her husband was actually dead. After a lengthy investigation, the Senate Intelligence Committee decided to keep its report secret. The mystery has never been solved.[21]

Meanwhile, the hard-line antidétente forces were roiling the waters on a number of fronts. In March 1976, Nitze, James Schlesinger, and former

Undersecretary of State Eugene Rostow had set in motion what in November would become the Committee on the Present Danger (CPD). A committee by that name had been established once before in 1950 to back Nitze's NSC 68. Three Team B members—Nitze, Pipes, and William Van Cleave—served on the executive committee. Among the early supporters were Mellon heir Richard Mellon Scaife and the future Director of Central Intelligence William Casey. Members included *Commentary* magazine editor Norman Podhoretz, Richard Perle, Dean Rusk, and Ronald Reagan. The CPD's founding statement warned that the Soviet Union sought dominance through "an unparalleled military buildup" and that under the cover of arms control, it was preparing to fight and win a nuclear war.[22]

The Team B and CPD efforts to subvert the intelligence community and drive the country to the right were cheered on by a network of newly formed foundations and think tanks funded, in part, by the Scaife family, the Coors family, and William Simon, president of the John M. Olin Foundation. Among the recipients of such largesse were the Heritage Foundation, the American Enterprise Institute, the Hudson Institute, the Manhattan Institute, the Federalist Society, the Washington Legal Foundation, the Institute for Justice, the Hoover Institute, Freedom House, and the Ethics and Public Policy Center. These interests backed a series of right-wing publications, including *National Interest/Public Interest, Commentary,* and *The American Spectator.*

This burgeoning right-wing network had little use for a relative moderate like Gerald Ford. Its members itched to put a real right winger like Reagan into the White House. Ford and his White House chief of staff, Donald Rumsfeld, attempted to mollify Ford's critics. They engineered a major cabinet shake-up in October 1975, known as the "Halloween Day Massacre." Rumsfeld took over for Schlesinger at Defense. General Brent Scowcroft replaced Kissinger as national security advisor. Bush replaced William Colby at the CIA. Dick Cheney, Rumsfeld's deputy, took over as White House chief of staff. And Vice President Nelson Rockefeller was informed that he was off the ticket in 1976. Kissinger, furious, drafted a letter of resignation that he never sent. Many saw Rumsfeld's fingerprints all over this shake-up. Nixon had described Rumsfeld as a "ruthless little bastard."[23] Kissinger later said Rumsfeld was the most ruthless man he'd ever met.

Spurning his once-moderate views, Rumsfeld had moved steadily to the right, positioning himself as a staunch defender of Team B and foe of Kissinger's détente policies. He helped block a new SALT treaty in early 1976. "The opposition came from Secretary of Defense Don Rumsfeld and the Joint Chiefs of Staff, and I recognized that they held the trump card," Ford later wrote.[24] Rumsfeld began warning that the Soviets threatened to overtake the United States in military strength and that détente was not in the United States' interests. Ford got

Trying to placate their critics on the right, Ford and his chief of staff,
Donald Rumsfeld, engineered a major cabinet shake-up in October
1975, known as the "Halloween Day Massacre." Among other changes,
Rumsfeld took over for James Schlesinger as secretary of defense. Many
saw Rumsfeld, whom Nixon had described as a "ruthless little bastard,"
behind the shake-up. From his new post at the Pentagon, Rumsfeld began
warning that the Soviets threatened to overtake the United States in
military strength and that détente was not in the United States' interests.

the message, announcing in March 1976, "We are going to forget the use of the word détente." [25]

That capitulation was not enough to placate the party's resurgent right wing. Ronald Reagan excoriated the "moderate" policies advocated by Nixon, Ford, and Kissinger, which, he believed, were weakening the United States in the fight against its mortal Communist foes. In late March, he accused Kissinger of saying "The day of the US is past and today is the day of the Soviet Union. . . . My job as Secretary of State is to negotiate the most acceptable second-best position available." [26] Kissinger, not surprisingly, denied having ever made such remarks. [27]

Ford managed to stave off the attack from the neocon-infused Republican Right but was narrowly defeated in November by former Governor Jimmy Carter, a millionaire peanut farmer and longtime Sunday school teacher from Plains, Georgia. Carter, an evangelical Baptist, ran as a populist and an outsider, appealing to blacks, farmers, and disaffected youth. More of a New South agribusinessman than a small farmer, Carter, as historian Leo Ribuffo pointed out, harked back to the pre–World War I progressives, who stressed scientific efficiency and public morality, more than to the New Deal and Great Society reformers, who

(**LEFT**) *Jimmy Carter leaves a church while campaigning in Jacksonville, Florida.* (**RIGHT**) *A Carter supporter holds up a campaign sign at the 1976 Democratic National Convention in New York City. A millionaire peanut farmer and longtime Sunday school teacher from Plains, Georgia, Carter narrowly defeated Ford. Running as a populist and an outsider, appealing to blacks, farmers, and disaffected youth, he promised to restore trust in government and heal the wounds resulting from divisions over Watergate, the Vietnam War, and years of generational, gender, and racial discord.*

wanted to strengthen the welfare state.[28] Carter promised to restore trust in government and heal the wounds resulting from divisions over Watergate, the Vietnam War, and years of generational, gender, and racial discord.

The little Carter knew about foreign policy came from meetings of the Trilateral Commission, an organization founded in 1972 by Chase Manhattan Bank Chairman David Rockefeller, who also headed the influential Council on Foreign Relations (CFR). Rockefeller and many of his establishment cronies were troubled by recent developments. Not only was the United States suffering a monumental defeat in Vietnam, it was facing a destabilizing economic crisis. Many found Nixon's response threatening. By abandoning the gold standard and imposing wage and price controls and a tariff on imports, Nixon was undermining the liberal internationalism that had reigned supreme since 1945. When Nixon's measures were viewed alongside labor's and Congress's efforts to limit imports and punish multilateral corporations that shipped jobs overseas, some members of the CFR feared the resurgence of economic nationalism and even the outbreak of an international trade war.[29]

Looking for a new instrument to help stabilize the international order—the CFR had been rendered largely ineffectual by a sharp split over Vietnam—Rockefeller seized upon the approach suggested by Columbia University Professor Zbigniew Brzezinski. In his 1970 book, *Between Two Ages*, Brzezinski called for a "community of developed nations" from Western Europe, the United States, and Japan to guide the international order.[30] The two New Yorkers, who vacationed near each other in Seal Harbor, mapped out the kind of organization that could bring this to fruition.

At the June 1972 annual meeting of the secretive Bilderberg Group, held at the Hotel de Bilderberg in Oosterbeek, the Netherlands, Rockefeller proposed forming an organization that would bolster the world capitalist order by strengthening ties among leaders on the three continents. Brzezinski, who was a member of both the Bilderberg Group and the CFR, enthusiastically seconded the proposal. Seventeen members attended a planning meeting at Rockefeller's New York estate the following month. Beginning with sixty members on each continent, they set up offices in New York, Paris, and Tokyo. Most rejected the CPD's knee-jerk anticommunism, hoping instead to lure the Soviets into an international system that promoted economic interdependence and free flow of trade and capital. Third-world economic and political problems would be addressed outside the Cold War framework.[31]

Brzezinski served as executive director of the commission's North American branch. The son of a Polish diplomat and probably the most unreconstructed anti-Communist among the founding members, he tapped Carter for membership.[32] He and Rockefeller saw in Carter a rising, though still little-known, southern governor who was eager to be educated about the world. Always confident and ambitious, Carter was already discussing a run for the presidency with his close advisors. He had yet to make a splash on the national scene. When he appeared on the television show *What's My Line?* in December 1973, none of the panelists, Arlene Francis, Gene Shalit, Soupy Sales, could identify what he did for a living. Perhaps Brzezinski was impressed that Carter had nominated hard-line anti-Communist and neocon favorite Senator Henry "Scoop" Jackson for president at the 1972 Democratic National Convention.

Brzezinski and Rockefeller saw something in Carter that convinced them that he was worth cultivating and got behind his candidacy early. Carter's deputy campaign manager Peter Bourne revealed that "David and Zbig had both agreed that Carter was the ideal politician to build on."[33] Brzezinski served as Carter's foreign policy advisor and speechwriter during the campaign. Carter filled out his administration with twenty-six fellow Trilateralists, including Vice President

Walter Mondale, Secretary of State Cyrus Vance, Secretary of Defense Harold Brown, Treasury Secretary Michael Blumenthal, and Federal Reserve Chairman Paul Volcker. At the CIA, Carter replaced Trilateral Commission member Bush with fellow member Stansfield Turner. Trilateralists, including Warren Christopher, Anthony Lake, and Richard Holbrooke, also populated the secondary ranks. Most significantly, Carter selected Brzezinski as his national security advisor. Trilateralist Kissinger was not offered a position in the administration.

Despite his inexperience, Trilateralist connections, and centrist instincts, Carter came into office with a moderately progressive vision of what the United States could become. Among his top priorities was cutting defense spending. During the campaign, he had denounced U.S. nuclear hypocrisy: "by enjoining sovereign nations to forgo nuclear weapons, we are asking for a form of self-denial that we have not been able to accept ourselves." Rejecting the typical double standard that powerful nations imposed on weaker ones, he recognized that the United States didn't have the "right to ask others to deny themselves such weapons" unless it was actively moving to eliminate its own nuclear arsenal. "The world is waiting, but not necessarily for long," he realized. "The longer effective arms reduction is postponed, the more likely it is that other nations will be encouraged to develop their own nuclear capability."[34]

Such honesty was refreshing, as was his promise to restore the United States' moral standing in the world and learn from Vietnam. He declared that "never again should our country become militarily involved in the internal affairs of another nation unless there is a direct and obvious threat to the security of the United States or its people."[35] He vowed never to repeat the "false statements and sometimes outright lies" that his predecessors had used to justify the U.S. invasion of Vietnam. He raised the hopes of mankind by announcing that the United States would "help shape a just and peaceful world that is truly humane. . . . We pledge . . . to limit the world's armaments. . . . And we will move this year a step toward the ultimate goal—the elimination of all nuclear weapons from this Earth. We urge all other people to join us, for success can mean life instead of death."[36]

Just how heartfelt Carter's comments on Vietnam were is difficult to ascertain. They clearly represented a welcome departure from the apologetics of his predecessors and successors. But they may have represented a kind of dissembling intended to make the new president seem much more liberal than he actually was or than his record as president would suggest. While campaigning in 1976, Carter responded to a reporter's question about Vietnam by asserting, "I called for a complete pullout" in March 1971, after having previously taken a more typical southern prowar position. However, in August of that year, he had written a column saying that he had supported the initial U.S. involvement in

Carter and Soviet leader Leonid Brezhnev sign SALT II. For all the treaty's fanfare, it was only a measured success. Both sides were actually allowed to continue their nuclear buildups at a reduced rate.

Vietnam to fight "Communist aggression," but now, "since we are not going to do what it takes to win, it is time to come home." The following year, he had supported Nixon's bombing of North Vietnam and mining of harbors and urged Americans to "give President Nixon our backing and support—whether or not we agree with that decision." Even as late as April 1975, with Saigon about to fall to the Communists and their supporters, he had told reporters that he supported giving the Saigon regime $500 million to $600 million in military aid for another year to help stabilize it.[37]

Thus, Carter may never have been as liberal on foreign policy as many assumed he was. But he did manage to rile the CPD crowd by selecting dovish Paul Warnke to head the Arms Control and Disarmament Agency, appointing liberal former Atlanta Mayor Andrew Young, an African American, as UN ambassador, and siding, at least initially, with Vance's lawyerly pragmatism and commitment to détente over the toxic anticommunism of Brzezinski. That allowed Carter to score some significant early successes. He successfully renegotiated the Panama Canal treaty. In 1978, he helped secure the Camp David Accords, which led to Israeli withdrawal from Egyptian territory captured in the 1967 war and the establishment of diplomatic relations between the two countries. He also made headway in arms control. Warnke negotiated the SALT II treaty with the Soviets, mandating a reduction in nuclear missiles and bombers, and helped convince Carter to resist the Pentagon's pressure to build the B-1 bomber. SALT II, for all the fanfare surrounding its signing in June 1979, was only a measured success, actually allowing both sides to continue their build-ups at a reduced rate. Both parties were permitted to add another four thousand warheads by 1985 and deploy one new weapons system over the five-year life of the treaty. CPDers denounced the treaty, claiming that it would give the Soviets "strategic superiority" and open a "window of vulnerability."[38] They called for massive growth in defense spending and civil defense. With the Scaife Foundation pouring over $300,000 into the CPD, foes of SALT II outspent treaty backers by fifteen to one.

But Carter's lack of foreign policy experience would come back to haunt him, and his growing reliance on Brzezinski and other hawkish advisors would doom his progressive agenda, leaving the administration's foreign policy awash in a sea of Cold War orthodoxy. Brzezinski quickly instituted a significant change in procedure that allowed him to exert inordinate influence on the president. Whereas in the past, a top CIA official had given the President's Daily Brief, Brzezinski arranged to do this himself, with no one else present. "From the very first day of the Presidency," he wrote, "I insisted that the morning intelligence briefing be given to the President by me and by no one else. The CIA tried to have me take a briefing officer with me, but I felt that this would inhibit candid talk." Brzezinski overruled Turner's objections.[39]

In his memoirs, Brzezinski outlined the deliberate, systematic process whereby he came to shape Carter's thinking on foreign policy issues:

> In effect, the morning briefing involved a touching of bases, some prodding of the President to think about problems that in my judgment needed attention, the planting of basic ideas, and—especially in the first months of his Presidency—some wider discussions of conceptual or strategic issues. This was particularly important in the initial stages, when we were defining our broad goals and setting our priorities. I also used the sessions occasionally to make suggestions to Carter as to what he ought to stress in his public statements, including possible formulations or wordings. He was extremely good at picking up phrases, and I was often amazed how after such a morning briefing he would use in a later press conference or public appearance words almost identical to those we had discussed.

Priding himself on being Carter's ventriloquist, Brzezinski outlined the additional steps he had taken to make sure that his lessons sank in. In addition to repeated daily conversations, he began sending Carter a weekly NSC report, which was "meant to be a highly personal and private document, for the

President alone." It usually opened with a one-page editorial from Brzezinski in which he "commented in a freewheeling fashion on the Administration's performance, alerted him to possible problems, conveyed occasionally some criticism, and attempted to impart a global perspective."[40]

Brzezinski noted that Carter sometimes disagreed with his analysis and was "irritated" by his reports. But the record of the administration shows that Brzezinski's obsessive anticommunism—he bragged about being "the first Pole in 300 years in a position to really stick it to the Russians"—eventually wore Carter down and won him to Brzezinski's point of view.[41]

Carter came to office committed to promoting human rights, but he used human rights as a vehicle for attacking the Soviet Union, causing relations between the two countries to chill. The Soviets, proud of the fact that they had expanded civil liberties and decreased the number of political prisoners in recent years, countered that Soviet citizens had rights that Americans didn't enjoy. The Kremlin instructed Ambassador Anatoly Dobrynin to ask Vance how the Americans would feel if the Soviets tied détente to ending U.S. racial discrimination or unemployment.[42]

Carter also overreacted to the USSR's support of Mengistu Haile Mariam in Ethiopia. Mengistu had come to power in a 1974 coup that had overthrown Emperor Haile Selassie. During those years, the Soviet Union was taking advantage of the turbulence throughout Africa and the rest of the third world to align with progressive forces and push socialist models of development. But third-world involvements would repeatedly trap the Soviets in their own quagmires economically, politically, and militarily. Ethiopia proved to be such a case. In late 1977, Soviet leaders, encouraged by Castro and his support for African liberation movements, responded to requests from Mengistu, who was facing invasion from neighboring Somalia and opposition from a Somali-supported Eritrean independence movement. Despite their criticism of Mengistu's often brutal behavior, the Soviets significantly increased support for Ethiopia's revolutionary government, providing over a billion dollars' worth of military equipment and a thousand military advisors. They also assisted in transporting 17,000 Cuban military and technical personnel to assist the Ethiopians. Most African nations applauded the Soviet intervention, viewing it as a legitimate response to Somali aggression.

Carter responded mildly at first, sharing Soviet leaders' sense that détente and arms control were the top priorities. Brzezinski, however, urged the president to stop being "soft" and stand up to the Soviets. "A president must not only be loved and respected; he must also be feared," the national security advisor argued. He urged Carter "to pick some controversial subject on which you will deliberately choose to act with a degree of anger, even roughness, designed to

Carter with Zbigniew Brzezinski, whose selection as national security advisor would help doom Carter's progressive agenda. The hawkish son of a Polish diplomat and an obsessed anti-Communist, Brzezinski set out to deliberately and systematically shape Carter's thinking on foreign policy.

have a shock effect."[43] Carter thought Ethiopia a good place to start. Despite Vance's strong objections, Carter accused the Soviets of "expanding their influence abroad" through "military power and military assistance."[44] Brzezinski was thrilled by Carter's denunciation of Soviet actions. He would later remark on several occasions that "SALT lies buried in the sands of the Ogaden."[45] The Right was more strident in its attack on Soviet adventurism in Africa. Reagan warned:

> If the Soviets are successful—and it looks more and more as if they will be—then the entire Horn of Africa will be under their influence, if not their control. From there, they can threaten the sea lanes carrying oil to western Europe and the United States, if and when they choose. More immediately, control of the Horn of Africa would give Moscow the ability to destabilize those governments on the Arabian peninsula which have proven themselves strongly anti-Communist . . . in a few years we may be faced with the prospect of a Soviet empire of protégés and dependencies stretching from Addis Ababa to Capetown.[46]

Soviet leaders did not anticipate such a strong response in light of similar U.S. actions in its sphere of influence. But they did overestimate U.S. willingness to accord them equal status. Many within the Soviet hierarchy and intelligentsia were already questioning the wisdom of Soviet involvement in countries such as Afghanistan, Angola, Ethiopia, Mozambique, Somalia, and South Yemen, given the repeated unwillingness of their repressive leaders to heed Soviet advice on political and economic issues.

Carter's support for human rights prompted Soviet countercharges. In July 1978, Carter "deplored" and "condemned" Soviet sentencing of dissident Anatoly Sharansky to thirteen years in prison for allegedly spying for the CIA. Carter's charges particularly galled the Soviet leaders because he and Brzezinski had been cozying up to China, whose human rights record was far, far worse. Brzezinski admitted to Carter that China was executing as many as twenty thousand prisoners a year. However, the sting of Carter's accusation was blunted by UN Ambassador Andrew Young's telling a French newspaper that there were "hundreds, maybe even thousands of people I would call political prisoners" in U.S. jails.[47]

Criticizing Soviet human rights lapses while supporting other egregious human rights offenders was a dangerous game to play and sometimes backfired. In 1967, Great Britain announced plans to withdraw its forces from east of Suez. The United States decided to fill the void. It built a military base on the island of Diego Garcia in the Indian Ocean, from which the British had expelled almost two thousand natives between 1968 and 1973. The United States would use the base as a launch pad to protect its interests in the Persian Gulf.[48] It also tied its fortunes even more closely to the shah of Iran, who, along with Israel, became the principal defender of U.S. economic and geopolitical interests in the Persian Gulf, which held 60 percent of the world's known oil reserves. During these years, the oil-rich Gulf states had begun to play an important role in world economic affairs, importing goods from the United States and Europe and investing billions of petrodollars in U.S. banks.

During the 1960s and '70s, the United States supplied Iran with an arsenal of sophisticated weapons. In what must seem a cruel irony to a later generation, the United States even urged Iran to begin a large-scale nuclear power program to save its abundant oil reserves. U.S. leaders' open embrace of the repressive shah so soon after the CIA had overthrown an extremely popular Iranian leader enraged most Iranians. One leading opponent of the shah and his modernization program, Ayatollah Ruhollah Khomeini, declared, "Let the American President know that in the eyes of the Iranian people, he is the most repulsive member of the human race today because of the injustice he has imposed on our Muslim nation."[49] For this and other outbursts, the shah's government exiled Khomeini from his homeland in 1964. Over the next fifteen years, the Iranian cleric kept up a steady stream of invective against both the shah and his U.S. backers from Iraq and Paris.

Iranian discontent continued to grow, fueled by the 1970s economic slow-down. Despite the shah's dismal human rights record, Carter had backed additional arms sales to Iran, which had already been receiving more than any other nation. Ties between Carter and the shah, whom the *New York Times* described as "a ruler as close to an absolute monarch as exists these days," seemed to be strengthening, provoking many to decry Carter's hypocrisy on human rights.[50] The Iranian royal couple paid a visit to the Carters in November 1977, staying at the White House. During their discussions, Carter gave preliminary approval to the sale of six to eight light-water nuclear reactors to Iran. When combined with the fourteen to sixteen that the shah was negotiating to buy from France and West Germany, Iran would have a substantial nuclear power program.

Hoping to show support for their beleaguered ally, President and Mrs. Carter shared an ornate and lavish New Year's Eve with the shah in Tehran as protesters demonstrated in both nations' capitals. Five crystal wineglasses adorned the place setting of each of the four hundred guests. Carter was effusive in his praise for his host: "Our talks have been priceless, our friendship is irreplaceable, and my own gratitude is to the Shah, who in his wisdom and with his experience has been so helpful to me, a new leader. There is no leader with whom I have a deeper sense of personal gratitude and personal friendship."[51]

In subsequent months, huge protests renewed across Iran. In September, the shah imposed martial law. Brzezinski urged Carter to either aggressively support the shah or support a military coup. Fearing that the Soviets would seize the opportunity to move into the Gulf, he asked the Pentagon to draw up plans for the United States to occupy Iran's oil fields. In December, he warned Carter that the United States faced "the most massive American defeat since the beginning of the Cold War, overshadowing in its real consequences the setback in Vietnam."[52] Brzezinski maneuvered behind the scenes to see if a coup was possible. Ambassador William Sullivan recalled, "I received a telephone call relaying a message from Brzezinski, who asked whether I thought I could arrange a military coup against the revolution. . . . I regret the reply I made is unprintable."[53]

In January 1979, the shah fled his country. Brzezinski feared a Communist takeover. In what turned out to be a colossal failure of intelligence, the CIA and State Department downplayed the threat posed by Islamic fundamentalism. Henry Precht, the State Department's Iran desk officer, recounted how he had figured out what was brewing:

> Late in November 1978, we called in all the experts on Iran . . . to discuss what to do about Iran and what was going to happen there . . . the night before I'd guest-lectured at a class at American University, and . . . there

were a lot of Iranian students there. . . . when I asked what they thought was going to happen in Iran, they all said: Islamic government. The next day, at our conference, we went around the room all saying what we thought would happen, and people were saying things like, "There will be a liberal government, with the National Front, and Khomeini will go to Qom." When my turn came I said, "Islamic government." I was the only one.[54]

In February, seventy-seven-year-old Ayatollah Khomeini returned to Tehran to a hero's welcome and set about establishing an Islamic republic based on Sharia law. The goal was to create a new caliphate. The head of the Iran branch at Langley assured the CIA's Tehran station: "Don't worry about another embassy attack. The only thing that could trigger an attack would be if the Shah was let into the United States—and no one in this town is stupid enough to do that."[55] No one, that is, except for Carter, who buckled under pressure from Kissinger, David Rockefeller, Brzezinski, and other friends of the shah. The Iranian public erupted in anger. In November, students burst into the embassy and seized fifty-two American hostages, whom they held for 444 days. Fearing Soviet intervention to quell the rising tide of Islamic fundamentalism, Carter rushed twenty-five warships to the Persian Gulf, including three nuclear-armed aircraft carriers, and 1,800 marines. He also blocked the release of Iranian assets in the United States and cut off oil imports from Iran.

When those measures didn't lead to the hostages' release, the American public grew restive. Chief of Staff Hamilton Jordan alerted Carter to the fact that "the American people are frustrated at our country's inability to do anything to free the prisoners and retaliate in a fashion that makes us feel better about ourselves."[56] But Carter continued to show restraint. Khomeini's mistrust of the Soviet Union and its left-wing Iranian allies limited the extent to which the Soviets could exploit the situation. Khomeini's anti-Soviet feelings deepened when the Soviet Union invaded Afghanistan in December 1979 and hardened further after Soviet-allied Iraq invaded Iran in September 1980.

The Americans were lucky in one regard in terms of Iran. As part of Eisenhower's "atoms for peace" program, the United States had sold dozens of research reactors to countries all over the world, including Iran, and had been supplying highly enriched uranium to fuel them. Some of the reactors used fuel enriched to 93 percent. Shortly before the shah's ouster, the United States had sold Iran fifty-eight pounds of weapons-grade uranium. Fortunately, the fuel had not yet been delivered when the revolutionary government seized power, and the sale was suspended.[57]

Crises seemed to be flaring all over. Central America, after suffering decades of poverty under U.S.-backed right-wing dictators, was ready to explode by the

Despite the Iranian ruler's dismal human rights record, President Carter never ceased to support the beleaguered shah, outraging most Iranians. At a lavish 1978 New Year's Eve celebration with the shah in Tehran, as protesters demonstrated in both nations' capitals, Carter offered his host this adulatory toast: "Our talks have been priceless, our friendship is irreplaceable, and my own gratitude is to the Shah, who in his wisdom and with his experience has been so helpful to me, a new leader. There is no leader with whom I have a deeper sense of personal gratitude and personal friendship." Riots broke out soon after the Carters left. In January 1979, the shah fled Iran.

Protest against the shah during the Iranian Revolution. In what turned out to be a colossal intelligence failure, the CIA and State Department downplayed the threat of Islamic fundamentalism.

late 1970s. In Nicaragua, the Sandinista National Liberation Front, named after martyred guerrilla leader Augusto Sandino, threatened to overthrow President Anastasio Somoza Debayle. The Somoza family's brutal and corrupt forty-three-year rule had united the impoverished citizens in opposition. Carter administration officials feared that a Sandinista victory would embolden revolutionary forces in neighboring countries, especially Guatemala, Honduras, and El Salvador. Brzezinski argued for military intervention, citing the humiliation of appearing "incapable of dealing with problems in our own backyard."[58] While Carter weighed his options, the Sandinistas seized power in July 1979—Latin America's first successful revolution since Cuba's twenty years earlier—and began an ambitious program of land, education, and health reform. They put out feelers for better relations with the United States, and Congress responded by appropriating $75 million in emergency aid to the new government. But as reports surfaced that Nicaragua was transferring arms from Cuba into El Salvador, Carter halted aid twelve days before Reagan took office in January 1981.

Carter also faced a moment of reckoning in El Salvador, where a small group of wealthy landowners—the Forty Families—had ruled for over a century, using any means at their disposal to subdue the impoverished masses. Death-squad murders increased in the 1970s to quell growing popular resistance. Following the 1980 assassination of Archbishop Oscar Romero, the various insurgent groups had coalesced to form the Frente Faribundo Martí para la Liberación Nacional (FMLN). By late 1980, with the FMLN insurgents poised to triumph, Carter, pressured by Brzezinski, opted to restore military aid to the dictatorship.

A storm was also gathering in Afghanistan, a backward nation with a per capita annual income of only $70 in 1974. In 1976, the State Department reported that the United States "is not, nor should it become, committed to, or responsible for the 'protection' of Afghanistan in any respect."[59] But things changed when pro-Soviet rebels led by Nur Muhammad Taraki and Hafizullah Amin seized power in April 1978. Taraki, the new head of state, proclaimed, "The future for the people looks very bright." *New York Times* reporter William Borders took issue with that assessment: "By the standards of almost any place else in the world, however, the future really does not look all that bright—not in a land where the life expectancy is 40 years, where infant mortality is 18 percent and no more than one person in ten can read." Borders continued, "Afghanistan has very few highways and not one mile of railway, and most of its people live either as nomads or as impoverished farmers in brown mud villages behind high walls, a life scarcely different from what it was when Alexander the Great passed this way 2,000 years ago."[60]

The Soviet Union, which had friendly relations with the previous government, actually opposed the coup, despite the prior government's repressive behavior toward Afghan Communists. The new government's reform policies—particularly educational programs for women, land reform, and plans for industrialization—and harshly repressive tactics animated the growing insurgency by Afghan mujahideen, Islamist holy warriors operating out of Pakistan. A civil war was soon raging.

The United States cast its lot with the mujahideen. Carter, uncomfortable with the religious zealotry and reactionary views of the insurgents, initially rejected Brzezinski's plans for covert operations against the new government. Brzezinski instead worked with the CIA to train and secure outside funding for the rebels. In February, Islamic extremists in Kabul kidnapped U.S. Ambassador Adolph "Spike" Dubs, who was killed when Afghan police and Soviet advisors stormed the hotel in which he was being held. The United States subsequently deepened its involvement in the country.

Brzezinski saw more opportunity than danger in the growing Islamic fundamentalism. For several years, the United States had been working with Iranian and Pakistani intelligence to develop a right-wing Islamic fundamentalist movement within Pakistan that would challenge governments sympathetic to the Soviet Union. Brzezinski later acknowledged that the United States had been supporting the mujahideen even before the Soviet invasion: "It was July 3, 1979, that President Carter signed the first directive for secret aid to the opponents of the pro-Soviet regime in Kabul. And that very day I wrote a note to the president in which I explained to him that in my opinion this aid was going to induce a Soviet military intervention."[61]

Brzezinski understood the Soviets' fear that the Afghan insurgency would spark an uprising by the 40 million Muslims in Soviet Central Asia. Afghan leaders had been pressing Moscow to send troops to quell the uprising and the Russians rebuffed their requests. Brezhnev instead urged them to ease repression of political opponents. Soviet leaders concluded correctly that the Americans were instigating the insurgency in cooperation with extremist elements in Iran and Pakistan. They figured that China might also be playing a role. But they still hesitated to intervene. Gromyko summed up their concerns: "We would be largely throwing away everything we achieved with such difficulty, particularly détente, the SALT-II negotiations would fly by the wayside, there would be no signing of an agreement (and however you look at it that is for us the greatest political priority), there would be no meeting of [Brezhnev] with Carter, . . . and our relations with Western countries, particularly the FRG, would be spoiled."[62]

The Soviets opted to oust Amin, the driving force behind the repression, and replace him with Taraki. But the plan backfired, leaving Taraki dead and Amin more firmly entrenched in power. Not only did Amin then widen the repression, he also reached out to the United States for help. Dreading the thought of a pro-American regime on their southern border, replete with U.S. troops and Per-shing II missiles, Soviet leaders decided to replace Amin with Babrak Karmal, despite knowing that the resulting instability might require them to send troops into the country. Military leaders opposed intervention, fearing that it would incite a unified Muslim response that would bog them down for years in a place they had no business being in. But Brezhnev foolishly insisted the war would be over in three to four weeks. His decision to send troops was made easier by the fact that détente with the West had already begun to unravel with growing U.S. opposition to ratifying SALT II and NATO's decision to deploy new intermedi-ate-range ballistic missiles in Europe. Still, as historian Melvyn Leffler reminded readers, "When they made their decision to intervene in Afghanistan, Soviet leaders saw threat, not opportunity."[63]

Defying his wary military advisors, Brezhnev deployed over 100,000 Soviet troops on Christmas Day 1979. Up to the very eve of the invasion, the CIA kept assuring Carter that no such action was forthcoming. The world scoffed at the Soviet claim that it was defending against covert U.S. efforts to destabilize a gov-ernment friendly to Moscow on the Soviet Union's border. Brzezinski cheered the invasion, believing he had lured Moscow into its own Vietnam trap.

In full Cold War mode by that point, Carter called the invasion of Afghani-stan "the greatest threat to peace since the Second World War"—a statement so hyperbolic that *New York Times* columnist Russell Baker felt compelled to remind him of the Berlin blockade, the Korean War, the Suez crisis, the Cuban Missile Crisis, and the war in Vietnam.[64] In his January 23, 1980, State of the Union address, Carter declared:

> The region which is now threatened by Soviet troops in Afghanistan is of
> great strategic importance: It contains more than two-thirds of the world's
> exportable oil. The Soviet effort to dominate Afghanistan has brought
> Soviet military forces to within 300 miles of the Indian Ocean and close to
> the Straits of Hormuz, a waterway through which most of the world's oil
> must flow. The Soviet Union is now attempting to consolidate a strategic
> position, therefore, that poses a grave threat to the free movement of
> Middle East oil. . . .
>   Let our position be absolutely clear: An attempt by any outside force to
> gain control of the Persian Gulf region will be regarded as an assault on the
> vital interests of the United States of America, and such an assault will be
> repelled by any means necessary, including military force.[65]

The final sentence, which became enshrined as the Carter Doctrine, was interpreted in the Kremlin as a clear threat of war—even nuclear war. Vance

*Zbigniew Brzezinski with Pakistani soldiers in March 1980. Although
Carter had cut off aid to Muhammad Zia-ul-Haq's repressive government in
1977 because of Zia's contempt for human rights and his nuclear weapons
program, the United States now offered Pakistan millions of dollars in
military and economic aid in return for supporting Islamic insurgents
fighting Soviet intervention in Afghanistan. Brzezinski traveled to Pakistan
and Saudi Arabia to work out financial and military collaboration.*

attempted to remove it from the address, striking it from the draft that the State
Department submitted to the White House. Brzezinski fought to keep it in, convincing Press Secretary Jody Powell that without it the speech was devoid of
content. Powell persuaded Carter that his national security advisor was right.[66]

Interviewed the following month on NBC News, Assistant Secretary of State
William Dyess reiterated the threat, pointing out that "the Soviets know that this
terrible weapon has been dropped on human beings twice in history and it was
an American president who dropped it both times."[67]

The Soviets thought that U.S. accusations of Soviet aggression in the Middle
East were preposterous, yet Carter withdrew the U.S. ambassador from Moscow
and took SALT II off the table. He cut trade between the two countries, banned
U.S. athletes from participating in the upcoming Moscow Olympics, increased
defense spending, and sent Secretary of Defense Harold Brown to China to
sound out Chinese leaders about establishing military ties.

As many of Brezhnev's advisors had warned, the Soviet intervention did spark
a much larger uprising on the part of Islamists both inside and outside Afghanistan. Resistance groups based in Peshawar, Pakistan, joined with madrassa-trained

Islamic zealots from Saudi Arabia, Egypt, and Pakistan to aid the Afghan resistance fighters. In Islamabad, thirty-five Muslim nations condemned the Soviet aggression. Brzezinski began looking for ways to fan the flames of potential discontent among Muslims in Soviet Central Asia. In earlier decades, the United States had employed Islamic fundamentalism as a weapon in the fight against secular Arab nationalism. It would now use Islamic extremism against the Soviet Union. But that meant cooperating with Pakistan's president, General Muhammad Zia-ul-Haq. Carter had cut off aid to his repressive government in 1977 because of Zia's contempt for human rights and his nuclear weapons program. Now, within days of the invasion, Carter offered Zia hundreds of millions of dollars' worth of military and economic aid in return for supporting the Islamist insurgents. In February 1980, Brzezinski traveled to Pakistan and Saudi Arabia to work out financial and military collaboration. Saudi Prince Turki al-Faisal told a CIA officer, "We don't do operations. We don't know how. All we know how to do is write checks." The Saudis agreed to match the U.S. contributions.[68]

Despite Carter's saber rattling, the United States would not have been able to repel a Soviet invasion of the Gulf, short of beginning a nuclear war. Carter therefore took measures to rectify that situation. He built up a rapid deployment force with new bases in Somalia, Kenya, and Oman from which several thousand U.S. troops could be quickly deployed to the Gulf in a crisis. He strengthened ties with friendly governments in the region, such as Saudi Arabia. And he made a major adjustment in nuclear strategy, issuing Presidential Directive 59, which changed the U.S. nuclear war-fighting strategy from fighting wars of mutually assured destruction to fighting "flexible" and "limited" nuclear wars that the United States could win. Not only did Carter's effort to eliminate nuclear weapons fall flat, PD-59 initiated a massive increase in conventional and nuclear arms. Under it, the United States prepared to fight a protracted nuclear war, first targeting Soviet leaders, while holding attacks on cities in abeyance.

Thus were dashed, once and for all, the hopes that Carter embodied for a safer and more peaceful world. During his one term in office, he managed to support research on the neutron bomb, authorize deployment of nuclear-armed cruise missiles to Europe, commission the first Trident submarine, and double the number of warheads aimed at the Soviet Union. Thus, despite having Carter in the White House, the CPD's campaign to defeat SALT II and increase defense spending had succeeded beyond its wildest dreams. In fact, by the end of his term, Carter had done a complete about-face and bought the CPD's view of an aggressive Soviet Union that had to be contained. Détente was dead. Carter even repudiated his earlier criticism of the Vietnam War. Vietnam veterans had long since become freedom fighters who "went to Vietnam without any desire to capture territory or to impose American will on other people."[69] Despite his best intentions, he had laid the groundwork for the extreme views that Reagan would bring to the White House. As Anne Cahn summarized in her book *Killing Détente:*

> By the 1980 presidential election, the choice in foreign and defense policy was between that of the Carter administration, which favored the MX missile, the Trident submarine, a Rapid Deployment Force, a "stealth" bomber, cruise missiles, counterforce targeting leading to a first-strike capability, and a 5 percent increase in defense spending, and that of the Republicans under Ronald Reagan, who favored all of these *plus* the neutron bomb, antiballistic missiles, the B-1 bomber, civil defense, and an 8 percent increase in defense spending.[70]

Not only did Carter not fulfill his promise to sharply reduce defense spending, he significantly increased it, from $115.2 billion in his first budget to $180 billion in his final one.[71] Nor was he apologetic about this reversal. During his reelection campaign, he even got into a proxy war with the Republicans over the issue. Appearing on the *Today* show in early July, Defense Secretary Harold Brown attacked the Republicans for cutting defense spending by more than 35 percent between 1969 and 1976, whereas the Carter administration had raised it by 10 percent during its time in office and planned to raise it an additional 25 percent during its second term. Former Secretary of Defense Melvin Laird challenged Brown's math but admitted that defense spending had gone up faster under Carter than under Nixon or Ford.[72]

From the Soviet vantage point, U.S. behavior was quite alarming. As future CIA director Robert Gates later admitted, "the Soviets saw a very different Jimmy Carter than did most Americans by 1980, different and more hostile and threatening."[73] At that point, Soviet leaders didn't know what to expect from Carter. In late 1979 and early 1980, the U.S. early-warning system malfunctioned on four occasions, triggering combat alerts of U.S. strategic forces. The KGB believed that they were not malfunctions but deliberate Pentagon ploys to lower Soviet anxiety and response time during future alerts by lulling them into a false sense of complacency, thereby making them vulnerable to a surprise attack. The Soviets weren't the only ones frightened by the episodes. Gates reported Brzezinski's account to him of the November 9, 1979, incident in his memoirs:

> Brzezinski was awakened at three in the morning by [his military assistant William] Odom, who told him that some 220 Soviet missiles had been launched against the United States. Brzezinski knew that the President's decision time to order retaliation was from three to seven minutes after a Soviet launch. Thus he told Odom he would stand by for a further call

to confirm a Soviet launch and the intended targets before calling the President. Brzezinski was convinced we had to hit back and told Odom to confirm that the Strategic Air Command was launching its planes. When Odom called back, he reported that he had further confirmation, but that 2,200 missiles had been launched—it was an all-out attack. One minute before Brzezinski intended to telephone the President, Odom called a third time to say that other warning systems were not reporting Soviet launches. Sitting alone in the middle of the night, Brzezinski had not awakened his wife, reckoning that everyone would be dead in half an hour. It had been a false alarm. Someone had mistakenly put military exercise tapes into the computer system. When it was over, Zbig just went back to bed. I doubt he slept much, though.[74]

The dangerous incident, which was leaked to the press, caused alarm in the Kremlin. Ambassador Dobrynin conveyed Brezhnev's "extreme anxiety" over what happened. Brzezinski and the Defense Department drafted the response, which senior State Department advisor Marshall Shulman characterized as "gratuitously insulting and inappropriate for the Carter/Brezhnev channel." Shulman considered it "kindergarten stuff—not worthy of the United States" and wondered, "Why do we have to be so gratuitously snotty?"[75]

Beset by a struggling economy and a series of poorly handled foreign policy crises, Carter appeared weak and out of touch as the 1980 election approached. Perhaps the final nail in his coffin came in April 1980, when the United States completely bungled a hostage rescue attempt, leaving eight Americans dead in the Iranian desert after a helicopter collided with a refueling plane. The Iranian government triumphantly displayed the charred bodies, adding to the humiliation. Secretary of State Cyrus Vance, who had consistently opposed this harebrained scheme, resigned in protest—something no secretary of state had done since William Jennings Bryan. He wrote his letter of resignation four days before the ill-fated raid. Columnist Mary McGrory noted that Vance had served in the Johnson administration during another war he had come to oppose and knew full well that his resignation would be divisive at a critical time. In fact, she wrote, "He apparently intends it to be. He found out a long time ago that keeping your mouth shut during discussions of madness is often the greatest disservice you can do your country."[76] Carter's approval rating plummeted to 40 percent.

Although widely recognized as the most respected member of the administration, Vance had been increasingly marginalized for quite some time as Brzezinski's hawkish views drowned out Vance's efforts at diplomacy. Vance's influence had steadily waned and, by the late 1970s, virtually disappeared. The *Washington Post* observed, "Mr. Vance had fallen out of phase with the president.

Brzezinski and Secretary of State Cyrus Vance. Although widely recognized as the most respected member of the administration, Vance was marginalized as Brzezinski's hawkish views drowned out the secretary of state's efforts at diplomacy. In April 1980, Vance resigned in protest after the United States completely bungled an attempt to rescue the American hostages in Tehran, leaving eight Americans dead in the Iranian desert after a helicopter collided with a refueling plane.

The secretary, and the early Carter, spoke for a benevolent and rationalistic world in which the United States, by accommodating certain legitimate imperatives of others, would find its proper place. The world to which Mr. Carter, much more than Mr. Vance, has sought to adjust recently is one in which factors of power and perversity loom large." [77] As the *Wall Street Journal* noted, the motivating force behind Vance's decision was "the increasingly hawkish tone in the administration's foreign policy," beginning in 1978 with the president "buying the case put by . . . Brzezinski." [78] Vance weighed in a few days later, telling an interviewer that the national security advisor should act as the coordinator of different views, "But he should not be the one who makes foreign policy or who expresses foreign policy to the public." [79]

Carter himself entered the fray a few days later. In what seemed a very petty reaction, he told a Philadelphia town meeting that his new secretary of state, Edmund Muskie, would be "a much stronger and more statesmanlike senior citizen figure who will be a more evocative spokesman for our nation's policy" than Vance had been. For Carter, who had been holed up in the White House throughout the Iran hostage crisis, a symbolic hostage of his own making, it was the first major public address outside Washington in over six months. [80]

Following the Iranian Revolution, U.S. officials cozied up to Iraqi dictator Saddam Hussein, whom they saw as a regional counterweight to the hostile

Iranian regime. They feared that Iranian-style Islamic fundamentalism could threaten pro-American regimes in Kuwait, Saudi Arabia, and Jordan. Brzezinski strategized ways to sever Iraq from the Soviet orbit. In September 1980, Saddam, with at least tacit U.S. approval, invaded neighboring Iran, attacking across the Shatt al-Arab waterway leading to the Persian Gulf. Iraq, however, did not secure the easy victory that U.S. intelligence sources had predicted. Within a week, the United Nations called for a cease-fire. In late October, Carter, playing both sides, announced that if the Iranians released the U.S. hostages, the United States would send the $300 million to $500 million in arms that had been purchased by the prior regime. Reaganites smelled an "October surprise" that would hand Carter the election. In what Carter White House Iran aide and Columbia University political scientist Gary Sick called "a political coup," a group of Reagan supporters were alleged to have cut a deal with the Iranian government. At the time, the presidential race was still tight. Some mid-October polls even had Carter in the lead. The details are murky and impossible to confirm, but it appears that Reagan campaign officials met with Iranian leaders and promised to allow Israel to ship arms to Iran if Iran would hold the hostages until Reagan won the election. In response to a 1992 query from Indiana Congressman Lee Hamilton, the Supreme Soviet's Committee on Defense and Security Issues reported that a series of secret meetings had taken place in Europe between top Reagan campaign officials and Iranian officials. The Soviet report identified Reagan campaign manager and future CIA Director William Casey, vice presidential candidate and former CIA Director George Bush as attending and offering substantially more military supplies than the Carter team was offering.[81] Iran released the embassy personnel on January 21, 1981, Reagan's first day in office. The United States continued arms sales to Iran via Israel, often channeled through private dealers, for several years. An early chance to end the war, which Saddam offered to do in return for Iraqi control of the Shatt al-Arab waterway and an Iranian promise not to interfere in Iraq, was also squandered. With the United States helping fuel the conflict, the Iran-Iraq War would continue for eight years, leaving, some estimate, over a million dead and costing over a trillion dollars.

Chapter 11

THE REAGAN YEARS:

Death Squads for Democracy

In 1987, President Ronald Reagan threw down the gauntlet in Berlin: "General Secretary Gorbachev, if you seek peace, if you seek prosperity for the Soviet Union and Eastern Europe, if you seek liberalization: Come here to this gate! Mr. Gorbachev, open this gate! Mr. Gorbachev, tear down this wall!"

And on November 9, 1989, less than two and a half years after Ronald Reagan spoke those stirring words, the wall came down. The Soviet Empire in Eastern Europe soon crumbled. In 1991, the Soviet Union itself collapsed. The Cold War was over. Many credit Reagan with winning the Cold War. And some lionize him as one of the United States' great presidents. But was Reagan really the heroic champion of freedom and democracy who brought closure to the most dangerous era in human history? Or was there a darker side to the man and his administration that made a mockery of his words? What really lay behind the smiling facade of this most unlikely of presidents?

Ronald Reagan, the folksy, homespun actor turned General Electric pitchman, had been California governor since 1967. He espoused strong family values but was estranged from his children and was the first president to divorce. A man of limited knowledge but deep religious beliefs and strong conservative convictions, he provided little guidance on policy and had no interest in or grasp of detail. His vice president, George H. W. Bush, confessed to Soviet Ambassador Anatoly Dobrynin that he at first found Reagan's views on international relations "almost unimaginable." Bush, Dobrynin wrote, was "simply amazed to see to what extent Reagan was dominated by Hollywood clichés and the ideas of his wealthy but conservative and poorly educated friends from California."[1] National Security Council Soviet expert Richard Pipes admitted that at NSC meetings the president seemed "really lost, out of his depth, uncomfortable." Very early in the new administration, counterterrorism coordinator Anthony Quainton was summoned to brief the president. In Quainton's words, "I gave that briefing to the President, who was joined by the Vice President, the head of CIA, the head of the FBI, and a number of National Security Council members. After a couple of jelly beans, the President dozed off. That . . . was quite unnerving."[2]

Jimmy Carter was deeply troubled by Reagan's complete lack of curiosity when he tried to brief the incoming president on the challenges he would face, assessments of world leaders, and command and control of nuclear weapons. Carter aide Jody Powell recounted, "The boss really thought it was important for Reagan to know this stuff before he was sworn in and as he ran through it he couldn't believe that Reagan wasn't asking any questions. He thought maybe Reagan wasn't taking any notes because he didn't have a pad and pencil and finally offered him one, but Reagan said, no thanks; he could remember it. It was just the damnedest thing."[3]

Many of Reagan's close associates were struck by the depth of his ignorance. Upon returning from his late 1982 Latin American tour, Reagan told reporters, "Well, I learned a lot. . . . You'd be surprised. They're all individual countries."[4] Canadian Prime Minister Pierre Trudeau wondered, "What planet is that man living on?" when the president told him that "the Soviets [had brought] an American priest to Moscow in order to send him back to be a spokesman for Actors Equity."[5] Speaker of the House Tip O'Neill was startled when Reagan, admiring O'Neill's desk that had belonged to Grover Cleveland, told him that he had played Cleveland in the movie *The Winning Season*. O'Neill reminded him that the desk had belonged to President Cleveland, not Grover Cleveland Alexander, the pitcher. O'Neill, who served in the House for thirty-four years, said that Reagan "knows less than any President I've ever known."[6]

Reagan's simplistic worldview seemed to be a pastiche stitched together from Hallmark greeting cards, Currier and Ives lithographs, Benjamin Franklin aphorisms, Hollywood epics, and Chinese fortune cookies. He wrote, "I'd always felt that from our deeds it must be clear to anyone that Americans were a moral people who . . . had always used our power only as a force for good in the world."[7]

He often displayed a striking inability to differentiate between reality and fantasy. In a late 1983 Oval Office meeting, he told Israeli Prime Minister Yitzhak Shamir that as a photographer during the Second World War he had filmed the Allies liberating the Nazi death camps and had been so moved by the suffering he witnessed that he had decided to keep a copy of the film in case he ever encountered a Holocaust skeptic. Shamir was so impressed with Reagan's story that he repeated it to his cabinet and it was printed in the Israeli paper *Ma'ariv*. Reagan later repeated a variant of the story to Simon Wiesenthal and Rabbi Marvin Hier, telling them he had been with the Signal Corps filming the camps and had shown

Ronald Reagan was one of the least intellectually curious men to ever occupy the White House. Counterterrorism coordinator Anthony Quainton recalled being summoned to the White House early in the new administration: "I gave that briefing to the President, who was joined by the Vice President, the head of CIA, the head of the FBI, and a number of National Security Council members. After a couple of jelly beans, the President dozed off. That . . . was quite unnerving."

the film to someone just a year after the war. Hearing the story, *Washington Post* reporter Lou Cannon noted that Reagan had never left the United States during or immediately after the war. The story was entirely fanciful.[8]

Reporters then had a field day revealing other Reagan whoppers. *Chicago Tribune* columnist Mike Royko, perhaps to dispel the notion that the president's flights of fancy were a product of old age or related to his diminishing mental powers, wrote that he first became aware of Reagan's habit of altering the truth in 1968 when, to highlight how lawless society was becoming, Reagan asserted that eight Chicago police officers had been killed in one recent month alone. Royko, curious, discovered that no cops had been killed in Chicago in months and only one or two in the entire year.[9] Reagan often repeated his story about the Chicago "welfare queen" with eighty names, thirty addresses, and twelve Social Security cards who had a tax-free income of over $150,000. The numbers would change—she sometimes had 127 names and received over one hundred different checks—but the point—an attack on greedy, dishonest blacks who stole from hardworking white Americans—remained the same.[10]

Compiling lists of Reaganisms became a national pastime. Reagan often made up apocryphal quotes from prominent individuals including Oliver Wendell

Holmes and Winston Churchill. Perhaps it was fitting, therefore, that his press spokesman, Larry Speakes, admitted that he had made up quotes and attributed them to Reagan, anticipating what he would have wanted to say.[11]

For meetings with visitors and even with his own cabinet officials, Reagan read from three-by-five-inch file cards provided by staffers. Visitors would be mortified on those occasions when he unknowingly read from the wrong set of cards. He extrapolated from personal experience to form his views of the world. Facts could be ignored or contradicted when they didn't support his preferred narrative. When William Clark, a former California Supreme Court justice, took over as national security advisor in 1982, he was shocked to discover how little Reagan actually knew about the world. He instructed the Pentagon and CIA to produce films explaining security issues and describing the world leaders Reagan would be meeting.[12]

Reagan's disengaged style and lack of foreign policy experience left the door open to palace intrigue among his subordinates, who were eager to fill the void. Vice President Bush displayed firm, if nefarious, establishment credentials, with long-standing family ties to Rockefeller, Morgan, and Harriman interests. After graduating from Yale, he had moved to Texas, become an oilman, and run unsuccessfully for the Senate in 1970. Richard Nixon had engineered his appointment as Republican Party chairman.

Jeane Kirkpatrick would also play a prominent role in shaping foreign policy. A conservative Democrat and Georgetown political scientist who supported Reagan because of his staunch anticommunism, she was rewarded with an appointment as ambassador to the United Nations. Kirkpatrick supplied the Reaganites with a justification for supporting right-wing dictatorships, calling them "authoritarian" regimes instead of "totalitarian" ones. Along with her colleague Ernest Lefever, who directed Georgetown's Ethics and Public Policy Center, she contemptuously dismissed Jimmy Carter's concern for human rights and reform programs. Lefever, a defender of repressive regimes from El Salvador to South Africa, became assistant secretary of state for human rights. The *New York Times* described him as "an ultraconservative who sneers at existing policy as sentimental nonsense and believes it is profound error to embarrass allies, however repressive, with talk about habeas corpus." He dismissed concerns about torture in Argentina and Chile because it was "a residual practice of the Iberian tradition." His center had recently been assailed for accepting a large contribution from Nestlé after conducting a study supportive of its campaign to convince mothers to replace breast-feeding with infant formula despite evidence that the switch had contributed to a tripling of infant malnutrition in underdeveloped nations.[13] In June, the Senate Foreign Relations Committee rejected Lefever as unqualified for the position. Five of the committee's nine Republicans joined

*Reagan meets with UN Ambassador Jeane Kirkpatrick. A conservative
Democrat and Georgetown political scientist who supported Reagan
because of his staunch anticommunism, Kirkpatrick played a large role
in supplying the Reaganites with a justification for supporting right-wing
"authoritarian" dictatorships instead of left-wing "totalitarian" ones.*

with all eight Democrats in the vote. He was replaced by the like-minded Elliott
Abrams.

Not everyone welcomed the opportunity for freelancing that resulted from
Reagan's inattention. General Colin Powell, the deputy to National Security
Advisor Frank Carlucci, recalled, "The President's passive management style
placed a tremendous burden on us. Until we got used to it, we felt uneasy implementing recommendations without a clear decision. . . . One morning . . . Frank
moaned . . . , 'My God, we didn't sign on to run this country!'" James Baker, who
served Reagan as campaign manager, White House chief of staff, and Treasury
secretary, described the resulting foreign policy structure as "a witches' brew of
intrigue . . . and separate agendas."[14] Though often at one another's throats over
control of policy, Reagan's top advisors shared an enthusiasm for covert operations. Together with Secretary of State Alexander Haig and Bush, they initiated
operations in Central America and Africa through the National Security Planning Group, while supporting Soviet-bloc dissidents and expanding Carter's
programs in Afghanistan.

Global economic travails made their job easier. The rapid economic growth
experienced by resource-rich third-world countries in the 1960s and early 1970s
ground to a halt by the mid-1970s as the worldwide economic decline undercut

income earned through raw-material exports. Third-world debt ballooned, crippling the prospects for continued development and devastating already impoverished populations. Revolutionary states that had overthrown colonialist regimes and experimented with socialism were among the hardest hit, leading many to question the viability of leftist development models. Reagan saw the resulting unrest as an opportunity to topple unfriendly governments and prove the superiority of capitalism.

The Soviet economy also hit the skids in the late 1970s, beginning a sustained period of stagnation and decline that only worsened when oil prices collapsed in 1982. Military expenditures, which absorbed almost a quarter of the gross domestic product (GDP), were further weakening the economy. Reagan was determined to exploit the situation. At his first press conference, on January 29, 1981, he unleashed an anti-Communist diatribe that reversed almost two decades of progress in easing Cold War tensions:

> Well, so far détente's been a one-way street that the Soviet Union has used
> to pursue its own aims . . . the promotion of world revolution and a one-
> world Socialist or Communist state, whichever word you want to use . . .
> they, at the same time, have openly and publicly declared that the only
> morality they recognize is what will further their cause, meaning they
> reserve unto themselves the right to commit any crime, to lie, to cheat, in
> order to attain that, and that is moral, not immoral, and we operate on a
> different set of standards.[15]

The CIA, which had largely been kept in check by Carter, played a major role in Reagan's new anti-Communist crusade. CIA analysts had long prided themselves on professionalism and distance from the operations side of the Agency. That would not fly with the Reagan team. The assault that began via Bush's Team B reached fruition under Casey. Administration hard-liners wanted intelligence that supported their view of a dangerous, hostile, and expansion-minded Soviet Union regardless of how far such a perception departed from reality. Casey, a multimillionaire Wall Street lawyer and devout Irish Catholic, had come to the CIA, according to his deputy Robert Gates, "to wage war against the Soviet Union." According to Gates, "the Reaganites saw their arrival as a hostile takeover."[16] Casey had read Claire Sterling's *The Terror Network* and was convinced that the Soviet Union was the fount of all international terrorism. According to Melvin Goodman, head of the CIA's office for Soviet analysis, "Several of us met with Casey to try to tell the director that much of Sterling's so-called evidence was in fact CIA 'black propaganda,' anticommunist allegations planted in the European press." But, he added, "Casey contemptuously noted . . . that

Reagan with CIA Director William Casey, a multimillionaire Wall Street lawyer and devout Irish Catholic, who had come to the CIA, according to his deputy Robert Gates, "to wage war against the Soviet Union." Under Casey, the CIA painted a picture of a hostile, expansionist USSR, an image that didn't accord with the facts.

he 'learned more from Sterling than from'" all of them. Others who touted the Sterling line included Haig, Wolfowitz, State Department consultant Michael Ledeen, and State Department official Robert "Bud" McFarlane.[17] CIA experts, however, knew that the Soviets, for all their faults, actually discouraged terrorism.

Casey and Gates began a purge of analysts who refused to knuckle under. If their reports failed to support the administration line, Casey just wrote his own conclusions. Goodman, who served as a senior CIA Soviet analyst from 1966 to 1986, observed, "The CIA caricature of a Soviet military octopus whose tentacles reached the world over supported the administration's view of the 'Evil Empire.'" Goodman blamed "the fact that the CIA missed the most important historical development in its history—the collapse of the Soviet Empire and the Soviet Union itself"—largely on "the culture and process that Gates established in his directorate."[18]

While CIA intelligence was being dismantled, operations were running amok. Colonel John Waghelstein, who headed the U.S. military advisory team in El Salvador, stated, "Real counterinsurgency techniques are a step toward the primitive." That description could be applied to the efforts of U.S.-backed and trained government forces in El Salvador and Guatemala and to the U.S.-run insurgency in Nicaragua. These "freedom fighters," as Reagan called them, routinely raped, tortured, castrated, mutilated, decapitated, and dismembered their victims.[19] To harden Guatemalan soldiers to the point where they were able to kill some 100,000 Mayan peasants between 1981 and 1983, army recruits were beaten, degraded, even submerged in sewage, and forced to remain covered in shit for extended periods of time. Broken and dehumanized, they carried out brutal acts. In December 1982, in the village of Dos Erres, the army slaughtered over 160 people, swinging the 65 child victims by their feet and smashing their heads against the rocks. Just the day before, Ronald Reagan had visited Guatemala as part of a tour of Latin America and complained that its president, General Efraín Ríos Montt, a born-again evangelical Christian who had recently seized power in a military coup, had received "a bum rap," assuring reporters that the dictator was "totally committed to democracy." Reagan called him "a man of great personal integrity and commitment."[20] In fact, he said that in light of Guatemala's improved human rights record, he was considering restoring military aid, which Carter had cut off in 1977 because of the government's deplorable human rights record. Reagan was apparently comfortable with Ríos Montt's explanation that "we have no scorched-earth policy. We have a policy of scorched communists."[21] U.S. Ambassador Frederic Chapin announced, "The killings have stopped.... The Guatemalan government has come out of the darkness and into the light."[22]

Reagan also met that day with Honduran President Roberto Suazo Córdova, who was waging his own U.S.-backed counterinsurgency war. According to the *Los Angeles Times,* the meeting occurred in a "drab building" at "a heavily guarded military airport in eastern Honduras. Soldiers manned anti-aircraft guns in the sugar cane fields bordering the runway, and military helicopters patrolled overhead.... The weather was hot and humid, and the pinstripe suits worn by White House officials looked conspicuously out of place." Secretary of State George Shultz whispered to one reporter, "This is the strangest thing I've ever seen."

The trip had its share of unscripted moments. In Costa Rica, Sergio Erick Ardón, head of the People's Revolutionary Movement, rose in the balcony of the National Theater and loudly indicted the U.S. president and his "militarization of Central America."[23]

In Colombia, Reagan was blindsided by President Belisario Betancur Cuartas, who used his toast to criticize Reagan's efforts to "isolate" and "exclude" Cuba and Nicaragua from hemispheric peace and development efforts while tolerating murder by right-wing governments: "Our responsibility as heads of state does not allow us to remain unmoved by the daily opening of gravesites in the ground of our common geography: 30,000 graves in El Salvador, to mention only one nation, shock the drowsy conscience of leaders." The Reagan entourage was furious with this attack. Nor were they pleased with the riots and demonstrations in downtown Bogotá or the crowds lining the streets greeting Reagan's speeding motorcade with shouts of "Fuera!" or "Yanqui go home!"[24] Unable to get all the "individual countries" straight, Reagan insulted his hosts in Brazil by saluting "the people of Bolivia."[25]

Reagan's sorry spectacle of giving absolution to murderous dictators did not go unremarked back home. *New York Times* columnist Anthony Lewis began an op-ed piece, appropriately titled "Howdy, Genghis," with "Under the name of 'anti-Communism,' the President of the United States has just had a friendly meeting with a tyrant who makes a policy of mass murder. That is what has happened, in Ronald Reagan's administration, to Americans' belief that their country stands for basic human decency in the world." Lewis described reports of Guatemalan soldiers descending on rural villages in helicopters, hacking women to death with machetes, torching huts, and gouging out eyes as part of a campaign to take the countryside back from the guerrillas. Lewis quoted the *Boston Globe's* assessment of this antiguerrilla campaign as falling "somewhere between a pogrom and genocide." He noted the fact that Reagan's embrace of "torturers and murderers" extended beyond the leaders of Guatemala and El Salvador to include recent visits to Washington from the dictators of South Korea and the Philippines and an upcoming one from Muhammad Zia-ul-Haq of Pakistan, who since taking power in 1977 "has eliminated the political opposition and resorted regularly to torture." Lewis ended with a poignant reminder that has rung true throughout all the decades of the American Empire: "The shame marks all of us. When the economic follies of the Reagan Administration have been forgotten, its insensitivity to human cruelty will still stain the name of the United States."[26]

The sense of outrage so eloquently expressed by Lewis was reinforced by reports released by Amnesty International, Americas Watch, the Council on Hemispheric Affairs, and other human rights groups, detailing the ongoing murders and atrocities, and by remarks by a Guatemalan Jesuit priest, Reverend Ricardo Falla, S.J., at a press conference arranged by the American Anthropological Association. Falla, who was trained at Georgetown, charged that the purpose of organized massacres of Indians was to leave "no survivors" and hence "no memory" of what happened. He elaborated, "That is why babies and children are killed. It's really incredible. These children, if they survive, will avenge the death of their parents. . . . These little ones are slit open with knives, or their heads are broken against rocks or beams of houses." Father Falla described a massacre at San Francisco de Nentón, which transpired over an eight-hour period and included a break for dinner: "After killing the women and children, they stopped to eat the steaks which they had roasted from a bull they killed shortly after their arrival. They laughed at old people who cried out like sheep when the blunt knives did not cut their throats. They sang while they listened to the radios they stole from the Indians later in the evening, when the massacre was finished."[27]

In January 1983, Reagan ended the embargo on military aid. He authorized sales of military hardware. But Congress's resistance forced Guatemala to rely on military aid primarily from close U.S. allies Israel and Taiwan. Israel was also providing military aid to El Salvador and the Nicaragua contras. CIA support for the Guatemalan military continued unabated. In August 1983, Óscar Humberto Mejía Victores overthrew Ríos Montt in a coup, ending the period known as "La Violencia" but not the violence itself. Following the coup, the CIA and State Department reported an increase in political killings and abductions. In February 1984, Ambassador Frederic Chapin cabled Washington about what he called "the horrible human rights realities in Guatemala."[28] The next day, officials in the State Department approved a secret report urging Congress to resume military aid to Guatemala in light of its improved human rights record.

In 1986, in a secret report, the State Department acknowledged a systematic campaign by "security forces and rightist paramilitary groups" to kidnap and murder potential rural social workers, medical personnel, and *campesinos* dating back to 1966 and peaking in 1984. Guatemala's official Historical Clarification Commission issued a report in 1999 detailing the 626 massacres of Mayan villages carried out by the Guatemalan army, which it termed a "genocide." It charged the CIA and other U.S. government agencies with providing direct and indirect support for the Guatemalan slaughter, whose death toll it estimated at 200,000.[29]

The United States was perpetrating atrocities of a different sort in Nicaragua. Former members of Somoza's thuggish Nicaraguan national guard had been gathering across the border in Honduras, where, with CIA Director Casey's assistance, they plotted a return to power. They called themselves the *contrarevolucionarios,* or "contras" for short. Here, as elsewhere, Casey transformed Carter's rudimentary covert operations into a massive undertaking. He set up a Central America Task Force to run things. He installed Duane Clarridge to head the Latin America division. Clarridge was the perfect foil. He knew nothing about Latin America, never having worked in the region, and spoke no Spanish.

U.S. Ambassador to Nicaragua Anthony Quainton pinpointed the start of the war for an interviewer: "The secret war began on March 15, 1982, when the CIA, using Nicaraguan agents, blew up the bridges that connected Nicaragua with Honduras." It had actually begun earlier. That December, Congress banned the use of government funds to overthrow the Sandinista government. In the administration, moderates like Shultz had little voice as hard-line right wingers increasingly set a ruthless foreign policy in Nicaragua and beyond. Reagan lied to Congress about what the CIA was up to. Casey lied repeatedly, deliberately misleading the House and Senate select intelligence committees. According to

Gates, "Casey was guilty of contempt of Congress from the day he was sworn in."[30] Shultz later said that he had complained to National Security Advisor Frank Carlucci in January 1987: "I told him that I had no confidence in the intelligence community, that I had been misled, lied to, cut out."[31] Congress nonetheless significantly expanded the intelligence budget, with much of the appropriation going to the CIA.

In order to make an end run around Congress, Casey and NSC official Oliver North concocted an elaborate illegal operation. Aided by Israeli arms dealers, the United States sold missiles to its enemies in Iran at exorbitant prices and used the profits to fund the contras, with Latin American drug dealers often serving as intermediaries and receiving easier access to U.S. markets in return. With U.S. funds and CIA guidance, the contra army grew to 15,000. The CIA also recruited contract mercenaries from countries like Guatemala and El Salvador who launched independent attacks from offshore, bombing and mining coastal targets and commercial ports.

Reagan defended the United States' covert war with a flight of fancy that bore little resemblance to the reality on the ground in 1984. "The Nicaraguan people," he said, "are trapped in a totalitarian dungeon, trapped by a military dictatorship that impoverishes them while its rulers live in privileged and protected luxury and openly boast their revolution will spread to Nicaragua's neighbors as well. It's a dictatorship made all the more insulting, all the more dangerous by the unwanted presence of thousands of Cuban, Soviet-bloc and radical Arab helpers."[32] Reagan went so far as to call the contras "the moral equivalent of the Founding Fathers," a comparison so odious that it drew a sharp rebuke from the Organization of American Historians. Reagan's "moral equivalents" were notorious for torturing, mutilating, and slaughtering civilians. Employing terrorist tactics, the contras destroyed schools, health care clinics, cooperatives, bridges, and power stations and were responsible for the deaths of most of the 30,000 civilians killed in the war. One advisor to the Joint Chiefs of Staff called them "the strangest national liberation organization in the world." In his view, they were "just a bunch of killers."[33] The U.S. Embassy reported one former contra leader's assertion that civilians who refused to join the contras were "shot or stabbed to death" and others were "burned to death in smelting ovens." He said that kidnapped young girls were "raped night and day."[34]

Atrocities were also committed in El Salvador, where U.S. leaders decided to test their new post-Vietnam counterinsurgency doctrines and try to defeat an uprising without a large commitment of U.S. forces. First they expanded and modernized the Salvadoran army, which, by 1983, reached 53,000 troops, many of whom were trained in Fort Benning, Georgia, or in the U.S.-run School of the

Americas in Panama. Former U.S. Ambassador Robert White, who served under both Carter and Reagan, testified before Congress:

> For 50 years El Salvador was ruled by a corrupt and brutal alliance of the rich and the military. The young officers revolt of 1979 attempted to break that alliance. It was then Reagan renewed tolerance and acceptance of the extreme right which led to the emergence of the National Republican Alliance, ARENA, and the rise of ex-Major Roberto D'Aubuisson.
>
> ARENA is a violent Fascist party modeled after the Nazis and certain revolutionary Communist groups. . . . The founders and chief supporters of ARENA are rich Salvadoran exiles headquartered in Miami and civilian activists in El Salvador. ARENA'S military arm comprises officers and men of the Salvadoran Army and security forces. . . . My Embassy devoted considerable resources to identifying the sources of rightwing violence and their contacts in Miami, Florida. . . . the Miami Six explained . . . that to rebuild the country, it must first be destroyed totally, the economy must be wrecked, unemployment must be massive, the junta must be ousted and a "good" military officer brought to power who will carry out a total cleansing—*limpieza*—killing 3 or 4 or 500,000 people. . . . Who are these madmen and how do they operate? . . . the principal figures are six enormously wealthy former landowners. . . . They hatch plots, hold constant meetings and communicate instructions to D'Aubuisson.[35]

In March 1981, the CIA informed Vice President Bush that D'Aubuisson, the "principal henchman for wealthy landlords," was running "the right-wing death squads that have murdered several thousand suspected leftists and leftist sympathizers during the past year." Three American Maryknoll nuns and a Catholic layperson who had been involved in humanitarian relief work had been raped and slaughtered shortly before Reagan's inauguration. UN ambassador-designate Jeane Kirkpatrick insisted, "the nuns were not just nuns" but FMLN "political activists." Secretary of State Alexander Haig called them "pistol-packing nuns" and suggested to a congressional committee that "perhaps the vehicle the nuns were riding in may have tried to run a roadblock."[36]

One atrocity particularly stands out. U.S.-trained and armed Salvadoran troops slaughtered the 767 inhabitants of the village of El Mozote in late 1981. The victims, including 358 children under age thirteen, were stabbed, decapitated, and machine-gunned. Girls and women were raped. When *New York Times* correspondent Raymond Bonner tried to expose what had occurred, the *Wall Street Journal* and other pro-Reagan newspapers assaulted Bonner's credibility.

Echoing Reagan, who anointed the contras "the moral equivalent of the Founding Fathers," the College Republicans distributed this flyer calling for support for "Nicaraguan Freedom Fighters." Those "Freedom Fighters" were notorious for torturing, mutilating, and slaughtering civilians.

The *Times* buckled under pressure and pulled Bonner out of El Salvador. Administration officials helped cover up the massacre. Conditions worsened. In late 1982, the Council on Hemispheric Affairs reported that El Salvador, along with Guatemala, had the worst record of human rights abuses in Latin America: "Decapitation, torture, disemboweling, disappearances and other forms of cruel punishment were reported to be norms of paramilitary behavior sanctioned by the Salvadoran government."[37] However, Elliott Abrams, assistant secretary of state for human rights, testified that the reports of death-squad involvement were "not credible."[38]

George Bush had trouble sympathizing with the suffering of the people in the United States' backyard. Before Pope John Paul II visited Central America, Bush said he couldn't understand how Catholic clergy could reconcile their religious beliefs with Marxist philosophy and tactics and support the insurgents. Reverend Theodore Hesburgh, president of Notre Dame, tried to explain that poverty and social injustice could easily lead priests to supporting Marxists or anyone else challenging the status quo. "Maybe it makes me a right-wing extremist," Bush replied, "but I'm puzzled. I just don't understand it."[39]

U.S. economic and military aid grew steadily during these years, spurred by the 1984 Kissinger Commission on Central America. Senator Jesse Helms was the point man for this effort in Congress. Administration officials deliberately concealed U.S. government documents implicating the Salvadoran National Police, the National Guard, and the Treasury Police so that congressional funding would continue. Under Carter and Reagan, Congress funneled nearly

$5 billion to the tiny country, making it the largest recipient of U.S. foreign aid, per capita, in the world. Meanwhile, the death squads continued to cleave a path of destruction. The death toll reached 70,000. Approximately half a million Salvadorans tried to escape the violence by migrating to the United States in the 1980s, but most were turned back. In 1984, U.S. immigration officials admitted approximately one in forty Salvadoran asylum seekers, while almost all the anti-Communist applicants fleeing Nicaragua were welcomed.

In 1980, *Commentary* magazine, the United States' leading neoconservative journal, published a series of essays decrying what conservatives called the "Vietnam syndrome"—the revulsion against the Vietnam War that made Americans squeamish about using force to resolve international conflicts. Reagan agreed: "For too long, we have lived with the 'Vietnam Syndrome.' . . . Over and over they told us for nearly 10 years that we were the aggressors bent on imperialistic conquests. . . . It is time we recognized that ours was, in truth, a noble cause. . . . We dishonor the memory of 50,000 young Americans who died in that cause when we give way to feelings of guilt." [40]

Bogged down in protracted proxy wars in Nicaragua and El Salvador, Reagan hungered for an easy military victory that would restore Americans' self-confidence and get the Vietnam monkey off America's back. His opportunity came in 1983 when a radical faction overthrew the revolutionary government of Maurice Bishop in Grenada, a tiny Caribbean island with 100,000 inhabitants, murdering its leaders. Before his death, Bishop had alleged that a campaign was under way to destabilize his nation by "the vicious beasts of imperialism"—the United States. [41] Using the resulting instability as a pretext for action, U.S. officials decided to invade and topple the new government, despite clear opposition from the United Nations, the Organization of American States (OAS), and even British Prime Minister Margaret Thatcher. They pressured reluctant Caribbean nations to call for U.S. intervention.

The timing proved fortunate for the administration. While preparing the invasion, the United States suffered a humiliating setback when a powerful truck bomb blew up a U.S. Marine Corps barracks in Lebanon, leaving 241 dead. Desperate for a distraction, Reagan announced that the invasion of Grenada was needed to rescue endangered American medical students on the island. The students, however, were in no immediate danger. When the dean of the medical school polled them, 90 percent said they wanted to stay. To avoid even the minimalist kind of scrutiny the United States had received in Vietnam, U.S. officials banned media from accompanying invading forces for their own "safety" and offered government footage. The 7,000 U.S. invaders encountered more resistance than they had bargained for from a small force of poorly armed Cubans. The entire operation was logistically bungled from the start. Twenty-nine U.S.

*Skulls of victims murdered by a death squad lie discarded in a lava
field in El Playon, El Salvador. In March 1981, the CIA informed
Vice President Bush that the Salvadoran leader Roberto D'Aubuisson
was running "the right-wing death squads that have murdered several
thousand suspected leftists and leftist sympathizers during the past year."
But with the United States funding and promoting counterinsurgency
in the Central American nation, neoconservative Reagan officials
denied reports tying atrocities to the Salvadoran government.*

soldiers died, and more than 100 were wounded. Nine helicopters were lost.
Most troops were quickly withdrawn.

Congressman Dick Cheney of Wyoming participated in the first post-
invasion congressional delegation and applauded the United States' new can-
do image around the world. When another delegation member, Representative
Don Bonker of Washington, derided claims that the students had been at risk,
Cheney blasted him in a *Washington Post* op-ed. As if in a dress rehearsal for lying
about Iraq two decades later, Cheney claimed that "the Americans were in imminent danger," "every effort was made to secure their evacuation by diplomatic
means," and the new Grenadan government posed "a threat to the security of
the entire region."[42] Fellow delegation member Representative Ron Dellums of
California challenged Cheney's distortions, calling the invasion "a thinly veiled
effort to use American students and a tiny black Caribbean country to mask
the further militarization of American foreign policy." Dellums also dismissed
the claim of protecting the students, noting "our delegation could not find one
confirmed instance in which an American was threatened or endangered before
the invasion. In fact, the . . . campus was a mere 20 meters from an unprotected
beach. If the safety of the students was the primary goal, why did it take the U.S.

forces three days to reach it?"[43] By a ten-to-one margin, the UN General Assembly "deeply deplor[ed]" the "armed intervention in Grenada," which it called "a flagrant violation of international law."[44]

Among the casualties were at least twenty-one mental patients killed in a misguided bombing attack on their hospital. General Edward Trobaugh, commander of the 82nd Airborne Division, told reporters that the Grenadan People's Revolutionary Army had been inept but that the small contingent of Cubans on the island, many of whom were there to build an airstrip, had fought well. He informed visiting congressmen that there was no indication that the medical students had ever been threatened. Reagan criticized the press for labeling the action an "invasion" when it was really a "rescue mission."[45]

In his address to the American people, Reagan emphasized the threat to U.S. security, pointing to "a warehouse of military equipment [that] contained weapons and ammunition stacked almost to the ceiling, enough to supply thousands of terrorists." Reagan dispelled the notion that Grenada was an idyllic tropical escape: "Grenada, we were told, was a friendly island paradise for tourism. Well, it wasn't. It was a Soviet-Cuban colony, being readied as a major military bastion to export terror and undermine democracy." "We got there just in time," he asserted, one step ahead of catastrophe.[46]

Afterward Reagan proudly announced, "Our days of weakness are over. Our military forces are back on their feet and standing tall."[47] Even the sting of humiliation in Vietnam had been alleviated. U.S. soldiers in Vietnam, he claimed, had been "denied permission to win." "We didn't lose the war," he insisted. "When the war was all over and we'd come home—that's when the war was lost." In December 1988, a National Defense Commission report concluded, "Our failure in Vietnam still casts a shadow over U.S. intervention anywhere."[48]

The U.S. attempt to avenge the killing of marines in Lebanon was badly bungled. Casey worked closely with the Saudis to assassinate the Hezbollah leader, Sheikh Muhammad Hussein Fadlallah, exploding a massive car bomb outside his residence in 1985. Eighty people died and two hundred were wounded, but Fadlallah escaped unharmed.[49]

While running roughshod over Central America and the Caribbean, Reagan also trampled the United States' working class and poor, who were sacrificed to the exigencies of a massive military buildup, which was cheered on by the more than fifty members of the Committee on the Present Danger who held official positions. Right after the 1980 election, former Defense Secretary Melvin Laird had warned that a "defense spending binge" would be "the worst thing that could happen" to the United States.[50] Reagan ignored that advice, having campaigned on the fiction that the United States was militarily weak and vulnerable to a Soviet attack,

In late 1983, the United States used instability in Grenada as a pretext to invade the tiny island nation and topple its revolutionary government. In a logistically bungled operation, nineteen U.S. soldiers died, and more than a hundred were wounded. Nine helicopters were lost. Most of the troops were quickly withdrawn.

Medical students wait to be evacuated during the U.S. invasion of Grenada. Reagan claimed that the invasion was necessary to rescue the endangered students, but the students were actually in little danger. When polled by the dean of the medical school, 90 percent said they wanted to stay.

saying "we're in greater danger today than we were the day after Pearl Harbor. Our military is absolutely incapable of defending this country." [51]

Reagan's scare tactics worked. By 1985, he had increased defense spending by a staggering 51 percent over 1980 expenditures. To finance this, he slashed federal support for discretionary domestic programs by 30 percent, effectively transferring $70 billion from domestic programs to the military. [52]

Senator Howard M. Metzenbaum praised Budget Director David Stockman's adroitness at cutting the budget, "but," he added, "I also think you've been cruel, inhumane and unfair." Four hundred eight thousand people lost their eligibility for Aid to Families with Dependent Children (AFDC) by 1983, and 299,000 saw their benefits cut. Reagan prodded Congress into cutting $2 billion out of the $12 billion food stamp budget and $1 billion from the $3.5 billion budget for school lunches. The budgets for Medicaid, child nutrition, housing, and energy assistance were also pared. Federal funds for cities were cut almost in half. [53] While waging war on the poor, Reagan cut the highest income tax rate, which was 70 percent when he took office, to 28 percent by the time he left.

New and upgraded weapons systems rolled off the assembly lines, including the long-delayed and very costly MX missile program, which moved missiles around loops that hid their precise location, making them largely invulnerable to a Soviet first strike. Reagan knew that the Soviets, whose economy was stagnant, would be hard pressed to keep pace.

The nuclear arms budget also grew by leaps and bounds. In 1981, George Kennan, the architect of U.S. containment policy, decried the continuing senseless buildup of nuclear weapons: "We have gone on piling weapon upon weapon, missile upon missile, new levels of destructiveness upon old ones. We have done this helplessly, almost involuntarily, like the victims of some sort of hypnotism, like men in a dream, like lemmings headed for the sea." [54]

Reagan and Bush were anything but helpless in their arms buildup. They rejected the widely held view that nuclear war would lead to mutual destruction and began planning to win such a war—an approach advocated by nuclear extremists like Colin Gray and Keith Payne, who declared in 1980, "The United States should plan to defeat the Soviet Union." They believed that the United States might lose 20 million citizens in the process. The key to surviving a nuclear attack, they posited, was an effective command-and-control structure to prevent chaos and keep lines of communication open. The military called this "C3": command, control, and communications. [55] Reagan invested heavily to ensure its invulnerability. Perversely, he projected such a war-winning strategy onto the Soviets. He pointed to a massive Soviet civil defense program as proof, even though no such program existed.

The Pentagon's master plan for 1984–1988 ranked defense of the Middle East second only to the defense of North America and Western Europe. The plan explained:

> Our principal objectives are to assure continued access to Persian Gulf oil and to prevent the Soviets from acquiring political-military control of the oil directly or through proxies. It is essential that the Soviet Union be confronted with the prospect of a major conflict should it seek to reach oil resources of the Gulf. Whatever the circumstances, we should be prepared to introduce American forces directly into the region should it appear that the security of access to Persian Gulf oil is threatened.[56]

To put this into effect, the United States spent a billion dollars modernizing military bases and deployed nuclear-armed cruise missiles to Comiso, Italy, from which they could reach targets throughout the Middle East. It inserted itself into the middle of the Iran-Iraq War. It provided arms to Iran, helping it turn the tide and begin advancing, by mid-1982, toward Basra, Iraq's second largest city. Administration officials then had a change of heart and decided to do "whatever was necessary and legal" to prevent an Iranian victory. They did so knowing full well that Iraq was using chemical weapons. On November 1, senior State Department official Jonathan Howe informed Secretary of State Shultz that Iraq was resorting to "almost daily use of CW" against Iran. In December 1983, Reagan sent special envoy Donald Rumsfeld to Baghdad to meet with Saddam Hussein. The U.S. Embassy reported that Saddam showed "obvious pleasure" at Rumsfeld's visit and the letter he presented from the president. Rumsfeld assured Saddam that the United States was doing all it could to cut off arms sales to Iran.[57]

Rumsfeld returned for a second visit the following March, partly to assure Saddam that the United States' priority was defeating Iran, not punishing Iraq for using chemical weapons. Howard Teicher, a Reagan administration NSC Iraq expert, later admitted in a sworn court affidavit that the United States had "actively supported the Iraqi war effort by supplying the Iraqis with billions of dollars of credits, by providing military intelligence and advice to the Iraqis, and by closely monitoring third country arms sales to Iraq to make sure Iraq had the military weaponry required." More than sixty officers at the Defense Intelligence Agency provided combat planning assistance. Teicher reported that Casey used a Chilean company to deliver cluster bombs, which could effectively repel Iran's human-wave attacks.[58] U.S., British, and German arms manufacturers happily supplied Iraq's growing needs. Under license by the Commerce Committee, U.S. companies shipped several strains of anthrax that were later used in Iraq's biological weapons program and insecticides that could be used for chemical war-fare. The Iraqi military brazenly warned in February 1984, "the invaders should know that for every harmful insect there is an insecticide capable of annihilating it whatever the number and Iraq possesses this annihilation insecticide." [59]

Iran asked for a UN Security Council investigation. Although U.S. intelligence reports confirmed Iran's charges, the United States remained silent for several more months, before finally criticizing the Iraqi use of chemical warfare in early March. But when Iran proposed a UN resolution condemning Iraq's use of chemi-cal weapons, U.S. Ambassador Kirkpatrick lobbied other countries to render "no decision." Upon the Iraqi ambassador's suggestion, the United States preempted the Iranian measure by getting a Security Council presidential statement in late March opposing the use of chemical weapons but not mentioning Iraq as the guilty party. In November 1984, the United States restored diplomatic relations with Iraq. Not only did the use of chemical warfare persist until the end of the war with Iran, but in late 1987, the Iraqi air force began dropping chemical weapons against Iraq's own Kurdish citizens, whom the government accused of supporting Iran. The attacks against rebel-controlled villages peaked with the chemical war-fare assault on the village of Halabjah in March 1988. Despite widespread outrage in the United States, including from many inside the administration, U.S. intel-ligence aid to Iraq actually increased in 1988 and, in December 1988, the govern-ment authorized a sale to Iraq of $1.5 million in insecticides by Dow Chemical, the manufacturer of the napalm used in Vietnam.

Infuriated by Iraq's use of chemical weapons and by U.S. tacit support for such heinous behavior, Ayatollah Ruhollah Khomeini, who had ended the shah's secret nuclear weapons program when he assumed power in 1979, condemning nuclear weapons as anti-Islamic, reversed course in 1984 and started the pro-gram back up again.

While the United States was strengthening its support for Saddam Hussein's Iraqi regime, Reagan continued his bombastic anti-Soviet rhetoric and provoca-tive behavior. In 1983, he urged his audience at the annual convention of the National Association of Evangelicals in Orlando, Florida, "to speak out against those who would place the United States in a position of military and moral infe-riority . . . [not] to ignore the facts of history and the aggressive impulses of an evil empire." [60] The United States deployed ground-launched cruise missiles to Great Britain and Pershing II missiles to West Germany in November 1983 and conducted Able Archer 83—a massive military test using nuclear weapons—that same month. By the end of 1983, U.S.-Soviet relations had reached their lowest point in more than two decades. The two nations were conducting proxy wars around the globe, and a real one seemed possible. Some Soviet officials were convinced that a U.S. attack was imminent.

Bellicose rhetoric frightened the public. *The Day After,* which was viewed by a huge television audience, and other nuclear-war movies heightened the sense of alarm and helped spark a massive nuclear freeze movement. Psychiatrists reported that children in both the United States and Soviet Union were experiencing an outbreak of nuclear nightmares not seen since the early 1960s.

Even nuclear weapons designers were not inured against the implications of the rising threat of nuclear war. Physicist Theodore Taylor had an epiphany during his first visit to the Soviet Union. He described the experience to psychiatrist Robert Jay Lifton, whose own probing scholarship had revolutionized the field of nuclear studies:

> Walking in Red Square in Moscow, Taylor saw many young people in wedding parties visiting Lenin's tomb and the Tomb of the Unknown Soldier and was impressed by how happy they looked. He experienced a flashback to the night of the birth of one of his children years before when, rather than being with his wife, he was at the Pentagon poring over intelligence data, including aerial photographs of central Moscow, in connection with potential plans for nuclear attack. Standing in Red Square, he began to weep uncontrollably: "It was seeing those happy-looking, specific people, going around, working their way up to the mausoleum. For any human being to contemplate setting off a bomb on top of all this, these people, is insane . . . a symptom of insanity." He had experienced such feelings before, but now for the first time "I literally set foot in the SU to see what it was that I was doing with all the details filled in." Before that, Moscow had been no more than "a set of lines at various levels of rads . . . and . . . pressures and calories . . . per square centimeter" that one had to "match" with "the bombs with those numbers."

Taylor decided to abandon weapons research and devote himself to more life-affirming research.[61]

Despite his bluster, Reagan too feared the possibility of nuclear war, although his knowledge of nuclear weapons was limited. In 1983, he shocked a group of congressmen when he said that bombers and submarines did not carry nuclear weapons. But his profound, gut-level aversion to nuclear weapons was sincere. He repeatedly told stunned advisors that he considered them "evil" and wanted to eradicate them. His fears were shaped, in large part, by his religious convictions, particularly his fascination with Armageddon, the biblical account of the bloody conflagration that ends history and augurs Jesus's return, which he believed might be coming. He associated it with nuclear war and thought it his responsibility to protect the American people. Bud McFarlane, who served as Reagan's deputy national security advisor, said, "From the time he adopted the Armageddon thesis, he saw it as a nuclear catastrophe. Well, what do you do about that? Reagan's answer was that you build a tent or a bubble and protect your country." [62]

Reagan decided to protect the United States from incoming missiles by building a high-tech, futuristic atmospheric shield around the nation. But such a seemingly benign defensive shield was actually a major provocation to the Soviets. Although such a shield, if it worked at all, would have done little to protect against a Soviet first strike, it might have offered a measure of protection against a limited retaliatory attack by a Soviet Union already crippled by a U.S. first strike.

Reagan also understood how easily a crisis could be provoked. In September 1983, when Soviet military personnel mistakenly took a Korean Air Lines passenger jet that had crossed into Soviet airspace for a spy plane and, after unheeded warnings, shot it down, killing all 269 people on board, including 61 Americans, Reagan railed against "the Korean Air Lines massacre" as an "act of barbarism" and a "crime against humanity." [63] But in his memoirs he drew a different lesson: "If anything, the KAL incident demonstrated how close the world had come to the precipice and how much we needed nuclear arms control: If, as some people speculated, the Soviet pilots simply mistook the airliner for a military plane, what kind of imagination did it take to think of a Soviet military man with his finger close to a nuclear push button making an even more tragic mistake?" [64]

His concerns about nuclear war came to the fore again the following month. After watching an advance copy of *The Day After,* he wrote in his diary: "It has Lawrence, Kansas wiped out in a nuclear war with Russia. It is powerfully done—all $7 mil. worth. It's very effective & left me very depressed." [65] The usually unflappable Reagan remained depressed for days. [66] His advisors became so concerned that they brought in Weinberger's Soviet expert, Assistant Secretary of Defense for National Security Policy Richard Perle, to talk sense into him.

Reagan's concerns didn't abate, although Perle and others could sometimes manipulate him into defending a nuclear buildup that was at odds with his deeper wishes. It was also during this time, in the fall of 1983, that he was beginning to grasp that Soviet leaders took his bellicose rhetoric and military escalation seriously and feared that he was preparing for an attack.

His diary entry for November 18 was revealing. He worried about the Soviets being "so paranoid about being attacked" that he planned to reassure them that "no one here has any intention of doing anything like that. What the h—l have they got that anyone would want." He then noted that Shultz would appear on ABC following *The Day After,* but now he was more concerned about making sure the film didn't further fuel the already strong public opposition to his nuclear policies: "We know it's 'anti-nuke' propaganda but we're going to take it over & say it shows why we must keep on doing what we're doing." In that same diary entry, he also wrote about "a most sobering experience with Cap. W. & Gen. Vessey in the situation room—a briefing on our complete plan in the event of a nuclear attack."[67]

Reagan later wrote in his memoirs, "Three years had taught me something surprising about the Russians: Many people at the top of the Soviet hierarchy were genuinely afraid of America and Americans. Perhaps this shouldn't have surprised me, but it did. In fact, I had difficulty accepting my own conclusion at first." When he came to office, it didn't dawn on him that the Soviets could actually fear a U.S. first strike. "But the more experience I had with the Soviet leaders and other heads of state who knew them, the more I began to realize that many Soviet officials feared us not only as adversaries but as potential aggressors who might hurl nuclear weapons at them in a first strike."[68]

Although Reagan might have found such an idea inconceivable, he did note that "there were still some people at the Pentagon who claimed a nuclear war was 'winnable.'" He concluded that they were "crazy," but he was beginning to understand why the Soviets might take them seriously. In October, he suggested to Shultz that "maybe I should go see [Yuri] Andropov and propose eliminating all nuclear weapons."[69]

The Soviet leaders not only feared the kind of decapitating first strike envisioned in Presidential Directive 59, drummed up by members of the Committee on the Present Danger, they took concrete steps to ensure the survivability of their nuclear deterrent—a form of subdelegation similar to that undertaken earlier by Eisenhower. Their fears were heightened by U.S. deployment of Pershing and cruise missiles in Europe in 1983, which meant that Soviet leaders would have even less time to launch a retaliatory strike. As David Hoffman details in his Pulitzer Prize–winning 2009 work, *The Dead Hand,* Soviet leaders contemplated constructing a fully automated system, the "Dead Hand," in which computers would launch a nuclear counterstrike if leaders were incapacitated. Frightened by this Strangelovian prospect—"It was complete madness," said Colonel Valery Yarynich of the Strategic Rocket Forces—they instead settled on a system in which a small number of duty officers in deep underground bunkers would authorize the launch. The system was tested in November 1984 and put into operation soon thereafter.[70]

Yarynich grappled with a profoundly troubling question that often plagued U.S. nuclear planners as well: he wondered if, knowing that their country was already destroyed, Soviet duty officers would actually decide to launch their weapons. He explained:

> We have a young lieutenant colonel sitting there, communications are
> destroyed, and he hears "boom," "boom," everything is shaking—he might

fail to launch. If he doesn't begin the launching procedure there will be no retaliation. What's the point of doing it if half the globe has already been wiped out? To destroy the second part? It makes no sense. Even at this point, this lieutenant colonel might say, "No, I won't launch it." No one will condemn him for it or put him before a firing squad. If I were in his place, I wouldn't launch.

Yarynich understood that it was the unpredictability of the officer's response that gave the system whatever limited deterrent effect it might have. He also thought it irrational that the Soviets were going out of their way to hide rather than broadcast the system's existence.[71]

Reagan traced his commitment to eradicating nuclear weapons to his earliest presidential briefings about nuclear weapons:

One of the first statistics I saw as president was one of the most sober and startling I've ever heard. I'll never forget it: The Pentagon said at least 150 million American lives would be lost in a nuclear war with the Soviet Union—even if we "won." For Americans who survived such a war, I couldn't imagine what life would be like. The planet would be so poisoned the "survivors" would have no place to live. Even if nuclear war did not mean the extinction of mankind, it would certainly mean the end of civilization as we knew it. No one could "win" a nuclear war.[72]

Despite his abhorrence of nuclear war, Reagan possessed a dark side that fantasized about using those weapons to defeat his enemies. Such thinking slipped out in shocking fashion when Reagan quipped during a sound check for a radio broadcast, "My fellow Americans, I am pleased to tell you today that I've signed legislation that will outlaw Russia forever. The bombing begins in five minutes." Reagan was unaware that the tapes were rolling as he spoke.[73] The reaction at home and abroad was quick and unsparing. Colorado Senator Gary Hart thought that Reagan's "poor judgment" might have been caused by the stress of his reelection campaign but worried that "more frighteningly, it's in moments of that sort that his real feelings come out, which is the most dismaying and distressing possibility."[74] The *New York Times* reported that the story was front-page news across Europe. Paris's *Le Monde* figured that psychologists would have to determine whether the comments were "an expression of repressed desire or the exorcism of a dreaded phantom." West Germany's Social Democrats dismissed Reagan— "The lord of life or combustion of all Western Europe"—as "an irresponsible old man . . . who probably can no longer distinguish whether he is making a horror movie or commanding a superpower," while the Greens exclaimed that the "perverse joke makes the blood of every reasonable person run cold."[75] TASS, the Soviet news agency, quoted a Western leader who described Reagan as a man "who smiles at the possibility of the mass extermination of people" and decried "the hypocrisy of his peace rhetoric." *Izvestia* called it a "monstrous statement."[76]

At home, the controversy refused to go away. Commentators raised doubts about Reagan's fitness for the job. White House Deputy Chief of Staff Michael Deaver's admission that Reagan often napped during cabinet meetings didn't help. John Oakes, a former senior *New York Times* editor, asked what kind of confidence the American people could have during a crisis in a man of such "shallow, rash, and superficial judgment?" He and others cited Reagan's confusion over fundamental policy issues, including contradictory statements about tax policy, and found him unqualified for the job.[77] Former MIT president Jerome Wiesner, who served as science advisor to both Kennedy and Johnson, described Reagan's "gallows humor" as a "verbal Rorschach test" and questioned his competence to continue with his finger on the nuclear button.[78] Some people even raised the question of the president's mental acuity. Reporters were particularly troubled by a recent photo opportunity at his ranch at which Reagan was asked a basic question about arms control. *Los Angeles Times* reporter Robert Scheer described the scene: "No answer came, and for an embarrassing few moments, the President of the United States seemed lost, gesturing but not speaking. Then his wife, Nancy, at his side, apparently saved him with an answer, uttered while barely moving her lips. 'Doing everything we can,' she said. Reagan repeated, 'We're doing everything we can.'"[79]

Those around Reagan ran interference and protected him as best they could. George Shultz nurtured the side of Reagan that preferred negotiations over belligerency. Backed by Nancy Reagan and Michael Deaver, Shultz battled against the administration zealots. Reagan gave Shultz the green light to improve relations with the Soviets. In mid-1982, the United States and the Soviets began negotiating a new treaty to dramatically reduce strategic forces: the Strategic Arms Reduction Treaty, or START. But Reagan continued the Committee on the Present Danger's campaign of bemoaning American weakness. "You often hear," he stated in late 1982, "that the United States and the Soviet Union are in an arms race. The truth is that while the Soviet Union has raced, we have not. . . . Today, in virtually every measure of military power the Soviet Union enjoys a decided advantage."[80] Despite the scare talk, the United States still maintained a small advantage. In 1985, the U.S. arsenal contained 11,188 strategic warheads to the Soviets' 9,907. In total warheads—strategic, intermediate-range, and tactical—the United States led 20,924 to 19,774. And global arsenals continued to grow, peaking in 1986 at more than 70,000 nuclear weapons with a total destructive capability equivalent to that of approximately 1.5 million Hiroshima bombs.[81]

Arms control gained renewed urgency when scientists calculated that even a small nuclear exchange would release enough smoke, dust, and ash into the atmosphere to block the sunlight, plunging the earth into a prolonged period of cooling that would kill off much of its plant life. Some predicted dire consequences, even the end of life on the planet, caused by the "nuclear winter" that would result from a nuclear war.

Tensions between the world's two military superpowers were running precariously high when an extraordinary development in the Soviet Union changed the course of history. In March 1985, Konstantin Chernenko became the third Soviet leader to die in office in two and a half years. His successor, fifty-four-year-old Mikhail Gorbachev, brought new energy and vision to the job. As a young man, he had witnessed the horrors of war. Later, as a Communist Party official, he had traveled widely in the West. As premier, he intended to realize his dream of revitalizing Soviet socialist democracy and improving the lives of the Soviet people. Like Khrushchev and other reformers before him, he knew that that could not be accomplished as long as military expenditures continued virtually unchecked.

He later described the situation he confronted: "Defense spending was bleeding the other branches of the economy dry." Visits to defense plants and agricultural production complexes drove home the point. "The defense production workshop making modern tanks . . . had the newest equipment. The one working for agriculture was making obsolete models of tractors on old-time conveyor belts." The cause of this disparity was obvious. "Over the previous five-year plans," Gorbachev wrote, "military spending had been growing twice as fast as national income. This Moloch was devouring everything that hard labor and strain produced." But even Gorbachev found it difficult to obtain the hard data needed to fully assess the situation. "What made matters worse," he explained, "was the fact that it was impossible to analyze the problem. All the figures related to the military-industrial complex were classified. Even Politburo members didn't have access to them." [82]

Precise figures are still hard to come by. Central Committee staffer Vitaly Katayev may have kept the most detailed and accurate records. He estimated that in 1985 the Soviet defense sector accounted for 20 percent of the economy. It incorporated nine ministries, not all of whose functions could be identified by their titles. The ministry dealing with the Soviet Union's nuclear programs, for example, was titled the "Ministry of Medium Machine Building." Defense production consumed the efforts of more than fifty cities and, according to NSA Director William Odom, ate up some 20 to 40 percent of the Soviet budget. [83]

To realize his goals of revitalizing the nation, Gorbachev needed to end the arms race and redeploy resources to productive purposes. He also needed to end the war in Afghanistan, a conflict he had thought from the beginning was a "fatal error" and now believed was a "bleeding wound." [84] Achieving those goals would go a long way toward refurbishing the Soviet Union's international image, which had been badly tarnished during the previous decade. One of his foreign policy advisors, Sergei Tarasenko, commented, "One of the first concerns of the Gorbachev administration was to repair this image so the Soviet Union wouldn't be viewed as the 'evil empire.'" Gorbachev braced for resistance from his own defense sector. [85]

Gorbachev wrote his first of several extraordinary letters to Reagan on March 24, 1985. It was a letter that might have been written by Henry Wallace forty years earlier:

> Our countries are different by their social systems, by the ideologies in them. But we believe that this should not be a reason for animosity. Each social system has a right to life, and it should prove its advantages not by force, not by military means, but on the path of peaceful competition with the other system. And all people have the right to go the way they have chosen themselves, without anybody imposing his will on them from outside.

Gorbachev also echoed Kennedy's American University commencement address when he wrote to Reagan in October that despite their differences, they must "proceed from the objective fact that we all live on the same planet and must learn to live together." [86]

One big question was whether Gorbachev would have a partner in the U.S. president to meet him partway in realizing his vision for a peaceful and prosperous world. Reagan had never disavowed what he told Richard Allen, who would become his first national security advisor, prior to taking office: "My idea of American policy toward the Soviet Union is simple, and some would say simplistic. It is this: We win and they lose." [87] But Reagan's initial response to Gorbachev was sufficiently positive to keep the doors open. He asked the Soviet leader to meet with a delegation of visiting Americans, including House Speaker Tip O'Neill.

Gorbachev sensed that winning the Cold War animated Reagan's stubborn devotion to his Strategic Defense Initiative, which came to be known as "Star Wars." The Soviet leader knew that such a system would do nothing to protect the United States if the Soviets launched thousands of missiles against it and reasoned that therefore its true purpose was to protect against a limited Soviet response after the United States had delivered a first strike. He also knew that the Soviets could render it even more ineffective by overwhelming it with additional missiles and warheads or by confusing it with undetectable decoys. And the cost of building more missiles and decoys was far less than the cost of SDI countermeasures. He wrote to Reagan that "the program of 'star wars' already

Reagan delivers a national television address explaining his Strategic Defense Initiative (SDI). Nicknamed "Star Wars," the cockamamie scheme for a missile defense shield would prove a deal breaker in Reagan's negotiations with Soviet leader Mikhail Gorbachev.

seriously undermines stability. We urgently advise you to wind down this sharply destabilizing and dangerous program." In October, Gorbachev decried SDI and overall U.S. militarism at a meeting of Warsaw Pact leaders: "They are planning to win over socialism through war or military blackmail. [SDI's] militaristic nature is obvious. . . . Its purpose is to secure permanent technological superiority of the West, not only over the socialist community, but over [U.S.] allies as well."[88]

Despite their serious differences over SDI, human rights, military buildups, and third-world conflicts, Gorbachev and Reagan held a friendly summit in Geneva in November. They connected on a human level, if not on a political or ideological one. Over dinners, they toasted each other warmly. Gorbachev mentioned the biblical adage that there is "a time to throw stones, and . . . a time to gather them." "Now is the time," he proffered, "to gather stones which have been cast in the past." Reagan noted that they were dining on the forty-third anniversary of the Soviet counterattack at the decisive Battle of Stalingrad and said he hoped that this summit would be "yet another turning point for all mankind—one that would make it possible to have a world of peace and freedom."[89]

After the meeting, both sides remained hopeful, though wary. Soviet leaders were baffled by Reagan's stubborn clinging to his Star Wars fantasy and feared that he might be lulling them into a dangerous complacency. Gorbachev feared that Reagan was just the mouthpiece of the U.S. military-industrial complex, as he had once been the mouthpiece for GE.

*Reagan and Gorbachev shake hands at a plenary
session during the 1985 Geneva summit.*

Gorbachev and his supporters were sincere in their desire for disarmament, détente, and democratic reform. Anatoly Chernyaev, who was one of Gorbachev's most trusted foreign policy advisors, later insisted that "détente was a sincere policy. We wanted détente, we wanted peace, we craved it. . . . Look at Central Committee Secretary Yegor Ligachev, he was a conservative, right? A reactionary, even, and yet he . . . would stand up, right in front of Gorbachev, and he would scream, 'How long will our military-industrial complex keep devouring our economy, our agriculture and our consumer goods? How long are we going to take this ogre, how long are we going to throw into its mouth the food of our children?'"[90]

Gorbachev decided to push his "peace offensive" even more aggressively. In January 1986, he wrote to Reagan, boldly offering "a concrete program . . . for the complete liquidation of nuclear weapons throughout the world . . . before the end of the present century."[91] In the interim, he proposed removing all U.S. and Soviet intermediate-range ballistic missiles from Europe, ending nuclear testing, sharply reducing strategic weapons, and changing the ABM treaty to allow the United States to continue research on SDI but banning deployment for fifteen years. He had already, the previous August, announced a unilateral nuclear testing moratorium.

The U.S. response reinforced Soviet doubts about Reagan's real intentions. The United States announced plans for a new series of nuclear tests. It also increased its support for the Afghan mujahideen and undertook provocative actions on other fronts.

On April 26, 1986, the devastating accident at the Chernobyl nuclear reactor in Ukraine gave Gorbachev further impetus to push his antinuclear campaign. The accident was devastating in itself, leaving 8,000 dead and directly affecting 435,000 more. The government's attempt to downplay its severity proved to be a huge international embarrassment as radioactive particles rained down across Western Europe and beyond. But most significantly, the accident drove home the danger posed by even a limited nuclear war. Marshal Sergei Akhromeyev, the head of the Soviet general staff, recalled that after Chernobyl, "a nuclear danger for our people ceased to be abstraction. It became a palpable reality."[92] Soviet Deputy Foreign Minister Alexander Bessmertnykh reflected on the fact that Chernobyl "was something like one-third of the smallest nuclear explosive. And if it caused such great damage to almost half of Europe, what would happen if we should use all those arsenals we now have in our hands?" Gorbachev told a Politburo meeting in July 1986, "Global nuclear war can no longer be the continuation of rational politics, as it would bring the end of all life, and therefore of all politics."[93]

Chernobyl offered concrete proof that the Soviet Union was floundering. In May, Shultz suggested to Reagan a way to both exploit Soviet weakness and push Reagan's nuclear arms control agenda. He told the president, "The Soviets, contrary to the Defense Department and the CIA line, are not an omnipotent, omnipresent power gaining ground and threatening to wipe us out. On the contrary, we are winning. In fact, we are miles ahead." Shultz stressed that the Soviets were ahead in only one area: ballistic missiles. Therefore, reducing the numbers of ballistic missiles was very much in the United States' interest.[94]

Reagan and Gorbachev met in Iceland in October 1986. Gorbachev brought along a stunningly bold set of disarmament proposals. In the opening session, the sweep of Gorbachev's vision caught Reagan unprepared, causing the president, as Gorbachev recalled, to fumble clumsily for a response:

> Reagan reacted by consulting or reading his notes written on cards. I tried to discuss with him the points I had just outlined, but all my attempts failed. I decided to try specific questions, but still did not get any response. President Reagan was looking through his notes. The cards got mixed up and some of them fell to the floor. He started shuffling them, looking for the right answer to my arguments, but he could not find it. There could be no right answer available—the American President and his aides had been preparing for a completely different conversation.[95]

Gorbachev offered to cut strategic offensive arms in half, eliminate all U.S. and Soviet IRBMs in Europe while allowing Britain and France to maintain their arsenals, freeze short-range missiles, stop nuclear testing, allow on-site inspections as the Americans demanded, and limit SDI testing to labs for the next ten years. Reagan initially failed to grasp the significance of what Gorbachev had proposed or the fact that he was acceding to long-standing U.S. demands, leaving the Soviet leader frustrated by his response. During the break, Reagan huddled with his advisors back at the U.S. Embassy. Paul Nitze observed that the Soviet proposal was "the best we have received in twenty-five years."[96]

The debate continued at the following session. Gorbachev pushed Reagan to seize this extraordinary opportunity. Reagan gave on some points but held tight to his vision of SDI. Gorbachev countered that he wouldn't be able to convince his people and his allies to make such dramatic reductions in strategic weapons if Reagan insisted on destroying the ABM treaty. Reagan offered to share SDI with the Soviets at some date in the future when it was ready. One of Reagan's advisors, Jack Matlock, recalled, "Gorbachev finally exploded. 'Excuse me, Mr. President,' he said, his voice rising, 'but I cannot take your idea of sharing SDI seriously. You are not willing to share with us oil well equipment, digitally guided machine tools, or even milking machines. Sharing SDI would provoke a second American revolution! Let's be realistic and pragmatic."[97]

Expert negotiating teams met through the night, hammering out an agreement both sides could live with. Nitze led the U.S. team. Marshal Sergei Akhromeyev led the Soviet team. Kenneth Adelman, associate director of the Arms Control and Disarmament Agency, proclaimed, "Defining strategic systems, excluding bomber weapons, and closing on limits is one amazing night's work, indisputably more progress than we achieved in thousands of hours in hundreds of meetings over the previous five years."[98]

But when they met the next morning, negotiations again ran aground. As Gorbachev summarized them, they agreed on reducing strategic weapons and on intermediate-range nuclear weapons but failed on the comprehensive nuclear test ban and on the ABM treaty. "Let's go home," the despondent Gorbachev said. "We've accomplished nothing." After discussing other matters, Gorbachev made one last-ditch effort, proposing that Shultz and Foreign Minister Eduard Shevardnadze meet over lunch to see if they could resolve the differences.[99]

Over lunch the Soviet foreign minister, objecting to the fact that the Soviets had thus far made all the concessions, pressed the United States for compromise on SDI. The United States came up with a formulation that would achieve the intended gains while allowing it to keep SDI. At the afternoon session, Gorbachev countered with a proposal that the ABM treaty remain in effect for ten years, with neither party having the right of withdrawal or the right to test any components of an ABM system outside laboratories, and a 50 percent reduction in strategic offensive weapons in five years, with the remainder to be eliminated in the next five years. After further wrangling over the details, each leader met with his close advisors. Reagan asked Perle, the most conservative member of his team, whether the United States could proceed with its SDI research under the constraints placed by the Soviets. Perle, who feared that a sweeping arms control deal would strengthen the Soviet economy and society, replied, "Mr. President, we cannot conduct the research under the terms he's proposing. It will effectively kill SDI." Reagan then solicited opinions from Shultz and Nitze, both of whom disagreed with Perle and urged Reagan to accept Gorbachev's wording.[100]

When they returned, Gorbachev realized that Reagan had changed the language from eliminating all strategic weapons to eliminating only all offensive ballistic missiles, the area in which the Soviets were strongest. Gorbachev objected. Reagan finally relented and asked, "Do we have in mind . . . that by the end of the two five-year periods all nuclear explosive devices would be eliminated, including bombs, battlefield systems, cruise missiles, submarine weapons, intermediate range systems, and so on?" Gorbachev agreed, "We can say that, list all those weapons." Shultz responded, "Then let's do it!" Gorbachev said he was ready to sign the agreement to eliminate nuclear weapons if Reagan restricted SDI testing to the laboratory. Reagan balked, heeding Perle's advice, and insisted on the right to conduct atmospheric tests. They had reached an impasse. Gorbachev made one last appeal:

> If we sign a package containing major concessions by the Soviet Union regarding fundamental problems, you will become, without exaggeration, a great president. You are now literally two steps from that. . . . If not, then let's part at this point and forget about Reykjavik. But there won't be another opportunity like this. At any rate, I know I won't have one.
>
> I firmly believed that we could come to an agreement. Otherwise I would not have raised the question of an immediate meeting with you; otherwise I would not have come here in the name of the Soviet leadership with a solid store of serious, compromising proposals. I hoped they would meet with understanding and support from your side, that we could resolve all issues. If this does happen, if we manage to achieve deep reductions and the destruction of nuclear arms, all of your critics will not dare open their mouths. They would then be going against the opinions of the overwhelming majority of people in the world, who would welcome our success. If, on the other hand, we are not able to come to an agreement, it

Gorbachev and Reagan meet during the summit in Reykjavík.
Catching Reagan completely off guard, Gorbachev arrived
with a strikingly bold set of disarmament proposals.

Disappointed, Reagan and Gorbachev depart from Reykjavík.
The two leaders had come remarkably close to completely
eliminating nuclear weapons, but Reagan's refusal to abandon
SDI shattered the prospect of total nuclear disarmament.

will obviously become the job of another generation of leaders; you and I have no more time.

The American side has essentially not made any concessions, not a single major step to meet us halfway. It's hard to do business on that basis.

Soviet Foreign Minister Shevardnadze then interjected "very emotionally" that future generations, reading the minutes of meetings and seeing how close the participants had come to eliminating nuclear weapons, would never forgive them if they didn't come to an agreement. Reagan said that adding the word "laboratory" would cause him great political damage at home. Gorbachev said that if he allowed the United States to take the arms race to space and deploy SDI after ten years, he would be viewed as foolish and irresponsible. Each asked the other to bend. Neither would.[101]

The meeting ended. The United States and the Soviet Union had come within a hairsbreadth—one word—of eliminating nuclear weapons. But the scourge of nuclear weaponry would continue to haunt the world. Reagan, egged on by arch-neocon Perle, sacrificed the hopes of humanity for an illusion—a Star Wars fantasy that, as Richard Rhodes wrote, represented little more than "a specious concern for testing outside the 'laboratory' systems that had hardly yet even entered the laboratory in 1986."[102]

Reagan and Gorbachev left the building. Gorbachev described the scene:

> It was already dusk. The mood was downcast. Reagan reproached me: "You planned from the beginning to come here and put me in this position!"
>
> "No. Mr. President," I replied. "I am prepared to go back inside right now and sign the document concerning the issues we already agreed upon if you will refrain from plans to militarize space."
>
> "I'm extremely sorry," Reagan answered.[103]

Gorbachev expressed optimism in public, highlighting how much progress the two sides had made. "For the first time we looked beyond the horizon," he declared. But in private he expressed profound disappointment at U.S. obstinancy. He explained to the Politburo that he was dealing not only with the "class enemy"—the capitalist United States—but with President Reagan, "who exhibited extreme primitivism, a caveman outlook, and intellectual impotence." That, however, was not the main impediment. The first problem, he averred, was tactical: the United States had miscalculated the extent of the Soviet Union's "internal difficulties" and therefore assumed that Gorbachev would be almost desperate to reach an agreement, even on U.S. terms. The second was strategic: the United States believed it might "exhaust us economically via arms race, create obstacles

Reagan with Lieutenant Colonel Oliver North and Nicaraguan contra leader Adolfo Calero in National Security Advisor Robert McFarlane's office. McFarlane and North, a gung-ho but unstable marine with delusions of grandeur and a knack for embellishment, were the principal plotters in the administration's illegal scheme to sell weapons to the Iranian government in order to fund the contras.

for Gorbachev and for the entire Soviet leadership, undermine its plans for resolving economic and social problems and thereby provoke popular discontent." The U.S. leaders, he said, hoped this would rupture Soviet relations with third-world nations and "with the help of SDI . . . achieve military superiority." In concluding his remarks, Gorbachev expressed his bitterness toward the U.S. negotiators: "representatives of American administration are people without conscience, with no morale. Their line is the one of pressure, deceit, or greedy mercantilism." [104]

Both sides hoped to revive the talks. But before that could happen, scandal rocked the Reagan-Bush administration. On October 5, 1986, the Sandinistas downed a plane manned by three Americans carrying supplies to Nicaragua's contras. The only survivor admitted to working for the CIA. Additional information slowly leaked out as hearings of the Senate Intelligence Committee and the Tower Commission lifted the veil from an administration up to its eyeballs in illegality, corruption, blundering, and subterfuge involving American hostages in Lebanon, arms sales to Iran, unsuccessful efforts to halt the torture and prevent the murder of the CIA station chief in Beirut, ill-fated attempts to cultivate nonexistent "moderates" in Tehran, support for Iraq in its war with Iran, and collaboration with a rogues' gallery of unsavory characters, including Panamanian strongman Manuel

Noriega, as it funneled war materiel to the contras in Nicaragua in flagrant violation of the 1982 Boland Amendment, which outlawed U.S. financial aid to efforts to defeat the ruling Sandinistas.

The principal operatives in the affair, aside from Reagan and Bush, were CIA Director Casey, National Security Advisor McFarlane, and Lieutenant Colonel Oliver North, a decorated Vietnam veteran who had suffered an apparent nervous breakdown upon returning from Vietnam and spent twenty-two days in Bethesda Naval Hospital. North, who was assigned to the NSC in 1981, was a gung-ho marine with a taste for hyperbole and a touch of megalomania, who had, after his return from Vietnam and hospitalization, become a fundamentalist Christian. North ran much of the operation on a day-to-day basis, putting together an unsavory network of right-wing fund-raisers, covert operatives, and conniving arms dealers to carry it out.

The CIA attempted to circumvent the congressional constraints upon its actions but did not do a very good job of hiding its involvement. It made the mistake of bringing in retired Special Forces veterans who had served in Vietnam. In one embarrassing episode, they convinced the Agency to translate into Spanish an old comic book instructing Vietnamese peasants on ways to take over a village by murdering the mayor, chief of police, and militia. The CIA distributed a Spanish-language version of this "Freedom Fighter's Manual" to the contras. Some ended up in the hands of opponents of the U.S. wars in Central America, who made them public.[105] Americans also learned that the CIA had mined Nicaraguan harbors, which provoked conservative icon Barry Goldwater to scold Casey. "I am pissed off," he wrote. "This is an act violating international law. It is an act of war.[106]

Congress reacted in October 1984 by strengthening the Boland Amendment and cutting off all aid to the contras. In order to tie Casey's hands, Congress explicitly prohibited any intelligence agency from soliciting funds from "any nation, group, organization, movement, or individual." Chief of Staff James Baker feared that administration "crazies" would nonetheless solicit funds from other countries, which Casey, McFarlane, and North proceeded to do. Saudi Arabia provided the lion's share, but other nations, including South Africa, Israel, and Taiwan, pledged millions of dollars more. Shultz had warned Reagan that approving further assistance would constitute an impeachable offense. But Casey, Bush, and Reagan all pooh-poohed that notion.[107]

Reagan instructed his top aides to do what they could. He told National Security Advisor McFarlane, "I want you to do whatever you have to do to help these people keep body and soul together."[108] McFarlane soon saw a way to carry that out. In summer 1985, he met with David Kimche, director general of the Israel Foreign Ministry. Kimche convinced him that he was working with Iranian "moderates," who were poised to take power when the elderly Ayatollah Khomeini passed from the scene. He suggested that in return for arms, the Iranians could help secure the release of U.S. hostages being held in Lebanon by Hezbollah, a pro-Iranian Shiite group. Included among the hostages was CIA Beirut station chief William Francis Buckley, who, unknown to the Americans, had been tortured to death in June. In mid-1985, Reagan, despite his public opposition to negotiating with hostage-takers, authorized Israel to transfer TOW antitank missiles to Iran. Israel continued to serve as the go-between in weapons sales for fourteen months. During that time, Iran released some American hostages but seized more so that it always had a steady supply to barter. Israel had also been secretly sending its own weapons to the ayatollah's regime.[109]

The notion of dealing with Iranian "moderates" had gained currency among top administration officials, who began to think about the shape of a post-Khomeini Iran. In June 1985, the CIA produced a National Intelligence Estimate on Iran titled "Iran: Prospects for a Near Term Instability," which suggested that conditions inside Iran were unstable and Khomeini's days might be numbered. The NSC picked up on this theme in a National Security Directive suggesting that Iranian "moderates" might be inclined toward the United States. Secretary of Defense Caspar Weinberger wrote on his copy of the report, "This is almost too absurd for comment. It's based on the assumption there's about to be a major change in Iran and that we can deal with that rationally. It's like inviting Kadafi over for a cozy lunch."[110]

The Iranians demanded and the United States sent HAWK antiaircraft missiles and other weapons. In 1986, the Iranians requested and received battlefield intelligence to assist them in their war with Iraq. They paid exorbitantly for the assistance.

Flush with money from the Iranian arms sales and from the Saudis, the CIA expanded its military support for the contras, with the anti-Castro Cubans Félix Rodríguez and Luis Posada Carriles playing a major part. Rodríguez was a close associate of Vice President Bush's national security advisor, Donald Gregg, a former CIA official. Posada had escaped incarceration in Venezuela for his role in killing seventy-three people in a Cuban passenger jet bombing in 1976. Congress also authorized $100 million to support Central American operations following the repeal of the Boland Amendment, a move instigated by Cheney.

On October 5, the operation began to come unglued. That day a young Nicaraguan soldier brought down the C-123 cargo plane carrying weapons to the contras. Former marine Eugene Hasenfus, the plane's only survivor, confessed to his Sandinista captors that he worked for the CIA and was supplying the contras. On election day, November 4, the speaker of the Iranian parliament, Ali Akbar Hashemi Rafsanjani, went public with the story of U.S.-Iranian dealings. Bush, the following day, recorded in his diary, "This is one operation that had been held very, very tight, and I hope it will not leak." [111]

It was much too late for that. Details of the murky, convoluted operation were splashed across the nation's newspapers and television screens. The White House issued clumsy denials. On November 13, Reagan admitted that "small amounts of defensive weapons" had been transferred but that "we did not—repeat did not—trade weapons or anything else for hostages; nor will we."

The lies continued when Casey and Rear Admiral John Poindexter testified before Congress. Several of those involved, including Poindexter, North, and General Richard Secord, began shredding thousands of pages of incriminating documents in their possession. On November 25, Reagan gave what historian Sean Wilentz described as "the worst performance of his presidency if not his entire career" when he told the press corps that based on the preliminary findings of Attorney General Edwin Meese, he "was not fully informed of the nature of one of the activities undertaken in connection with this initiative." He announced that Poindexter was stepping down as national security advisor and that North had been relieved of his duties. "As I've stated previously," he added, "I believe our policy goals toward Iran were well founded. However, the information brought to my attention yesterday, convinced me that in one aspect, implementation of that policy was seriously flawed." After reading this brief statement, he turned the session over to Meese and walked off as reporters kept yelling out questions. [112] One week later, Gallup reported that Reagan's approval ratings had plummeted 21 points to 46 percent in the course of the month.

Investigations were conducted, all directly implicating Reagan but making it apparent that he had little grasp of and less control over what his underlings were up to. The congressional investigating committee concluded, "If the President did not know what his National Security Advisors were doing, he should have." Independent counsel Lawrence Walsh declared, "President Reagan created the conditions which made possible the crimes committed by others by his secret deviations from announced national policy as to Iran and hostages and by his own determination to keep the contras together 'body and soul' despite a statutory ban on contra aid." [113]

Among those convicted of crimes were National Security Advisor Bud McFarlane, after an abortive suicide attempt; his successor, Rear Admiral William Poindexter; Lieutenant Colonel Oliver North, the mastermind behind the entire operation; and Assistant Secretary of State Elliott Abrams. Defense Secretary Caspar Weinberger was indicted but pardoned. CIA Director William Casey died of a brain tumor the day after the congressional hearings began. Vice President George H. W. Bush, though having figured prominently in the foolhardy scheme, managed to avoid prosecution. Deputy CIA Director Robert

Gates escaped prosecution, though the manipulation and politicization of intelligence on his watch paved the way for Reagan's disastrous policies.[114] McFarlane later regretted not having had the "guts" to warn Reagan. "To tell you the truth," he said, "probably the reason I didn't is because if I had done that, Bill Casey, Jeane Kirkpatrick and Cap Weinberger would have said I was some kind of commie."[115]

This sordid affair dashed hopes for renewing talks on nuclear disarmament. Gorbachev decided to salvage something by decoupling the intermediate-range ballistic missile issue from other long-term measures. He visited Washington in December 1987 and signed the Intermediate-Range Nuclear Forces Treaty, a major milestone in U.S.-Soviet relations. "This was the first agreement in history on the mutually agreed destruction of an entire class of nuclear weapons," Gorbachev noted.[116]

Meanwhile, Soviet operations were finally winding down in Afghanistan. Reagan and Casey had transformed Carter's tentative support for the Afghan insurgents into the CIA's largest covert operation to date, totaling more than $3 billion. The CIA channeled aid through Pakistan's President Zia, who funneled U.S. arms and dollars to the most extreme Afghan Islamist faction under Gulbuddin Hekmatyar, a man of legendary cruelty. According to James Forest, director of terrorism studies at West Point, Hekmatyar "was known . . . to patrol the bazaars of Kabul with vials of acid, which he would throw in the face of any woman who dared to walk outdoors without a full burka covering her face."[117] He was also known for skinning prisoners alive.[118] Senior State Department official Stephen Cohen admitted, "The people we did support were the nastier, more fanatic types of mujahdeen."[119] The CIA station chief in Islamabad, Pakistan, Howard Hart, recalled, "I was the first chief of station ever sent abroad with this wonderful order: 'Go kill Soviet soldiers.' Imagine! I loved it."[120] The CIA even provided between 2,000 and 2,500 U.S.-made Stinger missiles, some of which WikiLeaks revealed were used to down NATO helicopters three decades later.

From his early days in office, Gorbachev had made clear his intention to withdraw Soviet troops from Afghanistan and sought U.S. assistance in making that happen. He assured Reagan that his country had "no plan for using Afghanistan to gain access to a warm water port, to extend its influence to the Persian Gulf, or to impinge on U.S. interests in any way."[121]

The United States worked with the Saudis and Pakistanis to tie Soviet forces down as long as possible and did what it could to make sure that UN efforts to broker a settlement failed, funneling massive amounts of money and arms to the insurgents, who were also profiting immensely off the suddenly burgeoning opium production and sales. The Chinese, British, and Egyptians contributed millions of dollars' worth of weapons. The CIA delivered the money and

An Afghan fighter demonstrates the positioning of a handheld surface-to-air missile. Reagan and Casey transformed Carter's tentative support for the mujahideen into the CIA's largest covert operation to date, totaling more than $3 billion.

weapons to Pakistani intelligence. After taking their cut, the Pakistanis shipped the remainder to Afghan rebel leaders in Peshawar, who skimmed off their share before shipping the rest on to the front lines. Many of the stockpiled weapons would later be turned against the United States.[122]

Because of the fighting, approximately 3 million Afghans—one-third of the population—fled to Pakistan. In February 1988, Gorbachev announced that Soviet troops would withdraw from the country. The withdrawal began on May 15 and lasted for ten months. The Geneva Accords ending the fighting were signed by the United States, the Soviet Union, Afghanistan, and Pakistan. Only the Soviets adhered to their commitments. Zia promised Reagan that Pakistani supplies to the Afghan rebels would continue to flow unabated. "We'll just lie about it," he said. "That's what we've been doing for eight years. . . . Muslims have the right to lie in a good cause."[123]

Over a million Afghans were killed in the fighting. The Pakistani dictatorship profited, becoming the third largest recipient of U.S. foreign aid. The United States turned a blind eye toward Pakistan's progress in developing a nuclear bomb.

Tens of thousands of Arabs flooded into Pakistan to join the jihad against the infidels, including a wealthy Saudi named Osama bin Laden and Egyptian doctor Ayman al-Zawahiri. They and thousands of other future Islamist terrorists received military training in the Pakistani camps, learning such valuable skills as how to perform assassinations and detonate car bombs. Thousands more flocked to Pakistan's madrassas, where they were indoctrinated in radical Islam and recruited for jihad. The madrassas were one product of the $75 billion the Saudis spent during the 1980s to spread Wahhabi extremism. Casey ignored repeated warnings that the religious fanaticism he was helping unleash would eventually pose a threat to U.S. interests. He instead persisted in his view that the unholy partnership between Christianity and Islam would endure and could be used to bludgeon the Soviets throughout the region. In fact, in mid-decade, Casey unleashed mujahideen raids across the border into the Soviet Union in the hope of inciting Islamist uprisings by Soviet Muslims.[124]

Upon withdrawing from Afghanistan, the Soviets sounded out U.S. willingness to collaborate on curbing Islamic extremism in Afghanistan, but the Americans could not be bothered. The die-hard Islamists now in control of Afghanistan worked closely with Pakistani intelligence. Having achieved its goals, the United States washed its hands of the mess it had helped create. Former U.S. Ambassador to Saudi Arabia Charles Freeman complained, "We start wars without figuring out how we would end them. Afghanistan was lurching into civil war, and we basically didn't care anymore." He said that he and U.S. Ambassador to Pakistan Robert Oakley had tried to get CIA officials from Directors Robert Gates and William Webster on down to think seriously about ending the U.S., Saudi, and Pakistani involvement, but they were dealing with people who reasoned, "Why should we go out there and talk to people with towels on their heads?"[125] According to RAND expert Cheryl Benard, whose husband, Zalmay Khalilzad, served as U.S. ambassador to Afghanistan:

> We made a deliberate choice. At first, everyone thought, there's no way to beat the Soviets. So what we have to do is to throw the worst crazies against them that we can find, and there was a lot of collateral damage. We knew exactly who these people were, and what their organizations were like, and we didn't care. Then, we allowed them to get rid of, just kill all the moderate leaders. The reason we don't have moderate leaders in Afghanistan today is because we let the nuts kill them all. They killed the leftists, the moderates, the middle-of-the-roaders. They were just eliminated, during the 1980s and afterwards.[126]

Reagan left office a befuddled old man who claimed little knowledge of things going on under his nose, yet many people lionize him and credit him with having restored the United States' faith in itself after the failed presidencies of Johnson, Nixon, Ford, and Carter. Even before Reagan's second term, conservatives had begun anointing him one of the nation's great presidents. A 1984 Republican campaign memo read, "Paint Reagan as the personification of all that is right with or heroized by America. Leave Mondale in a position where an attack on Reagan is tantamount to an attack on America's idealized image of itself." [127]

But what is Reagan's real legacy? One of the most poorly informed and least engaged chief executives in U.S. history, he empowered a right-wing resurgence of hard-line anti-Communists who militarized U.S. foreign policy and rekindled the Cold War. He paid lip service to democracy while arming and supporting repressive dictators. He turned local and regional conflicts in the Middle East and Latin America into Cold War battlegrounds, unleashing a reign of terror to suppress popular movements. He spent enormous sums on the military while cutting social programs for the poor. He sharply reduced taxes on the wealthy, tripling the national debt and transforming the United States from the world's leading creditor in 1981 to its biggest debtor by 1985. In October 1987, he oversaw the worst stock market collapse since the Great Depression. He let the chance to rid the world of offensive nuclear weapons slip through his fingers because he wouldn't let go of a childish fantasy. And as for his much-vaunted role in ending the Cold War, as we will see, the lion's share of credit goes instead to his Soviet counterpart, Mikhail Gorbachev.

Chapter 12

THE COLD WAR ENDS:

Squandered Opportunities

"Suddenly, a season of peace seems to be warming the world," the *New York Times* exulted on the last day of July 1988. Protracted, bloody wars were ending in Afghanistan, Angola, Cambodia, and Nicaragua, and between Iran and Iraq.[1] Later that year, Palestine Liberation Organization leader Yasir Arafat, under pressure from Moscow, renounced terrorism and implicitly recognized Israel's right to exist. But the most dramatic development was still to come. In December 1988, Soviet leader Mikhail Gorbachev declared the Cold War over:

> the use or threat of force no longer can . . . be an instrument of foreign
> policy. This applies above all to nuclear arms. . . . let me turn to the main
> issue—disarmament, without which none of the problems of the coming
> century can be solved. . . . the Soviet Union has taken a decision to reduce
> its armed forces . . . by 500,000 men. . . . we have decided to withdraw by
> 1991 six tank divisions from East Germany, Czechoslovakia and Hungary,
> and to disband them. . . . Soviet forces stationed in those countries will be
> reduced by 50,000 men and their armaments, by 5,000 tanks. All Soviet
> divisions remaining . . . will become clearly defensive.

He promised to reveal Soviet plans for the "transition from the economy of armaments to an economy of disarmament" and called upon other military powers to do likewise through the United Nations. He proposed a 50 percent reduction in offensive strategic arms, asked for joint action to eliminate "the threat to the world's environment," urged banning weapons in outer space, and demanded an end to exploitation of the third world, including a "moratorium of up to 100 years on debt servicing by the least developed countries."

Still, he was not finished. He called for a UN-brokered cease-fire in Afghanistan as of January 1. In nine years of war, the Soviets had failed to defeat the Afghan insurgents despite deploying 100,000 troops, working closely with local Afghans, and building up the Afghan army and police. He proposed an international conference on Afghan neutrality and demilitarization and held out an olive branch to the incoming administration of George H. W. Bush, offering a "joint effort to put an end to an era of wars, confrontation and regional conflicts, to aggressions against nature, to the terror of hunger and poverty as well as to political terrorism. This is our common goal and we can only reach it together."[2]

The *New York Times* characterized Gorbachev's riveting hourlong speech as the greatest act of statesmanship since Wilson's Fourteen Points in 1918 or Roosevelt and Churchill's Atlantic Charter in 1941—"the basic restructuring of international politics." And, the *Times* proclaimed, "he promised to lead the way unilaterally. Breathtaking. Risky. Bold. Naive. Diversionary. Heroic. . . . his ideas merit—indeed, compel—the most serious response from President-elect Bush and other leaders." The *Washington Post* called it "a speech as remarkable as any ever delivered at the United Nations."[3]

Bush had not yet moved into the White House after trouncing Massachusetts Governor Michael Dukakis in the recent election. Trailing by 17 points during the summer, Bush struggled to overcome what was widely being described as the "wimp" factor. For a while, it looked like the election might turn on the issue of whether Bush was too much of a wimp to be president. Some thought it odd that Bush, a recipient of a Distinguished Flying Cross, who had flown fifty-eight combat missions in the Pacific during World War II, would be so derided. *Newsweek* considered it a "potentially crippling handicap—a perception that he isn't strong enough or tough enough for the challenges of the Oval Office."[4] Not even the fact that Bush captained Yale's baseball team earned him a pass. The *Washington Post's* Curt Suplee wrote, "Wimp. Wasp. Weenie. Every woman's first husband. Bland conformist. These now shop-worn pejoratives are the essence of George Bush's 'image problem'—the vague but powerful suspicion of many citizens that the vice president may be too feckless and insubstantial to be the leader of the free world."[5] "He's been reduced to a cartoon," his second son, Jeb Bush, complained.[6]

Commentators attributed the image to his wealthy, pampered upbringing and his Ivy League education. Always staid and reserved, he had been nicknamed "Poppy" as a boy. Despite resigning from the Council on Foreign Relations and Trilateral Commission, he couldn't shake the image of being the ultimate "Establishment" candidate—the man endorsed by David Rockefeller.[7] On top of that, most of his political offices had been appointments. None of

*Addressing the United Nations in New York, Soviet leader
Mikhail Gorbachev declared the Cold War over and announced
a series of peaceful reforms and steps toward disarmament in
a December 1988 speech that the* New York Times *called the
greatest act of statesmanship since Wilson's Fourteen Points in
1918 or Roosevelt and Churchill's Atlantic Charter in 1941.*

Reagan's charisma had rubbed off on him as Reagan's vice president. It turned out that Reagan didn't like Bush and hadn't wanted him on the ticket, but his preferred choices—Senator Paul Laxalt and Representative Jack Kemp—wouldn't fly. Bush's kowtowing to Reagan and the right-wing policies he had previously opposed, including what he called "voodoo economics," made him look weak and unprincipled. "I'm following Mr. Reagan—blindly," Bush told one reporter upon receiving the nomination.[8] He went so far as to call Oliver North, a man he would have once found contemptible, his "hero." One commentator noted that Bush tried on "the boorish philosophies of the political Right . . . to get closer to the Oval Office."[9] Bush's initial victory in the New Hampshire primary frustrated his principal opponent, Bob Dole, who fumed, "There's nothing there."[10]

People thought he lacked a home or community—he officially resided in a Houston hotel—and derided his tendency to end sentences with "muddy" phrases like "whatever it is" and "all that sort of stuff" and mocked his "speech disturbances: sentence incompletion, interruption of word sequences and tongue slips."[11] Feisty Texas Governor Ann Richards quipped at the Democratic National Convention, "Poor George. He was born with a silver foot in his mouth."[12]

When parading his war record, defending gun rights, frequenting barbecues, and shamelessly pandering to the Right did nothing to help Bush change his image, he tried a different strategy. He questioned Dukakis's patriotism and openly played the race card with a campaign ad about furloughed murderer Willie Horton that appealed to voters' fear of crime. But the coup de grâce came when CBS news anchor Dan Rather pressed him on his involvement in the Iran-Contra scandal. Bush was ready to pounce. He challenged the question's fairness and angrily retorted, "It's not fair to judge my whole career by a rehash on Iran. How would you like it if I judged your career by those seven minutes when you walked off the set in New York?" His strategy worked. Reporters referred to the "Rather Bushwhacking," calling Bush a "bully."[13] Few noticed that Rather's questions about Bush's role were entirely legitimate. During the campaign, Bush insisted that he had been "out of the loop—no operational role" in the illegal operation, but in his taped diary the former CIA director admitted, "I'm one of the few people that know fully the details."[14] Bush would later pardon former Secretary of Defense Caspar Weinberger to avoid testimony about Bush's role in the scandal.

Bush's foreign policy team included James A. Baker III at State, Dick Cheney at Defense, and General Brent Scowcroft as his national security advisor. Scowcroft chose Robert Gates as his number two man. Paul Wolfowitz took over as undersecretary of defense for policy.

While in New York to address the United Nations, Gorbachev met with Reagan and Bush, seeking help on arms control and troop withdrawal. But Bush's advisors remained skeptical and the CIA, whose intelligence capabilities had been degraded by years of unrelenting right-wing assault, completely misread what was occurring. As Gates later admitted in his memoirs, "the American government, including CIA, had no idea in January 1989 that a tidal wave of history was about to break upon us."[15] Gates and Cheney were most skeptical of Gorbachev's initiatives and sought ways to take advantage of his willingness to reform the Soviet system. For the most part, Cheney's opposition to working with Gorbachev prevailed. Cheney opposed an early summit, fearing that Gorbachev's initiatives would weaken Western resolve. Bush decided on a strategy that would further erode Soviet military strength: whereas Gorbachev was calling for eliminating tactical nuclear weapons in Europe—an offer most Europeans applauded—the United States countered that the Soviet Union should remove 325,000 troops in exchange for a U.S. cut of 30,000. Bush and Gorbachev did not meet again for another year.

While neglecting the Soviet Union, Bush continued to play the China card, building on the economic and political ties that Reagan had forged with Chinese leaders, who had assisted in toppling pro-Soviet governments in Afghanistan and Cambodia. As former ambassador to China, Bush intended to maintain

*Reagan and Bush meeting with Gorbachev on Governors Island during
Gorbachev's visit to New York for the UN address. Gorbachev sought
their help on arms control and troop withdrawal, but Bush's advisors
remained skeptical and the CIA, ravaged by right-wing "reformers,"
completely misread the changes occurring in the Soviet Union.*

close relations. His plans were almost derailed by Beijing's brutal crackdown on
prodemocracy demonstrators. As television viewers around the world looked on,
the People's Liberation Army slaughtered 3,000 demonstrators in Tiananmen
Square, wounding 10,000 more. But Bush resisted pressure to punish China's rulers, initially even opposing legislation allowing the 43,000 Chinese students in
the United States to remain in the country beyond their one-year visas.

Gorbachev hoped to jump-start the Soviet economy, which had been moribund since the late 1970s. He knew that the Soviet Union could no longer afford
war in Afghanistan, support for third-world allies, and a military establishment
that consumed more than 20 percent of GNP and more than half of total government expenditures. Soviet officials decided to cut their losses. They ended
support for Cuban troops in Angola and Ethiopia and Vietnamese troops in Cambodia and pulled Soviet troops out of Afghanistan in early 1989. The third world,
an arena that had looked so promising a decade earlier, was now unraveling. The
Soviet people had tired of expensive and ill-advised adventures. The Afghan war
had cost the lives of over 14,000 Soviets and hundreds of thousands of Afghans,
drained scarce resources, and inflamed anti-Communist feeling throughout the
Muslim world. Young Muslim radicals who had once turned to socialism now
looked to radical Islam. The faltering Soviet economy no longer provided a viable

model for development. Fed up with the repressive and costly policies of many of the Soviet Union's third-world allies, who resisted his demands to change their ways, Gorbachev proposed that the United States and the Soviet Union both stop interfering in third-world affairs and let nations settle their disputes amicably.

At the Moscow summit in May 1988, Gorbachev had asked Reagan to cosign a statement affirming peaceful coexistence and disavowing military interventions into other nations' internal affairs. Reagan refused to sign. Undeterred, Gorbachev acted unilaterally. Historian Odd Arne Westad grasped the significance of this extraordinary reversal: "Gorbachev and his advisors . . . developed an understanding of the significance of national self-determination that went beyond those of the leaders of any major power in the twentieth century. The Soviet president practiced what both liberals and revolutionaries had been calling for at the beginning of the century—a firm and idealist dedication to letting the peoples of the world decide their own fates without foreign intervention." [16]

Not only did the United States not accept this principle, it worked actively to subvert it, exploiting the openings Gorbachev had provided in the third world. The United States continued to fuel Islamic radicalism. Many of the U.S.-backed jihadis who had fought against the Soviets in Afghanistan joined the Islamist cause in Chechnya, Bosnia, Algeria, Iraq, the Philippines, Saudi Arabia, Kashmir, and elsewhere. Ethnic and tribal conflicts also erupted in Africa and the Balkans.

Gorbachev urged Eastern European governments to embrace the spirit of perestroika. Poland was the first to act. In April 1989, the government of General Wojciech Jaruzelski agreed to free elections. In June, candidates from the Solidarity trade union federation, with clandestine CIA support, soundly defeated the Communists, who peacefully relinquished power, agreeing to participate in a Solidarity-led coalition government. Unlike in Hungary in 1956 and Czechoslovakia in 1968, the Soviets did not intervene. In May, Estonia and Lithuania declared their sovereignty. Latvia followed in July. Gorbachev encouraged the reformers. In late July, Foreign Minister Eduard Shevardnadze explained the Soviet acceptance of these changes to Secretary of State Baker: "If we were to use force, then it would be the end of *perestroika*. We would have failed. It would be the end of any hope for the future, the end of everything we're trying to do, which is to create a new system based on humane values. If force is used, it will mean that the enemies of *perestroika* have triumphed. We would be no better than the people who came before us. We cannot go back." [17]

Other Eastern European nations followed suit. In October, the ruling Communists in Hungary declared themselves social democrats and established a republic. That month, following Gorbachev's visit to Berlin, demonstrators drove Erich Honecker from power in East Germany. And finally, on November 9, 1989, East and West Berliners jointly began tearing down the Berlin Wall, desecrating the Cold War's most reviled symbol. Gorbachev's foreign policy advisor, Anatoly Chernyaev, wrote in his diary, "The Berlin Wall has collapsed. This entire era in the history of the Socialist system is over. . . . This is the end of Yalta [and] the Stalinist legacy. . . . This is what Gorbachev has done. . . . He has sensed the pace of history and helped history to find a natural channel." But the transformation of Europe was far from over. The Czech parliament responded to demonstrations and a general strike by electing poet Václav Havel prime minister. One by one, all the Eastern European Communist governments fell. The world watched in disbelief. A peaceful revolution had occurred across the socialist bloc as citizens, burdened by decades of government repression and bureaucratic ineptitude, clamored for a better life. Gorbachev rejected the long-held view that controlling Eastern Europe was crucial to Soviet security. He believed that removing the drain of Eastern Europe would allow the Soviet Union and its allies to rapidly develop humane, democratic socialist systems.

Gorbachev saw this as a new beginning, but many U.S. policy makers hailed it as the ultimate vindication—the triumph of the capitalist West after decades of Cold War. It was "the end of history," State Department policy planner Francis Fukuyama declared, anointing Western liberal democracy "the final form of human government." In September 1990, Michael Mandelbaum, director of East-West studies at the Council on Foreign Relations, exulted, "the Soviets . . . have made it possible to end the cold war, which means that for the first time in 40 years we can conduct military operations in the Middle East without worrying about triggering World War III."[18] The United States would soon test that hypothesis.

When Bush traveled to Poland and Hungary in July, he deliberately avoided saying or doing anything that might provoke a Soviet response. Having previously derided "the vision thing," even the tearing down of the Berlin Wall failed to elicit a jubilant response on his part. He explained, "I am not an emotional kind of guy." He told Gorbachev, "I have conducted myself in ways not to complicate your life. That's why I have not jumped up and down on the Berlin Wall." "Yes, we have seen that" and "appreciate" it, Gorbachev replied.[19]

Though willing to allow for the radical transformation of Eastern Europe, Gorbachev hoped the end of the Cold War would lead to the dissolution of NATO as well as the Warsaw Pact. Recognizing that that might not happen, he insisted that NATO at least not expand farther to the east. He was even willing to allow for reunification of the two Germanys as long as NATO troops and weapons were not permitted on former East German soil. But he and other Russian leaders who believed they had received ironclad U.S. and German promises that eastward expansion by NATO would never be permitted were in for a rude awakening when the Clinton and second Bush administrations continued expanding right up to Russia's doorstep. Russian leaders expressed outrage and a sense of betrayal. Although U.S. officials, over the years, have insisted that no such promises were ever given, recently released documents appear to substantiate the Russian claims.

In February 1990, Bush, Baker, and German Chancellor Helmut Kohl sought ways to convince Gorbachev to remove the 380,000 Soviet troops in East Germany and renounce legal claims of occupation dating back to Germany's surrender in 1945. They wanted to avoid the growing demand from many of the newly liberated countries to demilitarize Central and Eastern Europe, a move that would have diminished the U.S. domination of Europe. Baker met with Gorbachev on February 9 and asked him, "Would you prefer to see a unified Germany outside of NATO, independent and with no U.S. forces or would you prefer a unified Germany to be tied to NATO, with assurances that NATO's jurisdiction would not shift one inch eastward from its present position?" Baker recorded Gorbachev's reply that "any extension of the zone of NATO would be unacceptable."

Helmut Kohl met with Gorbachev the following day and stated that "naturally NATO could not expand its territory" into East Germany. On February 10, German Foreign Minister Hans-Dietrich Genscher conveyed the same message to Eduard Shevardnadze, stating, "We are aware that NATO membership for a unified Germany raises complicated questions. For us, however, one thing is certain: NATO will not expand to the east." To make sure that his Soviet counterpart understood that this applied to all of Eastern Europe and not just Germany, Genscher added, "As far as the nonexpansion of NATO is concerned, this also applies in general."

Upon receiving Kohl's assurance, Gorbachev approved German reunification. But no legally binding papers were signed. The deal was not in writing. And Gorbachev later compounded the problem by agreeing in September to allow NATO expansion into East Germany in exchange for desperately needed financial assistance from Germany.

Clearly, Gorbachev thought there had been an agreement and felt that he had been blindsided. The United States and West Germany had promised not to expand NATO "as much as a thumb's width further to the East," he insisted. President Dmitri Medvedev was equally perturbed, contending in 2009 that the Soviet Union had gotten "none of the things that we were assured, namely that NATO would not expand endlessly eastwards and our interests would be continuously taken into consideration." U.S. Ambassador to Moscow Jack Matlock has agreed that the Soviet Union was given a "clear commitment." The German newsmagazine *Der Spiegel* conducted its own investigation in late 2009, finding that "after speaking with many of those involved and examining previously classified British and German documents in detail, *SPIEGEL* has concluded that there was no doubt that the West did everything it could to give the Soviets the impression that

Celebrants atop the falling Berlin Wall on November 9, 1989. Gorbachev saw Soviet communism's collapse as a new beginning, but many U.S. policy makers hailed it as the ultimate vindication.

NATO membership was out of the question for countries like Poland, Hungary or Czechoslavakia." Historian Mary Elise Sarotte, author of an award-winning book on this period, explained, "In summary, Gorbachev had listened to Baker and Kohl suggest to him for two days in a row that NATO's jurisdiction would not move eastward, and at the end he agreed to let Germany unify."[20]

The United States, for its part, appreciated Gorbachev's restraint in Eastern Europe but didn't hesitate to use force in its own backyard. Panamanian strongman Manuel Noriega had long been the United States' boy in Central America. He had twice attended the U.S. Army School of the Americas in the Panama Canal Zone and had been on the CIA payroll since the 1960s. Corrupt and unscrupulous, he profited from assisting Colombia's Medellín drug cartel, but he also fingered Medellín rivals to the U.S. Drug Enforcement Administration. His assistance to the contras in Nicaragua won him protection from top Reagan administration officials, including William Casey, Elliott Abrams, and Oliver North. But his 1988 indictment on U.S. federal drug charges and his overturning of Panama's 1989 presidential election finally convinced Bush that he was more of a liability than an asset. With U.S. encouragement, Panamanian military officers attempted a coup. The United States, however, offered no assistance.

The chair of the House Select Committee on Intelligence, David McCurdy, bemoaned the "resurgence of the wimp factor."[21]

In December 1989, Bush decided to act unilaterally, and bypass Congress, in violation of the War Powers Act of 1973. He sent 15,000 troops to assist the 12,000 already in the country to overthrow Noriega and take down his Panamanian Defense Forces and paramilitary units in what the United States called "Operation Just Cause." Bush attempted to defend the invasion, claiming that he had acted "only after reaching the conclusion that every other avenue was closed and the lives of American citizens were in grave danger."[22] One reporter pushed Cheney for an explanation: "Mr. Secretary, following the failed coup in Panama, you came into this room and you made a number of arguments justifying our decision not to get more heavily involved. You . . . said it wasn't up to the United States . . . to go willy-nilly around the world knocking off governments. . . . Why is your earlier assessment, which you made in this room two months ago, not valid anymore?" Cheney responded, apparently with a straight face, "I think we as a Government bent over backward to avoid having to take military action," only invading when it became clear that "American lives were at risk."[23]

Latin Americans angrily condemned the return to gunboat diplomacy. Mexico proclaimed that "fighting international crimes is no excuse for intervention in a sovereign nation."[24] Cuba denounced the "new imperialist aggression" and said it showed "the disdain of the United States for international law."[25] The Organization of American States voted 20–1 to "deeply deplore" the invasion.[26] Only a U.S. veto blocked similar UN Security Council action.

Latin Americans' bitterness about the invasion, which violated the charter of the OAS, would persist for years. Shortly after the 9/11 attacks by Al-Qaeda, the editors of the Nicaragua-based magazine *Envío* wrote that in December 1989, "the government of George Bush Sr. ordered the invasion of Panama, a military operation that bombed civilian neighborhoods and killed thousands of Panamanians just to flush out a single man, Manuel Noriega. . . ." "Was that not state terrorism?" they asked.[27]

Soviet U.S. expert Georgi Arbatov warned that the invasion would strengthen Soviet hard-liners, who would see through the hypocrisy of the United States' praising Soviet nonintervention while it was itself overthrowing governments. They had good reason to feel that way. The invasion was indeed a signal that Soviet inaction would not curb U.S. bellicosity; it might, in fact, embolden the United States to act more recklessly. The *Washington Post*'s Bob Woodward pointed to Colin Powell's support for the invasion as critical to Bush's decision making. Powell declared, "We have to put a shingle outside our door saying 'Superpower Lives Here,' no matter what the Soviets do, even if they evacuate from Eastern Europe."[28] Neocon Elliott Abrams concluded that the United

U.S. Drug Enforcement Agency (DEA) agents escort General Manuel Noriega onto a U.S. aircraft. Despite the fact that the Panamanian strongman had long enjoyed CIA funding and U.S. protection for assisting the contras in Nicaragua and fingering his drug cartel's rivals to the DEA, in December 1989, Bush sent some 15,000 troops to assist the 12,000 already in the country to overthrow Noriega and take down his Panamanian Defense Forces. Latin Americans angrily condemned the return to gunboat diplomacy.

States should have invaded sooner and speculated that "the reduced danger of escalation makes limited military action more rather than less likely."[29]

Noriega eluded U.S. forces for almost a week before seeking asylum at the Vatican Embassy. The United States surrounded the embassy with enormous speakers and, despite Vatican protests, blasted rock music—songs like "I Fought the Law (And the Law Won)," "Nowhere to Run," and "You're No Good"—around the clock. Noriega was sentenced to jail in the United States for drug trafficking. In the aftermath of the seemingly successful and popular military action, the supine Congress failed to challenge the president for flouting the War Powers Act, which requires the White House to seek congressional approval for the use of force in other countries.

But Bush wasn't finished. The Reagan administration had cozied up to Iraq's Saddam Hussein, removing Iraq from the State Department list of terrorist states and backing it in its war against Iran. Even Saddam's use of chemical weapons to crush Kurdish resistance had elicited little protest. Following a clumsy attempt by the United States to pin that crime on Iran, Bush extended an additional $1.2 billion in credits and loans to Saddam while Kuwait demanded that Iraq repay the money it had borrowed to wage war against Iran. Kuwait also refused to abide by the OPEC oil quotas, driving down the price of oil at a time when Iraq desperately needed the revenue to repay over $40 billion in accrued debts. Further angering Saddam, Kuwait, which had been part of Iraq until 1961, rejected Iraq's claims on their disputed border.

U.S. Ambassador April Glaspie met with Saddam in Baghdad on July 25, 1990, assuring him that Bush "wanted better and deeper relations" and had "no opinion" on its border dispute with Kuwait, which had been no friend of the United States.[30] Senator and former UN Ambassador Daniel Patrick Moynihan described Kuwait to fellow senators as "a particularly poisonous enemy of the United States" whose "anti-Semitism was at the level of the personally loathsome."[31] Saddam took Glaspie's remarks as a signal that the United States would acquiesce in his Kuwaiti takeover. The following week, three Iraqi divisions entered Kuwait, giving Iraq control of one-fifth of the world's oil supply. In September, Glaspie effectively confirmed that she had led Saddam on, telling the *New York Times*, "I didn't think—and nobody else did—that the Iraqis were going to take all of Kuwait."[32]

Cheney, Powell, and General Norman Schwarzkopf rushed to meet with Saudi Arabia's King Fahd. They showed him doctored photos of 150,000 Iraqi troops and 1,500 tanks poised just across his border in Kuwait and convinced him to allow a large U.S. military force onto Saudi soil, giving the United States its long-sought toehold in the region. The deception was soon exposed. A Japanese newspaper obtained satellite photos showing no Iraqi troop buildup in the area. American media took interest in the story. ABC News purchased additional satellite photos the following month, reconfirming the original assessment. *Newsweek* called it "the case of the 'missing' military presence." "In fact," *Newsweek* reported, "all they could see, in crystal-clear detail, was the U.S. buildup in Saudi Arabia." U.S. Ambassador to Saudi Arabia Charles Freeman warned, "This will never work. All it's going to take is one photo of some GI pissing on the wall of a mosque, and the Saudi government will be overthrown."[33] Despite Pentagon pressure to bury the story, Jean Heller, a highly respected reporter with the *St. Petersburg Times*, decided to pursue it, obtaining more photos that she showed to physicist and defense analyst Peter Zimmerman, who exposed the fraudulence of the U.S. claims. *Newsday* reported the comments of one senior U.S. commander who acknowledged, "There was a great disinformation campaign surrounding this war."[34]

There is no evidence that Saddam ever intended to invade Saudi Arabia. Powell acknowledged that for the first three weeks, Iraq could have marched unimpeded into Saudi Arabia if it had so desired. He agreed with Turkish and Arab leaders

*Secretary of Defense Dick Cheney meets with Crown Prince Sultan,
the Saudi minister of defense and aviation. Following Iraq's invasion
of Kuwait, Cheney, along with Generals Colin Powell and Norman
Schwarzkopf, rushed to meet with the Saudis, showing them doctored
photos of an alleged Iraqi troop buildup on their border with Kuwait.
Convincing King Fahd to allow a large U.S. military force onto Saudi
soil, the United States gained its long-sought toehold in the region.*

that sanctions would force Saddam to reverse course. Former Secretary of Defense
Robert McNamara urged the Senate to use sanctions, not war. In fact, UN-imposed
sanctions were taking a tremendous toll on Iraq. In October, CIA Director William
Webster reported that sanctions had curtailed 98 percent of Iraq's oil exports and
perhaps 95 percent of its imports. Zbigniew Brzezinski testified that an invasion
could be "highly counterproductive," turning the Arab world and European allies
against the United States and causing chaos in the region.[35]

Pressure mounted quickly for a strong response by Bush. The Israeli press led
the charge. An editorial in *Hadashot* was typical. "The pro-Iraqi puppet Government in Kuwait," it lashed out, "is an expression of U.S. impotence and the weakness of President George Bush. Bush, until now at least, resembles Chamberlain
in his knowing capitulation to Hitler."[36]

Bush turned the tired Munich analogy on its head. In an August 8 televised
address to the nation, he described Saddam as "an aggressive dictator threatening his neighbors" and compared him to Hitler.[37] He kept the rhetoric at a fever

pitch. *Washington Post* editor Charles Paul Freund dissected the Bush strategy: "Bush's major rhetorical device in constructing his argument against aggression was Hitler. . . . Saddam Hussein's sudden media Hitlerization was . . . another chapter in a process we have seen several times in recent years involving such figures as 'strongman' Noriega of Panama, the 'fanatical' Khomeini of Iran and Libya's 'madman' Gadhafi." [38]

Comparing Saddam Hussein to the most justly reviled figure of the twentieth century struck many observers as unreasonable, even absurd. At a campaign event in the Boston suburbs, Bush suggested that Saddam was worse than Hitler in using hostages as "human shields" at potential military targets. When asked how this could make him worse than the man responsible for the Holocaust, Bush equivocated, "I didn't say the Holocaust, I mean, that is outrageous. But I think brutalizing young kids in a square in Kuwait is outrageous, too. I was told that Hitler did not stake people out against potential military targets and that he did, indeed, respect—not much else, but he did, indeed respect the legitimacy of the embassies. So we've got some differences there." [39]

Bush also announced that U.S. troops were headed toward the Persian Gulf to take up positions in Saudi Arabia. He decided to act before the Saudis came up with their own solution to the crisis, fearing that a Saudi initiative might undermine U.S. domination of the region and its oil resources. Given the Saudis' disdain for the Kuwaiti oligarchy, he feared that an "Arab solution" would leave Iraq in a powerful position. [40]

Meanwhile, Kuwaiti officials hired the world's largest public relations firm, Hill & Knowlton, to sell the war. The firm's Washington director, Craig Fuller, had been Bush's chief of staff when he was vice president. Fuller helped orchestrate the largest foreign-funded effort ever undertaken to manipulate U.S. public opinion. On October 10, at hearings sponsored by Congress's Human Rights Caucus, a fifteen-year-old girl testified that she had been a volunteer in a Kuwaiti hospital when Iraqi troops burst in. She described what she had witnessed: "They took the babies out of the incubators, took the incubators, and left the babies on the cold floor to die." Bush cited the story repeatedly in making the case for war: "It turns your stomach to listen to the tales of those that have escaped the brutality of Saddam the invader. Mass hangings. Babies pulled from incubators and scattered like firewood across the floor." It was later discovered that not only was the young witness lying about having been at the hospital, she was the daughter of the Kuwaiti ambassador to the United States and a member of the ruling family. [41] By the time the fraud was exposed, U.S. bombing of Baghdad had already begun.

On November 29, the final UN Security Council resolution authorized use of "all necessary means" to force Iraqi evacuation from Kuwait. Votes for the resolution didn't come cheap. Egypt had almost $14 billion of debt written off by the United States and the Gulf states another $6.7 billion. Syria received over $2 billion from Europe, Japan, Saudi Arabia, and other Arab states. Saudi Arabia gave the Soviets $1 billion, and the United States offered credit guarantees. For not vetoing the resolution, China's foreign minister, who had been persona non grata after Tiananmen Square, was given a White House reception.

For joining Cuba in voting against the resolution, Yemen was punished severely. A senior U.S. diplomat informed the Yemeni ambassador, "That was the most expensive 'no' vote you ever cast."[42] Three days later, the United States cut $70 million in desperately needed aid to Yemen. The World Bank and the International Monetary Fund (IMF) started squeezing Yemen, and Saudi Arabia expelled 800,000 Yemeni workers.

While understanding the importance of marshaling international support to provide a "cloak of acceptability" to their invasion, U.S. leaders made it clear that they weren't about to relinquish control to the United Nations or anyone else. As Bush and Scowcroft explained in their memoirs, "It was important to reach out to the rest of the world, but even more important to keep the strings of control tightly in our hands."[43]

The U.S. public was also sharply divided. Approval of Bush's handling of the crisis had dropped by 30 percent in three months. Despite Bush's rhetoric about the nobility of the United States' motives, it was difficult to sell the despotic leaders of Saudi Arabia or Kuwait as paragons of democracy. Nor was it easy to make the case that crucial U.S. interests were at stake. The United States, unlike Western Europe and Japan, depended very little on Kuwaiti oil. In fact, Iraqi and Kuwaiti oil combined accounted for only 9 percent of U.S. imports. And neither the Europeans nor the Japanese were eager to go to war over Kuwait.

Confronted with growing opposition, administration officials seized upon another strategy to frighten both the American public and vacillating UN officials. In late November, Cheney and Scowcroft appeared on Sunday talk shows brandishing the nuclear threat. Cheney spoke about Iraq's nuclear weapons progress and its chances of achieving "some kind of crude device" in less than a year. Scowcroft told David Brinkley that Saddam might achieve that goal within "months." "One has to assume," he added, "that he might be more willing to use nuclear weapons than has any other power." Scowcroft had apparently forgotten which country it was that had previously dropped nuclear bombs on an adversary and had threatened to do so again dozens more times over the years. And as if the nuclear threat weren't frightening enough, Scowcroft added the terrorist threat for good measure. When asked, "What we have heard is that [Saddam] has gathered a whole raft of terrorists into his country and they are standing around awaiting instructions. Is that right?" "That's right," Scowcroft replied.[44]

Despite Cheney's insistence that congressional approval of the use of force was not needed, Bush decided to take the measure to Congress. With antiwar protesters filling the streets, the House passed the war resolution on January 12 by 250–183. The Senate passed it 52–47.

By mid-January, the United States had 560,000 troops in the region. Almost 700,000 would serve by the end of the war. This gargantuan force was justified by even larger estimates of the number of Iraqi troops. Powell estimated half a million, Cheney a million, and Schwarzkopf 1.5 million.

The Security Council resolution had given the Iraqis until January 15, 1991, to withdraw their forces. Had Saddam been more savvy, he might have outfoxed the Americans who were most bent on war. *New York Times* reporter Judith Miller had earlier described what one European diplomat termed the "nightmare scenario" for the Americans: an Iraqi withdrawal that would leave Saddam in power and his arsenal intact, especially if it were accompanied by calls for elections to determine Kuwait's future political structure. If that had happened, the carefully crafted U.S. game plan could have unraveled and Saddam would have survived. The Saudis would have felt compelled to request the removal of all international forces, whose stay in the country, Bush and King Fahd had promised, would last only as long as the danger persisted. The ruling Sabah family in Kuwait would either be toppled or have its powers sharply constrained. U.S. plans to establish a long-term presence in the Gulf region would be thwarted.[45]

The Iraqis would pay severely for Saddam's failure to snatch diplomatic victory from the jaws of military defeat. Operation Desert Storm began on January 17, 1991. The United States pummeled Iraqi facilities for five weeks with its new high-tech weapons, including cruise and Tomahawk missiles and laser-guided bombs. After having crippled Iraq's communications and military infrastructure, U.S. and Saudi forces attacked battered, demoralized, and outnumbered Iraqi troops in Kuwait, who put up little if any resistance. U.S. forces slaughtered escaping Iraqis along what became known as the "highway of death." They deployed a new category of weapons made out of depleted uranium, whose radioactivity and chemical toxicity would produce cancers and birth defects for years. Victims may have included U.S. soldiers, who suffered from what became known as Gulf War Syndrome. But enough of the Republican Guard escaped the slaughter to ensure that Saddam would retain his hold on power.

Bush and his advisors decided not to push to Baghdad to overthrow the regime, recognizing that such a move would bolster the regional hegemony of Iran, antagonize the United States' Arab allies, and embroil the United States in a costly and complicated occupation. Cheney warned, "Once we cross over the line and start intervening in a civil war . . . it raises the very real specter of getting

RIGHT: *Antiwar protesters filled the streets in January 1991.*

BELOW (LEFT TO RIGHT): *General Colin Powell, General Norman Schwarzkopf, and Paul Wolfowitz listen to Dick Cheney (not pictured) at a press conference during Operation Desert Storm. The United States' use of a gargantuan force of almost 700,000 troops during the war was justified by the massive estimates of Iraqi troops by Powell, Cheney, and Schwarzkopf, who predicted a half-million, a million, and 1.5 million, respectively.*

us involved in a quagmire figuring out who the hell is going to govern Iraq." On another occasion he elaborated:

> It's not clear what kind of government you would put in place of the one that's currently there now. Is it going to be a Shia regime, a Sunni regime or a Kurdish regime? Or one that tilts toward the Baathists, or one that tilts toward the Islamic fundamentalists? How much credibility is that government going to have if it's set up by the United States military when it's there? How long does the United States military have to stay to protect the people that sign on for that government, and what happens to it once we leave?[46]

Colin Powell agreed with Cheney. The United States didn't want to occupy Iraq, and there was no "Jeffersonian democrat waiting in the Ba'ath Party to take over." The United States, he argued, was better off not getting "mired down in a Mesopotamian mess."[47]

Wolfowitz and fellow State Department official I. Lewis "Scooter" Libby disagreed. But Bush resisted their urgings. "Trying to eliminate Saddam . . . would have incurred incalculable human and political costs," he later explained. "We would have been forced to occupy Baghdad and, in effect, rule Iraq." He added that "there was no viable 'exit strategy.'"[48]

U.S. officials urged the Iraqis to rise up and topple Saddam. Shiites and Kurds responded en masse. But the United States stood idly by while the Iraqi government crushed the uprising, using poison gas and helicopter gunships. Still, the war showcased U.S. military power. Bush proclaimed a new world order and gushed, "The ghosts of Vietnam have been laid to rest beneath the sands of the Arabian desert."[49] One White House speechwriter programmed his word processor so he could write "New World Order" by hitting a single command key.[50] Among those who dismissed this empty "burst of triumphalism" was conservative columnist George Will, who wrote, "If that war, in which the United States and a largely rented and Potemkin coalition of allies smashed a nation with the GNP of Kentucky, could . . . make America 'feel good about itself,' then America should not feel good about itself." He noted "how close Bush came to unilaterally amending the Constitution by stripping from Congress all right to involvement in the making of war. Bush only grudgingly . . . sought constitutional approval for launching the biggest military operation in U.S. history, an attack on a nation with which we were not at war."[51] In two months of bombing, the United States destroyed much of Iraq's infrastructure, including roads, bridges, sanitation facilities, waterways, railroads, communications systems, factories, and the electrical grid, and caused immense suffering. In March, the United Nations described the

Operation Desert Storm began on January 17, 1991. The United States pummeled Iraqi facilities for five weeks with its new high-tech weapons. After crippling Iraq's communications and military infrastructure, U.S. and Saudi forces attacked battered, demoralized, and outnumbered Iraqi troops in Kuwait, who put up little if any resistance. U.S. forces slaughtered escaping Iraqis along what became known as the "highway of death."

bombing as "near apocalyptic," driving Iraq back into the "pre-industrial age."[52] A Harvard team reported a "public health catastrophe."[53] The continuing UN sanctions exacerbated a miserable situation, reducing real wages by over 90 percent. Although estimates vary widely, credible sources report that over 200,000 Iraqis died in the war and its aftermath, approximately half of them women and children. The U.S. death toll stood at 158.

"By God, we've kicked the Vietnam syndrome once and for all!" Bush rejoiced. But privately he was more circumspect. As the war was coming to an end, he wrote in his diary that he was experiencing "no feeling of euphoria." "It hasn't been a clean end," he regretted. "There is no battleship *Missouri* surrender. This is what's missing to make this akin to WWII, to separate Kuwait from Korea and Vietnam."[54] And with Saddam Hussein remaining safely ensconced in power, victory seemed hollow and incomplete.

Gorbachev, meanwhile, had even less to celebrate. Just a few days after signing the START I treaty, on August 18, 1991, as he prepared to give even greater autonomy to the Soviet republics, Communist hard-liners placed him under house arrest. Boris Yeltsin, president of the Russian Republic, led a popular uprising that returned Gorbachev to power. But Gorbachev's days were numbered. He was determined to use whatever time he had left to pursue his nuclear arms control agenda. START I would limit both sides to 6,000 strategic nuclear warheads and 1,600 delivery systems. Gorbachev also pushed for elimination of the 45,000 smaller-yield tactical nuclear weapons that the United States and Soviet Union had placed primarily in Europe. Although less dangerous than the powerful strategic weapons that were being slowly reduced, some of these battlefield weapons could yield up to a megaton, which was the equivalent of almost seventy Hiroshima bombs. Joint Chiefs of Staff Chairman Colin Powell had commissioned a study that recommended eliminating the tactical nuclear weapons, but it was rejected by the Pentagon. "The report went up to the Pentagon policy staff, a refuge of Reagan-era hard-liners, who stomped all over it, from Paul Wolfowitz on down," Powell wrote in his memoirs. Cheney stomped, too.[55] Despite the setbacks, both sides made significant unilateral cuts in their nuclear arsenals that would reduce, though not eliminate, the danger of complete nuclear annihilation.

On Christmas Day, having lost his base of support, Gorbachev resigned. The Soviet Union was no more. The Cold War had ended. The most visionary and transformative leader of the twentieth century had yielded power. Even some people in the United States had come to appreciate the immensity of his contribution. James Baker had said to him in September 1990, "Mr. President . . . nobody in the world has ever tried what you and your supporters are trying today. . . . I've seen a lot, but I've never met a politician with as much bravery and courage as you have."[56]

As wasteful and dangerous as the Cold War was, it had brought a kind of structure and stability. What would happen now? Would peace and tranquility return? The United States had been blaming social and political upheaval on the Soviet Union for the previous forty-six years. In truth, though, the Soviets had more often than not exercised restraint upon their allies. And what would now become of the United States' vast military and intelligence establishment, which had been constructed to counter a deliberately exaggerated Soviet threat? How would the hawks justify the bloated military budget that for decades had diverted resources from needed development to expensive weaponry and gaudy defense sector profits? And what would come of Gorbachev's promise to reduce the once massive Soviet nuclear arsenal to less than 5,000 warheads?

The answers would soon be forthcoming. In 1992, Paul Wolfowitz oversaw the creation of a new "Defense Planning Guidance," forecasting future challenges to U.S. interests. An early draft insisted that the United States not allow any rival to emerge that could threaten U.S. global hegemony and that it take unilateral and preemptive action against states attempting to acquire weapons of mass destruction (WMD). The draft outlined seven potential war scenarios and warned that the United States must be prepared to simultaneously fight wars against North Korea and Iraq, while resisting a Russian incursion into Europe.

Bush and Gorbachev sign the START I treaty at the Kremlin in Moscow. The treaty would limit both sides to 6,000 strategic nuclear warheads and 1,600 delivery systems. Gorbachev also pushed for the elimination of tactical nuclear weapons, a move endorsed in a study commissioned by Joint Chiefs Chairman Colin Powell. But that was rejected by the Pentagon. Despite the setbacks, both sides made significant unilateral cuts in their nuclear arsenals that would reduce, though not eliminate, the danger of nuclear holocaust.

The *New York Times* reported that the classified "documents suggest levels of manpower and weapons that would appear to stall, if not reverse, the downward trend in military spending by the mid-1990s."[57]

The plan provoked a firestorm of criticism at home and abroad. It was a "Pax Americana," Senator Joseph Biden charged—"an old notion of the United States as the world's policeman." Senator Robert Byrd called the Pentagon strategy "myopic, shallow, and disappointing. The basic thrust of the document seems to be this: 'We love being the sole remaining superpower in the world and we want so much to remain that way that we are willing to put at risk the basic health of our economy and well-being of our people to do so.'" Future presidential candidate Pat Buchanan called it "a formula for endless American intervention in quarrels and war when no vital interest of the United States is remotely engaged." The *New York Times* decried its "chest-thumping unilateralism." The Pentagon backpedaled so fast that it tripped over its own lies. A Pentagon spokesman insisted that the plan hadn't been seen by Wolfowitz, who drafted it, or by Cheney, though he admitted that it was in line with Cheney's thinking.[58]

Bush's 91 percent approval rating at the end of the Persian Gulf War blinded leading Democrats to his electoral vulnerability, leaving the door open for Arkansas Governor Bill Clinton. Clinton, who chaired the centrist Democratic

Leadership Council, ran as a "new kind of Democrat"—one positioned midway between the liberals and the conservatives. He promised a business-friendly administration that would lower the deficit, cut middle-class taxes, strengthen the military, and "end welfare as we know it." With Ross Perot siphoning off 19 percent of the popular vote, Clinton trounced Bush in the electoral college.

The Democrats' euphoria over capturing the White House proved short-lived. Republicans weakened Clinton out of the gate by blocking his attempt to secure the open admission of gays into the military, but the much more telling blow would be struck in defeating his plan to overhaul the health care system. Among advanced industrial countries, only the United States and apartheid South Africa lacked a national health care system. The Republicans and their business allies spent $50 million to frighten the American public and deny health care coverage to tens of millions of citizens. Richard Armey, chair of the House Republican Conference, prepared for what he called "the most important domestic policy debate of the past half century . . . the Battle of the Bulge of big-government liberalism." Armey believed, "The failure of the Clinton plan will . . . leave the President's agenda weakened, his . . . supporters demoralized, and the opposition emboldened. Our market-oriented ideas will suddenly become thinkable, not just on health care, but on a host of issues. . . . Historians may mark it as . . . the start of the Republican renaissance."[59]

The 1994 midterm elections gave Republicans control of both branches of Congress for the first time in forty years. Both parties lurched further to the right. Succumbing to conservative pressure, Clinton ended Aid to Families with Dependent Children, which had helped poor families since the Great Depression, and supported a war on drugs and tough-on-crime legislation. The U.S. prison population exploded from a half million in 1980 to 2 million twenty years later. Forty-five percent of those incarcerated were African American, and 15 percent were Hispanic.

Post-Soviet Russia also moved to the right. Yeltsin turned to Harvard economist Jeffrey Sachs and other USAID-funded Harvard experts for help in privatizing the economy. Sachs had advised on Poland's initial transformation from socialism to capitalism, an effort that would double poverty in two years and, by some estimates, plunge over half of Poland's population into poverty by 2003. Sachs and company encouraged First Deputy Prime Minister Yegor Gaidar and Deputy Prime Minister Anatoly Chubais to subject Russia to even more intense "shock therapy" than Poland had experienced. Gorbachev had resisted similar demands by the G7, IMF, and World Bank. Another key player was Undersecretary of the Treasury Lawrence Summers. As the World Bank's chief economist, he had recently created a furor by signing a supposedly sarcastic memo, declaring, "The economic logic behind dumping . . . toxic waste in the lowest wage country is impeccable," adding, "I've always thought that under-populated countries in Africa are vastly UNDER-polluted." Brazil's secretary of the environment told Summers, "Your reasoning is perfectly logical but totally insane . . . a concrete example of the unbelievable alienation, . . . social ruthlessness and . . . arrogant ignorance of many conventional 'economists.'"[60]

Russia's flirtation with crony capitalism proved equally insane. Before the Russian people knew what hit them, Yeltsin had deregulated the economy, privatized state enterprises and resources, eliminated desperately needed subsidies and price controls, and established privately owned monopolies. The Western aid and debt relief that Sachs promised never materialized. Sachs later blamed Cheney and Wolfowitz for pursuing "long-term U.S. military dominance over . . . Russia."[61] Conditions worsened while Clinton was in office. In what Russians called the "great grab," the nation's factories and resources were sold off for a pittance to private investors, including former Communist officials, who became multimillionaires overnight.

Yeltsin responded to the popular outcry against his policies by dissolving parliament, suspending the Constitution, and ruling primarily by decree for the rest of the decade. The World Bank's chief economist for Russia told the *Wall Street Journal,* "I've never had so much fun in my life."[62]

The Russian people didn't share in the frivolity. Russia's economy collapsed. Hyperinflation wiped out people's life savings. Tens of millions of workers lost their jobs. Life expectancy plummeted from sixty-six to fifty-seven years. By 1998, more than 80 percent of Russian farms had gone bankrupt. Russian GDP had been almost cut in half. The Russian economy shrank to the size of Holland's. In 2000, capital investment stood at 20 percent of what it had been a decade earlier. Fifty percent of Russians earned less than $35 per month—the official poverty line—and many hovered just above. Russia was rapidly becoming a third-world nation. Embittered, Russians joked that they thought the Communists had been lying to them about socialism and capitalism, but it turned out they were only lying about socialism.

Sachsonomics worked similar miracles in the other former Soviet republics, where the number of people living in poverty jumped from 14 million in 1989 to 147 million—and that was before the crash of 1998. Famed Russian novelist Alexander Solzhenitsyn, who returned to Russia after being exiled for two decades, described the situation in 2000:

> As a result of the Yeltsin era, all the fundamental sectors of our state, economic, cultural, and moral life have been destroyed or looted. We live literally amid ruins, but we pretend to have a normal life. . . . great reforms . . . being carried out in our country . . . were false reforms because

they left more than half of our people in poverty.... Will we continue
looting and destroying Russia until nothing is left? ... God forbid these
reforms should continue.[63]

Popular disdain for Yeltsin fueled anti-Americanism. Russians also bristled
over U.S. involvement in the energy-rich Caspian Basin region and expansion
of NATO to include Hungary, Poland, and the Czech Republic—a move that
ninety-two-year-old George Kennan called "an enormous and historic strategic error." Russians condemned the U.S.-led NATO bombing of fellow Slavs in
Yugoslavia in 1999. One survey reported that 96 percent of Russians considered
the bombing a "crime against humanity." In 2000, 81 percent saw U.S. policy
as anti-Russian, most respondents believing that the United States was imposing a "reverse iron curtain" on Russia's borders.[64] Economically crippled, Russia
placed greater reliance on its nuclear arsenal as its last line of defense, broadened
the circumstances under which it would use nuclear weapons, and began modernizing its arsenal.

Dangerous incidents occurred. In 1995, Soviet radar operators mistook
a Norwegian rocket launch for an incoming ballistic missile. Yeltsin activated
his nuclear football for the first time. He and his top military advisors debated
whether to launch a nuclear counterattack against the United States until Russia's nine early-warning satellites confirmed that Russia was not under attack and
the crisis ended. By 2000, only two of those satellites were still operating, leaving
Russia blind for much of each day.

Polls showed Russians preferring order over democracy, with growing numbers pining for the "good old days" of Stalin. Though Clinton extolled Yeltsin as
the architect of democracy, the Russian people deplored his illegal shutdown
of and armed assault on the elected parliament, his launching of a bloody war
against the breakaway republic of Chechnya in 1994, and his stewardship of the
collapsing economy. Gorbachev denounced Yeltsin as a "liar" who had more
privileges than the Russian tsars.[65] Polling single-digit approval ratings, Yeltsin
resigned on December 31, 1999, and was replaced by former KGB officer Vladimir Putin.

Once Afghanistan's Russian-backed government fell in 1992, the United
States lost interest in that distant, barren land, where life expectancy stood at
forty-six years. A bloody civil war erupted between various Islamist factions and
ethnic groups. One consisted largely of Afghan refugees recruited from madrassas—Saudi-sponsored religious schools in Pakistan. These fanatical religious
students, or *talibs*, formed the Taliban—with help from the Pakistani intelligence service. Many had already received military training in CIA-financed
camps. Most had studied textbooks developed by the University of Nebraska

President Clinton and Russian leader Boris Yeltsin share a laugh during a press conference at FDR's home in Hyde Park, New York, in October 1995. Though Clinton extolled Yeltsin as the architect of democracy, the Russian people deplored his illegal shutdown of and armed assault on the elected parliament, his launching of a bloody war against the breakaway republic of Chechnya in 1994, and his stewardship of the collapsing economy. Gorbachev denounced Yeltsin as a "liar" who had more privileges than the Russian tsars.

at Omaha's (UNO) Center for Afghanistan Studies in a program funded by USAID to the tune of $51 million between 1984 and 1994. Published in Dari and Pashtu, the dominant Afghan languages, the books were designed to stoke Islamic fanaticism and spur resistance to the Soviet invaders. Page after page was filled with militant Islamic teachings and violent images. Children learned to count using pictures of missiles, tanks, land mines, Kalashnikovs, and dead Soviet soldiers. One leading Afghan educator said, "The pictures . . . are horrendous to school students, but the texts are even much worse." One, for example, shows a soldier adorned with a bandolier and a Kalashnikov. Above him is a verse from the Koran. Below is a statement about the mujahideen, who, in obedience to Allah, willingly sacrifice their lives and fortunes to impose Sharia law on the government. Students learned to read by studying stories about jihad. When the Taliban seized Kabul in 1996, they continued using the same violent jihadist texts, simply removing the human images, which they considered blasphemous.[66] Girls would be spared the indignity of seeing such texts, though; they were banned from school entirely. The Taliban subjected all Afghans to the most extreme Sharia law, banning visual images and instituting public amputations, beatings, and executions. Women lost all rights, including the rights to work and to go out in public without a male escort.

Also in 1996, the Taliban welcomed a young Saudi named Osama bin Laden back to Afghanistan. He returned as head of Al-Qaeda (The Base), an extremist organization committed to driving the United States and its allies out of the Muslim world and reestablishing the caliphate. He had been part of the CIA netherworld, recruiting and training the foreign militants who flooded into Afghanistan to battle the Soviet infidels. Funding came largely from Saudi royal family members eager to spread their strict Wahhabist form of Islam. Bin Laden's father was one of Saudi Arabia's wealthiest men. Above all else, bin Laden decried the presence of the United States' "infidel armies" in Saudi Arabia, Islam's holiest land, and condemned U.S. support for Israel. Openly pledging to expunge U.S. allies in Saudi Arabia, Jordan, Egypt, and Palestine, he issued his first fatwa in 1992, calling for jihad against the Western occupation of Islamic lands.

Bin Laden delivered on his threats. A 1995 Al-Qaeda bombing of a U.S. military base in Riyadh, Saudi Arabia, killed five U.S. airmen and wounded thirty-four. The following June, a powerful truck bomb destroyed a building in the Khobar Towers complex in Saudi Arabia, killing 19 U.S. airmen and wounding 372. The Saudi government, given its close ties to the bin Laden family, steered the U.S. investigation toward Saudi Shiites tied to Iran. FBI Director Louis Freeh met repeatedly with Saudi Ambassador Prince Bandar bin Sultan, who convinced him that Iran was involved, despite bin Laden's brazen claims of responsibility for both bombings. Bin Laden experts in the FBI and CIA were handcuffed in their investigations.

But the Saudi bombing, that year's bombing of the federal building in Oklahoma City by right-wing domestic terrorists, and the sarin gas attack in a Tokyo subway by Aum Shinrikyo caught the attention of some administration officials. In January 1996, the CIA's Counterterrorist Center opened a new office. Its sole responsibility was to track Osama bin Laden, who was setting up terrorist training camps in Afghanistan.

While barely acknowledging the Al-Qaeda threat, Clinton administration officials were alert to investment possibilities in the region. Clinton pushed for building pipelines to ship the oil and gas from former Soviet republics in Central Asia along routes that bypassed Iran and Russia. Studies placed the total value of Central Asian oil and gas reserves at between $3 trillion and $6 trillion. The administration supported efforts by the U.S. oil company Unocal to build a $2 billion pipeline to transport natural gas from Turkmenistan to Pakistan and India. "By Unocal prevailing," noted a State Department official, "our influence will be solidified, the Russians will be weakened and we can keep Iran from benefiting."[67] Counting on the Taliban to stabilize the war-torn country, Unocal celebrated the Taliban's seizure of Kabul. It was a "very positive" development,

Page from a Dari language textbook developed by University of Nebraska at Omaha's (UNO) Center for Afghanistan Studies. An excerpt from the book's next page reads, "Jihad is the kind of war that Muslims fight in the name of God to free Muslims and Muslim lands from the enemies of Islam. If infidels invade, jihad is the obligation of every Muslim." Many among Afghanistan's Taliban had studied such textbooks, whose development was funded by USAID to the tune of $51 million between 1984 and 1994.

said Unocal's executive vice president. Neocon Zalmay Khalilzad, a Unocal consultant who had worked in the State Department under Wolfowitz and in the Defense Department under Cheney, agreed. Pakistani journalist Ahmed Rashid explained that some U.S. diplomats "saw them as messianic do-gooders—like born-again Christians from the American Bible Belt." [68]

Unocal pulled out all the stops to win approval of its pipeline. It hired the University of Nebraska's Center for Afghanistan Studies to help it create goodwill and do some needed vocational training. The Center was to teach fourteen basic skills, at least nine of which would be of direct use in building the pipeline. To make this happen, the Center needed to be in the good graces of both of the major rival factions in Afghanistan: the Northern Alliance and the Taliban. The *Omaha World-Herald* reported that the Northern Alliance "has been criticized by the U.S. State Department, the United Nations and human-rights groups for terrorism, rape, kidnapping of women and children, torture of prisoners and indiscriminate killing of civilians during battles." And they, by most standards, were the good guys. The Taliban, which then controlled about 75 percent of the country, including the stretches where the pipeline was to run, were accused by Amnesty International of "gender apartheid" and of facilitating the growth of nearly half of the world's opium supply. When asked why an academic institution would accept such a role, aside from the substantial sum Unocal was paying, the Center's director Thomas Gouttierre replied, "I don't assume a private corporation is evil." Nor did he have much of an issue with the Taliban, whom he described as "the same sort of people who spawned William Jennings Bryan. They're populists. . . . They are not out there oppressing people." [69]

The victims of Al-Qaeda's 1998 bombings of U.S. embassies in Nairobi, Kenya, and Dar es Salaam, Tanzania, were not so certain about the Taliban or their guests. The bombs detonated ten minutes apart, killing more than two hundred people. Two years later, Al-Qaeda struck again with a suicide attack against the USS *Cole*. Clinton then gave the okay to kill bin Laden at his base camp in Afghanistan. After the bombings, Unocal pulled out of the pipeline deal, but others remained interested. Enron, whose chief executive Ken Lay was a major backer of George W. Bush, envisioned building a pipeline that could supply cheap natural gas to Enron's faltering Dabhol power plant in India. Dick Cheney, who had become CEO of Halliburton, also set his sights on oil reserves. He told a 1998 gathering of oil industry executives, "I can't think of a time when we've had a region emerge as suddenly to become as strategically significant as the Caspian."[70]

Although the United States faced no clear threat from hostile nations, the Clinton administration squandered the promised peace dividend in a new wave of military spending. In January 2000, it added $115 billion to the Pentagon's projected Five Year Defense Plan, bringing the total to $1.6 trillion and proving that Democrats were even more tough-minded on defense than their Republican adversaries. It continued spending profusely on missile defense, even though experts warned that the costly system would never function as envisioned and enemies and allies alike feared that its pursuit indicated that the United States was striving to achieve a dangerous first-strike capability. Clinton also refused to sign the Ottawa land mines treaty and oversaw an increase in U.S. arms sales from 32 percent of the world market in 1987 to 43 percent a decade later, the lion's share going to countries with deplorable human rights records.

The greatest pressure for increased military spending came from a single-minded group of neoconservatives, spearheaded by William Kristol and Robert Kagan, who, in 1997, formed the Project for the New American Century (PNAC). The PNAC harked back to Henry Luce's vision of unchallenged U.S. global hegemony. The group's founding statement of principles deplored the fact that the United States had lost its way under Clinton and called for return to "a Reaganite policy of military strength and moral clarity." The founders claimed a direct lineage from Scoop Jackson's bunker to Team B to the Committee on the Present Danger, with a few minor detours along the way. They were a far cry from Carter's Trilateralists. The original signers included Elliott Abrams, William Bennett, Jeb Bush, Dick Cheney, Eliot Cohen, Midge Decter, businessman Steve Forbes, Francis Fukuyama, Frank Gaffney, Fred Ikle, historian Donald Kagan, Zalmay Khalilzad, I. Lewis "Scooter" Libby, Norman Podhoretz, former Vice President Dan Quayle, Henry Rowen, Donald Rumsfeld, and Paul Wolfowitz.[71] They and other members and collaborators, including Richard Perle,

Kenneth Adelman, Richard Allen, Richard Armitage, John Bolton, Jeane Kirkpatrick, Charles Krauthammer, Daniel Pipes, and former Director of Central Intelligence James Woolsey, would dominate political discourse and policy making during the George W. Bush administration as completely as the Trilateralists had dominated Carter's. The consequences would prove even more damaging for humanity—far more damaging, in fact—than the misguided policies implemented by the Brzezinski-dominated Carter administration.[72]

PNACers laid out their program in a series of reports, letters, and statements. They demanded increased defense spending, completion of the United States' domination of space, and deployment of a sweeping missile defense system. They insisted that the United States be able to "fight and decisively win multiple, simultaneous major theater wars" and police "critical regions," especially the oil-rich Middle East. Their first order of business was toppling Saddam Hussein and establishing a new government under the aegis of Ahmed Chalabi and his Iraqi National Congress. In January 1998, PNACers urged Clinton to circumvent the UN Security Council and take unilateral military action. But Saddam hadn't provided sufficient provocation.

Since the Gulf War, UN weapons inspectors had been overseeing destruction of Iraq's WMD. U.S.- and British-enforced no-fly zones and harsh UN sanctions had caused immense suffering. In an interview with Secretary of State Madeleine Albright, Lesley Stahl noted, "We have heard that a half million children have died. . . . that's more children than died in Hiroshima," and asked, "is the price worth it?" Albright replied, "I think this is a very hard choice, but the price—we think the price is worth it."

Experts would debate the precise number of Iraqi children who died as a result of the sanctions. In December 1995, two UN-affiliated researchers, writing in the British medical journal *The Lancet,* placed the number at 567,000 but later lowered that estimate. In 2003, British Prime Minister Tony Blair, speaking at a joint press conference with George Bush, said, "Over the past five years, 400,000 Iraqi children under the age of five died of malnutrition and disease," using that as an excuse to justify an invasion that would add tens of thousands more to that total.[73]

Though Clinton resisted the pressure to invade, he and his secretary of state laid the rhetorical groundwork for Bush and Cheney. Albright warned, "Iraq is a long way from [the United States], but what happens there matters a great deal here. For the risks that the leaders of a rogue state will use nuclear, chemical or biological weapons against us or our allies is the greatest security threat we face."[74] On another occasion, Albright had the audacity to declare, "If we have to use force, it is because we are America; we are the indispensable nation. We stand tall and we see further than other countries into the future."[75]

Clearly, neither Albright nor Clinton saw very far into the past. In late October 1998, Clinton signed the Iraq Liberation Act, which asserted, "It should be the policy of the United States to support efforts to remove the regime headed by Saddam Hussein from power in Iraq and to promote the emergence of a democratic government to replace that regime."[76] Saddam immediately stopped inspections but backed down under the threat of war in mid-November and allowed the inspections to continue.

Albright's hawkishness rankled the more sober-minded members of the administration. During one discussion, Albright asked, "What's the point of having this superb military that you're always talking about if we can't use it?" Powell recalled, "I thought I would have an aneurysm. American GIs were not toy soldiers to be moved around on some sort of global game board."[77]

The 2000 election was the most scandalous in U.S. history. George W. Bush defeated John McCain in an ugly Republican primary that laid the groundwork for the tactics he would use in the general election. Bush shed his compassionate conservatism and attacked McCain furiously from the right. He reached out to the neo-Confederates, unreconstructed segregationists who fought to keep the rebel flag flying over the South Carolina state capitol. He spoke at Bob Jones University, whose claim to fame was its policy of banning interracial dating among students. But most notoriously, Karl Rove and the Bush brain trust planted the idea that McCain, "the fag candidate," had fathered an illegitimate black daughter and his wife, Cindy, was a drug addict. McCain responded, "The political tactics of division and slander are not our values . . . those who practice them in the name of religion or in the name of the Republican Party or in the name of America shame our faith, our party and our country."[78] McCain was correct, but the tactic worked among a Republican Party base that was moving sharply to the right.

For his running mate, Bush selected Dick Cheney, who had fortuitously been put in charge of vetting potential nominees. Republicans hoped that Cheney, a veteran of several administrations and six terms in Congress, would lend gravitas to a ticket headed by the lightly regarded, inexperienced former Texas governor. Cheney had made a fortune during his brief stint as CEO of Halliburton, retiring in 2000 with a $34 million severance package. In 1998, he merged Halliburton with Dresser Industries, forming the world's biggest oil services firm. Halliburton was also a major defense contractor through its subsidiary Brown & Root. Bush and Cheney faced off against Vice President Al Gore and Senator Joe Lieberman. The race was complicated by the participation of reformer Ralph Nader and conservative Pat Buchanan.

As the elections approached, polls indicated a tight outcome. Bush advisors feared their candidate would win the popular vote but lose in the electoral college. They readied plans to orchestrate a popular uprising accusing Gore of using the antiquated electoral college to thwart the public will.

The election was very close indeed. Nationally, Gore won the popular vote by 544,000. Winning Florida would have also given him victory in the electoral college. The majority of Florida voters clearly intended to vote for Gore. But confusing "butterfly ballots" in West Palm Beach caused many elderly Jewish voters to inadvertently vote for Buchanan, who was sometimes accused of anti-Semitism and whom those voters, in particular, despised, and antiquated punch card machines in poor, heavily Democratic districts caused state officials to invalidate 180,000 ballots either for not clearly identifying a candidate or for voting more than once. But most troubling was that tens of thousands of pro-Gore African-American voters had been purged from the voting lists and denied the right to vote by Republican election officials, who had been directed to do so by the Bush Florida campaign cochair, Secretary of State Katherine Harris, on the pretext, often incorrect, that they were convicted felons. In the end, more than 10 percent of African Americans were disqualified compared to only 2 percent of Republican-leaning whites. Had the rates been equal, more than 50,000 more African Americans would have voted in Florida, giving Gore an overwhelming lead and ensuring his election. But because of the irregularities and the 97,000 votes that went to Nader, Bush clung to a minuscule lead of less than 1,000 votes out of 6 million cast. If certified, Bush would win the election by 271–266 electoral college votes.

The deck was stacked against Gore. Bush's younger brother Jeb was governor. Harris, a fierce partisan, was in charge of certifying the results. Partial recounts cut Bush's lead below 600 votes. Fearing that the full state recount Gore demanded would sink him, Bush deployed family consigliere James Baker, his father's campaign manager and secretary of state, to use every available court challenge to block the recount. The Bush campaign also flew down a small army of members of Congress, congressional staffers, and lawyers to run the operation on the ground, many arriving in corporate jets leased to the campaign by Bush's friend "Kenny Boy" Lay of Enron and Cheney's friends at Halliburton.

The ground operation was overseen by House Republican Whip Tom DeLay. Some 750 Republican operatives swarmed into three predominantly Democratic counties that were considering recounts. At raucous rallies, they portrayed themselves as local citizens outraged that Gore was stealing the election, a theme echoed by Republican media allies. On November 22, the Republican field army, fortified by right-wing Cubans, physically disrupted the Miami-Dade canvassing board's attempt to examine almost 11,000 disputed ballots in what the *Wall Street Journal* called a "door-kicking, window-banging protest." The fifty-person mob, which included staffers of DeLay and Senator Trent Lott, was led by New York Congressman John Sweeney, who started them chanting "Shut it down!," "Three blind mice," and "Fraud, fraud, fraud." Members of the canvassing board were physically assaulted, and Supervisor of Elections David Leahy was punched. One thousand more Cuban Americans, they were told, were on the way. The Brooks Brothers Riot, as it was dubbed because of the well-dressed insurgents, achieved its goal, forcing frightened board members to abandon their recount, which, the *Journal* reported, was expected to help Gore "chip away" at Bush's lead.

The operatives repeated their performance in heavily Democratic Broward County, outnumbering Democratic protesters outside the courthouse by ten to one. Among those observing the shutdown of the Miami-Dade canvassing board was *Wall Street Journal* editorial writer Paul Gigot, who commented, "If it's possible to have a bourgeois riot, it happened here Wednesday. And it could end up saving the presidency for George W. Bush."[79]

Harris disallowed other recounts and certified Bush the winner by 537 votes. Though outspent in Florida by more than four to one, Gore continued to fight through the courts. On December 8, the Florida Supreme Court ordered a statewide recount of all ballots recorded as showing no vote or more than one vote in cases where names were both checked and written in. With his lead falling below 200 votes, Bush appealed to the U.S. Supreme Court to stop the recount. Seven of the nine justices had been appointed by Republican presidents and five of the seven by administrations in which Bush's father was either president or vice president. The Supreme Court voted 5–4 to stop the recount, handing Bush the election. Justices Ruth Bader Ginsburg and Stephen Breyer dissented, charging, "Although we may never know with complete certainty the identity of the winner of this year's presidential election, the identity of the loser is perfectly clear. It is the nation's confidence in the judge as an impartial guardian of the rule of law."[80] Others alleged that an outright coup had occurred.

Bush promised to govern as a "compassionate conservative." But Cheney's selection of right-wingers and neocons to fill key administration positions made clear that compassion and compromise would be in short supply. For defense secretary, the dour vice president–elect picked his mentor Donald Rumsfeld, whom Henry Kissinger had called "the most ruthless man I ever met."[81] Jim Baker reminded Bush, "you know what he did to your daddy," referring to Rumsfeld's effort to derail his father's political career in the 1970s.[82] But Bush took perverse pleasure in picking the man who had so openly defied his father. Rumsfeld, a man of prodigious arrogance, and Cheney, gloomy, dyspeptic, and pathologically secretive, would dominate foreign policy making, consistently riding roughshod over Secretary of State Colin Powell.

Cheney was on a mission to restore the power of the executive branch, which had steadily eroded, he believed, since the passage of the War Powers Act in 1973 and Watergate. Sharing Cheney's contempt for public opinion, Bush surrounded

*During the presidential election recount, on November 22, 2000,
Republican operatives, fortified by right-wing Cubans, physically
disrupted the Miami-Dade County canvassing board's attempt to examine
almost 11,000 disputed ballots in what the* Wall Street Journal *called
a "door-kicking, window-banging protest." The Brooks Brothers Riot,
as it was dubbed because of the well-dressed insurgents, achieved its
goal, forcing frightened board members to abandon their recount.*

himself with yes-men and true believers. He told Bob Woodward, "I do not need to explain why I say things. That's the interesting thing about being the President. Maybe somebody needs to explain to me why they say something, but I don't feel like I owe anybody an explanation."[83] He held fewer press conferences than any other modern president, addressed only prescreened audiences, and set up special zones to isolate protesters far from his appearances.

From the start, serious debate over domestic policy concerns was conspicuous by its absence. One of the few who tried to instigate such discussions was John DiIulio, whom Bush had chosen to head the White House Office of Faith-Based and Community Initiatives. DiIulio, a respected political scientist from the University of Pennsylvania who had previously taught at Harvard and Princeton, stuck out like a sore thumb in this administration. Not only were he and Treasury Secretary Norman Mineta the only Democrats in the administration, he was, according to journalist Ron Suskind, the administration's "big brain." Bush called him "one of the most influential social entrepreneurs in America." He was also one of the few who took seriously the commitment to "compassionate conservatism," speaking, for example, about the need to save "the least, the last and the lost."[84]

Surrounded by neoconservative ideologues and harassed constantly by the religious Right, DiIulio lasted barely eight months. In October 2002, he opened up in a letter to Suskind in which he expressed admiration for the president, who, he said, was "much, much smarter than some people . . . seem to suppose" but criticized the environment in the White House, where, from the president on down, there was virtually no discussion of substantive domestic policy concerns:

> There were no actual policy white papers on domestic issues [and] only a couple people in the West Wing who worried at all about policy substance and analysis. . . . [The] lack of basic policy knowledge [is] somewhat breathtaking. . . . This gave rise to what you might call Mayberry Machiavellis—staff, senior and junior, who consistently talked and acted as if the height of political sophistication consisted in reducing every issue to its simplest, black-and-white terms for public consumption, then steering legislative initiatives or policy proposals as far right as possible.[85]

Whereas the first President Bush and Clinton had made some efforts at diplomacy and coalition building, Bush 43 exhibited the kind of "chest-thumping unilateralism" that neocons had demanded for decades. He announced that he would not send the International Criminal Court treaty to the Senate for ratification, despite the fact that Clinton had signed it and virtually every other Western democracy had joined. Perhaps he and Cheney anticipated that membership in the world's first war crimes tribunal might interfere with their future plans. Bush then rejected the Comprehensive Nuclear Test Ban Treaty, which 150 nations had signed. He repudiated the Kyoto Protocol on global warming; abrogated the ABM Treaty with Russia, which freed him to expand the costly and unproven missile defense program; disavowed the Middle East peace process; and suspended talks with North Korea on its long-range missile program. Cheney strategically positioned loyalists throughout the bureaucracy and worked closely with Rumsfeld to expand the role and influence of the Pentagon. Though lacking any popular mandate, Bush and Cheney proceeded to ride roughshod over the opposition, taking advantage of the fact that Republicans controlled the presidency and both houses of Congress for the first time since the 1920s.

This Bush administration, as Ralph Nader put it, was "marinated in oil,"[86] with two oilmen at the helm and Chevron board member Condoleezza Rice, who had a double-hulled oil tanker named after her, as national security advisor. Cheney quickly put together an energy task force and began formulating a new national energy policy based on securing control of Persian Gulf and Caspian Sea oil. He later fiercely resisted efforts to force the disclosure of task force participants' names and their discussions. A top NSC official instructed NSC staff to cooperate with the task force as it tried to "meld" together its review of "policies toward rogue states" like Iraq and "actions regarding the capture of new and existing oil and gas fields."[87] Cheney told an audience of oil industry executives in 1999, "There will be an average of two percent annual growth in global oil demand over the years ahead along with conservatively a three percent natural decline in production from existing reserves. That means by 2010 we will need on the order of an additional fifty million barrels a day. So where is the oil going to come from? . . . the Middle East, with two-thirds of the world's oil and the lowest cost, is still where the prize ultimately lies."[88] The task force urged the administration to pressure Middle Eastern nations whose governments controlled their oil industries "to open up areas of their energy sectors to foreign investment."[89]

Congressman Dennis Kucinich spelled out the implications:

> Oil is a major factor in every aspect of U.S. policy in the Persian Gulf.
> Ask yourself: What commodity accounts for 83 percent of total exports
> from the Persian Gulf? What is the U.S. protecting with our permanent
> deployment of about 25,000 military personnel, 6 fighter squadrons, 6
> bomber squadrons, 13 air control and reconnaissance squadrons, one
> aircraft carrier battle group, and one amphibious ready group based at
> 11 military installations? . . . the disproportionate troop deployments in
> the Middle East aren't there to protect the people, who constitute only 2
> percent of the world population.[90]

Cheney and Bush spent their first eight months in office aggressively pursuing the PNAC agenda. They paid little if any heed to the terrorist threat. The attacks on September 11, 2001, could have and should have been prevented. NSC Counterterrorism Chief Richard Clarke tried to alert top administration officials, including Cheney, Rice, and Powell, to the Al-Qaeda threat from their very first days on the job. He warned that an attack was imminent. On January 25, he requested that Rice call an urgent cabinet-level "principals" meeting to discuss the threat. He finally got his meeting on September 4.

Warning signs abounded in the summer of 2001. Intercepted Al-Qaeda messages stated that "something spectacular" was about to occur.[91] FBI agents reported suspicious behavior by individuals who wanted to know how to fly passenger airplanes but were not interested in learning how to land. Tenet received an August briefing paper titled "Islamic Extremist Learns to Fly" about the arrest in Minnesota of Zacarias Moussaoui after officials at the flight school he was attending reported his strange behavior.[92] Clarke testified that CIA Director George Tenet was running around Washington with his "hair on fire," trying to get Bush's attention.[93] In late June, Tenet told Clarke, "I feel it coming. This is going to be the big one."[94] Intelligence agencies issued threat reports with headlines such as "Bin Laden Threats Are Real," "Bin Laden Planning High Profile Attacks," "Bin Laden Planning Multiple Operations," "Bin Laden Public Profile May Presage Attack," and "Bin Laden's Network's Plans Advancing."[95] Alerts warned of a high probability of near-term "spectacular" attacks resulting in numerous casualties and causing turmoil in the world. According to writer Thomas Powers, in the nine months before September 11, intelligence personnel "had warned the administration as many as forty times of the threat posed by Osama bin Laden, but that is not what the administration wanted to hear, and it did not hear it."[96]

The President's Daily Brief that Bush received at his Crawford, Texas, ranch on August 6 was headlined "Bin Laden Determined to Strike in US." It discussed the threat of Al-Qaeda operatives hijacking planes. Bush was as uninterested as ever, telling his CIA briefer, "All right. You've covered your ass, now."[97] Tenet later testified that "the system was blinking red."[98] Still, Bush had the temerity to tell a news conference in April 2004, "Had I any inkling whatsoever that the people were going to fly airplanes into buildings, we would have moved heaven and earth to save the country."[99]

Rice was equally culpable and equally disingenuous. During summer 2001, Tenet and CIA counterterrorism chief J. Cofer Black pushed her to adopt a plan to thwart bin Laden's pending attack, but Rice was preoccupied with ballistic missile defense. Frustrated, Black later remarked, "The only thing we didn't do was pull the trigger to the gun we were holding to her head."[100] Rice later commented, "I don't think anybody could have predicted . . . that they would try to use an airplane as a missile, a hijacked airplane as a missile."[101]

Bush and Rice's lack of interest was shared by others in the administration. Acting FBI Director Thomas Pickard told the 9/11 Commission that he had briefed Attorney General John Ashcroft twice that summer about the terrorist threat, but that, after the second briefing, Ashcroft told him he didn't want to hear about it anymore.[102] Deputy Secretary of Defense Paul Wolfowitz also discounted the warnings. Rumsfeld went further, threatening, as late as September 9, to get the president to veto Senate Armed Services Committee plans to transfer $600 million from the missile defense budget to counterterrorism.

Nor at that time did many predict that Bush, Cheney, Rice, Rumsfeld, Wolfowitz, and their cronies would use this criminal assault on the United States as an excuse to launch wars against two Islamic nations—wars that would cause far more damage to the United States than Osama bin Laden ever could—or to begin shredding the U.S. Constitution and the Geneva Convention.

Chapter 13

THE BUSH-CHENEY DEBACLE:

"The Gates of Hell Are Open in Iraq"

George W. Bush was legendary for his misstatements and malapropisms. But sometimes, through the mangled syntax, a bit of truth would slip out. Such was the occasion in 2004 when he declared, "Our enemies are innovative and resourceful, and so are we. They never stop thinking about new ways to harm our country and our people, and neither do we."[1]

When Bush's party was unceremoniously booted out of office in 2008, he was rated by historians as among the very worst presidents in U.S. history if not the absolute worst.[2] His popularity and approval ratings set new lows for the modern era but were actually higher than those of his even less popular vice president, Dick Cheney. Bush and Cheney left the country in shambles, its economy collapsing and its international reputation at an all-time low. After invading two countries, threatening many others, and undermining the rule of law at home and abroad, the once-admired United States was now universally feared and widely condemned. People wondered whether the wrongheaded policies of the Bush-Cheney administration had resulted from ineptitude, hubris, and blind ambition or if perhaps there was something more sinister about its plans for the United States and the world.

Although the ever-cautious Barack Obama chose not to investigate the crimes of his predecessor, others would adhere more closely to the strictures of international law. In February 2011, George W. Bush was forced to cancel a speaking engagement in Switzerland for fear of massive protests against his torture policies. Activists were also planning to file a criminal complaint with Swiss prosecutors. Katherine Gallagher of the Center for Constitutional Rights explained, "Waterboarding is torture, and Bush has admitted without any sign of remorse, that he approved its use. . . . Torturers—even if they are former presidents of the United States—must be held to account and prosecuted. Impunity for Bush must end."[3] Protest organizers urged demonstrators to bring a shoe in honor of the Iraqi journalist who was jailed for throwing his shoes at Bush in 2008. Referencing the 1998 London arrest of the late Chilean dictator Augusto Pinochet, Gavin Sullivan of the European Center for Constitutional and Human Rights said, "What we have in Switzerland is a Pinochet opportunity." Amnesty International announced that similar steps would be taken if Bush traveled to any of the 147 nations that were party to the UN Convention Against Torture.[4]

The events of September 11, 2001, and the United States' reaction to them changed the course of history. On that day, Islamic extremists dealt the United States a crushing blow. With the president and his top aides asleep at the switch, Al-Qaeda hijackers flew planes into the premier symbols of U.S. imperial power: the World Trade Center and Pentagon. More than 2,750 people were killed in New York City, including some 500 foreign nationals from 91 countries. The nation watched in horror as flames engulfed the twin towers before their stunning collapse. Another 125 perished at the Pentagon. But the damage to the United States would pale in comparison to the damage the Bush administration wreaked in response to Al-Qaeda's heinous attack.

Bush subsequently ignored demands to investigate how such a colossal intelligence and leadership failure could have occurred. When the pressure finally became too great, Bush turned to Henry Kissinger to produce an official whitewash. Even the *New York Times* wondered whether the choice of Kissinger, the "consummate Washington insider," with his "old friendships and business relationships," to chair the commission was anything more than "a clever maneuver by the White House to contain an investigation it long opposed."[5]

Kissinger received a visit from a group of New Jersey women who had been widowed in the attack. One asked him if he had any clients named bin Laden. Kissinger spilled his coffee and nearly fell off his office couch. While his visitors rushed to clean up his mess, Kissinger blamed his clumsiness on his "bad eye." The next morning, he resigned from the commission.[6]

Kissinger was replaced by former New Jersey Governor Thomas Kean, who, along with his cochair, former Indiana Congressman Lee Hamilton, delivered the largely exculpatory report in 2004. In his book on the commission, *New York Times* reporter Philip Shenon placed the principal blame for the commission's gentle treatment of the responsible parties in the White House on the guiding hand of the commission executive director and Condoleezza Rice confidant, Philip Zelikow.[7] *Washington Post* international correspondent Glenn

Soldiers brief President Bush on a heavy machine gun in July 2002.

Kessler described him as a "one-person think tank for Rice"—her "intellectual soul mate."[8] Rice's negligence in ignoring pre-9/11 warning signs that an attack was imminent was undeniable.

For most Americans, 9/11 was a terrible tragedy; for Bush and Cheney it was also an incredible opportunity—a chance to implement the agenda that their neo-conservative allies had been cooking up for decades. The Project for a New American Century's recent report "Rebuilding America's Defenses" had stated that "the process of transformation . . . is likely to be a long one, absent some catastrophic and catalyzing event—like a new Pearl Harbor."[9] Al-Qaeda had given PNACers their Pearl Harbor. Within minutes of the attack, the Bush team, minus the absent president, leapt into action. Vice President Cheney and his legal counsel David Addington took charge. Addington soon joined forces with Timothy Flanigan and John Yoo to argue that the president, as wartime commander in chief, could act virtually unfettered by legal constraints.[10] Proceeding on that basis, Bush would sharply increase the powers of the executive branch and curtail civil liberties, declaring "I don't care what the international lawyers say, we are going to kick some ass."[11]

Bush and the PNACers in his administration knew precisely whose ass they wanted to kick. On September 12, already looking past Al-Qaeda's Osama bin Laden and his Taliban collaborators in Afghanistan, Bush instructed

The smoldering rubble of the fallen World Trade Center buildings in New York City two days after the Al-Qaeda attacks of September 11, 2001.

counterterrorism chief Richard Clarke, "See if Saddam did this. See if he's linked in any way." Clarke, incredulous, responded, "But, Mr. President, al Qaeda did this." Bush persisted. Detailing the encounter, Clarke reported that when Bush walked away, Clarke's assistant Lisa Gordon-Haggerty "stared after him with her mouth hanging open." "Wolfowitz got to him," she said.[12]

Deputy Secretary of Defense Paul Wolfowitz had a lot of help. His boss, Donald Rumsfeld, had already ordered the military to draw up strike plans for Iraq. "Go massive," he said. "Sweep it all up. Things related and not."[13] Clarke assumed that Rumsfeld was joking when he said Iraq had better targets than Afghanistan. He wasn't. On the morning of September 12, CIA Director George Tenet ran into Richard Perle, who was leaving the West Wing of the White House. Perle declared, "Iraq has to pay a price for what happened yesterday. They bear responsibility."[14] On September 13, Wolfowitz announced that the response to the 9/11 attacks would extend well beyond Afghanistan to "ending states who sponsor terrorism."[15]

That afternoon, when Rumsfeld spoke of expanding the mission to "getting Iraq," Secretary of State Colin Powell insisted that they focus on Al-Qaeda. Clarke thanked him and expressed his befuddlement over the obsession with Iraq: "Having been attacked by al Qaeda, for us now to go bombing Iraq in response would be like our invading Mexico after the Japanese attacked us at

*As Ike looks on, Paul Wolfowitz speaks with Donald Rumsfeld, Colin Powell,
and Scooter Libby during a Cabinet Room meeting on September 12, 2001.*

Pearl Harbor." Knowing whom he was dealing with, Powell shook his head. "It's
not over yet," he said.[16]

Powell was right. The neocons would soon abandon the fig leaf of Iraqi
involvement in 9/11. On September 20, the PNAC wrote a letter to Bush stating
that "even if evidence does not link Iraq directly to the attack, any strategy aim-
ing at the eradication of terrorism and its sponsors must include a determined
effort to remove Saddam Hussein from power in Iraq."[17] The October 15 issue of
William Kristol's *Weekly Standard* ran a cover story making "The Case for American Empire" in which Max Boot blamed the September 11 attack on the fact that
the United States had not sufficiently imposed its will on the world. Boot knew
how to remedy that mistake: "The debate about whether Saddam Hussein was
implicated in the September 11 attacks misses the point. Who cares if Saddam
was involved in this particular barbarity?"[18]

Having been attacked by Al-Qaeda in Afghanistan, the United States was preparing to retaliate against Iraq, whose leader, Saddam Hussein, was an avowed
enemy of both Al-Qaeda and the anti-U.S. regime in Iran. Clarke admitted, "At
first I was incredulous that we were talking about something other than getting
al Qaeda. Then I realized with almost a sharp physical pain that Rumsfeld and
Wolfowitz were going to try to take advantage of this national tragedy to promote their agenda about Iraq."[19]

Clarke underestimated Bush, Cheney, Rumsfeld, and Wolfowitz. Their agenda went far beyond Iraq. From atop the rubble at the World Trade Center, Bush proclaimed, "Our responsibility to history is already clear. To answer these attacks and rid the world of evil." [20]

Cheney appeared on *Meet the Press* and said, "We also have to work, though, sort of the dark side. . . . We've got to spend time in the shadows in the intelligence world. A lot of what needs to be done here will have to be done quietly, without any discussion, using sources and methods that are available to our intelligence agencies, if we're going to be successful. That's the world these folks operate in, and so it's going to be vital for us to use any means at our disposal, basically, to achieve our objective." [21]

The administration moved to the "dark side" with alacrity. The following day, Bush authorized the CIA to establish detention facilities outside the United States where torture and other harsh interrogation techniques would be employed. Four days later Bush announced before a joint session of Congress that the United States was embarking on a global war on terrorism—extending to "any nation that continues to harbor or support terrorism." [22] Through its policy of extraordinary rendition, the CIA began seizing suspects without any legal proceedings being brought against them and flying them to secret "black sites" around the world.

The CIA requested and received presidential authorization to hunt down, capture, and kill members of Al-Qaeda and other terrorists anywhere in the world. In October, a senior official told the *Washington Post*'s Bob Woodward that the president had directed the CIA to "undertake its most sweeping and lethal covert action since the founding of the agency in 1947." "The gloves are off," the official said. "The president has given the agency the green light to do whatever is necessary. Lethal operations that were unthinkable pre–September 11 are now underway." Cheney noted another important change. "It is different than the Gulf War was," he told Woodward, "in the sense that it may never end. At least, not in our lifetime." [23]

In fact, many things that were unthinkable before September 11 were happening now. First and foremost, the White House began usurping unprecedented powers, powers that threatened the U.S. constitutional order. To make that possible, Bush exploited the post-9/11 climate of fear and uncertainty. In the days after 9/11, the government arrested and detained 1,200 men in the United States, most of whom were either Muslims or of Middle Eastern or South Asian extraction. Another 8,000 were sought for interrogation. Wisconsin Senator Russ Feingold demanded a halt to such profiling. "This is a dark hour for civil liberties in America," he warned. "What I'm hearing from Muslim Americans, Arab Americans, South Asians and others, suggests a climate of fear toward our government that is unprecedented." [24]

Bush rushed the USA PATRIOT Act through Congress. The Senate version was sent straight to the floor without discussion, debate, or hearings. In this crisis atmosphere, only Feingold had the courage to vote against it, insisting, "It is . . . crucial that civil liberties in this country be preserved, otherwise I'm afraid that terror will win this battle without firing a shot." It passed in the House by a vote of 337–79,[25] and Bush signed it into law on October 26, 2001. The PATRIOT Act expanded government surveillance and investigative powers. In 2002, Bush empowered the National Security Agency to conduct warrantless wiretaps in violation of the legal reviews required by the Foreign Intelligence Surveillance Act (FISA) courts and to monitor U.S. citizens' e-mail.[26]

To convince the American people to accept such blatant infringement on their privacy and civil liberties, the administration barraged the public with constant alerts, heightened security, and a five-tier system of color-coded warnings that fluctuated based on each day's danger of terrorist attack. The system was so obviously being manipulated by Rumsfeld and Attorney General John Ashcroft that Bush's secretary of homeland security, Tom Ridge, felt compelled to resign after one particularly egregious episode.[27] The administration also began identifying points of vulnerability, listing 160 sites as potential terrorist targets. By the end of 2003, the number climbed to 1,849. One year later, it stood at 28,360. It jumped to an astounding 78,000 in 2005 and 300,000 in 2007. Even the nation's heartland wasn't immune. Amazingly, Indiana led all states with the most potential targets—8,591—almost three times as many as California. The national database included petting zoos, doughnut shops, popcorn stands, ice cream parlors, and the Mule Day Parade in Columbia, Tennessee.[28]

Bush made it clear that this was a new kind of war—a war fought not against a nation or even an ideology but against a tactic: terrorism. As retired Ambassador Ronald Spiers pointed out, framing it that way was deliberate and pernicious. Choosing the "war" metaphor, he wrote in 2004, "is neither accurate nor innocuous, implying as it does that there is an end point of either victory or defeat. . . . A 'war on terrorism' is a war without an end in sight, without an exit strategy, with enemies specified not by their aims but by their tactics. . . . The President has found this 'war' useful as an all-purpose justification for almost anything he wants or doesn't want to do. . . . It brings to mind Big Brother's vague and never-ending war in Orwell's *1984*."[29]

It was also a new kind of war in that it would require no sacrifice from the overwhelming majority of Americans. The fighting would fall on the members of a volunteer army drawn largely from the lower ranks of society. The cost would be borne by future generations.

Whereas, at the start of World War II, Franklin Roosevelt had warned, "War costs money. . . . That means taxes and bonds and bonds and taxes. It means cutting luxuries and other non-essentials." [30] Bush saw things differently. He cut taxes on the wealthy and told Americans to visit "America's great destination spots . . . and enjoy life the way we want it to be enjoyed." [31] *New York Times* columnist Frank Rich captured the unreality: "No one is demanding that the rest of us pay for serious airline or bioterror security, or that we cut down on gas-guzzling to reduce our dependency on the oil of Saudi Arabia, whose other big export is terrorists. Instead we are told to go shopping, take in a show, go to Disneyland." [32]

Bush asked the American people to make a hard choice: whether to visit Disney World or Disneyland. He gave the Afghan Taliban a different choice: either turn over the Al-Qaeda leaders or be bombed back to the Stone Age, which much of Afghanistan had never left. "Bombing Afghanistan back to the Stone Age . . ." wrote Tamim Ansary, an Afghan living in the United States for thirty-five years and a bitter foe of bin Laden and the Taliban, "that's been done. The Soviets took care of it already. Make the Afghans suffer? They're already suffering. Level their houses? Done. Turn their schools into piles of rubble? Done. Eradicate their hospitals? Done. Destroy their infrastructure? Cut them off from medicine and health care? Too late. Someone already did all that. New bombs would only stir the rubble of earlier bombs. Would they at least get the Taliban? Not likely." [33]

Other critics of the rush to war pointed out that no Afghans were among the nineteen hijackers. Fifteen were Saudis, one Lebanese, one Egyptian, and two were from the United Arab Emirates. They had lived in Hamburg and trained and took flight lessons primarily in the United States.

On October 7, 2001, less than a month after the terrorist attacks, the United States and its allies launched Operation Enduring Freedom. The Taliban leaders quickly got the message and scrambled to negotiate. On October 15, Taliban foreign minister Wakil Ahmed Muttawakil, whom the U.S. Embassy in Islamabad considered to be very close to Taliban leader Mullah Muhammad Omar, offered to turn bin Laden over to the Organization of the Islamic Conference (OIC) for trial. Evidence suggests that Omar had been trying to rein in bin Laden for some time and that relations between the Afghans and Al-Qaeda had been frayed. U.S. representatives had actually had more than twenty meetings with Taliban officials during the previous three years to discuss their turning bin Laden over for trial. U.S. officials concluded that the Taliban were stalling. Milton Bearden, the former CIA station chief who oversaw the 1980s covert war in Afghanistan from his Pakistani base, disagreed, blaming U.S. obtuseness and inflexibility. "We never heard what they were trying to say," he told the *Washington Post*. "We had no common language. Ours was 'give up bin Laden.' They were saying 'do something to help us give him up.'" U.S. State Department and Embassy officials met with Taliban security chief Hameed Rasoli as late as August 2001. "I have no doubts they wanted to get rid of him," Bearden said in October 2001. But the United States never offered the face-saving measures the Taliban needed.[34]

Rumsfeld's high-tech warfare succeeded in sharply limiting U.S. casualties, but the lack of U.S. boots on the ground allowed bin Laden, Omar, and many of their supporters to slip away when the United States had them trapped at Tora Bora in December 2001. Afghan civilians didn't fare as well, suffering approximately four thousand deaths, according to University of New Hampshire Professor Marc Herold—more than the number killed at the World Trade Center and Pentagon combined.[35] Perhaps five times that number would die from disease and starvation in the months to follow.

Although Bush quickly lost interest in Afghanistan and turned his attention to Iraq, the war dragged on for the remainder of his presidency. Hamid Karzai ruled through brutal warlords and corrupt functionaries who turned Afghanistan into the world's biggest supplier of opium. By 2004, Afghanistan was supplying 87 percent of the world total.[36] In 2009, the country ranked second only to Somalia on the global corruption index.[37] Fed up with corruption and exhausted by war, many Afghans welcomed back the Taliban, despite their earlier disgust with repressive Taliban policies.

Though the 9/11 plotters slipped easily through their fingers, the CIA and military did round up thousands of others in Afghanistan and beyond. Their treatment would signal just how dark Bush and Cheney were willing to go in the name of the United States—a country that had always considered its humane treatment of prisoners a sign of its moral superiority. Bush branded the detainees "unlawful enemy combatants," not prisoners of war whose rights had to be respected, and threw them into the U.S. naval station at Guantánamo Bay, Cuba, or into the CIA's "black-site" prisons, where they could be held indefinitely. The least fortunate were delivered for even worse abuse by allied governments known for their cruelty, like Hosni Mubarak's Egypt and Bashar al-Assad's Syria. Bush waived the battlefield hearings required by the Geneva Convention to determine whether captives were civilians or combatants. As a result, many prisoners who had no connection to Al-Qaeda or the Taliban were rounded up by unscrupulous Iraqis and Afghans seeking U.S. cash bounties. Innocent prisoners had no means of appeal. On the advice of White House legal counsel Alberto Gonzales, Bush declared that the Geneva Conventions on the Treatment of Prisoners of War, which the United States ratified in 1955, did not apply to suspected Taliban and Al-Qaeda members.[38] Among those outraged by Bush's abrogation of the Geneva Conventions was Joint Chiefs of Staff Chairman General Richard Myers.

The CIA was instructed to employ ten enhanced interrogation methods, the product of five decades of research into psychological torture. The techniques were spelled out in the CIA's 1963 *Kubark: Counterintelligence Interrogation*

Manual and honed by U.S. allies in Asia and Latin America in the 1960s, '70s, and '80s. Such psychological torture had been abandoned at the end of the Cold War and repudiated in 1994, when the United States signed the UN Convention Against Torture. It was back in force after 9/11 and often went beyond the strictly "psychological."[39]

Arthur Schlesinger, Jr., told journalist Jane Mayer that he considered the new torture policy, as Mayer put it, "the most dramatic, sustained, and radical challenge to the rule of law in American history."[40] The CIA outlined the procedures in detail. Upon arrest, the suspect would be "deprived of sight and sound" with blindfold and earmuffs. If the detainee proved uncooperative, he would be stripped naked, flooded with constant bright light and high-volume noise up to 79 decibels, and kept awake for up to 180 hours. Once the prisoner was convinced that he had no control, serious interrogation would begin. After guards shackled the prisoner's arms and legs, placed a collar around his neck, and removed the hood covering his head, interrogators would slap him across the face, sometimes repeatedly, and, using the collar as a handle, slam his head into the wall up to thirty times. Subsequent methods included dousing the prisoner with water, denying him the use of toilet facilities, forcing him to wear dirty diapers, chaining him to ceilings, and requiring him to stand or kneel in painful positions for prolonged periods of time.[41] The International Committee of the Red Cross reported that prisoners at Guantánamo were told that they were being taken "to the verge of death and back."[42]

Waterboarding was employed in special cases—and sometimes repeatedly, despite the fact that the United States had prosecuted Japanese military interrogators for use of waterboarding against U.S. prisoners during World War II. The process was described by Malcolm Nance, an interrogation expert who had been an instructor with the U.S. military's Survival, Evasion, Resistance, and Escape (SERE) program to train U.S. soldiers to withstand interrogation:

> Unless you have been strapped down to the board, have endured the agonizing feeling of the water overpowering your gag reflex, and then feel your throat open and allow pint after pint of water to involuntarily fill your lungs, you will not know the meaning of the word. Waterboarding is a controlled drowning that, in the American model, occurs under the watch of a doctor, a psychologist, an interrogator and a trained strap-in/strap-out team. It does not simulate drowning, as the lungs are actually filling with water. There is no way to simulate that. The victim is drowning. How much the victim is to drown depends on the desired result (in the form of answers to questions shouted into the victim's face) and the obstinacy of the subject.[43]

*High-tech warfare during the first stage of Operation Enduring Freedom
succeeded in sharply limiting U.S. casualties. The Afghans were not
so lucky. And the lack of U.S. boots on the ground allowed Osama bin
Laden and other Al-Qaeda leaders to easily slip away.* (**TOP**) *A U.S.
Navy F-14D Tomcat prepares to refuel for a bombing mission over
Afghanistan.* (**ABOVE**) *A U.S. Air Force B-1 Lancer bomber takes off
for Afghanistan from the U.S. base on the island of Diego Garcia.*

Abu Zubaydah was waterboarded in Bangkok at least eighty-three times over
a four- or five-day period in August 2002, even though interrogators were convinced he was telling the truth. Still, CIA officials at the Counterterrorism Center at Langley demanded that the procedure be continued for a month, backing
down only when the interrogators threatened to quit. Upon Zubaydah's capture, Bush identified him as "al-Qaeda's chief of operations."[44] In reality, though,

Zubaydah turned out to be a minor operative—not even an official member of Al-Qaeda—who may very well have been mentally ill. The *Washington Post* reported in 2009, "The methods succeeded in breaking him, and the stories he told of al-Qaeda terrorism plots sent CIA officers around the globe chasing leads. In the end, though, not a single significant plot was foiled as a result of Abu Zubaida's tortured confessions, according to former senior government officials who closely followed the interrogations." And, the *Post* acknowledged, whatever information investigators extracted that might have had any marginal utility had come out before the waterboarding began. The waterboarding did yield an abundance of information, according to the *Post:* "Abu Zubaida began unspooling the details of various al-Qaeda plots, including plans to unleash weapons of mass destruction. Abu Zubaida's revelations triggered a series of alerts and sent hundreds of CIA and FBI investigators scurrying in pursuit of phantoms." One former intelligence official admitted, "We spent millions of dollars chasing false alarms."[45]

Purported 9/11 mastermind Khalid Sheikh Mohammed was waterboarded 183 times, as if he were going to disclose something on the 183rd time that he hadn't divulged in the previous 182.[46] Psychologists helped refine techniques, exploiting prisoners' phobias. Interrogators also exploited Arabs' cultural sensitivities by subjecting prisoners to public nudity and snarling dogs.[47]

In February 2004, Major General Antonio Taguba reported that his investigation had turned up numerous instances of "sadistic, blatant, and wanton criminal abuses"[48] at Abu Ghraib detention center, including rape of both male and female prisoners. Only four months earlier, Bush had announced, a bit prematurely perhaps, that "Iraq is free of rape rooms and torture chambers."[49]

After the Abu Ghraib exposé created an international uproar in 2004, the Justice Department withdrew the legal memo authorizing torture. The damage done to the United States' international reputation was incalculable. Arthur Schlesinger, Jr., confided, "No position taken has done more damage to the American reputation in the world—ever"[50] than Bush's torture policy. However, the CIA subsequently captured another Al-Qaeda suspect and again sought permission to employ brutal interrogation methods. Rice responded, "This is your baby. Go do it."[51]

Journalist Patrick Cockburn interviewed the senior U.S. interrogator in Iraq who had elicited the information that led to the capture of Iraqi Al-Qaeda leader Abu Musab al-Zarqawi. He told Cockburn that torture not only produces no useful information, but its use in Iraq "has proved so counterproductive that it may have led to the death of as many U.S. soldiers as civilians killed in 9/11."[52]

Although officials tried to pin the blame on a few "bad apples"—sadistic rogue interrogators who took matters into their own hands—torture was approved by top administration officials. Members of the National Security Council's Princi-

A protest poster compares waterboarding during the Spanish Inquisition to its modern-day practice by the United States at Guantánamo Bay, Cuba, under the Bush administration.

pals Committee—Cheney, Rice, Rumsfeld, Powell, Tenet, and Ashcroft—met repeatedly to specify which methods would be used on which prisoners. Ashcroft interrupted one NSC discussion and asked, "Why are we talking about this in the White House? History will not judge this kindly."[53] General Barry McCaffrey agreed: "We tortured people unmercifully. We probably murdered dozens of them during the course of that, both the armed forces and the C.I.A."[54] For years, the 770-plus prisoners at Guantánamo and thousands more in Iraq and Afghanistan were denied legal counsel and the right to call witnesses to defend themselves. As of late 2008, charges had been brought against only twenty-three. Over five hundred had been released without being charged, often after years of harsh and humiliating treatment.[55] One FBI counterterrorism expert testified that of the Guantánamo detainees, fifty at most were worth holding.[56] Major General Taguba said, "There is no longer any doubt as to whether the current administration has committed war crimes. The only question that remains to be answered is whether those who ordered the use of torture will be held to account."[57]

The legal groundwork, which dated back to the 1990s, was provided by Justice Department lawyers. In one particularly outrageous memo, John Yoo and Assistant Attorney General Jay Bybee defined torture as pain "equivalent in intensity to . . . organ failure, impairment of bodily function, or even death"[58] and then only if inflicting the pain was the deliberate purpose of the interrogation.

In 2004, when the Supreme Court ruled that detainees had the right to challenge the legality of their detention in the federal courts, Bush established the Combat Status Review Tribunal and an Annual Review Board to sidestep the ruling. Finally, in June 2008, the Supreme Court ruled that detainees had a right to federal court review of the basis for their detention.[59]

Americans' rights were often trampled on as well. In an effort to preempt protests, federal and local authorities conducted sweeping arrests of legal protesters on numerous occasions, including at the Republican conventions in both 2004 and 2008.

Bush did his best to avoid the protests that did occur. On the rare occasions when he ventured out in public, the Secret Service would quarantine critics in protest zones so far away that neither Bush nor the media could see them. Those holding protest signs outside the designated areas were subject to arrest. London's *Evening Standard* reported that when Bush visited London in 2003, the White House demanded that the British impose a "virtual three-day shutdown of central London in a bid to foil disruption of the visit by antiwar protesters."[60]

Taking his cue from Cheney, Bush cloaked White House deliberations in a veil of secrecy so impenetrable that it was unprecedented in U.S. history. Access to documents under the Freedom of Information Act was sharply curtailed, and documents once publicly available were reclassified and disappeared. The government repeatedly invoked "national security" and "state secrets" to thwart those attempting to bring lawsuits. Colonel Lawrence Wilkerson, chief of staff to Colin Powell, said he had never seen such secrecy and described it as a "cabal" between Cheney and Rumsfeld to bypass normal channels.[61] Conservatives, too, objected. "We see an unprecedented secrecy in this White House that . . . we find very troubling," said Judicial Watch director Larry Klayman in 2002. "True conservatives don't act this way."[62]

But repressive measures in the United States paled in comparison to the measures Bush inflicted on the rest of the world. And the worst was still to come as U.S. policy makers geared up for the invasion of Iraq, which had actually been on the drawing board long before 9/11. Wolfowitz's obsession with Iraq dated at least as far back as 1979, when he directed a Pentagon assessment of the Persian Gulf region that highlighted Iraq's threat to its neighbors, particularly Saudi Arabia and Kuwait, and proposed a buildup of U.S. forces in the region to counter this threat. The report began, "We and our major industrialized allies have a vital and growing stake in the Persian Gulf region because of our need for Persian Gulf oil and because events in the Persian Gulf affect the Arab-Israeli conflict."[63] Based on that report, the United States had begun positioning cargo ships laden with military equipment in the region.

Wolfowitz nurtured that obsession in the intervening years. He and his allies had made dealing with Iraq a top priority of the PNAC. He fixated relentlessly on Iraq as deputy secretary of defense. A senior administration official observed, "If you look around the world at other issues, he's nonexistent. He's not a major player on any other issue." In fact, the official commented, he doesn't even know the Defense Department position on other issues.[64]

Iraq rose to the top of administration concerns almost from the moment Bush took office. He opened his first National Security Council meeting on January

Detainees pray at the U.S. prison at Guantánamo Bay, Cuba. One FBI counterterrorism expert testified that of the nearly eight hundred detainees incarcerated at Guantánamo, fifty at most were worth holding.

30, 2001, by asking, "So Condi, what are we going to talk about today? What's on the agenda?" "How Iraq is destabilizing the region, Mr. President," Rice replied.[65]

Administration neocons were on board from the start. When the NSC principals met again two days later, Rumsfeld interrupted Powell's discussion of "targeted sanctions" against Iran. "Sanctions are fine," he blurted out. "But what we really want to think about is going after Saddam." He later added, "Imagine what the region would look like without Saddam and with a regime that's aligned with U.S. interests. It would change everything in the region and beyond it. It would demonstrate what U.S. policy is all about." Looking back, Treasury Secretary Paul O'Neill recognized that the die had been cast from the very beginning: "From the start, we were building the case against Hussein and looking at how we could take him out and change Iraq into a new country. And, if we did that, it would solve everything. It was all about finding *a way to do it*. That was the tone of it. The President saying, 'Fine. Go find me a way to do this.'"[66]

O'Neill told Ron Suskind that as early as March 2001, administration officials were discussing concrete plans for invading and occupying Iraq.[67] Cheney's Energy Task Force played an important part. Other invasion backers included Wolfowitz protégés I. Lewis "Scooter" Libby, who was Cheney's national security advisor; Stephen Hadley, who was Rice's deputy; and Richard Perle, now head of the Pentagon's Defense Policy Board. On September 19 and 20, Defense Policy Board members decided to put Iraq in the crosshairs as soon as they disposed of Afghanistan. The *New York Times* reported that the insiders promoting the invasion were called the "Wolfowitz cabal."[68]

Members of the cabal searched high and low for an Iraqi connection to 9/11. Rumsfeld asked the CIA to come up with evidence linking Iraq to 9/11 on at least ten separate occasions.[69] Prisoners were tortured in the hope that they would divulge such information. But none existed. Rumsfeld and Cheney reviled the CIA analysts who pointed out this inconvenient fact.

Lacking evidence, they manufactured their own. Cheney and Libby pointed repeatedly to a meeting in Prague between the hijacker Mohamed Atta and an Iraqi intelligence official, even though Tenet had proved that Atta was in the United States at the time of the alleged meeting, living in Virginia in the shadow of CIA headquarters.[70]

Wolfowitz turned to Laurie Mylroie, whose thoroughly discredited writings had tied Iraq to practically every terrorist episode in recent memory, including the 1995 Oklahoma City bombing. Mylroie complained that the Clinton administration had dismissed her as "a nut case."[71] CNN analyst Peter Bergen called her a "crackpot," a view shared by the intelligence community. He mocked her "unified field theory of terrorism." But Wolfowitz and Perle took her seriously, as did *New York Times* reporter Judith Miller, with whom she coauthored a 1990 book about Saddam Hussein. Wolfowitz sent former CIA Director James Woolsey on a wild-goose chase overseas to try to corroborate her cockamamie theories. Though most of the administration neocons stopped short of Mylroie's assertion that "Al Qaeda is a front for Iraqi intelligence,"[72] Bush and Cheney repeatedly alluded to Iraqi involvement in the 9/11 attacks. In September 2003, Cheney told *Meet the Press's* Tim Russert that Iraq was the "heart of the base, if you will, the geographic base of the terrorists who have had us under assault now for many years, but most especially on 9/11."[73]

The CIA, meanwhile, was conjuring up its own perverse and outlandish ways to discredit both Saddam and bin Laden. The CIA's Iraq Operations Group considered fabricating a video showing Saddam having sex with a teenage boy and then "flood[ing] Iraq with the videos." "It would look like it was taken by a hidden camera," said a former official. "Very grainy, like it was a secret videotaping of a sex session." The CIA did actually produce a video simulating bin Laden and his Al-Qaeda buddies around a campfire imbibing liquor and sharing tales of sexual encounters with boys.[74]

Such undertakings were only slightly less bizarre than the actual "intelligence" collected during the buildup to the war. One of the administration's favorite intelligence sources was Ahmed Chalabi, who headed the Iraqi National Congress (INC). The INC, which received millions of dollars from the Bush administration, relayed fanciful reports of ongoing WMD programs from Iraqi defectors, many of whom were clearly out to instigate a U.S. attack. Later, with the Americans occupying Baghdad, Chalabi boasted, "We are heroes in error. As far as we're concerned, we've been entirely successful."[75]

One former top Defense Intelligence Agency official, Colonel Patrick Lang, saw Defense Department fingerprints all over this. "The Pentagon has banded together to dominate the government's foreign policy, and they've pulled it off," he complained bitterly. "They're running Chalabi. The D.I.A. has been intimidated and beaten to a pulp. And there's no guts at all in the C.I.A."[76]

Using this kind of notoriously false information, the administration challenged the findings of CIA analysts and UN weapons inspectors and tirelessly made its case for invading Iraq. "We know they have weapons of mass destruction," Rumsfeld insisted. "There isn't any debate about it."[77] In early October 2002, Bush, echoing a similar warning from Rice the month before, announced, "we cannot wait for the final proof—the smoking gun—that could come in the form of a mushroom cloud."[78] But no one could outdo Cheney when it came to outright fabrications and dire prognostications:

> The Iraqi regime has . . . been very busy enhancing its capabilities in the field of chemical and biological agents, and they continue to pursue the nuclear program. . . . Armed with an arsenal of these weapons of terror and a seat at a top [*sic*] 10 percent of the world's oil reserves, Saddam Hussein could then be expected to seek domination of the entire Middle East, take control of a great portion of the world's energy supplies, directly threaten America's friends throughout the region and subject the United States or any other nation to nuclear blackmail. Simply stated, there is no doubt that Saddam Hussein now has weapons of mass destruction; there is no doubt that he is amassing them to use against our friends, against our allies and against us.[79]

Based upon this fictitious threat assessment, which the Intelligence Community echoed in its National Intelligence Estimate of October 2002, Bush readied for war while maintaining the facade of seeking a peaceful resolution.[80] In March 2002, he popped unexpectedly into a meeting between Rice and a bipartisan group of senators and exclaimed, "Fuck Saddam. We're taking him out."[81] In May, he told Press Secretary Ari Fleischer, "I'm going to kick his sorry motherfucking ass all over the Mideast."[82]

But some experts knew that Bush's claims about Iraqi WMD were grossly exaggerated if not completely false. Former chief UN weapons inspector Scott Ritter told CNN in 2002, "No one has substantiated the allegations that Iraq possesses weapons of mass destruction or is attempting to acquire weapons of mass destruction." CNN's Fionnuala Sweeney pointed out, "It is hard to account if you cannot get into the country." Ritter's response to that and subsequent questions shed important light on the administration's use of WMD as a casus belli:

> That's right. Then why did the United States pick up the phone in December 1998 and order the inspectors out—let's remember Saddam Hussein didn't kick the inspectors out. The U.S. ordered the inspectors out 48 hours before they initiated Operation Desert Fox—military action that didn't have the support of the U.N. Security Council and which used information gathered by the inspectors, to target Iraq. . . . As of December 1998 we had accounted for 90 to 95 percent of Iraq's weapons of mass destruction capability—"we" being the weapons inspectors. We destroyed all the factories, all of the means of production and we couldn't account for some of the weaponry, but chemical weapons have a shelf-life of five years. Biological weapons have a shelf-life of three years. To have weapons today, they would have had to rebuild the factories and start the process of producing these weapons since December 1998.

"How much access did you get to the weapons inspection sites?" Sweeney asked. "One-hundred percent," Ritter assured her.[83]

Though Ritter was persona non grata within the administration and could be easily dismissed, there was no excuse for ignoring the cautionary words of General Tommy Franks, the head of U.S. Central Command, whom Rumsfeld tasked with drawing up war plans. At a September 2002 meeting of the NSC, Franks stated bluntly, "Mr. President, we've been looking for Scud missiles and other weapons of mass destruction for ten years and haven't found any yet."[84]

Leading establishment figures, including several linked to the president's father, tried to convince Bush that an invasion would be pure folly. The dissenters included General Brent Scowcroft, who had been George H. W. Bush's national security advisor, James Baker, Lawrence Eagleburger, and George Kennan. Military opposition also ran deep. Marine Lieutenant General Gregory Newbold, director of operations for the Joint Chiefs of Staff, recalled, "I can't tell you how many senior officers said to me, 'What the hell are we doing?'" They asked, "Why Iraq? Why now?"[85]

British Prime Minister Tony Blair stepped forward to lend a hand. In September 2002, Blair, who would be widely mocked as "Bush's poodle," released a dossier about Iraq's weapons of mass destruction that was so riddled with falsehoods, it would later prove scandalous. Blair insisted, however, on getting a UN resolution to provide him with political cover in Britain, where antiwar sentiment remained strong.[86]

The UN Security Council voted to send inspectors into Iraq again. Saddam accepted unconditionally. Inspections began in November. Over the next three and a half months, UN inspectors visited five hundred sites, some repeatedly. The list included those identified by the CIA as the most likely locations for concealing WMD. Nothing turned up. UN chief weapons inspector Hans Blix wondered, "If this was the best, what was the rest? . . . could there be 100 percent certainty about the existence of weapons of mass destruction but zero percent knowledge about their location?"[87] Blix later compared Bush administration officials to medieval witch hunters, who "were [so] convinced there were witches, when they looked for them, they certainly found them."[88]

In the midst of this latest round of inspections, Iraq submitted its 11,800-page weapons dossier to the United Nations. "Iraq has no weapons of mass destruction," declared Lieutenant General Hossam Mohammed Amin. But Bush, having already stipulated that any weapons declaration that did not admit to having WMD would be fraudulent, dismissed it scornfully. "The declaration is nothing, it's empty, it's a joke," he told visiting Spanish Prime Minister José María Aznar. "At some point, we will conclude that enough is enough and take him out." Iraq's UN ambassador, Mohammed Aldouri, challenged the United States to provide evidence of its allegations. Not only did the United States have no reliable evidence, it edited out more than 8,000 pages from Iraq's report before passing it on to the ten nonpermanent members of the Security Council—in part to hide the role of the U.S. government and twenty-four major U.S. corporations in supporting Iraq's weapons programs.[89]

After rigorous inspections, Blix refused to charge Iraq with being in violation of UN Resolution 1441 requiring Iraq to disarm. *Newsweek* reported on March 3, 2003, that Saddam's son-in-law Hussein Kamel, who had run Iraq's WMD programs for ten years before defecting in 1995, told the CIA, British intelligence, and UN inspectors that Iraq had destroyed all its chemical and biological weapons after the Gulf War. Rolf Ekéus, who headed the UN inspections team from 1991 to 1997, said that Kamel's information was "almost embarrassing, it was so extensive."[90]

Between 1991 and 1998, UN inspectors supervised the destruction of 817 of Iraq's 819 proscribed medium-range missiles, 9 trailers, 14 launchers, and 56 fixed missile-launch sites. Iraq also destroyed 73 of 75 chemical or biological warheads, 163 warheads for conventional explosives, 88,000 filled and unfilled chemical munitions, 4,000 tons of precursor chemicals, more than 600 tons of weaponized and bulk chemical weapons agents, and 980 pieces of equipment essential for production of such weapons. The Iraqis destroyed Al Hakam, the main facility producing and developing biological weapons, plus 60 pieces of equipment taken from three other facilities and 22 tons of growth media for biological weapons.[91]

If Middle Eastern and South Asian countries having WMD were by itself sufficient reason to justify a U.S. invasion, there were several other potential targets in the area. In the 2002 report titled "Weapons of Mass Destruction in the Middle East," Anthony Cordesman of the Center for Strategic and International Studies listed Egypt (chemical), India (chemical, biological, nuclear), Iran (chemical, biological), Israel (chemical, biological, nuclear), Libya (chemical), Pakistan (chemical, biological, nuclear), and Syria (chemical, biological).[92]

In fact, Iraq posed no threat. It had destroyed so many weapons between 1991 and 1998 that it had become one of the weaker states in the region. Its military expenditures were just a fraction of that of some of its neighbors. In 2002, Iraq spent approximately $1.4 billion on its military. The United States spent more than three hundred times that amount.[93]

Nevertheless, the scare tactics worked. To make sure they would, the administration deliberately timed the congressional vote to occur before the 2002 midterm elections and threatened to brand all who opposed the rush to war as unpatriotic and cowardly at a time of grave national crisis. Many caved in to the pressure, including Hillary Clinton and John Kerry. On October 2, 2002, the Senate voted 77–23 to authorize the use of force. The House did likewise, 296–133. The resolution directly connected Iraq to Al-Qaeda and alleged that Iraq posed a threat to the United States.

Only one Republican—Lincoln Chafee of Rhode Island—voted against the resolution in the Senate. He later condemned the spinelessness of top Democrats who had succumbed to Bush's blackmail: "They were afraid that Republicans would label them soft in the post–September 11 world, and when they acted in political self-interest, they helped the president send thousands of Americans and uncounted innocent Iraqis to their doom." Chafee watched as cowering Democrats repeatedly "went down to the meetings at the White House and the Pentagon and came back to the chamber ready to salute. With wrinkled brows they gravely intoned that Saddam Hussein must be stopped. Stopped from what? They had no conviction or evidence of their own. They were just parroting the administration's nonsense."[94]

Among the groups lobbying Congress to support the war was the American Israel Public Affairs Committee (AIPAC), an influential organization that was considerably to the right of mainstream American Jewish opinion and generally in lockstep with the neocons on Middle East policy. In January 2003, AIPAC Executive Director Howard Kohr told the *New York Sun* that " 'quietly' lobbying Congress to approve the use of force in Iraq" had been one of "AIPAC's successes over the past year."[95]

Much has rightly been made of the administration neocons' fierce defense of what they perceived as Israeli interests, which, in their minds, included toppling

Saddam Hussein. Again, Wolfowitz led the way. The *Jerusalem Post* reported that Bush's appointment of Wolfowitz as deputy secretary of defense had "the Jewish and pro-Israel communities . . . jumping with joy." In 2002, the *Forward* described him as "the most hawkishly pro-Israel voice in the Administration." If his was the most hawkishly pro-Israel voice, others including Undersecretary of Defense Douglas Feith's, Perle's, Libby's, and Bolton's were close behind.[96]

Having pushed the resolution through Congress, the administration continued peddling fraudulent and thoroughly discredited claims. Bush unveiled one of the most infamous in the January 2003 State of the Union address, declaring, "The British government has learned that Saddam Hussein recently sought significant quantities of uranium from Africa,"[97] an allegation that Joseph Wilson, former Deputy Chief of Mission to Iraq and former ambassador to three African countries, had already shown to be false. When Wilson later exposed the administration's mendacity, top officials, including Libby, retaliated by illegally outing Wilson's wife as a covert CIA operative, destroying her career and putting many people in jeopardy.

Relying on "evidence" provided by Feith, which had been repeatedly refuted point by point by CIA and DIA analysts, Cheney and Libby made frequent visits to Langley, pressing CIA analysts to reconsider their assertion that Iraq had no ties to Al-Qaeda. Tension between administration hawks and intelligence analysts escalated. As national intelligence officer for the Middle East, Paul Pillar was in charge of the intelligence community's assessments on Iraq. He described the "poisonous atmosphere" in which administration supporters were accusing him and other intelligence officers of "trying to sabotage the president's policies."[98] On one occasion, when Hadley demanded that the deputy director for intelligence revise the "link" paper, Tenet phoned Hadley in a fit of pique and shouted, "We are not rewriting this fucking report one more time. It is fucking over. Do you hear me! And don't you ever fucking treat my people this way again. Ever!"[99]

But the most ignominious moment came on February 5, 2003, when Secretary of State Colin Powell, the most respected and trusted member of the administration, went before the United Nations and made the case for war. Bush had handpicked Powell for the job. "You have the credibility to do this," he told Powell. "Maybe they'll believe you."[100]

Powell spoke for seventy-five minutes. He brought an array of props, including tape recordings, satellite photos, artists' renderings, and a small vial of anthrax-like white powder to illustrate how little would be required to cause a tremendous loss of life. He assured the delegates:

> My colleagues, every statement I make today is backed up by sources,
> solid sources. These are not assertions. What we're giving you are facts and

conclusions based on solid intelligence.... We have firsthand descriptions
of biological weapons factories on wheels and on rails.... We know that
Iraq has at least seven of these mobile biological agent factories. The
truck-mounted ones have at least two or three trucks each ... the mobile
production facilities ... can produce anthrax and botulinum toxin. In fact,
they can produce enough dry biological agent in a single month to kill
thousands upon thousands of people.... Our conservative estimate is that
Iraq today has a stockpile of between 100 and 500 tons of chemical-weapons
agent.... [Saddam] remains determined to acquire nuclear weapons.... what
I want to bring to your attention today is the potentially much more sinister
nexus between Iraq and the Al Qaeda terrorist network.[101]

It was a thoroughly shameful performance that Powell later called a low point
in his career.[102] Many of the claims had already been rejected by both the intelligence community and UN inspectors. Others relied on information provided
by known fabricators like Chalabi and "Curveball," an alcoholic cousin of one of
Chalabi's aides. Curveball had earlier been exposed as a fraud by German intelligence, to which he had provided over a hundred false reports on WMD. "I had
the chance to fabricate something to topple the regime," Curveball later admitted. German officials alerted the CIA that Curveball could not be trusted. Powell
actually resisted pressure from Cheney's office to make an even more direct link
between Saddam and Al-Qaeda, dismissing many of the assertions sent over by
Libby and company as "bullshit." [103]

Members of the intelligence community were outraged over Pentagon neocons' hijacking, distorting, and fabricating intelligence. When the nonexistent
WMD later failed to materialize, *New York Times* columnist Nicholas Kristof
described them as "spitting mad" and eager to have their say. One lashed out, "As
an employee of the Defense Intelligence Agency, I know how this administration
has lied to the public to get support for its attacks on Iraq." [104]

Whereas Powell's speech largely fell flat overseas, it had the desired impact
on U.S. public opinion. The *Washington Post* described the evidence as "irrefut-
able." Prowar sentiment jumped from one-third of the public to one-half. When
Powell visited the Senate Foreign Relations Committee the next day, Joseph
Biden gushed, "I'd like to move the nomination of Secretary of State Powell for
President of the United States." [105]

The United States still needed to secure approval from nine of the fifteen Security Council members, and it needed to dissuade France from exercising its veto. It
applied enormous pressure on developing countries, which were all aware of what
happened to Yemen in 1990 after it joined Cuba in opposing the use of force against
Iraq. The UN gambit might have succeeded had not courageous young British

intelligence officer Katharine Gun, at great personal risk, exposed an illegal NSA operation to spy on and pressure UN delegates to support the war measure. The exposé shocked Britain but went almost unreported by the U.S. media.[106] Despite threats and bribes, and after weeks of unrelenting pressure, only the United States, Great Britain, Spain, and Bulgaria supported the resolution. Among those defying the United States were Cameroon, Chile, Guinea, Angola, and Mexico.[107]

U.S. officials sneered at France and Germany for opposing the war. Rumsfeld dismissed them as "old Europe."[108] In a move reminiscent of World War I vilification of all things German, the House of Representatives cafeteria renamed French fries "freedom fries." *New York Times* columnist Thomas Friedman called for replacing France on the UN Security Council with India: "France, as they say in kindergarten, does not play well with others."[109]

Bush remained bitter for years over "old Europe's" refusal to support the war. In his 2010 memoirs, he accused German Chancellor Gerhard Schroeder of having reneged on a January 2002 promise to back an invasion. Schroeder angrily refuted those charges, shooting back, "As we know today, the Bush administration's reasons for the Iraq war were based on lies." That view was seconded by other German officials. Uwe-Karsten Heye, who was Schroeder's spokesman at the time, disparaged Bush's understanding of the international situation: "We noticed that the intellectual reach of the president of the most important nation at the time was exceptionally low. For this reason, it was difficult to communicate with him. He had no idea what was happening in the world. He was so fixated on being a Texan. I think he knew every longhorn in Texas."[110]

The decision to invade on March 10 had already been made. Meeting with Blair five days before Powell's speech, Bush proposed several ways to provoke a confrontation, including painting a U.S. surveillance plane in UN colors to draw Iraqi fire, producing a defector to publicly disclose Iraq's WMD, and assassinating Saddam.[111]

As the drums of war beat louder, U.S. media abandoned any pretense of objectivity, trumpeting the militarists and silencing the critics, who vanished from the airwaves. MSNBC, which was owned by General Electric, canceled Phil Donahue's prime-time show three weeks before the invasion. An NBC memo explained that Donohue "seems to delight in presenting guests who are anti-war, anti-Bush and skeptical of the administration's motives." NBC officials feared that the show would provide "a home for the liberal anti-war agenda at the same time our competitors are waving the flag at every opportunity."[112]

And wave the flag they did. CNN, Fox, NBC, and other television networks and radio stations paraded a stream of retired generals who, it was later revealed, were being given Pentagon talking points. The Pentagon recruited over seventy-five officers, almost all of whom worked directly for military contractors that would profit from the war. Rumsfeld personally approved the list. Many were flown to Baghdad, Guantánamo, and other sites for special tours. A 2008 exposé in the *New York Times* reported, "Internal Pentagon documents repeatedly refer to the military analysts as 'message force multipliers' or 'surrogates' who could be counted on to deliver administration 'themes and messages' to millions of Americans 'in the form of their own opinions.'"

Victory would be easy, the former military officials assured gullible listeners and fawning television anchors, whose networks paid their faux informants between $500 and $1,000 per appearance. Brent Krueger, a senior aide to Torie Clarke, the assistant secretary of defense for public affairs who oversaw the effort, crowed, "You could see they were taking verbatim what the secretary was saying or what the technical specialists were saying. And they were saying it over and over and over." On some days, he noted, "We were able to click on every single station and every one of our folks were up there delivering our message. You'd look at them and say, 'This is working.'"

Some later regretted having peddled lies to sell a war. Fox analyst Major Robert Bevelacqua, a retired Green Beret, complained, "It was them saying, 'We need to stick our hands up your back and move your mouth for you.'" NBC military analyst Colonel Kenneth Allard called the program "psyops on steroids." "I felt we'd been hosed," he admitted.[113]

Major newspapers spouted the same drivel. In 2004, *New York Times* public editor Daniel Okrent savaged the *Times* for having printed stories that "pushed Pentagon assertions so aggressively you could almost sense epaulets sprouting on the shoulders of editors."[114]

For the neocons, Iraq was just the appetizer. After devouring Iraq, they planned to return for the main course. In August 2002, a senior British official told *Newsweek*, "Everyone wants to go to Baghdad. Real men want to go to Tehran."[115] Undersecretary of State John Bolton voted for Syria and North Korea. PNACer Norman Podhoretz urged Bush to think bigger still. "The regimes that richly deserve to be overthrown and replaced are not confined to the three singled-out members of the axis of evil," he wrote in his journal, *Commentary*. "At a minimum, the axis should extend to Syria and Lebanon and Libya, as well as 'friends' of America like the Saudi royal family and Egypt's Hosni Mubarak, along with the Palestinian Authority, whether headed by Arafat or one of his henchmen."[116] Michael Ledeen, a former U.S. national security official and neocon strategist, mused, "I think we're going to be obliged to fight a regional war, whether we want to or not. It may turn out to be a war to remake the world."[117]

When retired General Wesley Clark visited the Pentagon in November 2001, he discovered that this was more than a pipe dream. A senior military staff officer told him, "we were still on track for going against Iraq. . . . But there was more.

This was being discussed as part of a five year campaign plan, he said, and there were a total of seven countries, beginning with Iraq, then Syria, Lebanon, Libya, Iran, Somalia, and Sudan. So, I thought, this is what they mean when they talk about 'draining the swamp.'" [118]

People knowledgeable about the region, including those in the State Department and CIA, tried to dispel this neocon fantasy. "It's a war to turn the kaleidoscope, by people who know nothing about the Middle East," said former U.S. Ambassador to Saudi Arabia Charles Freeman. [119] "It may be excusable as a fantasy of some Israelis . . . ," said Anthony Cordesman. "As American policy, however, it crosses the line between neo-conservative and neo-crazy." [120] Princeton international relations expert G. John Ikenberry marveled at the "imperial ambition" of neocons who foresaw "a unipolar world in which the United States has no peer competitor" and in which "no state or coalition could ever challenge it as global leader, protector and enforcer." [121]

With war approaching, some noticed how few of the war enthusiasts had served their country during the Cold War or in Vietnam, earning them the label of "chickenhawks." Despite heartily supporting the Vietnam War, most went out of their way to avoid combat. Now they were blithely sending other young men and women off to Afghanistan and Iraq to kill and be killed. Republican Senator Chuck Hagel of Nebraska, a Vietnam veteran who opposed the administration's warmongering, remarked, "It is interesting to me that many of those who want to rush this country into war and think it would be so quick and easy don't know anything about war. They come at it from an intellectual perspective versus having sat in jungles or foxholes and watched their friends get their heads blown off." [122] Highly decorated Marine General Anthony Zinni found it "interesting to wonder why all the generals see it the same way, and all those that never fired a shot in anger and really hell-bent to go to war see it a different way. That's usually the way it is in history." [123]

It was even more so now. Dick Cheney called Vietnam a "noble cause," but after leaving Yale for Casper Community College in Wyoming, he applied for and received four student deferments and then another one for being married. "I had other priorities in the 60s than military service," he explained. [124] Some think it not accidental that the Cheneys had their first child in July 1966, nine months after the Johnson administration announced it would begin drafting married men without children. [125] George W. Bush used family connections to get into the National Guard, which was only 1 percent African American. Bush failed to complete his six-year commitment and got himself assigned to Alabama, where he engaged in politics. [126] Four-star General Colin Powell, the former chairman of the Joint Chiefs of Staff, wrote in his 1995 autobiography, "I am angry that so many of the sons of the powerful and well placed . . . managed to wangle slots in

Reserve and National Guard units. Of the many tragedies of Vietnam, this raw class discrimination strikes me as the most damaging to the ideal that all Americans are created equal and owe equal allegiance to their country."[127] Future House Speaker Newt Gingrich got a student deferment. He told a reporter that Vietnam was "the right battlefield at the right time." When asked why it wasn't right for him, he replied, "What difference would I have made? There was a bigger battle in Congress than in Vietnam."[128] But he wasn't elected to Congress until four years after the United States pulled out all its troops. John Bolton supported the Vietnam War while attending Yale but enlisted in the Maryland National Guard to avoid combat. He later wrote in his Yale twenty-fifth reunion book, "I confess I had no desire to die in a Southeast Asian rice paddy."[129] Paul Wolfowitz, Scooter Libby, Peter Rodman, Richard Perle, former White House Chief of Staff Andrew Card, John Ashcroft, George Will, former New York City Mayor Rudolph Giuliani, Phil Graham, former Speaker of the House Dennis Hastert, Joe Lieberman, Senator Mitch McConnell, Supreme Court Justice Clarence Thomas, Trent Lott, Richard Armey, and former Senator Don Nickles got deferments. John Ashcroft got seven of them. Elliott Abrams had a bad back, former Solicitor General Kenneth Starr psoriasis, Kenneth Adelman a skin rash, Jack Kemp a knee injury—though he managed to play quarterback in the NFL for another eight years. Superhawk Tom DeLay, the future Republican majority leader, had worked as a pest exterminator. He assured critics that he would have served but that minorities had already taken the best positions. Rush Limbaugh missed Vietnam because he had a pilonidal or anal cyst.[130]

As war drew near, protesters took over the streets of over 800 cities around the world. Estimates range from 6 million to 30 million. Three million came out in Rome alone in what *Guinness World Records* lists as the largest antiwar rally in history.[131] More than a million protesters marched in London. Hundreds of thousands marched in New York. In most of Europe, more than 80 percent opposed a U.S. invasion of Iraq. Ninety-four to 96 percent did in Turkey. Opposition in Eastern Europe ranged from the mid-60s in the Czech Republic to the high 70s in Poland.[132]

In the Arab world, where the United States waged an aggressive campaign for public opinion, opposition was greatest. Polling firm Zogby reported that the percentage of Saudis with an "unfavorable opinion" of the United States rose from 87 to 97 percent in one year.[133] A *Time* magazine survey of over 300,000 Europeans found that 84 percent considered the United States the greatest threat to peace and only 8 percent considered Iraq the greatest threat.[134] Columnist Robert Samuelson wrote, "To foreign critics, [Bush's] Rambo-like morality confirms their worst stereotypes of Americans: stupid, incautious and bloodthirsty."[135]

Contemptuous of global opinion, Bush unleashed a massive aerial assault on

Antiwar protesters gather at the Washington Monument. As the invasion of Iraq drew near, U.S. protesters were joined by millions around the world, including an estimated 3 million in Rome.

March 20. The strategy was labeled "Shock and Awe," based on a 1996 study by Harlan Ullman and James Wade, who wrote, "Shutting the country down would entail both the physical destruction of appropriate infrastructure and the shutdown and control of the flow of all vital information and associated commerce so rapidly as to achieve a level of national shock akin to the effect that dropping nuclear weapons on Hiroshima and Nagasaki had on the Japanese." The goal, they explained, was to "impose a regime of Shock and Awe through delivery of instant, nearly incomprehensible levels of massive destruction directed at influencing society writ large, meaning its leadership and public, rather than targeting directly against military or strategic objectives." They warned that this strategy will be "utterly brutal and ruthless," and "can easily fall outside the cultural heritage and values of the U.S." [136]

But under Bush and Cheney, the cultural heritage and values of the United States had fundamentally changed. NBC anchor Tom Brokaw effervesced, "One of the things we don't want to do is to destroy the infrastructure of Iraq because in a few days we're going to own that country." [137] Rumsfeld went to Baghdad to thank the troops for their sacrifice, declaring, perhaps a trifle prematurely, "unlike many armies in the world, you came not to conquer, not to occupy, but to liberate and the Iraqi people know this . . . many . . . came to the streets to welcome you. Pulling down statues of Saddam Hussein, celebrating their new-found freedom."[138]

The carefully orchestrated images of U.S. power and Iraqi jubilation to which Rumsfeld alluded quickly gave way to images of Iraqis looting ancient treasures from Baghdad museums. It turned out that even the jubilation wasn't so jubilant or so spontaneous. The famous scene of Iraqis toppling the Saddam Hussein statue in Firdos Square was actually staged by a U.S. Army psychological warfare team who recruited the Iraqis and brought the statue down for them.[139]

With Iraq in the win column, potential targets for future regime change included Iran, Syria, Saudi Arabia, Lebanon, the PLO, Sudan, Libya, Yemen, and Somalia. Perle had earlier gloated, "We could deliver a short message, a two-word message: 'You're next.'"[140] In *The War over Iraq*, William Kristol and Lawrence Kaplan wrote, "we stand at the cusp of a new historical era." They considered it "a decisive moment" that was "so clearly about more than Iraq. It is about more even than the future of the Middle East and the war on terror. It is about what sort of role the United States intends to play in the world in the twenty-first century." "The mission begins in Baghdad," they acknowledged, "but it does not end there."[141]

No wonder Syrian President Bashar al-Assad told an Arab League summit meeting on March 1, "We are all targeted. . . . We are all in danger."[142] North Korea drew a similar lesson but proposed a different solution. Kim Jong Il said that Iraq's big mistake was not having nuclear weapons. If it had had such weapons, he argued, the United States would never have invaded. North Korea's official party newspaper, *Rodong Shinmun,* insisted that North Korea would neither submit to inspectors nor disarm. North Korea, it decided, "would have already met the same miserable fate as Iraq's had it compromised . . . and accepted the demand raised by the imperialists and its [sic] followers for nuclear inspection and disarmament. . . . No one should expect [North Korea] to make any slightest concession or compromise."[143]

Besides possessing nuclear weapons, North Koreans had one other "advantage" over the Iraqis: they weren't sitting on top of the world's second largest known oil reserves. Iraqis had no illusions about the United States' motives. The more U.S. leaders spoke about freedom, the more Iraqis heard the word "oil." More than three-quarters of Iraqis told pollsters that the U.S. invasion was motivated by a desire to control Iraqi oil. In a November 2002 radio interview, Rumsfeld categorically denied this: "Nonsense. It just isn't. There are certain things like that, myths, that are floating around. . . . It has nothing to do with oil, literally nothing to do with oil."[144]

Alan Greenspan, the long-serving chair of the Federal Reserve Board of Governors, thought such denials absurd. "I am saddened," he wrote, "that it is

U.S. tanks roll through Baghdad in the wake of the U.S. invasion of Iraq. With the perceived mission so quickly "accomplished" in Iraq, neoconservatives both inside and outside the Bush administration began to look elsewhere for dragons to slay.

politically inconvenient to acknowledge what everyone knows: the Iraq war is largely about oil." [145]

Experts estimated that Saudi Arabia, with 259 billion barrels of proven reserves, and Iraq, with 112 billion barrels, sat atop approximately one-third of the world's total supply of oil. Some thought that Iraq might actually have over 400 billion barrels of reserves.[146]

PNAC cofounder Robert Kagan believed that securing that oil would likely require a long-term military presence. "We will probably need a major concentration of forces in the Middle East over a long period of time," he said. "When we have economic problems, it's been caused by disruptions in our oil supply. If we have a force in Iraq, there will be no disruption in oil supplies." [147] Michael Klare, who has written extensively on the subject, took a broader view than Kagan. "Controlling Iraq is about oil as power," he observed, "rather than oil as fuel. Control over the Persian Gulf translates into control over Europe, Japan, and China. It's having our hand on the spigot." [148]

Those who wanted to dismantle Iraq's state-run companies and turn the oil over to the international oil companies ran into a buzz saw of defiance, replete with sabotage by insurgents, resistance by unionized oil workers, and opposition by the Iraqi parliament. Kellogg, Brown & Root, the Halliburton subsidiary, did receive a $1.2 billion contract in 2004 to reconstruct Iraq's southern oil facilities, but the Iraqis retained operational responsibility. The United States continued to pressure the Iraqi government to pass the long-stalled petrochemical bill.

U.S. victory celebrations proved premature. Defeating Iraq's demoralized army was simple. Imposing order proved impossible. Arrogant war planners ignored warnings from civilians and military alike that governing an occupied Iraq would not be the cakewalk they anticipated. In January 2003, the National Intelligence Council produced two lengthy assessments of what to expect following the invasion based on the views of the sixteen different intelligence agencies. Titled "Principal Challenges in Post-Saddam Iraq" and "Regional Consequences of Regime Change in Iraq,"[149] they warned that a U.S.-provoked war would increase Iran's influence in the region, open the door to Al-Qaeda in Afghanistan and Iraq, awaken dormant and potentially violent sectarian rivalries, spark a resurgence of political Islam, and facilitate fund-raising by terrorist groups "as a result of Muslim outrage over U.S. actions." Establishing democracy would be "a long, difficult and probably turbulent challenge" because Iraq had "no concept of loyal opposition and no history of alternation of power."[150]

Similar conclusions had been drawn after a series of April 1999 war games known as Desert Crossing that were designed to assess the aftermath of a U.S. invasion.[151] General Zinni, who led the effort, became adamantly opposed to going to war. He lambasted hawks who belittled the importance of public opinion in the Muslim world: "I'm not sure which planet they live on, because it isn't the one that I travel."[152] Michael Scheuer, the first head of the CIA's bin Laden unit, concurred, noting that "the CIA repeatedly warned Tenet of the inevitable disaster an Iraq war would cause—spreading bin Ladenism, spurring a bloody Sunni-Shiite war and lethally destabilizing the region."[153]

This information apparently never entered into the calculations of the president when planning for war. Shortly before the invasion began, Bush met with three Iraqi Americans, one of whom later became postwar Iraq's first representative to the United States. As they elaborated on concerns about a post-Saddam Sunni-Shiite split, they realized that the president had no idea what they were talking about and explained to him that Iraqis were divided into two potentially hostile sects. Bush evidently did not understand that he might be handing a suddenly Shiite-dominated Iraq to Iran on a silver platter.[154]

Al-Qaeda leaders thanked Allah for the colossal blunders, both tactical and strategic, of the United States' neocon strategists. In September 2003, on the second anniversary of 9/11, Al-Qaeda leader Ayman al-Zawahiri exulted, "We thank God for appeasing us with the dilemmas in Iraq and Afghanistan. The Americans are facing a delicate situation in both countries. If they withdraw they will lose everything and if they stay, they will continue to bleed to death."[155] The following year, bin Laden drew on the same "bleeding" metaphor to explain his strategy, taking credit for having "bled Russia for 10 years until it went bankrupt and was forced to withdraw in defeat." He was, he claimed, "continuing this policy in bleeding America to the point of bankruptcy," noting that the half-million dollars Al-Qaeda spent on the 9/11 terrorist acts had resulted in a U.S. "economic deficit" of over a trillion dollars.[156]

Bush, Cheney, and Rumsfeld made a series of calamitous decisions. Overriding the State Department, the Pentagon flew neocon favorite Ahmed Chalabi and hundreds of his supporters back to Baghdad shortly after Saddam's fall. U.S. Lieutenant General Jay Garner, to his credit, refused to allow Chalabi to play the role Rumsfeld and Cheney envisioned.[157] The Americans would later learn how suspect Chalabi's organisation's loyalties really were. Evidence surfaced of their ties to Iranian leaders and to the Iranian-linked Shiite militant League of the Righteous, which was implicated in the kidnapping and murder of foreigners, including the 2007 execution-style slaying of five U.S. marines. The U.S. government severed its ties with Chalabi in May 2008. Three months later, it arrested one of his top aides on suspicion that he had served as a liaison to the League.[158]

From President Bush on down, administration officials were simply delusional. In April 2003, *Nightline*'s Ted Koppel was incredulous when Andrew Natsios, the administrator of the Agency for International Development, told him that the total cost to U.S. taxpayers would be $1.7 billion.[159] Wolfowitz insisted that Iraqi oil revenues would be sufficient to finance the postwar reconstruction. As he had observed, Iraq "floats on a sea of oil."[160] By the time Bush left office, the United States had spent some $700 billion on the war, not including interest payments on borrowed money and long-term care for veterans, many of whom suffered crippling physical and psychological injuries.

Conditions in Iraq went from bad to worse when L. Paul Bremer replaced Garner in early May. Bremer swiftly dissolved the Iraqi army and police force and ordered former Baath Party members fired from government posts. Looting swept Baghdad as undermanned coalition forces could not maintain order. While national treasures disappeared from Iraq's museums, U.S. troops and tanks protected only the Oil Ministry building. The country rapidly descended into chaos as electricity failed, water supplies dried up, sewage ran in the streets, and the sick and wounded overwhelmed hospitals. While Bremer and the Coalition Provisional Authority (CPA), operating out of the heavily fortified Green Zone, issued upbeat reports, the insurgency, fueled by armed and disgruntled former Iraqi soldiers, whom Rumsfeld contemptuously dismissed as "dead-enders," grew and war costs skyrocketed.[161] The Pentagon requested an additional $87 billion for Iraq and Afghanistan.

By November 2003, coalition forces were suffering thirty-five attacks per day. Angry insurgents flooded in from throughout the Islamic world intent upon ousting the infidels. Bin Laden and Zawahiri urged fellow Muslims to "bury [the Americans] in the Iraqi graveyard." In September, between one thousand and three thousand were thought to have arrived, with thousands more on the way. One highly placed U.S. official noted, "Iraq is now Jihad Stadium. It is the place for fundamentalists to go now, it is their Super Bowl, where you go to stick it to the West . . . there are an infinite number of potential new players." [162]

Bremer set about reorganizing the Iraqi economy, which essentially meant privatizing the national oil company and two hundred other state-owned companies. Planning for this had begun before the invasion, when the U.S. Agency for International Development drew up its "Vision for Post-Conflict Iraq." Contracts for $900 million had been awarded to five infrastructure engineering firms, including Kellogg, Brown & Root and Bechtel. The Treasury Department had been busy circulating a program for "broad-based Mass Privatization" among financial consultants.

On May 27, 2003, Bremer announced that Iraq is "open for business again" and began issuing orders. Order no. 37 set a flat tax rate of 15 percent, slashing the tax burden on wealthy individuals and on corporations, which had been paying around 45 percent. Order no. 39 privatized state enterprises and permitted 100 percent foreign ownership of Iraqi firms. The profits, in their entirety, could be removed from the country. Leases and contracts could last for forty years and then be eligible for renewal. Order no. 40 privatized the banks. Rumsfeld testified that those reforms created "some of the most enlightened—and inviting—tax and investment laws in the free world." With estimates of reconstruction costs reaching $500 billion, it is no wonder that *The Economist* called it "a capitalist dream." [163] According to Nobel Prize–winning former World Bank chief economist Joseph Stiglitz, Iraq was getting "an even more radical form of shock therapy than pursued in the former Soviet world." [164]

Caught off guard by the strength of the insurgency, the Pentagon sent U.S. troops into combat without sufficient armor to protect vehicles that were targeted with improvised explosive devices. The sheer incompetence of officials sent by the Bush administration sometimes strained credulity. The *Washington Post* reported that job seekers were chosen based on right-wing political views and loyalty to the Bush administration, not expertise in development, conflict resolution, or the Middle East. Jim O'Beirne, a Bush political appointee, asked job applicants if they had voted for Bush, if they approved of his war on terror, and even if they supported *Roe v. Wade*. According to the *Post,* "A twenty-four-year-old who had never worked in finance—but had applied for a White House job—was sent to reopen Baghdad's stock exchange. The daughter of a prominent neoconservative commentator and a recent graduate from an evangelical university for homeschooled children were tapped to manage Iraq's $13 billion budget, even though they didn't have a background in accounting." The *Post* reported that many of those tasked with rebuilding Iraq focused instead on "instituting a flat tax, . . . selling off government assets, . . . ending food rations," [165] while the economy collapsed and unemployment skyrocketed.

In May 2003, law enforcement experts from the Justice Department reported that Iraq needed six thousand foreign advisors to revamp its police forces. The White House sent former New York City Police Commissioner Bernard Kerik to be the interim interior minister, along with a dozen advisors. Kerik, who would later be imprisoned after pleading guilty to eight felony counts, lasted three months before departing, leaving Iraq in worse shape than he found it. The Bush appointees proved to be the Keystone Kops of nation building. With a gut-level belief that governments were not capable of providing for their people, they set out to prove their convictions right. By September 2004, conditions had deteriorated so dramatically that Amr Moussa, head of the Arab League, announced, "The gates of hell are open in Iraq." [166]

Lacking sufficient troops to carry out basic functions, the government hired an army of private security guards and civilian contractors to do much of the work, often at outrageous cost and with little oversight. By 2007, they numbered 160,000. Many Blackwater security guards had served in right-wing militaries in Latin America. [167] They and other foreign personnel had been granted immunity from arrest by Iraqi authorities. Other support operations were outsourced to companies like Halliburton, which raked in profits in Iraq, Afghanistan, and Kuwait. With 40,000 employees in Iraq alone, it earned more than $24 billion by 2008, much of it coming from questionable no-bid contracts. After the invasion, Halliburton jumped from number nineteen to the top spot on the U.S. Army's list of contractors. [168] When Senator Patrick Leahy confronted Cheney on the floor of the Senate about Halliburton's shameless profiteering, Cheney erupted, "Fuck yourself." [169] Not only were Halliburton and its subsidiary KBR found to have repeatedly overcharged the government, but KBR's shoddy electrical work on U.S. bases resulted in hundreds of electrical fires and the electrocution of numerous soldiers. [170]

Conditions deteriorated further on February 22, 2006, when a bomb destroyed the golden dome of the Shiite shrine in Samarra. Enraged Shiites attacked Sunnis and their religious sites throughout the country. [171] Suicide bombings and murders of civilians became commonplace. The country teetered on the edge of civil war.

Award-winning journalist Helen Thomas confronted George Bush: "Mr. President, you started this war, a war of your choosing, and you can end it alone, today. . . . Two million Iraqis have fled their country as refugees. Two million more are displaced. Thousands and thousands are dead. Don't you understand you brought the al Qaeda into Iraq?" "Actually, I was hoping to solve the Iraqi issue diplomatically," Bush responded. "That's why I went to the United Nations and worked with the United Nations Security Council, which unanimously passed a resolution that said disclose, disarm or face serious consequences." [172]

Bush had earlier said he invaded Iraq after giving Saddam "a chance to allow the inspectors in, and he wouldn't let them in." Even the *Washington Post* had felt compelled to comment: "The president's assertion that the war began because Iraq did not admit inspectors appeared to contradict the events leading up to war this spring: Hussein had, in fact, admitted the inspectors and Bush had opposed extending their work because he did not believe them effective." [173]

Bruce Bartlett, who served in both the Reagan and first Bush administrations, described George W. Bush's psychology to journalist Ron Suskind in 2004:

> This is why George W. Bush is so clear-eyed about Al Qaeda and the Islamic fundamentalist enemy. He believes you have to kill them all. They can't be persuaded, that they're extremists, driven by a dark vision. He understands them, because he's just like them.... This is why he dispenses with people who confront him with inconvenient facts. He truly believes he's on a mission from God. Absolute faith like that overwhelms a need for analysis. The whole thing about faith is to believe things for which there is no empirical evidence. But you can't run the world on faith.

Suskind noted that when people questioned Bush's policies that appeared to fly in the face of reality, "The president would say that he relied on his 'gut' or his 'instincts' to guide the ship of state, and then he 'prayed over it.'" One of Bush's senior advisors accused Suskind of being "in what we call the reality-based community." He informed him, "That's not the way the world really works anymore. We're an empire now, and when we act, we create our own reality.... We're history's actors ... and you, all of you, will be left to just study what we do." [174]

Not everyone was so sanguine about denying reality. Seven noncommissioned officers with the 82nd Airborne described the Iraqi situation to the *New York Times* in August 2007:

> Viewed from Iraq at the tail end of a 15-month deployment, the political debate in Washington is indeed surreal.... To believe that Americans, with an occupying force that long ago outlived its reluctant welcome, can win over a recalcitrant local population and win this counterinsurgency is far-fetched.... Sunnis ... now find themselves forming militias, sometimes with our tacit support.... The Iraqi government finds itself working at cross purposes with us on this issue because it is justifiably fearful that Sunni

militias will turn on it should the Americans leave. . . . a vast majority of Iraqis feel increasingly insecure and view us as an occupation force that has failed to produce normalcy after four years and is increasingly unlikely to do so as we continue to arm each warring side. . . . the most important front in the counterinsurgency, improving basic social and economic conditions, is the one on which we have failed most miserably. Two million Iraqis are in refugee camps in bordering countries. Cities lack regular electricity, telephone services and sanitation. . . . In a lawless environment where men with guns rule the streets, engaging in the banalities of life has become a death-defying act. Four years into our occupation, we have failed on every promise. . . . the primary preoccupation of average Iraqis is when and how they are likely to be killed. . . . our presence . . . has . . . robbed them of their self-respect. They will soon realize that the best way to regain dignity is to call us what we are—an army of occupation—and force our withdrawal.[175]

In early 2008, Joseph Stiglitz and Harvard economist Linda Bilmes calculated that the cost of the Iraq War would actually reach $3 trillion, or 1,765 times what Natsios had estimated.[176] What did Iraqi citizens and U.S. taxpayers receive in return? In 2008, the International Red Cross reported a humanitarian "crisis" in Iraq leaving millions without clean water, sanitation, or health care: "The humanitarian situation in most of the country remains among the most critical in the world." Twenty thousand of the 34,000 doctors who had practiced in Iraq in 1990 had left the country; 2,200 had been killed and 250 kidnapped.[177] In 2010, Transparency International ranked Iraq the fourth most corrupt country in the world, just behind Afghanistan, Myanmar, and Somalia.[178]

But the starkest display of what the United States achieved came in March 2008, a month in which Baghdad received two prominent visitors: Dick Cheney and Iranian President Mahmoud Ahmadinejad. Cheney sneaked into Baghdad under a veil of secrecy, protected by a massive security force, and then beat a hasty retreat before his presence was known. Ahmadinejad broadcast his plans in advance and drove in a motorcade from the airport. The *Chicago Tribune* reported:

Ahmadinejad was greeted with hugs and kisses on the first day of his historic visit to Iraq . . . , marking a dramatic break with the past for the two former foes and a new challenge to U.S. influence in Iraq. . . . Ahmadinejad . . . planned to spend two days in Baghdad. He is sleeping outside the relative safety of the Green Zone. . . . Iraq and Iran are expected Monday to announce a series of bilateral agreements concerning trade, electricity and oil. "There are no limits to the cooperation that we are going to open up with our neighbor Iran," al-Maliki told reporters. Ahmadinejad was the first national leader to be given a state reception by Iraq's government. Iraqi President Jalal Talabani and Ahmadinejad held hands as they inspected a guard of honor, while a brass band played brisk British marching tunes. Children presented the Iranian with flowers. Members of Iraq's Cabinet lined up to greet him. ... At every step, Ahmadinejad and his Iraqi hosts underlined the common interests of the two countries, whose long-hostile relationship has been transformed by the installation of a Shiite-led government following the U.S.-led invasion. ... "The two people, Iraqi and Iranian, will work together to bring Iraq out of its current crisis," Ahmadinejad pledged. "... Iraq is already in the hands of the Iranians. It's just a matter of time," said independent Sunni parliamentarian Mithal al-Alusi. "Ahmadinejad's message is: Mr. Bush, we won the game, and you are losing."

Standing in the U.S.-controlled Green Zone alongside the Iraqi prime minister, Ahmadinejad dismissed Bush's repeated allegations that Iranian agents were arming and training Shiite militias and demanded that the United States "accept the facts of this region: the Iraqi people do not like or support the Americans."[179]

He was right. The Americans were the big losers, and Iran turned out to be the big winner. Its principal enemy had been eliminated, and its influence was now paramount in the region.

Already bogged down in two disastrous wars, there was little the United States could do about Iran, a charter member of Bush's "axis of evil," besides repeatedly decrying its expanding nuclear program, its meddling in Iraq, its support for terrorism, and the inflammatory statements by its president. Because Bush was bent on confrontation with Iran, he missed a historic opportunity to mend relations in the early part of the decade and to do so on the United States' terms.

Following 9/11, Iran assisted the United States in its fight against the Taliban—their mutual enemy—in Afghanistan. Then, after extensive informal discussions, Iran proposed a grand bargain in May 2003. In exchange for enhanced security, mutual respect, and access to peaceful nuclear technology, Iran offered recognition of Israel as part of a two-state solution; "full transparency" on its nuclear program; help in stabilizing Iraq; action against terrorist groups in Iran; the halting of material support for Palestinian opposition groups, including Hamas, and pressuring them to "stop violent actions against civilians" in Israel; and a concerted effort to transform Hezbollah into a "mere political organization within Lebanon." But because the administration neocons were intent on toppling the Iranian regime, not improving relations with it, they rejected the Iranian initiative and girded for war.[180] It was a blunder of epic proportions.

In 2005, Philip Giraldi, a former senior CIA official, reported, "The Pentagon, acting under instructions from ... Cheney's office," had ordered the U.S. Strategic

Command to prepare plans for a "large-scale air assault on Iran employing both conventional and tactical nuclear weapons."[181] Nuclear weapons were reserved for hardened and underground facilities and the uranium enrichment plant at Natanz. Vehement objections by the Joint Chiefs forced Bush and Cheney to remove this option. In 2007, the Bush administration again began stirring the pot with Iran. As late as October of that year, Bush warned that Iran was intent on acquiring nuclear weapons and that its doing so might cause World War III. His effort to drum up war sentiment was derailed in early December when the intelligence community released a new National Intelligence Estimate concluding with "high confidence" that Iran had halted its nuclear weapons program in 2003, repudiating its findings of only two years earlier.[182]

The greater threat to U.S. interests came from neighboring Pakistan, which had played such a crucial role in creating and sustaining the Taliban. Pakistan's intelligence agency, the Directorate for Inter-Services Intelligence (ISI), had also maintained close ties with Al-Qaeda, even sending Islamic militants for training in Al-Qaeda camps. The militants were then deployed to wage a war of terror to dislodge Indian control of the disputed territory of Kashmir. Just two days after 9/11, Bush gave the Pakistanis an ultimatum. Deputy Secretary of State Richard Armitage handed General Mahmood Ahmad, head of the ISI, a list of seven nonnegotiable demands, including ending Pakistani support for and diplomatic relations with the Afghan Taliban, granting overflight rights to U.S. airplanes and access to naval bases and airports, and publicly condemning terrorism. According to President Pervez Musharraf, Armitage told Ahmad that Pakistan would be bombed "back to the Stone Age" if it didn't comply. Though the Pakistanis mistrusted the United States and blamed it for many of their problems—"After the Soviets were forced out of Afghanistan," said Shamshad Ahmad, Pakistan's UN ambassador and a former foreign secretary, "you left us in the lurch with all the problems stemming from the war: an influx of refugees, the drug and gun running, a Kalashnikov culture"[183]—Pakistan had little choice but to comply. Pakistan's acquiescence, though halfhearted at best, opened the door to a flood of U.S. military aid as Bush lifted the ban on arms sales to India and Pakistan that Clinton had put into place following their 1998 nuclear tests. Despite Pakistan's promise to assist U.S. efforts, its primary focus remained on India, and the ISI continued to support anti-U.S. Taliban fighters in Afghanistan.

Tensions between India and Pakistan had flared anew when Islamic militants staged an attack on the Indian parliament in December 2001. War between the two nuclear-armed states seemed imminent. A million soldiers confronted each other across the Line of Control in Kashmir. Experts feared that the Indian army would overrun its Pakistani counterpart and that Pakistan would retaliate, as it threatened, with nuclear weapons. The Pentagon estimated that 12 million people could die almost immediately if nuclear weapons were exchanged. The insanity of the situation was driven home by the comments of General Mirza Aslam Beg, a retired chief of Pakistan's armed forces, who said, "I don't know what you're worried about. You can die crossing the street, hit by a car, or you could die in a nuclear war. You've got to die someday anyway." [184] The Indians were almost as obtuse. General Sundararajan Padmanabhan, India's army chief, remarked, "If we have to go to war, jolly good. If we don't, we will still manage." [185]

The U.S. arms that began pouring into Pakistan further inflamed tensions. Though the crisis was temporarily resolved, large-scale U.S. arms transfers to Pakistan increased to over $3.5 billion in 2006 alone, ranking Pakistan first among U.S. arms recipients. This was even more galling following the disclosure, in 2003, that A. Q. Khan, the father of Pakistan's nuclear industry, had run a network that sold nuclear bomb designs and bomb-making materials to North Korea, Libya, Iran, and possibly other nations over a fifteen-year period. Khan and his associates were known to have also visited Syria, Saudi Arabia, Egypt, Chad, Mali, Nigeria, Niger, and Sudan. Evidence indicates that senior Pakistani military and government officials had supported Khan's activities. And the United States had turned a blind eye to Pakistan's bomb project in return for Pakistani aid against the Soviets in Afghanistan—a policy suggested by Brzezinski but enacted under Reagan. Khan confessed publicly to his transgressions, and, the very next day, Musharraf pardoned him, calling him "my hero." Khan remained under de facto house arrest for five years, but Pakistani authorities never brought charges and refused to allow U.S. officials to question him. A Pakistani senator chortled, "America needed an offering to the gods—blood on the floor. Musharraf told A.Q., 'Bend over for a spanking.'" [186]

That was more than the United States demanded of Musharraf. A former senior U.S. intelligence official complained to journalist Seymour Hersh, "Khan was willing to sell blueprints, centrifuges, and the latest in weaponry. He was the worst nuclear-arms proliferator in the world and he's pardoned—with not a squeak from the White House." [187] The United States instead lavished military aid and political support on Musharraf, who had seized power in a military coup in 1999 and ruled with an iron fist until he was ousted in 2008. U.S. support for the dictator and his military did little to win friends in that impoverished Islamic republic. A 2007 Pew poll found that only 15 percent of Pakistanis had a favorable view of the United States, significantly less than the 23 percent who the previous year had reported a favorable view of Pakistan's archenemy, India, against which Pakistan had fought four wars. [188] In 2007, 46 percent of Pakistanis held a favorable view of Osama bin Laden. Nine percent viewed Bush favorably. [189]

Nor was Bush making many friends in Russia. Although he said he had looked into Russian President Vladimir Putin's soul and liked what he saw, Bush,

A. Q. Khan, the father of Pakistan's nuclear industry, who, it was revealed in 2003, ran a network that sold nuclear bomb designs and bomb-making materials to North Korea, Libya, Iran, and possibly other nations over a fifteen-year period. The United States had turned a blind eye to Pakistan's bomb project in return for Pakistani aid in fighting the Soviets in Afghanistan.

as had Clinton before him, treated Russia with contempt. Shortly after taking office, Bush, ignoring strong Russian opposition, withdrew from the 1972 ABM Treaty to pursue his missile defense initiative. But he and Putin had a surprisingly friendly meeting in June 2001. After the September 11 attacks, Putin was one of the first foreign leaders to phone Bush and express condolences. On September 24, he announced a five-point plan to support the U.S. war on terrorism. Not only would he share intelligence and open Russian airspace to the United States, he said, but he would acquiesce in and even facilitate the stationing of U.S. troops in the Middle East, which many in Russia's military and intelligence community strongly opposed.

Bush repaid Putin's largesse by breaking his father's promise to Gorbachev and expanding NATO ever closer to Russia's borders, effectively encircling Russia with U.S. and NATO military bases, some in former Soviet territories. This second wave of expansion began in late 2002 and concluded with the admission of Bulgaria, Romania, Slovakia, Slovenia, Lithuania, Latvia, and Estonia in March 2004. The Russians objected vehemently. Extending NATO to former Warsaw Pact nations like Bulgaria and Romania was objectionable enough, but extending NATO to former Soviet republics like Lithuania, Latvia, and Estonia was adding insult to injury.

Openly contemptuous of Russian opinion, Bush pressed NATO to expand even farther. Croatia and Albania joined in 2008. And he made it clear that he also wanted to add Georgia and Ukraine, despite protests by Russia and warnings from other NATO members that this would seriously damage relations between Russia and the West. Russians were convinced that U.S. democracy programs in Ukraine, Georgia, and Belarus were simply a ploy to further expand NATO and isolate Russia.

U.S.-Russian relations, which had looked so promising in 2001, were badly damaged in 2003 when the United States decided to invade Iraq. Russian officials threatened to veto a war resolution in the United Nations if Bush chose to go that route. Russia's mistrust of the United States ran so deep that it withdrew the strategic arms treaty designed to eventually mandate substantial cuts in nuclear stockpiles.

In April 2005, Putin used his annual state of the nation address to parliament to lament the breakup of the Soviet Union as the "greatest geopolitical disaster of the last century." Given the Russians' hardships under capitalism, many ordinary Russians also looked back nostalgically to life in the Soviet Union.[190] In parts of Russia, a Stalin revival was even under way as many citizens wanted to honor his contribution to the Soviet Union's history, especially his role in World War II, and were willing to downplay his crimes. "They never miss a chance in the West to rewrite history and diminish our country's role in the victory over fascism, so that's even more reason not to forget Stalin now," said Lyubov Sliska, a parliamentary first deputy speaker.[191]

The Russians also felt threatened by Bush's nuclear policies. While inveighing against nonexistent WMD in Iraq, Bush substantially and dangerously lowered the threshold for the use of real WMD. His 2002 Nuclear Posture Review (NPR) deliberately blurred the line between nuclear and conventional weapons and began targeting nonnuclear nations, which not only eliminated the incentive for such nations not to acquire nuclear weapons, it encouraged them to do so to avoid being targeted. The NPR asserted that the United States had the right to use nuclear weapons (1) if WMD of any sort were used against the United States; (2) to penetrate hardened or underground targets that couldn't be destroyed with conventional weapons; and (3) if the United States encountered "surprising military developments."[192] Recognizing the terrifying implications of this new policy, the *New York Times* ran a powerful editorial on March 12, 2002, titled "America as Nuclear Rogue," which insisted, "If another country were planning to develop a new nuclear weapon and contemplating preemptive strikes against a list of nonnuclear powers, Washington would rightly label that nation a dangerous rogue state. Yet such is the course recommended to President Bush by a new Pentagon planning paper that became public last weekend. . . . Where the Pentagon review goes very wrong is in lowering the threshold for using nuclear weapons and in undermining the effectiveness of the Nuclear Nonproliferation Treaty."[193] According to the treaty, the United States and the other nuclear powers were legally obliged to move toward eliminating their nuclear arsenals. Not only did Bush ignore that provision, he advocated developing a new generation of miniature nuclear weapons and bunker-busting bombs whose smaller size would make them more usable in combat situations.

Bush's nuclear policy threatened to destabilize the entire nonproliferation regime. In his riveting Peace Declaration of August 6, 2003, Hiroshima Mayor Tadatoshi Akiba lashed out at the United States' recklessness: "The nuclear Non-Proliferation Treaty, the central international agreement guiding the elimination of nuclear weapons, is on the verge of collapse. The chief cause is U.S. nuclear policy that, by openly declaring the possibility of a pre-emptive nuclear first strike and calling for resumed research into mini-nukes and other so-called 'useable nuclear weapons,' appears to worship nuclear weapons as God." [194]

Russian leaders took issue with several aspects of the NPR, but their reaction was muted compared to the shock caused by a spring 2006 article in the March–April issue of *Foreign Affairs*, the journal of the Council on Foreign Relations, the seat of the nation's foreign policy establishment. In the article, Keir Lieber of Notre Dame and Daryl Press of the University of Pennsylvania analyzed the relative strengths and weaknesses of U.S., Russian, and Chinese nuclear forces and concluded that the dramatic post–Cold War improvement in U.S. nuclear capabilities, combined with the "precipitous decline of Russia's arsenal, and the glacial pace of modernization of China's nuclear forces," created a situation in which neither the Russians nor the Chinese could effectively retaliate against a U.S. nuclear attack. That gave the United States its long-sought first-strike capability. The United States could destroy Russia or China with impunity. The United States' long-standing adversaries were unable to retaliate and would remain so for the foreseeable future.

The authors also conjectured about the real reasoning behind U.S. insistence on a missile defense shield. Such a shield would not, as typically assumed, be of value in a defense context as a "stand-alone shield" against a large-scale Russian missile barrage. Its value would come in an offensive context, protecting the United States against a retaliatory attack by the tiny number of Russian or Chinese weapons that might survive a U.S. first strike. [195]

Lieber and Press had actually been floating these ideas for a couple of years in academic circles. But their publication in *Foreign Affairs* hit like a sledgehammer. The *Washington Post* reported that the article "sent heads spinning" in Russia "with visions of Dr. Strangelove." [196] Russian economist and former acting Prime Minister Yegor Gaidar wrote in the *Financial Times*, "The publication of these ideas in a respectable American journal has had an explosive effect. Even those Russian journalists and analysts who are not prone to hysteria or anti-Americanism took it as an outline of the official position of the U.S. Administration." [197]

Putin immediately announced that Russia would spend whatever was necessary to maintain its deterrent capability. But the publication was "a major blow to Putin's prestige," said Vitaly Shlykov, a strategic analyst formerly with the Soviet military intelligence agency GRU. "Now he will pull out all the stops and spend whatever necessary to modernize Russia's nuclear deterrent," Shlykov predicted. Some Russian experts pointed to the fact that a new generation of nuclear missiles capable of penetrating the U.S. missile defense system was about to come on line. They had been developed in response to Bush's abrogating the ABM treaty in 2001 and included Topol-M ICBMs and, a little later, Bulava missiles for nuclear submarines.[198]

Russian experts debated the article's timing and the message the CFR was trying to convey. "Many people think it's not a coincidence that such an article was 'ordered' by someone," explained Dmitri Suslov, an analyst with the independent Council on Foreign and Defense Policy in Moscow. Because it was substantially true, he said, it had made security experts "very nervous." He thought it odd that with all the nuclear powers in the world, only the United States and Russia still had arsenals pointed and primed to wipe each other out. But publication of the article meant that the situation was not about to change. "At the very least," he noted, "this article has postponed any chance of talking about removing the MAD framework from our relations with the US."

Others thought it was designed to send a warning about Russia's growing ties with China. Viktor Mikhaylov, director of the Institute of Strategic Stability and a former Russian nuclear energy minister, dismissed allegations that Russia's capabilities had deteriorated and offered an alternative explanation: "This was done during our president Vladimir Vladimirovich Putin's visit to the People's Republic of China . . . the Americans probably look at this drawing closer together by our two countries maliciously and malignly. . . . But it exists and it will be developing." If that was the intention, Gaidar thought, it would backfire. "If someone had wanted to provoke Russia and China into close cooperation over missile and nuclear technologies, it would be difficult to find a more skilful and elegant way of doing so," he wrote.[199]

The Bush administration scrambled to calm the tense situation. Assistant Secretary of Defense for International Security Policy Peter Flory released a statement in a follow-up forum in the September–October *Foreign Affairs* that took issue with both the article's accuracy and its interpretation. He claimed that the United States was actually weakening its first-strike capability. Keith Payne, deputy assistant secretary of defense for forces policy from 2002 to 2003, insisted that the United States had consistently rejected developing a "credible first-strike capability" since the days when Robert McNamara was secretary of defense. Payne charged angrily, "They cherry-pick and misstate information about U.S. force developments . . . to fit the policy they have so miscast, while ignoring or dismissing U.S. force reductions and glaring deficiencies that do not fit their characterization. . . . their message is a gross distortion of U.S. policy, and that distortion is destabilizing U.S.-Russian relations."[200]

Alexei Arbatov, director of the Center on International Security Studies at the Institute for World Economy and International Relations of the Russian Academy of Sciences, thought that Lieber and Press were making a very important point. He acknowledged that Russian nuclear weapons were mostly Cold War relics that had outlived their usefulness and would soon be removed from service. The modern arsenal consisted of three or four new ballistic-missile submarines and a hundred Topol-M missiles, which would suffice as a minimal deterrent but only if kept on dangerous hair-trigger alert. In light of this growing strategic imbalance, Arbatov feared that a crisis could easily result in an accidental nuclear war. He warned, "if Russia feared a U.S. first strike, Moscow might make rash moves (such as putting its forces on alert) that would provoke a U.S. attack. . . . Lieber and Press," he concluded, "are rightly concerned about that risk."[201]

Lieber and Press replied convincingly to Flory and Payne, as well as to Pavel Podvig, a Stanford expert on Russia's nuclear program, who argued that Russian capabilities were far more potent than suggested. Lieber and Press conceded that the Pentagon had cut the size of the ballistic-missile submarine fleet but pointed out that the yield of SLBM warheads had more than quadrupled and their accuracy had markedly increased. As a result, an SLBM warhead used to have a 12 percent chance of destroying a hardened Russian missile silo, whereas now one type of SLBM warhead had a 90 percent chance and the other had a 98 percent chance. A similar situation prevailed with the upgraded Minuteman III ICBMs.

They next responded to Payne by showing that the United States had retained first-strike options in its nuclear war plans, pointing to a recently declassified 1969 document containing five full-scale nuclear attack options, three of which were preemptive. In response to Podvig, they argued that the gap in Russia's early-warning system was large enough for the United States to launch SLBMs through and hit targets across Russia.[202] Their response did nothing to calm Russians' fears. Nor did U.S. plans to install a missile defense system in Eastern Europe.

Russia also took sharp issue with Bush administration efforts to weaponize space. Bush appeared to be realizing the vision of the head of the U.S. Space Command, who had predicted in 1996, "We will engage terrestrial targets someday—ships, airplanes, land targets—from space. . . . We're going to fight from space and we're going to fight into space. . . . That's why the U.S. has development programs in directed energy and hit-to-kill mechanisms."[203] The rest of the world united in opposition to U.S. plans to expand the realm of conflagration. In 2000, the United Nations, by a vote of 163–0, passed a resolution on the Prevention of an Outer Space Arms Race, with Micronesia, Israel, and the United States abstaining. Defying world opinion, in January 2001, a commission led by Rumsfeld warned that the United States could face a "Space Pearl Harbor" if it didn't dominate space and recommended that the military "ensure that the president will have the option to deploy weapons in space."[204] That year, Peter Teets, undersecretary of the air force, told a space warfare symposium, "We haven't reached the point of strafing and bombing from space—nonetheless, we are thinking about those possibilities."[205]

In 2006, UN members voted 166–1 in favor of the resolution, with only the United States opposed. At the UN Conference on Disarmament, the United States consistently thwarted efforts by Russia and China to ban weaponization. Among the more bizarre programs the air force was looking into was one called "Rods from God," which would deploy solid tungsten cylinders, twenty or thirty feet long and one or two feet in diameter, that would be fired from satellites at tremendous speeds, easily destroying any target on the earth.[206]

Between NATO expansion, U.S. nuclear and space policies, and wars in Iraq and Afghanistan, U.S.-Russian relations took a sharp turn for the worse. The hopes for Russian-American friendship and a different world so eloquently articulated by Gorbachev had now definitively been relegated to the junk heap of history. It was as if the Bush administration were creating the nightmarishly militarized nation that Eisenhower had so poignantly warned about in 1961. During Bush's years in office, military spending more than doubled to reach $700 billion. The Pentagon had increasingly usurped the role of the State Department in foreign policy making, a process that had begun under the Kennedy administration.

It also encroached upon CIA intelligence gathering and had become increasingly involved in overseas covert operations. After marginalizing the agency in the run-up to the invasion of Iraq, Bush largely completed the decades-old process of destroying the nation's intelligence-gathering capabilities when he appointed Congressman Porter Goss to replace George Tenet in July 2004. Goss had joined the Agency as a Yale undergraduate forty-five years earlier. But he had become an unbridled critic who, according to Howard Hart, denounced the agents as "a bunch of dysfunctional jerks" and "a pack of idiots."[207] As director, he undertook the biggest purge in the Agency's history. According to Tim Weiner in his Pulitzer Prize–winning history of the CIA, "The new director surrounded himself with a team of political hacks he had imported from Capitol Hill. They believed they were on a mission from the White House—or some higher power—to rid the CIA of left-wing subversives."[208] The agency was further emasculated later that year when Bush appointed John Negroponte to the newly created position of director of national intelligence (DNI).

When former CIA Director Robert Gates became secretary of defense late in 2006, generals were ensconced as director of the CIA, both undersecretary and deputy undersecretary of defense for intelligence, chief of the State Department's counterterrorism operations, and head of CIA covert operations—all positions long held by civilians. Retired Admiral Mike McConnell soon replaced Negroponte as DNI.

The Pentagon also owned or leased over 75 percent of all federal buildings.[209] And it ran a vast, far-flung network of over 700, by some counts over 1,000, bases in some 130 countries that spanned every continent but Antarctica, plus 6,000 bases in the United States and its territories. The Department of Defense Base Structure Report for FY 2008 stated, "The Department of Defense (DOD) remains one of the world's largest 'landlords' with a physical plant consisting of more than 545,700 facilities (buildings, structures and linear structures) located on more than 5,400 sites, on approximately 30 million acres."[210] Its thirteen naval task forces patrolled the oceans and seas. The American Enterprise Institute called for turning this network of overseas bases into a system of "frontier stockades," housing a "global cavalry," which, "like the cavalry of the Old West, . . . is one part warrior and one part policeman."[211]

Douglas Feith outlined the new military posture: "We are performing the most thorough restructuring of U.S. military forces overseas since" 1953, he informed the House Armed Services Committee. "We want . . . greater flexibility for our forces, their ability to deploy powerful capabilities rapidly anywhere in the world where they are needed." Feith regretted that September 11 had made the current posture obsolete. "Much of our current posture," he testified, "still reflects the mentality and reality of the Cold War—forward deployed forces configured as defensive, tripwire units and expected to fight near where they were based." But now those forces would be required to "project power into theaters that may be far from where they are based." "The lessons of the last 15 years tell us," he elaborated, "that we often are required to conduct military operations in places that were not predicted. . . . Our goal is to have forces deployed forward in such a way that they can quickly reach crisis spots as necessary in the future." This would require a rethinking of current basing arrangements. He noted, for example, "Our plans for our posture in Europe include lighter and more deployable ground capabilities, leading-edge air and naval power, advanced training facilities, and strengthened special operations forces, all positioned to deploy more rapidly to the Middle East and other hot spots."[212]

"The administration has instituted what some experts describe as the most militarized foreign policy machine in modern history," wrote James Sterngold in the *San Francisco Chronicle.* "The policy has involved not just resorting to military action, or the threat of action, but constructing an arc of new facilities in such places as Uzbekistan, Pakistan, Qatar and Djibouti that the Pentagon calls 'lily pads.' They are seen not merely as a means of defending the host countries—the traditional Cold War role of such installations—but as jumping-off points for future 'preventive wars' and military missions." [213]

The United States was not only the world's policeman, it was also the world's arms supplier, often fueling the conflicts in which it ultimately intervened on "humanitarian" grounds. In 2008, it signed agreements to sell $37.8 billion in arms, representing over 68 percent of the world total. Italy came in second at $3.7 billion. Almost $30 billion of that total went to developing nations, which purchased over 79 percent of their arms from the United States. [214]

It fell to none other than Zbigniew Brzezinski to accurately assess the toll taken on American democracy by Bush's disastrous war on terrorism. Brzezinski was in a good position to know, having played a similar role in stirring up Cold War fears of the Soviet Union. He wrote in March 2007 that the so-called war on terror, by deliberately creating a "culture of fear," had had a "pernicious impact on American democracy, on America's psyche and on U.S. standing in the world." The damage was "infinitely greater" than that inflicted on 9/11. He worried that the administration was exploiting public fear to justify war with Iran and contrasted the United States' "five years of almost continuous national brainwashing on the subject of terror" with the "more muted reactions of" other victims of terrorism, including Britain, Spain, Italy, Germany, and Japan. He mocked Bush's "justification for his war in Iraq" and his absurd claim "that he has to continue waging it lest al-Qaeda cross the Atlantic to launch a war of terror here in the United States." Bush's fearmongering was reinforced by "terror entrepreneurs . . . experts on terrorism [whose] task is to convince the public that it faces new threats. That puts a premium on the presentation of credible scenarios of ever-more-horrifying acts of violence." As a result, "America has become insecure and more paranoid." For proof, he pointed to Congress's ever-growing list of potential targets across the United States for would-be terrorists. He also deplored the madness of proliferating "security checks," "electronic billboards urging motorists to 'Report Suspicious Activity' (drivers in turbans?)," and television shows with "bearded 'terrorists' as the central villains" that "reinforce the sense of the unknown but lurking danger that . . . increasingly threaten[ed] the lives of all Americans." Television and films had stereotyped Arabs, he regretted, "in a manner sadly reminiscent of the Nazi anti-Semitic campaigns," opening Arab Americans to harassment and abuse.

He noted the impact that the Bush administration's appalling civil rights records had had on citizens at home and the grave damage the war on terror had done to the United States internationally. "For Muslims," he wrote, "the similarity between the rough treatment of Iraqi civilians by the U.S. military and of the Palestinians by the Israelis has prompted a widespread sense of hostility toward the United States in general." He singled out "a recent BBC poll of 28,000 people in 27 countries" that ranked Israel, Iran, and the United States "as the states with 'the most negative influence on the world.' Alas, for some," he emphasized, "that is the new axis of evil!"

Brzezinski concluded by asking "Where is the U.S. leader ready to say, 'Enough of this hysteria, stop this paranoia'?" and urged that "even in the face of future terrorist attacks, the likelihood of which cannot be denied, let us show some sense. Let us be true to our traditions." [215] As Brzezinski repeatedly made clear, terrorism was a tactic, not an ideology, and declaring war on a tactic made absolutely no sense.

Meanwhile, behind the ideological veil of free-market capitalism, the richest Americans continued to plunder the national wealth. Bush and Cheney did everything they could to facilitate the effort, knowing the consequences full well. Shortly before the 2000 presidential election, Bush joked with some of his wealthy followers, "This is an impressive crowd—the haves and the have-mores. Some people call you the elite; I call you my base." [216]

Within months of taking office, Bush signed a bill cutting taxes for the wealthiest Americans. He passed additional tax cuts in 2002 and 2003. Meanwhile, federal spending rose sharply, increasing 17 percent in his first term alone. Under Clinton, federal spending had increased by 11 percent in constant dollars over two terms. By 2004, Bush had turned the $128 billion surplus he inherited into a $413 billion deficit. The *New York Times* reported that for Wall Street, the Bush years were the new Gilded Age. Bankers, the *Times* revealed, celebrated their obscene bonuses with five-figure dinners. [217] The Government Accountability Office (GAO) reported that between 1998 and 2005, two-thirds of American corporations, at least a quarter of which had assets in excess of $250 million, paid no income taxes. [218] These years saw the sharpest rise in income inequality in the nation's history. The 44.3 percent of the nation's income that went to the top 10 percent in 2005 exceeded the 43.8 percent that had gone to the top 10 percent in 1929 and was a far cry from the 32.6 percent of 1975. [219] In 2005, the richest 3 million had as much income as the bottom 166 million, who comprised more than half of the population. [220] The ranks of American billionaires swelled from 13 in 1985 to more than 450 in 2008. Two hundred twenty-seven thousand people joined the ranks of millionaires in 2005 alone. But workers' wages barely kept pace with inflation, and 36 million were below the poverty line. Almost all the new wealth created went directly to the top 10 percent of the population, with most going to the top one-tenth of 1 percent. In 2006, the twenty-five top U.S. hedge fund managers earned an average of $570 million each.[221] In 2007, their average earnings jumped to $900 million.[222]

The International Labour Organization reported that between 2003 and 2007, executive managers' pay increased by 45 percent in real terms while that of the average executive grew by 15 percent and that of the average worker by only 3 percent. In 2003, executive managers in the top fifteen U.S. firms earned 300 times as much as the average American worker. By 2007, that number was up to more than 500 times.[223]

Bush cut the top tax rates on income, on capital gains, which were mostly stock profits, and on dividends, which typically fell from 39.6 percent to 15 percent. The 36 percent marginal tax rate on the richest Americans was the lowest it had been in over eighty years and a far cry from the 91 percent under Eisenhower. But few hedge fund or private equity managers paid the 36 percent rate. Treating their earnings as capital gains, they paid at an average rate of 17 percent. The situation got so bad that billionaires, including Bill Gates and Warren Buffett, publicly decried the "inequality gap." Buffett, the third richest man in the world, noted that he was taxed at 17.7 percent on his taxable income while his secretary was taxed at 30 percent of hers.[224] Estate taxes, which only the top 2 percent paid, had also been slashed.

Meanwhile, the minimum wage stagnated at $5.15 an hour from 1997 to 2007. In 2007, at the other end of the scale, some 2 million U.S. households were worth between $10 million and $100 million and thousands were worth more than that amount.

Labor Secretary Elaine Chao was the most openly antilabor occupant of that office in more than a hundred years. She effectively dismantled the Occupational Safety and Health Administration and the Mine Safety and Health Administration. Unions were put under unprecedented scrutiny by Department of Labor agents, while employers were allowed to flout regulations with impunity. As a result, union membership plummeted to record lows, as barely 12 percent of the workforce was represented at the end of the Bush presidency, most of whom were government workers.

Global inequality was even more extreme. A December 2006 report by economists in the United States, Canada, Great Britain, and Finland found that the richest 1 percent owned 40 percent of global wealth and the top 10 percent owned 85 percent, while the poorest 50 percent struggled to survive with only 1 percent. Per capita wealth ranged, in 2000, from $180,837 in Japan and $143,727 in the United States to $1,100 in India and $180 in the Democratic Republic of Congo. By 2008, the net worth of the world's richest 1,100 people—its billionaires—was approximately double that of the poorest 2.5 billion people.[225] Some analysts estimated that the world's richest 300 people had more wealth than the poorest 3 billion.

Despite the wildly erroneous perceptions of the American people, U.S. foreign aid was doing little to rectify this situation. In fact, according to the OECD, U.S. development aid in 2008 totaled less than .2 percent of gross domestic product, the lowest among twenty-two advanced industrial nations, which averaged .47 percent. Sweden gave at more than five times the rate the United States did, with Luxembourg, Norway, Denmark, and the Netherlands not far behind. Even Ireland gave at more than three times the U.S. rate.[226]

During Bush's tenure, administration officials and their allies on Wall Street and conservative groups like the American Enterprise Institute sang the praises of unregulated financial markets, which they trusted to generate economic abundance and private fortunes. They turned a blind eye to financial shenanigans and unbridled speculation as the national debt skyrocketed from $5.7 trillion at the end of the Clinton administration to over $10 trillion by the time Bush left office.[227]

Economic conditions declined precipitously with the downturn that began in December 2007. Income and wealth plummeted, and poverty registered a sharp increase. Harvard economist Lawrence Katz put the situation succinctly when he stated, "For the typical American family, the 2000s have been a disaster."[228] Even before the collapse of 2008, the Bush years had produced the lowest jobs and income growth in the postwar period.

By late 2009, over 40 million Americans were living in poverty. In 1988, 26 percent of Americans told Gallup pollsters that the country was divided between haves and have-nots, with 59 percent identifying themselves as haves and only 17 percent as have-nots. When Pew asked that same question in the summer of 2007, 48 percent responded that the country was so divided, with 45 percent considering themselves haves and 34 percent have-nots.[229]

The United States had become a plutocracy with almost a quarter of income going to the top 1 percent and the richest one-tenth of 1 percent earning as much as the poorest 120 million. Former Secretary of Labor Robert Reich identified the new plutocrats: "With the exception of a few entrepreneurs like Bill Gates, they're top executives of big corporations and Wall Street, hedge-fund managers, and private equity managers."[230]

By November 2008, it was clear to most Americans that Bush-Cheney foreign and domestic policies had been an unmitigated disaster. A CBS News/*New York Times* poll placed Bush's final approval rating at 22 percent, down from 90 percent following the 9/11 attack. Cheney's stood at an abysmal 13 percent.[231]

Americans hungered for change. They were fed up with the United States' wars, tired of runaway defense spending, concerned about assaults on consti-tutional rights, angry over policies that favored the very wealthy, and worried about the deepening economic collapse. But few people realized how powerful the beneficiaries of the United States' military-industrial complex and national security state had become and how fiercely they would resist any challenge to their rule. They would soon find out the hard way.

Chapter 14

OBAMA:

Managing a Wounded Empire

"We are an attractive empire, the one everyone wants to join," crowed neocon Max Boot in the aftermath of 9/11.[1] But now, after two long and disastrous wars, trillions of dollars in military spending, a network of more than 1,000 foreign military bases, torture and abuse of prisoners on several continents, assault on both international law and the U.S. Constitution, a near economic collapse, drone attacks killing alleged terrorists and civilians alike, disparities between rich and poor unheard of in an advanced industrial country, appallingly low test scores for students, government surveillance on an unprecedented scale, collapsing infrastructure, domestic uprisings on both the Left and the Right, and an international reputation left in tatters, the U.S. empire does not look all that attractive.

George W. Bush, who canceled his 2011 speaking engagement in Switzerland to avoid massive protests and the risk of being indicted as a war criminal, and his empire-friendly advisors bear a lot of responsibility for this sorry state of affairs. They saddled Barack Obama and the American people with an incredible mess. Obama confided to one of his closest aides: "I'm inheriting a world that could blow up any minute in a half dozen ways..."[2]

The country Obama inherited was indeed in shambles, but Obama took a bad situation and, in certain ways, made it worse. Swept into office on a wave of popular euphoria, he mesmerized supporters throughout the campaign with his exhilarating rhetoric, surpassing intelligence, inspiring biography, commitment to defending civil liberties, rejection of unilateralism, and strong opposition to the Iraq War—qualities that made him seem the antithesis of Bush. The election of Barack Hussein Obama, the child of a black Kenyan father and a white Kansan mother, who was raised in Indonesia as well as Hawaii and went on to graduate

Flanked by endorsers including Caroline Kennedy and Ted Kennedy (second and third from left, respectively), Barack Obama addresses supporters during a rally in Hartford, Connecticut, in February 2008. The youthful candidate's soaring rhetoric on the campaign trail inspired lofty expectations. But for progressives hoping he would become the heir to a tradition represented by Franklin Roosevelt, Henry Wallace, and the post–Cuban Missile Crisis John F. Kennedy, Obama's first three years in office were sorely disappointing.

from Columbia and become president of the *Harvard Law Review,* felt like a kind of expiation for the sins of a nation whose reputation had been sullied, as we have shown throughout this book, by racism, imperialism, militarism, nuclearism, environmental degradation, and unbridled avarice. The suffering caused by misguided U.S. policies had been immense. For many, Obama's election offered redemption. It attested to the other side of America and its place in history, a side marked by idealism, egalitarianism, constitutionalism, republicanism, humanism, environmentalism, and the embrace of freedom and democracy as universal principles. Progressives hoped Obama would become the heir to a tradition represented by Franklin Roosevelt and Henry Wallace and by the post–Cuban Missile Crisis John F. Kennedy.

Yet rather than repudiating the policies of Bush and his predecessors, Obama has perpetuated them. Rather than diminishing the influence of Wall Street and the major corporations in U.S. life, Obama has given them latitude to continue most of their predatory practices. Rather than restoring the civil liberties that Bush had eviscerated and limiting the executive powers that Bush usurped after 9/11, Obama, with few exceptions, has tightened the grip of the domestic security/surveillance apparatus, stifling civil liberties and the right to dissent.

In the brilliant 1939 film *Mr. Smith Goes to Washington*, director Frank Capra spends the first eleven minutes exposing a nefarious web of power, intrigue, and clandestine deal making to reveal the hidden world that the naive and idealistic Jefferson Smith will encounter when he tries to change the ways of Washington. Barack Obama would confront a similar nest of entrenched interests. But Obama was much more savvy and, apparently, more cynical than Smith. By knowingly surrounding himself with establishment insiders as domestic and foreign policy advisors, he preemptively closed the door on the kind of bold innovations and breaks with the past that his campaign had promised.

Having betrayed his earlier promises and become the first presidential candidate to turn down public campaign financing in the general election, Obama turned to Wall Street funders with deep pockets, like Goldman Sachs, Citigroup, JPMorgan Chase, Skadden Arps, and Morgan Stanley. Also high on the list of Obama contributors were General Electric and other defense contractors. And the pharmaceuticals industry—Big Pharma—reversed years of supporting Republicans, contributing more than three times as much to Obama as to McCain.[3]

Obama's grassroots supporters largely overlooked these disturbing facts. Progressives projected onto him their own hopes and expectations, conservatives their worst fears. Both were mistaken. He ran a centrist campaign, advancing safely pragmatic policy initiatives. He consistently championed the middle class. The working class and the poor—black, Hispanic, Asian, Native American and white—seemed an afterthought as Obama battled Hillary Clinton and then John McCain. Instead of seizing the opportunity to explain how the decline of manufacturing and other structural factors at the heart of a dysfunctional corporate- and Wall Street–dominated system had exacerbated the problems for all poor people and especially African Americans, he hectored poor blacks for not taking more "personal responsibility." He positioned himself to the left of Clinton by trumpeting his opposition to the Iraq War, which she had voted to support, but to the right of George Bush on Afghanistan, a position his supporters conveniently ignored. And his Senate vote for the Foreign Intelligence Surveillance Act, which gave legal immunity to telecommunications companies complicit in Bush's wiretapping, should have signaled that he might be unwilling to relinquish some of the powers that Bush and Cheney had appropriated.

The biggest winner under Obama was Wall Street. After wrecking the economy with speculative innovations, including credit-default swaps and collateralized debt obligations, bankers came begging for bailouts. Not surprisingly, Obama's economic advisors—almost all disciples of Bill Clinton's Treasury secretary Robert Rubin—were more than happy to assist with a $700 billion financial bailout program. Rubin, who had been systematically cultivating Obama since 2005, had cochaired Goldman Sachs prior to his stint at Treasury, where he had masterminded two of the policies that helped precipitate the financial crisis his protégés would now handle: the deregulation of the derivatives market and the 1999 repeal of the Glass-Steagall Act, which had separated investment banking from commercial banking. Having pushed through these changes at the Treasury, he was rewarded with a top job at Citigroup, where he received $126 million over the next eight years. The *New York Times* reported in late November 2008, "as Barack Obama fills out his economic team, a virtual Rubin constellation is taking shape." Rubin's Treasury chief of staff and fellow Citigroup exec Michael Froman was in charge of putting this team together. The two top positions went to Rubin protégés Timothy Geithner, the New York Fed chief, whom Obama named as Treasury Secretary, and Lawrence Summers, whom he named senior White House economic advisor. Geithner had worked under Rubin at Treasury and Summers had been Treasury Secretary at the time Glass-Steagall was repealed. Like Rubin, Summers, an avowed deregulator, had also cashed in on his service to Wall Street, earning $5.2 million working one day a week for the D. E. Shaw hedge fund in 2008, while raking in another $2.7 million in speaking fees, much coming from Wall Street firms. Goldman Sachs paid him $135,000 for one speech alone.[4] In light of how much Wall Street was going to profit from the Geithner-Summers stewardship of the economy, Goldman Sachs and the other "banksters" got off cheap. Obama tapped Rubin protégé Peter Orszag as budget director. According to the *Times*, "Geithner, Summers and Orszag have all been followers of the economic formula that came to be called Rubinomics: balanced budgets, free trade and financial deregulation." The lower echelons of economic decision making were also populated by Rubin allies. The glaring exceptions were Christine Romer, chair of the Council of Economic Advisors, and Jared Bernstein, Biden's chief economic policy advisor. The two of them fought unsuccessfully, during their brief tenures, against some of the Rubinites' neoliberal initiatives, but were ultimately outnumbered and outflanked.

Former Democratic strategist David Sirota aptly identified the ways Rubin's people would mold Obama's economic strategy: "Bob Rubin, these guys, they're classic limousine liberals. These are basically people who have made shitloads of money in the speculative economy, but they want to call themselves good Democrats because they're willing to give a little more to the poor. That's the model for this Democratic Party: Let the rich do their thing, but give a fraction more to everyone else."

On November 23, 2008, the Bush administration announced a potential $306 billion bailout of Citigroup, which was facing collapse. Citigroup had recently received $25 billion under the Troubled Asset Relief Plan, which provided a massive bailout to the financial sector. The *Times* made clear that Geithner played a "crucial role" in the negotiations and that Bush's Treasury Secretary, Henry Paulson, had worked very closely with Obama's transition team. Wall Street was so exuberant over the deal that the Dow posted its biggest two-day jump in over twenty years and Citigroup's stock, which had tumbled in price from $30 to $3.77 in the past year, shot up 66 percent in one day. "If you had any doubts at all about the primacy of Wall Street over Main Street," former Labor Secretary Robert Reich exclaimed, "your doubts should be laid to rest." Abundant proof would be forthcoming. The *Washington Post* reported in early April 2009 that the Treasury Department was bending the law and defying the will of Congress to avoid limiting executive pay: "The Obama administration is engineering its new bailout initiatives in a way that it believes will allow firms benefiting from the programs to avoid restrictions imposed by Congress, including limits on lavish executive pay, according to government officials."[5]

University of Texas economist James Galbraith lambasted Obama for meekly submitting to the bankers' demands as if there were no other way to solve the crisis:

> ... one cannot defend the actions of Team Obama on taking office. Law, policy and politics all pointed in one direction: turn the systemically dangerous banks over to Sheila Bair and the Federal Deposit Insurance Corporation. Insure the depositors, replace the management, fire the lobbyists, audit the books, prosecute the frauds, and restructure and downsize the institutions. The financial system would have been cleaned up. And the big bankers would have been beaten as a political force.
>
> Team Obama did none of these things. Instead they announced "stress tests," plainly designed so as to obscure the banks' true condition. They pressured the Federal Accounting Standards Board to permit the banks to ignore the market value of their toxic assets. Management stayed in place. They prosecuted no one. The Fed cut the cost of funds to zero. The President justified all this by repeating, many times, that the goal of policy was "to get credit flowing again."
>
> The banks threw a party. Reported profits soared, as did bonuses. With free funds, the banks could make money with no risk, by lending back to the Treasury. They could boom the stock market. They could make a mint on proprietary trading. Their losses on mortgages were concealed....[6]

Former Federal Reserve chairman Paul Volcker advised Obama to take strong action. "Right now," he said, "when you have your chance, and their breasts are bared, you need to put a spear through the heart of all these guys on Wall Street that for years have been mostly debt merchants." But rather than stand up to Wall Street, Obama prostrated himself before the CEOs of the thirteen largest banks in March 2009, telling them, "I want to help. I'm not out there to go after you. I'm protecting you. But if I'm going to shield you from public and congressional anger, you have to give me something to work with on these issues of compensation."[7] The bankers paid lip service to voluntary restraint and then proceeded with record bonuses. Thus, unlike the Europeans who limited bankers' compensation, the Obama administration did not even limit compensation to those whose companies were saved by government bailouts. Obscene profits ensued. The *Wall Street Journal* reported that total compensation and benefits at Wall Street banks, investment banks, hedge funds, money-management firms, and securities exchanges reached record levels of $128 billion in 2009 and $135 billion in 2010.[8] The greatest beneficiaries were the twenty-five top hedge fund managers, whose average earnings jumped from a paltry $570 million in 2006 to a more respectable $1 billion in 2009.[9] In 2010, one New York hedge fund manager, John Paulson, pulled in $4.9 billion.

Journalist Ron Suskind later reported that a more complicated internal negotiation had actually occurred behind the scenes in which Obama agreed with Romer and others that a fundamental restructuring of the banks was necessary, beginning with Citigroup. It was Geithner and Rahm Emanuel who effectively sabotaged this Citigroup effort. Geithner, Suskind contended, failed to come up with the plan that Obama had asked for and eventually convinced the president to go along with his own Wall Street–friendly approach. Emanuel, who had earned over $18 million in two and a half years working for the investment banking firm Wasserstein Perella after leaving the Clinton White House in 1999, insisted they all go along with Geithner. Obama rolled over without a fight.[10]

The financial crisis that began in 2008 did nothing to stanch the corporate bleeding of the middle and working classes. Average total compensation for CEOs of Standard & Poor's 500 Index companies rose 23 percent in 2010 to $11.4 million. CEO pay, which equaled 343 times that of the median worker in 2010, had risen more than eightfold since 1980, when it stood at a mere 42 times as much. By comparison, CEOs in other industrial countries earned far less. British and Canadian CEOs earned 22 times as much as the average British and Canadian worker, and Japanese only 11. Discovery Communications' CEO David Zaslav was among those who cashed in. His pay jumped from $7.9 million in 2008 to $11.7 million in 2009 to $42.6 million in 2010.

The rest of the workforce was left largely to fend for itself. Obama's economic stimulus program was only about half the $1.2 trillion advocated by Christine Romer, whose recommendation was left off the options submitted by Summers.[11] The economic recovery of the early Obama years was not only weak in terms of generating new jobs, its benefits went entirely to the wealthiest Americans. Economist Andrew Sum and his group of researchers at Northeastern University discovered that, from the second quarter of 2009 through the first quarter of 2011, national income grew by $505 billion dollars. Pretax corporate profits grew by $465 billion. Wages and salaries, however, declined by a sobering $22 billion.[12] In the nine months after hitting the nadir of the recession in the second quarter of 2009, they found, corporate profits accounted for 85 percent of the increase in profits and wages. For the same recovery period following the 1981–1982 recession, only 10 percent had gone to corporate profits. In 2010, 93 percent of income growth went to the top 1 percent of households, leaving a scant 7 percent for the other 99 percent to divide up. The top .01 percent, some 15,000 families, did even better, absconding with a stunning 37 percent of new earnings. Meanwhile, benefits continued to tumble. A 2010 survey found that over the previous year, employee health insurance premiums had increased 13.7 percent while employer contributions fell by 0.9 percent.[13]

What Chris Hedges termed "the corporate rape of America"[14] had been under way for decades. While executive pay skyrocketed, pay for the average nonsupervisory worker, according to the Bureau of Labor Statistics, had fallen more than 10 percent since the 1970s. The Congressional Budget Office estimated that between 1979 and 2005 income of the top 1 percent jumped 480 percent.[15]

By 2007, the top 1 percent was receiving 25 percent of national income and owned almost 40 percent of American wealth. With unions representing only 7 percent of the private work force in 2007, real wages, adjusted for inflation, were actually lower than they had been thirty years earlier. In 2007, the bottom 80 percent owned only 15 percent of all wealth. Overall, by 2011, the Economic Policy Institute reported, the richest 1 percent had more wealth than the bottom 90 percent. Families had, for the most part, managed to maintain standards of living since the 1970s by expanding female participation in the workforce (women with young children working outside the home jumped from 24 percent in 1966 to 60 percent in the late 1990s), sharply increasing the number of hours worked (100 more hours per year for the typical male worker and 200 more for the typical female over two decades earlier), and borrowing at inordinate, and ultimately unsustainable, rates (squeezing $2.3 trillion from homes between 2002 and 2007).[16]

A stunning measure of how far the United States had fallen came from the October 2011 Bertelsmann Stiftung Foundation report "Social Justice in the OECD—How Do the Member States Compare," which ranked the United States twenty-seventh out of the thirty-one OECD nations, only beating Greece,

Chile, Mexico, and Turkey. The report measured many factors, including poverty prevention, poverty rates for children and senior citizens, income inequality, expenditures on pre-primary education, health care, and other key metrics.
The United States came in twenty-ninth in overall poverty rate and twenty-
eighth in child poverty and income inequality.[17] Columbia University's National
Center for Children in Poverty reported that 42 percent of children lived in low-
income families, half of them below the poverty line. The Associated Press reported in December 2011 that almost half of all Americans were either in poverty
or subsisting on low incomes. The Census Bureau reported that in 2010, 46.2
million Americans were below the poverty line, which was the highest number
since it began publishing those figures fifty-two years earlier.

Not only were more Americans falling into poverty, fewer and fewer were
able to escape. Mobility studies shattered the myth that the United States was a
society with fluid class lines and easy upward mobility. In fact, the United States,
with its porous social safety net, failing schools, and low percentage of unionized
workers, had considerably less social mobility than any other advanced industrial society.[18]

These disparities had so infuriated Americans who were struggling to afford
health care and mortgage payments while feeding their families that Congress
reluctantly acted, passing the Dodd-Frank Wall Street Reform and Consumer
Protection Act in 2010. The act required corporate executives of publicly traded
companies to submit their pay to shareholders for nonbinding approval. Among
those who railed against efforts to curb corporate pay was Countrywide Financial CEO Angelo Mozilo, who pulled in more than $470 million in cash plus
proceeds from stock sales during the five years before the effects of his untrammeled greed and illegal dealings helped bring down the housing market. Mozilo
denounced "the left-wing press and the envious leaders of unions" for pressuring corporate boards and accused them of driving "entrepreneurship" out of the
public sector.[19]

The Dodd-Frank Act, though a step in the right direction, did little to correct
the underlying problems that caused the collapse, failing to address the incentive structures that encouraged risky behavior or to reverse the dynamics that
allowed banks to grow to the size where they were "too big to fail." As William
Isaac, former chairman of the Federal Deposit Insurance Corporation, acknowledged in *Forbes* magazine, the bill "would not have prevented the recent financial
crisis, and it will not prevent the next one." "In truth," Isaac wrote, "the bill does
almost nothing to change a dysfunctional regulatory system that drove three
very serious banking crises in the past 40 years."[20]

Washington Post financial staff writer Steven Pearlstein was stunned that
Obama could not "give voice to this populist outrage and constructively channel

A homeless man sleeps under an advertisement for luxury residences in the Bowery neighborhood of Manhattan. The Census Bureau reported that in 2010 a record 46.2 million Americans were below the poverty line, one of many indicators of expanding economic inequality in the United States.

this public anger" over Wall Street and Geithner's "let-them-eat-stuffing" attitude. For Pearlstein, a "telling moment" came in November 2009, when Geithner "gave a back-of-the-hand to the idea of a global tax on financial transactions as a way of raising money for economic stabilization while also discouraging high-volume, short-term speculation." If Obama really cared about the people instead of those who had plundered the economy, Pearlstein wrote, he could instruct the Justice Department to launch an antitrust inquiry into excessive Wall Street profits, pressure Congress to close the tax loophole allowing hedge fund and private-equity fund managers to pay lower taxes than their secretaries, and push the Group of 20 to "put the transaction tax back on the agenda."[21]

Pearlstein wondered, "Whose Side Is Obama On?" The question became more poignant as the 2012 elections approached. Anger over the economy had boiled over. Occupy Wall Street and allied protesters gathered in towns and cities across the nation in a grassroots uprising of a sort not seen since the 1930s. Obama walked a fine line, trying to signal both the anti–Wall Street protesters and the Wall Street tycoons, whom the protesters reviled, that he was with them. In June 2011, the *New York Times* reported that Obama had offended Wall Street's high rollers by calling them " 'fat cats' and criticizing their bonuses" and by having the audacity to propose any curbs at all on their rapaciousness. Now, according to the *Times*, Obama and his top aides, looking for Wall Street backing in his reelection bid, were trying to salve the bankers' wounded feelings.[22] Franklin Roosevelt had compared ungrateful capitalists to the drowning old man who berates his rescuer for not saving his hat; Obama came before them, hat in hand, and begged forgiveness. Unlike Roosevelt, who had made enemies of Wall Street financiers by implementing large-scale government job creation and sweeping regulatory reform, Obama not only privileged those Wall Street insiders over the working masses, he apologized for having hurt their feelings.

Obama also paid debts to other corporate donors. Nobel Prize–winning economist Joseph Stiglitz noted, "When pharmaceutical companies receive a trillion-dollar gift—through legislation prohibiting the government, the largest buyer of drugs, from bargaining over price—it should not come as cause for wonder. It should not make jaws drop that a tax bill cannot emerge from Congress unless big tax cuts are put in place for the wealthy. Given the power of the top 1 percent, this is the way you would *expect* the system to work." Stiglitz cited the response from banker Charles Keating, who was brought low by the 1980s savings and loan crisis. When asked by a congressional committee whether the $1.5 million he had contributed to elected officials could buy influence, he answered, "I certainly hope so."[23] The Supreme Court decision in the 2010 Citizens United case, which removed limits on corporate campaign spending, ensured that the influence of corporate and banking interests would mushroom.

Obama's failure to articulate a progressive vision was also apparent in the fight over health reform, which was to have been his signature initiative. Obama decided early on that he would avoid a fight with the health insurance and pharmaceutical industries, which not only had contributed heavily to his campaign but had played a major role in defeating Clinton's reform efforts. To win their support, he capitulated to demands that the legislation exclude core Democratic initiatives like drug reimportation and bulk price negotiations. He also took the single-payer issue off the table, although he admitted that a single-payer system represented the best option for providing affordable care for all, as most developed countries had long proven. Rather than leading the reform effort himself, he asked Congress to come up with the details. He further placated the health insurance industry by removing the public option and Medicare expansion, despite the fact that both received lopsided public support.

The medical industry did the rest. The massive effort to eliminate provisions that might reduce corporate profits was galvanized by 3,300 lobbyists representing more than 1,500 organizations, triple the number registered to lobby on defense. Fighting to shape policies that could affect 17 percent of the economy, the lobbyists, who outnumbered members of Congress six to one, spent $263.4 million in the first six months of 2009 alone. The resulting legislation expanded coverage for uninsured Americans but did so in a way that was a windfall for the insurance companies.[24]

The White House blamed congressional "centrists" like Joe Lieberman for forcing it to accept compromises that were anathema to most Democrats. Senator Russell Feingold, a strong supporter of the public option, wasn't buying these excuses. "This bill appears to be legislation that the president wanted in the first place, so I don't think focusing it on Lieberman really hits the truth," Feingold said.[25] Obama's bungled health care reform effort, marked by the inability to even refute Republican charges of death panels, was so unpopular that it became an albatross around the necks of Democrats in the 2010 election. As Robert Kuttner noted, "This battle should have been the president and the people versus the interests. Instead more and more voters concluded that it was the president and the interests versus the people." And the Democrats paid for that widely perceived sellout.[26]

Budget battles followed the same script. Obama continued to strive for bipartisanship with opponents who were out not only to defeat him but to discredit any notion that government was at all capable of solving social problems. As *Washington Post* columnist Harold Meyerson stated in April 2011, "If it does nothing else, the budget that House Republicans unveiled . . . provides the first real Republican program for the twenty-first century, and it is this: Repeal the twentieth century."[27]

Yet the final deal that Obama struck with the Republicans was actually worse than the Republican starting position—not only extending the Bush tax cuts for the wealthiest Americans, but slashing desperately needed social programs for the most vulnerable. Bush had "temporarily" instituted the tax cuts a decade earlier, knowing full well that they were never intended to expire. Dan Bartlett, Bush's former spokesman, admitted: "We knew that, politically, once you get it into law, it becomes almost impossible to remove it. That's not a bad legacy. The fact that we were able to lay the trap does feel pretty good, to tell you the truth."[28] The fact that the Obama-led Democrats walked blithely into the trap felt less good for the American public, which overwhelmingly opposed extending the tax cuts for the wealthiest Americans at a time of prodigious budget deficits.

Nobel Prize–winning Princeton economist Paul Krugman bemoaned the loss of Obama the "inspirational figure" and wondered, "Who is this bland, timid guy who doesn't seem to stand for anything in particular?" He described Obama's approach to bargaining with the Republicans as starting "by negotiating with himself, making preemptive concessions, then pursue a second round of negotiation with the G.O.P., leading to further concessions." Krugman criticized Obama for failing to challenge the new consensus, which he characterized as "a philosophy that says the poor must accept big cuts in Medicaid and food stamps; the middle class must accept big cuts in Medicare (actually a dismantling of the whole program); and corporations and the rich must accept big cuts in the taxes they have to pay. Shared sacrifice!"[29]

Rather than heed such criticism, Obama tacked further to the right. First he selected William Daley, a former JPMorgan Chase executive, as his chief of staff to replace Emanuel. Then, adding insult to injury, he chose GE chairman and CEO Jeffrey Immelt as chair of the President's Council on Jobs and Competitiveness, making him Obama's chief outside economic advisor. Obama could not have sent a clearer signal on where he stood. In 2010, GE made over $14.2 billion in profits but paid no federal taxes. In fact, GE actually received a $3.2 billion tax credit. The company had also received $16.1 billion from the Federal Reserve during the 2008 financial crisis. Obama's selection of Immelt as his chief advisor on job creation came at a time when GE was being lambasted for outsourcing jobs as well as for cutting health and retirement benefits for new employees. For so effectively privileging private greed over social responsibility, Immelt, an "old" employee, saw his total compensation jump from $9.89 million in 2009 to $21.4 million in 2010, a raise of well over 100 percent. In case Wall Street didn't get a clear enough message from Immelt's appointment, Obama followed up with a conciliatory address to the archnemesis of everything progressive in America, the U.S. Chamber of Commerce, and with an order to federal agencies to review regulations for the purpose of eliminating some.[30]

When the 2010 Congressional elections rolled around, the enthusiasm gap between Republicans and Democrats was enormous. Obama's temporizing and lassitude had so demoralized his base that the Republicans won in a landslide, prompting him to reach out even further across the aisle. He quickly reneged on his promise to implement tougher environmental standards, announcing that he would forgo new rules regarding smog and toxic emissions from boilers, leaving in place Bush administration policies.

Even this didn't placate the Wall Street and corporate elite, who repaid Obama's largesse by throwing their support behind Mitt Romney in the 2012 elections. By April 2012, top banking executives, hedge fund operators, and private equity investors—the same people who had backed Obama two to one in 2008—were contributing four times as much to Romney as to Obama, and that doesn't include the enormous sums they were lavishing upon pro-Romney "super PACs." As of summer 2012, General Electric employees, who had contributed five times as much to the Obama campaign as they did to McCain's in 2008, were backing Romney 4:1. And Immelt announced that he wouldn't be endorsing either candidate.[31]

Among the greatest disappointments to his followers was Obama's refusal to roll back the expanding national security state that so egregiously encroached on American civil liberties. He had actually gotten off to a promising start. On his first day in office, he rescinded a 2001 Bush executive order limiting access to former presidents' records and overturned a 2001 Ashcroft memo giving government agencies broad authority to reject public disclosure requests. He pledged his administration to a new transparency. "For a long time now, there's been too much secrecy in this city," he acknowledged. "This administration stands on the side not of those who seek to withhold information but with those who seek it to be known. The mere fact that you have the legal power to keep something secret does not mean you should always use it. Transparency and the rule of law will be the touchstones of this presidency."[32]

Obama's commitment to transparency did not last long. By summer 2010, the ACLU was warning about the "very real danger that the Obama administration will enshrine permanently within the law policies and practices that were widely considered extreme and unlawful during the Bush administration. There is a real danger, in other words, that the Obama administration will preside over the creation of a 'new normal.'"[33]

That was precisely what Obama has done—a far cry from his campaign promises to defend the Constitution against Bush's trespasses. He had, for example, criticized Bush's repeatedly invoking state secrets to block lawsuits. In office, he reversed himself, impeding prosecution of Bush-era torture and other abuses and advancing what the *New York Times* described as "a sweeping view of executive secrecy powers." He has invoked the "state secrets privilege" more often than any previous president to halt lawsuits involving torture, extraordinary rendition, and illegal NSA wiretapping. He has continued the CIA's extraordinary rendition program, denied habeas corpus rights to Afghan prisoners, sanctioned military commissions, and authorized, without due process, the CIA killing of a U.S. citizen in Yemen who was accused of having ties to Al-Qaeda.[34] His refusal to investigate and prosecute those in the Bush administration guilty of torture was itself a violation of international treaties.

Bush Justice Department official Jack Goldsmith quickly recognized that Dick Cheney's rebuke of Obama for reversing the Bush-era terrorism policies was flat out wrong. In fact, Goldsmith wrote in the *New Republic*, "The truth is closer to the opposite: The new administration has copied most of the Bush program, has expanded some of it, and has narrowed only a bit. Almost all of the Obama changes have been at the level of packaging, argumentation, symbol, and rhetoric. . . . The Obama strategy," he concluded, "can thus be seen as an attempt to make the core Bush approach to terrorism politically and legally more palatable, and thus sustainable."[35]

Civil libertarians were appalled, expecting so much more from this former professor of constitutional law. His University of Chicago law school colleague Geoffrey Stone, chairman of the board of the American Constitutional Society, decried the gap between Obama's policies and his campaign promises, regretting Obama's "disappointing willingness to continue in his predecessor's footsteps." George Washington University law professor Jonathan Turley observed disappointedly that "the election of Barack Obama may stand as one of the single most devastating events in our history for civil liberties."[36]

In many respects, Obama has been more secretive than the pathologically secretive Bush-Cheney administration. His government has classified more information and responded more slowly to Freedom of Information Act requests than his predecessor. It has prosecuted more government whistle-blowers than all previous administrations, employing the 1917 Espionage Act in six separate cases, compared to a total of three in the ninety-two years before he took office.

The most notorious case is that of Private Bradley Manning, a twenty-two-year-old army intelligence analyst in Iraq. Manning has been accused of leaking classified documents to WikiLeaks and was indicted on thirty-four counts, including violating the Espionage Act and "aiding the enemy," which was potentially punishable by death. Some of the leaked documents, allegedly including the "Collateral Murder" video that showed U.S. troops coldly and calculatingly gunning down a dozen Iraqi civilians, including two Reuters journalists, revealed U.S. war crimes. Manning also allegedly leaked Iraq War logs that detailed atrocities and civilian death tolls far in excess of official government figures.

Despite not having been convicted of any crime, Manning was kept naked for days and in solitary confinement for nine months in conditions that many considered torture. Among those who bristled at Manning's horrendous treatment was P. J. Crowley, the State Department's top spokesman. Crowley described the treatment of Manning to students at MIT as "ridiculous and stupid and counterproductive." Three days later, Crowley resigned after thirty years of government service.[37]

Finally, in December 2011, after nineteen months in military custody, Manning was given a military hearing to determine whether there was sufficient evidence to proceed with a court-martial. That the Obama administration had decided to prosecute Manning for disclosing the truth but to let Bush, Cheney, and their associates off the hook for lying, torture, invading sovereign nations, and committing other war crimes was a clear though sad indication of this administration's sense of justice and transparency. As law professor Marjorie Cohn observed, "If Manning had committed war crimes instead of exposing them, he would be a free man today."[38]

Equally outrageous was the Obama administration's reaction to Julian Assange's release through WikiLeaks of over 250,000 diplomatic cables that he allegedly got from Manning. Assange made the mistake of not redacting names on the first batch released. But the intense reaction was due to the fact that the cables exposed the depths of U.S. government mendacity on a broad range of crucial issues, including the invasions of Iraq and Afghanistan. Additional revelations of corruption and repression by U.S. allies helped spark the uprisings in Egypt, Libya, Yemen, and Tunisia that spurred what's become known as the Arab Spring. The impact on international journalism and public opinion was unprecedented. Articles based on the leaked documents appeared almost daily in leading newspapers throughout the world. As Glenn Greenwald correctly observed, "WikiLeaks easily produced more newsworthy scoops over the last year than every other media outlet combined." In recognition of this contribution, in November 2011, WikiLeaks received the award for "Most Outstanding Contribution to Journalism," Australia's equivalent of the Pulitzer Prize, from the Walkley Foundation. The Foundation trustees applauded WikiLeaks for revealing "an avalanche of inconvenient truths in a global publishing coup. Its revelations, from the way the war on terror was being waged, to diplomatic bastardry, high-level horse-trading and the interference in the domestic affairs of nations, have had an undeniable impact."[39]

Yet the Justice Department has been exploring ways to punish Assange and other individuals associated with the WikiLeaks release, possibly under the Espionage Act. Among the strongest backers of the "get Assange" campaign were some who had earlier decried China and other repressive societies for limiting Internet access and freedom of the press. Senate Intelligence Committee chair Dianne Feinstein demanded that Assange "be vigorously prosecuted for espionage."[40] Joe Lieberman agreed. Newt Gingrich called him an "enemy combatant." Sarah Palin wanted him targeted as if he were Al-Qaeda and hunted as an "anti-American operative with blood on his hands."[41] James Goodale, former *New York Times* general counsel in the Pentagon Papers case, described the corrosive effect such a prosecution would have on American press freedoms. "Charging Julian Assange with 'conspiracy to commit espionage,'" he warned, "would effectively be setting a precedent with a charge that more accurately could be characterized as 'conspiracy to commit journalism.' "[42]

Obama has tenaciously pursued whistle-blowers and "leakers." But his efforts were dealt a serious blow in June 2011, when the prosecutors dropped felony charges under the Espionage Act against Thomas Drake, an NSA employee who had courageously revealed to the *Baltimore Sun* that the NSA had wasted over a billion dollars on a flawed Trailblazer system for surveilling digital communications. He pleaded guilty to a misdemeanor for unauthorized use of a government computer and received no fine or jail time. The Drake case was the first the Obama Justice Department had brought under the Espionage Act. The Defense Department's internal watchdog issued a report exonerating Drake and upholding his allegations. The administration vowed to press on with its other cases, even though most were of equally dubious merit.[43]

Its vendetta against Pulitzer Prize–winning *New York Times* reporter James Risen, who broke the story about massive NSA wiretapping in 2005, sent a chilling message to all reporters who refused to name confidential sources—the lifeblood of information that the government wished to hide from the public. Furious with the embarrassing disclosures, Cheney had pressured the Bush Justice Department to investigate Risen's activities but failed to secure an indictment. Obama, once again, took a stalled Bush initiative and looked to pursue it in ways that the ham-fisted Bush administration only dreamed about. In April 2010, the Justice Department subpoenaed Risen to testify. Risen made clear that he would go to jail rather than divulge his sources. In January 2011, the administration indicted former CIA officer Jeffrey Sterling for allegedly leaking classified information to Risen about a bungled 2000 operation to sabotage Iran's nuclear program, which Risen reported on in his 2006 book, *State of War: The Secret History of the CIA and the Bush Administration*. Greenwald, a stalwart defender of civil liberties, condemned Obama's unparalleled assault. "As in so many other instances," Greenwald averred, "the Obama administration appears on the verge of fulfilling Dick Cheney's nefarious wish beyond what even Cheney could achieve."[44]

Political leaders and journalists around the world mocked America's democratic pretensions. Writers at London's *Guardian*, which, like the *New York Times* and *Der Spiegel*, had published the documents, led the assault. John Naughton assailed the "delicious irony" of trying to shut WikiLeaks down. Seumas Milne wrote that official U.S. reaction "is tipping over toward derangement." "Not much truck with freedom of information, then, in the land of the free," he chortled. Naughton observed that Hillary Clinton's 2009 rebuke of China for interfering with Internet freedom "reads like a satirical masterpiece."[45]

Nor did Obama do anything to restrain the enormous and rapidly proliferating security complex. In 2010, in a sobering four-part series, the *Washington Post* published the results of a two-year investigation into what it described as "an alternative geography of the United States, a Top Secret America hidden from public view and lacking in thorough oversight." In this world, 854,000 people with top-secret security clearances operate out of 1,271 government organizations and 1,931 private companies in about 10,000 U.S. locations, working on programs involving counterterrorism, homeland security, and intelligence. The Pentagon ran two-thirds of the programs. The intelligence budget reached well over $75 billion in 2009, more than two and a half times its size before 9/11. The NSA intercepts and stores an astounding 1.7 billion e-mails, phone calls, and other communications each day.[46]

In the final installment of the series, the *Post's* Dana Priest and William Arkin reported that "the United States is assembling a vast domestic intelligence apparatus to collect information about Americans, using the FBI, local police, state homeland security offices and military criminal investigators," and many of the targets of the probe "have not been accused of any wrongdoing" but were turned in for acting suspiciously. The monitoring was being done by 3,984 local, state, and federal organizations, often using methods introduced in Iraq and Afghanistan. The FBI had also collected 96 million sets of fingerprints at its data campus in Clarksburg, West Virginia. [47]

During the May 2011 congressional debate over extending the Patriot Act, Senate Democrats Ron Wyden and Mark Udall, both of whom were members of the Intelligence Committee, expressed outrage over the way the administration was interpreting certain provisions of the act. "When the American people find out how their government has secretly interpreted the Patriot Act, they will be stunned and they will be angry," Wyden warned, citing reactions to past abuses like 1970s domestic spying, the Iran-Contra affair, and Bush's warrantless surveillance. [48]

The American people weren't paying sufficient attention. Congress extended the Patriot Act's surveillance powers until 2015. The FBI significantly expanded the investigative powers of some 14,000 agents. The Supreme Court extended search and surveillance powers. Overall, Fourth Amendment guarantees of privacy and protections against unreasonable search and seizure, protections that were considered sacrosanct by the Founding Fathers, were being severely eroded. [49]

Civil libertarians were justifiably aghast at the new powers that the U.S. government had acquired since 9/11. Jonathan Turley listed ten: 1) presidential power to order the assassination of U.S. citizens; 2) indefinite detention; 3) presidential power to decide whether prisoners will be tried in federal courts or military tribunals; 4) warrantless surveillance; 5) use of secret evidence in detentions and trials and invoking the government's right to secrecy to force dismissal of cases against the United States; 6) refusal to prosecute war criminals; 7) increased use of secret Foreign Intelligence Surveillance Courts; 8) immunity from judicial review for companies involved in warrantless surveillance of U.S. citizens; 9) monitoring of citizens without court orders; 10) extraordinary renditions of individuals to other countries, including those that commit torture. While Obama has disavowed use of some of these powers, his forbearance would in no way constrain future occupants of the Oval Office. And, as Turley aptly noted, "An authoritarian nation is defined not just by the use of authoritarian powers, but by the ability to use them. If a president can take away your freedom or your life on his own authority, all rights become little more than a discretionary grant subject to executive will." [50]

As much of a disappointment as Obama was on domestic and security policy, his foreign policy may have been worse. His initial foreign policy advisors consisted primarily of Clinton Administration veterans, including National Security

Advisor Anthony Lake, Assistant Secretary of State Susan Rice, Navy Secretary Richard Danzig, Treasury Secretary Robert Rubin's chief of staff Michael Froman, and State Department official Gregory Craig. Also playing a significant role was Jimmy Carter's rabidly anti-Communist national security advisor Zbigniew Brzezinski. The *Washington Post* reported, however, that closest to Obama during the campaign were two newcomers—Samantha Power, a professor of public policy at Harvard's Kennedy School of Government, and retired Air Force Major General Scott Gration. Gration, a fighter pilot for most of his years in uniform, served as director of strategy and planning under Marine General James Jones when he was supreme allied commander in Europe.[51] Hopes for fresh thinking centered mostly on Power, who was best known for her book *"A Problem from Hell": America and the Age of Genocide,* which made a liberal interventionist argument in cases where genocide was occurring, and on Obama himself. Power was forced to resign from the campaign after calling Hillary Clinton a "monster" but returned as a senior aide on the National Security Council and aggressively pushed for U.S. intervention in Libya.

Obama's own foreign policy experience was quite limited and his views were conventional, if sometimes muddled. He told one campaign audience in Pennsylvania, "The truth is that my foreign policy is actually a return to the traditional bipartisan realistic policy of George Bush's father, of John F. Kennedy, of, in some ways, Ronald Reagan."[52] While untangling precisely what Obama meant by that bizarre conflation would be a challenge, what was clear was that he was not offering a decisive break with over a century of imperial conquest. His was a centrist approach to better managing the American empire rather than advancing a positive role for the United States in a rapidly evolving world. He intended to reduce U.S. involvement in the Middle East and increase U.S. engagement with Asia, where American hegemony was being challenged by a resurgent and ever more potent China. "We've been on a little bit of a Middle East detour over the course of the last ten years," Kurt Campbell, the assistant secretary of state for East Asian and Pacific Affairs, noted. "And our future will be dominated utterly and fundamentally by developments in Asia and the Pacific region." "The project of the first two years has been to effectively deal with the legacy issues that we inherited, particularly the Iraq war, the Afghan war, and the war against Al-Qaeda, while rebalancing our resources and our posture in the world," Benjamin Rhodes, one of Obama's deputy national security advisors, said. "If you were to boil it all down to a bumper sticker, it's 'Wind down these two wars, reestablish American standing and leadership in the world, and focus on a broader set of priorities, from Asia and the global economy to a nuclear-nonproliferation regime.'"[53]

With this in mind, Obama quickly moved to redress some of the more egregious aspects of Bush's policies. On his first day in office, he held discussions on withdrawal from Iraq and made clear his plans to be actively involved in Israeli-Palestinian peace negotiations. He signed orders preventing people in the executive branch from accepting gifts from lobbyists and from lobbying the executive branch upon leaving government. His second day was even better. He barred enhanced interrogations, closed the CIA's "black site" prisons and announced plans to shut the military prison at Guantánamo within one year.

For a variety of reasons, Obama would fail to deliver on many of these promises. Opposition would come from lockstep Republicans, conservative Democrats, and sometimes even his own advisors. The *Washington Post* described Obama's incoming foreign policy team as "experienced and centrist."[54] His chief advisors—Hillary Clinton as secretary of state, Bush Republican holdover Robert Gates as secretary of defense, General James Jones, a John McCain ally, as national security advisor, and Admiral Dennis Blair, the former chief of U.S. Pacific Command, as director of national intelligence (DNI)—may have been experienced but, unfortunately, "centrist" would prove to be a stretch.

Obama had said that if he had to take one book with him into the White House, it would be Doris Kearns Goodwin's *Team of Rivals,* which celebrated Abraham Lincoln's wisdom in bringing his political rivals and personal detractors into his Cabinet. Obama followed those guidelines in choosing the hawkish Clinton and Gates, but he neglected to balance them with equally forceful critics of American empire.

The results were predictable. In August 2009, neocon Elliot Cohen's *Wall Street Journal* op-ed titled "What's Different About the Obama Foreign Policy" reassured conservatives that very little had changed: "The underlying structure of the policy remains the same. . . . Moreover, because the Obama foreign policy senior team consists of centrist experts from the Democratic Party, it is unlikely to make radically different judgments about the world, and about American interests in it, than its predecessors."[55]

Gates was the principal guarantor of imperial continuity. A staunch Cold Warrior with close ties to the neocons, Gates had come off relatively unscathed in the public mind, despite involvement in several scandalous situations, which have never been fully investigated. During the Reagan years, he had facilitated arms sales to both Iraq and Iran during their disastrous war. He was instrumental in revamping CIA intelligence gathering, purging independent-minded analysts who wouldn't go along with the view of a menacing Soviet threat that justified an enormous U.S. military buildup. He was also a key proponent of Reagan's murderous policies in Central America, advocating illegal covert measures against the Sandinista regime in Nicaragua.[56]

Gates teamed with Clinton to frustrate those who hoped for reassessment of America's role in the world. "People are wondering what the future holds, at home and abroad," Clinton told the Council on Foreign Relations (CFR). "So let me say it clearly: The United States can, must, and will lead in this new century."[57] "We are still essentially, as has been said before, the indispensable nation," Gates concurred in November 2010.[58] But in declaring a "new American moment" before the CFR, Clinton offered a version of American history stunning in its simplicity and vapidity: "After the Second World War, the nation that had built the transcontinental railroad, the assembly line, the skyscraper, turned its attention to constructing the pillars of global cooperation. The third World War that so many feared never came. And many millions of people were lifted out of poverty and exercised their human rights for the first time. Those were the benefits of a global architecture forged over many years by American leaders from both political parties."[59]

In speeches in Prague, Cairo, Oslo, and elsewhere, Obama articulated a more nuanced understanding of America's role in the world. But his ultimate message was largely the same as that of Clinton and Gates. Nothing was more disappointing than his Nobel Peace Prize acceptance speech in December 2009. That a president waging two wars would receive the prize was preposterous in the first place. But the selection committee members must have been even more chagrined when they heard Obama's defense of American militarism in an address that came just days after announcing that he was sending additional forces to Afghanistan. An at times thoughtful speech about the complex problems facing the world was sullied by a defense of war, unilateralism, and preemption.

Obama asserted presidential power in ways that must have made Dick Cheney jealous. In 2011, Obama defied his own top lawyers, insisting that he did not need congressional approval under the War Powers Resolution to continue military activities in Libya beyond the sixty-day limits inscribed in the resolution. Offering a bizarre, some would say Orwellian, interpretation reminiscent of George W. Bush's definition of "torture" and Bill Clinton's definition of "sex," Obama insisted that the U.S. military engagement was outside the legal definition of "hostilities." Even hawkish House Speaker John Boehner was taken aback by Obama's contention that prolonged bombing of Libya as part of an effort to assassinate Muammar Gaddafi and overthrow his regime didn't constitute "hostilities." "The White House says there are no hostilities taking place," Boehner commented. "Yet we've got drone attacks under way. We're spending $10 million a day. We're part of an effort to drop bombs on Qaddafi's compounds. It just doesn't pass the straight-face test, in my view, that we're not in the midst of hostilities." Obama had rejected the views of Pentagon general counsel Jeh Johnson and acting head of the Justice Department's Office of Legal Counsel Caroline Krass. Disregarding the opinion of the Office of Legal Counsel in such affairs was almost unprecedented.[60]

*Secretary of State Hillary Clinton and Defense Secretary Robert Gates
confer during a Cabinet Room meeting. A holdover from the Bush
administration, Gates teamed with the hawkish Clinton to frustrate
those who hoped for a reassessment of America's role in the world.*

When asked, during the 2008 primary campaign, if a president could bomb
Iran without congressional authorization, Obama responded, "The president
does not have power under the Constitution to unilaterally authorize a military
attack in a situation that does not involve stopping an actual or imminent threat
to the nation."[61] NATO went far beyond the limited UN resolution authorizing
it to take steps to protect Libyan civilians, thereby establishing a very dangerous
precedent.

Despite regime change in Libya, signs abounded that the American empire
was in serious decline. U.S. ability to control events had eroded. WikiLeaks' November 2010 release of secret State Department cables prompted the *Guardian's* Simon Jenkins to decry the sheer ineptitude and wrongheadedness of U.S.
foreign policy: "The money wasting is staggering. . . . The impression is of the
world's superpower roaming helpless in a world in which nobody behaves as bid-
den. Iran, Russia, Pakistan, Afghanistan, Yemen, the United Nations are all per-
petually off script. Washington reacts like a wounded bear, its instincts imperial
but its power projection unproductive."[62]

Nowhere was this more apparent than Afghanistan, where U.S. forces had
been bogged down since 2001 with the stated goal of defeating Al-Qaeda.
Obama shared this commitment, having promised during the campaign to end
the war in Iraq so he could throw more resources into Afghanistan. Many tried
to dissuade him from such folly. On June 30, 2009, Obama dined in the White

House with nine of America's leading presidential historians, seeking their insights into what had enabled past presidents to succeed and what had caused them to fail. Because Obama indicated that he wanted such dinners to become an ongoing event, participants maintained their silence about what was discussed. More than a year later, Northwestern's Garry Wills finally broke his silence. "There has been no follow-up on the first dinner, and certainly no sign that he learned anything from it," Wills wrote in frustration. "The only thing achieved has been the silencing of the main point the dinner guests tried to make—that pursuit of war in Afghanistan would be for him what Vietnam was to Lyndon Johnson." As the meal was winding down, Obama had asked them to go around one more time for final words of advice. Wills recalled, "When my turn came, I joined those who had already warned him about an Afghanistan quagmire. I said that a government so corrupt and tribal and drug-based as Afghanistan's could not be made stable. He replied that he was not naive about the difficulties but he thought a realistic solution could be reached. I wanted to add 'when pigs fly,' but restrained myself."[63]

By the time of that June meeting, Obama had already doubled down on the mess he inherited from Bush, regarding which a senior U.S. military commander informed the *Washington Post* during the final days of the Bush administration, "We have no strategic plan. We never had one."[64] When Obama took office, the United States had 34,000 troops in the country. In February, he ordered 34,000 more "to stabilize a deteriorating situation."[65] In May, Gates, upon the urging of regional commander General David Petraeus, fired General David McKiernan as commander of U.S. forces in Afghanistan and replaced him with Lieutenant General Stanley McChrystal.

McChrystal appeared to have been cast for the part by Stanley Kubrick. The *Times* described him as an "ascetic who . . . usually eats just one meal a day, in the evening, to avoid sluggishness," operates "on a few hours' sleep," and runs "to and from work while listening to audiobooks on an iPod." He oversaw "secret commando operations" in Iraq for five years as head of the secret Joint Special Operations Command (JSOC), running what Sy Hersh called an "executive assassination wing" out of Cheney's office. According to the *Times*, "former intelligence officials say that he had an encyclopedic, even obsessive, knowledge about the lives of terrorists, and that he pushed his ranks aggressively to kill as many of them as possible." Some thought of him as a "warrior-scholar," others as a "driven workaholic."[66]

McChrystal implemented a Petraeus-like counterinsurgency strategy inside Afghanistan, though he took greater pains to limit civilian casualties and adopted a much more aggressive stance vis-à-vis Pakistan. Unlike McKiernan, McChrystal viewed Afghanistan and Pakistan as "one thorny problem," having supported commando attacks on Taliban sanctuaries in Pakistan.[67] Although McChrystal's days were numbered, targeted assassination would become the sine qua non of U.S. global strategy.

Obama understood the strategic importance of Pakistan. "The cancer is in Pakistan," Obama acknowledged at a November 25, 2009, Oval Office meeting. Succeeding in Afghanistan was necessary, he insisted, "so the cancer doesn't spread there."[68]

The U.S.-Pakistani relationship was marked by opportunism on both sides. In the 1980s, the United States worked closely with Pakistani intelligence— the Directorate for Inter-Services Intelligence (ISI)—to train and supply the "holy warriors" who battled the Soviets in Afghanistan. In appreciation for Pakistani assistance, the United States turned a blind eye toward Pakistan's then nascent nuclear program, which expanded at breakneck pace throughout the Bush/Obama years. By 2011, Pakistan possessed an arsenal estimated at 110 nuclear weapons with enough fissile material to make 40 to 100 more, replacing France as the world's fifth largest nuclear power. Despite substantial U.S. assistance in securing those weapons and materials, lax security made theft of bomb-making ingredients a real threat in a country rife with Islamic extremists, many of whom had been hardened, with U.S. backing, on the battlefields of Afghanistan.[69]

The U.S.-Pakistani alliance was a fragile one. Following Soviet withdrawal from Afghanistan, it took U.S.-backed mujahideen three more years to finally overthrow the Soviet-allied Najibullah government in 1992. Thereafter, U.S. interest in the region waned. President Pervez Musharraf, the former Pakistani army chief who took power in a 1999 coup, said that Pakistanis felt that they had been "used and ditched" by the United States. U.S. restoration of sanctions during the 1990s because of Pakistan's nuclear program further exacerbated tensions.[70]

After 9/11, the United States again sought Pakistani assistance. But this time the Pakistanis weren't so eager to lend a hand. The United States threatened to bomb them "back to the Stone Age" if they didn't comply with U.S. demands, including ending support for the Afghan Taliban.[71] The United States paid Pakistan over $2 billion per year for assistance in driving the Taliban out of sanctuaries in the remote frontier areas near the Afghan border, from which the Taliban waged war against NATO forces. Pakistan proved a reluctant partner, targeting insurgents who struck within Pakistan while covertly harboring the two largest Taliban groups operating in Afghanistan.

While the Pakistanis dragged their feet, the United States acted unilaterally. U.S. special forces and the CIA's Counterterrorism Pursuit Teams—a three-thousand-man Afghan secret army—launched assaults into the ungoverned tribal regions where insurgents clustered.[72] Pakistanis were outraged by U.S. violation of their sovereignty.

Pakistanis particularly bristled at increased U.S. drone attacks inside Pakistan, which, the *Washington Post* reported, had left between 1,350 and 2,250 dead in Obama's first three years in office. Drones, which could be used for surveillance or attack, when equipped with Hellfire missiles, had increasingly become the U.S. weapon of choice in both Pakistan and Afghanistan. Obama authorized as many drone attacks in his first nine months as Bush had in the preceding three years, leading to deaths of many innocent civilians.

David Kilcullen, who had served as a counterinsurgency advisor to General David Petraeus from 2006 to 2008, and Andrew Exum, an army officer in Iraq and Afghanistan from 2002 to 2004, provided insight into Pakistani rage in May 2009. They cited Pakistani press reports indicating that over the past three years U.S. drone strikes had killed 700 civilians and only 14 terrorist leaders, which equated to 50 civilians for every militant, "a hit rate of 2 percent." While noting that U.S. officials "vehemently" denied these figures and acknowledging that they likely exaggerated the proportion of civilian casualties, Kilcullen and Exum warned that "every one of these dead noncombatants represents an alienated family, a new desire for revenge, and more recruits for a militant movement that has grown exponentially even as drone strikes have increased" and that "visceral opposition" was being expressed in areas of Pakistan far from where the strikes were occurring.[73]

An accurate count of civilian casualties was hard to come by. Pakistan photographer Noor Behram, who hailed from the tribal region of Waziristan where most of the strikes were occurring, held an exhibition in London in summer 2011 of graphic and grisly photos from twenty-seven drone attacks. Behram lowered the ratio of civilians to terrorists a bit. "For every 10 to 15 people killed," he found, "maybe they get one militant." The New America Foundation placed the civilian toll at 20 percent. Behram's account of the aftermath sounds strikingly similar to the effects of U.S. bombing in other wars: "There are just pieces of flesh lying around after a strike. You can't find bodies. So the locals pick up the flesh and curse America. They say that America is killing us inside our own country, inside our own homes, and only because we are Muslims. The youth in the area surrounding a strike gets crazed. Hatred builds up inside those who have seen a drone attack. The Americans think it is working, but the damage they're doing is far greater."[74] Faisal Shahzad, the Pakistani-born U.S. citizen who is best known as "the Times Square bomber," is a case in point. Shortly after his arrest, he asked, "How would you feel if people attacked the United States? You are attacking a sovereign Pakistan." At his trial, when asked by the judge how he could risk killing innocent women and children, he responded that U.S.

drone strikes "don't see children, they don't see anybody. They kill women, children, they kill everybody."[75] To the Pakistanis, the victims were human beings. To the drone operators, they were "bug splats."[76]

No wonder 97 percent of Pakistanis told Pew researchers that they viewed U.S. drones negatively and the number who saw the United States as an enemy jumped from 64 percent in 2009 to 74 percent in 2012. No wonder so many were incensed at the smug indecency of President Obama's comment at the May 2010 White House Correspondents' Association dinner upon spotting the popular teenage Jonas Brothers band members in the audience. Referring to his daughters, Obama quipped, "Sasha and Malia are huge fans but, boys, don't get any ideas. Two words for you: predator drones. You will never see it coming." In spring 2012, only 7 percent of Pakistanis held a positive view of Obama.[77]

Obama's tasteless remarks were at least an attempt at humor, though one on a par with George Bush's feigned search for WMD under his oval office desk six years earlier. In June 2011, Obama's counterterrorism advisor John Brennan claimed with a straight face that for almost a year, "there hasn't been a single collateral death" from the drone attacks, an assertion that drone supporter Bill Roggio, who followed the strikes closely as editor of *The Long War Journal*, dismissed as "absurd." Shortly thereafter, Britain's Bureau of Investigative Journalism reported that based on interviews in the tribal areas, at least forty-five civilians had been killed in ten strikes in the past year.[78] Brennan could make such a ludicrous claim in part because Obama had classified any military-age male who happened to be in a strike zone as a combatant. That apparently included civilians who had tried to help rescue victims or had the bad judgment to attend funerals of combatants, dozens of whom had been killed by CIA drones, the Bureau reported in February 2012.[79]

In 2010, with Pakistani anger exploding, U.S. ambassador Cameron Munter complained that the operation was "out of control." "He didn't realize his main job was to kill people," a colleague said.[80] Obama and Biden saw increased use of drones as a way to punish the Taliban and Al-Qaeda without an expanded troop commitment, but others recognized the questionable legal status of such targeted assassinations and worried about the future implications of a world in which such lethal technology was widely dispersed. In fact, prior to 9/11, the United States had opposed "targeted killing" by other nations. In 2000, U.S. ambassador to Israel Martin Indyk condemned Israeli targeting of Palestinians. "The United States government," he said, "is very clearly on the record as being against targeted assassinations. They are extrajudicial killings and we do not support that."[81]

Obama signaled his intention to not only aggressively pursue Bush's war on terror, but to expand the use of drones in doing so even before he took office. A former CIA official disclosed that Obama's transition teams assured agency personnel that "they were going to be 'as tough if not tougher' than the Bush people. . . . They basically shitcanned the interrogation board. But they wanted to make it clear that they weren't a bunch of left-wing pussies—that they would be focusing and upping the ante on the Predator program."[82]

Drone usage would expand on Obama's watch from Pakistan—the only country targeted when Bush left office—to six countries over the next three plus years as the United States added Islamic rebels in the Philippines to the list in February 2012. Critics agreed with Tom Engelhardt's astute observation that "drones . . . put wings on the Bush-era Guantánamo principle that Washington has an inalienable right to act as a global judge, jury, and executioner, and in doing so remain beyond the reach of any court of law."[83]

What was not appreciated until later was the direct, hands-on involvement of the president himself in targeting specific individuals who were put on official "kill lists." In 2006, former vice president Al Gore expressed outrage over George Bush's exercise of powers and wondered whether there were any limits to what presidents could do. Gore asked: "If the president has the inherent authority to eavesdrop on American citizens without a warrant, imprison American citizens on his own declaration, kidnap and torture, then what can't he do?"[84] Obama's targeted assassinations provided a chilling answer. Glenn Greenwald warned that "the power to order people executed (including U.S. citizens) is far too extreme and dangerous to vest in one person without any checks, review, oversight or transparency." After all, he reminded readers, "it was a consensus among Democrats that George Bush should be forced to obtain judicial review before merely spying on or detaining people, let alone ordering them executed by the CIA."[85]

The Obama administration kept a tight veil of secrecy around the program, refusing to divulge information about targeting or casualties. The CIA, which conducted the attacks in Pakistan, even refused to acknowledge that such a program existed. But drone warfare had breathed new life into an agency that had been left for dead after 9/11. "You've taken an agency that was chugging along and turned it into one hell of a killing machine," one former official declared. In the decade after 9/11, the CIA's Counterterrorism Center staff had grown sevenfold. Approximately 20 percent of CIA analysts were now "targeters" and 35 percent supported drone operations.[86]

The overall cost and complexity of the operation was immense. Each combat drone required a team of at least 150 people to maintain it and ready it to strike its target. The Air Force, which ran the drones in Iraq and Afghanistan, was spending $5 billion per year to operate the program and the cost was increasing rapidly. The Pentagon requested an additional $5 billion for 2012. The JSOC carried out additional strikes in Yemen and Somalia. Strikes were being launched in late 2011 from more than sixty widely scattered bases, by "pilots" wearing the same green flight suits as fighter pilots and maneuvering drones with joysticks and video game–like computer screens. Plans were in the works to supplement these land-based drones with aircraft-carrier-based attack planes that could be deployed in the Pacific and strike targets from three times as far away as Navy fighter jets. The United States was working on miniaturizing these remotely operated intelligence gathering and killing machines to the size of birds and even insects and promoting them as the future face of warfare. In 2011, the Pentagon disclosed plans to spend close to $40 billion over the next decade to add more than 700 medium and large drones to a stockpile that in 2012 totaled more than 19,000, including mini-drones. The Air Force already had more pilots learning to fly drones than it had pilots training to fly aircraft. There were also plans to supply soldiers with thousands of hand-launchable mini-drones for sur-veying areas and dive-bombing enemy forces.[87]

But U.S. allies and UN officials questioned the legality of such targeted assas-sinations. Further concerns about legality were aroused when the United States killed U.S. born Al-Qaeda supporter Anwar al-Awlaki and Samir Khan, a natural-ized American citizen, in Yemen in late September 2011. The following month, another strike killed Awlaki's 16-year-old U.S.-born son. In July 2012, relatives of the victims joined with the ACLU and the Center for Constitutional Rights to file a wrongful death lawsuit against Secretary of Defense Leon Panetta, CIA Director Petraeus, and two senior commanders of the military's Special Opera-tions forces on the grounds that the "killings violated fundamental rights af-forded to all U.S. citizens, including the right not to be deprived of life without due process of law."[88]

The Awlakis and Khan were among the many victims of the Yemeni drone campaign. Much like in Pakistan, the drones were creating far more enemies than they were killing. When the U.S. began its Yemeni drone campaign in 2009, Al-Qaeda in the Arab Peninsula had fewer than 300 militants in Yemen. By mid-2012, that number had jumped to over 700. As the *Washington Post* reported, the stepped-up targeting in southern Yemen was "stirring increasing sympathy for al-Qaeda-linked militants and driving tribesmen to join a network linked to ter-rorist plots against the United States." The *Post* quoted one Yemeni businessman who lost two brothers—a teacher and a cellphone repairman—in a U.S. strike as stating, "These attacks are making people say, 'We believe now that al-Qaeda is on the right side.'" Hundreds of tribesman had also joined the fight not out of sympathy for Al-Qaeda but out of hatred toward the United States. "The drones are killing al-Qaeda leaders, but they are also turning them into heroes," warned a local human rights activist.[89]

For American policy makers, drones represented an ingenious low-cost, low-risk form of robotic warfare that kills enemies from thousands of miles away, without endangering U.S. forces. Critics, however, deplored this cowardly form of remote, long-distance killing. Thailand's *Nation* newspaper wrote acerbically that "drones . . . satisfy our selfish and rather lily-livered need to eavesdrop, kill and destroy without facing the slightest chance of reciprocation in kind."[90] The army was also experimenting with killer robots that could supplement or replace combat troops. One robot design being tested in Fort Benning, Georgia, operated in conjunction with surveillance drones and was equipped with a grenade launcher and a machine gun. Many feared that these new steps in mechanized warfare, by greatly limiting the numbers of Americans coming home in body bags, would lower the threshold for going to war. "Wars will be started very easily and with minimal costs," warned Wendell Wallach, who chaired the technology and ethics study group at Yale's Interdisciplinary Center for Bioethics.[91]

For Engelhardt, drones were simply the latest in a long line of "wonder weapons" guaranteed to ensure American military hegemony from atomic bombs to hydrogen bombs to the Vietnam-era electronic battlefield to Reagan's missile defense shield to the First Gulf War's "smart bombs."[92] Doubt was cast upon their wonder-weapon status in late 2011 when Iranians displayed an RQ-170 Sentinel that they had brought down intact while it was spying over their territory. More than two dozen others had crashed up to that point but none with so much fanfare or such embarrassing consequences.

Some expressed concern that the Iranians would reverse engineer the drone and learn its secrets. Dick Cheney demanded that Obama send planes to destroy the downed aircraft while it lay grounded. But it was too late. The cat was already out of the bag. More than fifty countries, some friendly and some hostile to the United States, had already purchased drones, and several had their own sophisticated drone programs in place. Most of those purchased were of the surveillance variety, but the United States had sold attack drones to close allies. In 2009, the United States punished Israel, which was second only to the United States in drone manufacture, for selling an attack drone to China. WikiLeaks revealed that Israel had angered U.S. authorities by selling advanced model drones to Russia. Among the other countries that claimed to have mastered manufacturing drones with lethal capabilities were Russia, India, and even Iran. In summer 2010, Iranian president Mahmoud Ahmadinejad displayed a model he called the "ambassador of death."

But the main challenge to U.S. ambitions and pretensions appeared to come from China, which had the most dynamic program outside the United States. By 2011, five years after publicly displaying its first drone, China boasted over two dozen varieties, with more on the way. And, most troubling, China appeared to have no compunctions about selling armed drones to other nations. China's

Aviation Industry Corp. offered customers a model comparable to the U.S. Predator called the Yilong ("pterodactyl" in English) that combined combat and surveillance capabilities. Among the countries lining up to buy combat models from China was sometime U.S. ally Pakistan.

Leading U.S. defense contractors like General Atomics Aeronautical Systems, whose advanced Predators and MQ9 Reapers sold for over $10 million each, clamored to get in on this market and pressured the U.S. government to ease export controls. Vice Admiral William Landay III, director of the Defense Security Cooperation Agency, which oversaw such sales, instructed his subordinates to determine in advance which countries could purchase drones with which capabilities,[93] so U.S. manufacturers would be ready to hit the ground running when they got the green light.

By using the rationale that it was engaged in a battle against Al-Qaeda and the Taliban that was not restricted to "hot battlefields" as a justification for targeted assassinations in multiple countries, the United States was establishing a dangerous precedent. As Human Rights Watch pointed out, what was to stop China from targeting Uighur activists living in New York City or Russia from killing Chechen militants in London?

Director of National Intelligence Admiral Dennis Blair, who had tried to curb drone attacks and other CIA covert activities, believing them a blot on America's reputation, was replaced in 2010 by retired Lieutenant General James Clapper, the former head of the National Geospatial-Intelligence Agency, who defended such actions. Blair complained that the White House's obsession with drone strikes had replaced serious strategizing about how to defeat Al-Qaeda. "The steady refrain in the White House was, 'This is the only game in town'— reminded me of body counts in Vietnam," Blair observed.[94]

In Afghanistan, U.S. officials touted drone attacks as an improvement over the aerial bombardment that marked the earlier stages of the war. In March 2010, the *New York Times* reported that "civilian deaths caused by American troops and American bombs have outraged the local population and made the case for the insurgency."[95] U.S. bombs had killed thousands of Afghan civilians. Many others were shot at checkpoints. Command Sergeant Major Michael Hall, the senior NATO enlisted man in Afghanistan, said that many of those imprisoned at the Bagram Air Base had joined the insurgency after the deaths of people they knew. "There are stories after stories about how these people are turned into insurgents," he told his troops. "Every time there is an escalation of force we are finding that innocents are being killed."[96]

Obama and his advisors had been reading *Lessons in Disaster,* Gordon Goldstein's cautionary study of the deepening U.S. involvement in Vietnam. Goldstein shows how foreign policy makers' failure to question basic assumptions about a monolithic Communist threat and the domino theory had led the U.S. astray. Obama determined not to make the same mistakes in dealing with Al-Qaeda and the Taliban.

Obama understood that getting bogged down in Afghanistan would doom his presidency, much as Vietnam had destroyed Johnson's. Having already increased the U.S. troop commitment and declared that winning the war was vital to America's national interests, he now sought options that would limit U.S. involvement and offer an exit strategy. But, as *Washington Post* staff writer Bob Woodward has skillfully shown, he was boxed in and outflanked by his top military advisors—Mike Mullen, Petraeus, McChrystal—who, with the aid of Secretaries Gates and Clinton, pushed for 40,000 additional troops, an expanded mission, including full-scale counterinsurgency organized around military-led nation building, and an open-ended commitment. Obama demanded they provide additional options. But at a September 30 meeting he eliminated the one option that made sense, telling his national security advisors, "I want to take off the table that we're leaving Afghanistan."[97] Still, he made clear he didn't want a commitment that would last ten years and cost $1 trillion. The military leaders, he charged angrily at the November 11, 2009, strategy review session, had presented only the one foolhardy option. To make matters worse, all three had publicly stated that anything less than their desired troop buildup would result in a humiliating defeat, a view that was immediately trumpeted by the leading neocons and their allies in the media.

New York Times and *Washington Post* editors did all they could to back the hawks. The media watch group Fairness & Accuracy in Media and Reporting (FAIR) surveyed all *Times* and *Post* op-eds during the first ten months of 2009 that addressed the direction of U.S. policy in Afghanistan. The *Times*, despite having been scandalized by Judith Miller's role in the lead-up to the invasion of Iraq, ran thirty-six columns supporting the war and only seven opposing it. The ratio was more than ten to one in the *Post*, whose editors were very explicit about where they stood. Breaking with McChrystal's war policy, the *Post* editorialized in September 2009, "would both dishonor and endanger this country."[98]

Biden and Marine General James Cartwright, the vice chairman of the Joint Chiefs, proposed a scaled-back approach that would still increase troops by 20,000 but reject nation building and population protection, thereby promising a much quicker exit. They wanted to focus on weakening and dividing the Taliban in hopes of reconciliation and on training Afghan forces. Gates and Mullen later punished Cartwright for his dissent by blocking his elevation to chairman of the Joint Chiefs, even after Obama had informed him that he had the job.[99]

What Afghanistan actually needed was economic aid and social reform, not more U.S. troops. The depths of Afghan poverty were staggering. As of 2009,

*MQ-1 Predator (**TOP**) and MQ-9 Reaper (**ABOVE**) drones fly combat missions above Afghanistan. U.S. officials touted these unmanned weapons as precise instruments for the targeted killing of enemy combatants, but their use led to numerous civilian deaths and helped usher in an era of drone proliferation across the globe.*

even with U.S. dollars flooding the country, Afghanistan was still the world's fifth poorest nation with one of the widest gaps between rich and poor. Per capita income stood at $426. Sixty-eighty percent of the population lived on less than a dollar per day. Only 23 percent had access to sanitary drinking water. Average life expectancy was 43 years. Twenty-four percent of adults could read and write, but only 14 percent of women. Even in 2011, a decade into the war, only 30 percent of girls attended school.[100] Despite such enormous need, the United States was spending over $100 billion annually on military efforts and only $2 billion on sustainable development. The Center for American Progress reported that "even the Soviet Union spent more on reconstruction" than the United States had.[101] But even that paltry sum was in shocking excess of what the Afghan government could generate. Anthony Cordesman of the Center for Strategic and International Studies, who was part of McChrystal's civilian advisory team in 2009, wrote that "outside aid is some 14 times higher than the Kabul government's revenue-generating capability."[102]

The condition of Afghan women was particularly deplorable. They had been suffering terribly ever since the United States and its allies overthrew the Soviet-backed regime, whose unpopularity was partly due to its egalitarian impulses toward women. Liberating women from Taliban repression had been one of the U.S. justifications for invading in the first place. But, as Atiq Sarwari and Robert Crews reminded readers, "within a twenty-five year period Afghan women became the object of emancipation at the hands of four separate regimes: the communists, the mujahideen, the Taliban, and the American-led coalition all presented the amelioration of the plight of women as an obligation that made their rule legitimate."[103] And in the rural areas, where the overwhelming majority of Afghans live, little had changed and infant and maternal mortality rates remained among the highest in the world, although they, like life expectancy, had recently shown signs of improving.[104] In some Taliban-controlled southern provinces, fewer than 1 percent of girls attended middle school. David Wildman and Phyllis Bennis wrote, "arming one group of men with a terrible record on rights so they could overthrow another group of men with a terrible record on women's rights has done little to improve the situation for women. Afghan women remain unequal in law, in health, and in life." In 2009, Afghanistan still ranked second worst on the UN's Gender-Related Development Index measuring, among other things, female literacy, access to education, and life expectancy.[105] And that was after eight years of U.S. occupation and reform.

Under the circumstances, more U.S. troops was the last thing Afghanistan needed, and many people tried to save Obama from making a colossal blunder. In early November, U.S. ambassador to Afghanistan Karl Eikenberry wrote two secret memos to Hillary Clinton warning that the counterinsurgency policy was failing and troop increases would backfire. Eikenberry, who had been the commander of U.S. troops in the country for 18 months in 2006 and 2007, cautioned: "The last time we sent substantial additional forces—a deployment totaling 33,000 in 2008–2009—overall violence and instability in Afghanistan intensified." And, he made clear, "More troops won't end the insurgency as long as the Pakistan sanctuaries remain." The corruption of Afghan president Hamid Karzai and the incompetence of the Afghan army and police only made the situation more hopeless.[106]

Others with knowledge of the region concurred. In September 2009, four former top intelligence officials warned the *New York Times'* Nicholas Kristof

*Obama and Afghan President Hamid Karzai converse during a March
2010 dinner at the Presidential Palace in Kabul. A shaky U.S. ally at best,
Karzai has led a government that has proven both brutal and corrupt.*

that "the very presence of our forces in the Pashtun areas is the problem" and a
buildup would only "prove to the Pashtuns that the Taliban are correct. The basic
ignorance by our leadership is going to cause the deaths of many fine American
troops with no positive outcome."[107] One of the four, Howard Hart, former CIA
station chief in Pakistan, campaigned for rapid withdrawal of U.S. forces. He told
students at the University of Virginia that the United States could send hundreds
of thousands of troops and spend "umpteen billion" dollars and it would still do
no good: "They will never stop fighting us," Hart said. "They never stopped fighting the Soviets. They've never stopped fighting each other."[108]

Not only did Afghans hate the presence of invading forces, they hated their
tactics, especially in the heightened counterinsurgency phase of the war. Afghans
resented night raids in which U.S. and Afghan troops forced their way into people's homes, kicking in doors, and breaking Afghan taboos about invading the privacy of women. The night raids, which increased exponentially once Obama took
office, targeted Taliban leaders and suspected insurgents in an attempt to destroy
the Taliban "shadow governments" that functioned throughout the country. What
the Israeli geographer Eyal Weizman said about such tactics in Palestine and Iraq
applies equally, if not more so, in Afghanistan: "unexpected penetration of war
into the private domain of the home has been experienced by civilians in Palestine, just like in Iraq, as the most profound form of trauma and humiliation."[109]

And, to make matters worse, nighttime raids, like the drones, often mistakenly targeted innocent civilians. In May 2011, a midnight NATO raid on a home

outside Jalalabad killed a local policeman mistakenly identified as a Taliban leader. Troops also killed his twelve-year old niece Nelofar, who was sleeping outside in the courtyard to escape from the sweltering indoor heat. A NATO official promptly apologized for the tragic accident. Nelofar's grieving father took little comfort in the apology. "They killed my twelve-year-old innocent daughter and my brother-in-law and then told me, 'We are sorry,'" he said. "What does it mean? What pain can be cured by this word 'sorry'?"[110] That the homegrown Taliban were guilty of killing more civilians than the foreign invaders that year did nothing to mitigate Afghans' anger toward NATO forces.

Reports surfaced repeatedly of American soldiers who went over the line, gratuitously killing innocent civilians in Afghanistan as was earlier the case in Iraq. One twenty-year-old soldier, who went AWOL in Canada, described the process that led to the erosion of human empathy:

> I swear I could not for a second view these people as anything but human. The best way to fashion a young hard dick like myself—"dick" being an acronym for "dedicated infantry combat killer"—is simple and the effect of racist indoctrination. Take an empty shell off the streets of L.A. or Brooklyn, or maybe from some Podunk town in Tennessee and these days America isn't in short supply. I was one of those no-child-left-behind products. Anyway, you take this empty vessel and you scare the living shit out of him, break him down to nothing, cultivate a brotherhood and camaraderie with those he suffers with, and fill his head with racist nonsense like all Arabs, Iraqis, Afghans are *Hajj*. *Hajj* hates you. *Hajj* wants to hurt your family. *Hajj* children are the worst because they beg all the time. Just some of the most hurtful and ridiculous propaganda, but you'd be amazed at how effective it's been in fostering my generation of soldiers.[111]

One group of deranged young men formed a twelve-person "kill team" that murdered innocent Afghans and then staged evidence to make it look as if they acted in self-defense. One of the accused confessed to the murders. U.S. authorities were not pleased when photos of the soldiers posing with the corpses appeared in *Der Spiegel*.

The damage done by American troop presence was only exacerbated by the deplorable behavior of Afghan leaders. When Matthew Hoh, a senior U.S. diplomat in Afghanistan's Zabul Province who had previously served as a Marine Corps captain in Iraq, resigned in September 2009, he wrote that Karzai's government is awash in "glaring corruption and unabashed graft" and that Karzai is "a President whose confidants and chief advisers comprise drug lords and war crimes villains, who mock our own rule of law and counter-narcotics effort."[112]

Ambassador Eikenberry too opposed throwing dollars and arms at the no-toriously corrupt Karzai regime, headed by Karzai's friends, family members, and political allies, who gorged themselves on the money that poured into the impoverished country, and warlords who were just as brutal, repressive, misogy-nistic, and undemocratic as the Taliban who preceded them—men who former Afghan parliament member and human rights crusader Malalai Joya described as "photocopies of the Taliban."[113] *The Economist* reported that in "parts of Af-ghanistan where insurgents have been driven out and the writ of the govern-ment has been restored, residents have sometimes hankered for the warlords, who were less venal and less brutal than Mr Karzai's lot."[114]

In 2010, Transparency International ranked Afghanistan the world's second most corrupt nation behind Somalia and two spots ahead of Iraq. The UN re-ported that in 2009 Afghans spent $2.5 billion to bribe police and government officials, which equaled approximately a quarter of Afghanistan's legitimate gross domestic product. The bribes averaged out to $158 per capita—a substantial amount in a country where the average annual GDP is only $426.[115]

The November 2010 release of part of the quarter million confidential dip-lomatic cables obtained by WikiLeaks proved quite revealing and profoundly embarrassing. Corruption was pervasive, engulfing almost everyone in leader-ship positions. Karzai's anti-corruption tsar, Izzatullah Wasifi, spent four years in a U.S. jail for selling heroin in Las Vegas. Karzai worked hard to protect family members and supporters, often seeing that charges were dropped even when they were caught red-handed.

The Commerce Minister told diplomats that the Transportation Ministry collected $200 million per year in trucking fees, but only $30 million of that total ended up in government coffers. People pay up to $250,000 to get jobs oversee-ing these operations. The American Embassy in Kabul reported that Afghani-stan's first vice president from 2004–2009, Ahmad Zia Massoud, was found by customs officials to be carrying $52 million in cash when he visited the United Arab Emirates in 2009. Massoud denied the charges but didn't explain how, on a salary of a few hundred dollars a month, he could afford to live in a waterfront house alongside other Afghan officials in Palm Jumeirah, a luxury Dubai com-munity. Another cable acknowledged that Ahmed Wali Karzai, the president's half brother and the most powerful man in Kandahar before his assassination in July 2011, who had long been on the CIA payroll, was "widely understood to be corrupt and a narcotics trafficker."[116] Other Hamid Karzai allies also gorged on the drug trade. British forces caught the governor of Helmand with 20,000 pounds of opium in his office. Though ousted from the governorship, he was later appointed to the Senate.[117]

The Taliban had actually done a good job keeping the drug trade under control when they were in power. But following the U.S. invasion, drugs had proliferated wildly. Opium production skyrocketed from 185 tons in 2001 to 8,200 tons in 2007, constituting 53 percent of the entire national economy and employing nearly 20 percent of the Afghan population.[118] The drug lords lived in opulent carnival-colored mansions called "poppy palaces" that were distinguished by their non-Afghan "narcotecture" styles. But many Afghans suffered from the resulting drug abuse. In 2005, 920,000 addicts were reported. The number increased substantially after that.[119]

Under Karzai, illicit drugs provided a steady flow of funds for the Taliban who taxed them at a rate of 10 percent and protected drug convoys for an additional fee. The Taliban also received hundreds of millions of dollars indirectly from the United States and NATO. Journalist Jean MacKenzie reported that in much of the country contractors factored at least a 20 percent cut on projects to the Taliban to let them proceed. One Afghan contractor reported, "I was building a bridge. The local Taliban commander called and said 'don't build a bridge there, we'll have to blow it up.' I asked him to let me finish the bridge, collect the money—then they could blow it up whenever they wanted. We agreed, and I completed my project."[120]

In 2010, American officials paid $2.2 billion to U.S. and Afghan trucking companies to transport supplies to U.S. bases. These trucking companies hired security firms that were often linked to top government officials to protect the trucks for between $800 and $2,500 per truck. The security firms, in turn, often faked fights to magnify the need for their services and bribed the Taliban to let the trucks pass without attacking them, leading one NATO official in Kabul to complain, "We're funding both sides of the war."[121]

Karzai's brother Mahmoud was exonerated by a commission appointed by Hamid Karzai to look into the massive fraud at Kabul Bank, the country's largest, where powerful insiders and shareholders received $925 million in loans often without either collateral or documentation. Among the recipients were government ministers and members of Parliament. The commission reported that Mahmoud Karzai had paid back his loans although a Central Bank governor informed parliament that Karzai still owed $22 million. He wasn't the only well-connected brother implicated. Abdul Hassin Fahim, the brother of the country's powerful first vice president, owed over $100 million but assured the commission that he would pledge enough property to cover that amount.

In June 2011, Abdul Qadeer Fitrat, the governor of Afghanistan's Central Bank, resigned and fled the country. He had come under increasing attack by Karzai's allies in the wake of his testimony to Parliament and subsequent investigation into the bank fraud and feared for his life. Afghanistan's attorney general brought charges against him. The allegations were supported by commission chairman Azizullah Ludin, who had earlier served Karzai as head of the Independent Electoral Commission that gave its stamp of approval to the hotly contested 2009 presidential elections, which was universally condemned as fraudulent.[122]

The extent of vote fraud in that and other elections had proved an outright embarrassment to the United States and NATO. The UN's Electoral Complaints Commission threw out more than a million votes, 28 percent of Karzai's total. Deputy UN envoy Peter Galbraith declared, "The fraud has handed the Taliban its greatest strategic victory in eight years of fighting the United States and its Afghan partners."[123] When the Afghan parliament subsequently rejected Karzai's attempt to replace the three foreign members of the five-member commission with hand-picked Afghans, Karzai threatened to join the Taliban.

Outright buying of votes is so pervasive in Afghanistan that it was barely hidden during the September 2010 parliamentary elections. Votes that cost as little as $1 in Kandahar might go for $18 in eastern Ghazni Province. Most were in the five- to six-dollar range. And with only 2,500 votes needed to win in certain districts, this seemed like a sound investment. The *New York Times* explained, "many well-heeled Afghan independent candidates are looking to buy their way into the lucrative sinecure of a seat in Parliament. That not only comes with a healthy salary—about $2,200 a month gross—but tremendous opportunities for graft." Registration cards for female voters were in particularly high demand both because they didn't contain photographs and because men often voted for women who were not permitted to leave the house.[124]

Much of this corruption and fraud was well-known to Obama while he was trying to decide which course of action to pursue in Afghanistan. On November 25, 2009, he met with Rahm Emanuel, national security advisor General Jones, and Jones's deputy Thomas Donilon and expressed his frustration: "It'd be a lot easier for me to go out and give a speech saying, 'You know what? The American people are sick of this war, and we're going to put in 10,000 trainers because that's how we're going to get out of there.'" Woodward contends that was precisely what Obama wanted to say if he had the courage to stand up to his military advisors.[125]

"It's not the number," Biden explained. "It's the strategy." Still wavering, Obama met with close National Security Council advisors over Thanksgiving weekend to weigh his options. "I don't see how you can defy your military chain here," Army Colonel John Tien warned him, implying that his entire military high command—Mullen, Petraeus, McChrystal, and Gates—might resign in protest. Donilon and CIA director Leon Panetta had been expressing similar views. "No Democratic president can go against military advice, especially if he asked for it," Panetta admonished. "So just do it," he recommended. "Do what they say."

Seeing that Obama was again being forced into a corner against his better judgment, General Douglas Lute, the NSC coordinator for Afghanistan and Pakistan, reminded him, "Mr. President, you don't have to do this." Just the day before, Colin Powell had offered the same advice. "You don't have to put up with this," he told the president. "You're the commander in chief. These guys work for you. Because they're unanimous in their advice doesn't make it right. There are other generals. There's only one commander in chief."

When it finally came down to decision time, Obama didn't have the courage or integrity of a post–Cuban Missile Crisis John F. Kennedy. He settled on a 30,000-troop increase, giving the military leaders almost everything they wanted and more than they expected.[126]

Borrowing a page from the Bush guidelines on patriotic atmospherics, Obama chose West Point for his December 1 speech outlining plans to increase U.S. troop levels to around 100,000. He explained that the United States and its allies had invaded Afghanistan because it had provided sanctuary for Al-Qaeda, which was responsible for 9/11. He forgot to mention at least three crucial facts. First, only fifty to one hundred of Al-Qaeda's worldwide total of 300 cadre were actually in Afghanistan, while the rest of its badly degraded force operated out of Pakistan and received most of its support from citizens of U.S.-backed regimes in Saudi Arabia, Kuwait, Yemen, and the United Arab Emirates. Second, Taliban leader Mullah Omar had actually opposed the 9/11 attack against U.S. targets. According to the official report of the 9/11 Commission, "As final preparations were under way during the summer of 2001, dissent emerged among al Qaeda leaders in Afghanistan over whether to proceed. The Taliban's chief, Mullah Omar, opposed attacking the United States. Although facing opposition from many of his senior lieutenants, bin Laden effectively overruled their objections, and the attacks went forward."[127] And, third, terrorists didn't need a safe haven replete with training camps to conduct clandestine operations. As Paul Pillar, the former deputy chief of the CIA's counterterrorism center, pointed out, "the operations most important to future terrorist attacks do not need such a home, and few recruits are required for even very deadly terrorism. Consider: The preparations most important to the Sept. 11, 2001, attacks took place not in training camps in Afghanistan but, rather, in apartments in Germany, hotel rooms in Spain and flight schools in the United States."[128]

Obama's logic befuddled CNN commentator Fareed Zakaria: "If Al Qaeda is down to 100 men there at the most, why are we fighting a major war?" Citing the 100 NATO troops who had been killed the previous month and the $100 billion plus annual cost, he determined that the war was costing "more than one allied death for each living Al Qaeda member in the country in just one month" and "a billion dollars for every member of Al Qaeda thought to be living in Afghanistan in one year." In response to those who justified the war because the Taliban were allies of Al-Qaeda, Zakaria observed, "this would be like fighting Italy in World War II after Hitler's regime had collapsed and Berlin was in flames just because Italy had been allied with Germany."[129]

Jim Lacey of the Marine Corps War College made his own calculations, based on the 140,000 coalition soldiers, and determined the cost was actually $1.5 billion annually per Al-Qaeda member in Afghanistan. "Did anyone do the math?" Lacey wondered. "In what universe do we find strategists to whom this makes sense?"[130]

Historian Andrew Bacevich pointed out the most glaring contradiction. If Afghanistan was really so critical to U.S. safety and security, which he considered "a preposterous notion," "then why set limits on U.S. involvement there? . . . Why not send 100,000 troops rather than 30,000? Why not vow to do 'whatever it takes,' rather than signal an early exit? Why not raise taxes and reinstate the draft . . . ? Why not promise 'victory'—a word missing from the president's address?"[131]

And the price tag was indeed astronomical and climbing. In 2006, congressional researchers estimated that it cost $390,000 per soldier per year in Afghanistan. By 2009, the figure had climbed to $1 million per year because of the heightened cost of mine-resistant troop carriers and surveillance equipment and the $400 per gallon cost of delivering fuel through insurgent-thick and forbidding mountainous terrain.[132]

Obama tried to mollify his progressive supporters by announcing that troop withdrawals would begin July 2011 with all troops out by 2014. In *The Promise*, Jonathan Alter reported that Obama said to Petraeus and Mullen: "I want you to be honest with me. You can do this in eighteen months?" Petraeus replied, "Sir, I'm confident we can train and hand over to the ANA [Afghan National Army] in that time frame." Obama pressed further, "If you can't do the things you say you can in 18 months, then no one is going to suggest we stay, right?" Petraeus assured him, "Yes, sir, in agreement" and Mullen chimed in, "Yes, sir."[133]

But, as *Washington Post* columnist Dana Milbank wryly observed, "President Obama's eighteen-month deadline for starting the Afghanistan pullout didn't survive its first eighteen hours." Administration officials testifying before the Senate Armed Services Committee the day after Obama's speech made clear that the pullout date was only aspirational. Gates set the tone when he testified: "Our current plan is that we will begin the transition . . . in July of 2011. We will evaluate in December 2010 whether we believe we will be able to meet that objective." Gates informed senators that the president had the prerogative to change his mind. Mullen agreed. Hillary Clinton added, "I do not believe we have locked ourselves into leaving."[134] In May 2010, at a dinner that Clinton hosted for Karzai and some top cabinet ministers, Gates assured the Afghans, "We're not leaving Afghanistan prematurely. In fact," he added, "we're not ever leaving at all."[135] Indeed, the Pentagon was planning to keep 10,000 to 30,000 troops in Afghanistan and believed it was in a strong position to get its way because of Afghan dependence on foreign aid.

Withdrawal was contingent upon training, arming, and equipping an ANA and police force that could provide security. McChrystal lobbied for a combined force of 400,000. Estimates of the annual cost of maintaining an Afghan security force that size ran to around $10 billion, but Afghan tax revenues only totaled some $2 billion, and three-quarters of the national budget came from foreign aid, leading John Kerry to ask: "So who will pay the bills to avoid having those armed soldiers and police mobilized as part of the next insurgency?"[136]

Internal government reviews made clear that building such a force was a daunting, if not impossible, task. After years of training, few Afghan army or police units could function independently, and leadership was lacking at all levels. Lieutenant General William Caldwell, the American who headed the NATO effort to train Afghan forces, reported in 2011 that 30 percent of Afghan soldiers deserted every year with the highest rates in the combat areas where they were most needed. A comparable percentage left the police each year. Caldwell put the literacy rate of army recruits at around 10 percent. Corruption ran rampant. Conditions were deplorable. Afghan soldiers damaged new buildings by tearing sinks off the walls to wash their feet before praying or building fires on barrack floors for cooking and heating in buildings that already contained kitchens and furnaces. Repairs were time-consuming and costly.[137]

Another issue was motivation. As Thomas Friedman observed in chiding Obama for not having the courage to reject a war that neither he nor his advisors wanted: "You know you're in trouble," he wrote, "when you're in a war in which the only party whose objectives are clear, whose rhetoric is consistent and whose will to fight never seems to diminish, is your enemy: the Taliban." "Why," he asked, "do we have to recruit and train our allies, the Afghan army, to fight? . . . If there is one thing Afghan males should not need to be trained to do, it's to engage in warfare. That may be the only thing they all know how to do after thirty years of civil war and centuries of resisting foreign powers. After all, who is training the Taliban? They've been fighting the U.S. Army to a draw—and many of their commanders can't even read."[138]

Those who wondered what government forces were doing if not reading or fighting got some disturbing insight in January 2011, when the Afghan government signed an agreement with the UN to stop recruiting children into the police force and to ban the common and, according to the *Washington Post*, growing practice of using young boys as sex slaves. The *New York Times* reported that "as part of the Afghan tradition of *bacha bazi*, literally 'boy play,' boys as young as nine are dressed as girls and trained to dance for male audiences, then prostituted in an auction to the highest bidder. Many powerful men, particularly commanders in the military and the police, keep such boys, often dressed in uniforms, as constant companions for sexual purposes." In Afghanistan, *bacha bazi* had actually become rampant among the insurgent mujahideen during their U.S.-backed campaign to oust Soviet forces. It was most openly practiced around Kandahar, where, the *Times* noted, the "Taliban originally came to prominence . . . when they intervened in a fight between two pedophile warlords over the possession of a coveted dancing boy." The Taliban had banned this practice when they were in power.[139]

While Afghan commanders cavorted, American troops were paying a tremendous price, both physically and psychologically. A study by doctors at the Landstuhl Regional Medical Center in Germany, where most wounded troops stopped before returning to the United States, found a dramatic increase in the percentage of injured troops who had lost limbs between 2009 and 2010 due to the widespread use of improvised explosive devices (IEDs). In 2010, 11 percent of the casualties had undergone amputations. Thirty-eight percent of the amputees had undergone multiple amputations.

Among the most gruesome were injuries to the genitals and urinary tract, the number of which almost tripled in just one year. Retired Army Colonel Dr. John Holcomb, who had had extensive combat medicine experience, called the findings of the study "unbelievable." "Everybody was taken aback by the frequency of these injuries: the double amputations, the injuries to the penis and testicles," said Holcomb. "Nothing like this has been seen before."[140]

Some injuries were going underreported. By mid-2010, the military reported 115,000 troops had suffered mild traumatic brain injuries from shock waves from roadside bombs. The injuries could cause long-term mental and physical damage. An investigation by ProPublica and National Public Radio discovered that such injuries were far more pervasive than the military indicated and that tens of thousands of other sufferers had gone uncounted.[141]

The psychological toll was also profound. In November 2009, Secretary of Veterans Affairs Erik Shinseki noted that "more veterans have committed suicide since 2001 than we have lost on the battlefields of Iraq and Afghanistan."[142]

Joseph Stiglitz and Harvard public policy professor Linda Bilmes reported in 2010 that 600,000 of the 2.1 million who had served in Iraq and Afghanistan had sought medical treatment from the Department of Veterans Affairs and that 500,000 had applied for disability benefits, which was approximately 30 percent higher than initially estimated. With treatment of post-traumatic stress disorder (PTSD) and other health issues only increasing over time and life expectancy rising, they estimated that the real cost of both wars could top $4 trillion. Considering that 9/11 cost Al-Qaeda approximately $50,000, the multitrillion-dollar U.S. response was indeed playing into bin Laden's goal of bankrupting the United States.[143]

Given the fundamental illogic of fighting a decade-long and immensely costly war in Afghanistan in order to defeat a debilitated enemy that was based in Pakistan, some concluded the United States must have an ulterior motive. They found a possible answer in 2010, when the Pentagon announced that its team of geologists and other investigators had confirmed the existence of vast Afghan mineral resources. The Pentagon projected that Afghanistan could become the "Saudi Arabia of lithium," a crucial ingredient in batteries for various electronic devices. London banker Ian Hannam, a mining expert with JPMorgan, went further, enthusing over the prospect that "Afghanistan could be one of the leading producers of copper, gold, lithium, and iron ore in the world." Petraeus, who would shortly replace McChrystal as commander of U.S. forces in Afghanistan, agreed. "There is stunning potential here," he said. Afghan officials estimated mineral worth at $3 trillion, a truly staggering figure for a country whose gross domestic product was around $12 billion and whose economy consisted largely of narcotics and foreign aid.[144]

Despite all the hoopla surrounding this "discovery," Afghanistan's mineral wealth was hardly a surprise. In January 1911, the *Chicago Daily Tribune* reported that Afghanistan "is rich in natural resources. It produces copper, lead, iron, and even gold."[145] In 1928, the newly formed Afghan-American Trading Company announced that it had acquired exclusive concessions to exploit Afghanistan's oil and minerals.[146] In 1941, the New York Times reminded readers that Afghan "mineral resources of oil, iron, coal, silver, lead and copper" were "largely underdeveloped."[147] Little was done to extract these resources in subsequent years, but both Afghans and foreign investors knew that day would eventually arrive.

While western investors waited for the security situation to stabilize before descending on the region, the resource-hungry Chinese pounced. A Chinese state-owned firm secured the rights to a copper mine in eastern Afghanistan. The Afghan minister who negotiated the deal, Mohammad Ibrahim Adel, was ousted after being accused by U.S. authorities of accepting a $30 million bribe from the Chinese.[148] He had been appointed by President Karzai in March 2006, when his predecessor refused to privatize the Ghori cement factory, Afghanistan's only operating cement plant, when approached by Mahmoud Karzai. Adel denies the charges.[149]

Investors also salivated over the potential energy resources in Central Asia. Atop that list was natural gas in Turkmenistan, which had potentially the fifth largest gas field yet discovered. Regional governments envisioned transporting that gas via a pipeline running through Afghanistan.

Meanwhile, the Pakistanis were maneuvering to undercut both the United States and India and make Pakistan the principal player in Afghanistan. They decided to exploit the growing rift between the United States and Karzai, who said he no longer felt the United States and NATO could win militarily and would eventually withdraw. Top Pakistani officials met repeatedly with Karzai, offering to deliver key Taliban leaders, including Sirajuddin Haqqani, Mullah Muhammad Omar, and Gulbuddin Hekmatyar, for a power-sharing arrangement that would end the conflict. Karzai's ouster of intelligence chief Amrullah Saleh and interior minister Hanif Atmar, both of whom had opposed such negotiations with Taliban fighters, showed that he too was interested, as was most of the country's Pashtun population.[150] However, such negotiations were fiercely opposed by the country's more pro-American Tajik, Uzbek, and Hazara communities, who constituted almost half the population. Having suffered the most during the reign of the Pashtun Taliban, they now constituted the most aggressive fighters in the ANA and their adamant opposition to such a deal raised the specter of civil war.[151]

After a decade of wasting blood and treasure, the American people had finally wearied of this futile war. In March 2011, an ABC News–*Washington Post* poll indicated that two-thirds of Americans did not believe the Afghanistan war was worth fighting. One year later, CNN reported, opposition had jumped to 72 percent.

Among the fiercest critics were the nation's mayors, who had seen their cities undergo draconian cuts due to declining revenues and shrinking federal aid. When they gathered in Baltimore in June 2011 for the annual meeting of the U.S. Conference of Mayors, they let the administration know how they felt. They called for a speedy end to the wars in Iraq and Afghanistan and for using the $126 billion annual savings to rebuild the nation's cities. Mayor Antonio Villaraigosa of Los Angeles said that the notion "that we would build bridges in Baghdad and Kandahar and not Baltimore and Kansas City absolutely boggles the mind."[152]

The pressure to leave had increased dramatically on May 1, 2011 when Navy SEALs killed Osama bin Laden, who was living comfortably in a home in Abbottabad, Pakistan, in the shadow of Pakistan's premier military academy. Believing Pakistani officials must have known of bin Laden's whereabouts, many Americans demanded that aid be cut off. Mistrust of Pakistani leaders ran so deep that the United States did not alert them that they had found bin Laden or were planning the attack, fearing that they would tip him off.

The raid proved to be a huge embarrassment to Pakistan, whose government was only a notch more stable than that of neighboring Afghanistan. U.S. ambassador to Pakistan Anne Patterson had reported in early 2010, "Pakistan's civilian government remains weak, ineffectual and corrupt." President Asif Ali Zardari,

America's principal ally, had earlier confided to Biden that the army and ISI, Pakistan's real power brokers, might "take me out."[153] Army Chief General Ashfaq Parvez Kayani was also in a tenuous position, facing a challenge from officers objecting to his ties to the United States. Under pressure, Kayani announced that Pakistan would no longer cooperate with U.S. drone attacks against insurgents operating from within Pakistan and would greatly restrict the latitude of U.S. intelligence operatives within the country.

Relations between the "allies" were dealt a further blow in November 2011 when a NATO air attack killed 24 Pakistani troops. When U.S. officials refused to apologize, the Pakistani government shut down supply routes to Afghanistan, forcing NATO to rely upon slower and more costly alternatives. The following May, a Pakistani court convicted a Pakistani doctor of treason for assisting the CIA in tracking down bin Laden and sentenced him to thirty-three years in prison. The U.S. Senate immediately retaliated by voting to cut $33 million in military aid on top of the $1.2 billion it was already withholding. Pakistan finally reopened the routes in early July 2012 after extracting an apology from Secretary of State Clinton.

In Congress, Republicans and Democrats alike used bin Laden's assassination to press for rapid withdrawal from Afghanistan. Richard Lugar, the ranking Republican on the Senate Foreign Relations Committee, argued that it was "no longer clear why we're there" and rejected the idea that the United States should be involved in "such grand nation-building."[154] Senator Dick Durbin, the Democratic Party whip, concurred. "If you believe that resolution of this conflict by military means is highly unlikely and not a realistic basis for US policy, how can we send one more American soldier to fight and die in Afghanistan?" he asked.[155]

The rift between the United States and the Karzai government also continued to widen. In mid-June 2011, Karzai denounced coalition forces in an address to the Afghanistan Youth International Conference. "You remember a few years ago I was saying thank you to the foreigners for their help; every minute we were thanking them," he said. "Now I have stopped saying that . . ." "They're here for their own purposes, for their own goals, and they're using our soil for that," he complained in the nationally televised broadcast. Karzai cited not only the mounting civilian casualties caused by NATO bombing but also the environmental damage, singling out the effect of depleted uranium weapons.[156] A few weeks earlier, Karzai had expressed outrage at a NATO bombing that killed several children and other civilians and threatened to take "unilateral action" against NATO if it continued to bomb Afghan homes. "If they continue their attacks on our houses. . . ." he warned, "history shows what Afghans do with trespassers and with occupiers."[157] U.S. officials were taken aback by such ingratitude. Outgoing

Obama and his national security team gather in the White House Situation Room to receive updates on the mission to assassinate Osama bin Laden.

Ambassador Eikenberry responded, "When we hear ourselves being called occupiers and worse, and our generous aid programs dismissed as totally ineffective and the source of all corruption, our pride is offended and we begin to lose our inspiration to carry on."[158]

Chastened by the angry response to his indelicate remarks, Karzai watched his words more carefully for a few months. But in October, he again infuriated his U.S. backers by telling a Pakistani journalist that "if war ever breaks [out] between Pakistan and America, we will side [with] Pakistan. I don't want any American soldier entering Afghans' homes anymore."[159]

Nor, as Senator Durbin suggested, was a military solution in the offing, troop surge or no troop surge. In July and August 2011 alone, the Taliban assassinated 181 high-ranking Afghan government officials, including Ahmed Wali Karzai. Other recent victims included Kandahar's mayor, the head of Kandahar's religious council, one of President Karzai's close advisors, and peace negotiator and former president Burhanuddin Rabbani.[160] In late July 2012, NATO released data showing that the number of insurgent attacks over the past three months had actually increased by 11 percent over the previous year, exposing the hollowness of repeated claims of success in defeating the insurgency.[161]

Bad news kept pouring out of the country. In September, Human Rights Watch reported that U.S.-trained and -funded members of the Afghan Local

Police (ALP) forces and militias known as *arbakai* had been abusing the villagers they were supposed to be protecting. Documented abuses included murder, rape, abductions, arbitrary detention, and forcible land grabs. Building up such forces was key to U.S. plans to stabilize the country. Petraeus had told the U.S. Senate that the ALP is "arguably the most critical element in our effort to help Afghanistan develop the capability to secure itself."[162]

The other pillar of future stability—the Afghan National Police (ANP)—was just as bad. Less than a month after the devastating Human Rights Watch report appeared, the UN Assistance Mission in Afghanistan found "compelling" evidence that the Afghan intelligence service, the National Directorate of Security, and the ANP were subjecting detainees, including children under the age of eighteen, to "systematic" torture during interrogation. Among the abuses highlighted in the report were twisting prisoners' genitals until they passed out, suspending them by their wrists and beating them with cables and rubber hoses, removing their toenails, subjecting them to electric shock and stress positions, and threatening them with sexual assault.[163]

The United Nations drug control agency reported that NATO efforts to slow the Afghan drug trade were failing. Opium poppy cultivation was up in 2011 for a second straight year, despite a 65 percent increase in antidrug efforts in 2011. Seven percent more land was under cultivation and, due to soaring prices, the expanded crop was bringing in $1.4 billion—double what it had the previous year. Cultivation, like the insurgency itself, had spread to the northern and eastern provinces from which it had previously been absent. Attacks on eradication teams had quadrupled from the previous year.[164]

Foreshadowing what would eventually be a miserable end to the U.S. invasion of Afghanistan, in October 2011 Obama announced that U.S. troops would be out of Iraq by year's end. The December 31 departure date had actually been negotiated by George W. Bush in 2008. Still, Obama took credit for fulfilling his campaign promise, and the majority of Americans applauded the end of the Iraq debacle.

Many within the Pentagon, however, found the announcement infuriating. After earlier insisting that a force of between 10,000 and 20,000 remain, military leaders had lowered their sights to between 3,000 and 5,000. They joined Obama and Clinton in pressuring the Iraqis to grant immunity from prosecution to U.S. troops remaining in the country. But, unmoved, the Shiite bloc in Parliament, led by Muqtada al-Sadr, refused and the final drawdown began.

To be sure, that would not entirely end U.S. presence in Iraq. The State Department estimated that as many as 16,000 or 17,000 U.S. personnel might remain, including 5,500 armed military contractors. The world's largest U.S. embassy, a 104-acre walled compound in Baghdad, and consulates in Basra and Irbil

The commander of the Afghan National Police (ANP) marches before cadets at the Afghan National Police Academy graduation ceremonies. No better at ensuring stability than the members of the Afghan Local Police (ALP)—who were accused of raping and murdering villagers whom they were supposed to be protecting—the UN Assistance Mission in Afghanistan found "compelling" evidence to conclude that members of the ANP were systematically torturing detainees.

would remain as constant reminders to Iraqis of U.S. invasion, devastation, conquest, and occupation. Colonel John S. Laskodi, commander of an army brigade that was assisting the State Department during the transition period, noted that "the Department of State is establishing its largest mission in its history." Senator John Kerry worried that the United States was "replacing a military presence with a private mercenary presence." The smaller number of remaining troops would oversee the $10 billion in U.S. contracts to arm the Iraqi military with tanks, fighter jets, and other weapons, $3 billion of which the U.S. government was paying for. The United States was also spending close to $1 billion per year to train the Iraqi police.[165]

The final tally would be almost 4,500 U.S. troops killed and more than 32,000 wounded. Tens of thousands more suffered from PTSD and other psychological ailments. Estimates of Iraqi deaths ranged from 150,000 to over 1 million. In October 2006, a team of U.S. and Iraqi epidemiologists reported 655,000 "excess" Iraqi deaths resulting from the U.S. invasion.[166] The United States had spent close to $1 trillion dollars, but that was a small down payment on what the final cost would amount to.

Obama welcomed the troops home at Fort Bragg. But instead of honestly

Villagers work to destroy a poppy field in the district of Por Chaman in Farah Province, Afghanistan. Such efforts had little effect, as the opium trade boomed during the years of the Karzai administration, leading to both spiraling addiction and rampant government corruption.

treating the Iraq War as the unmitigated disaster it had been for the United States, drawing some poignant lessons, and thanking those gathered for their sacrifice, Obama felt compelled to cloak the war's end in the kind of patriotic drivel that conjured up the powerfully haunting words of Rudyard Kipling, the erstwhile proponent of empire, who had convinced his son to enlist in the First World War, only to have him die his first day of combat. In his "Epitaphs of the War," Kipling wrote: "If any question why we died / Tell them, because our fathers lied."[167] Obama's lies would sear just as deeply and painfully. "We're leaving behind a sovereign, stable and self-reliant Iraq, with a representative government that was elected by its people," he told the troops, praising their "extraordinary achievement." The "most important lesson," he declared, was "about our national character . . . that there's nothing we Americans can't do when we stick together. . . . And that's why the United States military is the most respected institution in our land." He commended their willingness to sacrifice "so much for a people that you had never met," which, he insisted, was "part of what makes us special as Americans. Unlike the old empires, we don't make these sacrifices for territory or for resources. We do it because it's right. There can be no fuller expression of America's support for self-determination than our leaving Iraq to its people. That says something about who we are." Having rewritten the history of Iraq, he turned to Afghanistan, claiming that the troops had also "broken the momentum of the Taliban." The wars, he assured them, had made "America stronger and the world more secure." Reaching deep into the repository of America's sacred myths, he saluted the source of U.S. greatness, "the values that are written into our founding documents, and a unique willingness among nations to pay a great price for the progress of human freedom and dignity. This is who we are. That's what we do as Americans, together." He reminded them that they were "part of an unbroken line of heroes spanning two centuries—from the colonists who overthrew an empire, to your grandparents and parents who faced down fascism and communism, to you—men and women who fought for the same principles in Fallujah and Kandahar, and delivered justice to those who attacked us on 9/11."

One would be hard-pressed to know where to begin dissecting the distortions and debunking the myths, but, as we have shown throughout these pages, the notions of American altruism, benevolence, and self-sacrifice might be a good place to start, especially when combined with an explicit disavowal of interest in territories and resources. Obama identified America's uniqueness among nations as its "willingness . . . to pay a great price for the progress of human freedom and dignity." The wars, he absurdly claimed, had made the United States "stronger and the world more secure." He compared the troops who had slaughtered hundreds of Iraqi civilians in Fallujah to the American colonists "who overthrew an empire" and to the World War II generation who "faced down fascism." Perhaps he hadn't seen the American-flag burning jubilation of Fallujah's crowds during their Day of Resistance and Freedom that commemorated the U.S. departure from Iraq. Perhaps he hadn't read the accounts by U.S. marines of wanton and often indiscriminate killing of Iraqi civilians, including women and children, in Haditha and elsewhere throughout the country. Perhaps he hadn't seen the commander of U.S. forces in Anbar Province's explanation of why he didn't investigate U.S. troops' random killing of 24 Iraqi civilians in Haditha. "It happened all the time . . . ," he explained, "throughout the whole country." And in what was either the most contemptible lie since the early days of the Bush administration or unfortunately sloppy and careless phrasing, Obama congratulated the troops for having "fought for the same principles in Fallujah and Kandahar, and delivered justice to those who attacked us on 9/11," adding credence to the Bush-Cheney fabrication that the invasion of Iraq was somehow justified by Saddam's support for Al-Qaeda and perpetuating the dangerous illusion that the occupation of either country, as of 2011, had anything at all to do with that initial Al-Qaeda attack.[168]

The words were barely out of Obama's mouth before "stable" Iraq fell back into chaos. Within days, the country was wracked with a series of suicide bomb-ings that left scores dead and hundreds injured and the country on the verge of relapse into civil war. Sunnis were feeling particularly aggrieved. The coalition government that U.S. officials had finally managed to cobble together nearly eight months after the 2010 election had effectively collapsed. Prime Minister Nuri Kamal al-Maliki, a Shiite, had issued an arrest warrant for Vice President Tariq al-Hashimi, a Sunni, charging him with running a death squad out of his office, and had tried to unseat the Sunni deputy prime minister. Hashimi fled to the Kurdish region to escape arrest. Maliki's security forces had already arrested hundreds of Sunni opposition leaders and former Baathists in recent weeks while Maliki tightened his control over the army and police. Opponents accused him of becoming a dictator. Sunnis and secular critics boycotted Parliament. For months, Sunni provinces had been demanding greater autonomy, along the lines the Kurds had established in oil-rich Kurdistan, which had its own Parliament, president, and security forces. The country threatened to split into three separate regions.

Iraqi disdain for the American "sacrifice" that had disposed of a hated dic-tator but resulted in death and wounding of hundreds of thousands of Iraqi civilians was reflected in the fact that most senior Iraqis who were invited to what the *Washington Post* described as a "seemingly endless process of military ceremonies" did not attend. The United States had actually stopped holding large base-closing ceremonies the previous spring because insurgents were using them as an opportunity to launch attacks. One gathering particu-larly stood out. On December 17, U.S. and Iraqi officials assembled for a sign-ing ceremony to turn Contingency Operating Base Adder, the last U.S. base in Iraq, which once housed 12,000 U.S. troops and contractors, over to the Iraqi Air Force. The *Post's* Greg Jaffe described the scene. First, a "six-man Iraq band, clad in dirty blue uniforms, played a ragged marching song on dented trumpets and trombones." Following that, "an Iraqi military officer cheered in Arabic, clapped and stomped his feet. Soon the mostly Iraqi crowd was chanting and cheering with him." Jaffe noted that "an American military officer sat stiffly on the stage behind a sign marked 'colonel.'" The Iraqi speaker next shouted, "This is the end of the American occupation. May God have mercy on our martyrs." The remain-ing U.S. forces snuck off in the dead of night in what the paper described as "a secret predawn convoy to Kuwait."[169]

The two wars had been unmitigated disasters. Even Gates, on some level, ac-knowledged the indefensibility of ever again plunging the United States into the invasion of another country. In February 2011, he told West Point cadets, "In my opinion, any future defense secretary who advises the president to again send a

*Splattered with blood, five-year-old Samar Hassan cries
desperately after her parents were killed when they mistakenly
drove toward U.S. troops on dusk patrol in the Iraqi district
of Tal Afar. Estimates of civilian casualties vary widely.*

big American land army into Asia or into the Middle East or Africa should 'have his head examined,' as General MacArthur so delicately put it."[170]

The consequences of years of misguided and shortsighted U.S. policies were coming home to roost around the world. Nowhere was this more apparent than in the Middle East, where the United States was largely relegated to the role of bystander as the Arab Spring's extraordinary democratic upheaval was fundamentally transforming the region that the United States had done so much to shape. Decades of uncritically supporting Israel while arming, training, and propping up one Arab dictator after another, as well as the post-9/11 use of Egyptians, Libyans, and others as surrogate torturers, had stripped the United States of all moral authority. Its professions of democracy rang hollow. Nor could anyone take seriously U.S. outrage about repressive regimes using force against their citizens after U.S. forces in Iraq and Afghanistan had directly or indirectly been responsible for the killing and maiming of hundreds of thousands of civilians.

Even the goodwill generated by Obama's Cairo speech proved short-lived. Ghaith al-Omari, executive director of the American Task Force on Palestine, spoke for activists throughout the region: "It's become fashionable now to 'diss' the Americans," he said. "The prevalent mood now is to say that the United States is no longer relevant, that the Arab Spring is happening without the help of the United States."[171] Former International Atomic Energy Agency director and Nobel Peace Prize recipient Mohamed ElBaradei blamed the United States for decades of backwardness and repression throughout the region. "America," he charged, "is really pushing Egypt and pushing the whole Arab world into radicalization with this inept policy of supporting repression."[172]

United States support for regime change and the assassination of Muammar Gaddafi in Libya on the pretext of preventing threatened atrocities reeked of hypocrisy when stacked against prolonged U.S. inaction in the face of actual atrocities being perpetrated by governments in Bahrain, Yemen, Syria, and elsewhere or fierce internal repression in Saudi Arabia, where Wahhabi extremists continued to fund Al-Qaeda and other global jihadis. The lesson seemed to be that only U.S. allies were permitted to slaughter and repress their citizens.

In fact, when criticizing repressive Middle Eastern regimes, Obama pointedly omitted mention of Saudi Arabia, whose reactionary monarchy the United States had propped up for six decades in return for Saudi oil. Saudi Arabia had long been the largest purchaser of advanced U.S. weaponry. The *Wall Street Journal* projected that the sale Obama approved in 2010 might top $60 billion. Now with the Saudis helping thwart democratic reform throughout the region, intervening politically, monetarily, and, in the case of Bahrain, even militarily, the United States proved itself an unreliable ally for those seeking progressive change.

The United States was also trapped by its continued embrace of an Israeli government that had moved sharply to the right. Obama appeared to have more sympathy for the Palestinian position than his predecessors and his choice of George Mitchell as special envoy to the Middle East raised hopes that the United States would support an evenhanded settlement of the outstanding issues. Paramount among them was the presence of a half million Jewish settlers in Israeli-occupied East Jerusalem and the West Bank. Compounding this problem was the Israeli blockade of Gaza following Hamas's election in 2006. Everyone, with the exception of Israel's right-wing government under Bibi Netanyahu and members of the conservative Israel lobby in the United States, recognized that this was not only unjust and untenable, but that it threatened the continuation of Israel's increasingly tenuous democracy.

However, it was not Mitchell but Dennis Ross, Obama's chief Middle East advisor, who prevailed in internal debates. Ross, a Wolfowitz protégé and advisor to presidents going back to Reagan, was a staunch defender of Israel. In May 2011, King Abdullah II of Jordan complained that "we get good responses" from the State Department and Pentagon, "but not from the White House, and we know the reason why is because of Dennis Ross." Ross and Mitchell were at odds over whether the United States should propose a comprehensive peace plan for the region. Mitchell thought it might put needed pressure on a Netanyahu government that continued its illegal settlements policy and resistance to a meaningful two-state solution. Ross argued against pressuring Israel. The well-organized Israel lobby, which exercised inordinate influence in the United States, endorsed that view. Frustrated by Obama's buckling to pressure from the American Israel Public Affairs Committee (AIPAC), Mitchell resigned in April 2011.[173]

The United States again expressed contempt for world opinion over the Israeli-Palestinian conflict with its veto of the UN Security Council resolution condemning Israeli settlements on Palestinian territory not only as illegal but as an obstacle to peace. The resolution was sponsored by at least 130 nations and supported by all 14 other members of the Security Council. While the Obama administration sought to curry favor with AIPAC—the most conservative branch of the powerful Israel lobby—much of the world looked toward a UN vote to recognize an independent Palestinian state despite the vociferous opposition of the United States and Israel.

Though Israel and the United States managed to sidetrack that effort, the Israelis had grown increasingly isolated. The ouster of Hosni Mubarak in Egypt and growing Turkish support for the Palestinians had cost Israel two of its closest regional allies. Islamists were on the rise throughout the region. Thomas Friedman blamed this on "50 years of Arab dictatorship, in which only Islamists were allowed to organize in mosques while no independent, secular, democratic parties were allowed to develop in the political arena."[174] The uprising in neighboring Syria against the brutal Assad regime, although a major setback to Iran and Hezbollah, added another element of instability on Israel's border, exacerbated by the danger that Syria's large stockpile of chemical weapons might fall into the hands of Islamic extremists. Still, Netanyahu and his right-wing allies remained intransigent, expanding settlements in East Jerusalem and the West Bank in defiance not only of Obama but of universal opinion and knowing full well that such actions would undermine the prospects for a two-state solution.

Avraham Burg, former speaker of the Israeli Knesset, wondered if Israeli leaders had any intention of finding an equitable resolution. "Can we continue to exist without a perennial adversary, without being victims of persecution?" he asked. Distinguished Israeli intellectual Zeev Sternhell provided an answer in an article in *Haaretz* aptly titled "Israeli Right Needs Perpetual War."[175]

It was war with Iran that most captivated the right-wing Israeli imagination. Israeli hawks tried to build support for an attack on Iranian nuclear facilities, which they alleged were being used to produce a nuclear bomb. There was good reason to make sure that Iran did not reach that point, particularly because it might trigger a nuclear arms race throughout the region, with Saudi Arabia, Turkey, Egypt, Syria, and possibly others quickly following suit. In September 2011, Iran inaugurated the Middle East's first nuclear power plant at Bushehr, a Russian-built model. But other Middle Eastern nations were not far behind, with dozens of nuclear reactors set to come on line beginning in 2017 or 2018. Iran insisted it had no intention to build a bomb and continued to allow international monitors into the country. Israel, on the other hand, was widely believed to possess some 200 nuclear weapons. The U.S. intelligence committee stood by its 2007 National Intelligence Estimate, which concluded that Iran had stopped working on nuclear weapons in 2003 and not restarted the program. U.S. officials warned the Israelis that a preemptive attack would not only likely fail to achieve the desired results, it could lead to disastrous and destabilizing consequences in the region and beyond. They hoped that strengthening sanctions against Iranian oil exports and Iran's Central Bank would quiet the demand for military action.

Israel had come dangerously close to launching such an attack in 2010. In June 2011, Meir Dagan, who had headed the Israeli spy agency Mossad for eight years before stepping down the previous September, revealed that he, military chief of staff Gabi Ashkenazi, and Yuval Diskin, director of the Shin Bet internal security agency, had managed to block such reckless behavior on the part of Netanyahu and Israeli Defense Minister Ehud Barak. But now that all three were out of office, Dagan feared what Israel's leaders might do. Dagan explained, "I decided to speak out because when I was in office, Diskin, Ashkenazi and I could block any dangerous adventure. Now I am afraid that there is no one to stop Bibi and Barak." Other reports indicated that President Shimon Peres, Israeli Defense Forces Senior Commander Gadi Eisenkot, and recently retired chief of military intelligence Amos Yadlin had also opposed attacking Iran.[176]

A majority of Israelis also rejected a military strike. A November 2011 poll found that only 43 percent of Israeli Jews backed an attack although 90 percent believed that Iran would succeed in acquiring nuclear weapons. Sixty-four percent supported turning the region into a nuclear-free zone even though that would require Israel to give up its nuclear arsenal.[177]

The erosion of U.S. power and influence has also been obvious in Latin America, where, like in the Middle East, the effects of a century of supporting dictators who favored U.S. business and political interests over the well-being of their own people had resulted in a wave of anti-Americanism that swept the continent in the early years of the twenty-first century. Aside from tolerating the ousting of President Manuel Zelaya in Honduras, the United States had been largely unable to stop the leftist trend sweeping Central and South America. Even Colombia, the closest U.S. ally, had been reassessing its ties to the "colossus" of the north. Since taking office in 2010, Colombia's President Juan Manuel Santos has not only taken steps to reduce the enormous gap between Colombia's rich and poor, he has mended relations with Venezuela and Ecuador and now calls Hugo Chávez his "new best friend."[178]

In December 2011, Chávez convened a two-day summit of Latin American and Caribbean heads of state in Caracas. The colorful and controversial Venezuelan leader let it be known that his goal was to establish a hemispheric counterweight to the U.S.-dominated Organization of American States (OAS). Unlike the OAS, the new organization—the thirty-three-member Community of Latin American and Caribbean States (CELAC)—included Cuba and excluded the United States and Canada. Chávez proclaimed the summit "the most important political event in our America in 100 years or more." Cuban President Raul Castro was even more grandiose, anointing the new organization as potentially "the biggest event in our 200 years of semi-independence." The new organization was intended to further lessen U.S. influence in the region. "We are sentencing the Monroe Doctrine to death," announced Nicaraguan President Daniel Ortega, referring to President James Monroe's 1823 assertion that the Western Hemisphere was the United States' sphere of influence. "It's great to be here in the land of Bolívar," Paraguay's President Fernando Lugo told an interviewer, in reference to Simon Bolívar, the lionized Caracas-born nineteenth-century liberator of South America. "Bolívar's dream is becoming concrete little by little," he added.[179] Even U.S. allies like Presidents Felipe Calderón of Mexico, Juan Manuel Santos of Colombia, and Sebastián Piñera of Chile showed up for the inaugural event.

The United States was further isolated when Obama attended the Summit of the Americas in April 2012. Meeting in the Colombian coastal city of Cartagena, leaders of the Western Hemisphere, emboldened by the Caracas gathering, openly defied the United States in a way that was unprecedented and invigorating. Debate centered on two issues that were fundamental to hemispheric relations—the exclusion of Cuba and the U.S.-backed war on drugs. Whereas the United States had previously set the agenda and dictated the terms of the discussion, that was no longer the case. President Calderón described the change—the frankness with which the issues were discussed—as "radical and unthinkable." An article on the summit in the *Jamaica Observer* was headlined, "Summit shows how much Yanqui influence had waned."

Latin American leaders made clear that they had had it with U.S. efforts to ban Cuban participation, a stance defended only by the United States and

Canada. Members of the Bolivarian Alliance of the Americas (ALBA)—a group of Latin American states that had formed in 2004—said that they would not participate in another summit meeting without Cuba. Santos dismissed U.S. policy toward Cuba as "anachronistic" and "ineffective" and demanded Cuban inclusion, as did Brazil's Dilma Rousseff, who also indicated she would no longer attend without Cuba. Though defending U.S. policy, Obama noted that the discussion reminded him of "gunboat diplomacy and Yankees and the cold war."

Some of the leaders also challenged the United States on its drug policy, which Obama again defended despite his own admitted youthful indulgence. Guatemala's President Otto Perez Molina declared the forty-year-old war on drugs a failure and called for decriminalization. Santos noted that Colombia's own successful efforts to reduce coca cultivation had only resulted in a production spike in Peru and Bolivia and that drug violence, while lowered in Colombia, had now spilled over to Mexico, Guatemala, and Honduras.[180]

And in an act of unprecedented defiance, in August 2012, Ecuadorian President Rafael Correa outraged U.S., British, and Swedish authorities by offering political asylum to Julian Assange. Assange had holed up in the Ecuadorian embassy to avoid extradition to Sweden, where he was under investigation for sexual assault. He feared that once in Sweden, he would be extradited to the United States. The British were so disturbed by Ecuador's actions that they threatened to storm the Ecuadorian embassy and arrest Assange, which would constitute a flagrant violation of international law.

In June 2012, Paraguay's right-wing forces fought back with a parliamentary coup in that impoverished nation, impeaching left-leaning President Fernando Lugo, whose moderate program of land reform threatened Paraguay's wealthy landed interests and multinational agricultural corporations. The *International Herald Tribune* went out of its way to comment on the fact that the United States, which once called the shots in Latin America, had become irrelevant to political processes in the region.[181] However, by its refusal to join hemispheric neighbors in condemning the action, the United States was effectively sending a signal of support. Not so other Latin American nations. Argentina, Brazil, and Uruguay voted to suspend Paraguay from the South American free trade association Mercosur and invite Venezuela to join as a full member. Paraguay had been blocking Venezuela's membership in the trade organization, which operates by consensus.

Despite repeated setbacks in the Middle East and Latin America, U.S. military strength remained unchallenged. As Chalmers Johnson revealed years ago, the United States maintains its global hegemony not through an empire of colonies, but through an empire of bases strung across the planet. Journalist Nick Turse found it impossible to ascertain the exact number, but found evidence to indicate that the total was over 1,000. And the cost of maintaining this vast network was tens of billions of dollars. In 2010, the United States still had 124 bases in Japan, 38 of which were in Okinawa alone. South Korea still had 87.[182] In 2012, anthropologist David Vine confirmed that the total number of bases, despite the closure of 505 bases in Iraq, was still more than 1,000 and the annual cost of maintaining that global network of bases and 255,000 overseas troops was around $250 billion. Forces were being shifted, in large part, from mammoth Cold War–style bases to widely dispersed smaller bases known as "lily pads" that could serve as jumping-off points for highly mobile U.S. troops. Such bases were proliferating in the Middle East, Asia, and Latin America.[183] And the U.S. military was rapidly expanding its presence in Africa. China, America's new global rival, had no overseas bases.

The nation faced a quandary. The post–Cold War world refused to play by its rules. Neither its unprecedented military strength nor its overwhelming economic power translated into an ability to bend history in the ways U.S. leaders desired. The world seemed to be spinning increasingly out of U.S. control. Nothing symbolized this more than the rise of China, with its 1.3 billion people, booming economy (almost 40 percent of which remained state-owned), and authoritarian Communist Party–controlled political system. China's economic growth, while extraordinary under any circumstances, stood out even more starkly when measured alongside U.S. economic stagnation and decline. In 2011, China's per capita GDP, though still only 9 percent that of the United States, was double what it had been four years earlier. And Chinese leaders were projecting another doubling in the next four years. China had already replaced Japan as the world's second largest economy, having jumped remarkably from number seven in 2003. Indicative of future prospects, the Urban Land Institute and Ernst & Young reported that China devoted 9 percent of its GDP to infrastructure— more than triple the portion invested by the United States.[184]

China's new economic clout in October 2011 came into sharp relief when Europe asked China for help in saving the euro, inviting it to invest tens of billions of dollars in Europe's emergency stability fund. China was, in effect, being asked to assume the role long played by the United States as the world's financial leader. China had already bought up key economic assets in Europe, which had become China's largest trading partner. Although China balked at investing so heavily at a time when Europe's economic situation remained so precarious, the significance was unmistakable, especially coming just weeks after Timothy Geithner's advice to a gathering of European finance ministers had been so rudely dismissed. The *New York Times* aptly titled its front-page article "Advice on Debt? Europe Suggests U.S. Can Keep It."

Believing that recent developments had proven the superiority of its economic and political systems to those in the declining West, China had been asserting itself in other ways as well. Most troubling to U.S. leaders and Asian neighbors alike, China was rapidly modernizing its military. Defense spending had tripled to $160 billion in the course of one decade. It was building a blue-water navy. It added warships, submarines, fighter jets, and offensive missiles and armed its first aircraft carrier.

The military modernization would not have been so alarming to China's neighbors if China had not also aggressively pressed claims to disputed oil-, gas-, and mineral-rich islands and territories in the East and South China Seas. China's claims to the South China Seas alone conflicted with claims by Vietnam, Indonesia, the Philippines, Malaysia, Taiwan, and Brunei. In the East China Sea, tension remained high between China and Japan. Relations were punctuated with a series of confrontations that aroused passions on all sides. The rhetoric heated up. In October 2011, China's widely read and stridently nationalistic *Global Times* wrote threateningly, "If these countries don't want to change their ways with China, they will need to prepare for the sound of cannons. We need to be ready for that, as it may be the only way for the disputes in the sea to be resolved."[185]

China's military buildup, aggressive pursuit of energy and raw materials, and bullying of its weaker neighbors gave the United States the opening it was looking for. Instead of helping resolve the disputes amicably, U.S. leaders decided to exploit regional tensions and exaggerate the Chinese threat. In hyping China's military buildup, U.S. officials neglected to mention that China had in the past two decades substantially decreased the size of its army, the number of planes in its air force, and its fleet of submarines, and that the proportion of its GDP devoted to defense spending was in line with that of Japan, South Korea, and Taiwan.

The United States appeared ready to use this manufactured crisis not only to reassert U.S. hegemony in Asia and justify a bloated, if shrinking, defense budget, but to halt the overall decline in U.S. power and prestige. With all the trappings of a new cold war, the United States set out to "contain" China economically, militarily, and politically, and pressed other Asian nations to assist in the effort.

Secretary of State Hillary Clinton had thrown down the gauntlet with an article in the November 2011 issue of *Foreign Policy* magazine bluntly titled "America's Pacific Century." The article began, "As the war in Iraq winds down and America begins to withdraw its forces from Afghanistan, the United States stands at a pivot point." The dramatic change she heralded would be "a substantially increased investment—diplomatic, economic, strategic, and otherwise—in the Asia-Pacific region,"[186] which included the Indian Ocean as well as the Pacific.

Obama reinforced that message during his eight-day trip to the Pacific later that month. He informed the Australian Parliament, "In the Asia-Pacific century, the U.S. is all in. . . . I've therefore made a deliberate and strategic decision—as a Pacific nation the United States will play a larger and long-term role in shaping this region and its future." "The United States is a Pacific power, and we are here to stay," he said, even predicting the downfall of the Chinese Communist Party. Impending cuts in U.S. defense spending, he assured the Aussies, "will not—I repeat, will not—come at the expense of the Asia-Pacific." Proving his point, Obama announced that the United States would deploy 2,500 marines to Australia in what amounted to the first long-term U.S. troop increase in Asia since Vietnam, reversing decades of steady decline.[187] The increase would come on top of the 85,000 troops the United States already had in the Pacific, where seven of its eleven aircraft carriers and eighteen nuclear submarines were based.

From Australia, Obama went to Bali, Indonesia, for the annual meeting of the ten-nation Association of Southeast Asian Nations (ASEAN) and became the first U.S. president to attend the larger East Asia Summit meeting. During the summit, Obama joined with other participants in confronting Premier Wen Jiabao over China's South China Sea claims. Obama pledged to strengthen ties with each of the participants and announced that the United States was selling twenty-four F-16 fighters to the Indonesian air force. He also surprised attendees by unveiling plans to dispatch Secretary of State Clinton to Myanmar to repair U.S. relations with that Chinese ally.

Clinton was in the Philippines when Obama visited Australia. From the deck of a U.S. warship in Manila Bay, she signaled U.S. support for the Philippines' position in the South China Sea dispute. The United States had previously conducted joint naval exercises with the Philippines in June and then did so with Vietnam in July. In September, the United States and Vietnam signed a memorandum of understanding on defense cooperation. The once bitter enemies even discussed possible U.S. naval access to the port at Cam Ranh Bay. Vietnam announced a 35 percent increase in defense spending in 2012. The United States had also divulged plans to station some of its littoral combat ships in Singapore.

In December, the Philippines relaunched its biggest and most modern warship, a U.S. coast guard cutter. A Thai newspaper described the scene: "As a navy brass band played, Roman Catholic priests sprinkled holy water on the deck of the newly repainted warship, equipped with antiaircraft guns and a newly refurbished surveillance helicopter on the flight deck. Three navy planes flew past and officials broke a bottle of sugarcane wine on the bow as the ship went into commission." Officials also unveiled the Philippines' first troop- and tank-carrying ship and announced plans to purchase another coast guard cutter and fighter jets from the United States.[188] In July 2012, with tensions flaring anew over the disputed islands, President Benigno Aquino III announced plans to purchase helicopters and other aircraft that could be used in military confrontation. Malaysia, too, showed off its enhanced military strength by displaying its newly acquired submarines. Malaysia has extensive oil and gas resources in the South China Sea.

Admiral Robert Willard, commander of U.S. Pacific Command, indicated that efforts were also under way to fortify strategic ties with India to counter China's growing strength.[189] India loomed large in the effort to contain China. Despite the imposition of sanctions on India following its May 1998 nuclear tests, in March 2000 Bill Clinton became the first U.S. president to visit New Delhi in twenty-two years. The *New York Times* described the visit as a "lovefest." George W. Bush went much further to bolster U.S.-India ties. After 9/11, he lifted all sanctions and later established a military alliance. In 2006, he signed a nuclear cooperation agreement with India despite the fact that India was a nonsignatory to the Nuclear Nonproliferation Treaty (NPT). Though limited to civilian uses of nuclear power, this was a clear violation of the NPT and one that freed India to enhance its nuclear weapons program. The United States first had to gain approval of the forty-five nations that comprised the Nuclear Suppliers Group, a consortium that the United States had established following India's illegal 1974 test. "The administration bullied and wheedled international approval of the president's ill-conceived nuclear deal with India," charged a *Times* editorial. Ron Somers, president of the United States-India Business Council, called it a "tectonic shift" in relations between the two countries.[190] It was also a major setback to nonproliferation efforts.

Obama accelerated the strategic partnership, hosting the Indian prime minister at his first White House state banquet, pushing ahead with implementation of the nuclear agreement despite strong opposition from some of his own advisors, and solidifying the military alliance established by Bush. Hillary Clinton declared it the joint responsibility of the United States and India to "determine the course of the world."[191] Obama's three-day visit to India in November 2010 strengthened the partnership.

In November 2011, India's defense ministry approved a massive $12 billion military modernization program, which would include the Indian army's largest expansion on its border with China since the 1962 war. The Center for Strategic and International Studies estimated that India would spend a total of $80 billion by 2015. India had already been the world's leading arms importer between 2006 and 2011. To counter China's growing naval power, India planned to spend $45 billion on 103 new warships over the next twenty years.[192]

India's elevated levels of defense spending seemed even more objectionable in light of its persistent widespread poverty and the enormous gap between rich and poor. A survey of 73,000 households in nine of India's poorer states released in early 2012 found that 42 percent of children under the age of five were malnourished. "The problem of malnutrition is a matter of national shame," acknowledged Prime Minister Manmohan Singh, who continued to spend lavishly on unneeded weaponry.[193]

The United States had no patience for those who vacillated, as Japanese Prime Minister Yukio Hatoyama learned when he tried to renegotiate the agreement to relocate the large U.S. marine air base within Okinawa from Futenma to Henoko. Obama insisted that Japan abide by its commitment, despite fierce opposition by the Okinawans themselves. When Hatoyama caved to U.S. pressure, his government collapsed.

Hatoyama's successor, Naoto Kan, learned his lesson. In late December 2010, Japan announced a shift in military doctrine to deemphasize the threat from Russia to the north and shift resources to combating China and North Korea. Japan's Special Defense Forces would also cooperate much more closely with the United States, Australia, and South Korea. The new National Defense Program Guidelines called for increasing Japan's submarine fleet from sixteen to twenty-two, adding several new fighter jets, and cutting the number of tanks to create a more mobile force that could quickly dispatch troops to deal with crises in the China Seas or Korea. In December 2011, Japan announced purchase of some forty Lockheed Martin F-35 stealth fighter jets at a cost estimated at between $6 and $8 billion dollars, despite the desperate need for funds to rebuild after the previous March's devastating earthquake, tsunami, and nuclear accident.

Chinese leaders accused the United States of trying to encircle them, insisting that it was the United States, not China, that was projecting military power in the region. China, they maintained, had tried to peacefully resolve its disputes with its neighbors. They expressed outrage over Obama's approval of $5.8 billion in arms sales to Taiwan after having approved $6.4 billion the previous year. Congressional Republicans demanded even more, to which a senior administration official replied that compared to Bush, Obama had "provided twice the amount in half the time." The *People's Daily,* the official Chinese newspaper, informed the United States that it could forget about Chinese cooperation on other global issues: "American politicians are totally mistaken if they believe they can, on the one hand, demand that China behave as a responsible great power and cooperate with the United States on this and that issue, while on the other hand irresponsibly and wantonly harm China's core interests."[194] The Chinese were also angry over other perceived slights, including Obama's decision to meet with the Dalai Lama after choosing not to do so earlier in his administration when he was trying to improve relations with China.

The United States had also let slip that it was developing a new war strategy for Asia called the AirSea Battle Concept. Although highly classified, mention of it first appeared in the United States' 2010 Quadrennial Defense Review. It was designed as a way to coordinate U.S. naval and air forces to counter China's growing ability to disrupt the United States' high-tech weapons and communications systems and thereby interfere with its ability to project its military power in a conflict. U.S. military leaders pointed to the threat from China's "anti-access" strategy, which would limit U.S. ability to militarily aid allies. The fear, according to Andrew Krepinevich of the Center for Strategic and Budgetary Assessments (CSBA), was that such Chinese action would give it control of sea lanes in the Western Pacific.[195] Speaking at the U.S. Air Force Academy, Secretary of Defense Robert Gates said that such threats "appear designed to neutralize the advantages the US military has enjoyed since the end of the cold war—unfettered freedom of movement and the ability to project power to any region across the globe by surging aircraft ships, troops and supplies."[196]

Chinese leaders understood that it was actually their shipping that was being threatened by tightened U.S. control over the South China Sea through which tankers carrying most of China's oil imports passed. They pledged to resolve outstanding regional differences peacefully. But they also made clear that they would defend their interests. In a December address to China's Central Military Commission, President Hu Jintao told the navy to "make extended preparations for warfare."[197]

Also included in that calculation was war with the United States. When CSBA, one of the defense think tanks that had been gaming large-scale warfare with China for the Pentagon, issued a report on the topic in 2010, "the PLA (China's People's Liberation Army) went nuts," according to a U.S. official who had just returned from Beijing. An internal report prepared for the Marine Corps commandant warned that "an Air-Sea Battle-focused Navy and Air Force would be preposterously expensive to build," and, if used in war between the United States and China, would produce "incalculable human and economic destruction."[198]

In pushing the confrontation with China, the United States and its Pacific allies were playing a very dangerous game. Their economic dependence on China made them particularly vulnerable to retaliation. As the holder of over $1 trillion in U.S. treasury bonds, China had the U.S. economy by the throat. Could the United States really afford to risk a hostile relationship with its biggest creditor? And, complicating matters further, China had replaced the United States as the biggest trading partner of all the Asian nations. In 2004, the United States had been the largest trading partner of the ten nations that comprised ASEAN. By 2011, China was first and the United States had fallen to fourth. In December, Japan and China announced that their currencies would convert directly into each other, obviating the need for each to buy dollars before converting them into the other's currency. Such a move not only would expand trade between the two nations, it represented an important step toward making the yuan an alternate reserve currency to the dollar as China desired.

Undeterred, the United States persisted in the effort to bolster its economic position. In fall 2011, it formed a free trade group, the Trans-Pacific Partnership, with allies in Asia, Latin America, and North America. It did not invite China to join, which made Fred Hu, the former chairman of Goldman Sachs in greater China who now chaired the Primavera Capital Group financial advisory firm, wonder, "How can you have a credible trade organization if you exclude the biggest trading nation?"

In a parallel military move, the United States Pacific Command invited Russia and India to participate in a major naval exercise off Hawaii in June 2012. China was not invited to join.[199]

U.S. hegemonic pretensions remained lofty, but U.S. ability to police Asia and the rest of the globe was constrained by the dimensions of its budget crisis. By 2010, the U.S. was spending $1.6 trillion over revenues in its $3.8 trillion budget. The shortfall was borrowed largely from China and Japan. Debt service alone cost $250 billion. The military budget, including black operations, intelligence, foreign military aid, private contractors, and veterans' benefits, totaled over $1 trillion. Christopher Hellman of the National Priorities Project calculated that the U.S. actually spends over $1.2 trillion out of its $3 trillion annual budget on "defense," when all military- and security-related expenses are factored in.[200]

That figure approximately equaled what the rest of the world spent. Even during the height of the Cold War, the United States spent only 26 percent of the world total. As Congressman Barney Frank observed, "We have fewer enemies and we're spending more money." U.S. military spending consumed approximately 44 percent of all U.S. tax revenues. Maintaining bases cost approximately $250 billion. Hiring the Pentagon's vast army of private contractors, which, according to the *Washington Post*, totaled 1.2 million people, cost almost as much. New and costly high-tech weapons systems added to the burden. Did all this spending make Americans safer? Frank commented, "I don't think any terrorist has ever been shot by a nuclear submarine."[201]

In 2011, the Obama administration announced plans to reduce the Pentagon budget by at least $450 billion over the coming decade with additional cuts of $500 billion looming if Congress failed to meet other revenue goals. But Obama and Leon Panetta, who had moved from CIA to Defense, made clear that the restructuring would not impinge upon the U.S. shift toward Asia. They rejected proposals to cut the number of aircraft carriers from eleven to ten and planned to increase investment in the long-range stealth bombers and antimissile systems considered essential in combating China as well as armed drones, cyberspace systems, and rapid-deployment aircraft. In June 2012, Panetta notified a conference of defense officials from twenty-eight Asia-Pacific nations that the United States would "rebalance" its forces. By 2020, 60 percent of U.S. naval forces would be in the Pacific and only 40 percent in the Atlantic, a substantial shift from its 50-50 split in 2012. U.S. forces will include, Panetta explained, "six aircraft carriers in this region, a majority of our cruisers, destroyers, Littoral Combat Ships, and submarines." In case anyone missed the point, Panetta outlined some of the United States' spending priorities: "We are investing specifically in . . . an advanced fifth-generation fighter, an enhanced Virginia-class submarine, new electronic warfare and communications capabilities, and improved precision weapons—that will provide our forces with freedom of maneuver in areas in which our access and freedom of action may be threatened. We recognize the challenges of operating over the Pacific's vast distances. That is why we are investing in new aerial-refueling tankers, a new bomber, and advanced maritime patrol and anti-submarine warfare aircraft." And if that weren't sufficient, Panetta had the gall to remind listeners, including officials from China, the Philippines, Japan, Korea, Indonesia, Laos, Cambodia, and Vietnam, that "over the course of history, the United States has fought wars, we have spilled blood, we have deployed our forces time and time again to defend our vital interests in the Asia-Pacific region."[202] He insisted, with a straight face, that stepped-up U.S. efforts in the region were not aimed at containing China. Even the *New York Times* noted that "few in the audience said they believed that." Indonesia's foreign minister voiced the views of many who resented U.S. pressure to choose sides, a seeming throwback to John Foster Dulles's 1950s attacks on nations that refused to choose sides in the Cold War, commenting, "What worries us is having to choose—we don't want to be put in that position."[203]

U.S. plans to militarize the region were coming up against other obstacles as well. Some of America's Asian allies were confronting the same budgetary constraints that were impeding U.S. efforts. In May 2012, Australia, where Obama had kicked off his Asian tour a few months earlier, announced cuts in defense spending of 10.5 percent or $5.5 billion over the next four years, which, according to the Australian Strategic Policy Institute, would represent the lowest percentage of gross domestic product since 1938. The *Sydney (Australia) Morning Herald* warned that "Events in Canberra and Washington raise serious questions about the ability of the alliance partners to give effect to their grand pledges to each other. On the Australian side, it is stunningly clear what's happened. The Gillard government has chosen to reduce Australia's defence effort to its feeblest in 74 years. . . . The government weighed its priorities, and defence came in at the bottom."[204]

For the United States, with the Pacific off the table, defense savings would come, in part, from cutting the size of the army from 570,000 to 490,000 and lowering force levels in Europe. Joining Panetta at the Pentagon in early January 2012, Obama declared, "We're turning the page on a decade of war. . . . We'll be able to ensure our security with smaller conventional ground forces. We'll continue to get rid of outdated Cold War–era systems so that we can invest in the capabilities we need for the future."[205]

While cutting defense spending, pulling combat forces out of Iraq, and beginning the drawdown in Afghanistan represented a welcome retreat from the hypermilitarism of the Bush-Cheney years, they did not represent the sharp and definitive break with empire that the world needed to see from the United States and that Obama had been encouraged to pursue by the man who had engineered the end of the Soviet Empire: Mikhail Gorbachev. Gorbachev had pressed Obama to pursue the kind of bold initiatives that had allowed Gorbachev to change the course of history. "America needs perestroika right now . . . ," he said in 2009, "because the problems he has to deal with are not easy ones." Gorbachev called for ending the kind of unregulated free market policies that caused the global economic downturn and perpetuated the gap between the world's rich and poor. The United States, he warned, can no longer dictate to the rest of the world. "Everyone is used to America as the shepherd that tells everyone what to do. But this period has already ended." He condemned the Clinton and Bush administrations' dangerous militarization of international politics and urged the United States to withdraw from Afghanistan as Russia had done over twenty years ago when Gorbachev inherited a similarly disastrous and unpopular war.[206]

As 2012 dawned, the world was in extraordinary flux. U.S. global power had eroded, opening the door to an exciting array of possibilities, some fraught with dangers of their own. Recognizing the extraordinary upheaval that rattled ruling elites across the globe in 2011, *Time* magazine had just named "The Protester" its person of the year. The spark had actually been ignited in December 2010 when Mohamed Bouazizi, a twenty-six-year-old Tunisian street vendor, having been humiliated by police one too many times, set himself on fire. That simple and desperate act sparked a massive popular rebellion in Tunisia that overthrew the twenty-three-year rule of Zine El Abidine Ben Ali. The sight of ordinary Tunisians standing up fearlessly to their police state rulers struck a chord with millions who had suffered their own indignities at the hands of corrupt, dictatorial regimes that, more often than not, had been backed and armed by the United States. The movement spread quickly to Algeria, Egypt, and across the Arab world. The WikiLeaks release, beginning in February 2011, of a quarter million U.S. diplomatic cables poured fuel on an already burning fire. Protests in Libya, Syria, Yemen, and Bahrain were soon spiraling out of government control. Opposition to government- and banker-imposed austerity swept across Europe, most prominently in Spain, Greece, Italy, France, and Britain. Chinese citizens defied their government officials in protests against corruption and inequality. Russians rose up against vote fraud and Vladimir Putin's autocratic rule. Japanese expressed outrage over government and power company deception in the aftermath of the Fukushima nuclear disaster.

And in the United States, the Occupy Wall Street movement brought desperately needed attention to the tremendous and ever growing gap between the wealthiest 1 percent and the rest of the population—the 99 percent. The Pew Research Center reported in January 2012 that two-thirds of Americans believed that "strong" conflicts existed between rich and poor, a 19 percent increase since Pew's July 2009 survey. Thirty percent felt there were "very strong conflicts," a 50 percent jump in two and a half years.[207] This was no surprise given the fact that the net worth of the median American family had dropped 39 percent in three years from $126,400 in 2007 to just $77,300 in 2010, according to the Survey of Financial Resources issued every three years by the Federal Reserve. Those without high school diplomas saw their net worth plummet by 54 percent. In 2012, Joseph Stiglitz calculated that the combined $90 billion wealth of the six Walmart heirs equaled that of the bottom 30 percent of Americans.[208] The movement also raised profound and troubling questions about U.S. priorities in the aftermath of the financial meltdown. Budget cuts, though often ill-conceived, had forced Americans to reconsider the wisdom of the imperial project itself. At a time when unemployment soared, infrastructure decayed, and social services were decimated, could the United States really afford to maintain its vast global empire? Was it really in the U.S. interest to police the planet? Should the United States ever again invade countries that posed no threat to the American people?

The prospect for reform at home also brightened. The movement, harkening back to the workers' rights, social justice, and antiwar struggles of the 1930s and 1960s, ignited the imagination of millions across the country, especially America's youth. Suffused with a sense of utopian possibilities for the first time in decades, Americans began to ponder what a fair, equitable, and just society might look like. No longer would they tolerate the inordinate power and influence the wealthy exercised in dominating all spheres of public and private life. And the impact of the Occupy movement was felt far beyond its own ranks as its egalitarian and redistributionist sentiments reshaped political discourse in the United States. The broadening link between renewed U.S. activism and democratic strivings on a global scale augured well for the future.

But monumental problems exist that demand attention. Global warming threatens the future of life on the planet in ways that only nuclear war had done previously. It is already melting the Arctic and Antarctic ice caps, raising ocean levels, causing floods and droughts, expanding the reach of deadly diseases, and ruining global food and water supplies. The United States itself reels from the effects of record temperatures, disastrous hurricanes, floods, forest fires, and droughts rivaling the Dust Bowl of the 1930s. Nor has the nuclear threat by any means abated. The danger of nuclear proliferation, even nuclear anarchy, continues. Nuclear arsenals remain far in excess of the megatonnage that experts believe necessary to trigger a life-extinguishing nuclear winter. And despite Obama's professed commitment, the prospects for substantial reductions, let alone complete abolition, seem bleak.

In what would presage a remarkable turnaround if it continues, even Barack Obama began showing faint signs of returning to the transformational figure he had appeared to be during the 2008 campaign. Spurred by the Occupy Wall Street movement's success in getting out its message, continued Republican intransigence, economic stagnation, budgetary constraints, and tumbling approval ratings, by late 2011 Obama appeared to be regaining some of his old dynamism. Traces of populism crept into his speeches. He openly embraced ending the Iraq War and cutting defense spending, even though both developments had been forced upon him. Was there a chance that he might be undergoing a Kennedyesque road-to-Damascus conversion and realizing how poorly American militarism and imperialism had served the American people and the rest of the world? The prospects looked dim, and his Fort Bragg speech and willingness to sign the extremely dangerous 2012 Defense Authorization bill were not encouraging. What had become apparent was that the real hope for changing the United States—for helping it regain its democratic, egalitarian, and revolutionary soul—lay in U.S. citizens joining with the rebellious masses everywhere to deploy the lessons of history, their history, the people's history, which is no longer untold, and demand creation of a world that represents the interests of the overwhelming majority, not that of the wealthiest, greediest, and most powerful. Building such a movement is also the only hope to save American democracy from the clutches of an ever-expanding, ever-encroaching national security state. Such tyranny was a threat that America's revolutionary leaders understood very well. When a woman asked Benjamin Franklin in 1787, after the Constitutional Convention, "Well, Doctor, what have we got—a republic or a monarchy?" Franklin responded with words as timely today as when he uttered them, "A republic, Madam, if you can keep it."[209]

ACKNOWLEDGMENTS

A project of this scope required the support, assistance, and forbearance of a large number of people. On the film side, we'd like to thank the following: Fernando Sulichin for finding the financing and maintaining his composure through difficult times; Rob Wilson and Tara Tremaine were anchors from the beginning, culling archives around the world; Alex Marquez edited on and off through four years and many late nights, aided at various intervals by Elliot Eisman, Alexis Chavez, and Sean Stone; on the aural side, Craig Armstrong, Adam Peters, and Budd Carr—and Wylie Stateman; in the administrative grapple, Evan Bates and Suzie Gilbert; and Steven Pines for managing the money out of thin air. Many thanks to Showtime, through two different administrations—David Nevins for his insights; and the help of Bryan Lourd, Jeff Jacobs, Simon Green, and Kevin Cooper.

On the book side, we are indebted to Peter's colleagues and graduate students in American University's History Department. Max Paul Friedman lent his expertise on the history of U.S. foreign policy, reading the entire manuscript with painstaking care, challenging some of our interpretations and saving us from errors both large and small. Because U.S.-Soviet and U.S.-Russian relations figure so prominently in our story, we drew heavily on the expertise of Russian historian Anton Fedyashin, who was always ready to answer questions and check Russian language sources to make sure we got things right. Among Peter's other colleagues who responded with generosity to questions regarding their own fields of historical scholarship were professors Mustafa Aksakal, Richard Breitman, Phil Brenner, Ira Klein, Allan Lichtman, Eric Lohr, and Anna Nelson.

Among the graduate students, Eric Singer and Ben Bennett were indispensable. They took vast amounts of time out of their own research and writing to help with a variety of research tasks. Eric was a master at tracking down obscure information that no one else could find. Ben, among his many contributions, took charge of finding the visuals that add such an important dimension to this book. Other current and former Ph.D. students who worked extensively on this project include Rebecca DeWolf, Cindy Gueli, Vincent Intondi, Matt Pembleton, Terumi Rafferty-Osaki and Jay Weixelbaum. Additional research assistance and fertile leads were provided by Daniel Cipriani, Nguyet Nguyen, David Onkst, Allen Pietrobon, Arie Serota, and Keith Skillin.

Numerous friends and colleagues also provided invaluable assistance along the way. Daniel Ellsberg was extremely generous with his insights, suggestions, critical readings, and enthusiastic support. His knowledge of much of this history remains unsurpassed. Among the other scholars who gave generously of their time and expertise, answered questions, and suggested documents are Gar Alperovitz, Robert Berkowitz, Bill Burr, Bob Dreyfuss, Carolyn Eisenberg, Ham Fish, Michael Flynn, Irena Grudzinska Gross, Hugh Gusterson, Anita Kondoyanidi, Bill Lanouette, Milton Leitenberg, Robert Jay Lifton, Arjun Makhijani, Ray McGovern, Roger Morris, Satoko Oka Norimatsu, Robert Norris, Robert Parry, Leo Ribuffo, Jonathan Schell, Peter Dale Scott, Mark Selden, Marty Sherwin, Chuck Strozier, Janine Wedel, and Larry Wittner.

Because the project has taken as long as it has, we were sad to lose four of our biggest supporters along the way—Howard Zinn, Bob Griffith, Charlie Wiener, and Uday Mohan.

Barbara Koeppel provided additional assistance with the visuals and captions. Erin Hamilton offered valuable insights on Chile. Matt Smith and Clement Ho of the American University library were extremely helpful with finding sources and providing other assistance.

The team at Gallery Books did everything they could to meet our often unwieldy requests as we rushed to complete the two projects on schedule. We are especially indebted to our editor, Jeremie Ruby-Strauss, and his assistant, Heather Hunt. We would also like to thank Louise Burke, Jen Bergstrom, Jessica Chin, Emily Drum, Elisa Rivlin, Emilia Pisani, Tricia Boczkowski, Sally Franklin, Jen Robinson, Larry Pekarek, and Davina Mock.

Peter's daughter Lexie and his wife, Simki Kuznick, helped with research and footnoting and Simki pored patiently over numerous drafts of this manuscript with the skill of an editor and the eye of a poet.

NOTES

INTRODUCTION: ROOTS OF EMPIRE: "WAR IS A RACKET"

1   Lloyd C. Gardner, Walter F. LaFeber, and Thomas J. McCormick, *Creation of the American Empire,* vol. 1: *U.S. Diplomatic History to 1901* (Chicago: Rand McNally College Publishing, 1976), 108.

2   Alfred W. McCoy, Francisco A. Scarano, and Courtney Johnson, "On the Tropic of Cancer: Transitions and Transformations in the U.S. Imperial State," in *Colonial Crucible: Empire in the Making of the Modern American State,* ed. Alfred W. McCoy and Francisco A. Scarano (Madison: University of Wisconsin Press, 2009), 21.

3   J. M. Coetzee, *Waiting for the Barbarians* (London: Secker & Warburg, 1980), 133.

4   Sam Dillon, "U.S. Students Remain Poor at History, Tests Show," *New York Times,* June 15, 2011.

5   President Woodrow Wilson speaking on the League of Nations to a luncheon audience in Portland, OR. 66th Cong., 1st sess. *Senate Documents: Addresses of President Wilson* (May–November 1919), vol. 11, no. 120, p. 206.

6   Barack Obama, News Conference, April 4, 2009, www.presidency.ucsb.edu/ws/index .php?pid=85959&st=american+exceptionalism&st1=#axzz1RXk$VS7z.

7   Jonathan Martin and Ben Smith, "The New Battle: What It`¡ Means to Be American," August 20, 2010, www.politico.com/news/stories/0810/41273.html.

8   Nina J. Easton, "Thunder on the Right," *American Journalism Review* 23 (December 2001), 320.

9   Emily Eakin, "Ideas and Trends: All Roads Lead to D.C.," *New York Times,* March 31, 2002.

10   Ibid.

11   William Appleman Williams, *Empire as a Way of Life: An Essay on the Causes and Character of America's Present Predicament Along with a Few Thoughts About an Alternative* (New York: Oxford University Press, 1980), 62.

12   Samuel P. Huntington, *The Clash of Civilizations and the Remaking of World Order* (New York: Simon & Schuster, 1996), 51.

13   Max Boot, "American Imperialism? No Need to Run Away from Label," *USA Today,* May 6, 2003.

14   Niall Ferguson, *Colossus: The Price of America's Empire* (New York: Penguin, 2004), 14–15.

15   Paul Kennedy, "The Eagle Has Landed," *Financial Times,* February 22, 2002.

16   Jonathan Freedland, "Is America the New Rome?" *Guardian,* September 18, 2002.

17   "Joint Vision 2010," www.dtic.mil/jv2010/jvpub.htm; General Howell M. Estes III, USAF, United States Space Command, "Vision for 2020," February 1997, www.fas

.org/spp/military/docops/usspac/visbook.pdf; "Joint Vision 2020," www.dtic.mil/jointvision/jvpub2.htm.

18   Benjamin J. Cohen, *The Question of Imperialism: The Political Economy of Dominance and Dependence* (New York: Basic Books, 1973), 23.

19   Amiya Kumar Bacgchi, *Perilous Passage: Mankind and the Global Ascendance of Capital* (Lanham, MD: Rowman & Littlefield, 2005), 272.

20   Paul Kennedy, *The Rise and Fall of the Great Powers: Economic Change and Military Conflict from 1500 to 2000* (New York: Vintage Books, 1989), 150.

21   Lars Shoultz, *Beneath the United States: A History of U.S. Policy Toward Latin America* (Cambridge, MA: Harvard University Press, 1998), 86.

22   Walt Whitman, *Complete Poetry and Collected Prose* (New York: Viking, 1982), 1074.

23   Robert V. Bruce, *1877: Year of Violence* (Chicago: Ivan R. Dee, 1989), 225–226.

24   Philip Sheldon Foner, *The Great Labor Uprising of 1877* (New York: Monad Press, 1975), 157.

25   Philip Sheldon Foner, *History of the Labor Movement in the United States,* vol. 2: *From the Founding of the A.F. of L. to the Emergence of American Imperialism* (New York: International Publishers, 1975), 50.

26   Maury Klein, *The Life and Legend of Jay Gould* (Baltimore: Johns Hopkins University Press, 1997), 357.

27   Ida Minerva Tarbell, *All in the Day's Work: An Autobiography* (Urbana: University of Illinois Press, 2003), 82.

28   John D. Hicks, *Populist Revolt: A History of the Farmers' Alliance and the People's Party* (Minneapolis: University of Minnesota Press, 1931), 140, 440.

29   Walter LaFeber, *The New Empire: An Interpretation of American Expansion, 1860–1898* (Ithaca, NY: Cornell University Press, 1998), 366.

30   Robert L. Beisner, *Twelve Against Empire: The Anti-Imperialists 1898-1900* (New York: McGraw Hill, 1968), xiv.

31   William Roscoe Thayer, ed. "John Hay's Years with Roosevelt," *Harper's Magazine* 131 (1915), 578.

32   Homer Clyde Stuntz, *The Philippines and the Far East* (Cincinnati: Jennings and Pye, 1904), 144.

33   John Byrne Cooke, *Reporting the War: Freedom of the Press from the American Revolution to the War on Terrorism* (New York: Palgrave Macmillan, 2007), 78.

34   "Ratification of the Treaty Now Assured," *Chicago Tribune,* February 6, 1899.

35   "Treaty Wins in the Senate by One Vote," *Chicago Tribune,* February 7, 1899.

36   Stephen Kinzer, *Overthrow: America's Century of Regime Change from Hawaii to Iraq* (New York: Times Books, 2006), 49.

37   George Frisbie Hoar, *Autobiography of Seventy Years,* vol. 2 (New York: Charles Scribner's Sons, 1905), 304.

38   "Gain for the Treaty," *New York Times,* February 6, 1899.

39   Kinzer, *Overthrow,* 52–53.

40   David Howard Bain, *Sitting in Darkness: Americans in the Philippines* (New York: Houghton Mifflin, 1984), 84.

41   *Congressional Record,* Senate, 56th Cong., 1st Sess., 1900, vol. 33, pt. 1, 704.

42   William Jennings Bryan, *Speeches of William Jennings Bryan,* vol. 2 (New York: Funk & Wagnalls, 1909), 17, 24–26. For an excellent biography of Bryan, see Michael Kazin, *A Godly Hero: The Life of William Jennings Bryan* (New York: Alfred A. Knopf, 2006).

43   Stuart Creighton Miller, *Benevolent Assimilation: The American Conquest of the Philippines, 1899–1903* (New Haven, CT: Yale University Press, 1982), 211.

44   Henry Moore Teller, *The Problem in the Philippines* (Washington, DC: U.S. Government Printing Office, 1902), 52.

45   Epifanio San Juan, *Crisis in the Philippines: The Making of a Revolution* (South Hadley, MA: Bergin & Garvey, 1986), 19.

46   Some estimate that the death toll among Filipinos was higher than 600,000. See John M. Gates, "War-Related Deaths in the Philippines, 1898–1902," *Pacific Historical Review* 53 (1984), 367–378.

47   Eric Rauchway, *Murdering McKinley: The Making of Theodore Roosevelt's America* (New York: Hill & Wang, 2003), 102.

48   Howard C. Hill, *Roosevelt and the Caribbean* (Chicago: University of Chicago Press, 1927), 67.

49   Schoultz, *Beneath the United States,* 191.

50   Richard F. Grimmett, "Instances of Use of United States Armed Forces Abroad, 1798–2009," January 27, 2010, Congressional Research Service, www.fas.org/sgp/crs/natsec/RL32170.pdf.

51   Walter LaFeber, *Inevitable Revolutions: The United States in Central America* (New York: W. W. Norton, 1993), 42.

52   Ibid., 46.

53   Ibid., 50.

54   "The Republic of Brown Bros.," *Nation,* 114 (1922), 667.

55   LaFeber, *Inevitable Revolutions,* 69.

56   Howard Zinn and Anthony Arnove, *Voices of a People's History of the United States,* 2nd. ed. (New York: Seven Stories Press, 2009), 251–252.

CHAPTER 1: WORLD WAR I: WILSON VS. LENIN

1   William Appleman Williams, *The Tragedy of American Diplomacy* (New York: W. W. Norton, 1988), 72.

2   Richard Slotkin, *Gunfighter Nation: The Myth of the Frontier in Twentieth-Century America* (New York: HarperPerennial, 1992), 240.

3   Richard Hofstadter, *The American Political Tradition and the Men Who Made It* (New York: Alfred A. Knopf, 1949), 237–241.

4   Lloyd C. Gardner, *Wilson and Revolutions: 1913–1921* (New York: J. B. Lippincott, 1976), 12.

5   Walter LaFeber, *The American Age: United States Foreign Policy at Home and Abroad Since 1750* (New York: W. W. Norton, 1989), 262; Lloyd C. Gardner, Walter F. LaFeber, and Thomas J. McCormick, *Creation of the American Empire,* vol. 2: *U.S. Diplomatic History Since 1893* (Chicago: Rand McNally, 1976), 305.

6   George C. Herring, *From Colony to Superpower: U.S. Foreign Relations Since 1776* (New York: Oxford University Press, 2008), 390.

7   Gardner, LaFeber, and McCormick, *Creation of the American Empire,* vol. 2, 306–307; LaFeber, *The American Age,* 278.

8   Williams, *The Tragedy of American Diplomacy,* 70.

9   Lars Schoultz, *Beneath the United States: A History of U.S. Policy Toward Latin America* (Cambridge, MA: Harvard University Press, 1998), 246.

10   Nicholas D. Kristof, "Our Broken Escalator," *New York Times,* July 17, 2011.

11   Howard Zinn, *A People's History of the United States* (New York: Harper Colophon, 1980), 350.

12   Nell Irvin Painter, *Standing at Armageddon: The United States, 1877–1919* (New York: W. W. Norton, 1987), 293.

13   Ray Ginger, *The Bending Cross: A Biography of Eugene Victor Debs* (New Brunswick, NJ: Rutgers University Press, 1949), 328.

14   Herring, *From Colony to Superpower,* 399.

15   Kathryn S. Olmsted, *Real Enemies: Conspiracy Theories and American Democracy, World War I to 9/11* (New York: Oxford University Press, 2009), 34.

16   "Notes Linking Wilson to Morgan War Loans," *Washington Post,* January 8, 1936.

17   Herring, *From Colony to Superpower,* 403, 409–410.

18   "Scene in the Senate as President Speaks," *New York Times,* January 23, 1917.

19   "Amazement and Bewilderment Caused by Proposal of Wilson for Peace Pact for the World," *Atlanta Constitution,* January 23, 1917.

20   LaFeber, *The American Age,* 278; Carter Jefferson, *Anatole France: The Politics of Skepticism* (New Brunswick, NJ: Rutgers University Press, 1965), 195.

21   Thomas J. Knock, *To End All Wars: Woodrow Wilson and the Quest for a New World Order* (New York: Oxford University Press, 1992), 118.

22   Ibid., 120.

23   Ibid., 121, 131.

24   David M. Kennedy, *Over Here: The First World War and American Society* (New York: Oxford University Press, 1992), 184–185.

25   Ibid., 60–62.

26   William Graebner, *The Engineering of Consent: Democracy and Authority in Twentieth-Century America* (Madison: University of Wisconsin Press, 1987), 42.

27   Victor S. Clark, "The German Press and the War," *Historical Outlook* 10 (November 1919), 427.

28   "Shows German Aim to Control World," *New York Times,* December 3, 1917.

29   Stewart Halsey Ross, *Propaganda for War: How the United States Was Conditioned to Fight the Great War of 1914–1918* (Jefferson, NC: McFarland & Co., 1996), 241.

30   "Documents Prove Lenin and Trotzky Hired by Germans," *New York Times,* September 15, 1918.

31   Ross, *Propaganda for War,* 241.

32   "Creel Upholds Russian Exposure," *New York Times,* September 22, 1918.

33   "Spurns Sisson Data," *Washington Post,* September 22, 1918.

34   Ross, *Propaganda for War,* 241–242.

35   "The Sisson Documents," *Nation,* November 23, 1918, in Philip Sheldon Foner, *The Bolshevik Revolution: Its Impact on American Radicals, Liberals, and Labor* (New York: International Publishers, 1967), 137.

36   George F. Kennan, "The Sisson Documents," *Journal of Modern History* 28 (June 1956), 130–154.

37   Charles Angoff, "The Higher Learning Goes to War," *The American Mercury,* May–August 1927, 178.

38   Harold D. Lasswell, *Propaganda Technique in the World War* (New York: Alfred A. Knopf, 1927), 14–15.

39   "Oust Traitors, Says Butler," *New York Times,* June 7, 1917.

40   "Columbia Ousts Two Professors, Foes of War Plans," *New York Times,* October 2, 1917.

41   "The Expulsions at Columbia," *New York Times,* October 3, 1917.

42   "Quits Columbia; Assails Trustees," *New York Times,* October 9, 1917.

43   Ibid.

44   Horace Cornelius Peterson and Gilbert Courtland Fite, *Opponents of War, 1917–1918* (Madison: University of Wisconsin Press, 1957), 104–112.

45   Carol S. Gruber, *Mars and Minerva: World War I and the Uses of the Higher Learning in America* (Baton Rouge: Louisiana State University Press, 1975), 213–214.

46   "War Directed College Course to be Intensive," *Chicago Tribune,* September 1, 1918.

47   Gruber, *Mars and Minerva,* 217–218, 237–244; Kennedy, *Over Here,* 57–59.

48   "Bankers Cheer Demand to Oust Senator La Follette; 'Like Poison in Food of Army,'" *Chicago Tribune,* September 28, 1917.

49   Gruber, *Mars and Minerva,* 208.

50   Zinn, *A People's History of the United States,* 356.

51   Painter, *Standing at Armageddon,* 335; Kennedy, *Over Here,* 76.

52   "Sedition Act of 1918," www.pbs.org/wnet/supremecourt/capitalism/sources document1.html.

53   Nick Salvatore, *Eugene V. Debs: Citizen and Socialist* (Urbana: University of Illinois Press, 1982), 292.

54   Zinn, *A People's History of the United States,* 358.

55   Ibid., 358–359.

56   Ibid., 359.

57   "The I.W.W.," *New York Times,* August 4, 1917.

58   Kennedy, *Over Here,* 67–68; Knock, *To End All Wars,* 133; Alan Axelrod, *Selling the Great War: The Making of American Propaganda* (New York: Palgrave Macmillan, 2009), 181–182.

59   Painter, *Standing at Armageddon,* 335.

60   "Stamping Out Treason," *Washington Post,* April 12, 1918.

61   Zinn, *A People's History of the United States,* 355–356.

62   Painter, *Standing at Armageddon,* 336.

63   John D'Emilio and Estelle B. Freedman, *Intimate Matters: A History of Sexuality in America* (Chicago: University of Chicago Press, 1998), 212–213.

64   Barbara Meil Hobson, *Uneasy Virtue: The Politics of Prostitution and the American Reform Tradition* (Chicago: University of Chicago Press, 1990), 169, 176–177; Mark Thomas Connelly, *The Response to Prostitution in the Progressive Era* (Chapel Hill: University of North Carolina Press, 1980), 143–145.

65   Allan M. Brandt, *No Magic Bullet: A Social History of Venereal Disease in the United States Since 1880* (New York: Oxford University Press, 1987), 59–60, 101; Connelly, 140; Kennedy, *Over Here,* 186.

66   Brandt, *No Magic Bullet,* 101–106; Kennedy, *Over Here,* 186–187.

67   Brandt, *No Magic Bullet,* 116–119.

68   Randolph Bourne, "Unfinished Fragment on the State," in *Untimely Papers,* ed. James Oppenheim (New York: B. W. Huebsch, 1919), 145.

69   Jonathan B. Tucker, *War of Nerves: Chemical Warfare from World War I to Al-Qaeda* (New York: Pantheon Books, 2006), 10.

70   Wyndham D. Miles, "The Idea of Chemical Warfare in Modern Times," *Journal of the History of Ideas* 31 (April–June 1970), 300–303.

71   "Declaration (IV, 2) Concerning Asphyxiating Gases," Document 3 in Adam Roberts and Richard Guelff, ed. *Documents on the Laws of War,* 3rd ed. (New York: Oxford University Press, 2000), 60.

72   "Crazed by Gas Bombs," *Washington Post,* April 26, 1915.

73   "New and Peculiar Military Cruelties Which Arise to Characterize Every War," *Washington Post,* May 30, 1915.

74   "Topics of the Times," *New York Times,* May 8, 1915.

75   James Hershberg, *James B. Conant: Harvard to Hiroshima and the Making of the Nuclear Age* (New York: Alfred A. Knopf, 1993), 44.

76   David Jerome Rhees, "The Chemists' Crusade: The Rise of an Industrial Science in Modern America, 1907–1922," PhD Thesis, University of Pennsylvania, 1987, 169; Hershberg, *James B. Conant,* 45–49.

77   Hershberg, *James B. Conant,* 42.

78   James A. Tyner, *Military Legacies: A World Made by War* (New York: Routledge, 2010), 98–99.

79   Robert A. Millikan, "The New Opportunities in Science," *Science* 50 (September 26, 1919), 292.

80   John D. Moreno, *Undue Risk: Secret State Experiments on Humans* (New York: Routledge, 2001), 38–39; Andy Sagar, " 'Secret, Deadly Research': Camp AU Scene of World War Training Trenches, Drill Field," *Eagle,* American University, January 15, 1965.

81   Sagar, " 'Secret, Deadly Research.' "

82   Moreno, *Undue Risk,* 38–39; Sagar, " 'Secret, Deadly Research.' "

83   Martin K. Gordon, Barry R. Sude, Ruth Ann Overbeck, and Charles Hendricks, "A Brief History of the American University Experiment Station and U.S. Navy Bomb Disposal School, American University," Office of History, U.S. Army Corps of Engineers, June 1994, 12.

84   Hershberg, *James B. Conant,* 46–47.

85   Richard Barry, "America's Most Terrible Weapon: The Greatest Poison Gas Plant in the World Ready for Action When the War Ended," *Current History* (January 1919), 125, 127.

86   Robert Harris and Jeremy Paxman, *A Higher Form of Killing: The Secret History of Chemical and Biological Warfare* (New York: Random House, 2002), 35.

87   Barry, "America's Most Terrible Weapon," 127–128.

88   Dominick Jenkins, *The Final Frontier: America, Science, and Terror* (London: Verso, 2002), 38.

89   Tucker, *War of Nerves,* 19–20.

90   Barry, "America's Most Terrible Weapon," 128.

91   Yuki Tanaka, "British 'Humane Bombing' in Iraq During the Interwar Era," in Yuki Tanaka and Marilyn B. Young, ed. *Bombing Civilians: A Twentieth-Century History* (New York: New Press, 2009), 8, 11.

92   Spencer Tucker, ed., *Encyclopedia of World War I: A Political, Social and Military History* (Santa Barbara, CA: ABC-CLIO, 2005), 57.

93   Tanaka, "British 'Humane Bombing' in Iraq," 13–29.

94   Jenkins, *The Final Frontier,* 2–3.

95   Ibid., 12.

96   Will Irwin, *"The Next War": An Appeal to Common Sense* (New York: E. P. Dutton & Co., 1921), 37–38 (quotes in original).

97   "The Chemical Industry Show," *New York Times,* September 26, 1917.

98   Daniel P. Jones, "American Chemists and the Geneva Protocol," *Isis,* September 1980, 432, 438.

99   Ibid., 433, 438; Tucker, *War of Nerves,* 21–22.

100 Tucker, *War of Nerves,* 20.

101 Gardner, LaFeber, and McCormick, *Creation of the American Empire,* 336.

102 "President Wilson's Message to Congress on War Aims," *Washington Post,* January 9, 1918.

103 Gardner, LaFeber, and McCormick, *Creation of the American Empire,* 343.

104 Ibid., 343; Herring, *From Colony to Superpower,* 423.

105 Robert David Johnson, *The Peace Progressives and American Foreign Relations* (Cambridge, MA: Harvard University Press, 1995), 82–83.

106 "Our Men in Russia at Foch's Demand," *New York Times,* January 10, 1919.

107 Johnson, *The Peace Progressives and American Foreign Relations,* 84, 320 (Table A.1, "Votes on Anti-imperialist Issues," Section J).

108 H. G. Wells, *The Shape of Things to Come* (New York: Macmillan, 1933), 82.

109 Donald Kagan, *On the Origins of War: And the Preservation of Peace* (Doubleday, 1995), 285.

110 LaFeber, *The American Age,* 297.

111 Ibid., 299.

112 Ibid.

113 Woodrow Wilson, *Woodrow Wilson: Essential Writings and Speeches of the Scholar-President,* ed. Mario DiNunzio (New York: New York University Press, 2006), 36.

114 Paul F. Boller, Jr., *Presidential Anecdotes* (New York: Oxford University Press, 1981), 220.

115 Gardner, LaFeber, and McCormick, *Creation of the American Empire,* 340–341.

116 Herring, *From Colony to Superpower,* 418, 426.

117 Gardner, LaFeber, and McCormick, *Creation of the American Empire,* 341.

118 Knock, *To End All Wars,* 223–224, 329, note 76.

119 Boller, *Presidential Anecdotes,* 220–221.

120 John Maynard Keynes, *The Economic Consequences of the Peace* (New York: Harcourt, Brace and Howe, 1920), 36–37, 268.

121 John Lewis Gaddis, *Russia, The Soviet Union, and the United States: An Interpretive History* (New York: Alfred A. Knopf, 1978), 77; John M. Thompson, *Russia, Bolshevism, and the Versailles Peace* (Princeton, NJ: Princeton University Press, 1966), 2; Herring, *From Colony to Superpower,* 422.

122 Gardner, *Wilson and Revolutions,* 341–342.

123 Ibid., 338–339.

124 Robert K. Murray, *Red Scare: A Study in National Hysteria, 1919–1920* (New York: McGraw-Hill, 1955), 124–129.

125 Jeremy Brecher, *Strike!* (1972; reprint, Boston: South End Press, 1977), 126.

126 Olmsted, *Real Enemies,* 19.

127 66th Congress, 1st Session, *Senate Documents: Addresses of President Wilson,* 11, 120 (May–November 1919), 206.

128 Leroy Ashby, *The Spearless Leader: Senator Borah and the Progressive Movement in the 1920's* (Urbana: University of Illinois Press, 1972), 101.

129 Herring, *From Colony to Superpower,* 429.

130 Knock, *To End All Wars,* 186.

131 Ron Chernow, *The House of Morgan: An American Banking Dynasty and the Rise of Modern Finance* (New York: Simon & Schuster, 1990), 206–208.

132 Sally Marks, *The Illusion of Peace: International Relations in Europe, 1918–1933* (New York: St. Martin's Press, 1976), 13, 38–39.

133 David F. Schmitz, *Thank God They're on Our Side: The United States and Right-Wing Dictatorships, 1921–1965* (Chapel Hill: University of North Carolina Press, 1999), 31–45.

134 Daniel Yergin, *The Prize: The Epic Quest for Oil, Money, and Power* (New York: Simon & Schuster, 1991), 176–183.

135 Ibid., 233.

136 Darlene Rivas, "Patriotism and Petroleum: Anti-Americanism in Venezuela from Gómez to Chávez," in *Anti-Americanism in Latin America and the Caribbean,* ed. Alan L. McPherson (New York: Berghahn Books, 2006), 87.

137 Stephen G. Rabe, *The Road to OPEC: United States Relations with Venezuela, 1919–1976* (Austin: University of Texas Press, 1982), 22.

138 Yergin, *The Prize,* 233.

139 Rabe, *The Road to OPEC,* 17, 38, 43.

140 Ibid., 17–18, 36, 38.

141 Nikolas Kozloff, *Hugo Chávez: Oil, Politics, and the Challenge to the U.S.* (New York: Palgrave Macmillan, 2007), 15.

142 Yergin, *The Prize,* 233–236.

143 B. S. McBeth, *Juan Vicente Gómez and the Oil Companies in Venezuela, 1908–1935* (New York: Cambridge University Press, 1983), 70.

144 Rivas, "Patriotism and Petroleum," 93; Rabe, *The Road to OPEC,* 94–116; Yergin, *The Prize,* 436.

145 "Favors Body with Teeth," *New York Times,* August 29, 1920.

146 "The Republic of Brown Bros.," *Nation,* June 7, 1922, 667.

147 John Dos Passos, *Three Soldiers* (New York: George H. Doran, 1921), 209–211.

148 F. Scott Fitzgerald, *This Side of Paradise* (New York: Charles Scribner's Sons, 1920), 282.

149 Ernest Hemingway, *A Moveable Feast: The Restored Edition* (New York: Scribner, 2009), 61.

150 Kennedy, *Over Here,* 187–189; Loren Baritz, *The Servants of Power: A History of the Use of Social Science in American Industry* (New York: John Wiley & Sons, 1974), 43–46.

151 Kennedy, *Over Here,* 188.

152 Merle Curti, "The Changing Concept of 'Human Nature' in the Literature of American Advertising," *The Business History Review* 41 (Winter 1967), 337–353.

153 Noble T. Praigg. *Advertising and Selling: By 150 Advertising and Sales Executives* (New York: Doubleday, 1923), 442.

154 Roland Marchand, *Advertising the American Dream: Making Way for Modernity* (Berkeley: University of California Press, 1985), 69.

155 Ibid., 85.

156 H. L. Mencken, "The Husbandman," in H. L. Mencken, *A Mencken Chrestomathy* (New York: Alfred A. Knopf, 1967), 360–361.

157 Arthur M. Schlesinger, Jr., *The Cycles of American History* (New York: Houghton Mifflin Co., 1986), 16.

CHAPTER 2: THE NEW DEAL: "I WELCOME THEIR HATRED"

1 David M. Kennedy, *Freedom from Fear: The American People in Depression and War, 1929–1945* (New York: Oxford University Press, 1999), 163–164.

2 "Looking to Mr. Roosevelt," *New York Times,* March 4, 1933.

3 Arthur M. Schlesinger, Jr., *The Coming of the New Deal, 1933–1935* (New York: Houghton Mifflin Harcourt, 2003), 13.

4   "Text of New President's Address at Inauguration," *Los Angeles Times,* March 5, 1955.

5   "The Michigan 'Bank Holiday,'" *New York Times,* February 16, 1933; "More States Move to Protect Banks," *New York Times,* March 1, 1933; "Banks Protected in 5 More States," *New York Times,* March 2, 1933.

6   Anne O'Hare McCormick, "Main Street Reappraises Wall Street," *New York Times,* February 28, 1932.

7   "Mitchell Called in Senate Inquiry," *New York Times,* February 2, 1933.

8   Liaquat Ahamed, *Lords of Finance: The Bankers Who Broke the World* (New York: Penguin, 2009), 441; Jonathan Alter, *The Defining Moment: FDR's Hundred Days and the Triumph of Hope* (New York: Simon & Schuster, 2007), 150.

9   Barton J. Bernstein, "The New Deal: The Conservative Achievements of Liberal Reform," in *Towards a New Past: Dissenting Essays in American History,* ed. Barton J. Bernstein (New York: Pantheon, 1968), 268.

10   Francis Perkins, *The Roosevelt I Knew* (New York: Harper Colophon, 1946), 328.

11   Stephen K Shaw, William D. Pederson, and Frank J. Williams, ed. *Franklin D. Roosevelt and the Transformation of the Supreme Court,* vol. 3 (Armonk, NY: M. E. Sharpe, 2004), 83.

12   Robert S. McElvaine, *The Great Depression: America, 1929–1941* (New York: Times Books, 1983), 158; Gary Orren, "The Struggle for Control of the Republican Party," *New York Times,* August 17, 1976.

13   "The Nation: I've Had a Bum Rap," *Time,* May 17, 1976, 19.

14   "National Affairs: Not Since the Armistice," *Time,* September 25, 1933, 12.

15   Hugh S. Johnson, *Blue Eagle, from Egg to Earth* (New York: Doubleday, Doran, 1935), 405; Perkins, 206; McElvaine, 161.

16   Arthur G. Dorland, "Current Events: The Break Down of the London Economic Conference," *Quarterly Review of Commerce,* Autumn 1933, 36–37.

17   Michael Augspurger, "Henry Luce, *Fortune,* and the Attraction of Italian Fascism," *American Studies* 41 (Spring 2000), 115.

18   "Cites Harm to U.S. in 'Patriot Racket,'" *Baltimore Sun,* March 9, 1931.

19   Philip Jenkins, *Hoods and Shirts: The Extreme Right in Pennsylvania, 1925–1950* (Chapel Hill: University of North Carolina Press, 1997), 91.

20   Ibid., 118; "Ballot on Gold 283–5," *New York Times,* May 30, 1933.

21   Peter H. Amann, "A 'Dog in the Nighttime' Problem: American Fascism in the 1930s," *The History Teacher* 19 (August 1986), 572; Alan Brinkley, *Voices of Protest: Huey Long, Father Coughlin, and the Great Depression* (New York: Vintage Books, 1983), 266–277.

22   Michael Kazin, *The Populist Persuasion* (Ithaca, NY: Cornell University Press, 1998), 130.

23   Alan J. Lichtman, *White Protestant Nation: The Rise of the American Conservative Movement* (New York: Atlantic Monthly Press, 2008), 76; Leo P. Ribuffo, *The Old Christian Right* (Philadelphia: Temple University Press, 1983), 25–79, 80–127.

24   Lichtman, *White Protestant Nation,* 76; Jenkins, *Hoods and Shirts,* 101–104; Ribuffo, *The Old Christian Right,* 184–185.

25   Amann, "A 'Dog in the Nighttime' Problem," 566.

26　Kennedy, *Freedom from Fear*, 154; Raymond Moley, *After Seven Years* (New York: Harper & Brothers, 1939), 369–370.

27　"Defends Current Policy," *New York Times*, November 10, 1933; Franklyn Waltman, Jr., "Morgan Call on President Is Surprise," *Washington Post*, November 17, 1933; "More Loans Urged by Irénée DuPont," *New York Times*, December 31, 1933.

28　"Moley Says Banks Back Gold Policy," *New York Times*, December 4, 1933.

29　"Smith Hurls Broadside Against Gold Program," *Los Angeles Times*, November 25, 1933.

30　Howard Wood, "Fears for Nation's Future Lead Bankers to Speak Out," *Chicago Tribune*, September 29, 1934.

31　"Business Body Demands U.S. Return to Gold," *Washington Post*, November 4, 1933.

32　"Time to Stop Crying Wolf," *New York Times*, May 4, 1934.

33　"Business: Reassurance," *Time*, October 8, 1934, 56.

34　Kennedy, *Freedom from Fear*, 388–389; Douglas MacArthur, *Reminiscences* (New York: McGraw-Hill, 1964), 101.

35　Arthur Krock, "Tide Sweeps Nation," *New York Times*, November 7, 1934.

36　"Borah Demands a Rebuilt Party," *New York Times*, November 9, 1934.

37　Oswald Garrison Villard, "Russia from a Car Window," *Nation*, November 6, 1929, 517.

38　Louis Fischer, "Russia and the World Crisis," *Nation*, November 25, 1931.

39　"6,000 Artisans Going to Russia, Glad to Take Wages in Roubles," *Business Week*, September 2, 1931; "Amtorg Gets 100,000 Bids for Russia's 6,000 Skilled Jobs," *Business Week*, October 7, 1931.

40　Stuart Chase, "The Engineer as Poet," *New Republic*, May 20, 1931; Stuart Chase, *A New Deal* (New York: Macmillan, 1932), 252.

41　Edmund Wilson, *Travels in Two Democracies* (New York: Harcourt, Brace, 1936), 321.

42　Edmund Wilson, "The Literary Consequences of the Crash," *The Shores of Light: A Literary Chronicle of the Twenties and Thirties* (New York: Farrar, Straus & Young, 1952), 408; Peter J. Kuznick, *Beyond the Laboratory: Scientists as Political Activists in 1930s America* (Chicago: University of Chicago Press, 1987), 106–143.

43　"The Beleaguered City," *Los Angeles Times*, July 17, 1934.

44　"Strike Condemned by Coast Papers," *New York Times*, July 17, 1934.

45　Read Bain, "Scientist as Citizen," *Social Forces* 11 (March 1933), 413–414.

46　Kuznick, *Beyond the Laboratory*, 101–102.

47　Bernstein, "The New Deal," 271.

48　Frank A. Warren, *Liberals and Communism: The Red Decade Revisited* (Bloomington: Indiana University Press, 1966), 6.

49　John Dos Passos, "Whither the American Writer," *Modern Quarterly* 6 (Summer 1932), 11–12.

50　For a chilling account of the murderous policies of Hitler and Stalin, see Timothy Snyder, *Bloodlands: Europe Between Hitler and Stalin* (New York: Basic Books, 2010). Millions of people died in Stalin's deliberately induced Ukrainian famine of 1932 and 1933, during which thousands resorted to cannibalism.

51   Kennedy, *Freedom from Fear*, 278–279.

52   "Text of Roosevelt's Closing Campaign Speech at Madison Square Garden," *Baltimore Sun*, November 1, 1936.

53   Kennedy, *Freedom from Fear*, 286.

54   "President Sets a Record with Electoral Vote," *Chicago Tribune*, November 4, 1936.

55   "Politics and Health," *Nation*, July 30, 1938, 101.

56   "National Health Program Offered by Wagner in Social Security Bill," *New York Times*, March 1, 1939.

57   Peter Kuznick, "Healing the Well-Heeled: The Committee of Physicians and the Defeat of the National Health Program in 1930's America" (1989), unpublished paper; also see Kuznick, *Beyond the Laboratory*, 86–87.

58   Lichtman, *White Protestant Nation*, 68.

59   Ibid., 60–62.

60   Ibid., 69–70.

61   Arthur M. Schlesinger, Jr., *The Politics of Upheaval* (New York: Houghton Mifflin, 1960), 83. "Gen. Butler Bares Fascist Plot to Seize Government by Force," *New York Times*, November 21, 1934.

62   Lichtman, *White Protestant Nation*, 70.

63   Kathryn S. Olmsted, *Real Enemies: Conspiracy Theories and American Democracy, World War I to 9/11* (New York: Oxford University Press, 2009), 30.

64   "Probing War's Causes," *Washington Post*, April 14, 1934.

65   Wayne Cole, *Senator Gerald P. Nye and American Foreign Policy* (Minneapolis: University of Minnesota Press, 1962), 71–73.

66   John E. Wilz, *In Search of Peace: The Senate Munitions Inquiry, 1934–36* (Baton Rouge: Louisiana State University Press, 1963), 37.

67   "Arms and the Men," *Fortune*, March 1934, 53.

68   "Congress Gets Message," *New York Times*, May 19, 1934.

69   "Greed, Intrigue Laid to War Materials Ring," *Washington Post*, June 23, 1934.

70   "Munitions Control by the Government Favored by Senatorial Inquiry Group," *New York Times*, August 30, 1934.

71   "$1,245,000,000 Work to Du Ponts in War," *New York Times*, September 13, 1934.

72   Robert C. Albright, "Du Ponts Paid 458 Per Cent on War Profits," *Washington Post*, September 13, 1934.

73   Robert Albright, "Reich Builds Big Air Force with U.S. Aid, Inquiry Hears," *Washington Post*, September 18, 1934.

74   "Plan of Legion to Curb Profits of War Hailed," *Washington Post*, September 25, 1934.

75   "Nye Plans to Abolish War Profit," *Los Angeles Times*, September 27, 1934.

76   "Arms Inquiry Just Starting, Nye Declares," *Washington Post*, September 29, 1934.

77   "Look Before Leaping," *Washington Post*, October 1, 1934.

78   "Nye Asks 98% Tax for War Incomes," *New York Times*, October 4, 1934.

79   Constance Drexel, "State Ownership Not Arms Problem Remedy," *Washington Post*, December 4, 1934.

80   "The Problem of Munitions," *Chicago Tribune*, December 18, 1934; Walter Lippmann, "Today and Tomorrow," *Los Angeles Times*, December 16, 1934.

81   "Roosevelt Asks Laws to Remove Profit from War," *Los Angeles Times*, December 13, 1934.

82   Raymond Clapper, "Between You and Me," *Washington Post*, December 14, 1934.

83   Cole, *Senator Gerald P. Nye and American Foreign Policy*, 80, 82.

84   "800% War Profit Told at Inquiry; Du Pont Deal Up," *Washington Post*, December 14, 1934.

85   "Senator Nye's Third Degree," *Chicago Tribune*, December 24, 1934.

86   "Roosevelt Backs Munitions Inquiry," *New York Times*, December 27, 1934.

87   "Urge Continuing Munitions Inquiry," *New York Times*, January 11, 1935.

88   "Grace Challenges 100% War Tax Plan," *New York Times*, February 26, 1935; "Huge War Profits Laid to Bethlehem," *New York Times*, February 27, 1935.

89   Eunice Barnard, "Educators Assail Hearst 'Influence,'" *New York Times*, February 25, 1935; Eunice Barnard, "Nye Asks for Data for Press Inquiry," *New York Times*, February 28, 1935.

90   L. C. Speers, "Issue of War Profits Is Now Taking Form," *New York Times*, March 24, 1935; Robert C. Albright, "President Hears Drastic Plan to Take Profit Out of War," *Washington Post*, March 24, 1935; Cole, *Senator Gerald P. Nye and American Foreign Policy*, 85.

91   "House and Senate Clash on Drastic Bills to End All Profiteering in War," *New York Times*, April 3, 1935.

92   "Hostility to War Rules House Votes as Army Parades," *New York Times*, April 7, 1935.

93   Arthur Krock, "In the Nation," *New York Times*, April 11, 1935.

94   "Hedging on Aims Denied by Baruch," *New York Times*, April 17, 1935.

95   "Nye Submits Bill for Big War Taxes," *New York Times*, May 4, 1935.

96   "The Communistic War Bill," *Chicago Tribune*, September 18, 1935.

97   Newton D. Baker, "Our Entry into the War," *New York Times*, November 13, 1935.

98   Thomas W. Lamont, "Mr. Lamont Excepts," *New York Times*, October 25, 1935.

99   "2 Morgan Aides Deny Blocking Arms Inquiry," *Washington Post*, January 7, 1936.

100   Ibid; "Morgan Testifies as Nye Bares Data on War Loans Curbs," *New York Times*, January 8, 1936.

101   Felix Bruner, "Nye Assailed as Senators Leave Arms Investigation," *Washington Post*, January 17, 1936.

102   "Southerner Shakes with Rage as He Defends Chief in Senate," *Washington Post*, January 18, 1936.

103   "Funds Spent, Nye Declares Arms Inquiry Is Postponed," *Washington Post*, January 20, 1936.

104   "Senate Votes Funds for Nye Wind-up," *New York Times*, January 31, 1936.

105   Ray Tucker, "Hard Road to Peace Revealed by Inquiry," *New York Times*, February 9, 1936.

106   "An Inquiry Ends Well," *New York Times*, February 9, 1936.

107   "Nye Denies Inquiry 'Cleared' Morgan," *New York Times*, February 10, 1936.

108   George Gallup, "82% Majority Votes to End Profit of War," *Washington Post*, March 8, 1936.

109   "Munitions Report May Challenge Arms Industry," *Atlanta Constitution*, March 8, 1936.

110   "On Nationalizing Munitions," *Washington Post*, March 9, 1936.

111   Cole, *Senator Gerald P. Nye and American Foreign Policy*, 91–92.

112   "Nye Group Urges U.S. Set Up Its Own Gun Plants," *Chicago Tribune*, April 21, 1936.

113   Max Wallace, *The American Axis: Henry Ford, Charles Lindbergh, and the Rise of the Third Reich* (New York: St. Martin's Press, 2003), 226.

114   Richard S. Tedlow, *The Watson Dynasty: The Fiery Reign and Troubled Legacy of IBM's Founding Father and Son* (New York: HarperCollins, 2003), 129.

115   "British, Nazi Trade Groups Reach Accord," *Chicago Tribune*, March 17, 1939.

116   Theodore J. Kreps, "Cartels, a Phase of Business Haute Politique," *American Economic Review* 35 (May 1945), 297.

117   Kevin Maney, *The Maverick and His Machine: Thomas Watson Sr. and the Making of IBM* (New York: John Wiley & Sons, 2003), 206.

118   "Ford Says It's All a Bluff," *New York Times*, August 29, 1939; Wallace, *The American Axis*, 219.

119   GM spokesman John Mueller claimed that the company had lost day-to-day control over its German operations in September 1939. See Michael Dobbs, "Ford and GM Scrutinized for Alleged Nazi Collaboration," *Washington Post*, November 30, 1998; Wallace, *The American Axis*, 332; Bradford Snell, "American Ground Transport," U.S. Senate, Committee on the Judiciary, February 26, 1974, 17–18.

120   Snell, "American Ground Transport," 16.

121   Edwin Black, *Nazi Nexus: America's Corporate Connections to Hitler's Holocaust* (Washington, DC: Dialog Press, 2009), 9.

122   Ibid., 10; Dobbs, "Ford and GM Scrutinized."

123   Paul A. Lombardo, *A Century of Eugenics in America* (Bloomington: Indiana University Press, 2011), 100; Robert N. Proctor, *Racial Hygiene: Medicine Under the Nazis* (Cambridge, MA: Harvard University Press, 1988).

124   Black, *Nazi Nexus*, 34–35.

125   Daniel J. Kevles, *In the Name of Eugenics: Genetics and the Uses of Human Heredity* (New York: Alfred A. Knopf, 1985), 111; Black, *Nazi Nexus*, 25.

126   Kevles, *In the Name of Eugenics*, 116.

127   Ben Aris and Duncan Campbell, "How Bush's Grandfather Helped Hitler's Rise to Power," *Guardian*, Sep. 25, 2004; Wallace, *The American Axis*, 349.

128   Black, *Nazi Nexus*, 119; Snell, "American Ground Transport," 22.

129   *Research Findings About Ford-Werke Under the Nazi Regime* (Dearborn, MI: Ford Motor Company, 2001), 7, 121–122, http://media.ford.com/events/pdf/0_Research_ Finding_Complete.pdf.

130   Jason Weixelbaum, "The Contradiction of Neutrality and International Finance: The Presidency of Thomas H. McKittrick at the Bank for International Settlements in Basle, Switzerland 1940–1946," http://jasonweixelbaum.wordpress.com/#_ftn85.

131   Dobbs, "Ford and GM Scrutinized."

132   Johnson, *The Peace Progressives*, 292.

133   George C. Herring, *From Colony to Superpower: U.S. Foreign Relations Since 1776* (New York: Oxford University Press, 2008), 503–504.

134   Kennedy, *Freedom from Fear*, 395–396.

135   William L. Shirer, *The Rise and Fall of the Third Reich: A History of Nazi Germany* (New York: Simon & Schuster, 1960), 293.

136   Dominic Tierney, *FDR and the Spanish Civil War: Neutrality and Commitment in the Struggle that Divided America* (Durham, NC: Duke University Press, 2007), 68–69.

137   Kennedy, *Freedom from Fear*, 398–400.

CHAPTER 3: WORLD WAR II: WHO REALLY DEFEATED GERMANY?

1   "The Debate in Commons," *New York Times*, October 4, 1938.

2   David Reynolds, *From Munich to Pearl Harbor: Roosevelt's America and the Origins of the Second World War* (New York: Ivan R. Dee, 2001), 42–49.

3   United States Holocaust Memorial Museum, http://www.ushmm.org/wlc/en/article .php?ModuleId=10007411.

4   Frank L. Kluckhohn, "Line of 4,500 Miles," *New York Times*, September 4, 1940.

5   David M. Kennedy, *Freedom from Fear: The American People in Depression and War, 1929–1945* (New York: Oxford University Press, 1999), 456.

6   John C. Culver and John Hyde, *American Dreamer: The Life and Times of Henry A. Wallace* (New York: W. W. Norton, 2000), 123–125.

7   Arthur Schlesinger, Jr., "Who Was Henry A. Wallace? The Story of a Perplexing and Indomitably Naïve Public Servant," *Los Angeles Times*, March 12, 2000.

8   Peter J. Kuznick, *Beyond the Laboratory: Scientists as Political Activists in 1930s America* (Chicago: University of Chicago Press, 1987), 184–186, 205–206.

9   Samuel I. Rosenman, *Working with Roosevelt* (New York: Harper & Brothers, 1952), 218.

10   Culver and Hyde, *American Dreamer*, 222–223.

11   Charles Hurd, "President Moves," *New York Times*, March 31, 1940.

12   George Bookman, "President Says Program Would Eliminate 'Silly Foolish Dollar Sign,'" *Washington Post*, December 18, 1940.

13   "Mrs. Roosevelt Rebukes Congressmen of G.O.P.," *Los Angeles Times*, January 8, 1941.

14   "Hoover Scores Surrender of Congress," *Washington Post*, January 11, 1941.

15   "Wheeler Sees War in Bill," *Los Angeles Times*, January 13, 1941.

16   Ibid.

17   Robert C. Albright, "President Calls Senator's 'Plow Under . . . Youth' Remark 'Rotten,'" *Washington Post*, January 15, 1941.

18   "Wheeler Asserts Bill Means War," *New York Times*, January 13, 1941.

19   George C. Herring, *Aid to Russia 1941–1946: Strategy, Diplomacy, the Origins of the Cold War* (New York: Columbia University Press, 1973), 5.

20 Kennedy, *Freedom from Fear*, 475.

21 "Basic Fear of War Found in Surveys," *New York Times*, October 22, 1939.

22 David Kennedy pushed the number up to 3.6 million; cf. Kennedy, *Freedom from Fear*, 482.

23 "Text of Pledge by Churchill to Give Russia Aid," *Chicago Tribune*, June 23, 1941.

24 Turner Catledge, "Our Policy Stated," *New York Times*, June 24, 1941.

25 Herring, *Aid to Russia 1941–1946*, 12.

26 "Our Alliance with Barbarism," *Chicago Tribune*, September 2, 1941, 14.

27 Arthur Krock, "US Aid to Soviet Is Found Lagging," *New York Times*, December 3, 1941.

28 Charles A. Beard, *President Roosevelt and the Coming of the War* (Hamden, CT: Archon Books, 1968), 139.

29 Ibid., 141–142.

30 Walter LaFeber, *The American Age: United States Foreign Policy at Home and Abroad Since 1750* (New York: W. W. Norton, 1989), 381–382.

31 Justus D. Doenecke and John E. Wilz, *From Isolation to War, 1931–1941* (American History Series) (Arlington Heights, IL: Harlan Davidson, 1991), 159–161, 168–176.

32 Ronald H. Spector, *In the Ruins of Empire: The Japanese Surrender and the Battle for Postwar Asia* (New York: Random House, 2007), 95.

33 Henry R. Luce, "The American Century," *Life*, February 1941, 61–65.

34 LaFeber, *The American Age*, 380.

35 Henry A. Wallace, *The Price of Vision: The Diary of Henry A. Wallace 1942–1946*, ed. John Morton Blum (New York: Houghton Mifflin, 1973), 635–640.

36 Herring, *Aid to Russia 1941–1946*, 56, 58.

37 Herbert Feis, *Churchill, Roosevelt, Stalin: The War They Waged and the Peace They Sought* (Princeton, NJ: Princeton University Press, 1957), 42.

38 Lloyd C. Gardner, Walter F. LaFeber, and Thomas J. McCormick, *Creation of the American Empire*, vol. 2: *U.S. Diplomatic History Since 1893* (Chicago: Rand McNally, 1976), 425.

39 John Lewis Gaddis, *Russia, The Soviet Union, and the United States* (New York: McGraw-Hill, 1990), 149.

40 Kennedy, *Freedom from Fear*, 573.

41 Allan M. Winkler, *Franklin D. Roosevelt and the Making of Modern America* (New York: Longman, 2006), 235.

42 Kennedy, *Freedom from Fear*, 574.

43 Edward T. Folliard, "Molotov's Visit to White House, Postwar Amity Pledge Revealed," *Washington Post*, June 12, 1942.

44 "US Pledges Europe Attack," *Los Angeles Times*, June 12, 1942.

45 Kennedy, *Freedom from Fear*, 575–576.

46 Mark Sullivan, "A Military Question," *Washington Post*, August 5, 1942.

47 Mark Sullivan, "Mark Sullivan," *Washington Post*, July 12, 1942.

48 John Lewis Gaddis, *The United States and the Origins of the Cold War, 1941–1947* (New York: Columbia University Press, 1972), 69.

49 George C. Herring, *From Colony to Superpower: U.S. Foreign Relations Since 1776* (New York: Oxford University Press, 2008), 547.

50 Mark A. Stoler, *The Politics of the Second Front: American Military Planning and Diplomacy in Coalition Warfare, 1941–1943* (Westport, CT: Greenwood Press, 1977), 55–58, 110.

51 Kennedy, *Freedom from Fear*, 579.

52 "Hull Lauds Soviet Stand," *New York Times*, December 12, 1941.

53 Ralph Parker, "Russian War Zeal Lightens Big Task," *New York Times*, April 4, 1942.

54 Orville Prescott, "Books of the Times," *New York Times*, June 22, 1942.

55 Barnett Nover, "Twelve Months," *Washington Post*, June 22, 1942.

56 Robert Joseph, "Filmland Salutes New Tovarichi," *New York Times*, July 5, 1942.

57 Leland Stowe, "Second Front Held Vital," *Los Angeles Times*, July 7, 1942.

58 Leland Stowe, "Second Front Decision Held Imperative Now: All Signs Point to Powerful Resistance in West if Allies Wait Until Spring," *Los Angeles Times*, August 25, 1942.

59 George Gallup, "Allied Invasion of Europe Is Urged," *New York Times*, July 17, 1942.

60 June Austin, "Letter to the Editor," *Washington Post*, July 10, 1942.

61 "C.I.O. Leaders Ask President to Open Second Front at Once," *Los Angeles Times*, July 18, 1942.

62 "C.I.O. Rally to Ask 2d Front," *New York Times*, July 13, 1942.

63 "Moscow's Newspapers Highlight Second Front," *Atlanta Constitution*, August 2, 1942; "Sees Stand Vindicated," *New York Times*, June 13, 1942.

64 "500 Writers Ask 2d Front," *New York Times*, September 15, 1942.

65 "2d Front Demand Made at Red Rally," *New York Times*, September 25, 1942.

66 "43 May Be Too Late for 2nd Front—Wilkie," *Chicago Tribune*, September 27, 1942.

67 A. J. P. Taylor, *The Second World War: An Illustrated History* (New York: G. P. Putnam's Sons, 1975), 168.

68 Melvyn P. Leffler, *For the Soul of Mankind: The United States, the Soviet Union and the Cold War* (New York: Hill and Wang, 2007), 26.

69 Susan Butler, ed. *My Dear Mr. Stalin: The Complete Correspondence of Franklin D. Roosevelt and Joseph V. Stalin* (New Haven, CT: Yale University Press, 2005), 63.

70 Frances Perkins, *The Roosevelt I Knew* (New York: Harper & Row, 1946), 83–85.

71 Lloyd C. Gardner, *A Covenant with Power: America and World Order from Wilson to Reagan* (New York: Oxford University Press, 1984), 63.

72 Winston Churchill, *Triumph and Tragedy: The Second World War*, vol. vi (Boston: Houghton Mifflin Company, 1953), 214–215; Gaddis, *Russia, The Soviet Union, and the United States*, 154.

73 Edward S. Mason and Robert E. Asher, *The World Bank Since Bretton Woods: The Origins, Policies, Operations, and Impact of the International Bank for Reconstruction* (Washington, DC: Brookings Institution, 1973), 29.

74   Elizabeth Borgwardt, *A New Deal for the World: America's Vision for Human Rights* (Cambridge, MA: Belknap Press, 2005), 252.

75   Warren F. Kimball, *Forged in War: Roosevelt, Churchill, and the Second World War* (New York: William Morrow, 1997), 140.

76   Elliott Roosevelt, *As He Saw It* (New York: Duell, Sloan and Pearce, 1946), 37.

77   Warren F. Kimball, *The Juggler: Franklin Roosevelt as Wartime Statesman* (Princeton, NJ: Princeton University Press, 1991), 144.

78   Lloyd C. Gardner, *Approaching Vietnam: From World War II through Dienbienphu* (New York: W. W. Norton, 1988), 25.

79   Kimball, *The Juggler*, 149, 154.

80   Stephen F. Vogel, *The Pentagon: A History: The Untold Story of the Wartime Race to Build the Pentagon—and to Restore It Sixty Years Later* (New York: Random House, 2007), 42.

81   *New York Times* described it as a "great concrete doughnut of a building." *Newsweek* criticized the building's exterior as "penitentiary-like." Years later, Norman Mailer would observe that the "pale yellow walls" of the Pentagon, which he anointed "the true and high church of the military-industrial complex," were "reminiscent of some plastic plug coming out of the hole made in flesh by an unmentionable operation." See "Mammoth Cave, Washington, DC," *New York Times,* June 27, 1943; Vogel, *The Pentagon: A History,* 306; Norman Mailer, *The Armies of the Night: History as a Novel, the Novel as History* (New York: Signet, 1968) 116, 132.

82   Churchill, *Triumph and Tragedy,* 227–228; Paul Johnson, *Modern Times: The World from the Twenties to the Nineties* (New York: Perennial, 2001), 434.

83   LaFeber, *The American Age,* 413.

84   Howard Jones, *Crucible of Power: A History of American Foreign Relations from 1897* (Lanham, MD: Rowman & Littlefield, 2008), 219.

85   Churchill, *Triumph and Tragedy,* 338.

86   Gaddis, *The United States and the Origins of the Cold War, 1941–1947,* 163.

87   H. W. Brands, *The Devil We Knew: Americans and the Cold War* (New York: Oxford University Press, 1993), 6.

88   Kenneth W. Thompson, *Cold War Theories: World Polarization, 1943–1953* (Baton Rouge: Louisiana State University Press, 1981), 103.

89   "Report of President Roosevelt in Person to the Congress on the Crimea Conference," *New York Times,* March 2, 1945.

90   Robert E. Sherwood, *Roosevelt and Hopkins: An Intimate History* (New York: Harper & Brothers, 1950), 870.

91   Tsuyoshi Hasegawa, *Racing the Enemy: Stalin, Truman, and the Surrender of Japan* (Cambridge, MA: Harvard University Press, 2005), 43.

92   William E. Leuchtenberg, *In the Shadow of FDR: From Harry Truman to George W. Bush* (Ithaca, NY: Cornell University Press, 1983), 1.

93   Harry S. Truman, *Memoirs by Harry S. Truman: 1945: Year of Decisions* (New York: New American Library, 1955), 31.

94   Lloyd C. Gardner, *Architects of Illusion: Men and Ideas in American Foreign Policy, 1941–1949* (New York: Quadrangle Books, 1970), 56.

95   Walter Millis, ed., *The Forrestal Diaries* (New York: The Viking Press, 1951), 36–37.

96   LaFeber, *The American Age*, 417–418.

97   Truman, *Memoirs by Harry S. Truman: 1945*, 25–26.

98   Donald C. Watt, *Succeeding John Bull: America in Britain's Place, 1900–1975* (New York: Cambridge University Press, 1984), 105.

99   Robert H. Ferrell, ed. *Off the Record: The Private Papers of Harry S. Truman* (Columbia: University of Missouri Press, 1980), 17.

100   Truman, *Memoirs by Harry S. Truman: 1945*, 21, 104.

101   Gar Alperovitz, *The Decision to Use the Atomic Bomb and the Architecture of an American Myth* (New York: Alfred A. Knopf, 1995), 197.

102   Hasegawa, *Racing the Enemy*, 57.

103   Truman, *Memoirs by Harry S. Truman: 1945*, 86; Gardner, *Architects of Illusion*, 58–59.

104   Truman, *Memoirs by Harry S. Truman: 1945*, 95.

105   "Memorandum by Mr. Charles E. Bohlen, Assistant to the Secretary of State, of a Meeting at the White House, April 23, 1945," in *Foreign Relations of the United States, 1945*, vol. 5 (Washington, DC: U.S. Government Printing Office, 1967), 253.

106   Truman, *Memoirs by Harry S. Truman: 1945*, 87.

107   "WPB Aide Urges U.S. to Keep War Set-up," *New York Times*, January 20, 1944.

108   Robert H. Ferrell, *Harry S. Truman: A Life* (Columbia: University of Missouri Press, 1994), 200.

109   Truman, *Memoirs by Harry S. Truman: 1945*, 99.

110   Arnold A. Offner, *Another Such Victory: President Truman and the Cold War, 1945–1953* (Stanford, CA: Stanford University Press, 2002), 33.

111   Gaddis, *The United States and the Origins of the Cold War, 1941–1947*, 205.

112   Truman, *Memoirs by Harry S. Truman: 1945*, 102–103.

113   Gaddis, *Russia, The Soviet Union, and the United States*, 157.

114   Gaddis, *The United States and the Origins of the Cold War, 1941–1947*, 227.

115   Martin J. Sherwin, *A World Destroyed: Hiroshima and the Origins of the Arms Race* (New York: Vintage, 1987), 172–174, 180–183; Elizabeth Kimball MacLean, *Joseph E. Davies: Envoy to the Soviets* (New York: Praeger, 1992), 136–140; Walter Isaacson and Evan Thomas, *The Wise Men: Six Friends and the World They Made: Acheson, Bohlen, Harriman, Kennan, Lovett, McCloy* (New York: Simon & Schuster, 1986), 279.

116   "Durable World Peace Fervent Aim of Stalin," *Atlanta Constitution*, June 22, 1945; "Russia Seen Eager for Lasting Peace," *New York Times*, June 22, 1945.

117   Don Whitehead and John Beals Romeiser, *Beachhead Don: Reporting the War from the European Theater, 1942–1945* (New York: Fordham University Press, 2004), 355–356.

118   Harold Denny, "First Link Made Wednesday by Four Americans on Patrol," *New York Times*, April 28, 1945.

119   Leffler, *For the Soul of Mankind*, 34.

120   C. L. Sulzberger, "What the Russians Want—and Why," *New York Times*, June 10, 1945.

121   Editorial, "Russia's Children," *Washington Post*, January 1, 1945.

122   "First Lady Gathers Books for Russians," *New York Times*, July 1, 1945.

123 "'I Am an American' Is Powerful Password in Poland or Russia," *Washington Post*, March 4, 1945.

124 George Gallup, "New Confidence in Russian Aims Shown in Poll," *Los Angeles Times*, March 11, 1945.

125 Melvyn P. Leffler, "Inside Enemy Archives: The Cold War Reopened," *Foreign Affairs* 75 (July–August 1996), 123.

126 Alexander Werth, *Russia at War* (New York: Dutton, 1964), 768.

127 Anita Kondoyanidi, "The Liberating Experience: War Correspondents, Red Army Soldiers, and the Nazi Extermination Camps," *Russian Review* 69 (July 2010), 438.

128 Leffler, *For the Soul of Mankind*, 29.

129 Offner, *Another Such Victory*, 54.

130 "America and Russia," *Life*, July 30, 1945, 20.

131 Gardner, *Architects of Illusion*, 58.

CHAPTER 4: THE BOMB: THE TRAGEDY OF A SMALL MAN

1 Paul Fussell, "Thank God for the Atom Bomb: Hiroshima: A Soldier's View," *New Republic*, August 26 and 29, 1981, 28–30.

2 Robert E. Sherwood, *Roosevelt and Hopkins: An Intimate History* (New York: Harper & Brothers, 1950), 605.

3 Roger M. Macklis, "The Great Radium Scandal," *Scientific American* 269 (1993), 94–99; Spencer R. Weart, *Nuclear Fear: A History of Images* (Cambridge, MA: Harvard University Press, 1988), 50–52.

4 H. G. Wells, *The World Set Free* (New York: E. P. Dutton, 1914), 152.

5 Barton J. Bernstein, "Introduction" in *Toward a Livable World: Leo Szilard and the Crusade for Nuclear Arms Control*, ed. Helen S. Hawkins, G. Allen Greb, and Gertrud Weiss Szilard (Cambridge, MA: MIT Press, 1987), xxvi.

6 Allan M. Winkler, *Life Under a Cloud: American Anxiety About the Atom* (New York: Oxford University Press, 1993), 36.

7 Arthur Holly Compton, *Atomic Quest: A Personal Narrative* (New York: Oxford University Press, 1956), 49.

8 Jeremy Bernstein, *Hans Bethe, Prophet of Energy* (New York: Basic Books, 1980), 73.

9 Nuel P. Davis, *Lawrence and Oppenheimer* (New York: Da Capo Press, 1986), 130.

10 Compton, *Atomic Quest*, 128.

11 William Lanouette with Bela Silard, *Genius in the Shadows: A Biography of Leo Szilard, the Man Behind the Bomb* (Chicago: University of Chicago Press, 1992), 245.

12 Kai Bird and Martin J. Sherwin, *American Prometheus: The Triumph and Tragedy of J. Robert Oppenheimer* (New York: Vintage Books, 2005), 185.

13 Michael S. Sherry, *The Rise of American Air Power: The Creation of Armageddon* (New Haven, CT: Yale University Press, 1987), 172, 236.

14 Henry A. Wallace, "The Price of Free World Victory," in Henry A. Wallace, *The Price of Vision: The Diary of Henry A. Wallace, 1942–1946*, ed. John Morton Blum (Boston: Houghton Mifflin, 1973), 636.

15   Anthony Cave Brown, *"C": The Secret Life of Sir Stewart Graham Menzies* (New York: Macmillan, 1987), 481–484; Wallace, *The Price of Vision*, 385. In October 1945, Wallace recorded the following about Dahl in his diary: "He is a nice boy and I am very fond of him but necessarily he is working out problems from the standpoint of British policy, and British policy clearly is to provoke the maximum distrust between the United States and Russia and thus prepare the groundwork for World War III." Wallace, *The Price of Vision*, 492–493.

16   Culver and Hyde, *American Dreamer*, 298-300; "Costa Ricans Mass to Cheer Wallace," *New York Times*, March 19, 1943; "Wallace Sees Evil If Few Hold Riches," *New York Times*, April 20, 1943.

17   George Gallup, "The Gallup Poll," *Washington Post*, March 19, 1943.

18   Edwin W. Pauley, "Why Truman Is President," as told to Richard English. Copy in Harry S. Truman Library, Papers of Harry S. Truman, White House Central Files, Confidential Files. Referring to it as "The Pauley Conspiracy," he comments, "If it was a conspiracy, I am proud to have been its organizer."

19   Steve Kettmann, "Politics 2000," www.salon.com/politics2000/feature/2000/03/20/rice.

20   Robert J. Lifton and Greg Mitchell, *Hiroshima in America: A Half Century of Denial* (New York: Avon Books, 1995), 196–197.

21   Harry S. Truman, *Dear Bess: The Letters from Harry to Bess Truman, 1910–1959*, ed. Robert H. Ferrell (Columbia: University of Missouri Press, 1998), 80, 83; Ronald Takaki, *Hiroshima: Why America Dropped the Atomic Bomb* (Boston: Little, Brown, 1995), 109–111; Merle Miller, *Plain Speaking: An Oral Biography of Harry S. Truman*, 34–35, 51. One of the neighborhood boys, Morton Chiles, recalled that they "used to call Harry a sissy. He wore glasses and didn't play our games. He carried books, and we'd carry a baseball bat. So we called him a sissy." When, years later, a young questioner asked him if he was "popular" as "a little boy," Truman replied honestly, "Why, no, I was never popular. The popular boys were the ones who were good at games and had big, tight fists. I was never like that. Without my glasses I was blind as a bat, and to tell the truth, I was kind of a sissy. If there was any danger of getting into a fight, I always ran."

22   Arnold A. Offner, *Another Such Victory: President Truman and the Cold War, 1945–1953* (Stanford, CA: Stanford University Press, 2002), 8.

23   Ibid., 9.

24   Arthur Sears Henning, "How Boss Rule and Roosevelt Named Truman," *Chicago Tribune*, July 25, 1944.

25   Culver and Hyde, *American Dreamer*, 364.

26   Harry S. Truman, *Memoirs of Harry S. Truman*, vol. 1 (New York: Signet/New American Library, 1955), 21.

27   Henry L. Stimson and McGeorge Bundy, *On Active Service in Peace and War* (Harper & Brothers, 1948), 635–636.

28   Harry S. Truman, "Why I Dropped the Bomb," *Parade*, December 4, 1988. Bart Bernstein, who brought this article to my attention, cautions that Margaret Truman's editing may have influenced the wording.

29   Barton J. Bernstein, "A Postwar Myth: 500,000 U.S. Lives Saved," *Bulletin of the Atomic Scientists*, June–July 1986, 38; David M. Kennedy, *Freedom from Fear: The American People in Depression and War, 1929-1945* (New York: Oxford University Press, 1999), 834.

30   Henry L. Stimson, "The Decision to Use the Atomic Bomb," *Harper's Magazine*, February 1947, 97–107.

31   Tsuyoshi Hasegawa, *Racing the Enemy: Stalin, Truman, and Japan's Surrender in the Pacific War* (Cambridge, MA: Harvard University Press, 2005), 37.

32   Gar Alperovitz, *The Decision to Use the Atomic Bomb and the Architecture of an American Myth* (New York: Vintage Books, 1996), 328.

33   Richard B. Frank, *Downfall: The End of the Imperial Japanese Empire* (New York: Penguin, 1999), 354.

34   "Roosevelt in North Africa: The President Interrupts Historical Conference of Anglo-American High Command to Review U.S. Troops," *Life*, February 8, 1943.

35   Sherwood, *Roosevelt and Hopkins*, 696.

36   John W. Dower, *Embracing Defeat: Japan in the Wake of World War II* (New York: W. W. Norton, 1999), 282–283.

37   Hasegawa, *Racing the Enemy*, 52–53.

38   U.S. Department of Defense, *The Entry of the Soviet Union into the War Against Japan* (Washington, DC: U.S. Government Printing Office, 1955), 84.

39   John W. Dower, *Cultures of War: Pearl Harbor/Hiroshima/9-11/Iraq* (New York: W. W. Norton, 2010), 227.

40   Magic Diplomatic Summary SRS-1727, July 13, 1945, Records of the National Security Agency, Magic Files, Box 18, RG 457, National Archives.

41   Barton J. Bernstein, "The Perils and Politics of Surrender: Ending the War with Japan and Avoiding the Third Atomic Bomb," *Pacific Historical Review*, February 1977, 5.

42   "Senator Urges Terms to Japs Be Explained," *Washington Post*, July 3, 1945.

43   "Fatal Phrase," *Washington Post*, June 11, 1945.

44   Alperovitz, *The Decision to Use the Atomic Bomb*, 20.

45   Hasegawa, *Racing the Enemy*, 72–73.

46   Combined Chiefs of Staff, 643/3, "Estimate of the Enemy Situation (as of 6 July)" July 8, 1945, RG 218, Central Decimal Files, 1943–1945, CCS 381 (6/4/45), sec. 2, pt. 5.

47   Allan Nevins, "How We Felt About the War," in *While You Were Gone: A Report on Wartime Life in the United States*, ed. Jack Goodman (New York: Simon & Schuster, 1946), 13.

48   Lisle Abbott Rose, *Dubious Victory: The United States and the End of World War II* (Kent, Ohio: Kent State University Press, 1973), 58.

49   John W. Dower, *War Without Mercy: Race and Power in the Pacific War* (New York: Pantheon, 1986), 54, 78, 79, 85; "World Battlefronts, THE ENEMY: Perhaps He Is Human," *Time*, July 5, 1943, 29.

50   Dower, *War Without Mercy*, 51–52.

51   Truman, *Dear Bess*, 39.

52   Peter Kuznick, "We Can Learn a Lot from Truman the Bigot," *Los Angeles Times*, July 18, 2003; Miller, 183.

53   Edgar Jones, "One War's Enough," *Atlantic Monthly*, February 1946, 49.

54   Greg Robinson, *By Order of the President: FDR and the Internment of Japanese Americans* (Cambridge, MA: Harvard University Press, 2001), 89–90; John Morton Blum, *V Was*

for Victory: Politics and American Culture During World War II (New York: Houghton Mifflin Harcourt, 1976), 158.

55 Lillian Baker, *The Concentration Camp Conspiracies, A Second Pearl Harbor* (Lawndale, CA: AFHA Publications, 1981), 156.

56 Harry N. Scheiber, *Earl Warren and the Warren Court: The Legacy in American and Foreign Law* (New York: Lexington Books, 2007), 41; Roger Daniels, Sandra C. Taylor, Harry H. L. Kitano, and Leonard J. Arrington, *Japanese Americans, from Relocation to Redress* (Seattle: University of Washington Press, 1991), 242; "Bay City Warned Raid Peril Real," *Los Angeles Times,* December 10, 1941; Lawrence E. Davies, "Carrier Is Hunted off San Francisco," *New York Times,* December 10, 1941.

57 Kennedy, *Freedom from Fear,* 749–751.

58 Robert Asahina, *Just Americans: How Japanese Americans Won a War at Home and Abroad* (New York: Gotham, 2006), 20.

59 "Epilogue to a Sorry Drama," *Life,* April 28, 1967, 6; Kennedy, *Freedom from Fear,* 753.

60 John Howard, *Concentration Camps on the Home Front: Japanese Americans in the House of Jim Crow* (Chicago: University of Chicago Press, 2008), 120; Dower, *War Without Mercy,* 82.

61 Kennedy, *Freedom from Fear,* 751.

62 Eddie Yamaoka, "Sport Tidbits," *Heart Mountain Sentinel,* July 7, 1945.

63 Susan Lynn Smith, "Women Health Workers and the Color Line in the Japanese American 'Relocation Centers' of World War II," *Bulletin of the History of Medicine* 73 (Winter 1999), 585–586.

64 Linda Gordon and Gary Y. Okihiro, *Impounded: Dorothea Lange and the Censored Images of Japanese American Internment* (New York: W. W. Norton, 2008), 19–20.

65 Asahina, *Just Americans,* 43, 161–193.

66 "A Jap's a Jap," *Washington Post,* April 15, 1943.

67 Blum, *Victory,* 163, 166; Charles McClain, *The Mass Internment of Japanese Americans and the Quest for Legal Redress* (New York: Taylor & Francis, 1994), 189.

68 *Hirabayashi v. United States,* 320 U. S. 81, 1943, http://supreme.justia.com/us/320/81/case.html.

69 J. Burton, M. Farrell, F. Lord, and R. Lord, "Closing the Relocation Centers," www.nps.gov/history/history/online_books/anthropology74/ce3o.htm.

70 Michi Nishiura Weglyn, *Years of Infamy: The Untold Story of America's Concentration Camps* (Seattle: University of Washington Press, 1996), 268, 281–282.

71 Dower, *War Without Mercy,* 39.

72 Greg Mitchell, "On the Death of 'Hiroshima Bomb' Pilot Paul Tibbets," *Editor and Publisher,* November 1, 2007, http://editorandpublisher.com/Article/UPDATE-On-the-Death-of-Hiroshima-Bomb-Pilot-Paul-Tibbets. For a fuller discussion of Tibbets, see Peter J. Kuznick, "Defending the Indefensible: A Meditation on the Life of Hiroshima Pilot Paul Tibbets, Jr.," *The Asia Pacific Journal: Japan Focus,* January 22, 2008, http://japanfocus.org/-Peter_J_-Kuznick/2642.

73 Yuki Tanaka and Marilyn B. Young, *Bombing Civilians: A Twentieth-Century History* (New York: New Press, 2009), 5, 84–85, 117.

74 Lifton and Mitchell, *Hiroshima in America,* 133; Sherry, *The Rise of American Air Power,* 295.

75 Robert S. McNamara, "We Need International Rules for War," *The Gazette* (Montreal, Quebec), August 9, 2003.

76 Bird and Sherwin, *American Prometheus*, 291.

77 Alperovitz, *The Decision to Use the Atomic Bomb*, 352.

78 Ronald Schaffer, *Wings of Judgment: American Bombing in World War II* (New York: Oxford University Press, 1985), 154.

79 Sherwin, *A World Destroyed*, 298.

80 Alperovitz, *The Decision to Use the Atomic Bomb*, 147.

81 Sherwin, *A World Destroyed*, 62.

82 Bird and Sherwin, *American Prometheus*, 284.

83 Truman, *Memoirs by Harry S. Truman:1945*, 104.

84 For the full report, see the appendix to Alice Kimball Smith, *A Peril and A Hope: The Scientists' Movement in America: 1945–47* (Chicago: University of Chicago Press, 1965), 560–572.

85 Lanouette with Silard, *Genius in the Shadows*, 273.

86 Ibid., 527–528, note 42. Seventy-two percent favored a demonstration before use and 11 percent favored a demonstration and no use.

87 Bird and Sherwin, *American Prometheus*, 300.

88 Sherwin, *A World Destroyed*, 235; Harry S. Truman, *Off the Record: The Private Papers of Harry S. Truman*, ed. Robert H. Ferrell (New York: Harper & Row, 1980), 53.

89 Hasegawa, *Racing the Enemy*, 133–134.

90 Allen Dulles, *The Secret Surrender* (New York: Harper & Row, 1966), 255–256.

91 "Russo-Japanese Relations (13–20 July 1945)," Publication of Pacific Strategic Intelligence Section, Commander-in-Chief United States Fleet and Chief of Naval Operations, 21 July 1945, SRH-085, Record Group 457, Modern Military Branch, National Archives.

92 Alperovitz, *The Decision to Use the Atomic Bomb*, 27.

93 Truman, *Off the Record*, 53.

94 Truman, *Dear Bess*, 519.

95 Henry L. Stimson, diary, May 15, 1945, Sterling Memorial Library, Yale University.

96 Bird and Sherwin, *American Prometheus*, 304.

97 Ibid., 309.

98 Alperovitz, *The Decision to Use the Atomic Bomb*, 250–251.

99 Stimson, diary, July 21, 1945.

100 Ibid.

101 Stimson, diary, July 22, 1945.

102 Alperovitz, *The Decision to Use the Atomic Bomb*, 259.

103 Truman, *Off the Record*, 55.

104 Stimson, diary, May 31, 1945.

105 "Ike on Ike," *Newsweek*, November 11, 1963, 107.

106 Barton J. Bernstein, "Ike and Hiroshima: Did He Oppose It?," *Journal of Strategic Studies* 10 (September 1987), 377–389.

107 Alperovitz, *The Decision to Use the Atomic Bomb,* 271.

108 Robert L. Messer, *The End of an Alliance: James F. Byrnes, Roosevelt, Truman and the Origins of the Cold War* (Chapel Hill: University of North Carolina Press, 1982), 105.

109 Truman, *Off the Record,* 54.

110 Andrei Gromyko, *Memoirs* (New York: Doubleday, 1989), 110.

111 Hasegawa, *Racing the Enemy,* 177.

112 Fletcher Knebel and Charles W. Bailey, "The Fight over the Atom Bomb," *Look,* August 13, 1963, 20. For Groves's denial to Truman that he said this, see Alperovitz, *The Decision to Use the Atomic Bomb,* 780, note 39.

113 Alperovitz, *The Decision to Use the Atomic Bomb,* 415.

114 Dorris Clayton James, *The Years of MacArthur: 1941–1945,* vol. 2 (Boston: Houghton Mifflin, 1975), 774.

115 Richard Goldstein, "Paul W. Tibbets Jr., Pilot of Enola Gay, Dies at 92," *New York Times,* November 2, 2007.

116 Kuznick, "Defending the Indefensible."

117 Merle Miller and Abe Spitzer, *We Dropped the A-Bomb* (New York: Thomas Y. Crowell, 1946), 42–45.

118 Ibid., 45.

119 Hasegawa, *Racing the Enemy,* 179–180.

120 Robert Jay Lifton, *Death in Life: Survivors of Hiroshima* (New York: Random House, 1967), 441–442.

121 Miller and Spitzer, *We Dropped the A-Bomb,* 47. For a fuller discussion of the crewmembers and their reactions to the Hiroshima and Nagasaki bombings, see Kuznick, "Defending the Indefensible."

122 Truman, *Memoirs by Harry S. Truman: 1945,* 465.

123 Lifton and Mitchell, *Hiroshima in America,* 169–170.

124 David Holloway, *Stalin and the Bomb: The Soviet Union and Atomic Energy 1939–1956* (New Haven, Conn.: Yale University Press, 1994), 127.

125 Georgii Konstantinovich Zhukov, *The Memoirs of Marshal Zhukov* (New York: Delacorte Press, 1971), 674–675; Vladislav M. Zubok, *A Failed Empire: The Soviet Union in the Cold War from Stalin to Gorbachev* (Chapel Hill: University of North Carolina Press, 2007), 27, 354, notes 120 and 121.

126 Ralph B. Levering, Vladimir O. Pechatnov, Verena Botzenhart-Viehe, and C. Earl Edmondson, *Debating the Origins of the Cold War: American and Russian Perspectives* (Lanham, MD: Rowman & Littlefield, 2001), 105; Zubok, 354 (notes 120 and 121).

127 Hasegawa, *Racing the Enemy,* 197.

128 Miller and Spitzer, *We Dropped the A-Bomb,* 57–59.

129 Lifton and Mitchell, *Hiroshima in America,* 162.

130 Sherwin, *A World Destroyed,* 237.

131 Hasegawa, *Racing the Enemy,* 237.

132 Stimson, diary, August 10, 1945.

133 Dower, *Cultures of War,* 239.

134 Tsuyoshi Hasegawa, "The Atomic Bombs and the Soviet Invasion: What Drove Japan's Decision to Surrender?," *The Asia-Pacific Journal: Japan Focus,* www.japanfocus .org/-Tsuyoshi-Hasegawa/2501.

135 Ibid.

136 Memorandum for Chief, Strategic Policy Section, S&P Group, Operations Division, War Department General Staff, from Ennis, Subject: Use of Atomic Bomb on Japan, April 30, 1946, "ABC 471.6 Atom (17 August 1945), Sec. 7," Entry 421, RG 165, National Archives.

137 William D. Leahy, *I Was There: The Personal Story of the Chief of Staff to Presidents Roosevelt and Truman Based on His Notes and Diaries Made at the Time* (New York: Whittlesey House, 1950), 441.

138 Alperovitz, *The Decision to Use the Atomic Bomb,* 326.

139 Douglas MacArthur, memorandum to Herbert Hoover, December 2, 1960, Herbert Hoover Presidential Library, Post-Presidential Papers, Individual File Series, Box 129 G, Douglas MacArthur 1953–1964, folder [3212 (3)]. MacArthur's insistence on this point never wavered over the years. After a long talk with MacArthur in May 1946, Hoover had written in his diary, "I told MacArthur of my memorandum of mid-May 1945 to Truman, that peace could be had with Japan by which our major objectives would be accomplished. MacArthur said that was correct and that we would have avoided all the losses, the Atomic bomb, and the entry of Russia into Manchuria." Alperovitz, *The Decision to Use the Atomic Bomb,* 350–351.

140 H. H. Arnold, *Global Mission* (New York: Harper & Brothers, 1949), 598.

141 "Giles Would Rule Japan a Century," *New York Times,* September 21, 1945; Alperovitz, *The Decision to Use the Atomic Bomb,* 336.

142 Alperovitz, *The Decision to Use the Atomic Bomb,* 343.

143 Ibid., 329.

144 Sidney Shalett, "Nimitz Receives All-Out Welcome from Washington," *New York Times,* October 6, 1945.

145 Alperovitz, *The Decision to Use the Atomic Bomb,* 331. Testifying before Congress in 1949, Halsey said, "I believe that bombing—especially atomic bombing—of civilians, is morally indefensible." Alperovitz, *The Decision to Use the Atomic Bomb,* 720, note 52.

146 Ibid., 359.

147 Lifton and Mitchell, *Hiroshima in America,* 11.

148 "Japan Beaten Before Atom Bomb, Byrnes Says, Citing Peace Bids," *New York Times,* August 30, 1945.

149 "Oxnam, Dulles Ask Halt in Bomb Use," *New York Times,* August 10, 1945.

150 Gerald Wendt and Donald Porter Geddes, ed. *The Atomic Age Opens* (New York: Pocket Books, 1945), 207.

151 Sadao Asada, "The Mushroom Cloud and National Psyches," in *Living with the Bomb,* ed. Laura Hein and Mark Selden (Armonk, NY: M. E. Sharpe, 1997), 182.

152   Leahy, *I Was There,* 384–385.

153   Stimson, "The Decision," 107.

154   Asada, "The Mushroom Cloud and National Psyches," 179.

155   Wayne Phillips, "Truman Disputes Eisenhower on '48," *New York Times,* February 3, 1958.

156   John Toland, *The Rising Sun: The Decline and Fall of the Japanese Empire, 1936–1945* (New York: Random House, 1970), 766 note.

157   Bird and Sherwin, *American Prometheus,* 332.

158   Freeman J. Dyson, *Weapons and Hope* (New York: Harper & Row, 1985), 121.

159   Dwight McDonald, *Memoirs of a Revolutionist: Essays in Political Criticism* (New York: Farrar, Straus, and Cudahy, 1957), 97.

160   Margaret Truman, *Harry S. Truman* (New York: William Morrow, 1973), 555.

CHAPTER 5: THE COLD WAR: WHO STARTED IT?

1   Arthur Schlesinger, Jr., "Some Lessons from the Cold War," *Diplomatic History* 16 (January 1992), 47–53.

2   Paul Boyer, *By the Bomb's Early Light: American Thought and Culture at the Dawn of the Atomic Age* (New York: Pantheon, 1985), 7, 15.

3   Gerald Wendt and Donald Porter Geddes, ed. *The Atomic Age Opens* (New York: Pocket Books, 1945), 159.

4   "Everyman," *New York Times,* August 18, 1945.

5   "Last Judgment," *Washington Post,* August 8, 1945.

6   "Text of Kennedy's Address Offering 'Strategy of Peace' for Easing the Cold War," *New York Times,* June 11, 1963.

7   Gregg Herken, *The Winning Weapon: The Atomic Bomb in the Cold War* (New York: Vintage Books, 1982), 48.

8   Henry L. Stimson and McGeorge Bundy, *On Active Service in Peace and War* (New York: Harper & Brothers, 1948), 643–644.

9   Felix Belair, Jr., "Plea to Give Soviet Atom Secret Stirs Debate in Cabinet," *New York Times,* September 22, 1945.

10   "The Reminiscences of Henry Agard Wallace," Columbia University Oral History, p. 4379.

11   Arthur Compton to Henry A. Wallace, September 27, 1945, Arthur Compton Papers, Washington University in St. Louis Archives; Arthur Holly Compton, *The Cosmos of Arthur Holly Compton,* ed. Marjorie Johnston (New York: Alfred A. Knopf, 1967), 440.

12   Henry A. Wallace, *The Price of Vision: The Diary of Henry A. Wallace, 1942–1946,* ed. John Morton Blum (Boston: Houghton Mifflin, 1973), 489–490.

13   "Harry S. Truman, Press Conference, Oct. 8, 1945," www.presidency.ucsb.edu/ws/index.php?pid=12319#axzz1aJSeeAQ2.

14   Samuel A. Tower, "Truman for Civil Control over Atomic Energy in U.S.," *New York Times,* February 1, 1946.

15   "Secretary of Commerce Warns of Danger of Fascism Under Army," *Washington Post,* March 13, 1946.

16   Memorandum by the Commanding General, Manhattan Engineer District (Groves), January 2, 1946, *Foreign Relations of the United States, 1946,* vol. 1 (Washington, DC: U.S. Government Printing Office, 1972), 1197–1198.

17   Wallace, *The Price of Vision,* 496–497.

18   Ibid., 502–503, 517.

19   Melvyn P. Leffler, *A Preponderance of Power: National Security, the Truman Administration, and the Cold War* (Stanford, CA: Stanford University Press, 1992), 6.

20   Fraser J. Harbutt, *The Iron Curtain: Churchill, America, and the Origins of the Cold War* (New York: Oxford University Press, 1986), 152.

21   Melvyn P. Leffler, *For the Soul of Mankind: The United States, the Soviet Union and the Cold War* (New York: Hill and Wang, 2007), 55–56.

22   John Lewis Gaddis, *The United States and the Origins of the Cold War, 1941–1947* (New York: Columbia University Press, 1972), 119.

23   Arnold Joseph Toynbee, *Survey of International Affairs,* vol. 2: *The Middle East in the War* (New York: Oxford University Press, 1954), 1.

24   Geoffrey Wawro, *Quicksand: America's Pursuit of Power in the Middle East* (New York: Penguin, 2010), 5; Michael T. Klare, *Blood and Oil: The Dangers and Consequences of America's Growing Dependency on Imported Petroleum* (New York: Owl Books, 2004), 33; Edward W. Chester, *United States Oil Policy and Diplomacy: A Twentieth Century Overview* (Westport, CT: Greenwood Press, 1983), 234.

25   Klare, *Blood and Oil,* 32.

26   James A. Bill, *The Eagle and the Lion: The Tragedy of American-Iranian Relations* (New Haven, CT: Yale University Press, 1988), 18.

27   Ibid., 19.

28   "Text of Churchill Plea for Alliance," *Los Angeles Times,* March 6, 1946.

29   "Soviet Chief Calls Churchill Liar, Warmonger," *Chicago Tribune,* March 14, 1946.

30   "Mr. Churchill's Warning," *New York Times,* June 7, 1946.

31   "Testament," *Washington Post,* March 6, 1946.

32   "Mr. Churchill's Plea," *Chicago Tribune,* March 7, 1946.

33   "Senators Shy from Churchill Alliance Plan," *Chicago Tribune,* March 6, 1946; "Senators Cold to Churchill's Talk of Alliance," *Los Angeles Times,* March 6, 1946.

34   "Churchill Plea Is 'Shocking' to 3 Senators," *Washington Post,* March 7, 1946.

35   John D. Eddy, "Churchill's Speech," *Washington Post,* March 8, 1946.

36   Francis M. Stephenson, "Churchill's 'Attack on Peace' Denounced by James Roosevelt," *New York Herald Tribune,* March 15, 1946.

37   Marquis Childs, *Witness to Power* (New York: McGraw-Hill, 1975), 45.

38   "Ickes, Truman Feud Flames Hotter in Two New Letters," *Chicago Tribune,* February 14, 1946; "Ickes Flays Truman as He Quits," *Los Angeles Times,* February 14, 1946; Thomas J. Hamilton, "Ickes Resigns Post, Berating Truman in Acid Farewell," *New York Times,* February 14, 1946.

39   Bill Henry, "Ickes Blowup Rocks Capital like Atom Bomb," *Los Angeles Times,* February 14, 1946.

40   Henry Wallace, April 12, 1946, RG 40 (Department of Commerce); Entry 1, General Records of the Department of Commerce, Office of the Secretary, General Correspondence; Box 1074, File "104251/6" (2 of 7), National Archives, Washington, D.C.

41   "Dr. Butler Urges Iran Oil Sharing," *Los Angeles Times,* March 25, 1946.

42   "Russia and Iran," *Washington Post,* March 7, 1946.

43   Robert C. Albright, "Pepper Urges Big 3 to Meet on 'Confidence,'" *Washington Post,* March 21, 1946.

44   E. Brook Lee, "Relations with Russia," *Washington Post,* March 20, 1946.

45   "Nation: Good Old Days," *Time,* January 28, 1980, 13.

46   Boyer, *By the Bomb's Early Light,* 30.

47   David E. Lilienthal, *The Atomic Energy Years, 1945–1950,* vol. 2: *The Journals of David E. Lilienthal,* ed. Helen M. Lilienthal (New York: Harper & Row, 1964), 10, 27.

48   Ibid., 30; Herken, *The Winning Weapon,* 160–162.

49   Lilienthal, *The Atomic Energy Years, 1945–1950,* vol. 2, 59; Robert C. Grogin, *Natural Enemies: The United States and the Soviet Union in the Cold War* (New York: Lexington Books, 2001), 95.

50   Drew Middleton, "Baruch Atom Plan Spurned by Pravda," *New York Times,* June 25, 1946.

51   Lloyd J. Graybar, "The 1946 Atomic Bomb Tests: Atomic Diplomacy or Bureaucratic Infighting?," *Journal of American History* 72 (1986), 900.

52   "Red Sees Atom Test as Effort to Better Bomb," *Chicago Tribune,* July 4, 1946.

53   Lewis Mumford, "Gentlemen: You Are Mad!" *Saturday Review of Literature,* March 2, 1946, 5.

54   Wallace, *The Price of Vision,* 589–601.

55   James A. Hagerty, "Wallace Warns on 'Tough' Policy Toward Russia," *New York Times,* September 12, 1946.

56   Henry A. Wallace, "The Way to Peace," September 12, 1946, in Wallace, *The Price of Vision,* 661–668.

57   James Reston, "Wallace Speech Is Seen Embarrassing to Byrnes," *New York Times,* September 13, 1946.

58   "Hillbilly Policy, British Reaction," *Los Angeles Times,* September 15, 1946.

59   Eleanor Roosevelt, "My Day," September 17, 1946, www.gwu.edu/~erpapers/myday/ displaydoc.cfm?_y=1946&_f=md0 00445.

60   Wallace, *The Price of Vision,* 593.

61   Robert J. Donovan, *Conflict and Crisis: The Presidency of Harry S Truman* (New York: W. W. Norton, 1977), 227.

62   Wallace, *The Price of Vision,* 630.

63   Richard J. Walton, *Henry Wallace, Harry Truman, and the Cold War* (New York: Viking, 1976), 114.

64   Clifford-Elsey Report, Septembner 24, 1946, Conway Files, Truman Papers, Truman Library.

65   Leffler, *A Preponderance of Power,* 130–138; Offner, *Another Such Victory,* 178–182.

66   Clifford-Elsey Report.

67   Walter Isaacson and Evan Thomas, *The Wise Men: Six Friends and the World They Made* (New York: Simon & Schuster, 1986), 376.

68   Offner, *Another Such Victory,* 180–181.

69   Lloyd C. Gardner, *Three Kings: The Rise of an American Empire* (New York: New Press, 2009), 48.

70   "Plan to Split U.S. Charged," *Baltimore Sun,* May 29, 1946.

71   Robert L. Beisner, *Dean Acheson: A Life in the Cold War* (New York: Oxford University Press, 2006), 53, 57.

72   Gardner, *Architects of Illusion,* 204.

73   Dean Acheson, *Present at the Creation: My Years in the State Department* (New York: Signet, 1969), 293.

74   "Text of President Truman's Speech on New Foreign Policy," *New York Times,* March 13, 1947.

75   Lawrence S. Wittner, *Cold War America: From Hiroshima to Watergate* (New York: Holt, Rinehart and Winston, 1978), 34.

76   "Henry Wallace Answers President Truman [advertisement]," *New York Times,* March 18, 1947; "Truman Betraying U.S. Wallace Says," *New York Times,* March 14, 1947; Culver and Hyde, *American Dreamer,* 436–437.

77   "Pravda Opens Bitter Attack on U.S. Loans," *Washington Post,* March 16, 1947.

78   Gardner, *Architects of Illusion,* 221; Anne O'Hare McCormick, "Open Moves in the Political War for Europe," *New York Times,* June 2, 1947.

79   Herring, *From Colony to Superpower,* 616.

80   Lawrence S. Wittner, *American Intervention in Greece, 1943–49* (New York: Columbia University Press, 1982), 262–263.

81   Lorraine M. Lees, *Keeping Tito Afloat: The United States, Yugoslavia and the Cold War* (University Park, PA: Pennsylvania State University Press, 1993), 54; John Lewis Gaddis, *Russia, The Soviet Union, and the United States: An Interpretive History* (New York: Alfred A. Knopf, 1978), 192.

82   Lloyd C. Gardner, *Spheres of Influence: The Great Powers Partition Europe, From Munich to Yalta* (Chicago: I. R. Dee, 1993), 265.

83   Offner, *Another Such Victory,* 209–211.

84   Walter LaFeber, *The American Age: United States Foreign Policy at Home and Abroad Since 1750* (New York: W. W. Norton, 1989), 479–480.

85   Offner, *Another Such Victory,* 213.

86   Gaddis, *The United States and the Origins of the Cold War,* 322–323.

87   Vladislav Zubok and Constantine Pleshakov, *Inside the Kremlin's Cold War: From Stalin to Khrushchev* (Cambridge, MA: Harvard University Press, 1996), 276–277; Melvyn P. Leffler, "Inside Enemy Archives: The Cold War Reopened," *Foreign Affairs* 75 (July–August 1996).

88   Gary Wills, *Bomb Power: The Modern Presidency and the National Security State* (New York: Penguin, 2010), 63.

89   Walter Lippmann, *The Cold War: A Study in U.S. Foreign Policy* (New York: Harper & Brothers, 1947), 15–16, 19, 44.

90   Ellen Schrecker, *Many Are the Crimes: McCarthyism in America* (Princeton, NJ: Princeton University Press, 1998), 287; Wills, *Bomb Power,* 74.

91   Offner, *Another Such Victory,* 202.

92   Ibid., 192.

93   Mark Perry, *Four Stars* (Boston: Houghton Mifflin, 1989), 88; Townsend Hoopes and Douglas Brinkley, *Driven Patriot: The Life and Times of James Forrestal* (New York: Alfred A. Knopf, 1992), 310–312; "NSC 10/2," June 18, 1948, in William M Leary, ed., *The Central Intelligence Agency: History and Documents* (Birmingham, AL: University of Alabama Press), 133.

94   Colonel R. Allen Griffin, recorded interview by James R. Fuchs, staff interviewer, February 15, 1974, Harry S. Truman Library, Oral History Program; Wills, *Bomb Power,* 78, 88–89; Tim Weiner, *Legacy of Ashes: The History of the CIA* (New York: Doubleday, 2007), 28–29.

95   Norman J. W. Goda, "Nazi Collaborators in the United States: What the FBI Knew," in *U.S. Intelligence and the Nazis,* ed. Richard Breitman, Norman J. W. Goda, Timothy Naftali, and Robert Wolfe (New York: Cambridge University Press, 2005), 249–253.

96   Weiner, *Legacy of Ashes,* 43–45.

97   Wills, *Bomb Power,* 87.

98   Christopher Simpson, *Blowback: America's Recruitment of Nazis and Its Effects on the Cold War* (New York: Weidenfeld & Nicholson, 1988), 65.

99   Walter A. McDougall, *The Heavens and the Earth: A Political History of the Space Age* (Baltimore: John Hopkins University Press, 1997), 88.

100 Leffler, *A Preponderance of Power,* 238–239.

101 Avi Shlaim, "The Balfour Declaration and Its Consequences," in *Yet More Adventures with Britannia: Personalities, Politics and Culture in Britain,* ed. W. Roger Lewis (London: I. B. Tauris, 2005), 251.

102 Herring, *From Colony to Superpower,* 569.

103 Wawro, *Quicksand,* 37–38.

104 Wallace, *The Price of Vision,* 607.

105 Steven M. Gillon, *The American Paradox: A History of the United States Since 1945* (Boston: Wadsworth, 2012), 25.

106 Daniel Yergin, *The Prize,* 408.

107 William Stivers, "The Incomplete Blockade: Soviet Zone Supply of West Berlin, 1948–1949," *Diplomatic History* 21(Fall 1997), 569–570; Carolyn Eisenberg, "The Myth of the Berlin Blockade and the Early Cold War," in Ellen Schrecker, ed. *Cold War Triumphalism: The Misuse of History After the Fall of Communism* (New York: New Press, 2004), 174–200.

108 Carolyn Woods Eisenberg, *Drawing the Line: The American Decision to Divide Germany, 1944–1949* (New York: Cambridge University Press, 1998), 440.

109   James Carroll, *House of War: The Pentagon and the Disastrous Rise of American Power* (New York: Houghton Mifflin, 2006), 148.

110   John C. Culver and John Hyde, *American Dreamer: The Life and Times of Henry A. Wallace* (W. W. Norton, 2000), 456–457.

111   Ibid., 466–467.

112   Ibid., 464–470.

113   Ibid., 502.

114   PPS/23, "Review of Current Trends: U.S. Foreign Policy," February 24, 1948, *Foreign Relations of the United States, 1948,* vol. 1, Part 2 (Washington, DC: U.S. Government Printing Office, 1975), 524–525.

115   "The Tragedy of China," *New York Times,* January 24, 1949.

116   "Duel for Asia," *New York Times,* December 18, 1949.

117   "Chennault Sees War in Loss of China," *Washington Post,* June 26, 1949.

118   Margaret Truman, *Harry S. Truman* (New York: William Morrow, 1973), 412.

119   Harry Truman, "Statement by the President on Announcing the First Atomic Explosion in the U.S.S.R., September 23, 1949," *Public Papers of the Presidents: Harry S. Truman, 1945–1953,* Truman Library.

120   "Groves of Illusion," *Los Angeles Times,* February 28, 1946.

121   Kai Bird and Martin J. Sherwin, *American Prometheus: The Triumph and Tragedy of J. Robert Oppenheimer* (New York: Vintage Books, 2005), 417.

122   Gerard J. DeGroot, *The Bomb: A Life* (Cambridge, MA: Harvard University Press, 2005), 145–147.

123   "Public Was Deluded on Bomb, Dewey Says," *New York Times,* September 24, 1949.

124   "Lucas Blasts Gutter Politics over Red Atom," *Chicago Tribune,* October 10, 1949.

125   "Who Is Winning?," *New York Times,* October 9, 1949.

126   "Russ Bomb Heralds New Atom Era—as Predicted," William Laurence, *Los Angeles Times,* September 25, 1949.

127   Lilienthal, *The Atomic Energy Years, 1945–1950,* vol. 2, 584–585.

128   "Forrestal Hopes to Keep His Job," *Los Angeles Times,* October 10, 1948; Drew Pearson, "Pearson Replies," *Washington Post,* May 30, 1949.

129   "Four Forrestal Suicide Bids, Says Pearson," *Los Angeles Times,* May 23, 1949; Carroll, *House of War,* 151.

130   Marquis Childs, "Washington Calling: Food for Propaganda," *Washington Post,* May 5, 1949.

CHAPTER 6: EISENHOWER: A NOT SO PRETTY PICTURE

1   Melvyn P. Leffler, *For the Soul of Mankind: The United States, the Soviet Union and the Cold War* (New York: Hill and Wang, 2007), 91.

2   Gerard J. DeGroot, *The Bomb: A Life* (Cambridge, MA: Harvard University Press, 2005), 153.

3   Gregg Herken, *The Winning Weapon: The Atomic Bomb in the Cold War* (New York: Vintage Books, 1982), 279, 293–297.

4   David E. Lilienthal, *The Atomic Energy Years, 1945–1950*, vol. 2: *The Journals of David E. Lilienthal*, ed. Helen M. Lilienthal (New York: Harper & Row, 1964), 582.

5   Priscilla J. McMillan, *The Ruin of J. Robert Oppenheimer and the Birth of the Modern Arms Race* (New York: Viking, 2005), 24.

6   "USAEC General Advisory Committee Report on the 'Super,' October 30, 1949," in *The American Atom: A Documentary History of Nuclear Policies from the Discovery of Fission to the Present, 1939–1984*, ed. Robert C. Williams and Philip L. Cantelon (Philadelphia: University of Pennsylvania Press, 1984), 124–127.

7   Kai Bird and Martin J. Sherwin, *American Prometheus: The Triumph and Tragedy of J. Robert Oppenheimer* (New York: Vintage Books, 2005), 427.

8   Albert Einstein, *Einstein on Politics: His Private Thoughts and Public Stands on Nationalism, Zionism, War, Peace, and the Bomb*, ed. David E. Rowe and Robert Schulmann (Princeton, NJ: Princeton University Press, 2007), 404.

9   Leo Szilard, *Toward a Livable World*, ed. Helen S. Hawkins, G. Allen Greb, and Gertrud Weiss Szilard (Cambridge, MA: MIT Press, 1987), 84.

10   William Faulkner, Nobel Prize Banquet Speech, December 10, 1950, http://www.nobelprize.org/nobel_prizes/literature/laureates/1949/faulkner-speech.html.

11   "NSC 68: United States Objectives and Programs for National Security (April 14, 1950)," in *American Cold War Strategy: Interpreting NSC 68*, ed. Ernest R. May (New York: St. Martin's Press, 1993), 25, 28, 38, 55.

12   Robert Griffith, *The Politics of Fear: Joseph R. McCarthy and the Senate* (Lexington: University Press of Kentucky, 1970), 49.

13   Ellen Schrecker, *Many Are the Crimes: McCarthyism in America* (Princeton, NJ: Princeton University Press, 1998), 206.

14   Michael S. Sherry, *In the Shadow of War: The United States Since the 1930s* (New Haven, CT: Yale University Press, 1995), 174.

15   Schrecker, *Many Are the Crimes*, xiii, 267–268.

16   Mary McCarthy, "Naming Names: The Arthur Miller Case," in Mary McCarthy, *On the Contrary* (New York: Farrar, Straus, and Cudahy, 1961), 154.

17   I. F. Stone, "Must Americans Become Informers?," in I. F. Stone, *The Truman Era* (1953; reprint, New York: Random House, 1972), 99.

18   Richard H. Pells, *The Liberal Mind in a Conservative Age: American Intellectuals in the 1940s and 1950s*, 2nd ed. (Middletown, CT: Wesleyan University Press, 1989), 322.

19   Larry Ceplair and Steven Englund, *The Inquisition in Hollywood: Politics in the Film Community, 1930–1960* (New York: Anchor Press/Doubleday, 1980), 386–388, 403–407, 418–422.

20   Schrecker, *Many Are the Crimes*, 369–370.

21   Vincent Joseph Intondi, "From Harlem to Hiroshima: African Americans and the Bomb, 1945–1968," PhD dissertation, American University, 2009.

22   David K. Johnson, *The Lavender Scare: The Cold War Persecution of Gays and Lesbians in the Federal Government* (Chicago: University of Chicago Press, 2004), 166–168.

23   Schrecker, *Many Are the Crimes*, 208, 212, 216, 227.

24   Melvyn P. Leffler, *A Preponderance of Power: National Security, the Truman Administration, and the Cold War* (Stanford, CA: Stanford University Press, 1992), 365.

25   "War in Korea," *New York Times*, June 26, 1950.

26   David Halberstam, *The Coldest Winter: America and the Korean War* (New York: Hyperion, 2007), 2.

27   Lloyd C. Gardner, "The Dulles Years: 1953–1959," in *From Colony to Empire: Essays on the History of American Foreign Relations*, ed. William Appleman Williams (New York: John Wiley & Sons, 1972), 375–376.

28   Ibid., 371–372.

29   Halberstam, *The Coldest Winter*, 92–93.

30   Deborah Welch Larson, "Bandwagon Images in American Foreign Policy: Myth or Reality?" in *Dominoes and Bandwagons*, ed. Robert Jervis and Jack Snyder (New York: Oxford University Press, 1991), 96.

31   "Truman Lauds 'Brilliant' Victory by MacArthur," *Los Angeles Times*, September 30, 1950.

32   Robert L. Beisner, *Dean Acheson: A Life in the Cold War* (New York: Oxford University Press, 2006), 404.

33   Vladislav M. Zubok, *A Failed Empire: The Soviet Union in the Cold War from Stalin to Gorbachev* (Chapel Hill: University of North Carolina Press, 2007), 78.

34   Harry S. Truman, *Memoirs: Years of Trial and Hope* (New York: Doubleday, 1956), 375.

35   Halberstam, *The Coldest Winter*, 14–16, 386, 390–391.

36   "Statement by Gen. MacArthur," *New York Times*, November 29, 1950.

37   Bruce Cumings, *Korea's Place in the Sun* (New York: W. W. Norton, 1997), 272; Joseph Gerson, *Empire and the Bomb: How the U.S. Uses Nuclear Weapons to Dominate the World* (London: Pluto Press, 2007), 288; Drew Pearson, "Korea Briefing Startled British," *Washington Post*, December 8, 1950.

38   Alan Brinkley, *The Publisher: Henry Luce and His American Century* (New York: Alfred A. Knopf, 2010), 365.

39   "Speeches by Warren Austin of U.S. and Wu Hsiu-chuan of Red China in Security Council," *New York Times*, November 29, 1950.

40   Arthur Veysey, "Attlee to Tell Truman: Don't Use Atom Bomb," *Chicago Tribune*, December 2, 1950.

41   Cumings, *Korea's Place in the Sun*, 272; Gerson, *Empire and the Bomb*, 81; Bruce Cumings, *The Origins of the Korean War*, vol. 2: *The Roaring of the Cataract, 1947–1950* (Princeton, NJ: Princeton University Press, 1990), 749–750.

42   Michael H. Hunt, *Crises in U.S. Foreign Policy* (New Haven, CT: Yale University Press, 1996), 217–218.

43   "Rivers Urges A-Bomb Against Reds," *Miami Daily News*, November 28, 1950.

44   "Congressmen Split on Use of Atom Bomb," *Chicago Tribune*, December 1, 1950.

45   Richard Lee Miller, *Under the Cloud: The Decades of Nuclear Testing* (The Woodlands, TX: Two Sixty Press, 1991), 101.

46   A. M. Rosenthal, "U.N. Circles Wary on Atom Bomb Use," *New York Times*, December 1, 1950.

47   Cumings, *The Origins of the Korean War*, 750.

48   C. L. Sulzberger, "U.S. Prestige Ebbs on Korea, Europe-Asia Survey Shows," *New York Times,* December 7, 1950.

49   Bruce Cumings, *The Korean War: A History* (New York: Modern Library, 2010), 156.

50   Arnold A. Offner, *Another Such Victory: President Truman and the Cold War, 1945–1953* (Stanford, CA: Stanford University Press, 2002), 402.

51   Max Hastings, *The Korean War* (New York: Simon & Schuster, 1987), 201.

52   Cumings, *The Origins of the Korean War,* 750–751.

53   Halberstam, *The Coldest Winter,* 607.

54   "McCarthy Charges Treason with Bourbon," *Los Angeles Times,* April 13, 1951.

55   Richard H. Rovere and Arthur Schlesinger, Jr., *General MacArthur and President Truman: The Struggle for Control of American Foreign Policy* (1951; reprint, New Brunswick, NJ: Transaction Publishers, 1992), 276–277.

56   Halberstam, *The Coldest Winter,* 609.

57   Beisner, *Dean Acheson,* 432.

58   Ibid., 433, 446.

59   George Barrett, "Radio Hams in U.S. Discuss Girls, So Shelling of Seoul Is Held Up," *New York Times,* February 9, 1951.

60   I. F. Stone, *The Hidden History of the Korean War* (New York: Monthly Review Press, 1969), 313.

61   Bruce Cumings, "American Airpower and Nuclear Strategy in Northeast Asia Since 1945," in *War and State Terrorism: The United States, Japan, and the Asia-Pacific in the Long Twentieth Century,* ed. Mark Selden and Alvin Y. So (Lanham, MD: Rowman & Littlefield, 2004), 76.

62   Bruce Cumings, *Dominion from Sea to Sea: Pacific Ascendancy and American Power* (New Haven, CT: Yale University Press, 2009), 340–341.

63   John Lewis Gaddis, *Russia, The Soviet Union, and the United States: An Interpretive History* (New York: Alfred A. Knopf, 1978), 212.

64   Thomas C. Reeves, *The Life and Times of Joe McCarthy* (1982; reprint, Lanham, MD: Madison Books, 1997), 451.

65   Ibid., 436.

66   Stephen E. Ambrose, *Eisenhower: The President,* vol. 2 (New York: Simon & Schuster, 1984), 55.

67   Samuel Shaffer, "Behind Nixon's Speech," *Newsweek,* October 6, 1952, 25.

68   Stephen E. Ambrose, *Eisenhower: Soldier and President* (New York: Simon & Schuster, 1990), 218.

69   Dwight D. Eisenhower, "The Long Pull for Peace: Extracts from the Final Report of the Chief of Staff General of the Army Dwight D. Eisenhower," *The Army Information Digest,* April 1948, 41.

70   Ira Chernus, *Apocalypse Management: Eisenhower and the Discourse of National Security* (Stanford, CA: Stanford University Press, 2008), 30–31.

71   Walter LaFeber, *America, Russia, and the Cold War, 1945–2006* (Boston: McGraw-Hill, 2008), 147.

72   Leffler, *For the Soul of Mankind*, 104.

73   Klaus Larres, *Churchill's Cold War: The Politics of Personal Diplomacy* (New Haven, CT: Yale University Press, 2002), 189–193.

74   "Text of Speech by Eisenhower Outlining Proposals for Peace in World," *New York Times*, April 17, 1953.

75   "Highway of Peace," *New York Times*, April 17, 1953, 24.

76   "Eisenhower's Peace Program," *Washington Post*, April 17, 1953, 26.

77   Lloyd Gardner, "Poisoned Apples: John Foster Dulles and the 'Peace Offensive,'" in *The Cold War After Stalin's Death*, ed. Klaus Larres and Kenneth Osgood (Lanham, MD: Rowman & Littlefield, 2006), 85.

78   Arthur M. Schlesinger, Jr., *The Cycles of American History* (Boston: Houghton Mifflin, 1999), 399.

79   H. R. Haldeman with Joseph DiMona, *The Ends of Power* (New York: Dell, 1978), 121–122; Richard Nixon, *The Real War* (New York: Simon & Schuster, 1990), 255.

80   Jon Halliday and Bruce Cumings, *Korea: The Unknown War* (New York: Penguin, 1990), 203.

81   Ibid., 204.

82   Dwight MacDonald, "America! America!," in *50 Years of Dissent*, ed. Nicolaus Mills and Michael Walzer (New Haven, CT: Yale University Press, 2004), 50.

83   McMillan, *The Ruin of J. Robert Oppenheimer*, 142.

84   DeGroot, *The Bomb*, 179.

85   "Text of Eisenhower Inaugural Address Pledging Search for Peace," *New York Times*, January 21, 1953.

86   Edgar Snow, *Journey to the Beginning* (New York: Random House, 1958), 360–361.

87   "Ike Scouts Bomb as Full Defense," *Baltimore Sun*, February 25, 1947.

88   David Alan Rosenberg, "The Origins of Overkill: Nuclear Weapons and American Strategy 1945–1960," *International Security* 7 (Spring 1983), 27.

89   Peter J. Kuznick, "Prophets of Doom or Voices of Sanity? The Evolving Discourse of Annihilation in the First Decade and a Half of the Nuclear Age," *Journal of Genocide Research* 9 (2007), 424.

90   "The Central Problem," *New York Times*, September 19, 1953.

91   Richard H. Immerman, *Empire for Liberty: A History of American Imperialism from Benjamin Franklin to Paul Wolfowitz* (Princeton, NJ: Princeton University Press, 2010), 164–172.

92   Ronald W. Pruessen, *John Foster Dulles: The Road to Power* (New York: Free Press, 1982), 123–132.

93   Stephen Kinzer, *Overthrow: America's Century of Regime Change from Hawaii to Iraq* (New York: Times Books, 2006), 114.

94   Sherman Adams, *Firsthand Report: The Story of the Eisenhower Administration* (Westport, CT: Greenwood Press, 1974), 364.

95   John Prados, *The Sky Would Fall: Operation Vulture: The U.S. Bombing Mission in Indochina, 1954* (New York: Dial Press, 1983), 30.

96 Memorandum of Discussion at a Special Meeting of the National Security Council on Tuesday, March 31, 1953, *Foreign Relations of the United States, 1952–1954: Korea,* vol. 15 (Washington, DC: U.S. Government Printing Office, 1984), 827.

97 Appu K. Soman, *Double-edged Sword: Nuclear Diplomacy in Unequal Conflicts: The United States and China, 1950–1958* (New York: Praeger, 2000), 88.

98 Fred Kaplan, *The Wizards of Armageddon* (1983; reprint, Stanford, CA: Stanford University Press, 1991), 183–184.

99 Schlesinger, *Cycles of History,* 401.

100 Chernus, *Apocalypse Management,* 96.

101 Edward T. Folliard, "U.S. to Use A-Weapons in Any War," *Washington Post,* March 17, 1955; "President Says Atom Bomb Would Be Used like 'Bullet,'" *New York Times,* March 17, 1955.

102 "Record Shows U.S. Stands Ready to Use Its Nuclear Weapons Against Aggressor," *New York Times,* January 2, 1956.

103 Chernus, *Apocalypse Management,* 78–79.

104 William Lanouette, "Looking Back: Civilian Control of Nuclear Weapons," *Arms Control Today,* May 2009, 45.

105 "Text of Eisenhower's Address to the U.N. Assembly," *New York Times,* December 9, 1953.

106 Hanson W. Baldwin, "Eisenhower's Bid Hailed," *New York Times,* December 10, 1953.

107 Shane J. Maddock, *Nuclear Apartheid: The Quest for American Atomic Supremacy from World War II to the Present* (Chapel Hill: University of North Carolina Press, 2010), 91.

108 David Holloway, *Stalin and the Bomb: The Soviet Union and Atomic Energy, 1939–1956* (New Haven, CT: Yale University Press, 1994), 349–350.

109 John Foster Dulles, "The Evolution of Foreign Policy," *Department of State Bulletin* 30, no. 761 (January 25, 1954), 108.

110 William Henry Chamberlin, "The New Strategy," *Wall Street Journal,* March 22, 1954.

111 James Reston, "Washington: 'Massive Atomic Retaliation' and the Constitution," *New York Times,* January 17, 1954.

112 Kaplan, *The Wizards of Armageddon,* 212.

113 DeGroot, *The Bomb,* 190.

114 Leffler, *For the Soul of Mankind,* 112.

115 Gardner, "The Dulles Years," 391.

116 Kinzer, *Overthrow,* 122.

117 Beisner, *Dean Acheson,* 538; Kinzer, 117–118.

118 The Ambassador in Iran (Grady) to the Department of State, July 1, 1951, *Foreign Relations of the United States, 1952–1954,* vol. 10 (Washington, DC: U.S. Government Printing Office, 1989), 80.

119 Daniel Yergin, *The Prize: The Epic Quest for Oil, Money, and Power* (New York: Simon & Schuster, 1991), 457.

120 Ibid., 458.

121 Odd Arne Westad, *The Global Cold War: Third World Interventions and the Making of Our Times* (New York: Cambridge University Press, 2007), 121.

122 Beisner, *Dean Acheson,* 546.

123 Christopher Andrew, *For the President's Eyes Only: Secret Intelligence and the American Presidency from Washington to Bush* (New York: HarperCollins, 1995), 203.

124 The Ambassador in Iran (Henderson) to the Department of State, July 28, 1952, *Foreign Relations of the United States, 1952–1954,* vol. 10 (Washington, DC: U.S. Government Printing Office, 1989), 417.

125 Tim Weiner, *Legacy of Ashes: The History of the CIA* (New York: Doubleday, 2007), 86.

126 LaFeber, *America, Russia, and the Cold War, 1945–2006,* 162.

127 Piero Gleijeses, *Shattered Hope: The Guatemalan Revolution and the United States, 1944–1954* (Princeton, NJ: Princeton University Press, 1991), 150.

128 "The Guatemalan Cancer," *New York Times,* June 8, 1951.

129 "Red Cell in Guatemala," *Washington Post,* March 4, 1952.

130 Kinzer, *Overthrow,* 134–135.

131 Nick Cullather, *Secret History: The CIA's Classified Account of Its Operations in Guatemala 1952–1954* (Stanford, CA: Stanford University Press, 1999), 28.

132 Peter Chapman, *Bananas: How the United Fruit Company Shaped the World* (New York: Canongate, 2007), 131–132.

133 Richard H. Immerman, *The CIA in Guatemala: The Foreign Policy of Intervention* (Austin: University of Texas Press, 1982), 181; Stephen C. Schlesinger and Stephen Kinzer, *Bitter Fruit: The Untold Story of the American Coup in Guatemala* (New York: Doubleday, 1982), 137–138.

134 Cullather, *Secret History,* 26.

135 John W. Young, "Great Britain's Latin American Dilemma: The Foreign Office and the Overthrow of 'Communist' Guatemala, June 1954," *International History Review* 8 (November 1986), 575.

136 Weiner, *Legacy of Ashes,* 461.

137 Walter H. Waggoner, "U.S. Wants Rio Pact Inquiry on Arms Sent to Guatemala," *New York Times,* May 19, 1954.

138 Weiner, *Legacy of Ashes,* 98.

139 "Guatemala Lifts Ban; Allows *Times* Correspondent to Re-enter Country," *New York Times,* May 21, 1954.

140 Sydney Gruson, "U.S. Stand on Arms Unites Guatemala," *New York Times,* May 21, 1954.

141 Sydney Gruson, "Guatemala Says U.S. Tried to Make Her Defenseless," *New York Times,* May 22, 1954.

142 Sydney Gruson, "U.S. Arms Stand Alienates Guatemalan Foes of Reds," *New York Times,* May 24, 1954.

143 Kinzer, *Overthrow,* 140.

144 Young, "Great Britain's Latin American Dilemma," 584.

145 Kinzer, *Overthrow,* 145.

146 Schlesinger and Kinzer, *Bitter Fruit,* 206.

147 "The Text of Dulles' Speech on Guatemalan Upset," *New York Times,* July 1, 1954.

148 Young, "Great Britain's Latin American Dilemma," 588.

149 Stephen Kinzer, "Revisiting Cold War Coups and Finding Them Costly," *New York Times,* November 30, 2003.

150 Kinzer, *Overthrow,* 147; "Dulles Hails Upset of Reds," *Chicago Tribune,* July 1, 1954.

151 Philip C. Roettinger, "For a CIA Man, It's 1954 Again," *Los Angeles Times,* March 16, 1986.

152 Westad, *The Global Cold War,* 149.

153 "Text of Talk by President Eisenhower at Governors' Conference," *New York Times,* August 5, 1953.

154 "Speech by Vice-President Nixon, December 23, 1953," transcribed in *Conflict in Indo-China and International Repercussions: A Documentary History, 1945–1955,* ed. Allan B. Cole (Ithaca, NY: Cornell University Press, 1956), 171.

155 "Why U.S. Risks War for Indochina: It's the Key to Control of All Asia," *U.S. News & World Report,* April 4, 1954, 21.

156 McGeorge Bundy, *Danger and Survival: Choices About the Bomb in the First Fifty Years* (New York: Vintage, 1990), 267.

157 Prados, *The Sky Would Fall,* 145–157; Fawn M. Brodie, *Richard Nixon: The Shaping of His Character* (New York: W. W. Norton, 1981), 322.

158 Frederick W. Marks, *Power and Peace: The Diplomacy of John Foster Dulles* (New York: Praeger, 1993), 197, note 41.

159 Bundy, *Danger and Survival,* 78.

160 Schlesinger, *Cycles of History,* 400.

161 "Cat in the Closet," *Chicago Tribune,* April 13, 1954.

162 Chalmers M. Roberts, "Our 25 Years in Vietnam," *Washington Post,* June 2, 1968.

163 Richard H. Immerman, *John Foster Dulles: Piety, Pragmatism, and Power in U.S. Foreign Policy* (Wilmington, DE: Scholarly Resources, 1999), 93.

164 Walter Lippmann, "Surrender Demands by Both Sides Make Vietnam Settlement Difficult," *Los Angeles Times,* April 4, 1965.

165 William L. Ryan, "Real Leader Needed to Rally Vietnamese," *Washington Post,* April 24, 1954.

166 Hans Morgenthau, "Vietnam Chief a Multi-Paradox," *Washington Post,* February 26, 1956.

167 Dwight D. Eisenhower, *Mandate for Change: The White House Years* (New York: Doubleday, 1963), 372.

168 Wittner, *Resisting the Bomb,* 147.

169 Robert T. Hartmann, "AEC Chief Bares Facts on H-Bomb," *Los Angeles Times,* April 1, 1954; "Text of Statement and Comments by Strauss on Hydrogen Bomb Tests in the Pacific," *New York Times,* April 1, 1954.

170 Chernus, *Apocalypse Management,* 87.

171 Maddock, *Nuclear Apartheid,* 96.

172   Chernus, *Apocalypse Management*, 88.

173   Bundy, *Danger and Survival*, 271–273.

174   John Swenson-Wright, *Unequal Allies: United States Security and Alliance Policy Toward Japan, 1945–1960* (Stanford, CA: Stanford University Press, 2005), 181. For a fuller discussion of this effort, see Peter J. Kuznick, "Japan's Nuclear History in Perspective: Eisenhower and Atoms for War and Peace," *Bulletin of the Atomic Scientists*, April 13, 2011, http://www.thebulletin.org/web-edition/features/japans-nuclear-history-perspective-eisenhower-and-atoms-war-and-peace, or Toshiyuki Tanaka and Peter Kuznick, *Genpatsu to hiroshima—genshiryoku heiwa riyo no shinso (Nuclear Power and Hiroshima: The Truth Behind the Peaceful Use of Nuclear Power)* (Tokyo: Iwanami Shoten, 2011).

175   Stanley Levey, "Nuclear Reactor Urged For Japan," *New York Times*, September 22, 1954, 14.

176   "A Reactor for Japan," *Washington Post*, September 23, 1954, 18; Foster Hailey, "Tokyo Press Stirs Ire of Americans," *New York Times*, June 8, 1956.

177   William L. Laurence, "Now Most Dreaded Weapon, Cobalt Bomb, Can Be Built; Chemical Compound That Revolutionized Hydrogen Bomb Makes It Possible," *New York Times*, April 7, 1954.

178   "Russ Reported Making Deadly Nitrogen Bomb," *Los Angeles Times*, April 9, 1954.

179   "Cobalt Bomb's Peril to All Life Stressed," *Washington Post*, February 14, 1955.

180   DeGroot, *The Bomb*, 198.

Chapter 7: JFK: "The Most Dangerous Moment in Human History"

1   "Shedding New Light on the Stalin Regime," *Manchester Guardian*, March 17, 1956.

2   Gerald J. DeGroot, *Dark Side of the Moon: The Magnificent Madness of the American Lunar Quest* (New York: New York University Press, 2006), 64, 67–68.

3   Ibid., 69.

4   Martin Walker, *The Cold War: A History* (New York: Macmillan, 1995), 114.

5   Lloyd C. Gardner, "The Dulles Years: 1953–1959," in *From Colony to Empire*, ed. William Appleman Williams (New York: John Wiley & Sons, 1972), 418.

6   DeGroot, *Dark Side of the Moon*, 73.

7   "Science: Sputnik's Week," *Time*, October 21, 1957, 51.

8   Fred Kaplan, *The Wizards of Armageddon* (1983; reprint, Stanford, CA: Stanford University Press, 1991), 135.

9   Mathew Brzezinski, *Red Moon Rising: Sputnik and the Hidden Rivalries that Ignited the Space Age* (New York: Macmillan), 180.

10   David Halberstam, *The Fifties* (New York: Villard, 1993), 621.

11   "Khrushchev Speaks on Economic and Technical Progress," *Bulletin of the Atomic Scientists*, December 1957, 360.

12   Dwight D. Eisenhower: *Public Papers of the President of the United States: Dwight D. Eisenhower* (Washington, DC: U.S. Government Printing Office, 1961), 789–792.

13   William J. Broad, "U.S. Planned Nuclear Blast on the Moon, Physicist Says," *New York Times*, May 16, 2000.

14 Keay Davidson and Carl Sagan, *Carl Sagan: A Life* (New York: John Wiley & Sons, 1999), 86.

15 Special National Intelligence Estimate Number 11-10-57, "The Soviet ICBM Program," December 10, 1957, National Security Archive, Digital Collection, Soviet Estimate, 2.

16 Richard Rhodes, *Arsenals of Folly: The Making of the Nuclear Arms Race* (New York: Alfred A. Knopf, 2007), 109.

17 Chalmers M. Roberts, "Enormous Arms Outlay Is Held Vital to Survival," *Washington Post*, December 20, 1957.

18 DeGroot, *Dark Side of the Moon*, 69.

19 Joseph Alsop, "Matter of Fact: Untruths on Defense," *Washington Post*, August 1, 1958.

20 John G. Norris, "Power Shifts to Soviet, Kennedy Warns," *Washington Post*, August 15, 1958.

21 Michael S. Sherry, *The Rise of American Air Power: The Creation of Armageddon* (New Haven, CT: Yale University Press, 1987), 218.

22 Tim Weiner, *Legacy of Ashes: The History of the CIA* (New York: Doubleday, 2007), 162–163.

23 "Texts of Appeal by Noted Scientists for Abolition of War," *New York Times*, July 10, 1955.

24 Otto Nathan and Heinz Norden, ed. *Einstein on Peace* (New York: Schocken Books, 1960), 681.

25 "Policies Averted 3 Wars, Dulles Quoted as Saying," *New York Times*, January 12, 1956.

26 William S. White, "Rayburn Assails Stand by Dulles," *New York Times*, January 17, 1956.

27 "Dulles Risking U.S. Safety, Adlai Charges," *Washington Post*, January 15, 1956; Richard J. H. Johnston, "Stevenson Bids President Repudiate or Oust Dulles," *New York Times*, January 18, 1956.

28 Chalmers M. Roberts, "Political Pot-Shots Beset Dulles," *Washington Post*, January 17, 1956.

29 "Protest to Ike over Dulles' Step to the Brink," *Chicago Tribune*, January 29, 1956.

30 John Lewis Gaddis, "The Unexpected John Foster Dulles: Nuclear Weapons, Communism, and the Russians," in *John Foster Dulles and the Diplomacy of the Cold War*, ed. Richard H. Immerman (Princeton, NJ: Princeton University Press, 1990), 53–58.

31 "What the President Saw: A Nation Coming into Its Own," *Time*, July 29, 1985, 50.

32 Warren Unna, "Atoms and Politics," *Washington Post*, October 10, 1956; Bradford Jacobs, "Stevenson," *Baltimore Sun*, October 27, 1956.

33 Bradford Jacobs, "Democrat Again Urges Testing Ban," *Baltimore Sun*, October 16, 1956.

34 Henry R. Lieberman, "Nehru Again Asks End of Bomb Tests," *New York Times*, May 18, 1957.

35 "Focus on Atoms," *New York Times*, May 19, 1957.

36 Lawrence S. Wittner, *Resisting the Bomb: A History of the World Nuclear Disarmament Movement, 1954–1970* (Stanford, CA: Stanford University Press, 1997), 52–53.

37 Ibid., 35–36.

38 Warren Unna, "Libby Believes Man Can Tap Energy Sealed in Mountain by A-Bomb Blast," *Washington Post*, December 3, 1957.

39 Richard G. Hewlett and Jack M. Holl, *Atoms for Peace and War, 1953–1961: Eisenhower and the Atomic Energy Commission* (Berkeley: University of California Press, 1989), 529.

40 Gladwin Hill, "A.E.C. Considers Deep A-Blasting for Oil and Ore," *New York Times*, March 14, 1958.

41 "Underground Atom Blast Planned for U.S. for 1961," *New York Times*, March 17, 1960.

42 "'Plowshare' Seeks Uses for H-Bomb Explosions," *Washington Post*, August 23, 1959.

43 "Excerpts from Message by Schweitzer," *New York Times*, April 24, 1957; "Schweitzer Urges World Opinion to Demand End of Nuclear Tests," *New York Times*, April 24, 1957.

44 "Focus on Atoms," *New York Times*, May 19, 1957.

45 George Gallup, "Public Favors H-Tests' Halt, If—," *Washington Post*, May 19, 1957.

46 Earle P. Brown, "The Facing of Certain Death," *Washington Post*, July 28, 1957.

47 Gerard J. De Groot, *The Bomb: A Life* (Cambridge, MA: Harvard University Press, 2005), 211.

48 Bosley Crowther, "Screen: On the Beach," *New York Times*, December 18, 1959.

49 Spencer R. Weart, *Nuclear Fear: A History of Images* (Cambridge, MA: Harvard University Press, 1988), 218–219.

50 Kenneth D. Rose, *One Nation Underground: The Fallout Shelter in American Culture* (New York: New York University Press, 2001), 43.

51 Rhodes, *Arsenals of Folly*, 101.

52 Robert S. Norris and William M. Arkin, "Estimated U.S. and Soviet/Russian Nuclear Stockpiles, 1945–94," *Bulletin of the Atomic Scientists*, November–December 1994, 58–59; Robert S. Norris and William M. Arkin, "Global Nuclear Stockpiles, 1945–2006," *Bulletin of the Atomic Scientists*, July–August 2006, 66.

53 Daniel Ellsberg, personal communication with Peter Kuznick.

54 David A. Rosenberg, "The Origins of Overkill: Nuclear Weapons and American Strategy, 1945–1960," *International Security* 7 (Spring 1983), 8.

55 Daniel Ellsberg, *Secrets: A Memoir of Vietnam and the Pentagon Papers* (New York: Viking, 2002), 58–59.

56 David Talbot, *Brothers: The Hidden History of the Kennedy Years* (New York: Free Press, 2007), 36.

57 W. H. Lawrence, "President Describes Nixon Role in Administration's Decisions," *New York Times*, August 25, 1960.

58 Charles J. G. Griffin, "New Light on Eisenhower's Farewell Address," *Presidential Studies Quarterly* 22 (Summer 1992), 472.

59 Milton Leitenberg, personal communication with Peter Kuznick, December 2010.

60 "Text of Eisenhower's Farewell Address," *New York Times*, January 18, 1961.

61 Walter Lippmann, "Today and Tomorrow: Eisenhower's Farewell Warning," *Washington Post*, January 19, 1961.

62 Griffin, "New Light on Eisenhower's Farewell Address," 475.

63 Jack Raymond, "The 'Military-Industrial Complex': An Analysis," *New York Times*, January 22, 1961.

64 Talbot, *Brothers*, 35–36.

65 Desmond Ball, *Politics and Force Levels: The Strategic Missile Program of the Kennedy Administration* (Berkeley: University of California Press, 1980), 18–19.

66 Christopher A. Preble, "Who Ever Believed in the 'Missile Gap'?: John F. Kennedy and the Politics of National Security," *Presidential Studies Quarterly* 33 (December 2003), 805–806.

67 "Text of President Kennedy's Inaugural Address," *Washington Post,* January 21, 1961.

68 David Halberstam, *The Best and the Brightest* (New York: Random House, 1972), 60.

69 Kenneth P. O'Donnell and David F. Powers, *"Johnny, We Hardly Knew Ye": Memories of John Fitzgerald Kennedy* (Boston: Little, Brown, 1970), 14.

70 Talbot, *Brothers,* 45.

71 Talbot, *Brothers,* 50–51.

72 "Curtains for Now in Cuba," *Chicago Tribune,* April 22, 1961.

73 "The Collapse in Cuba," *Wall Street Journal,* April 21, 1961.

74 "A Policy on Cuba," *New York Times,* April 27, 1961.

75 Douglas Brinkley, *Dean Acheson: The Cold War Years* (New Haven, CT: Yale University Press, 1994), 127; Jim Heath, *Decade of Disillusionment: The Kennedy-Johnson Years* (Bloomington, IN: Indiana University Press, 1975), 83.

76 Halberstam, *The Best and the Brightest,* 69.

77 "Kennedy's Address," *Baltimore Sun,* April 21, 1961.

78 Jack Raymond, "Gore Would Oust the Joint Chiefs," *New York Times,* May 20, 1961; "C.I.A. Under the Microscope," *New York Times,* May 9, 1961.

79 Arthur M. Schlesinger, Jr., *A Thousand Days: John F. Kennedy in the White House* (New York: Houghton Mifflin, 1965), 292.

80 Ibid., 258.

81 Benjamin C. Bradlee, *Conversations with Kennedy* (New York: W. W. Norton, 1975), 122.

82 Talbot, *Brothers,* 50–51.

83 Weiner, *Legacy of Ashes,* 180.

84 Ibid., 178–179.

85 Talbot, *Brothers,* 51.

86 W. J. Rorabaugh, *Kennedy and the Promise of the Sixties* (New York: Cambridge University Press, 2002), 24.

87 Schlesinger, *A Thousand Days,* 391.

88 T. Christopher Jespersen, ed. *Interviews with George F. Kennan* (Jackson: University Press of Mississippi, 2002), 88.

89 Halberstam, *The Best and the Brightest,* 76.

90 Melvyn P. Leffler, *For the Soul of Mankind: The United States, the Soviet Union and the Cold War* (New York: Hill and Wang, 2007), 163–164.

91 Kaplan, *The Wizards of Armageddon,* 297.

92 Heather A. Purcell and James K. Galbraith, "Did the U.S. Military Plan a Nuclear First Strike for 1963?," *American Prospect* 19 (Fall 1994), 88–96.

93 Dean Rusk, *As I Saw It* (New York: W. W. Norton, 1990), 246–247.

94　Roger Hilsman, *From Nuclear Military Strategy to a World Without War: A History and Proposal* (New York: Praeger, 1999), 52.

95　"Text of Kennedy Appeal to Nation for Increases in Spending and Armed Forces," *New York Times,* July 26, 1961.

96　James Carroll, *An American Requiem: God, My Father, and the War That Came Between Us* (Boston: Houghton Mifflin, 1996), 82–83.

97　Michael R. Beschloss, *The Crisis Years: Kennedy and Khrushchev 1960–1963* (New York: Edward Burlingame Books, 1991), 278.

98　Shane J. Maddock, *Nuclear Apartheid: The Quest for American Atomic Supremacy from World War II to the Present* (Chapel Hill: University of North Carolina Press, 2010), 131.

99　Ibid., 162–163.

100　"Fallout Defense Seen in 'Deplorable Shape,'" *Washington Post,* March 29, 1960.

101　"Fire Wrecks Libby's Bel Air Fallout Shelter," *Washington Post,* November 10, 1961.

102　Rose, *One Nation Underground,* 190; "Atom Shelter Builders Finding Business Poor," *Los Angeles Times,* June 4, 1961.

103　Rose, *One Nation Underground,* 97, 94.

104　L. C. McHugh, "Ethics at the Shelter Doorway," *America,* September 30, 1961, 826.

105　Louis Cassels, "Private A-Shelters Held 'Unjust' by Bishop Dunn," *Washington Post,* October 14, 1961.

106　Rose, *One Nation Underground,* 98.

107　Arthur Gelb, "Political Satire Invades Capital," *New York Times,* January 30, 1962; Emma Harrison, "Priest Unmoved on Shelter View," *New York Times,* November 22, 1961.

108　"U.S. Bares Atomic Might," *Chicago Tribune,* October 22, 1961; Beschloss, *The Crisis Years,* 331.

109　The U.S. had one Titan and sixty-two Atlas ICBMs by December 31, 1961, according to the December 7, 1991, SAC report "Alert Operations and the Strategic Air Command, 1957–1991."

110　Roy F. Houchin, *US Hypersonic Research and Development: The Rise and Fall of Dyna-Soar, 1944–1963* (New York: Routledge, 2006), 140; Robert S. Norris and William M. Arkin, "Global Nuclear Stockpiles, 1945–2006," *Bulletin of the Atomic Scientists,* July–August 2006, 66.

111　Kaplan, *The Wizards of Armageddon,* 246.

112　Ibid., 254–257.

113　James G. Blight and Philip Brenner, *Sad & Luminous Days: Cuba's Struggle with the Superpowers after the Missile Crisis* (Lanham, MD: Rowman & Littlefield, 2002), 8.

114　Ibid.

115　Gregg Herken, *Counsels of War* (New York: Oxford University Press, 1987), 37.

116　Allan M. Winkler, *Life Under a Cloud: American Anxiety About the Atom* (New York: Oxford University Press, 1993), 175.

117　Talbot, *Brothers,* 95.

118　Weiner, *Legacy of Ashes,* 184–185.

119 "Justification for U.S. Military Intervention in Cuba," March 13, 1962, National Security Archive, www.gwu.edu/~nsarchiv/news/20010430/doc1.pdf.

120 John F. Kennedy, "Remarks of Senator John F. Kennedy at the Fourth Annual Rockhurst Day Banquet of Rockhurst College in Kansas City, Missouri, Saturday, June 2, 1956," www.findingcamelot.net/speeches/1956/remarks-of-senator-john-f -kennedy -at-the-fourth-annual-rockhurst-day-banquet-of-rockhurst-college-in-kansas -city-missouri-Saturday-June-2-1956/.

121 Douglas A. Borer, *Superpowers Defeated: Vietnam and Afghanistan Compared* (New York: Frank Cass Publishers, 1999), 102.

122 Halberstam, *The Best and the Brightest,* 135.

123 Schlesinger, *A Thousand Days,* 547.

124 Despite having a seventeen-to-one advantage in nuclear weaponry during the Cuban Missile Crisis, Kennedy considered the possibility of even one or two Soviet bombs striking U.S. cities too high a price to pay even if the United States could obliterate the Soviet Union in retaliation.

125 Maddock, *Nuclear Apartheid,* 197.

126 Blight and Brenner, *Sad & Luminous Days,* 36. We are grateful to Phil Brenner for clarifying the reference to Khrushchev's planned "December" visit.

127 Weiner, *Legacy of Ashes,* 201.

128 Richard Rhodes, *Dark Sun: The Making of the Hydrogen Bomb* (New York: Simon & Schuster, 1995), 574.

129 O'Donnell and Powers, *"Johnny, We Hardly Knew Ye,"* 318.

130 Ernest R. May and Philip D. Zelikow, *The Kennedy Tapes: Inside the White House During the Cuban Missile Crisis* (Cambridge, MA: Belknap Press, 1997), 178.

131 "Text of Kennedy's Address on Moves to Meet the Soviet Build-up in Cuba," *New York Times,* October 23, 1962.

132 Robert S. McNamara, *Blundering into Disaster: Surviving the First Century of the Nuclear Age* (New York: Pantheon, 1987), 10; Dobbs, *One Minute to Midnight,* 163.

133 Marion Lloyd, "Soviets Close to Using A-Bomb in 1962 Crisis, Forum Is Told," *Boston Globe,* October 13, 2002.

134 Alexander Mozgovoi, "The Cuban Samba of the Quartet of Foxtrots: Soviet Submarines in the Caribbean Crisis of 1962," *Military Parade,* Moscow, 2002, National Security Archive, www.gwu.edu/~nsarchiv/nsa/cuba_mis_cri/020000%20Recollections;%20 of%20Vadim%20Orlov.pdf.

135 "Khrushchev Note," *Los Angeles Times,* November 2, 1962.

136 Mimi Alford, *Once Upon a Secret: My Affair with President John F. Kennedy and Its Aftermath* (New York: Random House, 2012), 94; Andreas Wegner, *Living with Peril: Eisenhower, Kennedy, and Nuclear Weapons* (Lanham, MD: Rowman & Littlefield, 1997), 201; J. Anthony Lukas, "Class Reunion," *New York Times,* August 30, 1987.

137 William Taubman, *Khrushchev: The Man and His Era* (New York: W. W. Norton, 2003), 347.

138 Nikita S. Khrushchev, *Khrushchev Remembers* (Boston: Little, Brown, 1970), 552.

139 Aleksandr Fursenko and Timothy Naftali, *Khrushchev's Cold War: The Inside Story of an American Adversary* (New York: W. W. Norton, 2006), 500.

140 On October 25, Kennedy learned that the Soviets had installed Luna missiles, which could be used as tactical nuclear weapons or as conventional weapons. Kennedy and his advisors assumed that the Lunas were conventional. When Admiral George Anderson asked permission to load equivalent nuclear missiles on U.S. ships, Kennedy refused because he believed that the Soviet Lunas were not nuclear.

141 Robert S. McNamara, *In Retrospect: The Tragedy and Lessons of Vietnam* (New York: Vintage, 1996), 338–342; Jon Mitchell, "Okinawa's First Nuclear Missile Men Break Silence," *Japan Times*, July 8, 2012.

142 J. Anthony Lukas, "Class Reunion," *New York Times*, August 30, 1987.

143 Maddock, *Nuclear Apartheid*, 198.

144 Ibid.

145 Message from Chairman Khrushchev to President Kennedy, October 30, 1962, *Foreign Relations of the United States, 1961–1963*, vol. 11 (Washington, DC: U.S. Government Printing Office, 1997), 309–317.

146 Wittner, *Resisting the Bomb*, 416.

147 Leffler, *For the Soul of Mankind*, 161.

148 Arthur M. Schlesinger, Jr., *Robert Kennedy and His Times* (New York: Houghton Mifflin Harcourt, 2002), 596.

149 Leffler, *For the Soul of Mankind*, 184.

150 Beschloss, *The Crisis Years*, 624.

151 For a discussion of the Atmospheric Test Ban Treaty, see Wittner, *Resisting the Bomb*, 416–421.

152 Gareth Porter, *Perils of Dominance: Imbalance of Power and the Road to War in Vietnam* (Berkeley: University of California Press, 2005), 169–170.

153 John M. Newman, *JFK and Vietnam: Deception, Intrigue, and the Struggle for Power* (New York: Warner Books, 1992), 319–320.

154 James W. Douglass, *JFK and the Unspeakable: Why He Died and Why It Matters* (Maryknoll, NY: Orbis, 2008), 181.

155 For a fuller discussion of McNamara and Kennedy's maneuvering, see Porter, *Perils of Dominance*, 165–179.

156 Tad Szulc, "Crisis in Vietnam: Repercussions Are Felt Throughout Asia," *New York Times*, August 25, 1963.

157 Kai Bird, *The Color of Truth: McGeorge and William Bundy: Brothers in Arms* (New York: Touchstone, 1988), 261.

158 Ellsberg, *Secrets*, 195–196.

159 Douglass, *JFK and the Unspeakable*, 182.

160 John F. Kennedy, *Public Papers of the Presidents of the United States: John F. Kennedy, 1963* (Washington, DC: U.S. Government Printing Office, 1964), 459–464.

161 Talbot, *Brothers*, 206.

162 Wittner, *Resisting the Bomb*, 421–422.

163 Memorandum from the Joint Chiefs of Staff to Secretary of Defense McNamara: Nuclear Test Ban Issue, April 20, 1963, *Foreign Relations of the United States, 1961–1963*, vol. 7 (Washington, DC: U.S. Government Printing Office, 1995), 684.

164 "Transcript of President Kennedy's News Conference," *Washington Post*, March 22, 1963.

165 Beschloss, *The Crisis Years*, 632.

166 Talbot, *Brothers*, 213.

167 Andrei Gromyko, *Memoirs* (New York: Doubleday, 1989), 137.

168 Walter A. McDougall, *The Heavens and the Earth: A Political History of the Space Age* (New York: Basic Books, 1985), 221–222.

169 "Transcript of Kennedy Address to Congress on U.S. Role in Struggle for Freedom," *New York Times*, May 26, 1961.

170 "Excerpts from the Speech of President John F. Kennedy Before the United Nations General Assembly, September 20," *Bulletin of the Atomic Scientists*, November 1963, 45.

171 Douglass, *JFK and the Unspeakable*, 69–70; William Attwood, *The Twilight Struggle: Tales of the Cold War* (New York: Harper & Row, 1987), 257–262.

172 Jean Daniel, "Unofficial Envoy: An Historic Report from Two Capitals," *New Republic*, December 14, 1963, 16.

173 Douglass, *JFK and the Unspeakable*, 84–89.

174 Jules Dubois, "Kennedy Soft on Reds: Rocky," *Chicago Tribune*, November 14, 1963; Donald Janson, "Rockefeller Says Kennedy's Policy Imperils Peace," *New York Times*, November 17, 1963; Foster Hailey, "Governor Scores U.S. on Atom Use," *New York Times*, November 21, 1963.

175 Talbot, *Brothers*, 151.

Chapter 8: LBJ: Empire Derailed

1 Jean Daniel, "When Castro Heard the News," *New Republic*, December 7, 1963, 7–8.

2 David Talbot, *Brothers: The Hidden History of the Kennedy Years* (New York: Free Press, 2007), 33.

3 James W. Douglass, *JFK and the Unspeakable: Why He Died and Why It Matters* (Maryknoll, NY: Orbis, 2008), 381.

4 Melvyn P. Leffler, *For the Soul of Mankind: The United States, the Soviet Union and the Cold War* (New York: Hill and Wang, 2007), 192; Michael Dobbs, *One Minute to Midnight: Kennedy, Khrushchev, and Castro on the Brink of Nuclear War* (New York: Random House, 2009), 350.

5 Jim F. Heath, *Decades of Disillusionment: The Kennedy-Johnson Years* (Bloomington, IN: Indiana University Press, 1975), 36.

6 Doris Kearns Goodwin, *Lyndon Johnson and the American Dream* (New York: Harper & Row, 1976), 95.

7 David Halberstam, *The Best and the Brightest* (New York: Random House, 1972), 298.

8 Goodwin, *Lyndon Johnson and the American Dream*, 230, 251.

9 John McCone, Memorandum, November 24, 1963, http://www.presidency.ucsb.edu/vietnam/showdoc.php?docid=7.

10 Gareth Porter, *Perils of Dominance: Imbalance of Power and the Road to War in Vietnam* (Berkeley: University of California Press, 2005), 182–183.

11 Tim Weiner, *Legacy of Ashes: The History of the CIA* (New York: Doubleday, 2007), 237–239.

12   Leffler, *For the Soul of Mankind,* 213.

13   John Prados, *The Hidden History of the Vietnam War* (New York: Ivan R. Dee, 1995), 15.

14   Sidney Lens and Howard Zinn, *The Forging of the American Empire* (London: Pluto Press, 2003), 422.

15   Carl Oglesby and Richard Shaull, *Containment and Change* (New York: Macmillan, 1967), 116.

16   Jeffrey P. Kimball, ed. *To Reason Why: The Debate About the Cause of U.S. Involvement in the Vietnam War* (Philadelphia: Temple University Press, 1990), 271.

17   Lloyd Gardner, *Pay Any Price: Lyndon Johnson and the Wars for Vietnam* (New York: Ivan R. Dee, 1995), 233.

18   Marilyn B. Young, *The Vietnam Wars, 1945–1990* (New York: HarperPerennial, 1991), 120.

19   John Prados, *Vietnam: The History of an Unwinnable War, 1945–1975* (Lawrence: University Press of Kansas, 2009), 114.

20   Young, *The Vietnam Wars,* 129.

21   Fredrik Logevall, *Choosing War: The Lost Chance for Peace and the Escalation of War in Vietnam* (Berkeley: University of California Press, 1999), 357.

22   Loren Baritz, *Backfire: A History of How American Culture Led Us into Vietnam and Made Us Fight the Way We Did* (Baltimore: Johns Hopkins University Press, 1998), 156.

23   Prados, *The Hidden History of the Vietnam War,* 296.

24   Halberstam, *The Best and the Brightest,* 533.

25   Gardner, *Pay Any Price,* 203.

26   Robert M. Gates, *From the Shadows: The Ultimate Insider's Story of Five Presidents and How They Won the Cold War* (New York: Simon & Schuster, 1996), 566.

27   Daniel Ellsberg, *Secrets: A Memoir of Vietnam and the Pentagon Papers* (New York: Viking, 2002), 92.

28   "Russia Says U.S. Claims Right to Start A-War," *Washington Post,* April 27, 1965.

29   "Red Raps U.S. in U.N.," *Chicago Daily Defender,* April 27, 1965.

30   Rupert Cornwell, "Obituary: William Bundy," *Independent,* October 12, 2000; "Ky Warns of Fight If 'Reds' Win Vote," *New York Times,* May 14, 1967; "Ky Is Said to Consider Hitler a Hero," *Washington Post,* July 10, 1965; James Reston, "Saigon: The Politics of Texas and Asia," *New York Times,* September 1, 1965.

31   Neil Sheehan, *A Bright Shining Lie: John Paul Vann and America in Vietnam* (New York: Random House, 1988), 524.

32   Ellsberg, *Secrets,* 96.

33   Ibid., 97.

34   Christian G. Appy, *Patriots: The Vietnam War Remembered from All Sides* (New York: Viking, 2003), 122–123.

35   Rowland Evans and Robert D. Novak, *Lyndon B. Johnson: The Exercise of Power* (New York: New American Library, 1966), 539.

36   Young, *The Vietnam Wars,* 141.

37   Weiner, *Legacy of Ashes,* 285.

38   David J. Garrow, *Bearing the Cross: Martin Luther King, Jr., and the Southern Christian Leadership Council* (New York: William Morrow, 1986), 560.

39   Halberstam, *The Best and the Brightest,* 633.

40   Ibid., 434.

41   John Dumbrell, *President Lyndon Johnson and Soviet Communism* (Manchester, England: Manchester University Press, 2004), 12.

42   Overall, the 1967 ghetto uprisings left 88 dead, 1,397 injured, 16,389 arrested, and 2,157 convicted and resulted in almost $665 million in damage; see Weiner, *Legacy of Ashes,* 286.

43   Walter Lippmann, "Today and Tomorrow: The CIA Affair," *Washington Post,* February 21, 1967.

44   Weiner, *Legacy of Ashes,* 278–280; Tim Weiner, "Angleton's Secret Policy," *New York Times,* June 26, 2007.

45   Nhu Tang Trường, David Chanoff, and Van Toai Doan, *A Vietcong Memoir: An Inside Account of the Vietnam War and Its Aftermath* (New York: Harcourt Brace Jovanovich, 1985), 167.

46   "Wilson Warns Against Use of Nuclear Arms," *Los Angeles Times,* February 12, 1968.

47   General William C. Westmoreland, *A Soldier Reports* (New York: Doubleday, 1976), 338.

48   Jules Boykoff, *The Suppression of Dissent: How the State and Mass Media Squelch USAmerican Social Movements* (New York: Routledge, 2006), 202.

49   Jules Boykoff, *Beyond Bullets: The Suppression of Dissent in the United States* (Oakland, CA: AK Press, 2007), 180–181.

50   Walter LaFeber, *The Deadly Bet: LBJ, Vietnam and the 1968 Election* (Lanham, MD: Rowman & Littlefield, 2005), 60.

51   Robert D. Schulzinger, *A Time for War: The United States and Vietnam, 1941–1975* (New York: Oxford University Press, 1997), 266.

52   John Gerassi, *The Great Fear in Latin America* (New York: Collier, 1965),19–20, 129.

53   Britta H. Crandall, *Hemispheric Giants: The Misunderstood History of U.S.-Brazilian Relations* (Lanham, MD: Rowman & Littlefield, 211), 98; David F. Schmitz, *Thank God They're on Our Side: The United States and Right-Wing Dictatorships, 1921–1965* (Chapel Hill: University of North Carolina Press, 1999), 272–273.

54   Schmitz, *Thank God They're on Our Side,* 265.

55   Joseph Smith, *Brazil and the United States: Convergence and Divergence* (Athens: University of Georgia Press, 2010), 161.

56   Noam Chomsky, *Hegemony or Survival: America's Quest for Global Dominance* (New York: Henry Holt, 2003), 92.

57   William Blum, *Killing Hope: U.S. Military and CIA Interventions Since World War II* (Monroe, ME: Common Courage Books, 1995), 168.

58   James N. Green, *We Cannot Remain Silent: Opposition to the Brazilian Military Dictatorship in the United States* (Durham, NC: Duke University Press, 2010), 22.

59   H. W. Brands, *The Wages of Globalism: Lyndon Johnson and the Limits of American Power* (New York: Oxford University Press, 1995), 49.

60   Guian A. McKee, ed. *The Presidential Recordings: Lyndon B. Johnson,* vols. 4–6 (New York: W. W. Norton, 2007), 18.

61 Ronald G. Hellman and H. Jon Rosenbaum, *Latin America: The Search for a New International Role* (New York: Wiley, 1975), 80.

62 Michael Wines, "William F. Raborn Is Dead at 84; Led Production of Polaris Missile," *New York Times,* March 13, 1990.

63 Weiner, *Legacy of Ashes,* 250–251.

64 Schmitz, *Thank God They're on Our Side,* 284.

65 "Text of Johnson's Address on U.S. Moves in the Conflict in the Dominican Republic," *New York Times,* May 3, 1965.

66 Thomas J. Hamilton, "Sharp U.N. Clash," *New York Times,* May 4, 1965.

67 "Dominican Issues," *New York Times,* May 9, 1965.

68 Homer Bigart, "Bosch Gives His Version of Revolt," *New York Times,* May 8, 1965.

69 Odd Arne Westad, *The Global Cold War: Third World Interventions and the Making of Our Times* (New York: Cambridge University Press, 2005), 152.

70 Melvyn P. Leffler, *A Preponderance of Power: National Security, the Truman Administration, and the Cold War* (Stanford, CA: Stanford University Press, 1992), 260.

71 Blum, *Killing Hope,* 102.

72 Weiner, *Legacy of Ashes,* 151.

73 Blum, *Killing Hope,* 103; "Aid to Indonesian Rebels," *New York Times,* May 9, 1958.

74 Weiner, *Legacy of Ashes,* 142–154.

75 Douglass, *JFK and the Unspeakable,* 259; Evan Thomas, *The Very Best Men: Four Who Dared: The Early Years of the CIA* (New York: Touchstone, 1995), 232–233.

76 Douglass, *JFK and the Unspeakable,* 257–259, 376.

77 Westad, *The Global Cold War,* 186.

78 Samuel B. Griffith, *The Chinese People's Liberation Army* (New York: McGraw-Hill, 1967), 286.

79 David F. Schmitz, *The United States and Right-Wing Dictatorships, 1965–1989* (New York: Cambridge University Press, 2006), 45.

80 Blum, *Killing Hope,* 193–196.

81 Schmitz, *The United States and Right-Wing Dictatorships,* 48.

82 Bradley R. Simpson, *Economists with Guns: Authoritarian Development and U.S.-Indonesian Relations, 1960–1968* (Stanford, CA: Stanford University Press, 2008), 171.

83 Edward C. Keefer, ed. *Foreign Relations of the United States, 1964–1968: Indonesia, Malaysia-Singapore, Philippines* (Washington, DC: U.S. Government Printing Office, 2001), 571.

84 Schmitz, *The United States and Right-Wing Dictatorships, 1965–1989,* 48.

85 Weiner, *Legacy of Ashes,* 261.

86 Philip Shenon, "Indonesia Improves Life for Many but the Political Shadows Remain," *New York Times,* August 27, 1993.

87 Young, *The Vietnam Wars,* 106.

88 Goodwin, *Lyndon Johnson and the American Dream,* 251–252, 259–260.

CHAPTER 9: NIXON AND KISSINGER: THE "MADMAN" AND THE "PSYCHOPATH"

1   Stephen E. Ambrose, *Nixon: Ruin and Recovery, 1973–1990* (New York: Simon & Schuster, 1991), 488; Lawrence Martin, *The Presidents and the Prime Ministers: Washington and Ottawa Face to Face* (Toronto: Doubleday, 1982), 259.

2   H. R. Haldeman with Joseph Dimona, *The Ends of Power* (New York: Dell Books, 1978), 108, 111.

3   Robert Dallek, *Nixon and Kissinger: Partners in Power* (New York: HarperCollins, 2007), 93, 250.

4   Walter LaFeber, *The American Age: United States Foreign Policy at Home and Abroad Since 1750* (New York: W. W. Norton, 1989), 602; Henry A. Kissinger, *American Foreign Policy,* exp. ed. (New York: W. W. Norton, 1974), 183.

5   Walter Isaacson, *Kissinger: A Biography* (New York: Simon & Schuster, 2005), 764.

6   "Dr. Kirk Urges U.S. to Leave Vietnam," *New York Times,* April 13, 1968.

7   Rick Perlstein, *Nixonland: The Rise of a President and the Fracturing of America* (New York: Scribner, 2008), 265.

8   Dallek, *Nixon and Kissinger,* 68.

9   John Prados, *Vietnam: The History of an Unwinnable War, 1945–1975* (Lawrence: University Press of Kansas, 2009), 288.

10   Joseph A. Califano, Jr., *The Triumph and Tragedy of Lyndon Johnson* (New York: Simon & Schuster, 1992), 328; Jules Witcover, *The Making of an Ink-Stained Wretch: Half a Century Pounding the Political Beat* (Baltimore: Johns Hopkins University Press, 2005), 131.

11   Isaacson, *Kissinger,* 127–128.

12   Seymour M. Hersh, *The Price of Power: Kissinger in the Nixon White House* (New York: Summit Books, 1983), 20.

13   Ibid, 14.

14   Dallek, *Nixon and Kissinger,* 99.

15   Carolyn Eisenberg, "Remembering Nixon's War," in *A Companion to the Vietnam War,* ed. Marilyn B. Young and Robert Buzzanco (Maiden, MA: Blackwell, 2002), 263.

16   Anne Hessing Cahn, *Killing Détente: The Right Attacks the CIA* (University Park: Pennsylvania State University Press, 1998), 21.

17   Henry Kissinger, *White House Years* (Boston: Little, Brown, 1979), 26.

18   Odd Arne Westad, *The Global Cold War: Third World Interventions and the Making of Our Times* (New York: Cambridge University Press, 2007), 196.

19   Hersh, *The Price of Power,* 111.

20   Isaacson, *Kissinger,* 160.

21   Haldeman with DiMona, *The Ends of Power,* 122.

22   Fawn M. Brodie, *Richard Nixon: The Shaping of His Character* (New York: W. W. Norton, 1981), 322.

23   William Shawcross, *Sideshow: Kissinger, Nixon and the Destruction of Cambodia* (New York: Simon & Schuster, 1979), 30–32.

24   Isaacson, *Kissinger,* 213.

25   Jeffrey Kimball, *Nixon's Vietnam War* (Lawrence: University Press of Kansas, 1998), 159.

26   Ibid., 163; Young, *Vietnam Wars,* 239.

27   Hersh, *The Price of Power,* 127.

28   Kimball, *Nixon's Vietnam War,* 163; Hersh, *The Price of Power,* 126, 129.

29   Hersh, *The Price of Power,* 124.

30   Henry A. Kissinger, Memorandum for the President, "Contingency Military Operations Against North Vietnam," October 2, 1969, http://www.gwu.edu/~nsarchiv/NSAEBB/ NSAEBB195/VN-2.pdf.

31   "Editorial Note," *Foreign Relations of the United States, 1969–1976,* vol. 7, Vietnam, January 1969–July 1970, Document 125, http://history.state.gov/historicaldocuments/ frus1969-76v06/d125.

32   Richard Nixon, *RN: The Memoirs of Richard Nixon* (New York: Grosset & Dunlap, 1978), 398.

33   Hersh, *The Price of Power,* 124–125.

34   Tom Wells, *The War Within: America's Battle over Vietnam* (Berkeley: University of California Press, 1994), 358.

35   Gregg Herken, *Counsels of War* (New York: Oxford University Press, 1987), 217.

36   Nixon, *RN,* 401.

37   AAAS, Minutes of the Meeting of the AAAS Council, December 30, 1965, AAAS Archives, Washington, D.C.

38   "Scientists Protest Viet Crop Destruction," *Science,* January 21, 1966, 309.

39   Bryce Nelson, "Military Research: A Decline in the Interest of Scientists?" *Science,* April 21, 1967, 365.

40   Bryce Nelson, "Scientists Plan Research Strike at M.I.T. on 4 March," *Science,* January 25, 1969, 373.

41   Max Tishler, "The Siege of the House of Reason," *Science,* October 3, 1969, 193; Bryce Nelson, "M.I.T.'s March 4: Scientists Discuss Renouncing Military Research," *Science,* March 14, 1969, 1175–1178.

42   Hersh, *The Price of Power,* 134.

43   Christian G. Appy, *Patriots: The Vietnam War Remembered from All Sides* (New York: Viking, 2003), 122–123.

44   Robert S. McNamara, *In Retrospect: The Tragedy and Lessons of Vietnam* (New York: Vintage, 1996), 32–33.

45   Appy, *Patriots,* 243–244.

46   Ibid., 348–349.

47   Hersh, *The Price of Power,* 135.

48   Ibid.

49   Robert Parry and Norman Solomon, "Colin Powell's My Lai Connection," 1996, www .consortiumnews.com/2009/120209b.html.

50   Thomas S. Langston, ed. *The Cold War Presidency: A Documentary History* (Washington, DC: Congressional Quarterly Press, 2007), 297.

51   Perlstein, *Nixonland,* 482.

52   Isaacson, *Kissinger,* 269.

53   Bernard D. Nossiter, "Thousands of Students Protest War," *Washington Post,* May 6, 1970.

54   Kissinger, *White House Years,* 511, 513.

55   We are grateful to Daniel Ellsberg for this information.

56   Isaacson, *Kissinger,* 280.

57   Wells, *The War Within,* 579.

58   Testimony of Tom Charles Huston, *Hearings before the Select Committee to Study Governmental Operations with Respect to Intelligence Activities of the United States Senate,* 94th Cong., 1st Sess., "Huston Plan," September 23, 1975, 20.

59   Ambrose, *Nixon,* 508.

60   Stephen Kinzer, *Overthrow: America's Century of Regime Change from Hawaii to Iraq* (New York: Times Books, 2006), 175–176.

61   Ibid., 176.

62   Tim Weiner, *Legacy of Ashes: The History of the CIA* (New York: Doubleday, 2007), 307–308.

63   "New Kissinger 'Telecons' Reveal Chile Plotting at Highest Levels of U.S. Government," National Security Archive, www.gwu.edu/~nsarchiv/NSAEBB/NSAEBB255/index.htm.

64   Peter Kornbluh, *The Pinochet File: A Declassified Dossier on Atrocity and Accountability* (New York: New Press, 2003), 1–2, 18, 36; Westad, *The Global Cold War,* 201; Weiner, *Legacy of Ashes,* 309.

65   Kornbluh, *The Pinochet File,* 11.

66   Ibid., 8.

67   Weiner, *Legacy of Ashes,* 355.

68   Westad, *The Global Cold War,* 201.

69   Seymour M. Hersh, "Censored Matter in Book About C.I.A. Said to Have Related Chile Activities," *New York Times,* September 11, 1974.

70   "World: Chile: The Expanding Left," *Time,* October 19, 1970, 23.

71   Michael Dodge, Letter to the Editor, *Time,* November 16, 1970, 13.

72   Kornbluh, *The Pinochet File,* 17, 20–21, 58–59.

73   Ibid., 25, 26, 28–29, 64, 72.

74   Ibid., 79, 119.

75   Weiner, *Legacy of Ashes,* 364.

76   Kinzer, *Overthrow,* 187.

77   Ibid., 189.

78   James D. Cockcroft and Jane Carolina Canning, ed. *Salvador Allende Reader: Chile's Voice of Democracy* (Melbourne, Australia: Ocean Press, 2000), 201–220.

79   Robert Alden, "Allende, at U.N., Charges Assault by U.S. Interests," *New York Times,* December 5, 1972; Kinzer, *Overthrow,* 189; Joseph Zullo, "Allende Hits U.S., I.T.T.," *Chicago Tribune,* December 5, 1972; Don Shannon, "Chile President Accuses U.S. Firms of 'Indirect Aggression,'" *Los Angeles Times,* December 5, 1972.

80   Kinzer, *Overthrow*, 190.

81   Ibid., 194.

82   Tim Weiner, "Word for Word/Covert Action," *New York Times*, September 13, 1998.

83   "TelCon: 9/16/73 (Home) 11:50, Mr. Kissinger/The President," National Security Archive, www.gwu.edu/~nsarchiv/NSAEBB/NSAEBB123/Box%2022,%20File%20 3,%20Telcon,%209-16-73%2011,50%20Mr.%20Kissinger-The%20Pres%20 2.pdf.

84   Kornbluh, *The Pinochet File*, 265.

85   ARA Monthly Report (July), "The 'Third World War' and South America," August 3, 1976, National Security Archive, www.gwu.edu/~nsarchiv/NSAEBB/NSAEBB125/ condor05.pdf.

86   Ambassador Harry W. Shlaudeman to Secretary Kissinger, action memorandum, "Operation Condor," August 30, 1976, Department of State, National Security Archive, www.gwu.edu /~nsarchiv/NSAEBB/NSAEBB312/1_19760830_Operation_Condor.PDF.

87   FM USDEL Secretary in Lusaka to Henry Kissinger, cable, "Actions Taken," September 16, 1976, Department of State, National Security Archive, www.gwu.edu/~nsarchiv/ NSAEBB/NSAEBB312/2_19760916_Actions_Taken.pdf.

88   John Dinges, "Pulling Back the Veil on Condor," *Nation*, July 24, 2000, www.thenation .com/article/pulling-back-veil-condor.

89   Raymond L. Garthoff, *Détente and Confrontation: American-Soviet Relations from Nixon to Reagan* (Washington, DC: Brookings Institution, 1985), 290.

90   Richard Nixon, "Address to a Joint Session of the Congress on Return From Austria, the Soviet Union, Iran, and Poland," June 1, 1972, www.presidency.ucsb.edu/ws/index .php?pid=3450#axzz1aJSeeAQ2.

91   For a discussion of Okinawa, see Gavan McCormack, "Ampo's Troubled 50th: Hatoyama's Abortive Rebellion, Okinawa's Mounting Resistance and the U.S.-Japan Relationship (Part 1)," *The Asia-Pacific Journal: Japan Focus*, 22-3-10, May 31, 2010, www.japanfocus.org/-Gavan-McCormack/3365/; Gavan McCormack and Satoko Oka Norimatsu, *Resistant Islands: Okinawa Confronts Japan and the United States* (Lanham, MD: Rowman & Littlefield, 2012), 55–57.

92   Herring, *From Colony to Superpower*, 783–784.

93   Kurt M. Campbell and Tsuyoshi Sunohara, "Japan: Thinking the Unthinkable," in *The Nuclear Tipping Point: Why States Reconsider Their Nuclear Choices*, ed. Kurt M. Campbell, Robert J. Einhorn, and Mitchell B. Reiss (Washington, DC: Brookings Institution, 2004), 221–222.

94   Ibid., 225.

95   "The New Equilibrium," *New York Times*, June 3, 1972.

96   Jacob Heilbrunn, *They Knew They Were Right: The Rise of the Neocons* (New York: Anchor Books, 2009), 122.

97   Henry Kissinger, *Years of Upheaval* (Boston: Little, Brown, 1982), 249.

98   Daniel Ellsberg, *Secrets: A Memoir of Vietnam and the Pentagon Papers* (New York: Viking, 2002), 255–256, 258–260.

99   Ibid., 398.

100   Ibid., 408.

101   Ibid., 434, 440.

102   Ibid., 418.

103   Herring, *From Colony to Superpower*, 793.

104   Ellsberg, *Secrets*, 419.

105   Isaacson, *Kissinger*, 459.

106   "Transcript of the Speech by President on Vietnam," *New York Times*, January 24, 1973.

107   Robert McNamara lecture to Peter Kuznick's class at American University, October 21, 1999.

108   Mr. Kissinger/The President (tape) [telephone conversation], December 9, 1970, 8:45 p.m., National Security Archive, www.gwu.edu/~nsarchiv/NSAEBB/NSAEBB123/ Box%2029,%20File%202,%20Kissinger%20%96%20President%20Dec%209,%20 1970%208,45%20pm%20%200.pdf.

109   Mr. Kissinger/General Haig (tape) [telephone conversation], December 9, 1970, 8:50 p.m., National Security Archive, www.gwu.edu/~nsarchiv/NSAEBB/NSAEBB123/ Box%2029,%20File%202,%20Kissinger%20%96%20Haig,%20Dec%209,%201970%20 8,50%20pm%20106-10.pdf.

110   Ben Kiernan, *The Pol Pot Regime: Race, Power, and Genocide Under the Khmer Rouge* (New Haven, CT: Yale University Press, 2003), 23.

111   Kiernan, *The Pol Pot Regime*, xi, note 3.

112   Shawcross, *Sideshow*, 389.

113   Georges Chapelier and Joysane Van Malderghem, "Plain of Jars: Social Changes Under Five Years of Pathet Lao Administration," *Asia Quarterly* 1 (1971), 75.

114   Marilyn B. Young, *The Vietnam Wars, 1945–1990* (New York: HarperPerennial, 1991), 234–236; Fred Branfman, *Voices from the Plain of Jars: Life Under an Air War* (New York: Harper & Row, 1972), 3, 18–20.

115   Daniel Ellsberg, personal communication with Peter Kuznick.

116   "Excerpts from Mitchell's Testimony," *Los Angeles Times*, July 11, 1973.

117   *New Yorker*, vol. 49, 1973, 173.

118   Mark H. Lytle, *America's Uncivil Wars: The Sixties Era from Elvis to the Fall of Richard Nixon* (New York: Oxford University Press, 2006), 1.

119   Eisenberg, "Remembering Nixon's War," 263.

Chapter 10: Collapse of Detente: Darkness at Noon

1   "Carter Criticizes Bush and Blair on War in Iraq," *New York Times*, May 20, 2007.

2   Walter LaFeber, *America, Russia, and the Cold War, 1945–2006* (Boston: McGraw-Hill, 2008), 293.

3   Marilyn B. Young, *The Vietnam Wars, 1945–1990* (New York: HarperPerennial, 1991), 239.

4   Gregory D. Cleva, *Henry Kissinger and the American Approach to Foreign Policy* (Lewisburg, PA: Bucknell University Press, 1989), 40.

5   Jonathan Schell, *The Real War: The Classic Reporting on the Vietnam War* (New York: Da Capo Press, 2000), 53.

6   Ibid., 55.

7   Graham Hovey, "He Calls '73 Pledge of Aid to Hanoi Invalid," *New York Times,* May 20, 1977.

8   "Vietnam Report Details Unexploded Ordnance," *New York Times,* August 1, 2009.

9   Douglas Brinkley, *Gerald R. Ford* (New York: Macmillan, 2007), 91.

10 Odd Arne Westad, *The Global Cold War: Third World Interventions and the Making of Our Times* (New York: Cambridge University Press, 2007), 247; Clair Apodaca, *Understanding U.S. Human Rights Policy: A Paradoxical Legacy* (New York: Routledge, 2006), 60.

11 Robert Hotz, "Beam Weapon Threat," *Aviation Week & Space Technology,* May 2, 1977, 11.

12 Anne Hessing Cahn, *Killing Détente: The Right Attacks the CIA* (University Park, PA: Pennsylvania State University Press, 1998), 138.

13 Ibid., 152.

14 Richard Pipes, "Team B: The Reality Behind the Myth," *Commentary,* October 1986, 29, 33.

15 Thom Hartmann, "Hyping Terror for Fun, Profit—and Power," www.commondreams .org/views04/1207-26.htm.

16 Cahn, *Killing Détente,* 158.

17 Nicholas Thompson, *The Hawk and the Dove: Paul Nitze, George Kennan, and the History of the Cold War* (New York: Henry Holt, 2009), 260.

18 Ibid., 260–261.

19 Tom Nugent and Steve Parks, "New Evidence Clouds Paisley 'Suicide' Verdict," *Baltimore Sun,* April 2, 1979; "Paisley's Death Believed Linked to CIA, Majority Security Breach," *Baltimore Sun,* January 26, 1979; James Coates, "CIA Spy Mystery: How Did He Die and Why?," *Chicago Tribune,* October 8, 1978.

20 Coates, "CIA Spy Mystery."

21 Nugent and Parks, "New Evidence Clouds Paisley 'Suicide' Verdict"; "Wife Probing Death of Ex-CIA Official," *Los Angeles Times,* November 26, 1978; "The Paisley Mystery," *Baltimore Sun,* May 22, 1979; Timothy S. Robinson, "Full Report on Paisley to Be Secret," *Washington Post,* April 24, 1980.

22 Cahn, *Killing Détente,* 188.

23 Alexander Cockburn, *Rumsfeld: His Rise, Fall, and Catastrophic Legacy* (New York: Simon & Schuster, 2007), 20, note 18.

24 Gerald R. Ford, *A Time to Heal: The Autobiography of Gerald R. Ford* (New York: Harper & Row, 1979), 357.

25 Sean Wilentz, *The Age of Reagan: A History, 1974–2008* (New York: HarperCollins, 2008), 64.

26 Westad, *The Global Cold War,* 247–248.

27 Ibid., 443, note 102.

28 Leo P. Ribuffo, "Writing About Jimmy Carter as if He Was Andrew Jackson: The Carter Presidency in (Deep) Historical Perspective," delivered January 2007 at the University of Georgia, http://gwu.academia.edu/leoribuffo/Papers/168463/.

29 John B. Judis, "Twilight of the Gods," *Wilson Quarterly,* Autumn 1991, 46–47.

30 Zbigniew Brzezinski, *Between Two Ages: America's Role in the Technetronic Era* (Westport, CT: Greenwood Press, 1982), 297.

31 Judis, "Twilight of the Gods," 47–50.

32 Zbigniew Brzezinski, *Power and Principle: Memoirs of the National Security Adviser, 1977–1981* (New York: Farrar, Straus and Giroux, 1983), 5.

33 Howard Zinn, *A People's History of the United States* (New York: Harper Colophon, 1980), 551.

34 Jimmy Carter, *A Government as Good as Its People* (New York: Simon & Schuster, 1977), 99–100.

35 Walter L. Hixson, *The Myth of American Diplomacy: National Identity and U.S. Foreign Policy* (New Haven, CT: Yale University Press, 2008), 258, n. 23.

36 Lawrence S. Wittner, *Towards Nuclear Abolition: A History of the World Nuclear Disarmament Movement, 1971–Present* (Stanford, CA: Stanford University Press, 2003), 41.

37 Rowland Evans and Robert Novak, "Jimmy Carter: No Apology on Vietnam," *Washington Post,* July 7, 1976.

38 Alan Lichtman, *White Protestant Nation: The Rise of the American Conservative Movement* (New York: Atlantic Monthly Press, 2008), 334.

39 Brzezinski, *Power and Principle,* 64.

40 Ibid., 65–66.

41 LaFeber, *America, Russia,* 300.

42 Melvyn P. Leffler, *For the Soul of Mankind: The United States, the Soviet Union, and the Cold War* (New York: Hill and Wang, 2007), 268–269.

43 Ibid., 284.

44 "Speech of the President on Soviet-American Relations at the U.S. Naval Academy," *New York Times,* June 8, 1978.

45 Brzezinski, *Power and Principle,* 189.

46 Westad, *The Global Cold War,* 283.

47 John Drumbell, *The Carter Presidency: A Re-evaluation* (Manchester, England: Manchester University Press, 1995), 102.

48 David Vine, *Island of Shame: The Secret History of the U.S. Military Base on Diego Garcia* (Princeton, NJ: Princeton University Press, 2009).

49 Westad, *The Global Cold War,* 292.

50 "Tears and Sympathy for the Shah," *New York Times,* November 17, 1977; *see also* Ronald Lee Ridenhour, "America Since My Lai: 10 Years on a Tightrope," *Los Angeles Times,* March 19, 1978.

51 Lloyd C. Gardner, *The Long Road to Baghdad: A History of U.S. Foreign Policy from the 1970s to the Present* (New York: New Press, 2008), 51.

52 Leffler, *For the Soul of Mankind,* 301.

53 Gardner, *The Long Road to Baghdad,* 54–55.

54 Robert Dreyfuss, *Devil's Game: How the United States Helped Unleash Fundamentalist Islam* (New York: Henry Holt, 2005), 221.

55 Tim Weiner, *Legacy of Ashes: The History of the CIA* (New York: Doubleday, 2007), 371.

56   Leffler, *For the Soul of Mankind,* 308.

57   "Nuclear Know-how: A Close Call," *Los Angeles Times,* March 12, 1979.

58   Robert A. Pastor, *Condemned to Repetition: The United States and Nicaragua* (Princeton, NJ: Princeton University Press, 1987), 148.

59   Steve Galster, "Afghanistan: The Making of U.S. Policy, 1973–1990," National Security Archive, www.gwu.edu/~nsarchiv/NSAEBB/NSAEBB57/essay.html.

60   William Borders, "Afghanistan Vows 'Active Neutrality,'" *New York Times,* May 5, 1978.

61   Chalmers Johnson, *Blowback: The Costs and Consequences of American Empire* (New York: Henry Holt, 2004), xiii.

62   Leffler, *For the Soul of Mankind,* 310–311.

63   Ibid., 332.

64   Russell Baker, "A Bone in the Throat," *New York Times,* May 3, 1980.

65   Jimmy Carter, State of the Union Address 1980, January 23, 1980, www.jimmycarter library.gov/documents/speeches/su80jec.phtml.

66   Robert M. Gates, *From the Shadows: The Ultimate Insider's Story of Five Presidents and How They Won the Cold War* (New York: Simon & Schuster, 1996), 113.

67   Robert J. Lifton and Greg Mitchell, *Hiroshima in America: A Half Century of Denial* (New York: Avon Books, 1995), 220, 402.

68   Geoffrey Wawro, *Quicksand: America's Pursuit of Power in the Middle East* (New York: Penguin, 2010), 382.

69   "Transcript of President's News Conference on Foreign and Domestic Affairs," *New York Times,* March 25, 1977.

70   Cahn, *Killing Détente,* 49.

71   David Walsh, *The Military Balance in the Cold War: US Perception and Policy* (Abingdon: Routledge, 2008), 183.

72   Melvin R. Laird, "Defense Secretaries Shouldn't Play Politics," *Washington Post,* August 17, 1980.

73   Gates, *From the Shadows,* 113.

74   Ibid., 114–115.

75   State Department cable 295771 to U.S. Embassy Moscow, "Brezhnev Message to President on Nuclear False Alarm," 14 November 1979; Marshal Shulman memo to Secretary of State Cyrus Vance, 16 November 1979; Marshal Shulman memo to Cyrus Vance, 21 November 1979, National Security Archive Electronic Briefing Book No. 371, March 1, 2012, http://www.gwu.edu/~nsarchiv/nukevault/ebb371/index.htm.

76   Mary McGrory, "Vance Departs Knowing the Full Implications," *Baltimore Sun,* April 30, 1980.

77   "The Vance Resignation," *Washington Post,* April 29, 1980.

78   "Leaving Well," *Wall Street Journal,* April 29, 1980.

79   "Vance Says National Security Adviser Should Stop Making Foreign Policy," *Washington Post,* May 5, 1980.

80   Steven R. Weisman, "Carter Sees Muskie as 'Much Stronger' in the Job than Vance," *New York Times,* May 10, 1980.

81 Robert Parry, "The Crazy October Surprise Debunking," November 6, 2009, www .consortiumnews.com/2009/110609.html.

CHAPTER 11: THE REAGAN YEARS: DEATH SQUADS FOR DEMOCRACY

1 Anatoly Dobrynin, *In Confidence: Moscow's Ambassador to America's Six Cold War Presidents (1962–1986)* (New York: Times Books, 1995), 530.

2 Melvyn P. Leffler, *For the Soul of Mankind: The United States, the Soviet Union and the Cold War* (New York: Hill and Wang, 2007), 349; Tim Weiner, *Legacy of Ashes: The History of the CIA* (New York: Doubleday, 2007), 388.

3 Bob Schieffer and Gary Paul Gates, *The Acting President* (New York: E. P. Dutton, 1989), 91.

4 Lou Cannon, "Latin Trip an Eye-Opener for Reagan," *Washington Post,* December 6, 1982.

5 William E. Pemberton, *Exit with Honor: The Life and Presidency of Ronald Reagan* (Armonk, NY: M. E. Sharpe, 1997), 150.

6 Schieffer and Gates, *The Acting President,* 175.

7 Ronald Reagan, *An American Life* (New York: Simon & Schuster, 1990), 588.

8 Joanne Omang, "President, Nazi Hunter Discuss the Holocaust," *Washington Post,* February 17, 1984; Lou Cannon, "Dramatic Account About Film of Nazi Death Camps Questioned," *Washington Post,* March 5, 1984.

9 Mike Royko, "What Prez Says Ain't Necessarily So," *Chicago Tribune,* April 6, 1984.

10 James M. Perry, ". . . While Candidate Stays True to Form by Spreading the Word, and the Words," *Wall Street Journal,* January 15, 1988; Carl P. Leubsdorf, "Cornerstone of Reagan Election Appeal Is Promised Return to 'Good Old Days,'" *Baltimore Sun,* April 30, 1980.

11 Larry Speakes, *Speaking Out: The Reagan Presidency from Inside the White House* (New York: Scribner, 1988), 136.

12 Lou Cannon, *President Reagan: The Role of a Lifetime* (New York: Simon & Schuster, 1991), 156–157.

13 "Wrong Turn on Human Rights," *New York Times,* February 6, 1981; John M. Goshko, "Ultraconservative May Get Human Rights Post at State," *Washington Post,* February 5, 1981; Jack Anderson, "U.S. Human Rights Post Goes to a Foe," *Washington Post,* February 28, 1981; "The Case Against Mr. Lafever," *New York Times,* March 2, 1981.

14 Pemberton, *Exit with Honor,* 151.

15 Cannon, *President Reagan,* 241.

16 Robert M. Gates, *From the Shadows: The Ultimate Insider's Story of Five Presidents and How They Won the Cold War* (New York: Simon & Schuster, 1996), 191, 199.

17 Melvin Goodman, *Failure of Intelligence: The Decline and Fall of the CIA* (Lanham, MD: Rowman & Littlefield, 2008), 303.

18 Robert Parry, *Secrecy & Privilege: Rise of the Bush Dynasty from Watergate to Iraq* (Arlington, VA: Media Consortium, 2004), 192–193.

19 Colman McCarthy, "They Are Less than Freedom Fighters," *Washington Post,* March 2, 1985.

20 George Skelton, "Reagan Pledges to Back Guatemala," *Los Angeles Times,* December 5, 1982; Greg Grandin, *Empire's Workshop: Latin America, the United States, and the Rise of the New Imperialism* (New York: Holt Paperbacks, 2006), 101.

21 Mary McGrory, "Learning Diplomacy from Movies," *Chicago Tribune,* December 9, 1982.

22 Walter LaFeber, *Inevitable Revolutions: The United States in Central America* (New York: W. W. Norton, 1993), 322.

23 Skelton, "Reagan Pledges to Back Guatemala"; Lou Cannon, "Reagan Praises Guatemalan Military Leader," *Washington Post,* December 5, 1982.

24 Steven R. Weisman, "Reagan Criticized by Colombia Chief on Visit to Bogota," *New York Times,* December 4, 1982; Anthony Lewis, "Howdy, Genghis," *New York Times,* December 6, 1982.

25 Lou Cannon, " 'Unseemly Pressure' from Nofziger Reported to Annoy Reagan," *Washington Post,* December 6, 1982.

26 Lewis, "Howdy, Genghis."

27 Frank P. L. Somerville, "Guatemala Atrocities Reported by a Jesuit," *Baltimore Sun,* December 8, 1982.

28 Eric Alterman, *When Presidents Lie: A History of Official Deception and Its Consequences* (New York: Penguin Books, 2004), 246.

29 "Secret Guatemala's Disappeared," Department of State, 1986, Kate Doyle and Jesse Franzblau, "Historical Archives Lead to Arrest of Police Officers in Guatemalan Disappearance," March 17, 2009, National Security Archive Electronic Briefing Book No. 273, http://www.gwu.edu/~nsarchiv/NSAEBB/NSAEBB273/index.htm.

30 Gates, *From the Shadows,* 213.

31 George P. Shultz, *Turmoil and Triumph: My Years as Secretary of State* (New York: Scribner, 1993), 864.

32 Ronald Reagan, "Remarks to an Outreach Working Group on United States Policy in Central America," July 18, 1984, www.reagan.utexas.edu/archives/speeches/1984/71884d .htm.

33 Grandin, *Empire's Workshop,* 115, n. 75.

34 Harry E. Bergold, Jr., to United States, "Ex-FDN Mondragon Tells His Story," May 8, 1985, Department of State, http://gateway.proquest.com/openurl?url_ver=Z39.88 -2004&res_d at=xri:dnsa&rft_dat=xri:dnsa:article:CNI02471.

35 Robert S. Leiken and Barry Ruin, ed. *The Central American Crisis Reader* (New York: Summit Books, 1987), 562–563.

36 Walter LaFeber, "Salvador," in *Oliver Stone's USA: Film, History, and Controversy,* ed. Robert Brent Toplin (Lawrence: University Press of Kansas, 2000), 101.

37 "Research Group Calls Salvador, Guatemala Worst Rights Violators," *Baltimore Sun,* December 30, 1982.

38 Sean Wilentz, *The Age of Reagan: A History, 1974–2008* (New York: HarperCollins, 2008), 156.

39 John M. Goshko, "Catholic Aid to Marxists Puzzles Bush," *Washington Post,* March 3, 1983.

40 Ronald Reagan, "Peace: Restoring the Margin of Safety," delivered at the Veterans of Foreign Wars Convention, Chicago, IL, August 18, 1980, www.reagan.utexas.edu/archives /reference/8.18.80.html.

41 Stephen Kinzer, *Overthrow: America's Century of Regime Change from Hawaii to Iraq* (New York: Times Books, 2006), 227.

42 Dick Cheney, "What Bonker Missed," *Washington Post,* November 14, 1983.

43 Ronald V. Dellums, "And Then I Said . . . ," *Washington Post,* November 15, 1983.

44 Richard Bernstein, "U.N. Assembly Adopts Measure 'Deeply Deploring' Invasion of Isle," *New York Times,* November 3, 1983.

45 "Grenada Act a 'Liberation,' Not Invasion, Reagan Insists," *Los Angeles Times,* November 3, 1983.

46 Ronald Reagan, "Address to the Nation on Events in Lebanon and Grenada," October 27, 1983, www.reagan.utexas.edu/archives/speeches/1983/102783b.htm.

47 Robert Timberg, " 'Days of Weakness Over,' Reagan Tells War Heroes," *Baltimore Sun,* December 13, 1983.

48 Marilyn B. Young, *The Vietnam Wars, 1945–1990* (New York: HarperPerennial, 1991), 316.

49 Bob Woodward, "CIA Told to Do 'Whatever Necessary' to Kill Bin Laden," *Washington Post,* October 21, 2001.

50 Martin F. Nolan, "American Defense: Spending," *New York Times,* June 28, 1981.

51 Michael Kramer, "When Reagan Spoke from the Heart," *New York,* July 21, 1980, 18.

52 Wilentz, *The Age of Reagan,* 274.

53 Pemberton, *Exit with Honor,* 140.

54 Anthony Lewis, "Abroad and at Home: Nuclear News in Moscow," *New York Times,* June 4, 1981.

55 Colin S. Gray and Keith Payne, "Victory Is Possible," *Foreign Policy,* Summer 1980, 18, 21, 25.

56 Richard Halloran, "Special U.S. Force for Persian Gulf Is Growing Swiftly," *New York Times,* October 25, 1982.

57 Joyce Battle, ed. "Shaking Hands with Saddam Hussein: The U.S. Tilts Toward Iraq, 1980–1984," National Security Archive, www.gwu.edu/~nsarchiv/NSAEBB/NSAEBB82/.

58 Declaration of Howard Teicher before the United States District Court, Southern District of Florida, January 31, 1995, National Security Archive, www.gwu.edu/~nsarchiv/NSAEBB/NSAEBB82/iraq61.pdf.

59 Jonathan B. Tucker, *War of Nerves: Chemical Warfare from World War I to Al-Qaeda* (New York: Pantheon, 2006), 256.

60 "Excerpts from President's Speech to National Association of Evangelicals," *New York Times,* March 9, 1983.

61 Robert Jay Lifton and Eric Markusen, *The Genocidal Mentality: Nazi Holocaust and Nuclear Threat* (New York: Basic Books, 1990), 272.

62 Cannon, *President Reagan,* 290.

63 Robert Timberg, "Reagan Condemns 'Massacre' by Soviets, Spells Out Sanctions," *Baltimore Sun,* September 6, 1983.

64 David E. Hoffman, *The Dead Hand: The Untold Story of the Cold War Arms Race and Its Dangerous Legacy* (New York: Doubleday, 2009), 86.

65   Ronald Reagan, *The Reagan Diaries,* ed. Douglas Brinkley (New York: HarperCollins, 2007), 186.

66   Edmund Morris, *Dutch: A Memoir of Ronald Reagan* (New York: Random House, 1999), 498–499.

67   Reagan, *The Reagan Diaries,* 199.

68   Reagan, *An American Life,* 588; Hoffman, *The Dead Hand,* 96.

69   Reagan, *An American Life,* 586; Hoffman, *The Dead Hand,* 92.

70   Hoffman, *The Dead Hand,* 152–153.

71   Ibid., 153–154.

72   Reagan, *An American Life,* 550.

73   "Reagan in Radio Test, Jokes About Bombing Russia," *Baltimore Sun,* August 13, 1984.

74   Fay S. Joyce, "Mondale Chides Reagan on Soviet-Bombing Joke," *New York Times,* August 14, 1984.

75   "President's Joke About Bombing Leaves Press in Europe Unamused," *New York Times,* August 14, 1984; "European Reaction Is Uniformly Grim," *Baltimore Sun,* August 14, 1984.

76   Dusko Doder, "Moscow Calls Reagan's Quip 'Self-Revealing,'" *Washington Post,* August 15, 1984; "Soviets Hit 'Hostility' of Reagan Joke," *Los Angeles Times,* August 15, 1984.

77   John B. Oakes, "Mr. Reagan Bombs," *New York Times,* August 18, 1984.

78   Jerome B. Wiesner, "Should a Jokester Control Our Fate?," *Los Angeles Times,* August 30, 1984.

79   Robert Scheer, "White House Successfully Limits News," *Los Angeles Times,* August 20, 1984.

80   "Transcript of President's Address on Nuclear Strategy Toward Soviet Union," *New York Times,* November 23, 1982.

81   Gerard J. DeGroot, *The Bomb: A Life* (Cambridge, MA, Harvard University Press, 2005), 308–309.

82   Hoffman, *The Dead Hand,* 207–208.

83   Richard Rhodes, *Arsenals of Folly: The Making of the Nuclear Arms Race* (New York: Alfred A. Knopf, 2007), 205.

84   Wilentz, *The Age of Reagan,* 247.

85   Leffler, *For the Soul of Mankind,* 377.

86   Ibid., 380.

87   Wilentz, *The Age of Reagan,* 151.

88   Vladislav M. Zubok, *A Failed Empire: The Soviet Union in the Cold War from Stalin to Gorbachev* (Chapel Hill: University of North Carolina Press, 2007), 284; Leffler, *For the Soul of Mankind,* 380.

89   Leffler, *For the Soul of Mankind,* 385.

90   Rhodes, *Arsenals of Folly,* 129.

91   Ibid., 4.

92   Zubok, *A Failed Empire,* 288.

93 Rhodes, *Arsenals of Folly,* 26.

94 Shultz, *Turmoil and Triumph,* 716–717.

95 Rhodes, *Arsenals of Folly,* 242.

96 Ibid., 248.

97 Jack F. Matlock, *Reagan and Gorbachev: How the Cold War Ended* (New York: Random House, 2004), 222.

98 Kenneth L. Adelman, *The Great Universal Embrace: Arms Summitry—a Skeptic's Account* (New York: Simon & Schuster, 1989), 53.

99 Rhodes, *Arsenals of Folly,* 257–258.

100 Jay Winik, *On the Brink: The Dramatic, Behind-the-Scenes of the Saga of the Reagan Era and the Men and Women Who Won the Cold War* (New York: Simon & Schuster, 1996), 515.

101 Russian transcript of Reagan-Gorbachev Summit in Reykjavík, October 12, 1986 (afternoon), in FBIS-USR-93-121, September 20, 1993, "The Reykjavik File," National Security Archive, www.gwu.edu/~nsarchiv/NSAEBB/NSAEBB203/index.htm.

102 Rhodes, *Arsenals of Folly,* 266–269.

103 Mikhail Gorbachev, *Alone with Myself (Reminiscences and Reflections)* (Moscow, 2010), unpublished memoir without page numbers.

104 "Session of the Politburo of the CC CPSU," October 14, 1986, National Security Archive, www.gwu.edu/~nsarchiv/NSAEBB/NSAEBB203/Document21.pdf.

105 Philip Geyelin, "And CIA Comics," *Washington Post,* August 12, 1984; Weiner, *Legacy of Ashes,* 399.

106 Wilentz, *The Age of Reagan,* 167.

107 Ibid., 212, 214–215.

108 Pemberton, *Exit with Honor,* 173.

109 Lloyd C. Gardner, *The Long Road to Baghdad: A History of U.S. Foreign Policy from the 1970s to the Present* (New York: New Press, 2008), 67.

110 Doyle McManus and Michael Wines, "Schultz Said to Seek Ouster of Poindexter," *Los Angeles Times,* November 21, 1986.

111 Weiner, *Legacy of Ashes,* 403–408.

112 Wilentz, *The Age of Reagan,* 228; "Reagan: I Was Not Fully Informed," *Washington Post,* November 26, 1986.

113 Pemberton, *Exit with Honor,* 191–192.

114 Robert Parry, "The Mysterious Robert Gates," May 31, 2011, http://consortiumnews .com/2011/05/31/the-mysterious-robert-gates.

115 Pemberton, *Exit with Honor,* 174; Lawrence E. Walsh, *Firewall: The Iran-Contra Conspiracy and Cover-up* (New York: W. W. Norton, 1998), 120.

116 Gorbachev, *Alone with Myself.*

117 James J. F. Forest, ed. *Countering Terrorism and Insurgency in the 21st Century: International Perspectives,* vol. 2 (Westport, CT: Greenwood Publishing Group), 468.

118 Robert Dreyfuss, *Devil's Game: How the United States Helped Unleash Fundamentalist Islam* (New York: Henry Holt, 2005), 267.

119   Stephen Buttry and Jake Thompson, "UNO's Connection to Taliban Centers on Education UNO Program," *Omaha World-Herald,* September 16, 2001, 1.

120   Weiner, *Legacy of Ashes,* 384.

121   Leffler, *For the Soul of Mankind,* 405.

122   Alfred W. McCoy, "Can Anyone Pacify the World's Number One Narco-State? The Opium Wars in Afghanistan," March 30, 2010, www.tomdispatch.com/blog/175225; Weiner, *Legacy of Ashes,* 384.

123   Leffler, *For the Soul of Mankind,* 411.

124   Steve Coll, *Ghost Wars: The Secret History of the CIA, Afghanistan, and Bin Laden, from the Soviet Invasion to September 10, 2001* (New York: Penguin, 2004), 104; Thomas L. Friedman, "Bad Bargains," *Washington Post,* May 10, 2011.

125   Dreyfuss, *Devil's Game,* 290.

126   Ibid., 291.

127   Wilentz, *The Age of Reagan,* 173.

CHAPTER 12: THE COLD WAR ENDS: SQUANDERED OPPORTUNITIES

1   "Stirrings of Peace," *New York Times,* July 31, 1988.

2   "Excerpts from Speech to U.N. on Major Soviet Military Cuts," *New York Times,* December 8, 1988.

3   Robert G. Kaiser, "An Offer to Scrap the Postwar Rules," *Washington Post,* December 8, 1988.

4   Jennifer Lowe, "Whither the Wimp?," *Washington Post,* November 30, 1987.

5   Curt Suplee, "Sorry, George, But the Image Needs Work," *Washington Post,* July 10, 1988.

6   Margaret Garrard Warner, "Bush Battles the 'Wimp Factor,'" *Newsweek,* October 19, 1987, 28.

7   Sidney Blumenthal, "George Bush: A Question of Upbringing," *Washington Post,* February 10, 1988.

8   Sean Wilentz, *The Age of Reagan: A History, 1974–2008* (New York: HarperCollins, 2009), 265.

9   Thomas Hardy, "'Wimp Factor,' Joins Poor George Bush at the Starting Line," *Chicago Tribune,* October 18, 1987.

10   Wilentz, *The Age of Reagan,* 266.

11   Suplee, "Sorry, George, But the Image Needs Work."

12   "Transcript of the Keynote Address by Ann Richards, the Texas Treasurer," *New York Times,* July 19, 1988.

13   Tom Shales, "Rather, Bush and the Nine-Minute War," *Washington Post,* January 26, 1988; Richard Cohen, "The 'Wimp' Becomes a Bully," *Washington Post,* November 1, 1988.

14   Tim Weiner, *Legacy of Ashes: The History of the CIA* (New York: Doubleday, 2007), 408.

15   Robert M. Gates, *From the Shadows: The Ultimate Insider's Story of Five Presidents and How They Won the Cold War* (New York: Simon & Schuster, 1996), 449.

16   Odd Arne Westad, *The Global Cold War: Third World Interventions and the Making of Our Times* (New York: Cambridge University Press, 2007), 386–387.

17   Richard Rhodes, *Arsenals of Folly: The Making of the Nuclear Arms Race* (New York: Alfred A. Knopf, 2007), 287.

18   Leffler, *For the Soul of Mankind*, 436; Clifford Krauss, "U.S. Officials Satisfied with Soviets' Gulf Role," *New York Times*, September 20, 1990; Daniel T. Rogers, *Age of Fracture* (Cambridge, MA: Harvard University Press, 2011), 246.

19   Leffler, *For the Soul of Mankind*, 450.

20   Mary Elise Sarotte, "Enlarging NATO, Expanding Confusion," *New York Times*, November 30, 2009, 31; Uwe Klussman, Matthias Schepp, and Klaus Wiegrefe, "NATO's Eastward Expansion: Did the West Break Its Promise to Moscow?," www .spiegel.de/international/world/0,1518,druck-663315,00.html; Noam Chomsky, *Hopes and Prospects* (Chicago: Haymarket Books, 2010), 278–280.

21   Stephen Kinzer, *Overthrow: America's Century of Regime Change from Hawaii to Iraq* (New York: Times Books, 2006), 253.

22   "A Transcript of Bush's Address on the Decision to Use Force in Panama," *New York Times*, December 21, 1989.

23   "Cheney's Reasons for Why the U.S. Struck Now," *New York Times*, December 21, 1989.

24   R. W. Apple, "War: Bush's Presidential Rite of Passage," *New York Times*, December 21, 1989.

25   James Brooke, "U.S. Denounced by Nations Touchy About Intervention," *New York Times*, December 21, 1989.

26   John B. Quigley, *The Invasion of Panama and International Law* (Vienna: International Progress Organization, 1990), 3.

27   Noam Chomsky, *Hegemony or Survival: America's Quest for Global Dominance* (New York: Owl Books, 2004), 107.

28   Gary J. Dorrien, *Imperial Designs: Neoconservatism and the New Pax Americana* (New York: Routledge, 2004), 26.

29   Elliott Abrams, "Better Earlier," *Washington Post*, December 22, 1989.

30   "Excerpts from Iraqi Document on Meeting with U.S. Envoy," *New York Times*, September 23, 1990.

31   George F. Will, "Gorbachev, Hussein and Morality," *St. Petersburg Times*, January 16, 1991.

32   Elaine Sciolino, "Deskbound in U.S., the Envoy of Iraq Is Called Scapegoat for a Failed Policy," *New York Times*, September 12, 1990.

33   Lloyd C. Gardner, *The Long Road to Baghdad: A History of U.S. Foreign Policy from the 1970s to the Present* (New York: New Press, 2008), 81.

34   Ned Zeman, "Where Are the Troops?" *Newsweek*, December 3, 1990, 6; Craig Unger, *House of Bush, House of Saud* (New York: Scribner, 1994), 139–140.

35   Andrew J. Bacevich, *American Empire: The Realities and Consequences of U.S. Diplomacy* (Cambridge, MA: Harvard University Press, 2002), 63–64; David Hoffman, "Baker Calls Iraqi Threat to 'Economic Lifeline,' " *Washington Post*, November 14, 1990.

36   Joel Brinkley, "Israelis Praising Decision by Bush," *New York Times*, August 9, 1990.

37   R. W. Apple, Jr., "Bush Draws Line," *New York Times*, August 9, 1990.

38   Charles Paul Freund, "In Search of a Post-Postwar Rhetoric," *Washington Post*, August 12, 1990.

39   Maureen Dowd, "President Seeks to Clarify Stand," *New York Times*, November 2, 1990; Lloyd Gardner, "The Ministry of Fear: Selling the Gulf Wars," in *Selling War in a Media Age: The Presidency and Public Opinion in the American Century*, ed. Kenneth Osgood and Andrew K. Frank (Gainesville: University Press of Florida, 2010), 232–233.

40   Gardner, *The Long Road to Baghdad*, 77.

41   Ibid., 83–84.

42   Thomas L. Friedman, "How U.S. Won Support to Use Mideast Forces," *New York Times*, December 2, 1990.

43   George Bush and Brent Scowcroft, *A World Transformed* (New York: Knopf, 1998), 491.

44   Ruth Marcus, "U.N. Debate to Cap U.S. Lobby Effort," *Washington Post*, November 26, 1990.

45   Judith Miller, "Iraqi Pullout? Election in Kuwait? Prospects Worry Hawks," *New York Times*, October 8, 1990.

46   Patrick E. Tyler, "U.S. Juggling Iraq Policy," *New York Times*, April 13, 1991.

47   Dorrien, *Imperial Designs*, 35.

48   Bush and Scowcroft, *A World Transformed*, 489.

49   George C. Herring, *From Colony to Superpower: U.S. Foreign Relations Since 1776* (New York: Oxford University Press, 2008), 912.

50   Gardner, *The Long Road to Baghdad*, 78.

51   George F. Will, "The Emptiness of Desert Storm," *Washington Post*, January 12, 1992.

52   Paul Lewis, "U.N. Survey Calls Iraq's War Damage Near-Apocalyptic," *New York Times*, March 22, 1991.

53   Patrick E. Tyler, "U.S. Officials Believe Iraq Will Take Years to Rebuild," *New York Times*, June 3, 1991.

54   "Quotation of the Day," *New York Times*, March 2, 1991; Bacevich, *American Empire*, 62.

55   Rhodes, *Arsenals of Folly*, 292.

56   Ibid., 296.

57   Patrick E. Tyler, "Pentagon Imagines New Enemies to Fight in Post-Cold-War Era," *New York Times*, February 17, 1992; Patrick E. Tyler, "Lone Superpower Plan: Ammunition for Critics," *New York Times*, March 10, 1992.

58   Barton Gellman, "Keeping the U.S. First," *New York Times*, March 11, 1992; "America's Not the Only Cop," *New York Times*, June 7, 1992.

59   Alan Lichtman, *White Protestant Nation: The Rise of the American Conservative Movement* (New York: Atlantic Monthly Press, 2008), 410.

60   Jim Vallette, "Larry Summers' War Against the Earth," *CounterPunch*, June 15, 1999, www.counterpunch.org/1999/06/15/larry-summers-war-against-the-earth/; "Furor on Memo at World Bank," *New York Times*, February 7, 1992.

61   Jeffrey Sachs, *The End of Poverty: Economic Possibilities for Our Time* (New York: Penguin Books, 2005), 139.

62   Naomi Klein, *The Shock Doctrine: The Rise of Disaster Capitalism* (New York: Metropolitan Books, 2007), 291.

63   Stephen F. Cohen, *Failed Crusade: America and the Tragedy of Post-Communist Russia,* updated ed. (New York: W. W. Norton, 2001), 4–5.

64   Ibid., 36–37.

65   "Yeltsin Is a Liar, Says Gorbachev," *Times* (London), December 26, 2001.

66   Joe Stephens and David B. Ottaway, "From the U.S., the ABCs of Jihad," *Washington Post,* March 23, 2002; Stephen Buttry, "UNO's Afghan Textbooks Face Criticism," *Omaha World-Herald,* March 23, 2002.

67   Kenneth Freed, "Odd Partners in UNO's Afghan Project," *Omaha World-Herald,* October 26, 1997.

68   Ahmed Rashid, *Taliban: Militant Islam, Oil and Fundamentalism in Central Asia* (New Haven, CT: Yale University Press, 2000), 176.

69   Freed, "Odd Partners in UNO's Afghan Project."

70   Marjorie Cohn, "The Deadly Pipeline War: U.S. Afghan Policy Driven by Oil Interests," *Jurist,* December 8, 2001, www.commondreams.org/views01/1208-04.htm.

71   Project for the New American Century, "Statement of Principles," www .newamericancentury.org/statementofprinciples.htm.

72   Dorrien, *Imperial Designs,* 142–143. Of the eighteen people who signed the 1998 PNAC letter to Clinton calling for "removing Saddam Hussein and his regime from power," eleven took positions in the George W. Bush administration. Among the PNACers and prominent neocons who staffed the administration were Dick Cheney (vice president), Donald Rumsfeld (secretary of defense), Paul Wolfowitz (deputy secretary of defense), Richard Armitage (deputy secretary of state), Elliott Abrams (senior director for Near East, Southwest Asian, and North African Affairs on the National Security Council), John Bolton (undersecretary of state for Arms Control and International Security and UN ambassador), Paula Dobriansky (undersecretary of state for Global Affairs), Zalmay Khalilzad (president's special envoy to Afghanistan and ambassador at large for free Iraqis), Richard Perle (chair of the Pentagon's semiautonomous Defense Policy Board), Peter Rodman (assistant secretary of defense for International Security Affairs), William Schneider, Jr. (chair of the Pentagon's Defense Science Board), Robert B. Zoellick (U.S. trade representative), Stephen Cambone (director of the Pentagon Office of Program Analysis and Evaluation), Eliot Cohen (Defense Policy Board), Devon Gaffney Cross (Defense Policy Board), I. Lewis Libby (Vice President Cheney's chief of staff), William Luti and Abram Shulsky (directors of the Pentagon's Office of Special Plans), James Woolsey (Defense Policy Board), and David Wurmser (special assistant to the undersecretary of state for Arms Control).

73   John W. Dower, *Cultures of War: Pearl Harbor/Hiroshima/9-11/Iraq* (New York: W. W. Norton, 2010), 91–92.

74   "Transcript: Town Hall Meeting on Iraq at Ohio State February 18," February 20, 1998, www.fas.org/news/iraq/1998/02/20/98022006_tpo.html.

75   Gardner, *The Long Road to Baghdad,* 111.

76   Ibid., 112.

77   Colin Powell with Joseph Persico, *My American Journey* (New York: Random House, 1995), 576.

78   "Excerpt from McCain's Speech on Religious Conservatives," *New York Times*, February 29, 2000.

79   Nicholas Kulish and Jim Vandehei, "Politics & Economy: Protest in Miami-Dade Is a Well-Organized GOP Effort," *Wall Street Journal*, November 27, 2000; Paul Gigot, "Burgher Rebellion: GOP Turns Up Miami Heat," *Wall Street Journal*, November 24, 2000; Wilentz, *The Age of Reagan*, 423–424.

80   Edward Walsh, "Ruling Marked by the Words of a Dissenter," *Washington Post*, December 17, 2006.

81   "Profile: Washington Hawk Donald Rumsfeld," http://news.bbc.co.uk/2/hi/americas /2247256.stm.

82   Robert Draper, *Dead Certain: The Presidency of George W. Bush* (New York: Free Press, 2007), 282.

83   Bob Woodward, "A Course of 'Confident Action,'" *Washington Post*, November 19, 2002.

84   Elizabeth Becker, "Head of Religion-Based Initiative Resigns," *New York Times*, August 18, 2001; Ron Suskind, "Why Are These Men Laughing?," *Esquire*, January 2003, 97.

85   "John Dilulio's Letter," October 24, 2002, www.esquire.com/features/dilulio.

86   Joel Achenbach, "Nader Puts His Mouth Where the Money Is," *Washington Post*, August 4, 2000.

87   Jane Mayer, "Contract Sport: What Did the Vice-President Do for Halliburton?," *New Yorker*, February 16, 2004, www.newyorker.com/archive/2004/02/16/040216fa_fact.

88   "Full Text of Dick Cheney's Speech at the IP Autumn Lunch," http://web.archive.org/web /20000414054656/http://www.petroleum.co.uk/speeches.htm.

89   Antonia Juhasz, "Whose Oil Is It, Anyway?," *New York Times*, March 13, 2007.

90   Dennis Kucinich, "Obviously Oil," March 11, 2003, www.alternet.org/story/15359/.

91   Herring, *From Colony to Superpower*, 940.

92   David Johnston and Jim Dwyer, "Pre-9/11 Files Show Warnings Were More Dire and Persistent," *New York Times*, April 18, 2004.

93   "Clarke 'Would Welcome' Open Testimony," www.msnbc.msn.com/id/4619346/ns/us _news-security/t/clarke-would-welcome-open-testimony/#.TpJrlajEMhA.

94   Richard A. Clarke, *Against All Enemies: Inside America's War on Terror* (New York: Free Press, 2004), 235.

95   Johnston and Dwyer, "Pre-9/11 Files Show Warnings Were More Dire and Persistent."

96   Thomas Powers, "Secret Intelligence and the 'War on Terror,'" *New York Review of Books*, December 16, 2004, www.nybooks.com/articles/archives/2004/dec/16/secret -intelligence-and-the-war-on-terror.

97   Ron Suskind, *The One Percent Doctrine: Deep Inside America's Pursuit of Its Enemies Since 9/11* (New York: Simon & Schuster, 2006), 2.

98   Wilentz, *The Age of Reagan*, 440.

99   "Transcript of Bush's Remarks on Iraq: 'We Will Finish the Work of the Fallen,'" *New York Times*, April 14, 2004.

100   "Two Months Before 9/11, an Urgent Warning to Rice," *Washington Post*, October 1, 2006.

101   Frank Rich, "The Jack Welch War Plan," *New York Times*, September 28, 2002.

102   Johnston and Dwyer, "Pre-9/11 Files Show Warnings Were More Dire and Persistent."

CHAPTER 13: THE BUSH-CHENEY DEBACLE: "THE GATES OF HELL ARE OPEN IN IRAQ"

1   George W. Bush, *Public Papers of the Presidents of the United States: George W. Bush, 2004, Book 2, July 1 to September 30, 2004* (Washington, DC: Government Printing Office, 2004), 1494.

2   Robert S. McElvaine, "HNN Poll: 61% of Historians Rate the Bush Presidency Worst," History News Network, March 5, 2009, http://hnn.us/articles/48916.html.

3   Devin Dwyer, "George W. Bush Cans Swiss Trip as Groups Promise Prosecution for War Crimes," February 7, 2011, http://abcnews.go.com/Politics/george-bush-cancels-swiss -trip-rights-activists-vow/story?id=12857195.

4   Ewen MacAskill and Afua Hirsch, "George Bush Calls Off Trip to Switzerland," *Guardian* (London), February 6, 2011.

5   "The Kissinger Commission," *New York Times*, November 29, 2002.

6   Philip Shenon, *The Commission: The Uncensored History of the 9/11 Investigation* (New York: Twelve, 2008), 9–14.

7   Ibid., 39, 107, 324.

8   Glenn Kessler, "Close Adviser to Rice Plans to Resign," *Washington Post*, November 28, 2006.

9   "Rebuilding America's Defenses: Strategy, Forces, and Resources for a New Century," Project for the New American Century, September 2000, www.newamericancentury .org/RebuildingAmericasDefenses.pdf, 51.

10   David Cole, "What Bush Wants to Hear," *New York Review of Books*, November 17, 2005, www.nybooks.com/articles/archives/2005/nov/17/what-bush-wants-to-hear/; Chitra Ragavan, "Cheney's Guy," *U.S. News & World Report*, May 21, 2006, www.usnews.com /usnews/news/articles/060529/29addington.htm.

11   Joseba Zulaika, *Terrorism: The Self-Fulfilling Prophecy* (Chicago: University of Chicago Press, 2009), 214.

12   Richard A. Clarke, *Against All Enemies: Inside America's War on Terror* (New York: Simon & Schuster, 2004), 32.

13   Paul Krugman, "Osama, Saddam and the Ports," *New York Times*, February 24, 2006.

14   George Tenet, *At the Center of the Storm: My Years at the CIA* (New York: HarperCollins, 2007), xix.

15   Elisabeth Bumiller and Jane Perlez, "Bush and Top Aides Proclaim Policy of 'Ending' States That Back Terror," *New York Times*, September 14, 2001.

16   Clarke, *Against All Enemies*, 30–31.

17   Michael Cooper and Marc Santora, "Mideast Hawks Help to Develop Giuliani Policy," *New York Times*, October 25, 2007.

18   Max Boot, "The Case for American Empire," *Weekly Standard*, October 15, 2001, 30.

19   Clarke, *Against All Enemies*, 30.

20   Robert D. McFadden, "A Day of Mourning," *New York Times*, September 15, 2001.

21   "Vice President Dick Cheney Discusses the Attack on America and Response to Terrorism," NBC News Transcript, *Meet the Press*, September 16, 2001.

22   "Transcript of President Bush's Address," *Washington Post*, September 21, 2001.

23   Bob Woodward, "CIA Told to Do 'Whatever Necessary' to Kill Bin Laden," *Washington Post,* October 21, 2001.

24   Ruth Rosen, "Could It Happen Again?," *San Francisco Chronicle,* May 12, 2003.

25   Robin Toner, "Not So Fast, Senator Says, as Others Smooth Way for Terror Bill," *New York Times,* October 10, 2001.

26   In 1975, Senator Frank Church had warned of the dangers posed by much more limited NSA surveillance during that era: "That capability at any time could be turned around on the American people, and no American would have any privacy left, such is the capability to monitor everything: telephone conversations, telegrams, it doesn't matter. There would be no place to hide. . . . I know the capacity that is there to make tyranny total in America, and we must see to it that this agency [NSA] and all agencies that possess this technology operate within the law and under proper supervision." Marjorie Cohn, *Cowboy Republic: Six Ways the Bush Gang Has Defied the Law* (Sausalito, CA: PoliPointPress, 2007), 100–101.

27   The warning system would become an easy target for comics. Conan O'Brien joked, "Champagne-fuchsia means we're being attacked by Martha Stewart." Jay Leno quipped, "They added a plaid in case we were ever attacked by Scotland." John Schwartz, "U.S. to Drop Color-Coded Terror Alerts," *New York Times,* November 25, 2010.

28   Eric Lipton, "Come One, Come All, Join the Terror Target List," *New York Times,* July 12, 2006; Zbigniew Brzezinski, "Terrorized by 'War on Terror,'" *Washington Post,* March 25, 2007.

29   Katrina vanden Heuvel, "With Osama bin Laden Dead, It's Time to End the 'War on Terror,'" The Nation Blogs, May 2, 2011, www.thenation.com/blog/160310/osama-bin -laden-dead-its-time-end-war-terror.

30   H. W. Brands, *Traitor to His Class: The Privileged Life and Radical Presidency of Franklin Delano Roosevelt* (New York: Random House, 2008), 650.

31   George W. Bush, *Public Papers of the Presidents of the United States, George W. Bush, 2001, Book 2, July 1 to December 31, 2001* (Washington, DC: U.S. Government Printing Office, 2004), 1172.

32   Frank Rich, "Journal: War Is Heck," *New York Times,* November 10, 2001.

33   Tamim Ansary, *West of Kabul, East of New York: An Afghan American Story* (New York: Picador, 2003), 291.

34   David B. Ottaway and Joe Stephens, "Diplomats Met with Taliban on Bin Laden," *Washington Post,* October 29, 2001; Gareth Porter, "U.S. Refusal of 2001 Taliban Offer Gave bin Laden a Free Pass," May 3, 2011, http://ipsnews.net/news.asp?idnews=55476; Gareth Porter, "Taliban Regime Pressed bin Laden on Anti-U.S. Terror," February 11, 2001, http://ipsnews.net/news.asp?idnews=50300.

35   Karen DeYoung, "More Bombing Casualties Alleged,'" *Washington Post,* January 4, 2002.

36   Stephen Kinzer, *Overthrow: America's Century of Regime Change from Hawaii to Iraq* (New York: Times Books, 2006), 310.

37   Transparency International, Corruption Perceptions Index 2009, www.transparency.org /policy_research/surveys_indices/cpi/2009/cpi_2009_table.

38   James P. Pfiffner, *Power Play: The Bush Presidency and the Constitution* (Washington, DC: Brookings Institution Press, 2008), 146–149.

39   Alfred W. McCoy, *A Question of Torture: CIA Interrogation, from the Cold War to the War on Terror* (New York: Metropolitan Books, 2006), 10–11, 25–50, 101–107, 108–150;

Jane Mayer, *The Dark Side: The Inside Story of How the War on Terror Turned into a War on American Ideals* (New York: Doubleday, 2008), 159–181.

40 Mayer, *The Dark Side*, 8.

41 Joby Warrick, Peter Finn, and Julie Tate, "CIA Releases Its Instructions for Breaking a Detainee's Will," *Washington Post*, August 26, 2009.

42 Joby Warrick, Peter Finn, and Julie Tate, "Red Cross Described 'Torture' at CIA Jails," *Washington Post*, March 16, 2009.

43 Karen J. Greenberg, "Visiting the Torture Museum: Barbarism Then and Now," February 21, 2008, www.tomdispatch.com/post/174897/karen_greenberg_barbarism_lite.

44 George W. Bush, *Decision Points* (New York: Crown, 2010), 169.

45 Peter Finn and Joby Warrick, "Detainee's Harsh Treatment Foiled No Plots," *Washington Post*, March 29, 2009.

46 Scott Shane, "2 Suspects Waterboarded 266 Times," *New York Times*, April 20, 2009.

47 McCoy, *A Question of Torture*, 132–135.

48 Seymour M. Hersh, "Torture at Abu Ghraib," *New Yorker*, May 10, 2004.

49 "Remarks by the President at the 2003 Republican National Committee Presidential Gala," October 8, 2003, http://georgewbush-whitehouse.archives.gov/news/releases /2003/10/20031008-9.html.

50 Mayer, *The Dark Side*, 8.

51 "Sources: Top Bush Advisors Approved 'Enhanced Interrogation,'" April 9, 2008, http://abcnews.go.com/TheLaw/LawPolitics/Story?id=4583256&page=3.

52 Noam Chomsky, *Hopes and Prospects* (Chicago: Haymarket Books, 2010), 265–266.

53 George Hunsinger, ed. *Torture Is a Moral Issue: Christians, Jews, Muslims, and People of Conscience Speak Out* (Grand Rapids, MI: William B. Eerdmans, 2008), 71; "Decisions from on Low," *Star-Ledger* (Newark), April 15, 2008.

54 Glenn Greenwald, "The Suppressed Fact: Deaths by U.S. Torture," June 30, 2009, www .salon.com/news/opinion/glenn_greenwald/2009/06/30/accountability; Antonio Taguba, "Preface to 'Broken Laws, Broken Lives,'" June 2008, http://brokenlives.info /?page_id=23.

55 Roger Cohen, "A Command of the Law," *New York Times*, November 27, 2008.

56 Mayer, *The Dark Side*, 187.

57 Taguba, "Preface to 'Broken Laws, Broken Lives.'"

58 Seymour M. Hersh, *Chain of Command: The Road from 9/11 to Abu Ghraib* (New York: HarperCollins, 2004), 5.

59 Linda Greenhouse, "Justices, 5–4, Back Detainee Appeals for Guantánamo," *New York Times*, June 13, 2008.

60 Patrick Sawer, "Yard Fury over Bush Visit," *London Evening Standard*, October 11, 2003.

61 Sidney Blumenthal, "Dick Cheney Was Never a 'Grown Up': A Hard Look at How One Man Changed the Face of Neoconservatism," April 14, 2008, www.salon.com /2008/04/14/cheney_10/.

62 Alan Lichtman, *White Protestant Nation: The Rise of the American Conservative Movement* (New York: Atlantic Monthly Press, 2008), 447.

63   James Mann, *Rise of the Vulcans: The History of Bush's War Cabinet* (New York: Penguin Books, 2004), 80.

64   Sam Tanenhaus, "Bush's Brain Trust," *Vanity Fair,* July 2003, 169.

65   Ron Suskind, *The Price of Loyalty: George W. Bush, the White House, and the Education of Paul O'Neill* (New York: Simon & Schuster, 2004), 72.

66   Ibid., 85–86.

67   Ibid., 129.

68   Elaina Sciolino and Patrick E. Tyler, "A National Challenge: Saddam Hussein," *New York Times,* October 12, 2001.

69   Daniel Eisenberg, "We're Taking Him Out," *Time,* May 5, 2005, www.time.com/time/world /article/0,8599,235395,00.html.

70   Ron Suskind, *The One Percent Doctrine: Deep Inside America's Pursuit of Its Enemies Since 9/11* (New York: Simon & Schuster, 2006), 23, 189–191; Lloyd C. Gardner, *The Long Road to Baghdad: A History of U.S. Foreign Policy from the 1970s to the Present* (New York: New Press, 2008), 134–135, 202–203.

71   Dilip Hiro, *Secrets and Lies: Operation "Iraqi Freedom" and After* (New York: Nation Books, 2004), 8.

72   Peter Bergen, "Armchair Provocateur: Laurie Mylroie: The Neocons' Favorite Conspiracy Theorist," *Washington Monthly,* December 2003, www.washingtonmonthly .com/features/2003/0312.bergen.html.

73   *Meet the Press,* September 14, 2003.

74   Jeff Stein, "Spy Talk," *Washington Post,* May 25, 2010.

75   Jack Fairweather and Anton La Guardia, "Chalabi Stands by Faulty Intelligence That Toppled Saddam's Regime," *Daily Telegraph* (London), February 19, 2004.

76   Seymour Hersh, "Selective Intelligence," *New Yorker,* May 6, 2003.

77   Tim Weiner, *Legacy of Ashes: The History of the CIA* (New York: Doubleday, 2007), 486.

78   David E. Sanger, "Threats and Responses: The President's Speech," *New York Times,* October 8, 2002.

79   "In Cheney's Words: The Administration Case for Removing Saddam Hussein," *New York Times,* August 27, 2002.

80   Gardner, *The Long Road to Baghdad,* 153–154.

81   Todd S. Purdum and New York Times staff, *A Time of Our Choosing: America's War in Iraq* (New York: Henry Holt, 2003), 37.

82   Michael Isikoff and David Corn, *Hubris: The Inside Story of Spin, Scandal, and the Selling of the Iraq War* (New York: Crown, 2006), 3.

83   "Scott Ritter: Facts Needed Before Iraqi Attack," http://archives.cnn.com/2002/WORLD /meast/07/17/saddam.ritter.cnna/.

84   Kinzer, *Overthrow,* 294.

85   Thomas Ricks, *Fiasco: The American Military Adventure in Iraq* (New York: Penguin Press, 2006), 40–41.

86   Gardner, *The Long Road to Baghdad,* 141–143, 154.

87   Hans Blix, *Disarming Iraq* (New York: Pantheon Books, 2004), 156–157.

88   Lloyd C. Gardner, "Present at the Culmination: An Empire of Righteousness?," in *The New American Empire: A 21st Century Teach-in on U.S. Foreign Policy,* ed. Lloyd C. Gardner and Marilyn B. Young (New York: New Press, 2005), 3.

89   Rajiv Chadrasekaran, "Baghdad Delivers Weapons Data to U.N.," *Washington Post,* December 8, 2002; Kinzer, *Overthrow,* 295; Chalmers A. Johnson, *The Sorrows of Empire: Militarism, Secrecy, and the End of the Republic* (London: Verso, 2004), 224.

90   John Barry, Howard Fineman, Jonathan Adams, Tara Pepper, William Underhill, and Michael Isikoff, "Periscope," *Newsweek,* March 3, 2003.

91   Walter Pincus, "U.S. Lacks Specifics on Banned Arms," *Washington Post,* March 16, 2003.

92   Anthony H. Cordesman, Weapons of Mass Destruction in the Middle East: Regional Trends, National Forces, Warfighting Capabilities, Delivery Options, and Weapons Effects (Washington, DC: Center for Strategic and International Studies, 2002), 17–19, 22, 27–31, 37–40, 53–59, 90–94, 98–103.

93   Paul Krugman, "Things to Come," *New York Times,* March 18, 2003.

94   Frederik Logevall, "Anatomy of an Unnecessary War," in *The Presidency of George W. Bush: A First Historical Assessment,* ed. Julian E. Zelizer (Princeton, NJ: Princeton University Press, 2010), 110.

95   John J. Mearsheimer and Stephen M. Walt, *The Israel Lobby and U.S. Foreign Policy* (New York: Farrar, Straus and Giroux, 2008), 242–243. A broad range of Jewish groups jumped onto the prowar bandwagon. AIPAC continued to support the war vociferously even when most Americans, including most Jewish Americans, had turned against it. In 2007, Democratic Representative Jim Moran of Virginia noted, "Jewish Americans, as a voting bloc and as an influence on American foreign policy, are overwhelmingly opposed to the war. There is no ethnic group as opposed to the war as much as Jewish Americans. But, AIPAC is the most powerful lobby and has pushed this war from the beginning." In fact, Gallup reported that year, based on thirteen polls taken since 2005, that 77 percent of American Jews opposed the war compared to 52 percent of all Americans. AIPAC's former Director of Foreign Policy Issues Steven Rosen bragged that he could deliver the votes of seventy senators on any issue. "Representative Jim Moran on the Power of AIPAC," *Tikkun,* September–October 2007, 76; Mearsheimer and Walt, *The Israel Lobby and U.S. Foreign Policy,* 240–243. Jeffrey Goldberg, "Real Insiders: A Pro-Israel Lobby and an F.B.I. Sting," *New Yorker,* July 4, 2005, www.newyorker.com / archive/2005/07/04/050704fa_fact#ixzz1LilbqLAj.

96   Mearsheimer and Walt, *The Israel Lobby and U.S. Foreign Policy,* 238–240.

97   "President's State of the Union Message to Congress and the Nation," *New York Times,* January 29, 2003.

98   Paul R. Pillar, "Intelligence, Policy, and the War in Iraq," *Foreign Affairs,* March–April 2006, 24.

99   Ron Suskind, *The One Percent Doctrine,* 191.

100 Karen DeYoung, *Soldier: The Life of Colin Powell* (New York: Alfred A. Knopf, 2006), 439.

101 "Powell's Address, Presenting 'Deeply Troubling' Evidence on Iraq," *New York Times,* February 6, 2003.

102 "Colin Powell on Iraq, Race, and Hurricane Relief," *20/20,* September 8, 2005, http://abcnews.go.com/2020/Politics/story?id=1105979.

103   Ivo H. Daalder and James M. Lindsay, *America Unbound: The Bush Revolution in Foreign Policy* (Washington: DC: Brookings Institution Press, 2003), 158; Martin Chulov and Helen Pidd, "Curveball: How US Was Duped by Iraqi Fantasist Looking to Topple Saddam," *Guardian* (London), February 16, 2011; Gardner, *The Long Road to Baghdad,* 157.

104   Nicholas D. Kristof, "Cloaks and Daggers," *New York Times,* June 6, 2003, 33.

105   DeYoung, *Soldier,* 450–451.

106   For a full account of the Katharine Gun affair, see Marcia and Thomas Mitchell, *The Spy Who Tried to Stop a War: Katharine Gun and the Secret Plot to Sanction the Iraq Invasion* (Sausalito, CA: PoliPointPress, 2008).

107   Colum Lynch, "U.S. Pushed Allies on Iraq, Diplomat Writes," *Washington Post,* March 23, 2008.

108   Steven R. Weisman, "U.S. Set to Demand That Allies Agree Iraq Is Defying U.N.," *New York Times,* January 23, 2003.

109   Thomas L. Friedman, "Vote France off the Island," *New York Times,* February 9, 2003.

110   Toby Harnden, "Gerhard Schroeder Accuses George W. Bush of 'Not Telling Truth' in Memoirs," *Telegraph* (London), November 10, 2010.

111   Don Van Natta, Jr., "Bush Was Set on Path to War, Memo by British Adviser Says," *New York Times,* March 27, 2006.

112   Matthew Yglesias, "Democrats and the World," in *In Search of Progressive America,* ed. Michael Kazin with Frans Becker and Menno Hurenkamp (Philadelphia: University of Pennsylvania Press, 2008), 13.

113   David Barstow, "Behind TV Analysts, Pentagon's Hidden Hand," *New York Times,* April 20, 2008; "Instruments of War: Transcript," April 25, 2008, www.onthemedia .org/transcripts/2008/04/25/01.

114   Daniel Okrent, "The Public Editor: Weapons of Mass Destruction? Or Mass Distraction?," *New York Times,* May 30, 2004.

115   John Barry, "Beyond Baghdad: Expanding Target List," *Newsweek,* August 18, 2002.

116   Norman Podhoretz, "In Praise of the Bush Doctrine," *Commentary,* September 2002, 19.

117   Linda Diebel, "Bush Doctrinaires," *Toronto Star,* April 13, 2003.

118   Wesley K. Clark, *Winning Modern Wars: Iraq, Terrorism, and the American Empire* (New York: PublicAffairs, 2004), 130.

119   Robert Dreyfuss, "Just the Beginning: Is Iraq the Opening Salvo in a War to Remake the World?," *American Prospect,* April 1, 2003, 26.

120   Barbara Slavin, "Iraq a Harsh Climate to Try to Grow Democracy," *USA Today,* November 11, 2002.

121   G. John Ikenberry, "America's Imperial Ambition," *Foreign Affairs,* September–October 2002, 49–50.

122   Michael Hirsh, "Hawks, Doves and Dubya," *Newsweek,* September 2, 2002, 25.

123   Anthony Zinni, "Comments of Gen. Anthony Zinni (ret.) During a Speech before the Florida Economic Club, August 23, 2002," www.npr.org/programs/morning/zinni.html.

124   George C. Wilson, "Cheney Believes Gorbachev Sincere," *Washington Post,* April 5, 1989.

125   Phil McCombs, "The Unsettling Calm of Dick Cheney," *Washington Post,* April 3, 1991.

126 Robert H. Swansbrough, *Test by Fire: The War Presidency of George W. Bush* (New York: Palgrave Macmillan, 2008), 27; James E. Westheider, *Fighting on Two Fronts: African Americans and the Vietnam War* (New York: New York University Press, 1997), 29–30.

127 Colin L. Powell with Joseph E. Persico, *My American Journey* (New York: Random House, 1995), 148.

128 Stephen J. Whitfield, "Still the Best Catch There Is: Joseph Heller's *Catch 22*," in *Rethinking Cold War Culture*, ed. Peter J. Kuznick and James Gilbert (Washington, DC: Smithsonian Institution Press, 2001), 188.

129 Ross Goldberg and Sam Kahn, "Bolton's Conservative Ideology Has Roots in Yale Experience," *Yale Daily News*, April 28, 2005.

130 Paul D. Colford, *The Rush Limbaugh Story: Talent on Loan from God* (New York: St. Martin's Press, 1993), 14–20; Whitfield, "Still the Best Catch There Is," 188.

131 Craig Glenday, ed. *Guinness World Records 2010: Thousands of New Records in the Book of the Decade!* (New York: Bantam, 2010), 47.

132 Robert J. Samuelson, "The Gulf of World Opinion," *Washington Post*, March 27, 2003.

133 Michael Dobbs, "Persuasion: Why Success Requires More than Victory," *Washington Post*, March 30, 2003.

134 Nicholas D. Kristof, "Flogging the French," *New York Times*, January 31, 2003.

135 Samuelson, "The Gulf of World Opinion."

136 Harlan K. Ullman and James Wade, *Shock and Awe: Achieving Rapid Dominance* (Washington, DC: NDU Press, 1996), www.au.af.mil/AU/AWC/AWCGATE/ndu/shocknawe.

137 Arundhati Roy, *An Ordinary Person's Guide to Empire* (Cambridge, MA: South End Press, 2004), 64.

138 Donald Rumsfeld, "Remarks as Delivered by Secretary of Defense Donald H. Rumsfeld, Baghdad, Iraq, Wednesday, April 30, 2003," www.defense.gov/speeches/speech .aspx?speechid=382.

139 Gardner, *The Long Road to Baghdad*, 170; John W. Dower, *Cultures of War: Pearl Harbor/ Hiroshima/9-11/Iraq* (New York: W. W. Norton, 2010), 397–398.

140 Richard Perle, "Next Stop, Iraq: Remarks of the Hon. Richard Perle at the FPRI Annual Dinner," November 14, 2001, www.fpri.org/transcripts/annualdinner.20011114.perle .nextstopiraq.html.

141 Lawrence F. Kaplan and William Kristol, *The War over Iraq: Saddam's Tyranny and America's Mission* (San Francisco: Encounter Books, 2003), vii–viii, 124.

142 Robert Fisk, "American Billions Keep Arab Regimes Sweet," *Independent* (London), March 2, 2003.

143 Doug Struck, "Citing Iraq, N. Korea Signals Hard Line on Weapons Issue," *Washington Post*, March 30, 2003.

144 Gardner, *The Long Road to Baghdad*, 223.

145 Alan Greenspan, *The Age of Turbulence: Adventures in a New World* (New York: Penguin, 2007), 463.

146 Robert Dreyfuss, "The Thirty-Year Itch," *Mother Jones*, March–April 2003, http:// motherjones.com/politics/2003/03/thirty-year-itch?page=2.

147   *Congressional Record, Proceedings and Debates of the 108th Congress, First Session,* April 3, 2003, 8544.

148   Dreyfuss, "The Thirty-Year Itch."

149   "Report on Prewar Intelligence Assessments About Postwar Iraq," Select Committee on Intelligence, United States Senate, 110th Cong., May 25, 2007, 27, 57, http://intelligence.senate.gov/11076.pdf.

150   Walter Pincus and Karen DeYoung, "Analysts' Warnings of Iraq Chaos Detailed," *Washington Post,* May 26, 2007.

151   Roger Strother, "Post-Saddam Iraq: The War Game," November 4, 2006, National Security Archive, www.gwu.edu/~nsarchiv/NSAEBB/NSAEBB207/index.htm.

152   Nicholas D. Kristof, "War and Wisdom," *New York Times,* February 7, 2003.

153   Michael F. Scheuer, "Tenet Tries to Shift the Blame. Don't Buy It," *Washington Post,* April 29, 2007.

154   Peter W. Galbraith, *The End of Iraq: How American Incompetence Created a War Without End* (New York: Simon & Schuster, 2006), 83.

155   Bruce Hoffman, *Inside Terrorism* (New York: Columbia University Press, 2006), 292.

156   "Bin Laden: Goal Is to Bankrupt U.S.," November 1, 2004, http://articles.cnn.com/2004-11-01/world/binladen.tape_1_al-jazee ra-qaeda-bin?_s=PM:WORLD.

157   Aram Roston, *The Man Who Pushed America to War: The Extraordinary Life, Adventures, and Obsessions of Ahmad Chalabi* (New York: Nation Books, 2008), 252–253, 255–256; Gardner, *Long Road to Baghdad,* 205.

158   Eli Lake, "Chalabi Aide Tied to Shi'ite Terrorists," *Washington Times,* August 28, 2009.

159   "Interview with Andrew Natsios, Administrator for the US Agency for International Development, with Ted Koppel, *Nightline,* ABC News, 23 April 2003 on the Costs of Iraqi Reconstruction," www.mtholyoke.edu/acad/intrel/iraq/koppel.htm.

160   Bruno Coppieters and Boris Kashnikov, "Right Intentions," in *Moral Constraints on War: Principles and Cases,* ed. Bruno Coppieters and Nick Fotion (Lanham, MD: Rowman & Littlefield, 2008), 94.

161   Eric Schmitt, "2 U.S. Officials Liken Guerrillas to Renegade Postwar Nazi Units," *New York Times,* August 23, 2003.

162   James Risen and David Johnston, "Bin Laden Is Seen with Aide on Tape," *New York Times,* September 11, 2003.

163   For a discussion of U.S. privatization plans, see Dower, *Cultures of War,* 411–416.

164   Naomi Klein, *The Shock Doctrine: The Rise of Disaster Capitalism* (New York: Henry Holt, 2007), 432–436.

165   Rajiv Chandrasekaran, "Ties to GOP Trumped Know-how Among Staff Sent to Rebuild Iraq," *Washington Post,* September 17, 2006.

166   "'Gates of Hell' Are Open in Iraq, Warns Arab League Chief," Agence France Presse, September 19, 2004.

167   Jeremy Scahill, *Blackwater: The Rise of the World's Most Powerful Mercenary Army* (New York: Nation Books, 2008), 59–60.

168   James Risen, "U.S. Splits Controversial Contractor's Iraq Work 3 Ways, but Costs May Soar," *New York Times,* May 24, 2008; Robert O'Harrow, Jr., "Halliburton Is a Handy Target for Democrats," *Washington Post,* September 18, 2004.

169   Helen Dewar and Dana Milbank, "Cheney Dismisses Critic with Obscenity," *Washington Post,* June 25, 2004.

170   James Risen, "Electrical Risks Worse than Said at Bases in Iraq," *New York Times,* July 18, 2008.

171   Robert F. Worth, "Blast Destroys Shrine in Iraq, Setting Off Sectarian Fury," *New York Times,* February 22, 2006.

172   Gardner, *The Long Road to Baghdad,* 245.

173   Dana Priest and Dana Milbank, "President Defends Allegation on Iraq," *Washington Post,* July 15, 2003.

174   Ron Suskind, "Without a Doubt," *New York Times Magazine,* October 17, 2004, 44, 51.

175   Buddhika Jayamaha, Wesley D. Smith, Jeremy Roebuck, Omar Mora, Edward Sandmeier, Yance T. Gray, and Jeremy A. Murphy, "The War as We Saw It," *New York Times,* August 19, 2007.

176   Joseph E. Stiglitz and Linda Bilmes, *The Three Trillion Dollar War: The True Cost of the Iraq Conflict* (New York: W. W. Norton, 2008).

177   *Iraq: No Let-up in the Humanitarian Crisis* (Geneva: International Committee of the Red Cross, 2008), 3.

178   Transparency International, "Corruption Perceptions Index 2010 Results," www .transparency.org/policy_research/surveys_indices/cpi/2010/results.

179   Liz Sly, "In Iraq, Ex-Foe Is New Friend: Historic Visit by Iran Leader Showcases Ties," *Chicago Tribune,* March 3, 2008.

180   Gareth Porter, "Burnt Offering," *American Prospect,* May 25, 2006, www.prospect.org/cs /articles?articleId=11539.

181   Philip Giraldi, "Deep Background: In Case of Emergency, Nuke Iran; Give Tenet Another Medal; Iraq's Police Brutality," *American Conservative,* August 1, 2005, www .amconmag.com/article/2005/aug/01/00027/.

182   "Iran: Nuclear Intentions and Capabilities," National Intelligence Estimate, November 2007, www.dni.gov/press_releases/20071203_release.pdf, 6.

183   James Risen and Judith Miller, "A Nation Challenged," *New York Times,* October 29, 2001; Tim Reid, "We'll Bomb You to Stone Age, US Told Pakistan," *Times* (London), September 22, 2006, www.timesonline.co.uk/tol/news/world/middle_east/article 647188.ece.

184   Celia W. Dugger, "The World: Unthinkable," *New York Times,* June 2, 2002.

185   Roger D. Hodge, "Weekly Review," *Harper's Magazine,* January 15, 2002.

186   Hersh, *Chain of Command,* 291, 312; Statement of Leonard Weiss, Ph.D., to the House Subcommittee on International Terrorism and Nonproliferation, "The A. Q. Khan Network: Case Closed?: Hearing before the Subcommittee on International Terrorism of the Committee on International Relations," 109th Cong., 2nd Sess., May 25, 2006, 10; John Lancaster and Kamran Khan, "President Won't Submit to Nuclear Inspections," *Washington Post,* February 6, 2004.

187   Seymour M. Hersh, "The Deal: Why Is Washington Going Easy on Pakistan's Nuclear Black Marketers?," *New Yorker,* March 8, 2004, 32.

188   Pew Research Center, "Pew Global Attitudes Project: Spring 2007 Survey of 47 Publics" (Washington, DC: Pew Research Center for the People & the Press, 2007), 88; Pew Research Center, "Publics of Asian Powers Hold Negative Views of One Another," September 21, 2006, http://pewglobal.org/2006/09/21/publics-of-asian-powers-hold -negative-views-of-one-another/.

189   "Poll: Bin Laden tops Musharraf in Pakistan," September 11, 2007, http://articles.cnn .com/2007-09-11/politics/poll.pakistanis_1_approval-rating-poll-qaeda?_s=PM :POLITICS.

190   Nick Allen, "Soviet Break-up Was Geopolitical Disaster, Says Putin," *Daily Telegraph* (London), April 26, 2005.

191   Nick Allen, "Why Russia Is Putting Stalin Back on His Pedestal," *Daily Telegraph* (London), April 20, 2005.

192   William M. Arkin, "Secret Plan Outlines the Unthinkable," *Los Angeles Times,* March 9, 2002.

193   "America as Nuclear Rogue," *New York Times,* March 12, 2002.

194   Tadatoshi Akiba, "Peace Declaration, August 6, 2003," www.pcf.city.hiroshima.jp/declaration /English/2003/index.html.

195   Keir A. Leiber and Daryl G. Press, "The Rise of U.S. Nuclear Primacy," *Foreign Affairs,* March–April 2006, 42, 52.

196   Peter Finn, "Russians Sense the Heat of Cold War," *Washington Post,* April 3, 2006.

197   Yegor Gaidar, "Nuclear Punditry Can Be a Dangerous Game," *Financial Times* (London), March 29, 2006.

198   "Russian and U.S. Citizens See Each Other as Potential Enemies?," *Pravda,* April 24, 2006.

199   "National Security," program broadcast by Radio Russia on April 5, 2006, supplied by BBC Worldwide Monitoring; Fred Weir, "In Moscow, Buzz over Arms Race II," *Christian Science Monitor,* April 24, 2006; Gaidar, "Nuclear Punditry Can Be a Dangerous Game."

200   Peter C. W. Flory, "Does Washington Really Have (Or Want) Nuclear Primacy?," *Foreign Affairs,* September–October 2006, 149–150; Keith Payne, "A Matter of Record," *Foreign Affairs,* September–October 2006, 152.

201   Alexei Arbatov, "Cutting a Deal," *Foreign Affairs,* September–October 2006, 153–154.

202   Keir A. Lieber and Daryl G. Press, "Lieber and Press Reply," *Foreign Affairs,* September– October 2006, 154–157.

203   William B. Scott, "USSC Prepares for Future Combat Missions in Space," *Aviation Week & Space Technology,* August 5, 1996, 51.

204   *Report of the Commission to Assess United States National Security Space Management and Organization* (Washington, DC: U.S. Government Printing Office, 2001), viii, xii.

205   Sean Kay, *Global Security in the Twenty-First Century: The Quest for Power and the Search for Peace* (Lanham, MD: Rowman & Littlefield, 2006), 187.

206   Jonathan Shainin, "Rods from God," *New York Times Magazine,* December 10, 2006, 70.

207   Weiner, *Legacy of Ashes,* 502.

208   Ibid., 503.

209 Nick Turse, "Planet Pentagon How the Pentagon Came to Own the Earth, Seas, and Skies," July 11, 2007, www.tomdispatch.com/post/174818.

210 "Department of Defense Base Structure Report, Fiscal Year 2008 Baseline," www.acq .osd.mil/ie/download/bsr/BSR2008Baseline.pdf.

211 Thomas Donnelly and Vance Serchuk, "Toward a Global Cavalry: Overseas Rebasing and Defense Transformation," American Enterprise Institute for Public Policy Research, July 1, 2003, www.aei.org/outlook/17783.

212 Douglas J. Feith, "Prepared Statement Before the House Armed Services Committee," June 23, 2004, www.defense.gov/speeches/speech.aspx?speechid=133.

213 Tom Engelhardt, *The American Way of War: How Bush's Wars Became Obama's* (Chicago: Haymarket Books, 2010), 42.

214 Thom Shanker, "Despite Slump, U.S. Role as Top Arms Supplier Grows," *New York Times,* September 7, 2009.

215 Brzezinski, "Terrorized by 'War on Terror.'"

216 Mike Allen and Edward Walsh, "Presidential Rivals Feast on Jokes, Jabs," *Washington Post,* October 20, 2000.

217 Louise Story, "Wall St. Profits Were a Mirage, but Huge Bonuses Were Real," *New York Times,* December 18, 2008.

218 David Goldman, "Most Firms Pay No Income Taxes—Congress," August 12, 2008, http://money.cnn.com/2008/08/12/news/economy/corporate_taxes.

219 Lichtman, *White Protestant Nation,* 446.

220 James T. Patterson, "Transformative Economic Policies: Tax Cutting, Stimuli, and Bailouts," in Zelizer, *The Presidency of George W. Bush,* 130.

221 Paul Harris, "Welcome to Richistan, USA," *Observer* (London), July 22, 2007.

222 Louise Story, "Top Hedge Fund Managers Do Well in a Down Year," *New York Times,* March 25, 2009.

223 International Labour Organization, *World of Work Report 2008: Income Inequalities in the Age of Financial Globalization* (Geneva: International Institute for Labour Studies, 2008), www.ilo.org/public/english/bureau/inst/download/world08.pdf, xi.

224 Tomoeh Murakami Tse, "Buffett Slams Tax System Disparities," *Washington Post,* June 27, 2007.

225 David Rothkopf, "They're Global Citizens. They're Hugely Rich. And They Pull the Strings," *Washington Post,* May 4, 2008; David Brown, "Richest Tenth Own 85% of World's Assets," *Times* (London), December 6, 2006, www.timesonline.co.uk/tol/news /world/asia/article661055.ece.

226 "Giving More Generously: What Rich Countries Gave in Foreign Aid Last Year," *Economist,* March 31, 2009, www.economist.com/node/13400406?story_id=13400406.

227 Mark Knoller, "President Bush by the Numbers," February 11, 2009, www.cbsnews .com/stories/2009/01/19/politics/bush_legacy/main4735360.shtml.

228 Carol Morello and Dan Keating, "Millions More Thrust into Poverty," *Washington Post,* September 11, 2009.

229 Jodie T. Allen, "A Nation of 'Haves' and 'Have-Nots'?," Pew Research Center, September 13, 2007, http://pewresearch.org/pubs/593/haves-have-nots.

230   Robert Reich, "America Is Becoming a Plutocracy," October 18, 2010, www.salon.com /news/feature/2010/10/18/the_perfect_storm.

231   "Bush's Final Approval Rating: 22 Percent," www.cbsnews.com/stories/2009/01/16 /opinion /polls/main4728399.shtml.

CHAPTER 14: OBAMA: MANAGING A WOUNDED EMPIRE

1   Emily Eakin, "Ideas & Trends: All Roads Lead to D.C.," *New York Times,* March 31, 2002.

2   Bob Woodward, *Obama's Wars* (New York: Simon & Schuster, 2010), 11.

3   Steven S. Clark, "Pharma Makes a Pragmatic Left Turn in this Election," WTN News, November 3, 2008, wtnnews.com/articles/5185.

4   Glenn Greenwald, "Larry Summers, Tim Geithner and Wall Street's Ownership of Government," April 4, 2009, http://www.salon.com/2009/04/04/summers; Dan Froomkin, "White House Watch," Washington Post, April 6, 2009.

5   Matt Taibbi, "Obama's Big Sellout," December 13, 2009, *Rolling Stone,* www.common dreams.org/headline/2009/12/13-8; Jackie Calmes, "Obama's Economic Team Shows Influence of Robert Rubin—With a Difference," *New York Times,* November 24, 2008; Eric Dash, "Citigroup to Halt Dividend and Curb Pay," *New York Times,* November 23, 2008; Amit R. Paley and David Cho, "Administration Seeks an Out on Bailout Rules for Firms," *Washington Post,* April 4, 2009.

6   James K. Galbraith, "It Was the Banks," November 5, 2010, www.commondreams.org/ view/2010/11/05-13.

7   Dan Froomkin, "Suskind's 'Confidence Men' Raises Questions About Obama's Credibility," *Huffington Post,* December 2, 2011, www.commondreams.org/view/2011 /12/02-8.

8   Eric Alterman, "The Ingrates of Wall Street," *Nation,* June 15, 2011, www.thenation.com /article/161447/ingrates-wall-street.

9   Nelson D. Schwartz and Louise Story, "Pay of Hedge Fund Managers Roared Back Last Year," *New York Times,* April 1, 2010.

10   Michael Luo, "In Banking, Emanuel Made Money and Connections," *New York Times,* December 4, 2008.

11   Ryan Lizza, "Inside the Crisis: Larry Summers and the White House Economic Team," *New Yorker,* October 12, 2009, www.newyorker.com/reporting/2009/10/12/091012fa _fact_lizza?printable=true#ixzz1Q gGbqGCw.

12   Andrew Sum, Ishwar Khatiwada, Joseph McLaughlin, and Sheila Palma, "The 'Jobless and Wageless' Recovery from the Great Recession of 2007–2009: The Magnitude and Sources of Economic Growth Through 2011 and Their Impacts on Workers, Profits, and Stock Values," May 2011, www.clms.neu.edu/publication/documents/Revised_ Corporate_Report_May_27th.pdf; Jeff Madrick, "When Will Obama Sound the Alarm About Jobs?" June 9, 2011, www.huffingtonpost.com/jeff-madrick/when-will-obama -sound-the_b_874426.html.

13   Harold Meyerson, "The Unshared Recovery," *Washington Post,* September 6, 2010; Steven Rattner, "The Rich Get Even Richer," *Washington Post,* March 25, 2012.

14   Chris Hedges, "Nader Was Right: Liberals Are Going Nowhere With Obama," August 10, 2009, www.truthdig.com/report/item/20090810_nader_was_right_liberals_are _going_nowhere_with_obama.

15   Paul Krugman, "The Social Contract," *New York Times,* September 23, 2011.

16   Robert B. Reich, "How to End the Great Recession," *New York Times,* September 3, 2010; Edward N. Wolff, "Recent Trends in Household Wealth in the United States," March 2010, www.levyinstitute.org/pubs/wp_589.pdf, 11.

17   Charles M. Blow, "America's Exploding Pipe Dream," *New York Times,* October 29, 2011; www.sgi-network.org/pdf/SGI11_Social_Justice_OECD.pdf.

18   Jason DeParle, "Harder for Americans to Rise from Economy's Lower Rungs," *New York Times,* January 5, 2012.

19   Peter Whoriskey, "Executive Incentives," *Wall Street Journal,* November 20, 2008, online .wsj.com/public/resources/documents/st_ceos_20081111.html.

20   William M. Isaac, "Obama's Financial Reform Weak and Ineffective," *Forbes,* April 22, 2010, www.forbes.com/2010/04/22/financial-reform-barack-obama-chris-dodd -opinions-contributors-william-m-isaac.html.

21   Steven Pearlstein, "Whose Side Is Obama On?" *Washington Post,* November 25, 2009.

22   Nicholas Confessore, "Obama Seeks to Win Back Wall St. Cash," *New York Times,* June 13, 2011.

23   Joseph E. Stiglitz, "Of the 1%, By the 1%, For the 1%," *Vanity Fair,* May 2011, www .vanityfair.com/society/features/2011/05/top-one-percent-201105.

24   Jonathan D. Salant and Lizzie O'Leary, "Six Lobbyists Per Lawmaker Work on Health Overhaul (Update 2)," Bloomberg.com, August 14, 2009, www.bloomberg.com/apps/ news?pid=newsarchive&sid=aqMce51JoZWw.

25   Glenn Greenwald, "White House as Helpless Victim on Healthcare," December 16, 2009, www.salon.com/news/opinion/glenn_greenwald/2009/12/16/white_house.

26   Robert Kuttner, "A Wake Up Call," January 17, 2010, www.huffingtonpost.com/robert -kuttner/a-wake-up-call_b_426467.html.

27   Harold Meyerson, "Who's Hurt by Paul Ryan's Budget Proposal," *Washington Post,* April 5, 2011.

28   Thomas L. Friedman, "Still Digging," *New York Times,* December 7, 2010.

29   Paul Krugman, "The President Is Missing," *New York Times,* April 10, 2011.

30   Doug Cameron, "GE's Immelt Receives Cash Bonus," *Wall Street Journal,* March 14, 2011, online.wsj.com/article/SB10001424052748704893604576200850366030310 .html; Sheryl Gay Stolberg, "Obama Sends Pro-Business Signal with Adviser Choice," *New York Times,* January 21, 2011.

31   Harold Meyerson, "Wall St. Attacks Obama for Tactic It Uses," *Washington Post,* April 4, 2012; Zachary A. Goldfarb, "Obama Support for GE, Boeing, JPMorgan Doesn't Always Go Both Ways," *Washington Post,* July 19, 2012.

32   Margaret Talev, "Obama Retakes the Oath of Office After Busy First Day," *McLatchy News,* January 21, 2009, www.mcclatchydc.com/2009/01/21/60448/obama-retakes-the -oath-of-office.html.

33   "Obama Administration in Danger of Establishing 'New Normal' with Worst Bush-Era Policies, Says ACLU," July 29, 2010, www.aclu.org/national-security/obama -administration-danger-establishing-new-normal-worst-bush-era-policies-says-a.

34   Charlie Savage, "Court Dismisses a Case Asserting Torture by C.I.A.," *New York Times,* September 9, 2010.

35   Jack Goldsmith, "The Cheney Fallacy," *New Republic,* May 18, 2009, www.tnr.com /article/politics/the-cheney-fallacy?page=0,0&id=1e733cac-c273-48e5-9140 -80443ed1f5e2&p=1.

36   Jonathan Turley, "Taking Liberties: Obama May Prove Disastrous in Terms of Protecting Our Rights," *Los Angeles Times,* September 29, 2011.

37   Paul Richter, "State Department Spokesman P. J. Crowley Resigns," *New York Times,* March 14, 2011.

38   Marjorie Cohn, "Bradley Manning: Traitor or Hero," *Consortium News,* December 24, 2011, www.consortiumnews.com/2011/12/24/bradley-manning-traitor-or-hero.

39   "WikiLeaks Wins Australian Journalism Award," AFP, November 27, 2011, www.google .com/hostednews/afp/article/ALeqM5gQRUCe6qxRkV8J7Q8Ix6HUPcD_Eg; Glenn Greenwald, "WikiLeaks Wins Major Journalism Award in Australia," November 27, 2011, www.salon.com/2011/11/27/wikileaks_wins_major_journalism_award_in _australia.

40   Robert Scheer, "From Jefferson to Assange," *Nation,* December 28, 2010, www.thenation .com/article/156909/jefferson-assange.

41   Thomas R. Eddlem, "Gingrich Calls Assange an 'Enemy Combatant,'" *New American,* December 9, 2010, www.thenewamerican.com/usnews/foreign-policy/5454-gingrich -calls-assange-an-enemy-combatant; Martin Beckford, "Sarah Palin: Hunt WikiLeaks Founder Like al-Qaeda and Taliban Leaders," *Telegraph* (London), December 26, 2011, www.telegraph.co.uk/news/worldnews/wikileaks/8171269/Sarah-Palin-hunt -WikiLeaks-founder-like-al-Qaeda-and-Taliban-leaders.html.

42   James C. Goodale, "WikiLeaks Probe: Pentagon Papers Injustice Déjà Vu," *Daily Beast,* June 12, 2011, www.thedailybeast.com/articles/2011/06/13/wikileaks-probe-spoils -pentagon-papers-anniversary.html; Trevor Timm, "Cablegate One Year Later: How WikiLeaks Has Influenced Foreign Policy, Journalism, and the First Amendment," Electronic Freedom Foundation, November 28, 2011, www.eff.org/deeplinks/2011/11/ cablegate-one-year-later-how-wikileaks-has-influenced-foreign-policy-journalism.

43   R. Jeffrey Smith, "Classified Pentagon Report Upholds Thomas Drake's Complaints About NSA," *Washington Post,* June 23, 2011.

44   Glenn Greenwald, "Climate of Fear: Jim Risen v. the Obama Administration," June 23, 2011, www.salon.com/news/opinion/glenn_greenwald/2011/06/23/risen.

45   Steven Erlanger, "Europeans Criticize Fierce U.S. Response to Leaks," *New York Times,* December 10, 2010.

46   Dana Priest and William M. Arkin, "A Hidden World, Growing Beyond Control," *Washington Post,* July 19, 2010.

47   Dana Priest and William M. Arkin, "Monitoring America," *Washington Post,* December 20, 2010.

48   Charlie Savage, "Senators Say Patriot Act Is Being Misinterpreted," *New York Times,* May 27, 2011.

49   Charlie Savage, "F.B.I. Agents Get Leeway to Push Privacy Bounds," *New York Times,* June 13, 2011; David K. Shipler, "Free to Search and Seize," *New York Times,* June 23, 2011.

50 Jonathan Turley, "Ten Reasons We're No Longer the Land of the Free," *Washington Post,* January 15, 2012.

51 Karen DeYoung, "Familiar Faces and Some Prominent Newcomers," *Washington Post,* March 3, 2008.

52 Joshua E. Keating, "The Audacity of What?" *Foreign Policy,* January 24, 2011, www .foreignpolicy.com/articles/2011/01/24/the_audacity_of_what.

53 Ryan Lizza, "How the Arab Spring Remade Obama's Foreign Policy," *New Yorker,* May 2, 2011, www.newyorker.com/reporting/2011/05/02/110502fa_fact_lizza?currentPage =all.

54 Michael Abramowitz, Shailagh Murray, and Anne E. Kornblut, "Obama Close to Picking Clinton, Jones for Key Posts," *Washington Post,* November 22, 2008.

55 Eliot Cohen, "What's Different About the Obama Foreign Policy," *Wall Street Journal,* August 2, 2009, online.wsj.com/article/SB10001424052970203946904574300402608 475582.html.

56 Robert Parry, "The Secret World of Robert Gates," November 9, 2006, www.consortium news.com/2006/110906.html; Robert Parry, "How the War Hawks Caged Obama," November 30, 2009, www.consortiumnews.com/2009/113009.html; Robert Parry, *Secrecy & Privilege: Rise of the Bush Dynasty from Watergate to Iraq* (Arlington, VA: Media Consortium, 2004).

57 Mark Landler, "Clinton Speech Offers Policy Overview," *New York Times,* September 8, 2010.

58 Elisabeth Bumiller, "Gates on Leaks, Wiki and Otherwise," *New York Times,* November 30, 2010.

59 Andrew J. Bacevich, "Hillary Clinton's 'American Moment' Was Nothing But American Blather," *New Republic,* September 13, 2010, www.tnr.com/blog/foreign-policy/77612/ hillary-clintons-american-moment-was-nothing-american-blather.

60 Charlie Savage, "2 Top Lawyers Lost to Obama in Libya War Policy Debate," *New York Times,* June 18, 2011.

61 Charlie Savage, "Mostly in Echo, Rivals Discuss Reach of Power," *New York Times,* December 30, 2011; Steve Chapman, "Mirror Images," *Chicago Tribune,* January 5, 2012.

62 Simon Jenkins, "U.S. Embassy Cables: The Job of the Media Is Not to Protect the Powerful from Embarrassment," *Guardian,* November 28, 2010.

63 Garry Wills, "Obama's Legacy: Afghanistan," *New York Review of Books,* July 27, 2010, www.nybooks.com/blogs/nyrblog/2010/jul/27/obamas-legacy-afghanistan/.

64 Karen DeYoung, "Afghan Conflict Will Be Reviewed," *Washington Post,* January 13, 2009.

65 White House Press Release, February 17, 2009, www.whitehouse.gov/the_press_office/ Statement-by-the-President-on-Afghanistan.

66 Elisabeth Bumiller and Mark Mazetti, "A General Steps from the Shadows," *New York Times,* May 12, 2009; Tom Engelhardt, *The American Way of War: How Bush's Wars Became Obama's* (Chicago: Haymarket Books, 2010), 141.

67 Eric Schmitt and Mark Mazetti, "Switch Signals New Path for Afghan War," *New York Times,* May 12, 2009.

68 Bob Woodward, "Obama: 'We Need to Make Clear to People That the Cancer Is in Pakistan,'" *Washington Post,* September 29, 2010.

69   David E. Sanger and Eric Schmitt, "Pakistani Nuclear Arms Pose Challenge to U.S. Policy," *New York Times,* February 1, 2011.

70   K. Alan Kronstadt, "Pakistan-U.S. Relations," February 6, 2009, Congressional Research Service, www.fas.org/sgp/crs/row/RL33498.pdf.

71   Tim Reid, "We'll Bomb You to Stone Age, US Told Pakistan," *Times* (London), September 22, 2006, www.timesonline.co.uk/tol/news/world/middle_east/article 647188.ece.

72   Woodward, "Obama: 'We Need to Make Clear to People That the Cancer Is in Pakistan.'"

73   David Kilcullen and Andrew McDonald Exum, "Death from Above, Outrage down Below," *New York Times,* May 17, 2009.

74   Saed Shah and Peter Beaumont, "Human Face of Hellfire—Hidden Cost of America's Remote-Controlled Missiles," *Guardian* (London), July 18, 2011; Jemima Khan, "Under Fire from Afar: Harrowing Exhibition Reveals Damage Done By Drones in Pakistan," *Independent* (London), July 29, 2011.

75   Mehdi Hasan, "U.S. Drone Attacks Are No Laughing Matter, Mr. Obama," *Guardian* (London), December 29, 2010.

76   Glenn Greenwald, "Bravery and Drone Pilots," July 10, 2012, www.salon.com/2012/07 /10/bravery_and_drone_pilots.

77   Nico Hines, "Obama Schmoozes the Fourth Estate with Gags and Gaffes at Charity White House Bash," *Times* (London), May 3, 2010; Jamie Crawford, "Pakistani View of U.S. Reaches New Low," CNN, June 29, 2012, security.blogs.cnn.com/2012/06/29/ pakistani-view-of-u-s-reaches-new-low/?iref=allsearch.

78   Scott Shane, "C.I.A. Is Disputed on Civilian Toll in Drone Strikes," *New York Times,* August 12, 2011.

79   Chris Woods and Christina Lamb, "Obama Terror Drones," Bureau of Investigative Journalism, February 4, 2012, www.thebureauinvestigates.com/2012/02/04/obama -terror-drones-cia-tactics-in-pakistan-include-targeting-rescuers-and-funerals.

80   Karen DeYoung, "Secrecy Defines Obama's Drone War," *Washington Post,* December 20, 2011; Jo Becker and Scott Shane, "Secret 'Kill List' Proves a Test of Obama's Principles and Will," *New York Times,* May 29, 2012.

81   Tom Junod, "The Lethal Presidency of Barack Obama," *Esquire,* July 9, 2012, www .esquire.com/features/obama-lethal-presidency-0812-3.

82   Ibid.

83   Akbar Ahmed and Frankie Martin, "Deadly Drones Come to the Muslims of the Philippines," Al-Jazeera, March 5, 2012; Tom Engelhardt, "Obama's Bush League World," July 12, 2011, www.tomdispatch.com/post/175416/tomgram%3A_engelhardt %2C_making_earth_a_global_free-fire_zone.

84   Glenn Greenwald, "Excuses for Assassination Secrecy," July 12, 2012, www.salon.com /2012/07/12/excuses_for_assassination_secrecy.

85   Glenn Greenwald, "Obama's Killings Challenged Again," July 18, 2012, www.salon.com /2012/07/18/obamas_killings_challenged_again.

86   Greg Miller and Julie Tate, "Since Sept. 11, CIA's Focus Has Taken Lethal Turn," *Washington Post,* September 2, 2011.

87 Michael Hastings, "The Rise of the Killer Drones: How America Goes to War in Secret," *Rolling Stone,* April 26, 2012, www.rollingstone.com/politics/news/the-rise-of-the-killer-drones-how-america-goes-to-war-in-secret-20120416?print=true.

88 Charlie Savage, "Relatives Sue Officials Over U.S. Citizens Killed by Drone Strikes in Yemen," *New York Times,* July 18, 2012.

89 Sudarsan Raghavan, "In Yemen, U.S. Airstrikes Breed Anger, and Sympathy for Al-Qaeda," *Washington Post,* May 29, 2012.

90 "As Nature Is Displaying More Bipolar Behaviour—Floods One Day, Drought the Next—and Man Is Traversing More into the Realm of Boundless Greed and Shamelessness, Mutants Calling Themselves Politicians Are Saying Things Unplugged from Logic and Unlinked," *Nation* (Thailand), December 15, 2011.

91 John Markoff, "War Machines: Recruiting Robots for Combat," *New York Times,* November 29, 2010.

92 Tom Engelhardt, *The American Way of War: How Bush's Wars Became Obama's* (Chicago: Haymarket Books, 2010), 172–174; Elisabeth Bumiller and Thom Shaker, "War Evolves with Drones, Some Tiny as Bugs," *New York Times,* June 20, 2011.

93 William Wan and Peter Finn, "Global Rush Is On to Match U.S. Drones," *Washington Post,* July 5, 2011.

94 Becker and Shane, "Secret 'Kill List' Proves a Test of Obama's Principles and Will."

95 Thom Shanker, "Joint Chiefs Chairman Readjusts Principles on Use of Force," *New York Times,* March 3, 2010.

96 Richard A. Oppel, Jr., "Tighter Rules Fail to Stem Deaths of Innocent Afghans at Checkpoints," *New York Times,* March 26, 2010; Ben Kiernan and Taylor Owen, "Roots of U.S. Troubles in Afghanistan: Civilian Bombing Casualties and the Cambodian Precedent," *Asia-Pacific Journal,* June 28, 2010, www.japanfocus.org/-Ben-Kiernan/3380.

97 Peter Baker, "How Obama Came to Plan for 'Surge' in Afghanistan," *New York Times,* December 6, 2009.

98 Steve Rendell, "In Afghan Debate, Few Antiwar Op-Eds," *FAIR,* December 2009, www.fair.org/index.php?page=3949; "Wavering on Afghanistan?" *Washington Post,* September 22, 2009.

99 Craig Whitlock, "Gen. Cartwright, Poised to Lead Chiefs, Had His Shot Derailed by Critics," *Washington Post,* May 28, 2011.

100 World Food Program data, www.wfp.org/countries/afghanistan; Anthony H. Cordesman and Adam Mausner, "Is a 'Population-centric' Strategy Possible?" Center for Strategic & International Studies, April 26, 2010, csis.org/publication/agriculture-food-and-poverty-afghanistan; John Hanrahan, "About Living Standards in Afghanistan," December 3, 2009, niemanwatchdog.org/index.cfm?fuseaction=ask_this.view&askthisid=00435; Karin Brulliard, "Affluent Afghans Make Their Homes in Opulent 'Poppy Palaces,'" *Washington Post,* June 6, 2010.

101 David Wildman and Phyllis Bennis, *Ending the US War in Afghanistan: A Primer* (Northampton, MA: Olive Branch Press, 2010), 72–74.

102 Anthony H. Cordesman, "What's Our Long-Range Afghan Plan?," *Washington Post,* September 23, 2011.

103 Atiq Sarwari and Robert D. Crews, "Afghanistan and the Pax Americana," in *The Taliban and the Crisis of Afghanistan,* ed. Robert D. Crews and Amin Tarzi (Cambridge, MA: Harvard University Press, 2008), 315–16.

104 "Afghan Life Expectancy Rising as Healthcare Improves, Survey Shows," *Guardian* (London), November 30, 2011.

105 Wildman and Bennis, *Ending the US War in Afghanistan: A Primer,* 88–90, 94; Dana Burde, "It Takes a Village To Raise a School," *New York Times,* September 17, 2010.

106 Karl Eikenberry, memo to Hillary Clinton, November 6, 2009, documents.nytimes.com /eikenberry-s-memos-on-the-strategy-in-afghanistan.

107 Nicholas D. Kristof, "The Afghanistan Abyss," *New York Times,* September 6, 2009.

108 Andrew Shurtleff, "Former CIA Station Chief in Afghanistan Calls for Withdrawal," *Daily Progress,* www.votersforpeace.us/press/index.php?itemid=3419.

109 Conn Hallinan, "Afghanistan: Killing Peace," January 12, 2011, dispatchesfromtheedge blog.wordpress.com; Wildman and Bennis, *Ending the US War in Afghanistan: A Primer,* 160.

110 Alissa J. Rubin, "Girl, 12, Killed in NATO Raid on Wrong Afghan Home," *New York Times,* May 13, 2011.

111 Tariq Ali, "Operation Enduring Disaster: Breaking with Afghan Policy," November 16, 2008, www.tomdispatch.com/post/175003/tariq_ali_flight_path_to_disaster_in _afghanistan.

112 Matthew P. Hoh, letter to Ambassador Nancy J. Powell, September 10, 2009, *Washington Post,* www.washingtonpost.com/wp-srv/hp/ssi/wpc/ResignationLetter.pdf?sid =ST2009102603447.

113 Chris Hedges, "Opium, Rape and the American Way," November 2, 2009, www.truthdig .com/report/item/20091102_opium_rape_and_the_american_way/.

114 "Losing Afghanistan?" *Economist,* August 20, 2009, www.economist.com/node /14258750?story_id=14258750

115 "UN Afghanistan Survey Points to Huge Scale of Bribery," *BBC News,* January 19, 2010, news.bbc.co.uk/2/hi/8466915.stm; Alfred W. McCoy, "America and the Dictators: From Ngo Dinh Diem to Hamid Karzai," April 16, 2010, www.tomdispatch.com/blog /175233.

116 Scott Shane and Andrew W. Lehren, "Leaked Cables Offer Raw Look at U.S. Diplomacy," *New York Times,* November 28, 2010; Scott Shane, Mark Mazzetti, and Dexter Filkins, "Cables Depict Afghan Graft, Starting at Top," *New York Times,* December 2, 2010; Declan Walsh, "Flower Power," *Guardian,* August 16, 2008, www.guardian.co.uk/lifeandstyle /2008/aug/16/drugstrade.afghanistan; Dexter Filkins, Mark Mazzetti, and James Risen, "Brother of Afghan Leader Said to Be Paid by C.I.A.," *New York Times,* October 28, 2009.

117 Alissa J. Rubin and Matthew Rosenberg, "U.S. Efforts Fail to Curtail Trade in Afghan Opium," *New York Times,* May 26, 2012.

118 James Risen, "Propping Up a Drug Lord, Then Arresting Him," *New York Times,* December 11, 2010; "New Measures Against the Afghan Opium Tsunami," *United Nations Information Service,* October 31, 2007, www.unis.unvienna.org/unis/pressrels /2007/unisnar1013.html; Alfred W. McCoy, "Can Anyone Pacify the World's Number One Narco-State? The Opium Wars in Afghanistan," March 30, 2010, www.tomdispatch .com/blog/175225.

119 Walsh, "Flower Power"; Brulliard, "Affluent Afghans Make Their Homes in Opulent 'Poppy Palaces.'"

120 Jean MacKenzie, "Funding the Afghan Taliban," August 7, 2009, www.globalpost.com/dispatch/taliban/funding-the-taliban; Hugh Gusterson, "Why the War in Afghanistan Cannot Be Won," *Bulletin of the Atomic Scientists,* September 21, 2009, www.thebulletin.org/web-edition/columnists/hugh-gusterson/why-the-war-afghanistan-cannot-be-won.

121 Dexter Filkins, "Convoy Guards in Afghanistan Face an Inquiry," *New York Times,* June 6, 2010.

122 Rod Nordland, "Afghan Bank Commission Absolves President's Brother in Fraud Case," *New York Times,* May 29, 2011.

123 Ben Farmer, "U.S. Diplomat Claims UN Tried to Gag Him," *Telegraph* (London), October 4, 2009, www.telegraph.co.uk/news/6259530/US-diplomat-claims-UN-tried-to-gag-him.html.

124 Rod Nordland, "Afghan Votes Come Cheap, and Often in Bulk," *New York Times,* September 17, 2010.

125 Bob Woodward, "Military Thwarted President Seeking Choice in Afghanistan," *Washington Post,* September 27, 2010.

126 Bob Woodward, "Biden Warned Obama During Afghan War Review Not to Get 'Locked into Vietnam,'" *Washington Post,* September 28, 2010; Bob Woodward, *Obama's Wars,* 247, 311.

127 "Final Report of the National Commission on Terrorist Attacks Upon the United States," www.9-11commission.gov/report/911Report_Exec.htm.

128 Paul R. Pillar, "Who's Afraid of a Terrorist Haven?," *Washington Post,* September 16, 2009.

129 "Fareed Zakaria Criticizes 'Disproportionate' Afghanistan War on CNN," July 4, 2010, www.huffingtonpost.com/2010/07/04/fareed-zakaria-criticizes_n_635170.html.

130 George F. Will, "The War That Wasn't," *Washington Post,* May 3, 2011.

131 Andrew J. Bacevich, "Obama's Afghanistan Speech and Strategy," *Washington Post,* December 2, 2009.

132 Christopher Drew, "One Million Dollars to Keep One Soldier in Afghanistan for One Year," *New York Times,* November 16, 2009.

133 Robert Dreyfuss, "Getting Out in 2010," *Nation,* June 17, 2010, www.thenation.com/blog/getting-out-2011.

134 Dana Milbank, "A Deadline Written in Quicksand, Not Stone," *Washington Post,* December 3, 2009.

135 Woodward, *Obama's Wars,* 354.

136 Karen DeYoung and Scott Wilson, "With bin Laden Dead, Some Escalate Push for New Afghan Strategy," *Washington Post,* May 11, 2011; Wildman and Bennis, *Ending the US War in Afghanistan: A Primer,* 72–74.

137 David E. Sanger and Thom Shanker, "Military Seeks to Make Case Against Too-Hasty Reduction of Troops," *New York Times,* June 7, 2011; Thom Shanker and John H. Cushman, Jr., "Reviews Raise Doubt on Training of Afghan Forces," *New York Times,* November 6, 2009.

138   Thomas L. Friedman, "What's Second Prize?" *New York Times,* June 22, 2010.

139   Rod Nordland, "Afghans Plan to Stop Recruiting Children as Police," *New York Times,* January 29, 2011; Ernesto Londono, "Afghanistan Sees Rise in 'Dancing Boys' Exploitation," *Washington Post,* April 4, 2012.

140   Tony Perry, "U.S. Troops in Afghanistan Suffer More Catastrophic Injuries," *Los Angeles Times,* April 6, 2011.

141   T. Christian Miller and Daniel Zwerding, "Brain Injuries Remain Undiagnosed in Thousands of Soldiers," June 7, 2010, www.propublica.org/article/brain-injuries-remain -undiagnosed-in-thousands-of-soldiers.

142   Wildman and Bennis, *Ending the US War in Afghanistan: A Primer,* 28.

143   Leo Shane III, "Study: Wars Could Cost $4 Trillion to $6 Trillion," *Stars and Stripes,* September 29, 2010, www.stripes.com/blogs/stripes-central/stripes-central-1.8040/ study-wars-could-cost-4-trillion-to-6-trillion-1.120054.

144   James Risen, "U.S. Identifies Vast Riches of Minerals in Afghanistan," *New York Times,* June 13, 2010.

145   George A. Dorsey, "Ikyber Pass Key of Nations' Fate," *Chicago Tribune,* January 24, 1911.

146   "Americans acquire Afghanistan Oil" *New York Times,* May 8, 1928.

147   Announced by Radio New York Times (1923–current file); Oct 20, 1941; ProQuest Historical Newspapers, *New York Times* (1851–2001, page 4).

148   James Risen, "World's Mining Companies Covet Afghan Riches," *New York Times,* June 17, 2010.

149   Joshua Partlow, "Afghan Minister Accused of Taking Bribe," *Washington Post,* November 18, 2009.

150   Jane Perlez, Eric Schmitt, and Carlotta Gall, "Pakistan Is Said to Pursue Foothold in Afghanistan," *New York Times,* June 24, 2010; Joshua Partlow, "Haqqani Insurgent Group Proves Resilient Foe in Afghan War," *Washington Post,* May 29, 2011; Jane Perlez, "Official Admits Militancy's Deep Roots in Pakistan," *New York Times,* June 2, 2010.

151   Alissa J. Rubin, "Pakistan Urged Afghanistan to Distance Itself from the West, Officials Say," *New York Times,* April 28, 2011.

152   Michael Cooper, "Mayors See End to Wars as Fix for Struggling Cities," *New York Times,* June 18, 2001.

153   Jane Perlez, David E. Sanger, and Eric Schmitt, "Nuclear Fuel Memos Expose Wary Dance with Pakistan," *New York Times,* November 30, 2010.

154   John T. Bennett, "Pressure Builds to End Afghan War," May 4, 2011, thehill.com/ homenews/administration/159123-pressure-builds-to-end-the-afghan-war.

155   George Zornick, "Senator Dick Durbin Questions Sending 'One More' Soldier to Die in Afghanistan," May 3, 2011, www.thenation.com/blog/160377/senator-dick-durbin -questions-sending-one-more-soldier-die-afghanistan.

156   Rod Nordland, "Karzai Takes Another Shot at NATO Coalition," *New York Times,* June 19, 2001.

157   Ray Rivera and Ginger Thompson, "Karzai Is Testing U.S. Patience, Envoy Says," *New York Times,* June 20, 2011.

158 Ray Rivera and Ginger Thompson, "U.S. Envoy Responds to Karzai's Criticisms," *New York Times*, June 19, 2011.

159 Laura King, "Karzai Quote Taken Wrong Way, Aide Says," *Los Angeles Times*, October 25, 2011.

160 Alissa J. Rubin and Taimoor Shah, "Attack Kills Police Officers in Afghanistan," *New York Times*, September 29, 2011.

161 "NATO: Militant Attacks in Afghanistan Up 11 Percent in Past Three Months," *Washington Post*, July 27, 2012.

162 Human Rights Watch, "Afghanistan: Rein in Abusive Militias and Afghan Local Police," September 12, 2011, www.hrw.org/news/2011/09/12/afghanistan-rein-abusive-militias-and-afghan-local-police.

163 UN News Centre, "Systematic Torture in Afghan Detention Facilities—UN Report," October 10, 2011, www.un.org/apps/news/story.asp?NewsID=39985.

164 Jack Healy, "Afghanistan Sees Increase in Cultivation of Poppies," *New York Times*, October 12, 2001.

165 Tim Arango, "Premier Places Power-Sharing at Risk in Iraq," *New York Times*, December 22, 2011; "Iraq Withdrawal: After Troops Leave, A Substantial American Presence," *International Business Times News*, December 9, 2011; Farirai Chubvu, "Iraq—Uncle Sam's Unfinished War," *Herald* (Harare, Zimbabwe), December 15, 2011; Michele Keleman, "Huge Embassy Keeps US Presence in Iraq," National Public Radio, December 11, 2011.

166 David Brown, "Study Claims Iraq's 'Excess' Death Toll Has Reached 655,000," *Washington Post*, October 11, 2006.

167 David Gilmour, *The Long Recessional: The Imperial Life of Rudyard Kipling* (New York: Farrar, Straus and Giroux, 2002), 251.

168 "Obama's Speech to Troops at Fort Bragg," *New York Times*, December 15, 2011; Michael S. Schmidt, "Junkyard Gives Up Secret Accounts of Massacre," *New York Times*, December 15, 2011.

169 Greg Jaffe, "A War Without an Iconic Ending," *Washington Post*, December 25, 2011.

170 Thom Shanker, "Warning Against Wars Like Iraq and Afghanistan," *New York Times*, February 26, 2011.

171 Helene Cooper and Ethan Bronner, "Focus Is on Obama as Tensions Soar Across Mideast," *New York Times*, May 19, 2011.

172 David D. Kirkpatrick and Michael Slackman, "Egyptian Youths Drive the Revolt Against Mubarak," *New York Times*, January 27, 2011.

173 Helene Cooper and Mark Landler, "Obama's Peace Tack Contrasts with Key Aide, Friend of Israel," *New York Times*, May 22, 2011.

174 Thomas L. Friedman, "The Arab Awakening and Israel," *New York Times*, November 30, 2011.

175 Ira Chernus, "Israel and the Palestinians Through the Looking Glass," May 26, 2011, www.tomdispatch.com/blog/175397/tomgram%3A_ira_chernus,_ass-backwards_in_the_middle_east.

176 Ethan Bronner, "A Former Spy Chief Questions the Judgment of Israeli Leaders," *New York Times*, June 4, 2011; Gareth Porter, "Obama Seeks To Distance U.S. from Israeli Attack," January 3, 2012, ipsnews.net/news.asp?idnews=106361.

177   Shibley Tehlami and Steven Kull, "Preventing a Nuclear Iran, Peacefully," *New York Times,* January 16, 2012.

178   Simon Romero, "Colombia Leader Seeks Wide-Ranging Changes, and Looks Beyond the U.S.," *New York Times,* March 5, 2011.

179   Tom Phillips and Virginia Lopez, "US Not Invited as Chávez Launches Latin Group," *Guardian* (London), December 3, 2011; "Venezuela: New Regional Group Meets," *New York Times,* December 3, 2011; "New Americas Summit Dominated by Criticism of US," Agence France Press, December 2, 2011.

180   Sibylla Brodzinsky, "Cuba and Drug Policy Headline Summit of the Americas," *Christian Science Monitor,* April 16, 2012; Scott Wilson, "Americas Summit Ends Without an Agreement," *Washington Post,* April 16, 2012; Noam Chomsky, "Cartagena Beyond the Secret Service," *In These Times,* May 2, 2012, inthesetimes.com/article/13136/cartagena _beyond_the_secret_service_scandal.

181   Francisco Toro, "The Incredible Shrinking State Department," *International Herald Tribune,* July 5, 2012.

182   Nick Turse, "Empire of Bases 2.0," January 9, 2011, www.tomdispatch.com/blog /175338; Engelhardt, *The American Way of War,* 53.

183   David Vine, "The Lily-Pad Strategy," July 15, 2012, www.tomdispatch.com/post /175568/tomgram%3A_david_vine%2C_u.s._empire_of_bases_grows/?utm_source =TomDispatch&utm_campaign=d027c16bb5-TD_Vine7_15_2012&utm_medium =email#more.

184   Charles M. Blow, "For Jobs, It's War," *New York Times,* September 27, 2011.

185   "Don't Take Peaceful Approach for Granted," *Global Times,* October 25, 2011, www .globaltimes.cn/NEWS/tabid/99/ID/680694/Dont-take-peaceful-approach-for -granted.aspx.

186   Hillary Clinton, "America's Pacific Century," *Foreign Policy,* November 2011, www .foreignpolicy.com/articles/2011/10/11/americas_pacific_century?page=full.

187   Matthew Franklin, "Obama Pledges Leadership," *Australian,* November 18, 2011; Peter Harcher, "Toothless Among Asian Tigers," *Sydney Morning Herald,* July 21, 2012.

188   "Philippines Launches Its Most Modern Warship," *Nation* (Thailand), December 15, 2011.

189   Bill Gertz, "Military to Bolster Its Forces in Pacific," *Washington Times,* February 18, 2011.

190   Celia W. Dugger, "U.S. Envoy Extols India, Accepting Its Atom Status," *New York Times,* September 7, 2001; "A Bad Deal," *New York Times,* September 9, 2008; Peter Baker, "Senate Approves Indian Nuclear Deal," *New York Times,* October 2, 2008.

191   Plenary Session of the U.S.-India Strategic Dialogue, June 3, 2010, www.state.gov/ secretary/rm/2010/06/142623.htm.

192   "Arms Race Growing in Asia," *Toronto Star,* December 3, 2011.

193   Jim Yardley, "Malnutrition Widespread in Indian Children, Report Finds," *New York Times,* January 10, 2012.

194   Frank Ching, "China-US Power Play That Confuses Audiences," *New Straits Times* (Malaysia), September 29, 2011.

195   Paul McLeary, "Securing the Western Pacific," *Defense Technology International,* June 1, 2010.

196   Greg Torode, "Beijing Wary as New US Military Strategy Emerges," *South China Morning Post,* April 25, 2011.

197   "Hu Tells Navy to Prepare to Fight," *Hobart Mercury* (Australia), December 8, 2011.

198   Greg Jaffe, "U.S. Model for a Future War Fans Tensions with China and Inside Pentagon," *Washington Post,* August 1, 2012.

199   Jane Perlez, "Clinton Makes Effort to Rechannel the Rivalry with China," *New York Times,* July 7, 2012.

200   Christopher Hellman, "The Real U.S. National Security Budget," March 1, 2011, www .tomdispatch.com/post/175361/tomgram%3A_chris_hellman%2C_%241.2_trillion _for_national_security/.

201   Eric Margolis, "Obama the President Is Fighting Battles His Country Cannot Afford," *Toronto Sun,* February 7, 2010, www.torontosun.com/comment/columnists/eric_ margolis/2010/02/05/12758511-qmi.html; Lawrence Wittner, "How Much Is Enough? America's Runaway Military Spending," August 23, 2010, www.huffingtonpost.com/ lawrence-wittner/how-much-is-enough-americ_b_683600.html.

202   William Wan, "Panetta, in Speech in Singapore, Seeks to Lend Heft to U.S. Pivot to Asia," *Washington Post,* June 1, 2012; Leon E. Panetta, Speech to Shangri-La Security Dialogue, June 2, 2012, www.defense.gov/Speeches/Speech.aspx?SpeechID=1681.

203   Jane Perlez, "Panetta Outlines New Weaponry for Pacific," *New York Times,* June 2, 2012.

204   Harcher, "Toothless Among Asian Tigers."

205   Greg Jaffe, "Obama Announces New, Leaner Military Approach," *Washington Post,* January 5, 2012.

206   Amanda Andrews, "America Is in Urgent Need of Its Own 'Perestroika,' Says Gorbachev," *Telegraph* (London), March 12, 2009, www.telegraph.co.uk/finance/g20 -summit/4980262/America-is-in-urgent-need-of-its-own-peristrokia-says-Gorbachev .html; Anton Fedyashin, "Gorbachev's Great Expectations," *Washington Post,* April 13, 2009.

207   "Rising Share of Americans See Conflict Between Rich and Poor," Pew Research Center Publications, January 11, 2012, pewresearch.org/pubs/2167/rich-poor-social-conflict -class.

208   Binyamin Appelbaum, "Family Net Worth Drops to Level of Early '90s, Fed Says," *New York Times,* June 11, 2012; Joseph E. Stiglitz, "The 1 Percent's Problem," *Vanity Fair,* May 31, 2012, www.vanityfair.com/politics/2012/05/joseph-stiglitz-the-price-on-inequality.

209   Turley, "Ten Reasons We're No Longer the Land of the Free."

PHOTO CREDITS

Associated Press: page 264

Benutzer: Fb78 via Wikimedia Commons: page 525

Chris Hondro / Getty Images: page 599

Corbis Images: pages 358, 363, 375, 379, 415, 465, 495

Courtesy of Daniel Ellsberg and Danny Schechter: page 386

Courtesy of Los Alamos National Laboratory: pages 144, 174

Courtesy of U.S. Department of Energy: page 137

David Shankbone via Wikimedia Commons: page 557

Federal Bureau of Investigation: page 235

Franklin D. Roosevelt Presidential Library / National Archives: pages 49, 51, 52, 58, 95, 99, 100, 153

George Bush Presidential Library and Museum/ National Archives: page 483

George W. Bush Presidential Library / National Archives: page 503

Gerald R. Ford Presidential Library: pages 393, 394, 400

German Federal Archive: pages 89, 97, 228

Getty Images: pages 293, 435

Harry S. Truman / National Archives: page 121

Harry S. Truman Presidential Library: pages 140, 142, 207, 225, 231

Harry S. Truman Presidential Library / National Archives: pages 119, 165, 191, 202, 237

Information of New Orleans via Wikimedia Commons: page 479

Ixtlan: page xviii

Jim Kuhn via Wikimedia Commons: page 511

Jimmy Carter Library / National Archives: pages 407, 411

Jimmy Carter Presidential Library / National Archives: page 419

John F. Kennedy Presidential Library: pages 292, 307

John F. Kennedy Presidential Library / National Archives: pages 297, 311, 317

Library of Congress: pages xx, xxi, xxvi, xxix, 9, 13, 15, 17, 29, 33, 40, 47, 59, 67, 85, 107, 127, 133, 179, 198, 211, 280, 345, 351, 401

Library of Congress, University of Minnesota, National Archives: page 150

Library of Congress, Wikimedia Commons / Public Domain: pages 158, 159

Lyndon Baines Johnson Presidential Library: pages 326, 327

Lyndon Baines Johnson Presidential Library / National Archives: pages 333, 337, 339, 340, 342, 353

Nasser Sadeghi via Wikimedia Commons / Public Domain: page 261

National Archives: pages xxviii, 34, 118, 136, 155, 169, 170, 171, 183, 210, 245, 269, 274, 301, 306, 331, 341, 347, 361, 404, 502

National Archives, Wikimedia Commons / Public Domain: page 170

National Museum of the U.S. Air Force: pages 229, 331

New Yorker Magazine: page xxvii

New York Times: page 109

Official White House Photograph: pages 569, 581, 593

Oliver Stone Personal Collection: page 336

Peter Kuznick Personal Collection: page 336

Photos of the Great War: World War I Image Archive: pages 25, 27

Public Domain: pages xix, xxiii, 28, 35, 37, 81, 183, 234, 433, 489

Ragesoss via Wikimedia Commons: page 550

Richard Nixon Presidential Library / National Archives: pages 357, 359, 371, 381

Ronald Reagan Presidential Library: pages 423, 425, 427, 449, 453, 455

Ronald Reagan Presidential Library / National Archives: pages 448, 453, 467

Sue Ream via Wikimedia Commons: page 471

U.S. Air Force: pages 509, 579, 595, 596

U.S. Army: pages 239, 291, 369

U.S. Department of Defense: pages 199, 275, 437, 460, 473, 475, 479, 481, 501, 527

U.S. Information Agency: pages 107, 243

U.S. Marine Corps: pages xxxii, 174, 395, 437

U.S. Navy: page 513

U.S. State Department: page 537

Utilizator:Mihai.1954 via Wikimedia Commons: page 115

Wikimedia Commons / Public Domain: pages 135, 167, 233, 411

William J. Clinton Presidential Library / National Archives: page 487

INDEX

Page numbers in *italics* refer to illustrations.